Party Politics In America

Party Politics In America

NINTH EDITION

PAUL ALLEN BECK
The Ohio State University

MARJORIE RANDON HERSHEY
Indiana University

Longman

New York San Francisco Boston
London Toronto Sydney Tokyo Singapore Madrid
Mexico City Munich Paris Cape Town Hong Kong Montreal

Senior Acquisitions Editor: Eric Stano
Marketing Manager: Megan Galvin-Fak
Supplements Editor: Kristinn Muller
Production Manager: Ellen MacElree
Project Coordination, Text Design, and Electronic Page Makeup: Electronic Publishing
    Services Inc., NYC
Cover Design Manager: Nancy Danahy
Manufacturing Buyer: Al Dorsey
Printer and Binder: Courier
Cover Printer: Coral Graphics Services, Inc.

Library of Congress Cataloging-in-Publication Data

Beck, Paul Allen.
    Party politics in America / Paul Allen Beck, Marjorie Randon Hershey.--9th ed.
        p.   cm.
    Includes index.
    ISBN 0-321-05273-0
    1. Political parties--United States. I. Hershey, Marjorie Randon. II. Title.
JK2265.S65   2000   00-058118
324.273—dc21   CIP

Please visit our website at http://www.awl.com

ISBN 0-321-05273-0

1 2 3 4 5 6 7 8 9 10—CRW—03 02 01 00

Contents in Brief

Contents in Detail

Preface

One of the truths of the twentieth century, expressed by E. E. Schattschneider, is that "the political parties created democracy and... modern democracy is unthinkable save in terms of the parties." Another of those truths, at least according to large numbers of Americans, is "I don't vote for the party; I vote for the person." It is clear that we stand a better chance of preserving our democracy when the parties are thriving; that can be seen in the current struggles of other nations to develop democratic institutions. But in the classic American tradition, that doesn't mean we have to like them.

This long-running conflict between our need for parties and our dislike of them has given us a party system unique among democracies. No other nation's parties are so hamstrung by government regulation. No other parties have their candidates selected for them by whoever chooses to vote in a primary election. (Imagine the interesting—and real—predicament of a Democratic Party organization in Southern California when voters in a crowded primary race handed the party a high-ranking official of the local Ku Klux Klan as its congressional candidate.) Examining these and other features of the American parties gives us a fuller picture of the American version of democracy. That is one of the reasons why political parties are such a compelling and fascinating field of study.

It is a pleasure to thank the many people who helped in the development of this book. One of the easiest ways to reach high, of course, is to stand on the shoulders of giants. In preparing this edition of *Party Politics in America,* I have had the great privilege of building on the work of two remarkable scholars. A leading analyst of political parties, Frank Sorauf, originated this book, which was so influential in my learning about political parties and that of so many others, and sustained and strengthened it for two decades. Paul Allen Beck faced the challenge of moving this definitive work into the late 1980s and 1990s, and did so with the intellectual vision and the meticulous care that has marked his research on parties and voting.

The previous editions of this book by Sorauf and then Beck have long been known as the "gold standard" of books on political parties. They have been valued by instructors and students because they have, quite simply, provided the most comprehensive and definitive coverage of the field. From party history to the tripartite nature of the American parties, from conceptions of realignment to the fascinating details of campaign finance, these editions of *Party Politics in America* have been both an essential reference and an invitation to a generation of students.

The intent of the current edition has been to maintain the book's great strengths while making it shorter and even easier and more interesting for students to read. The writing has been streamlined without, I hope, sacrificing the book's conceptual strength and careful attention to detail. The additional years since the last edition have also made it possible for this edition to provide more perspective on the heralded "Republican revolution" of 1994 and to clarify the broader story of party change—realignment, dealignment, decline, revitalization—that has been a major focus of American political observers for so long. At the same time, this edition continues the comparative perspective on the American parties that the book has offered so effectively.

The ninth edition also makes extensive use of examples from the 2000 presidential primaries in chapters ranging from the nature of the nominating process to the nature of the two-party system. It features new information on campaign fund-raising practices and updates the discussion of congressional party leadership. Tables and figures, of course, have been extensively updated as have been many of the boxed features intended to draw students into particularly intriguing aspects of the parties. Finally, this edition includes a new section guiding students into the world of political parties on the Internet. In addition to the major parties' Web sites, this section introduces students to third parties ranging from the Greens to the Southern party as well as a variety of sites that offer valuable data on party politics and campaign finance; it provides an extensive list of suggested class assignments using these sites as well.

In addition to Sorauf and Beck, there are many other people whose contributions deserve public mention. I am grateful to my colleagues in the Department of Political Science at Indiana University, and especially to Bob Huckfeldt, Ted Carmines, John Williams, Leroy Rieselbach, Jerry Wright, Yvette Alex-Assensoh, Ken Bickers, and Pat Sellers. Members of the department's staff have been indispensable to my efforts: Margaret Anderson, Fern Bennett, Doris Burton, Scott Feickert, Steve Flinn, Loretta Heyen, Sharon LaRoche, Nancy Nicoll, Jan Peterson, and James Russell.

I owe so much to Gary Hetland, who has been a wonderfully efficient research assistant, and to all my students, graduate and undergraduate, for helping me understand the difference between the language of social science and that of normal people. It is an honor for me to recognize Austin Ranney, Murray Edelman, Leon Epstein, and Jack Dennis, who were most responsible for my interest in party politics and for the strength of the training I received in political science. Other colleagues and friends have also been among my best and favorite teachers: Bruce Oppenheimer, Gerry Pomper, Tony Broh, Jennifer Hochschild, Burdett Loomis, Richard Fenno, Jeffrey Berry, Ada Finifter, Anthony King, John Kingdon, Mike Kirn, Brian Silver, Jim Stimson, and Brian Vargus. And I appreciate the help of Walter Dean Burnham and Howard Scarrow.

I benefited from the reviewers of the most recent edition of the book: E. D. Dover of Western Oregon University; Richard Fox at Union College; John Hughes at Monmouth University; and James L. McDowell at Indiana State University. And it has been a pleasure to work with the people at Addison Wesley Longman and others, who endured a challenging production schedule to get the book into print: Editor Eric Stano, Kelly Villella, Ellen MacElree, and Scott Hitchcock and Gill Kent of Electronic Publishing Services Inc.

Most of all, I am deeply grateful to my family: my husband Howard, our daughters Katie, Lissa, and Lani, and Hong Hanh, our daughter in Vietnam. Anything I've ever accomplished has been due to their love and support.

MARJORIE RANDON HERSHEY
BLOOMINGTON, INDIANA
APRIL, 2000

Part 1

Parties and Party Systems

*I*f the writers of the American constitution were to return today for a look at the government they had designed, they would probably be stunned at its size and scope. Imagine James Madison's reaction to the news that federal and state governments were debating rules to govern taxes on the Internet or the ownership of frozen embryos created in an in vitro fertilization clinic. Government activity touches every part of our lives, from the level of bacteria allowed in our hamburgers to the nature of the airbags in our cars. Who makes these decisions? How can we hold them responsible if their decisions cause us harm? It is the political system that plays the crucial role in deciding, in Harold Lasswell's phrase, "who gets what, when, how."[1]

Because government decisions affect almost everything we do, large numbers of groups have mobilized to try to influence these decisions as well as the selection of the men and women who will make them. In a democracy, the political party is one of the oldest and most important of these groups. It has a great deal of competition, however. Organized interests such as the National Association of Realtors, the Environmental Defense Fund, and their fund-raising political action committees (PACs) also try to get their views adopted by government. So do pro-life and pro-choice groups, the Christian Coalition, and People for the Ethical Treatment of Animals. Even organizations whose main purpose is nonpolitical, such as universities, beer manufacturers, and teachers' unions, frequently try to influence government decisions that affect their livelihoods.

All these political organizations serve as *intermediaries* between individual citizens and the people in government who make these policy decisions (Figure I.1). By bringing together people who have shared interests, they amplify these people's voices in speaking to government. They raise issues that they want government to solve. They bring back information about what government is doing. In a very real sense, then, the parties and organized interests, along with television and the other media, are the links between citizens and political power.

These groups tend to specialize in certain political activities. Parties focus on nominating candidates, helping to elect them and organizing those who win. Most organized interests represent narrower groups; they are unlikely to win majorities so they try instead to influence the views of elected officials, administrators, and even

1

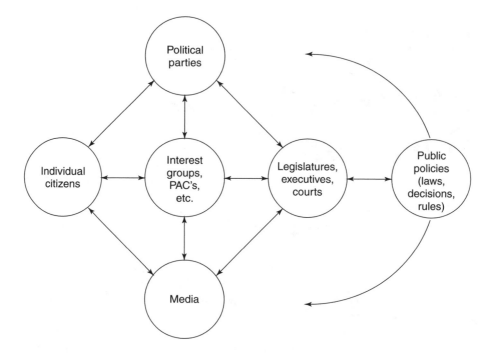

FIGURE I.1 Political organizations as intermediaries in the political system.

other organized interests. Still others work mainly to affect public opinion and media portrayals of an issue. Groups like these in other democracies may play different roles. The American parties, for example, are more preoccupied with election activities than are parties in Europe, which have been more committed to spreading ideologies and disciplining their legislators.

Intermediary groups are in constant competition as they fight to win political power. Parties, of course, compete with one another. They compete with powerful interest groups for the attention of legislators and for a dominant role in political campaigns; in fact, the American parties are not nearly as dominant in the business of campaigning as they were a century ago. They vie with one another for access to the scarce resources of money, expertise, and volunteer help and then, with those resources in hand, for the support of individual citizens and elected officials. Parties, in short, share a number of activities with other kinds of political groups and resemble these groups in some important ways.

They do so, however, in an environment full of very mixed feelings about their capabilities—and even about their very existence. On the one hand, many analysts have celebrated the American parties as the agents through which a democratic citizenry governs itself and even as the architects of a democratic government. They have been called "distinguishing marks" of modern government[2] and the guarantors of democracy in nations just beginning to make the transition to a democratic system.[3]

On the other hand, this heroic view of parties conflicts starkly with the antiparty sentiment that has existed since the nation began. James Madison and the other founders were very wary of organized factions in their new republic. About a century later, the Progressive movement—reformers intent on rooting out political corruption and returning power to middle-class people like themselves—targeted the entrenched political parties as the enemy to overcome. Disgust with party power in the 1960s and 1970s led to another series of party reforms that has helped to reshape current politics. Many Americans remain skeptical of the value of parties and may even see them as hazardous to a democracy's health.[4]

The hostile climate of public opinion has led, in turn, to a hostile climate of institutional rules. Faced with the challenge of adapting to these circumstances, the parties have responded over time with change in the form of their organization and the nature of their activities. Political parties as they existed a century ago can scarcely be found today, and the political parties we know today may not exist even twenty years from now.

The aim of this book is to explore the American parties: how they have developed, what they are, what they do, and what they are capable of contributing to a democratic politics. If many other organizations now perform several of the activities once regarded as the exclusive domain of the parties, are they really as central to the survival of a democratic system as many have assumed? To begin, let us examine the parties as they evolved in and adapted to the American political environment.

Chapter 1
....
In Search of the Political Parties

*T*ry to picture American politics without political parties. Many have found it an attractive thought; George Washington, for example, stated in his Farewell Address: "Let me warn you in the most solemn manner against the baneful effects of the spirit of party," which he considered the "worst enemy" of popular government. A lot of contemporary Americans agree; in survey after survey, many respondents say that they think of political parties with suspicion—like the cat at the bird feeder—when they think of them at all.

Imagine the next presidential campaign, then, as one in which Washington's message has been heeded. There will be no party organizations to run the primary elections and no party leaders to select or support the candidates. Would the process of selecting a president work better?

Of course, another way will have to be found to sort through the few hundred thousand presidential wanna-bes and select a very few to run in the general election. Without party primaries and caucuses, who would make that decision? Members of Congress? Not in a system designed to have separated powers. A convention of organized interests, including single-issue groups? A panel of judges selected by *People* magazine? The answer is not obvious, though it is obviously vital to our future.

Assuming that problem is solved, many other challenges remain. Strong party organizations help bring voters to the polls. Without any political parties, will voter turnout, already remarkably low in the United States, drop even further? Given the low levels of political interest, how will voters decide on a candidate if they do not have the guidance that party labels provide? Will they select a president based on extensive research into the candidates' stands on issues? Or will they choose based on the candidates' advertising, personalities, and appearance? When the new president takes office, how will he or she gain majority support for new programs from a Congress elected as individuals, with no party loyalties to link them?

What is this political organization that is so necessary and yet so distrusted? How can a party be distinguished from a temporary alliance of like-minded officials, an interest group, or a mass movement? What is included in the concept of party? Is it the politicians who share a party label in seeking and filling public offices? The activists who work in the headquarters and on the campaigns? The ordinary citizens who regularly vote for candidates bearing one party's label? Or is a party any grouping that chooses to call itself a party, whether Democratic or Boston Tea?

Political parties can be different things to different people, as the sample of alternative definitions in the following box illustrates. How they are defined matters for scholarly purposes, for it identifies the object of study and differentiates it from its environment. Because of the important role political parties have played in the workings of democracies, determining their essential features is more than an academic matter; it is a way of understanding what democracy requires and whether the politics we now practice is likely to protect or to undermine American democracy.

What is a Political Party? Some Alternative Definitions[1]

[A] party is a body of men united, for promoting by their joint endeavors the national interest, upon some particular principle in which they are all agreed.

Edmund Burke (1770)

In the broadest sense, a political party is a coalition of men seeking to control the governing apparatus by legal means. By coalition, we mean a group of individuals who have certain ends in common and cooperate with one another to achieve them. By governing apparatus, we mean the physical, legal, and institutional equipment which the government uses to carry out its specialized role in the division of labor. By legal means, we mean either duly constituted elections or legitimate influence.

Anthony Downs (1957)

[W]hat is meant by a political party [is] any group, however loosely organized, seeking to elect governmental office-holders under a given label. Having a label (which may or may not be on the ballot) rather than an organization is the crucial defining element.

Leon Epstein (1979)

[A] political party in the modern sense may be thought of as a relatively durable social formation which seeks offices or power in government, exhibits a structure or organization which links leaders at the centers of government to a significant popular following in the political arena and its local enclaves, and generates in-group perspectives or at least symbols of identification or loyalty.

William Nisbet Chambers (1967)

A fundamental difficulty in talking about political party is that the term is applied without discrimination to many types of groups and near-groups.... Within the body of voters as a whole, groups are formed of persons who regard themselves as party members.... In another sense the term party may refer to the group of more or less professional political workers.... At times party denotes groups within the government.... Often

(box continued)

> it refers to an entity which rolls into one the party-in-the-electorate, the professional political group, the party-in-the-legislature, and the party-in-the-government.... In truth, this all-encompassing usage has its legitimate applications for all the types of groups called party interact more or less closely and at times may be as one.
>
> *V. O. Key (1958)*
>
> Political parties can be seen as coalitions of elites to capture and use political office.... (But) a political party is ... more than a coalition. A major political party is an institutionalized coalition, one that has adopted rules, norms, and procedures.
>
> *John H. Aldrich (1995)*

TOWARD A TRIPARTITE DEFINITION OF PARTIES

These various views of party reduce easily to a few major themes. The ideological approach, seen in Edmund Burke's statement, envisions a party as a group of like-minded people who share a common set of values or stands on issues. This view has not enjoyed much favor among students of the American political parties. Parties in the United States have not been known for their ideological unity and coherence, at least in comparison with some traditional European parties, particularly those on the left. Defining parties solely as groups of ideologically like-minded people also makes it hard to distinguish parties from single-issue and splinter groups.

Most definitions of parties focus on other dimensions. Many scholars, such as Anthony Downs and Leon Epstein, see parties as teams of leaders unified in their effort to control government by winning elections and other means. Others, like William Nisbet Chambers and V. O. Key, Jr., prefer a broader definition that includes not only leaders and activists but also ordinary voters. These dimensions are important enough to the American party system to deserve fuller exploration.[2]

At a minimum, the major American parties include current or prospective office-holders who are willing to be identified together under the same label. Many parties in democratic nations, including the United States, were first formed as groups of political leaders who organized to promote certain programs. It is understandable, then, why some definitions of party center on elected leaders and their organized supporters.

But most observers see the American parties as broad-based organizations that go beyond candidates and officeholders. In some communities the parties have offices and phone listings, and virtually everywhere they have official standing under state law (see box on p. 8). Interested individuals can join them, work within them, become officers, and take part in setting their goals and strategies just as one would do in an Eagles Lodge or a Teamsters Union local. Some of these activists are even selected as the official representatives of the party under the statutory authority of the state. These activists and organizations are central parts of the party, too.

Many scholars are tempted to consider their definition complete at this point: to view the American parties as teams of political specialists actively involved in competing for and exercising political power. It is a common view among citizens as well, who may

What is Not a Political Party: West Virginia Law

Under West Virginia law, a party that receives at least 1 percent of the vote for governor has the right to place its nominees on the ballot in the subsequent statewide election. After a write-in candidate for governor received 7 percent of the vote in 1992, the political action committee that had organized her campaign declared itself the Mountaineer Party and claimed direct access to the 1994 ballot rather than having to gain it through a petition drive. The West Virginia Supreme Court ruled that this so-called party did not qualify for an automatic ballot position because it did not have a partylike organization prior to the 1992 election, had not presented itself as a party to the electorate in 1992, and did not include its 1992 candidate as a party member.

This incident is a reminder that the definition of a party is not only a matter for scholarly debate. Through their laws, the American states define what political parties are—and are not—and can thereby determine which groups will have the privileges generally accorded to official political parties, such as a listing on the ballot and access to public funding where it is available.[3]

prefer to see themselves as remaining on the outside of these not-so-beloved organizations. Further, it has allowed scholars to define parties in a neat, well-structured fashion and to analyze changes in the form they have taken over the course of American history.[4]

Limiting the definition of parties to political leaders, organizations, and activists has an attractive simplicity. Yet it ignores an important reality about political parties, especially in the United States. As intermediaries between government and the public, parties live among citizens as well as among activists. Many ordinary voters develop such strong and enduring attachments to a particular party that they are willing to make their commitment public by registering to vote as a Democrat or a Republican and continuing to support their chosen party's candidates. In a system where there are no requirements for formal membership in a party, such as paying dues, this is a strong measure of belonging. Moreover, when observers refer to a "Republican realignment" or a "Democratic state," they are envisioning the party as including voters as well as officeholders, office seekers, and activists.

The tradition of the reform-minded Progressive movement of the early 1990s, by instituting party registration and nomination through primary elections as regular practices, has strengthened the case for including a citizen base in a definition of American parties. Voters in party primaries in the United States are directly involved in what is probably the single most important party decision: selecting which candidates will run under the party label in elections. In other democratic nations, only a thin layer of party activists and leaders has the power to make this choice.

Because voters are involved directly in the nomination process, the line between leaders and followers that characterizes political parties in some other nations is blurred in the American setting. Thus voters as consumers not only choose among competing products (candidates) in the political marketplace but also assume the management responsibility to determine just what products will be introduced in the first place—an arrangement that would revolutionize market economies just as it has transformed political parties. This makes for a messier concept of political party, but a more realistic one for the American parties.

In short, the major American political parties are most accurately seen as having three interacting parts. These three are the *party organization,* which includes party leaders and the many activists who work for candidates and party causes; the *party in government,* comprising the men and women elected to office on the party's label, and the *party in the electorate,* or those citizens who loyally vote for the party's candidates (see Figure 1.1).[5] We will explore each of these parts of the parties separately, but it is important to keep in mind that much of the character of the American parties is defined by the ways in which they interact. This interaction pervades the American parties and is especially noticeable in the electoral process.[6]

The Party Organization

Party organizations include the formally chosen party leaders, the informally anointed ones, the legions of local ward and precinct workers, and the members and activists of the party—that is, the leaders and followers who give their time, money, and skills

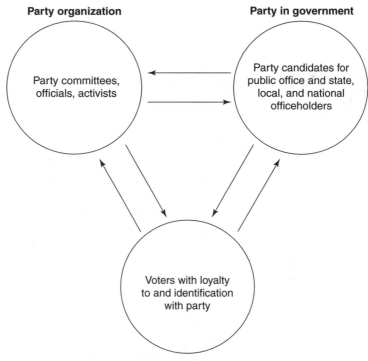

FIGURE 1.1 The three-part political party.

to the party. The organization operates in part through the formal machinery of committees and conventions set by the laws of the fifty states and in part through its own informal apparatus. Here we find the party bureaucracy, and also the face-to-face relationships that characterize any organization.

The Party in Government

The party in government is made up of people who have been elected to public office on that party's label. The major figures here are chief executives and legislators who share that party affiliation at the state and national level: presidents, governors, mayors, Congress members, and state legislators. The party organization may not be able to control or discipline them, but they do, in the broadest sense, speak for the party. Statements made by a president or the party's leader in Congress, for example, will get more attention than the pronouncements of the party's national chairperson.

Although the party organization and the party in government regularly work together to achieve their many common goals, the needs of particular officeholders may not always mesh with the party organization's aims. A member of Congress may seek a big victory to boost her presidential hopes, while the party's leaders and activists are trying to direct money and time to vulnerable party candidates in the hope of winning a majority in Congress. These tensions, when the party organization and the party in government compete for scarce resources in pursuit of somewhat different goals, demonstrate the need to treat them as separate parts of the party.

The Party in the Electorate

The party in the electorate is the least well defined of the three parts. It consists of the men and women who *see themselves* as Democrats or Republicans: those who feel some degree of loyalty to the party, who normally vote for its candidates in primaries and the general election, even if they have never set foot in the party's headquarters or dealt with its leaders and activists. Many of these *partisans* have declared themselves to be a Democrat or Republican when they registered to vote; more than half the states prescribe party registration. But many others comprise the party in the electorate even though they have not registered to vote under a party label.

These members of the electoral party are not under the control of the party organization; in fact, in nomination struggles, they may thumb their noses at the party organization's efforts. They can be seen as the regular consumers of the party's candidates and appeals. They may accept one candidate, reject another, and frustrate the party organization and party candidates with the fickleness of their affections. But they are vitally important because they are the core of the voting coalition necessary for effective power in American politics.

This relationship between the party organization and party in government, on the one hand, and the electoral party, on the other, is perhaps the most telling characteristic of the major American parties. Other political organizations, such as interest groups, try to attract supporters beyond their members and workers, but these supporters remain outside the political organization. That is not true of American parties.

The party in the electorate is more than an external group to be mobilized. State laws usually give it a voice in choosing the parties' candidates through the direct primary, and in many states it helps select local party officials such as ward and precinct committee leaders. So the major American party is an open, inclusive, semipublic, political organization

In their three-part structure, therefore, the major American parties include varied and even conflicting components. Each party is a reasonably clearly defined political organization with active, often disciplined participants. It is also an unorganized, public collection of partisans who may jeer some of their own party's candidates. The party encompasses a tremendous range of involvement and commitment. In its combination of organization and electorate, the American political party stands apart from other political organizations and from parties in other democracies.

A complicating reality of American politics is that each major party differs from state to state in the relationships among its three parts. The Republicans and the Democrats are so decentralized and so diverse that almost every state party has its own distinctive mix. In a few states, for instance, the party organization may dominate the party in government, whereas in others the reverse is the case. In some states the two parties in the electorate divide roughly along social-class lines, but in others they do not. The parties also differ from state to state in their openness with regard to nominating candidates for office. In some states, a voter can participate in a party's nomination process merely by voting for a candidate of that party on a ballot that includes candidates from both parties. In others, a voter must register with the party before election day in order to take part in that party's nomination of candidates. State parties are distinctive in many ways, not least in the form, makeup, and interrelationships among their three component parts.

THE PARTY AS A SET OF ACTIVITIES

What do political parties do? In varying degrees, the competitive political parties of every democracy perform three sets of activities: They select candidates and contest elections, they propagandize on behalf of a party ideology or program, and they try to influence elected officials to provide particular policy or patronage benefits.[7] Parties and party systems differ in the degree to which they emphasize these individual activities, but no party can completely ignore any of them.

Parties as Electors

Parties often seem to be completely absorbed by their efforts to elect candidates. Electoral activity so dominates the life of the American party that its metabolism follows almost exactly the cycles of the election calendar. Party activity reaches a peak at election time; between elections most parties go into hibernation. Parties are goal-oriented, and in American politics achieving one's goals ultimately depends on winning elections. The three parts of parties may sometimes differ in their specific goals, but they are brought together in their shared intention to elect party candidates.

Parties as Propagandizers

Second, the American parties carry on a series of loosely related activities that perhaps can best be called education or propagandizing. Some argue that the major American parties are allergic to ideology and perhaps even to a sincere commitment to specific ideas. Clearly, the Democrats and Republicans do not promote all-inclusive ideologies like those of a European Marxist party. They do, however, represent the interests and issue preferences of the groups that identify with and support them. In this sense, the Republicans and Democrats can be seen as the parties of business or labor, of the advantaged or the disadvantaged. Further, party differences have become clearer since the 1960s, even to the extent of approaching purer ideological differences. In presidential politics alone, the Goldwater conservatism of 1964, the McGovern liberalism of 1972, and the Reagan conservatism of the 1980s show how ideas can guide the major parties' political activities.

Parties as Governors

Almost all American national and state elected officials ran for office as either Democrats or Republicans. Not surprisingly, their partisan perspectives affect every aspect of the way government works. The legislatures of forty-nine states (the exception is nonpartisan Nebraska, but even there clear partisan ties are obvious to close observers and to many voters) and the United States Congress are organized along party lines, and the voting of their members shows considerable party discipline and cohesion. When legislatures face controversial issues, that party cohesion may break down. Yet in general, there is a surprising degree of party discipline. In executive branches, presidents and governors tend to appoint their copartisans as cabinet officers and agency heads, and count on their party loyalty to bind them to the executive's programs. Even the judicial branch cannot escape the organizing and directing touch of the parties, although in more subtle form.

These, then, are the main activities that the American parties, and democratic parties generally, set out consciously to perform. But the American parties do not have a monopoly on campaigning, propagandizing, or even taking part in governing. They compete regularly with interest groups, other political organizations, and even the media in all three areas. Although the American parties organize the legislatures, they battle constantly and often unsuccessfully against interest groups and constituency pressures for legislators' votes on major bills. In nominating candidates, especially at the local level, parties face tremendous competition from interest groups and powerful local personalities, who may each be sponsoring pet candidates. In promoting issues, the major parties are often overshadowed by the fervor of minor (third) parties, rafts of interest groups and other political groupings, individual public figures, and the media.

The nature of any party's activities affects the balance of power among the party's three parts. American parties' emphasis on election activities, for example, gives the party in government an unusual degree of power, even dominance. It can often leave the party organization in the shadows when competing for the attention of the party in the electorate. In parties more strongly linked to issues and ideologies—European parties, for instance—party organizations are more likely to be able to dictate to the legislative parties.

On the other hand, individuals from all three sectors of the party may come together for specific activities. Party organization activists committed to a particular elected official may join with other members of the party in government and with loyal party voters to return that official to office. When the election is won or lost, they will probably drift apart again. These groups of individuals from different parts of a party, drawn together to achieve a particular goal, are like the nuclei of the party.[8] They are small and informal task groups cutting across the differences in structure and goals that characterize the three party sectors. In American politics, alliances and coalitions are far more common within the parties than between them.

THE INDIRECT CONSEQUENCES
OF PARTY ACTIVITY

Behavior designed to reach a particular goal has indirect effects as well—and not all of these are intended. Congressional passage of a welfare reform bill, for example, might jump-start the formation of new welfare-rights groups in reaction to the changes. There is a long tradition in the study of the American parties of examining the indirect consequences of party activities. It produces rich insights into the parties' contributions to American politics yet it can be a frustrating enterprise, because it is much easier to examine a party activity than to prove which results or consequences it brings about.

Scholars of the American parties have noted a number of different consequences of party activity. Each of these indirect effects, or functions, as they are often called, contributes in important ways to the operation of American politics and the democratic process.[9] These are some of the most frequently mentioned consequences:

> Parties take part in the political socialization—political learning—of the American electorate by transmitting political values and information to large numbers of current and future voters. They preach the value of political commitment and activity. They simplify, and often oversimplify, the political world so that uninformed and not-very-well informed citizens can make more comprehensible choices. Voters can use attachment to the party as a perceptual screen, which can provide a key for assessing issues and candidates. By helping citizens form political judgments and make political choices, parties make it easier for people to be politically active.

> The American parties also help aggregate and organize political power. They put together masses of individuals and groups into blocs that are powerful enough to govern or to oppose those who govern. Thus, both within the individual and in the political world more broadly, political parties help to focus political loyalties on a small number of alternatives and then to accumulate support for them.

Because they devote so much effort to contesting elections, the parties dominate the recruitment of political leaders. Biographies of the members of any legislature, a cabinet, or even the courts will show how many of them entered public service through a political party or through partisan candidacy for office. Because the parties work at all levels of government from local to national, they may encourage the movement of leaders from one level to another. Further, because they are constants in the election process, parties help to make political change, and especially changes in government leadership, routine and orderly. This is in sharp contrast to the disruptive leadership changes that can occur in nations where the parties are not stable from one election to the next.

Finally, the American parties help unify a divided American political system. The United States government was designed to fragment political power, to make sure that no single group could gain enough of it to become a dictator. The division between the national government and the fifty states, multiplied by the threefold separation of powers in each, does an impressive job of fragmenting power. The challenge, of course, is to make it possible for these fragmented units to work together to solve problems. The two great national parties bring a unifying force into American politics. Their ability to do so has limits; for example, they often fail to link the president and the Congress together in causes that can bridge the separation of powers. The major parties, however, can provide a basis for cooperation in governmental institutions marked by decentralization and division.

THE SPECIAL CHARACTERISTICS OF POLITICAL PARTIES

The previous sections have discussed what political parties are and what they do.[10] Yet *all* political organizations, not just parties, exist to organize and mobilize their supporters either to capture public office or to influence the activities of those already in office. If the term *political party* is to have any meaning, it is important to determine what sets parties apart from other political organizations, especially the large national interest (or pressure) groups. The differences are sometimes subtle but they are important and interesting.

Commitment to Electoral Activity ...

Above all, a political party can be distinguished from other political organizations by its focus on contesting elections. Other political organizations may be involved in electoral politics, even extensively involved. Interest groups encourage candidates to run (and discourage others from running), support and contribute to them, and get their members to the polls on election day. Other nonparty groups may do the same. The parties, however, are preeminent among political groups in contesting elections. Their names and symbols are the ones the states recognize for inclusion on most ballots. Candidates are listed on the ballot as "Democrat" or "Republican," not as "Handgun Control, Inc." or "National Rifle Association."

... and to *Political* Activity

The major American parties and similar parties elsewhere are characterized by a full commitment to political activity. They operate solely as political organizations, as instruments of political action. Interest groups and most other political organizations, by contrast, move freely and frequently from political to nonpolitical activities and back again. The AFL-CIO, for example, seeks many of its goals outside the public political sphere, especially through collective bargaining. It may turn to political action to support sympathetic candidates or to lobby Congress when politics seems to be the best or only way to achieve its goals. Every organized group in the United States is a potential political organization. Still, interest groups almost always remain involved in some form of nonpolitical action as well. Parties live entirely in the political world.

Mobilization of Numbers

Because winning elections is so vital to the goals of parties, they must recruit an enormous range of supporters. An interest group whose goal is to influence a legislative committee or the rule-making in an administrative agency may succeed with a few strategists and the support of only a small, well-mobilized clientele. The political parties, to win elections, must be able to mobilize large numbers of citizens. Party appeals must be broad and inclusive; the party cannot afford to be exclusive or to represent only a narrow range of concerns. It is at the opposite pole from a "single-issue" group. The major political party has committed itself through its focus on electoral politics to mobilizing large numbers of citizens in large numbers of elections, and from that commitment flow many of its other characteristics.

Endurance

Political parties, at least in the United States, are also unusually stable and persistent. Personal cliques, factions, campaign organizations, and even many interest groups are fleeting by comparison. The size and the abstractness of the political parties, their relative independence from personalities, and their continuing symbolic strength for thousands of voters give them a far longer life. Both major American parties can trace their histories for much more than a century, and the major parties of other Western democracies have impressive, if shorter, life spans. This remarkable endurance adds to their value as political symbols. The parties are there as points of reference year after year, election after election, and candidate after candidate, giving continuity to the choices Americans face and the issues they debate.

Political Symbols

Finally, political parties differ from other political organizations by the extent to which they operate as symbols, or emotion-laden objects of loyalty. For millions of Americans, the party label is the chief cue for their decisions about candidates or issues. It is the point of reference that allows them to organize and simplify the buzzing confusion of political life. It shapes their perceptions and structures their choices; it relates their political values to the real options of American politics.

Resemblance to Other Organizations

Remember, however, that the differences between parties and other political organizations are differences of degree. Interest groups do become involved in elections, and the larger organized interests have achieved considerable stability and symbolic status. They can recruit candidates and give political cues to their members and friends. The unique American nominating process lets them play an important role in influencing the choice of party candidates. Interest groups also promote issue positions, try to influence officeholders, and (through their political action committees) give money to campaigns. They do not, however, and in most localities cannot, offer their names and symbols for candidates to use on the ballot.

Yet there are enough similarities that the major parties resemble some large organized interests, such as the Chamber of Commerce and the AFL-CIO, more closely than they do the minor or third parties. Most minor political parties are electoral organizations in name only. With the possible exception of the ever-changing Reform Party, the great majority of minor party candidates are in no danger of needing a victory speech on election night. Most minor parties do not have large numbers of local organizations. Their membership base, often dependent on a single issue, may be just as narrow as that of most interest groups. Even so, minor parties can appear on the ballot, and their candidates can receive public funding where it is available—assuming that they have qualified, typically by winning a certain number of votes in previous elections. In these ways (and sometimes *only* in these ways), they are more like the major parties than are the large interest groups.

THE EVOLUTION OF AMERICAN PARTIES

To see how the role and character of political parties have changed in relation to their environment, it is useful to look at their origins and evolution in the United States—the country credited with the development of the world's first parties. This history is one of a more than 200-year alliance with popular democracy. (For a summary of American party history, see the box "The American Major Parties" in Chapter 2.) The American parties grew up in response to the expansion of the adult suffrage and to all the changes it brought to American politics. It is also a history of change in the relative positions of the three different parts of the party, as first the party in government, then the party organizations, and then both the parties in government and in the electorate enjoyed their period of ascendancy.[11]

The Founding of American Parties

In the first years of the Republic, the vote was limited in almost every state to those free men who could meet property-holding or taxpaying requirements. Even these relatively small numbers of voters had limited power, as the writers of the Constitution intended. The president was to be chosen not directly by the voters but indirectly by the electoral college. Each state legislature was permitted to choose its own method of selecting that state's electors. Although election to the House of Representatives was entrusted to a direct popular vote, the Senate was not. Senators were to be chosen by the respective state legislatures. It was a cautious and limited beginning for democratic self-government.

In their first years, the organizations that were to become the American parties reflected this politics of a limited suffrage and indirect elections. They began as caucuses of like-minded members of Congress, concerned only with the political issues that preoccupied the nation's capital. These congressional caucuses nominated presidential candidates and mobilized groups of political figures to support or oppose the administration of the time. Gradually, during the 1790s, these factions began to take more enduring form as they struggled to keep their members focused on their collective purpose. The Federalists, as the dominant group came to be called, were organized around Alexander Hamilton and championed some degree of centralized control over the economy. The opposition, rallying around Thomas Jefferson and James Madison (see box below), wanted to protect the states' rights from national government

James Madison: Antiparty Theorist, Party Founder

James Madison, the fourth president of the United States and one of the most important framers of the American Constitution, was a paradoxical combination of theorist and activist when it came to political parties.

Writing in No. 10 of *The Federalist* to justify a new Constitution of which he was one of the prime architects, Madison railed against political parties in his famous warning against the "mischiefs of faction":

> Complaints are everywhere heard from our most considerate and virtuous citizens, equally the friends of public and private faith and of public and personal liberty, that our governments are too unstable, that the public good is disregarded in the conflicts of rival parties, and that measures are too often decided, not according to the rules of justice and the rights of the minor party, but by the superior force of an interested and overbearing majority.[12]

Just a few years later, locked in conflict with the administration over deep policy disagreements, however, Madison became a founder and key organizer of what some scholars have seen as the world's first political party, the Democratic-Republicans. He was the leader of the congressional opposition to the Washington administration in the early 1790s and especially to its guiding figure, Alexander Hamilton. After leaving Congress in mid-decade, he worked with his lifelong friend and ally, Thomas Jefferson, to organize the increasing opposition to the administration in the countryside. Their efforts met with extraordinary success—with Jefferson's presidential victory in 1800 and with the ensuing dominance of their Democratic-Republican party into the 1820s.

Madison probably would not have seen any contradiction between his thoughts and actions. In *The Federalist,* he justified the Constitution as necessary to contain the natural emergence of factions and to prevent them from undermining democracy. In founding the Democratic-Republicans, he was exercising his right to oppose the policies of one faction by organizing another.

interference. These nascent "parties" were dominated by their party in government at the national level.

Officeholders communicated with the voters at home in two ways. Party organization at the grass roots began as "committees of correspondence" between national and local leaders, and each side established a newspaper to propagandize on behalf of its cause. These were the first forms of outreach to the electorate. But the flow of communication was not wholly one-sided, from the Capitol to the grass roots. Organized popular protest against the Jay Treaty and other unpopular administration measures, as well as conflict within the various states, provided fertile ground for the development of parties on a national scale.

One of these incipient parties, the Democratic-Republicans (led by Jefferson), began to look more like a modern-style party by organizing efforts in the states and localities in time for the 1800 presidential elections. The more elitist Federalists failed to follow suit; the result was that they virtually disappeared in most states soon after the defeat of their last president, John Adams, in 1800. In short, the pressures for democratization were already powerful enough by the early 1800s to scuttle an infant party whose leaders in the government could not adapt to the need to organize a mass electorate, especially in the growing states of the frontier.[13]

The Democratic-Republicans, who were the party of agrarian interests and the frontier, quickly established their electoral superiority and enjoyed a one-party monopoly for twenty years. So thorough was their domination by the time of James Monroe's presidency that the absence of party and political conflict was called the "Era of Good Feelings." Despite the decline of one party and the rise of another, however, the nature of the parties did not change. It was a time when government and politics were the business of an elite of well-known, well-established men, and the parties reflected the politics of the time. In both of his successful races for the presidency (1816 and 1820), Monroe was the only nominee of the Democratic-Republican caucus in the Congress. The absence of party competition, moreover, made extensive grassroots organization unnecessary, thus stalling further development of the parties.

The nation's politics began to undergo sharp changes in the 1820s. By that decade, most states had eliminated the requirement that only landowners could vote, so the suffrage was extended to all white males, at least in state and federal elections. (Property qualifications lingered in local elections, in some places into the twentieth century, where revenues were raised from assessments on property.) The growing tide of democratization also made more public officials subject to popular election.[14]

The most obvious change in the 1820s, occurring so quickly at the national level that its evolution in the states is often obscured, was the emergence of the presidential election process that has lasted to this day. The framers of the Constitution had crafted a curious arrangement for selecting the president, known as the electoral college. Each state, in a manner chosen by its legislature, would choose a number of presidential electors equal to the size of its congressional delegation. These electors would meet in the state to cast their votes for president; the national winner was the candidate who received a majority of the states' electoral votes. If no candidate received a majority, the president was to be selected by the House of Representatives, with each state casting one vote.

By creating an electoral college, the Constitutional Convention was able to side-step some difficult and divisive questions about selecting a president. By leaving the choice of electors to the state legislatures, the convention avoided having to set uniform election methods and suffrage requirements, issues on which the framers were divided (and which involved, of course, the contentious matter of slavery). This also eliminated the need for federal intervention in a question where the states had previously made their own decisions, and which might have produced state opposition. Requiring electors to meet simultaneously in their respective states had the further virtue of preventing a cabal among electors from different states to put forward their own choice for president.

In the early years of the Republic, state legislatures adopted various methods for selecting presidential electors. A few states used popular elections from the beginning, even though voting rights were typically limited to property-owners or taxpayers. This number grew during the next three decades, although unevenly as partisan majorities within the state legislatures used the time-honored practice of manipulating election laws to their short-term advantage. Lame-duck Federalist legislatures were especially active around 1800 in turning to popular election to avoid the sure results of a transition in legislative control to the Democratic-Republicans. By the 1820s, popular election was most common, and after 1828 only in South Carolina were presidential electors selected by the state legislature.[15]

As the states moved toward popular election of presidential electors, the congressional caucus began to lose its power in the presidential selection process and its role as the predominant force within the parties. Growing enthusiasm for democratization led to increasing criticism of the practice of caucus nominations of presidential candidates, which came to be seen as the work of a narrow and self-perpetuating elite in the nation's capital.

The caucus system began to decline from its own infirmities as well. The Democratic-Republicans' attempt to nominate a presidential candidate in 1824 was a shambles. The chosen candidate of the caucus, William Crawford, ran fourth in the actual election, and because no candidate won a majority in the electoral college, it was left to the House of Representatives to choose among John Quincy Adams, Henry Clay, and Andrew Jackson. The House chose Adams over Jackson, the popular and electoral-vote front-runner in the election. When Jackson in turn defeated Adams in 1828, the nation entered a new phase of party politics.

The Emergence of a National Two-Party System

The nonparty politics of the Era of Good Feelings gave way to a two-party system that has prevailed ever since. The Democratic-Republicans had developed wings or factions, which chose divorce rather than reconciliation. Andrew Jackson led the frontier and agrarian wing of the Democratic-Republicans, the inheritors of the Jeffersonian tradition, into what is now thought of as the Democratic Party. The National Republicans, another faction of the old Democratic-Republicans who promoted Henry Clay for president in 1832, merged with the Whigs, and two-partyism in the United States was born.

Second, and just as important, the parties as political institutions began to change. The Jacksonian Democrats held the first national nominating convention in 1832 which, appropriately, nominated Jackson himself for a second term. (The Whigs and the smaller Anti-Masonic Party had both held more limited conventions a year before.) The campaign for the presidency also became more concerned with public outreach and less dominated by a national political leadership; new campaign organizations and tactics brought the contest to more and more people. As a consequence, Jackson came to the White House for a second term with a popular mandate as the leader of a national political party. Larger numbers of citizens were voting. The move to democratize parties and politics seemed irresistible.

In turn, party organization in the states expanded. Candidates for state and local office were increasingly nominated by conventions of state and local leaders rather than by the narrower caucuses. By the middle of the century, then, party organization was developing throughout the nation, and the party convention—a gathering of state and local party leaders held both in the states and nationally—had become an increasingly common way of picking party candidates. By 1840, the Whigs and the Democrats were established in the first truly national party system, and were competitive in all the states.

Modern political parties similar to those we know today—with their characteristic organizational structures, bases of loyal voters, and lasting alliances among governmental leaders—had thus arrived by the middle of the nineteenth century. The American parties were the first modern parties in Western history, and their arrival reflected, above all, the early expansion of the electorate in the United States. The comparable development of parties in Great Britain did not occur until the 1870s, after further extension of the adult male electorate in the Reform Acts of 1832 and 1867.[16]

The Golden Age of the Parties

Just as the parties were reaching their maturity, they and American politics received another massive infusion of voters from a new source: immigration from Europe. Hundreds of thousands of Europeans—the great majority from Ireland and Germany—immigrated to the United States before the Civil War. So many arrived, in fact, that their very appearance and their entry into American politics became a political issue. The newcomers found a ready home in the Democratic Party, and an anti-immigrant third party, the American Party (the so-called Know-Nothing Party), sprang up in response in the 1850s.

The tide of immigration was only temporarily halted by the Civil War. After the war ended, new nationalities came in a virtually uninterrupted flow from 1870 until Congress closed the door to mass immigration in the 1920s. More than five million arrived in the 1880s (equal to one tenth of the 1880 resident population), and ten million came between 1905 and 1914 (one eighth of the 1900 resident population).

The political parties played an important role in assimilating these huge waves of immigrants. They gravitated toward the American cities, where industrial jobs were available. It was in the cities that a new kind of party organization, the city "machine," developed in response to the immigrants' needs and vulnerabilities. The machines were impressively efficient organizations. They were also social-service systems that helped the new arrivals cope with a new country and with the problems of urban, industrial society. They softened the hard edge of poverty, they smoothed the way with government and the law, and they taught the immigrants the ways and customs of their new home. The political machines were often indistinguishable from the government of the city; they were the classic instance of "party government" in the American experience. They also were the vehicle by which the new urban working class won control of the cities away from the largely Anglo-Saxon, Protestant elites who had prevailed for so long. The parties again became an instrument of the hopes of new citizens, just as they had been in the 1830s. In doing so, they achieved their high point of power and influence in American history.

The American parties—with the party organization now their dominant part—reached their zenith, something of a "golden age," by the beginning of the twentieth century. Party organization now existed in all the states and localities; it positively flourished in the industrial cities. Parties achieved an all-time high in discipline in the Congress and in most state legislatures. They controlled campaigns for public office; they held rallies, canvassed door-to-door, and brought the voters to the polls. They controlled access to a lot of government jobs, ranging from street inspectors to members of the U.S. Senate. They were an important source of information and guidance for a largely uneducated and often illiterate electorate. They rode the crest of an extraordinarily vital American politics; the latter half of the nineteenth century featured the highest voter turnouts in the history of American presidential elections. The parties suited the needs and limitations of the new voters and the problems of creating majorities in the new and raw industrial society. If ever a time and a political organization were well matched, this was it.[17]

Parties after Their Golden Age

The drive to democratize American politics continued after the turn of the century. Women and blacks finally gained the right to vote, and the voting age was lowered to eighteen. With the adoption of the Seventeenth Amendment, U.S. senators came to be elected directly by the voters rather than by the state legislatures. Just as important for the parties, however, were changes that would be imposed on them in the name of egalitarianism and popular democracy.

The period that parties saw as their "golden age"—the height of their influence in American politics—did not seem so golden to groups of reformers. To them, party control of politics had led to rampant corruption and government inefficiency.[18] Fat, powerful, and even arrogant at the end of the nineteenth century, the parties fell under attack by Progressive reformers. The Progressives enacted the direct primary to give citizens a voice in party nominations, and large numbers of state legislatures wrote laws to define and limit party organizations. The business of nominating a president was made more open to the public by establishing presidential primaries in the states, and activists within the parties reformed their national conventions. In all, the Progressive reforms succeeded in wresting control of the parties from their professional organizations.

These reforms were shaped by the impulse to fix the problems of a democratic political system by further democratizing the system. Because party "bosses" and party power were seen by the Progressives as the culprit, the reforms were intended in part to lessen the power that the parties, and especially the party organizations, had achieved by the end of the 1800s. In that they succeeded; the parties would never regain the exalted position they had enjoyed in the three decades after the Civil War. So the expectations of the democratic ethos, which first shaped the parties by making them more public, more decentralized, and more active at the grass roots, later rendered the party organization increasingly incapable of playing the role it once played in American politics. The theme of the decline of the parties runs through many commentaries on the American parties, and it certainly will be addressed in this one.[19]

It would be too pat to conclude that these changes mark the next shift in power within the party, starting with the party in government, moving to the party organization during the golden age of the parties, and now to the party in the electorate. The Progressive reforms did give ordinary citizens new power in party affairs at the expense of the party organizations and their leaders. But in many cases, these citizens had little attachment to the party itself, making it difficult to view them as the party electorate. Further, the Progressive reforms also had the effect of freeing candidates for office from party control and, by weakening the party's campaign capabilities overall, made the party less relevant to them. Some would argue that this change strengthened the position of candidates relative to the party organization and perhaps even made them less vulnerable to popular control.

Not all reforms in traditional party practices have undermined the party organizations. Beginning many decades ago and reaching a peak in the 1960s, party rules for the selection of candidates, especially the presidency, have become more uniform across the nation. The Democratic Party, through its national committee and national convention, took the lead in this nationalization of party practices. At the same time, the Republicans were enhancing the capacity of their national party organization to support candidates throughout the country, an activity the Democrats soon tried to match. The result of these two nationalizing thrusts, one rules-based and the other organizational, was to strengthen the national party organizations at a time when state and particularly local organizations had grown weaker. Whether this new nationalization of the parties represents a basic change in their nature is not yet clear, but it has shifted the balance of organizational power from the grass roots to the party's national center.

Even with all these changes, the parties remain to a significant extent what they were eighty or a hundred years ago: the leading political organizations of mass, popular democracy. They developed and grew with the expansion of the suffrage and the popularizing of electoral politics. They were and remain the invention by which large numbers of voters come together to control the selection of their representatives. They rose to prominence at a time when a new electorate of limited knowledge and limited political sophistication needed the guidance of their symbols. So it was that the modern American political party was born and reached its time of glory in the nineteenth century. When one talks today of the decline of the parties, it is the standard of that golden age against which the decline is measured.

THE PARTY IN ITS ENVIRONMENT

This brief excursion into the parties' history is a reminder that forces in their environment shape both their form and their activities. Looking at the parties in isolation can be useful in focusing our attention, but it is clear that we cannot understand the American parties without examining the environmental pressures that affect them. The next section will consider the most influential and insistent of these environmental forces.

Electorates and Elections

As we have seen, the expansion of the right to vote shaped the very origin and development of the parties. Each new group of voters that enters the electorate challenges the parties to readjust their appeals. As they compete for the support of these new voters, the parties must reconsider their strategies for building coalitions that can win elections. Parties in states where black citizens had finally gained the right to vote, for example, learned to campaign differently from the days when they had to appeal to an all-white clientele.

The parties' fortunes are also bound up with the *nature* of American elections. The move from indirect to direct election of U.S. senators, for instance, transformed both the contesting of these elections and the parties that contested them. If the electoral college system is ever abolished and American presidents come to be chosen by direct popular vote, that change, too, would affect the parties.

A state's election machinery is, in effect, a form of extensive regulation of the parties' main political activity. Consider, for example, the change from parties' use of conventions to nominate state and congressional candidates to the use of the direct primary. This is a major addition to American election machinery and also an important regulation of the way a party selects its candidates, aimed by its Progressive originators at diminishing party power. Even the relatively minor differences in primary law from one state to another—such as differences in the form of the ballot or the time of the year in which the primary occurs —have effects on the parties. In short, the electoral institutions of the nation and the states set a matrix of rules within which the parties compete for votes.

The Political Institutions

Very little in the American political system escapes the influence of the two most prominent American institutional features: federalism and the separation of powers. At the national level and in the states, American legislators and executives are elected independently of one another, so it is possible, and in recent decades fairly frequent, for the legislature and the governor's or president's office to be controlled by different parties. Most other democracies, in contrast, have parliamentary systems in which the legislative majority chooses the officials of the executive branch from among its own members. When that parliamentary majority dissolves, its control of the executive ends, and a new government must be formed. An important result of this system is that American legislative parties can rarely achieve the degree of party discipline and cohesion that is common in parliamentary systems.

This separation between the American executive and the legislature also increases the conflict between executives and legislators of their own party. One reason is that the chief executive and the cabinet secretaries are not also legislative party leaders, as they are in a parliamentary system. Another is that legislative defiance of the executive on key party issues does not threaten to bring down the entire government and force new elections. Support for and opposition to executive programs has often cut across party lines in Congress and the state legislatures to a degree rarely found in parliamentary democracies.

The decentralization of American federalism, with its islands of state autonomy from national control, has also left an imprint on the American parties. It has instilled in them local political loyalties and generations of local political traditions. It has spawned an awesome range of public offices to fill, creating an electoral politics that dwarfs that of all other democracies in size and diversity. By permitting local rewards, local traditions, even local patronage systems, it has nurtured a large set of semi-independent local parties within the two national parties. The existence of these local centers of power has worked mightily against the development of strong, permanent, national party organs.

Statutory Regulation

No other parties among the world's democracies are as entangled in legal regulations as are the American parties. It was not always this way. Before the Progressive reforms a century ago, American parties were self-governing organizations, almost unrestrained by state or federal law. For most of the 1800s, for example, the parties printed, distributed, and often—with a wary eye on one another—even counted the ballots. The "Australian" (or secret) ballot reform changed all of this, vesting the responsibility for running elections in government, where it has remained ever since. As noted earlier, during their golden age, the parties nominated candidates for office using their own rules. The arrival of the direct primary around 1900 and recent reforms of the presidential nomination process, created by national party commissions but under state laws, have severely limited this autonomy. The parties even played an active role in hiring workers for government jobs, a practice that has largely disappeared due to waves of civil service reform and recent judicial intervention.

Both state and, to a still-limited degree, federal laws govern the parties today, producing an almost bewildering fifty-state variety of political parties. The forms of their organization are prescribed by the states in endless, often finicky detail. State laws set up elaborate layers of party committees and often chart the details of who will compose them, when they will meet, and what their agenda will be. State laws define the parties themselves, often by defining the right to place candidates on the ballot. Most states try to regulate party activities; many, for example, regulate party finances, and most place at least some limits on their campaign practices. In some states the parties have tried various strategies to evade the worst of these regulatory burdens. More recently, the federal government has added burdens of its own, regulating parties' campaign practices and finances, and outlawing certain state practices, especially involving primary and general elections.[20]

The Political Culture

It is much easier to detail the tangible aspects of the parties' environment, such as regulations and election systems, than it is to pin down so elusive a feature of the party environment as the political culture. A nation's political culture is the all-enveloping network of the political norms, values, and expectations of its people. It is, in other words, the people's view of what the political system is, what it should be, and what their place is in it.[21]

One of the most persistent components of the American political culture is the feeling that party politics is a compromising, underhanded, dirty business. Public opinion polls continue to provide evidence of that hostility toward partisan politics. A number of polls have found, for example, that American parents hope their children will not choose politics as their career. Politics as a vocation seems to rank slightly below used-car sales. Polls report that popular support for the parties is similarly low, even in comparison with other governing institutions such as Congress, the Supreme Court, or the president—none of which is venerated either. A 1998 survey demonstrated that enthusiasm for the two parties was so limited that when given a "feeling thermometer" ranging from 0 to 100 degrees on which to indicate their level of positive feeling, respondents could muster no more than an average rating of 55 for either the Democrats or the Republicans—a temperature that could best be termed chilly.[22]

Continuing suspicion of the parties is one element in a multifaceted political culture that helps shape the American parties. For example, the widespread view that legislators ought to vote in Congress on the basis of the interests of their local district certainly makes it harder to achieve party discipline in American legislatures. Even the question of what we regard as fair campaigning simply reflects the values and expectations of large numbers of Americans. Whether a strongly worded campaign ad is seen as "negative" or as hard-hitting and informative depends on cultural values, not on some set of universal standards. These cultural values affect citizens' feelings about the parties' behavior, and as a result they influence the behavior itself.

The Nonpolitical Environment

Parties' environment is broader than their *political* environment. Changes in levels of education in the United States, for example, affect the political culture, the skills of the electorate, and their levels of political information. The more educated Americans are, the more likely they are to pay attention to politics and to go to the polls on election day. On the other hand, if less-educated Americans tend to accept party loyalty more easily than do the better-educated, overall educational levels should make a difference in the electorate's dependence on political parties.

Perhaps no force has been more important for party politics than the emergence of the modern mass media, especially television and the Internet. Because the media can provide so much information about politics and candidates, voters need not depend on the parties to learn about elections and issues. Just as important, candidates can contact voters directly through the media, rather than having to depend on the parties to convey the message for them. The result has been to weaken party control over candidates' campaigns. To add insult to injury, media coverage tends not to place much emphasis on the parties themselves. Television attaches great importance to visual images, of course, so it is much more likely to cover individuals—candidates and public officials—than to cover institutions, such as parties, that do not have a "face."

Economic trends can also have a strong and often disruptive impact on the parties. When an economic recession occurs, for example, parties will find it harder to raise money, the patronage positions the party has to offer may become more attractive, and the positions the party takes on such questions as taxes, unemployment, and aid to the poor may need to be reevaluated. If the crisis is especially severe, as was the Great Depression of the 1930s, it may even fracture and reorganize the pattern of enduring party loyalties, end the careers of prominent party leaders, and make a majority party into an enfeebled minority.

This chapter began as a search for the nature of parties and their activities; it has concluded by looking at how they became what they are. It is important to understand what a political party is and what it does, and especially to understand its peculiar three-part nature: the party organization, the party in the electorate, and the party in government. The search for the parties, however, also requires a grasp of the environment in which they are set and by which they are shaped.

Chapter 2

The American Two-Party System

*M*ost nations' party systems have either one dominant political party or many parties competing for control of government. One-party systems have appeared in such diverse places as China, where the Communist Party continues to exercise undiluted control; the Soviet Union and Eastern Europe, which the Communist Party dominated until the 1990s; and Mexico, where the Partido Revolucionario Institucional's (or PRI) decades-long monopoly of elections has been seriously challenged only recently. By contrast, European democracies typically have multiparty systems in which three, four, or more parties compete with one another, often without any single party being able to win a majority of the votes.[1]

One-party and multiparty systems have been part of the American experience as well. Some states and cities have had a long tradition of one-party rule that, if not as total as that characterizing the old Soviet Union or China today, nonetheless rivals the single-party control enjoyed by Mexico's PRI. In other areas, at certain times several parties have flourished. Minor or third parties and independent candidates have played important roles in American politics, and they are increasingly important today. Several third-party or independent candidates have run for president in the last few decades. George C. Wallace came within thirty-two electoral votes of throwing the presidential race into the unpredictable hands of the House of Representatives in 1968. In 1980 John Anderson, running without any party label, won almost 6 million popular votes. Ross Perot's independent presidential bid in 1992 gained the support of almost 20 million Americans—and the third highest percentage of the popular vote for a candidate outside the major parties in history—and was transformed into a third party in 1996. Two years later, a former professional wrestler named Jesse "The Body" Ventura won the governorship of Minnesota as the candidate of Perot's Reform Party.

These campaigns are colorful enough to capture a lot of media attention; not many governors are nicknamed "The Body," or have worn a pink feather boa into a public arena. For better or for worse, however, they are rare. For most of American history, most elections have been contested by two parties, and only two parties. Even the rapid rise of the Republican Party from its founding in 1854 to become one of two major parties two years later, displacing the Whig Party in the process, is the exception that proves the rule. First Democrat versus Whig and then, since 1856, Democrat versus Republican, the United States has had a two-party system in national party competition.

Classifying party systems as one-party, two-party, and multiparty can be limiting. Because it focuses simply on counting the number of parties that compete in elections, this classification overlooks the ways in which minor parties can compete ideologically with the major parties, even if they cannot actually elect candidates. It draws attention to the size of the party's electorate rather than to differences among party organizations, and it ignores the full range of competition among all kinds of political groups. Yet it is a classification that is deeply ingrained in both everyday use and scholarly literature in spite of its limitations. So as we explore the roots of the two-party system, keep in mind that this classification scheme oversimplifies a more complex political reality.[2]

THE NATIONAL PARTY SYSTEM

The American party system has been essentially a two-party system for more than 160 years. That is a remarkable fact; since the 1830s, almost all partisan political conflict in the United States has been channeled through two major political parties. They rise and fall, they establish areas of strength, they suffer local setbacks and weaknesses, but they endure. Perhaps even more remarkable is that it is so hard to find another democracy in which two parties have dominated a nation's politics so thoroughly for so long.

Note that this two-party dominance did not exist consistently before 1836 (see box on p. 29). The American party system was unstable until that time. As Chapter 1 showed, the Federalists established a short period of superiority during the presidency of George Washington but failed to organize at the state and local level and quickly faded. Their rivals, the Democratic-Republicans, were left with no competition for a time, producing the one-party (or nonparty) politics of James Monroe's presidential terms. As the Washington-centered caucus method of nominations crumbled in the 1820s, however, new national parties appeared, and by 1836 a stable two-party system had emerged. One party, the Democrats, has kept its place in the party system ever since that time. The other party, the Whigs, survived until the 1850s and was replaced almost immediately by the infant Republican Party. Both the Democratic and the Republican parties were briefly divided along sectional lines by the events of the Civil War, but the old party labels have survived to this day.

Thus the two-party drama is long, but its cast of major characters is short. Minor parties have briefly pushed themselves into electoral competition but have not yet been able to sustain themselves at a major-party level over several elections. The Democratic and Republican parties also have changed, of course, in their issues and appeals and in the coalitions of voters that they assemble. Nevertheless, the Democratic and Republican parties have together made up the American two-party system for the great majority of American history.

The two major parties have been very close competitors during this time, at least at the national level. Of the thirty-three presidential elections from 1868 through 1996, only six were decided by a popular vote spread of more than 20 percent between the two major parties. In other words, in twenty-seven of these presidential elections, a shift of 10 percent of the vote or less would have given the other party's candidate the lead. No president during this time has ever received more than the 61 percent of the popular vote that Lyndon Johnson won in 1964.[3] Fourteen of these thirty-three presidential elections were decided by a spread of less than 7 percent of the popular vote.

The American Major Parties

The list of the American major parties is short and select. In over two hundred years of history, only five political parties have achieved a competitive position in American national politics, and one of these five does not fully qualify as a party. Three lost this status; the Democrats and Republicans maintain it to this day.

1. **The Federalist Party, 1788–1816.** The champion of the new Constitution and strong national government, it was the first American political institution to resemble a political party, although it failed to fulfill all of the conditions of a full-fledged party. Its strength was rooted in the Northeast and the Atlantic Seaboard, where it attracted the support of merchants, landowners, and established families of wealth and status. Limited by its narrow electoral base, it quickly fell before the success of the Democratic-Republicans.

2. **The Democratic-Republican Party, 1800–1832.** Opposed to the extreme nationalism of the Federalists, although many of its leaders had been strong proponents of the Constitution, it was a party of the small farmers, workers, and less-privileged citizens who preferred the authority of the states. Like its leader, Thomas Jefferson, it shared many of the ideals of the French Revolution, especially the extension of the suffrage and the notion of direct popular self-government.

3. **The Democratic Party, 1832–Present.** Growing out of the Jacksonian wing of the Democratic-Republicans, it was initially Andrew Jackson's party and the first really broad-based, popular party in the United States. On behalf of a coalition of less-privileged voters, it opposed such commercial goals as national banking and high tariffs; it also welcomed the new immigrants and opposed nativist (anti-immigrant) sentiment.

4. **The Whig Party, 1836–1854.** This party, too, had roots in the old Jeffersonian party—in the Clay-Adams faction and in enmity to the Jacksonians. Opposed to the strong presidency of Jackson, its greatest leaders, Henry Clay and Daniel Webster, were embodiments of legislative supremacy. For its short life, the Whig Party was an unstable coalition of many interests, among them nativism, property, and the new business and commerce.

5. **The Republican Party, 1854–Present.** Born as the Civil War approached, this was the party of Northern opposition to slavery and its spread to the new territories. Therefore it was also the party of the Union, the North, Lincoln, the freeing of slaves, victory in the Civil War, and the imposition of Reconstruction. From the Whigs it also inherited a concern for business, mercantile, and propertied interests.

Some of the closest presidential contests in American history have taken place in the last forty years (1960, 1968, 1976).

Elections to Congress have been even closer. If we turn to percentages of the two-party vote for ease of comparison, we see that the total vote cast for all Democratic candidates for the House of Representatives in a given election is not markedly different from the total vote for Republican candidates; the two parties have stayed roughly in balance for almost seventy years (Table 2.1). In House elections from 1932 through 1998, there has never been a difference greater than 17 percentage points

TABLE 2.1 Percentage of Two-Party Vote Won by Republican Candidates and Spread in Percentage of Total Votes, for President and House of Representatives: 1932–98

Year	Presidential Elections		House Elections	
	% Republican of Two-party Vote	% Republican Minus % Democratic of Total Vote	% Republican of Two-party Vote	% Republican Minus % Democratic of Total Vote
1932	40.8	−17.8	43.1	−13.1
1934			43.8	−11.9
1936	37.5	−24.3	41.5	−16.2
1938			49.2	−1.6
1940	45.0	−9.9	47.0	−5.7
1942			52.3	4.5
1944	46.2	−7.5	48.3	−3.4
1946			54.7	9.3
1948	47.7	−4.4	46.8	−6.4
1950			49.9	0
1952	55.4	10.7	50.1	−.4
1954			47.5	−5.5
1956	57.8	15.4	49.0	−2.4
1958			43.9	−12.8
1960	49.9	−.2	45.0	−8.8
1962			47.4	−4.9
1964	38.7	−22.6	42.5	−15.3
1966			48.7	−2.7
1968	50.4	.7	49.1	−1.7
1970			45.6	−8.3
1972	61.8	23.2	47.3	−5.3
1974			43.0	−17.0
1976	48.9	−2.1	42.8	−14.1
1978			45.6	−8.7
1980	55.3	9.7	48.7	−2.4
1982			43.8	−12.7
1984	59.2	18.2	47.2	−5.1
1986			44.9	−9.9
1988	53.9	7.8	46.0	−7.8
1990			46.0	−7.9
1992	46.5	−5.6	47.3	−5.2
1994			52.4	4.7
1996	45.3	−8.4	50.1	.3
1998			50.4	.8

Sources: Presidential data in 1932 from the *Statistical Abstract of the United States: 1992.* Congressional data for 1932 through 1992 and presidential data for 1936 through 1992 calculated from Harold Stanley and Richard G. Niemi, *Vital Statistics on American Politics* (Washington, DC: CQ Press, 1994), Tables 3-13 (President) and 3-17 (House). Remaining data are from *Congressional Quarterly Weekly Report*—for 1994: December 3, 1994, p. 3460; for 1996, President: November 9, 1996, p. 3190; for 1996, House: November 23, 1996, p. 3319. House election data for 1998 computed from the Federal Election Commission Web page: www.fec.gov/pubrec/fe98/pghchart.htm

between the two parties' overall votes; in twenty-six of the thirty-four elections, the spread was less than 10 percent. Further, in all but five of these elections, the difference between the two parties' percentage of the major party congressional votes was smaller than the difference between their presidential candidates' votes.

The closeness and persistence of party competition in national politics is apparent, then, in even the quickest survey of recent electoral history. Even more impressive is the resilience of the major parties. Although one party has gained great advantage from time to time, in the long run the other party has been able to restore the balance. The Democrats recovered quickly from their failures of the 1920s and regained the White House after their electoral reversals in the 1980s. By the same token, the GOP (or Grand Old Party, a nickname that developed for the Republican Party in the late 1800s) confounded the pessimists by springing back from the Roosevelt victories of the 1930s, landslide defeat in 1964, and the Watergate-related setbacks of the mid-1970s.

The overall national pattern of party victories and defeats is an important part of the story of the American two-party system. After all, the struggle for the presidency every four years is the one occasion on which we actually do have national parties and a national party system. On the other hand, these national trends may hide varying levels of party competition at the state and local levels. The degree to which voters can count on two competitive parties in state and local elections is an important issue in the party system.

THE FIFTY AMERICAN PARTY SYSTEMS

The closeness of presidential elections and the aggregate vote for the House of Representatives have often been the result of a great deal of one-party dominance below the national level. It was not until 1964, for example—176 years after the Republic formed—that Georgia cast its first electoral votes ever for a Republican presidential candidate and Vermont voted Democratic for the first time since the Civil War. And when we look at individual congressional races, we find that large numbers of candidates win election to the House of Representatives with at least 60 percent of the total vote. In 1998, for example, almost three quarters of the winning House candidates got at least 60 percent of the vote, and a full ninety-five of these candidates were elected without any major-party opposition.[4]

To develop a good measure of the varying degrees of competitiveness of the fifty state party systems, however, several practical problems must be resolved. First, which offices should be counted to determine a state's level of party competition: the vote for president, governor, senator, statewide officials, state legislators, or some combination of these? The competitiveness of a state's U.S. Senate seats may be strikingly different from that of its state legislative races. Second, should we count the candidates' vote totals and percentages, or simply the number of offices each party wins? Do we regard a party that averages 45 percent of the vote but never wins office any differently from one that averages around the 25 percent mark but occasionally elects a candidate?

The Ranney Index

The most familiar approach to measuring interparty competition below the national level is an index originated by Austin Ranney.[5] The Ranney index is an average of three indicators of party success during a particular time period: the percentage of the popular vote for the parties' gubernatorial candidates, the percentage of seats held by the parties in each house of the legislature, and the length of time plus the percentage of the time the parties held both the governorship and a majority in the state legislature. The resulting scores range from 1.00 (complete Democratic success) through 0.50 (Democratic and Republican parity) to 0.00 (complete Republican success).

Like any other summary measure, the Ranney index oversimplifies and sometimes distorts the nature of competition. One reason is that it is based wholly on state elections. This protects the measure from being distorted by landslide victories and other unusual events at the national level. Yet those national events may foreshadow what will occur in voting for state offices. In the South, for example, growing GOP strength appeared first in competition for national offices and only later worked its way down to the state and local level. In these states, the Ranney index has shown less interparty competition than really exists. A second problem is that the dividing lines between categories are purely arbitrary. There is no magic threshold that separates the category "competitive" from that of "one-party." Finally, any index score will vary, of course, depending upon the years on which it is calculated and the offices it covers. Nevertheless, snapshots of a particular time can provide helpful description, even if they cannot capture fully a dynamic reality.

Table 2.2 presents the calculations for the Ranney index through the 1998 elections. It shows much more balanced party competition at the state level than had appeared in Ranney index compilations for earlier years in the period since World War II. Note especially that no states are classified as fully one-party. The main change has been the development of two-party competition in the Southern states, which used to be one-party Democratic, and a parallel movement of formerly one-party Republican states to competitive status. Some regional patterns can still be seen; most states of the Mountain West, for example, remain largely Republican. In fact, these most recent Ranney scores show a shift toward Republican success in the states more generally, with the tipping point coming at the time of the 1994 elections. The result, however, seems to be greater interparty competition throughout the fifty states than has existed before.[6]

The differences in two-party competition from state to state can help provide explanations as to how competition develops and is sustained. Not so long ago, the states with the most competition were those with a more educated citizenry, stronger local party organizations, and larger and more urbanized populations. As the states have become more similar in their degree of interparty competition, the social and political differences between the more and less competitive states surely have narrowed as well.[7]

Competitiveness and Candidate Security

If you were a candidate for elective office, what would these findings about party competition in the states say about your likelihood of winning? For much of the history of the United States, especially throughout the nineteenth century, a candidate's chances of winning depended on what party he or she represented. Candidates of the dominant party in one-party areas were virtually assured of victory. In more competitive areas, candidates' fates were tied to the national or statewide forces that affected their parties. Even though American candidates have been better able to insulate themselves

TABLE 2.2 The Fifty States Classified According to Degree of Interparty Competition: 1995–98

One-Party Democratic (none)	Florida (.487)
Modified One-Party Democratic	Connecticut (.486)
	Maine (.464)
Hawaii (.775)	South Carolina (.461)
Arkansas (.774)	New York (.461)
Maryland (.720)	Indiana (.448)
West Virginia (.689)	Colorado (.425)
Rhode Island (.688)	Oregon (.413)
Georgia (.681)	Alaska (.374)
Louisiana (.680)	Iowa (.371)
Kentucky (.672)	Michigan (.369)
Missouri (.665)	Wisconsin (.364)
Two-Party	Illinois (.363)
Vermont (.648)	*Modified One-Party Republican*
Massachusetts (.634)	Pennsylvania (.325)
Alabama (.629)	New Jersey (.307)
Mississippi (.625)	New Hampshire (.304)
Oklahoma (.579)	Arizona (.298)
New Mexico (.578)	Utah (.290)
Delaware (.572)	South Dakota (.287)
Tennessee (.566)	Kansas (.264)
North Carolina (.562)	Ohio (.261)
Minnesota (.540)	North Dakota (.245)
Virginia (.536)	Wyoming (.242)
California (.532)	Montana (.225)
Nevada (.516)	Idaho (.199)
Texas (.507)	*One-Party Republican (none)*
perfect competition (.500)	
Washington (.493)	

Source: John F. Bibby and Thomas M. Holbrook, "Parties and Elections," in Virginia Gray, Russell L. Hanson and Herbert Jacob, eds., *Politics in the American States, Seventh Edition* (Washington, DC: CQ Press, 1999).

from their party's misfortunes than have candidates in many other democracies, during the nineteenth century many American constituencies could easily turn to the other party as the political winds changed. The result was considerable party turnover in seats and insecurity for many candidates.

Candidates for office in the twentieth century, particularly in the years since World War II, have had greater electoral security, mainly because incumbency has become so valuable a political resource. Between 1954 and 1992, the average success rates for incumbents seeking reelection were 93 percent in the House of Representatives and 82 percent in the Senate. These rates peaked in 1988 for the House when 99 percent of a historically high 409 incumbents were reelected, and in 1990 for the Senate when thirty of thirty-one senators running for reelection won. Incumbents in most state legislatures enjoyed similarly high rates of success. Researchers do not have definitive answers as to why incumbency came to be such a valuable resource in running for office. Incumbents certainly benefit from the "perks" of congressional office, their name recognition and the attention they receive from the media, the services they can provide to constituents, their relative ease in raising campaign money, and their experience in having run previous successful campaigns. No matter what the reason, it is clear that incumbency has provided great electoral security during this period, even though interparty competition was increasing.

Incumbency was not quite the valuable electoral resource in the early 1990s that it had been just a few years before. In 1990, the aggregate popular vote for incumbent House members dropped below the percentages won in the 1980s, even though most incumbents were still reelected at a rate that most challengers would have given their right arm to achieve. The elections of 1992 and 1994 were even less favorable to incumbents. Because of redistricting, special incentives for retirement, especially strong challengers, and a prevailing mood of anti-incumbency, fewer incumbents sought reelection to the House of Representatives in 1992 than at any time since 1954. Those who did met with a success rate of 88 percent in the primaries and general election, which, although still impressive, was the lowest since the post-Watergate election in 1974. More House incumbents sought reelection in 1994, but "only" 91 percent were reelected in both the primaries and general election. (Note, however, that all of the losing candidates were Democrats, suggesting that party considerations overrode incumbency.) The reelection rate returned to 94 percent in '96 and 98 percent in '98.[8] Yet these high rates of reelection can overstate the security of running as an incumbent. Many losing incumbents had been accustomed to winning their districts comfortably in previous years, leading their colleagues to wonder whether incumbents really enjoyed the kind of long-term security that their rates of return to office would suggest.[9]

THE CAUSES AND CONDITIONS OF TWO-PARTYISM

One of the most interesting puzzles in understanding American politics is this one: Why have we had a two-party system for so long, when most other democracies do not? Scholars have offered several different explanations for this uniquely American system.

Institutional Theories

By far the most widespread explanation of the two-party system, often called Duverger's law, ties it to the effects of American electoral and governmental institutions.[10] It argues that single-member districts with plurality elections tend to produce two-party systems. Plurality election in a single-member district means simply that one candidate is elected to each office, and that the winner is the person who receives the largest number of votes, even if it is not a majority. There are no rewards for parties or candidates that run second, third, or fourth. The American election system is, for most offices, a single-member district system with plurality election; it offers the reward of winning office only to the single candidate who gets the most votes and, so the theory goes, thus discourages the minority parties.[11]

A corollary of Duverger's law is that multimember constituencies and proportional representation result in multiparty systems. A system with multimember constituencies means that a particular legislative district will be represented by, say, four elected legislators. Each party prepares a slate of candidates for these positions, and the number of party candidates who win is proportional to the overall percentage of the vote won by the party slate (see box below).

Plurality versus Proportional Representation: How it Works in Practice

One way to examine the difference between plurality and proportional representation (PR) rules for electing candidates is to look for an election in which both rules are used. In American politics, the best places to look are presidential primaries, in which party voters select delegates to the national parties' nominating conventions. The Democrats use proportional representation in selecting delegates (with at least 15 percent of the vote needed to elect one delegate) and the Republicans generally use plurality election (also called winner-take-all).

Consider a congressional district that can elect four delegates to the convention, in which candidates A, B, C, and D get the following percentages of the vote. The candidates would win the following numbers of delegates, depending on whether the plurality or PR rule was used:

		Delegates Won	
	% of vote	PR	Plurality
Candidate A	40%	2	4
Candidate B	30%	1	0
Candidate C	20%	1	0
Candidate D	10%	0	0

It is clear that the plurality rule boosts the delegate strength of the leading candidate at the expense of all other candidates. The second-place candidate wins nothing but will still probably compete for the office because he or she has a chance of overtaking the victor. Under PR rules, three candidates win delegates in rough proportion to their popular support. In the 1992 presidential nomination contests, to cite a real-life example, winning about 20 percent of the popular vote won Jerry Brown more than 600 delegates under the Democrats' PR rules, but got Republican Pat Buchanan fewer than one hundred delegates under the Republicans' plurality rules. (There was no contest in the Democratic Party in 1996.) We can see an even sharper contrast between PR and plurality election rules by comparing single-member district elections in the United States and Britain with the multimember district systems of most European legislative elections. The use of PR in the European elections promotes multiparty politics and coalition governments in which two or more different parties often share control of the executive. In the British parliamentary system, by contrast, single-member districts operating under plurality rules typically produce a parliamentary majority for one party, giving it sole control of the executive, even if it fails to win a majority of the popular vote.

Many institutional theorists also argue that the importance of the single executive office in the American system strengthens the tendencies toward two-party politics. The American presidency and the state governorships are the main prizes of American politics and they are indivisible offices that go only to a single party. Minor parties rarely have a chance to compete effectively for president or governor. That they can be won with a plurality rather than a majority[12] further advantages the strongest contenders at the expense of the weaker ones. In contrast, the governing "cabinet" in a parliamentary system, which is the system used by many other democracies, is made up of a number of officeholders. Thus it may be formed by a coalition that includes representatives of several parties, including minority parties. In fact, even the main prize of chief executive in the cabinet can go to a small party if it provided the crucial votes to produce the majority. (Giovanni Spadolini, the premier of Italy in the early 1980s, came from a party that held less than 3 percent of the parliamentary seats.)

In a system with a single executive office, like the American, then, local or regional parties, even those that may elect candidates in their own bailiwicks, will typically find it unrealistic to compete for the office of the national executive. The result is to deny a minor party a number of other important opportunities as well. Without a presidential candidate, it is unlikely to gain the national attention that major parties get and to establish the national spokespersons who increasingly dominate the politics of democracies. Some minor parties, of course, may try for the presidency anyway. In fact, in recent years there have been some minor parties—the Reform Party in 1996, for example—whose primary focus has been the presidential race. Its candidate, however—Ross Perot, a billionaire who was willing to spend tens of millions on his campaign—is clearly not typical of most minor parties, as much as they may dream of such an opportunity.

Political scientist Leon Epstein identifies a third often neglected institutional factor that has prevented the development of third parties in areas of single-party dominance during the twentieth century—the direct primary.[13] By offering dissident groups an opportunity to compete for nominations within the dominant party, the direct primary keeps them from forming a third party. Thus in the one-party Democratic South or the one-party Republican Wisconsin of an earlier era, where traditional animosities kept most voters from supporting the other major party, factional disputes that under other conditions would have led to third-party development were contained within the dominant party by the existence of a direct primary. Similarly, the movement that developed around Ross Perot could be absorbed by a major party if Perot chose to seek that major party's nomination for president.

Dualist Theories

Some theorists argue that a basic duality of interest in American society has sustained the two-party system. V. O. Key suggested that the initial tension between the Eastern financial and commercial interests and the Western frontiersmen stamped itself on the parties as they were forming, and fostered two-party competition. Later, the dualism shifted to the North-South conflict over the issue of slavery and the Civil War and then to urban-rural and socioeconomic divisions. A related line of argument points to a natural dualism within democratic institutions: government versus opposition, those favoring and opposing the status quo, and even the ideological dualism of liberal and conservative. So, the argument goes, social and economic interests or the very processes of a democratic politics tend to reduce the contestants to two great camps, and that dualism gives rise to two political parties.[14]

We can see tendencies toward dualism even in multiparty systems, in that the constructing of governmental coalitions clearly separates the parties that make up the government from those that remain in opposition. In France and Italy, for example, the Socialists and other parties of the left or the various parties of the right and center often compete against one another in elections but then come together along largely ideological lines to contest runoff elections or to form a government. What distinguishes two-party from multiparty systems, in short, may be whether this basic tendency toward dualism is expressed in every aspect of the electoral process or only in the creation and functioning of a government.

The two major American parties play an important role in protecting a two-party system. Their openness to new groups and their adaptability to changing conditions—qualities rare among democratic parties—undermine the development of strong third parties. Just when a third party rides the crest of a new issue to the point where it can challenge the two-party monopoly, one or both of the major parties is likely to absorb the new movement. The experience of the Populists and the Progressives is a good example, as is the reaction of some Perot followers after the 1996 election. As discussed earlier, such absorption has become even more likely in the twentieth century as the direct primary has come to be the main method for selecting party candidates. When disgruntled groups have the opportunity to make their voices heard within one of the major parties and may even succeed in getting a candidate nominated in a primary, the resulting taste of power will probably discourage them from breaking away to pursue a third-party course.

Social Consensus Theories

Finally, the American two-party system has been explained in terms of the existence of a broad American social consensus. Even given their highly diverse social and cultural heritage, Americans early reached a consensus on the fundamentals that divide other societies. Almost all Americans have traditionally accepted the prevailing social, economic, and political institutions. They accepted the Constitution and its governmental structure, a regulated but free enterprise economy, and (perhaps to a lesser extent) American patterns of social class and status.

In traditional multiparty countries such as France and Italy, large chunks of public opinion have favored radical changes in those and other basic institutions. They have supported fundamental constitutional change, the socialization of the economy, or the disestablishment of the national church. Perhaps American politics escaped these divisions on fundamental matters because Americans did not have a history of the rigid class structure of feudalism. Perhaps the early expansion of the right to vote made it unnecessary for workers and other economically disadvantaged citizens to organize in order to gain some political power. Or perhaps it was the expanding economic and geographic frontiers that allowed Americans to concentrate on claiming a piece of a growing pie rather than on battling one another. Because the matters that divide Americans are secondary, so the argument goes, the compromises needed to bring them into one of two major parties are easier to make.[15]

How can we assess these explanations that have been offered for the existence of two-party politics in the U.S.? Are the factors they propose really causes of the two-party system, or are they effects of it? The chances are that they are, at least in part, effects. Certainly, two major parties will choose and maintain election systems (such as single-member districts) that do not offer easy entry to minor parties. Through their control of Congress and state legislatures, the Democrats and Republicans have made it difficult for third parties to qualify for the ballot or for third-party candidates to receive public funding when it is available. The major parties do what they can to move public opinion into their dual channels. The two-party system will also create and perpetuate the political attitudes that justify itself. It will even encourage some measure of social consensus by denying opportunities to movements that challenge this consensus.

Yet these effects of the two-party system can also be seen as causes to some degree. Clearly the most important cause is the institutional arrangement of American electoral politics. Without single-member districts, plurality elections, and an indivisible executive, it would have been much easier for third parties to break the near-monopoly enjoyed by the two major parties. The other Anglo-American democracies such as Britain and Canada, which share the American institutional arrangements, also tend to be dominated by two parties—though third parties are not quite as hobbled in these systems as in the American party system.

The other forces, especially the long-run American consensus on fundamental beliefs and its resulting lack of deep ideological splits, have contributed to the development of the American two-party system as well. Once the two-party system was launched, its very existence fostered the values of moderation, compromise, and pragmatism that helped keep it going. It also created deep loyalties within the American public to one party or the other and attachments to the two-party system itself.

DEVIATIONS FROM TWO-PARTYISM

As we have seen, the American two-party system can harbor pockets of one-party politics within some states and localities. There have been other deviations from the two-party pattern. Some areas have experienced a uniquely American brand of no-party politics, and third parties or independent candidates have occasionally made their presence felt, most recently in the 2000 presidential campaign. Any exploration of the nature of the American party system is incomplete without discussing these deviations from the predominant two-party mode.

Nonpartisan Elections

One of the crowning achievements of the Progressive movement was to restrict the role of parties in elections by removing party labels from many ballots, mostly in local elections. Roughly three quarters of American towns and cities conduct their local elections on a nonpartisan basis. One state, Nebraska, elects state legislators on a nonpartisan ballot, and many states elect judges in this manner.

Yet even removing party labels from the ballot has probably not removed partisan influences where parties are already strong. The nonpartisan ballot did not prevent the development of a powerful political party machine in Chicago. A resourceful party organization can still select its candidates and work in elections where party labels are not on the ballot, even though it must obviously try much harder to let voters know which are the party's candidates. Nonpartisanship, though, has contributed to the erosion of local party strength.

It is not easy to assess the effects of nonpartisanship because it has typically been adopted in areas and at times when partisanship has already been weakened. The reform was most likely to take root in cities and towns with weak parties and for offices, such as judgeships and school boards, where the traditional American aversion to party politics is most pronounced. Most Northeastern cities, where strong party machines were the most visible targets of the Progressives, by contrast were able to resist the reforms and retain partisan local elections to this day.

Beyond removing the party label from ballots, what are the effects of nonpartisanship? The traditional view among political scientists was that a move to nonpartisan elections shifts the balance of power in a pro-Republican direction rather than making politics any less partisan or more high-minded. Without party labels on the ballot, the voter is more dependent on other cues. Higher-status candidates tend to have more resources and visibility in the community, which can fill the void left by the absence of party. In current American politics, these higher-status candidates are more likely to be Republicans.[16] On the other hand, a study of council races in cities across the nation has challenged this conventional wisdom by showing that the GOP advantage disappears once the partisan nature of the city is taken into account.[17]

Pockets of One-Party Monopoly

Vestiges of one-party politics remain to this day in some states and localities. In the past, the states of the Deep South were the country's most celebrated area of one-party domination, but the same could be said of the rocklike Republicanism of Maine, New Hampshire, and Vermont. Today, scattered throughout the country are thousands of one-party cities, towns, and counties in which the city hall or county courthouse is virtually the property of one party.

Pockets of one-partyism in a nation with two competitive parties often seem to be linked with an unusual distribution of the voter characteristics that typically divide the parties. Since the 1930s, the major parties, especially in national elections, have divided the American electorate roughly along socioeconomic lines—income, education, and job status. A local constituency may be too small to contain the wide range of socioeconomic status (SES) characteristics that leads to competitive politics. Thus we can find "safe" and noncompetitive Democratic congressional districts in the older, less affluent, or black neighborhoods of large cities and "safe" Republican districts in the wealthier suburbs. In other words, the less diverse are its people, the more likely the district is to foster one-party politics.

Alternatively, there may be some local basis of party loyalty so powerful that it overrides the relationship between SES and partisanship. In the classic one-party politics of the American South, regional loyalties long overrode the factors that were dividing Americans into two parties in most of the rest of the country. Reaction to the Republicans as the party of abolition, Lincoln, the Civil War, and the hated Reconstruction was so intensely negative, even generations after the fact, that it overwhelmed the impact of socioeconomic differences. Competitiveness may also reflect the influences of community leaders, local traditions, or local political conflict, such as that between a dominant industry and its disgruntled employees.

Once one party has established dominance in an area, it can be very hard for the weaker party to overcome its disadvantages. These disadvantages begin with stubborn party loyalties. Voters are not easily moved from their attachments to a party, even though the reasons for the original attachment have long passed. Also, a party trying to become competitive may find itself caught in a vicious circle. Its inability to win elections limits its ability to raise money and recruit attractive candidates, because as a chronic loser it offers so little chance of achieving political goals. It may even find itself without an effective appeal to the electorate. The Republican Party in the South, for example, found for many years that the Democrats had recruited the region's most promising politicians and had preempted its most powerful appeals.

Today, the would-be competitive party finds disadvantage taking another form: its local appeals are limited by voters' perceptions of its national political stance. If the Democratic Party is identified nationally with the hopes of the poor and minority groups, its appeal in an affluent suburb may be limited. So a nationalized politics may increasingly rob the local party organization of the chance to develop strength based on its own issues, personalities, and traditions. To the extent that party loyalties grow out of national politics, as many Democrats in the South have learned in recent years, competitiveness may be beyond the reach of some local party organizations.

As if this were not enough, the weaker party faces other hurdles in its struggle to become competitive. At the beginning of each decade, state legislatures must redraw legislative district boundaries, as the Supreme Court required in the 1960s, to keep the districts roughly equal in population. The Court halted the decades-old practice of malapportioning those districts to protect or improve the chances of majority party candidates. But majority parties have been ingenious in finding ways to draw districts that preserve their advantage. This is why parties are especially concerned with winning state legislative majorities in the years when district lines must be redrawn. In the past, Southern Democrats were able to stifle competition by maintaining election laws that kept blacks and poor whites from voting. In addition to these institutional forces that can entrench one-party politics, the normal processes of social conformity can make it very hard for the weaker party to improve its standing in closely knit, socially sensitive communities.

The Third Parties

Two-partyism is occasionally challenged from the other side—by the emergence of a new party or a particularly attractive independent candidate. During most of American history, these challenges have come from other parties, understandably dubbed "third" or, referring to their impact, "minor" parties. The appearance of "independent" candidates running alone without any party label is a more recent challenge to two-party politics; it will be considered separately below.

Except for the rapid movement of the Republicans from third-party to major-party status between their founding in 1854 and the 1856 presidential election, third-party challenges have been short-lived, and the attention they have received exaggerates their electoral impact. Only seven minor parties in all of American history have carried so much as a single state in a presidential election, and only one (the Progressive Party) has done so twice (see box below). No minor party has come close to winning the presidency. Theodore Roosevelt and the Progressives in 1912 were the only minor-party candidacy ever to run ahead of one of the major-party candidates in either electoral or popular votes.

The Big Little Parties

There have been hundreds of minor parties in American politics. Which have been the strongest? If we choose as a test of strength the ability to carry just *one* state in a presidential election, only eight minor parties in American history qualify:

1. **Anti-Masonic Party, 1832:** seven electoral votes; 8 percent of the popular vote. A party opposed to the alleged secret political influence of the Masons; later part of an anti-Jackson coalition that formed the Whig party.

2. **American (Know-Nothing) Party, 1856:** eight electoral votes; 22 percent of the popular vote. A nativist party, often in alliance with the fading Whigs, opposed to open immigration and in favor of electing native-born Americans to public office.

3. **Constitutional Union Party, 1860:** thirty-nine electoral votes; 13 percent of the popular vote. The Southern remnant of the former Whig Party, organized to deny Lincoln and the Republicans an electoral college victory and dedicated to preserving the Union by preventing the abolition of slavery.

4. **People's (Populist) Party, 1892:** twenty-two electoral votes; 8 percent of the popular vote. An outgrowth of a movement of agrarian protest opposed to the economic power of bankers, railroads, and fuel industries and in favor of a graduated income tax, government regulation, and currency reform (especially free silver coinage).

5. **Progressive (Bull Moose) Party, 1912:** eighty-eight electoral votes; 27 percent of the popular vote. An offshoot of the Republican Party organized around the candidacy of former Republican President Theodore Roosevelt, it favored liberal reforms such as expanded suffrage, improved working conditions, conservation of resources, and antimonopoly laws.

6. **Progressive Party, 1924:** thirteen electoral votes; 17 percent of the popular vote. A continuation of the 1912 Progressive tradition with the candidacy of Robert La Follette, who had been one of its founders and leaders.

7. **States Rights Democratic (Dixiecrat) Party, 1948:** thirty-nine electoral votes; 2 percent of the popular vote. A Southern splinter of the Democratic Party, it ran as the Democratic Party in some Southern states on a conservative, segregationist platform.

8. **American Independent Party, 1968:** forty-six electoral votes; 14 percent of the popular vote. The party of George Wallace; traditionalist, segregationist, and opposed to the authority of the national government.

If we adopt a more stringent measure, the ability to draw at least 10 percent of the popular vote for president, only six minor parties qualify: numbers 2, 3, 5, 6, and 8 above plus the Free Soil candidacy of Martin Van Buren in 1848.

At the state level, the best examples of third-party power existed in the states of the upper Midwest. In the 1930s and 1940s, remnants of the Progressive movement—the Progressive Party in Wisconsin, the Farmer-Labor Party in Minnesota, and the Non-Partisan League in North Dakota—competed with some success against the major parties. But in these and a few other similar cases, multiparty competition lasted only briefly and ended with a return to two-party politics. Even the independent candidacy of Ross Perot in 1992 did not lead to multiparty competition at the state level in that year. Although he polled between 9 and 30 percent of the popular vote across the fifty states, he ran alone. Perot's Reform Party ran eight U.S. Senate and twenty-five U.S. House candidates in the 1996 elections, but none of them were elected.

In short, between the peaks of third-party influence are the long valleys. In most presidential elections, minor parties have received barely noticeable shares of the popular vote. The combined minor-party vote for president, excluding votes for independent candidates, was only slightly more than 600,000 in 1992, or about 0.6 percent of the total popular vote (Table 2.3). In 1996 this total jumped to 9.6 million, or 10 percent, but slightly more than 8 million of those votes (8.4 percent) were for Ross Perot as the Reform Party candidate. Even including Perot's votes, these are not figures likely to give much hope to third-party candidacies.

Third-party successes can also be found below the presidential level but they are as rare as they are captivating. For every example of third-party victory in local elections, there are thousands of races with no minor-party challenge. Of more than a thousand governors elected since 1875, fewer than twenty ran solely on a third-party ticket, and another handful ran as independents.[18] Jesse Ventura's successful candidacy in Minnesota in 1998 received enormous media attention precisely because it was so unusual.

TABLE 2.3 Popular Votes Cast for Minor Parties in 1992 and 1996 Presidential Elections

1992		1996	
Parties	*Vote*	*Parties*	*Vote*
Libertarian	291,628	Reform	8,085,402
Populist	107,002	Green	685,128
New Alliance	73,708	Libertarian	485,798
U.S. Taxpayers	43,398	U.S. Taxpayers	184,820
Natural Law	39,163	Natural Law	113,670
Socialist Workers	23,091	Workers World	29,083
Grassroots	3,875	Peace and Freedom	25,332
Socialist	3,064	Socialist Workers	8,476
Workers League	3,050	Others and Scattered	23,806
Others and Scattered	17,042		
Total	605,021	Total	9,641,515

Note: In 1988 and in 1992 there were six independent candidates including Ross Perot. Their totals (25,530 for LaRouche in 1988; 19,741,048 for Perot, and 61,356 for the others in 1992) and those for write-in candidates are not included in this table.

Sources: Federal Election Commission, *Federal Elections '92* (Washington, D.C.: Federal Election Commission, 1993), pp. 15–32; and FEC data on the 1996 election from http://www.fec.gov/pubrec/summ.htm.

Third-party candidates have been more successful in running for Congress, but in only seven election years have they won more than ten seats, and the most recent of those elections was in 1936. In all, the Democratic and Republican parties have monopolized American electoral politics even more fully at the state and local level than at the national level.

We use the term *third party* to designate all minor parties in the two-party system, but it would be a mistake to treat them as indistinguishable. They differ in origin, purpose, and activities. Their variety is as plain as a look at their labels: Socialist Workers, Green Party, Libertarian.[19]

Differences in Scope of Ideological Commitment   Although most minor parties are parties of ideology and issue, they differ in the scope of that commitment. The narrow, highly specific commitment of such parties as the Prohibition, Vegetarian, and Right to Life parties is apparent in their names. At the other extremes are those with the broadest ideological commitments: the Marxist parties and the recent profusion of conservative parties. One leading minor party in recent years, the Libertarian Party, for example, advocates a complete withdrawal of government from most of its present programs and responsibilities.[20] In the middle ground between specific issues and total ideologies, the examples are infinitely varied. The farmer-labor parties of economic protest—the Greenback and Populist parties—ran on an extensive program of government regulation of the economy and social welfare legislation. The U.S. Taxpayers Party (now the Constitution Party) in 2000 argues for less government regulation, lower taxes, and state and local control.

Difference of Origins   The minor parties differ, too, in their origin. Some were literally imported into the United States. Much of the early Socialist Party strength in the United States came from the freethinkers and radicals who fled Europe after the failed revolutions of 1848. Socialist strength in cities such as Milwaukee, New York, and Cincinnati reflected the concentrations of liberal German immigrants there. Other parties, especially the Granger and Populist parties and their successors, were homegrown channels of social protest, born of social inequality and economic hardship in the marginal farmlands of America.

Some minor parties began as splinters or factions of one of the major parties. For example, so great were the objections of the Progressives (the Bull Moose Party) of 1912 and the Dixiecrats of 1948 to the platforms and candidates of their parent parties that they ran their own slates and presented their own programs in presidential elections. In fact, the Dixiecrats, an anti-civil-rights faction within the Democratic Party, substituted their own candidate for the one chosen by the party's national convention as the official Democratic presidential candidate in the state. The same sentiment resulted in George Wallace's presence on the 1968 Alabama ballot as the Democratic candidate for president, in place of the national party's chosen candidate.

Differing Tactics   Finally, third parties differ in their tactics. For some, their mere existence is a protest against what they believe is the lack of choice provided by the major parties. They use their status as a party to try to educate citizens about their issues. The publicity value of the ballot is useful, and with it often comes media attention the party could not otherwise hope for. Indeed, many of these parties have freely accepted their election losses because they have chosen not to compromise their ideological principles for electoral success. The Prohibition Party, for example, has run candidates in presidential elections since 1872 with unflagging devotion to the cause of temperance, but without apparent concern for the fact that its highest proportion of the popular vote was 2 percent, and that came in 1892.

Some minor parties do have serious electoral ambitions. Often their goal is local, although today they find it difficult to control an American city, as the Socialists once did, or an entire state, like the Progressives. More realistically, they may hope to hold a balance of power in the presidential election between the major parties, as was the goal of the Dixiecrats of 1948 and George C. Wallace's American Independent Party of 1968. Both parties hoped that by carrying a number of states, most likely Southern states, they might prevent the major party tickets from winning the necessary majority of electoral college votes, thus throwing the stalemated election into the House of Representatives. Ross Perot even claimed to be looking for an outright victory in both 1992 and 1996.

The Question of Impact   Their variety is endless, but what have minor parties contributed to American politics? For better or for worse, they have influenced, perhaps even altered, the courses of a few presidential elections. By threatening about once a generation to deadlock the electoral college, they have probably kept alive movements to reform it. Beyond their role as potential electoral spoiler, however, can they count any significant accomplishments?

Some argue that minor parties deserve the credit for a number of public policies— programs that were first suggested by a minor party and then adopted by a major party when they reached the threshold of political acceptability. The proponents of this argument point to Socialist Party platforms that advocated such measures as a minimum wage for twenty or thirty years before the minimum wage law was enacted in the 1930s. Did the Democratic Party steal the Socialist Party's idea, or would it have proposed a minimum wage for workers even if there had been no Socialist Party? There is no way to be sure. The evidence suggests, however, that the major parties grasp new programs and proposals in their "time of ripeness," when large numbers of Americans have accepted the idea and it is thus politically useful for the major party to do so. But the major party might have picked up the new proposal from any of a number of groups: not only minor parties, but also interest groups, the media, influential public figures, or major-party factions. More than one commentator has noted that the cause of prohibition in the United States was served far more effectively by interest groups such as the Anti-Saloon League than by the Prohibition Party.

If the impact of third parties is so limited, then what attracts some voters to them? Note that there are few such voters; the self-fulfilling prophecy that a vote for a third party is a wasted vote is very powerful in American politics.[21] Yet some voters do cast third-party ballots. To Steven Rosenstone and his colleagues, who have investigated third-party presidential voting from 1840 to 1980, this results from the failure of major parties "to do what the electorate expects of them—reflect the issue preferences of voters, manage the economy, select attractive and acceptable candidates, and build voter loyalty to the parties and the political system."[22]

Continued dissatisfaction with the major parties has certainly provided an opening for a formidable third party. When this occurs, however, the normal workings of the American electoral system make it likely that the "third" party will displace one of the major parties (as the Republicans did with the Whigs) or be absorbed by changes in one of the major parties (as happened with the Democrats in 1896 and 1936). So alternatives to the two major parties tend to develop and expand only when the major parties are failing.

The Rise of Independent Candidates

In recent years, dissatisfaction with the two major parties has been vented in a new way—in support for candidates running as independents rather than on third-party tickets. The independent campaign of John Anderson in 1980 drew more than 5.7 million votes; he polled four times the votes of the minor parties combined and almost 7 percent of the popular vote nationwide. The independent candidacy of Ross Perot in 1992 received a larger share of the popular vote than any "third" candidate in history who was not a former president. With 19.7 million popular votes, Perot also outdrew the combined total of all of his third-party opponents in that race—by more than19 million ballots. Perot failed to win a single state, however, and much of his support seemed to come from voters who were more dissatisfied with Bush and Clinton than they were drawn into an enduring commitment to another party or candidate.[23]

Some third-party candidates have seemed more like independent candidates, in that they have run more as individuals than as leaders of an organized political party. George Wallace's American Independent Party in 1968 was dedicated to his own ambitions and had little more than the degree of organization required by the states for a place on the ballot. When Wallace sought the Democratic presidential nomination in 1972, the American Independent Party faded into the shadows. Similarly, Lowell Weicker won the governorship of Connecticut in 1990 as the candidate of A Connecticut Party, but he proved unable to build it into an organization capable of sustaining itself in later elections.

The common denominator in all these efforts is that they were vehicles for a single candidate; they did not try to run candidates for other offices or build a party organization. In this important way, independent candidates differ from earlier third-party movements, including the Republicans, the Populists several decades later, and the Progressive campaigns early in the twentieth century—all of which were aimed at creating a new major party. These recent independent (rather than truly third-party) presidential bids may signal a change in the very nature of third-party politics.

Because of its record success in the 1990s and its continuing presence, the Perot movement deserves special attention. In 1992, it achieved a degree of organization that other independent candidacies and even minor parties have lacked. Through his organizational efforts, Perot got on the ballot in all fifty states and mounted an active campaign throughout the nation. The key ingredient in the Perot challenge, however, was money— the millions of dollars from his own personal fortune that Perot was willing to invest in his quest for the presidency. This money financed the organizational efforts at the grass roots and, more important, purchased large blocks of expensive television time for the candidate's widely viewed "infomercials."[24] No other minor party or independent candidate for president in at least a century has achieved Perot's national visibility.

The Perot movement has remained a major force in American presidential politics, but in varying forms. Its first organizational expression, United We Stand America, grew to the point of having paid executive directors in all fifty states, elected state chairs, elected leaders in many of the nation's congressional districts, and dues-paying members across the nation. As a nonprofit educational organization, United We

Stand did not endorse or field candidates in the 1994 midterm elections, although Perot did urge his followers to vote against Democrats for Congress. By 1996 Perot forces sought to qualify for the ballot as a third party—the Reform Party. But as its presidential candidate, Perot was not able to match his 1992 showing. And following the election, some Reform activists sought new leadership. The 2000 presidential campaign began with the Reform Party entertaining the candidacies of former Republican Pat Buchanan, Governor Jesse Ventura, and real estate developer/celebrity Donald Trump, among others, and with an anti-Perot splinter party, the *American* Reform Party, planning its own presidential candidate. These contests did little to enhance the party's ideological clarity. Nevertheless, with so many Americans willing to consider supporting candidates outside the mainstream of the major parties, independent candidacies, in particular, should become more and more prominent.

WHITHER THE AMERICAN TWO-PARTY SYSTEM?

This look at two-party politics and its alternatives leads us to some conflicting conclusions about the future of the two-party system. In important respects, two-party dominance seems to be increasing. The competition between the Democrats and the Republicans, both nationally and within the states, is more spirited than it has been in decades. Below the presidential level, one-party politics and third-party successes seem to be less common.

Yet recent developments threaten the two-party dominance. Voter loyalties to the two major parties and support for the two-party system have declined in recent decades, providing an opening to independent candidates and contributing to greater volatility in election results. The barriers to ballot access for minor-party and independent candidates, once so formidable, have been lowered in recent years to make it even easier for alternatives to emerge. What will be the result?

The Decline of Minor Parties and the Rise of Independents

The record is clear: even with Ross Perot's bankroll, third parties are not gaining ground. Third-party members of Congress, common in the early decades of the two-party system, were rare throughout the twentieth century, and especially in recent years (Figure 2.1). Since 1952, only one member of Congress has been elected on a third-party ticket— James Buckley in 1971 as a Conservative Party senator from New York, and he aligned himself with the Republicans after taking office. (One other, Bernard Sanders of Vermont, has served in the 1980s and 1990s as an independent member of the House of Representatives, but he caucuses with the Democrats.) Minor-party candidates have also fared poorly in state legislative contests during this period, and local enclaves of minor-party strength have been reduced to a small though colorful handful.

As minor-party strength has declined, independent candidates have become more successful. The presence of independents was responsible for major-party candidates receiving the lowest percentage of the 1992 congressional vote since the 1930s, although this percentage remained in the high 90s.[25] In presidential politics, independents Anderson and Perot, not minor-party candidates, have mounted the most effective challenges to the major-party candidates in recent years. Several major figures (Perot and Anderson among them) considered running for president as independents

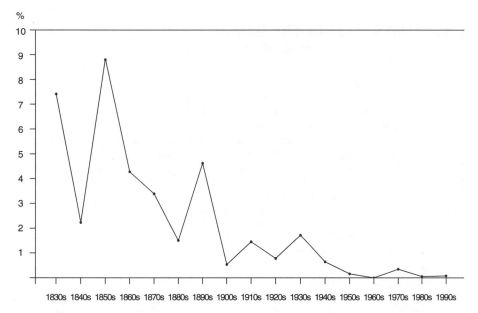

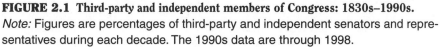

FIGURE 2.1 **Third-party and independent members of Congress: 1830s–1990s.**
Note: Figures are percentages of third-party and independent senators and representatives during each decade. The 1990s data are through 1998.

in 2000. There is probably no better gauge of the candidate-centered nature of recent American politics than voters' recent preferences for independents rather than minor-party candidates when they are inclined to deviate from a major-party vote.

It is ironic that although third parties have battled so long to overcome legal barriers to listing their candidates on the ballot, recent reductions in these barriers have benefited independent candidates to a greater extent than third parties. In many states, third-party and independent candidates have traditionally had to gather thousands of signatures just to earn a place on the ballot (see box on p. 48). A minor-party or independent presidential candidate must still satisfy a patchwork of different state requirements to qualify for the ballot nationwide, but the process has been eased by court decisions. Even so, the electoral process remains far less open to minor-party or independent candidates than to those of the major parties, who automatically qualify for the ballot.[26]

The financial hurdles faced by third-party and independent candidates are also coming down. The Wallace campaign astounded experts by raising and spending $7 million in 1968, then the largest sum ever spent by a minor-party campaign in American history. His achievement demonstrated that a nationwide third-party campaign could attract substantial financial backing, just as Perot's showed the advantages of great personal wealth. Public funding of presidential campaigns adds another possibility for funding by opening the public treasury to candidates outside the major-party mainstream. John Anderson was the first "outside" candidate to receive such federal financing. By polling more than 5 percent of the popular vote as an independent, he qualified for more than $4 million in public funds. This money was dispersed to him

Gaining Access to The Ballot:
A Tale of Four Candidates

George Wallace, 1968
George Wallace had to devote considerable resources to gaining a position on the ballot in his presidential bid in 1968. In most states, his supporters organized the petition drives necessary to gain the required number of signatures. In Ohio, where the difficulties in gaining ballot access were particularly great, he took his battle to the courts. To gain a place on the ballot under Ohio law, Wallace would have needed 433,000 signatures very early in his campaign. He sued instead. The Ohio law had been passed, the state argued in its defense, for legitimate purposes: to preserve the two-party system and to make sure small pluralities would not win elections. By a vote of six to three, the Court disagreed. It ruled that the Ohio law violated the equal protection clause of the Fourteenth Amendment in restricting the rights of voting and association of supporters of minor parties.[27]

John Anderson, 1980
A substantial part of John Anderson's independent campaign for the presidency in 1980 involved extensive efforts to gain a position on each of fifty state ballots. Petitions with large numbers of signatures were required in most states, and formal legal action was necessary in at least ten. The Anderson campaign in many states was built around the drive to gain access to the ballot in the hope that these activities would gain attention and help to create a strong organization. Unfortunately, the ballot access campaign spent $2.5 million and left little money for candidate advertising in the general election. Anderson also faced a second hurdle. Some states imposed early filing deadlines on nonparty, independent candidates. Ohio was one of them, and Anderson took the state to court. The issue was finally resolved in Anderson's favor in 1983, three years after the election, when the Supreme Court ruled that Ohio and other states could not discriminate against independent candidates seeking a place on the presidential ballot by imposing early deadlines.[28]

H. Ross Perot, 1992
The Perot independent candidacy for president benefited from the gains made in ballot access by previous independent and minor-party candidates. It still faced a difficult task when Perot declared to the Federal Election Commission that he was interested in organizing a run for the presidency in April 1992. In his home state of Texas, for example, Perot had to collect nearly 40,000 signatures by a May 11 deadline from registered voters who had not voted in the March 10 primary. In New York, 20,000 signatures from registered voters who had not voted in the April 7 primary were necessary, but they had to be gathered no sooner than July and no later than August 18. By mid-September, after spending $18 million to collect about 5.5 million signatures nationwide, he had qualified for a place on the ballot in all fifty states and the District of Columbia. Ironically, while his petition campaign was winding up its efforts, Perot had withdrawn as a presidential candidate, only to return to the race in October.

(box continued)

H. Ross Perot, 1996

As the 1996 presidential election approached, Ross Perot was at it again. This time his goal was to qualify a new political party for the ballot in all fifty states——a much more formidable task than qualifying as an independent candidate. He started too late to gain the 890,000 petition signatures necessary to meet the October 1995 deadline for the prized California ballot, and his petition drive initially fell short in Ohio. Only California and Ohio, with a November 20 deadline, required a new party to qualify before the election year had begun, and no other state required nearly as many signatures or registrants as California. Qualifying deadlines for new parties came much later in the remaining states——no earlier than April in the election year——so the new Perot-led party had better chances there. In states where it failed to qualify as a third party, though, the Perot movement pursued the presidency via the comparatively easier independent route.

after the election, but his vote total made him eligible for public funding in the next election—an opportunity he passed up by choosing not to run. Offsetting the advantages of this new campaign finance environment, though, is the enormous cost of modern campaigns, which probably restricts the opportunities to only a few highly visible or personally wealthy third-party or independent candidates.

Nevertheless, for non-major-party candidates with money to spend, the modern campaign environment offers new advantages. Television and the Internet provide a national audience to a candidate or party that can pay for it. Although traditional third parties were regionally based, organizing around local grassroots loyalties and concerns, minor party and independent candidates can now reach voters throughout the United States without the need for grassroots organizations—if they can pay for the media time or the Web page design. In fact, they can command attention through the very same channels used by the two major parties' candidates.

Quirks in local election laws continue to support a few local third parties. The classic instance is the New York minor parties—notably the Liberals and Conservatives—that survive because they can nominate candidates of a major party to run under their parties' own labels as well.[29] For national impact, minor parties must generally ride the coattails of a well-known, charismatic candidate. But given recent history, such candidates may find it more effective to run as independents or, if they run as third-party candidates, to stand alone on the party ticket. The challenge of fielding a full slate of candidates is not one that recent third parties have accepted. What seems most likely, then, is that minor parties and independents will follow different paths as they compete for space in the electoral arena.[30]

Increasing Major-Party Competitiveness

Along with the unprecedented successes of independent candidates, we have seen increasing competitiveness between the Republican and Democratic parties. No regions of the country and very few states can be seen as one-party areas any longer. Contests for state offices are more competitive now than they have been in decades, perhaps ever (see Table 2.2), and presidents have been winning with popular vote percentages that vary less and less from one state to another. They are no longer carrying some states by fat margins while losing others in a similarly lopsided way. The result is a more competitive two-party politics throughout the nation.

Increases in major-party competitiveness have the same roots as the challenges faced by local third parties: the nationalization of life and politics in the United States. It is harder and harder for one major party to maintain its dominance on the basis of regional appeals and traditions as the Democrats did in the South from 1876 to 1950. Further, the social and economic conditions that support one-party politics are disappearing. As Americans move more frequently, as industry comes to formerly agrarian states, as more and varied people move to the cities, each state gains the diversity of life and interests that supports national party competition. National mass media and national political leaders bring the conflict between the Democrats and the Republicans to all corners of the country. Party voters are increasingly recruited by the appeals of national candidates and issues regardless of the special appeals made by the local party. Most states have moved gubernatorial and other statewide elections to non-presidential-election years in order to mute the influence of these national forces. But this is only a small counterweight to the powerful pull of national politics.

This increase in two-party competition may create some new risks for the American parties. The reduction in pockets of one-party strength has the effect of removing a source of stability in the party system. When a party has unchallenged dominance in some areas, it can survive even a catastrophic national loss because it is still winning in its own strongholds. Without those one-party strongholds to fall back on, a losing party in the future may find its loss more sweeping and devastating. Further, the increase in competition expands the scope of party activity and thus makes extra demands on party resources. When one-party areas could be written off in a presidential campaign, the area of political combat was reduced. Now the parties must mobilize and organize more resources than ever across more of the states.

As we pass the 145th anniversary of the birth of competition between the Democrats and the Republicans, the two-party system faces a new challenge. The major parties' popularity may not be what it was, but their resilience and their dominance of the electoral system continues. The threat to their longevity comes not from third parties, which have been unable to cut into their strength; instead it has come from independent candidates such as Ross Perot, Jesse Ventura, and John Anderson.

Independents pose a different sort of threat to the two-party system from the threat of minor-party candidacies. The presence of strong independent candidates at the presidential level and below makes elections more unpredictable and may occasionally make governing coalitions more unstable. Running by themselves, without anyone else on their "tickets," and often with no clear indication that they stand for anything more than alternatives to the major-party candidates, their very independence keeps them from developing a stable and enduring challenge to the Democrats and Republicans. Unless these independents organize to confront the major parties across the ballot, therefore, they will probably remain no more than periodic threats to the major parties' candidates—major publicity draws but not capable of making a sustained challenge that could fundamentally transform the parties or the party system. On the other hand, creating such a sustained and nationwide challenge, difficult at any time, is extraordinarily difficult in current American politics; independent candidates are a natural accompaniment of candidate-centered politics.

Part 2

The Political Party as an Organization

*T*he parties have a life, as we have seen, that goes beyond the activities and personalities of their candidates. The party is a network of organizations, typically prescribed by state law, that exists at all the levels at which Americans elect public officials: precincts, townships, wards, cities, counties, congressional districts, and the states themselves. Both major parties have also set up national committees that concern themselves with presidential and congressional elections. All these party organizations have the official responsibility for making the party's rules and organizing its activities. The next three chapters examine these organizations and the activists and leaders who give them life.

We will focus in these chapters on the "private life" of the party organization, as opposed to its "public life" of recruiting and supporting candidates for office and promoting solutions to public problems. In particular, we will explore these questions: Where does the power lie in the party organizations? How do they find and use resources? What kinds of people are drawn to become party activists? How have the organizations changed over time? These internal characteristics of the party influence its ability to act effectively in the larger political system.

American party organizations vary tremendously. Party activists differ in the values and goals that bring them to the party organizations. Parties in different parts of the nation have ranged, throughout American history and even now, from elaborate organizations to complete somnolence. But by the standards of most Western democracies, the American party organizations would be judged to be fairly weak.

The weakness stems from the peculiar nature of the American party. The three sectors of any party—its organization, its candidates and elected officials, and its electorate—compete for dominance. They each have different sets of goals and they each seek control of the party to achieve their own ends. In the American system, the party organizations find it difficult to hold their own in this competition and to get the resources they need to influence elections and promote policies. Weakened by state regulations, the party organizations have rarely been able to exercise any real influence over the party's candidates and officeholders or over party voters. In fact, it is the organizations that are influenced. American party organizations depend on their party in government, which, after all, writes the laws that regulate the organization. They must also devote a great deal of energy to courting and mobilizing the party electorate, who are not formally party members nor, in many cases, even especially loyal to the party in their voting.

This lack of integration among the party's three sectors is typical of *cadre* parties—one of two common types into which parties are classified. In the cadre party, the organization is run by a relatively small number of leaders and activists. These officials and activists make the organization's decisions, choose its candidates, and select the strategies they believe voters will find appealing. In the other common type, the *mass-membership* party, the three party sectors are closely linked, with the party organization often the dominant force. In the mass-membership party, large numbers of party voters are dues-paying members of the party organization; they are likely to participate in its activities between elections as well as during campaigns.

Thus the party in the electorate becomes an integral part of the party organization in a mass-membership party, with the right to choose its leaders and vote on its policies. The party organization grows out of the party membership. It may even provide the members such nonpolitical benefits as insurance and leisure-time activities. And because the membership-based party organization has great power over candidate selection—it is not limited by the need to give less-involved voters the right to choose party candidates, as happens in a primary election—it can also exercise much greater control over the party in government. The mass-membership party, then, is a continuous, participatory organization; the cadre party, on the other hand, is a more pragmatic coalition of people and interests brought together temporarily to win elections, only to wither to a small core once the elections are over (see Table II.1).

In important ways the major American parties can be considered cadre parties. Even the parties' voters are not normally dues-paying members. Traditionally, party leaders and activists seldom considered their involvement in the party organization to be a full-time job; most are volunteers. The party's activities are almost exclusively election-related. The organization makes relatively little effort to control its candidates and elected officials, nor is it likely to succeed if it tries.

Recent changes have clearly strengthened the American party organizations. The parties now have the resources to employ full-time professional staffers in their

TABLE II.1 Comparison of Cadre and Mass-Membership Party Organizations

Organizational Feature	Cadre Party	Mass Membership Party
Members	Generally few	Many dues-paying members
Activities	Primarily electoral	Ideological and educational as well as electoral
Organizational life	Active mainly at elections	Continuously active
Leadership	Few full-time workers or leaders	Permanent bureaucracy and full-time leadership
Party organization's role	Usually subordinate to party in government	Generally has some influence on party in government

national and state offices. Party organizational power is less decentralized than it used to be. The parties solicit the party electorate more frequently, if only to raise money. Most primary elections are closed primaries in which voters have to declare a party affiliation before they are allowed to select the party's nominees.

Nevertheless, the major American parties are still more like cadre than mass-membership parties. Their organizations are focused almost completely on winning elections in an electoral system in which they must appeal to majorities. In a diverse nation the result is that the parties have not been very concerned with ideology or, at times, even with taking very specific stands on political issues. And in contrast to systems with mass-membership parties, the American parties do not monopolize the organization of political interests; rather, they work in a political system in which the electorate is already organized by a wealth of interest groups and other nonparty political organizations.

In spite of their comparative weakness and varying health, the American party organizations nonetheless command our attention, for they are at the very center of the political parties. More than the party in government or the party in the electorate, they control the parties' lives, their names, and their symbols. If their organizations are in decline, it may change the nature of American politics. If they become more robust, the consequences could be profound.

Chapter 3

The State and Local Party Organizations

*T*he traditional image of party organization in the United States is more military than democratic. It calls up a vision of "machines" headed by "bosses" who mobilize "armies" of workers to seek "spoils" through election victories. This image grows out of the long-standing American distrust of politics and politicians. In it, the party organization or "machine" is the prime villain in a wider net of political intrigue and corruption.

It is an entertaining picture, but a misleading one. Actual experience with American state and local party organizations will show that the pit bull of these descriptions can often be a poodle in disguise. The image of a powerful machine may have accurately characterized the party organizations of some major American cities and an occasional rural area at the beginning of the twentieth century. Even in their heyday, however, most state and local party organizations could be considered powerful machines only by believing the exaggerated claims of their leaders or their opponents. Now, with the last remnants of party machines all but gone, the "political machine" is like the Cheshire cat: only the smile remains.

When this tenacious myth is swept away, we can get a clear view of the real state and local party organizations. That requires a look from three different angles: the party organizations as they are constructed by state law, the party machines as they have traveled into modern times, and the party organizations as they do their work in major cities and in little towns.

THE PARTY ORGANIZATIONS IN STATE LAW

A good place to start looking at the reality of the party organizations is in the constitutions and laws of the fifty states. States have chosen a kaleidoscopic variety of ways to regulate the party organizations. Some almost bulge with detail, defining everything from the offices in the party organization's leadership to the rules with which party meetings must be conducted. In other states, the constitution and laws dispose of the parties in a few sentences or paragraphs.

State Regulations

A study by the Advisory Commission on Intergovernmental Relations (ACIR) indicates the rich variety found in these regulations as recently as the 1980s.[1] (See Table 3.1.) Most states have tried to regulate both internal party organization and the party role in the electoral process (as will be discussed later). At the organizational level, the study shows that the state party committees are regulated lightly in only twelve states; at the other extreme, in nineteen others—including California and New York—

TABLE 3.1 State Laws Regulating Political Parties

	State Committee Rules				Local Committee Rules			Cumulative
State	Selection[a]	Composition[b]	Meeting Date[c]	Internal Rules[d]	Selection[e]	Composition[f]	Internal Rules/ Activities[g]	Regulatory Index Score[h]
Light Regulators[i]								
Alaska								0
Delaware								0
Hawaii								0
Kentucky								0
North Carolina								0
Alabama							X	1
Georgia							X	1
Minnesota							X	1
New Mexico							X	1
Oklahoma							X	1
Virginia							X	1
Connecticut						X	X	3
Maine	X			X	X		X	4
New Hampshire	X				X		X	4
Moderate Regulators[i]								
Arkansas	X				X		X	5
Florida		X	X	X		X	X	5
Nebraska	X				X		X	5
Rhode Island				X	X	X	X	6
Pennsylvania	X	X	X	X			X	7
Colorado	X	X	X	X	X	X	X	8
Idaho	X	X			X	X	X	8
Iowa	X	X			X	X	X	8
South Carolina	X	X		X		X	X	8
South Dakota	X	X			X	X	X	8
Utah	X	X		X	X	X	X	8
Mississippi	X	X		X	X	X	X	9
Montana	X	X			X	X	X	9
Nevada	X	X		X	X	X	X	9
Vermont	X	X	X	X	X	X	X	9
Washington	X	X			X	X	X	9
Wisconsin	X	X			X	X	X	9

TABLE 3.1 (continued)

State	State Committee Rules				Local Committee Rules			Cumulative Regulatory Index Score[h]
	Selection[a]	Composition[b]	Meeting Date[c]	Internal Rules[d]	Selection[e]	Composition[f]	Internal Rules/ Activities[g]	
Heavy Regulators[i]								
Indiana	X	X	X	X	X	X	X	10
Michigan	X	X		X	X	X	X	10
New York	X		X	X	X	X	X	10
North Dakota	X	X	X	X	X	X	X	10
Oregon	X	X	X	X	X	X	X	10
Arizona	X	X	X	X	X	X	X	11
California	X	X		X	X	X	X	11
Maryland	X	X	X	X	X	X	X	11
Massachusetts	X	X	X	X	X	X	X	11
Missouri	X	X	X	X	X	X	X	11
Tennessee	X	X	X	X	X	X	X	11
West Virginia	X	X	X	X	X	X	X	11
Kansas	X	X	X	X	X	X	X	12
New Jersey	X	X	X	X	X	X	X	12
Texas	X	X	X	X	X	X	X	12
Wyoming	X	X	X	X	X	X	X	12
Illinois	X	X	X	X	X	X	X	13
Ohio	X	X	X	X	X	X	X	13
Louisiana	X	X	X	X	X	X	X	14

[a]Does state allow or require the manner of selecting the parties' state central committees?

[b]Does state law require the composition of the parties' state central committees?

[c]Does state law regulate when the parties' state central committees will meet?

[d]Does state law regulate any of the internal procedures of the parties' state central committees?

[e]Does state law regulate the manner of selecting the parties' local organizations?

[f]Does state law regulate the composition of the parties' local organizations?

[g]Does state law regulate any of the internal rules or activities of the parties' local organizations?

[h]Scores are determined by state regulatory actions in the seven areas examined. Scores of 0 (no regulation), 1 (medium regulation), or 2 (strong regulation) are possible on each action. Minimum score is 0; maximum score is 14.

[i]"Light" regulators are defined as having an index score of 0–4; "moderate" regulators are those states having index scores of 5–9; and "heavy" regulators are those states having index scores above 10.

Source: Modified from Timothy Conlan, Ann Martino, and Robert Dilger, *The Transformation in American Politics* (Washington, DC: Advisory Commission on Intergovernmental Affairs, 1986), pp. 141–142.

lawmakers have felt it necessary to tell the state parties even the dates on which their central committees must meet. Yet some of the strongest party organizations in the nation are also the most tightly regulated, so extensive state legal regulation does not necessarily weaken the parties.

The party organizations do not face similar kinds of regulations from the federal government. The United States Constitution makes no mention of parties—not even an oblique reference. Nor has the Congress tried very often to define or regulate party organizations. Only in the 1970s legislation on campaign finance is there a substantial body of national law that affects the parties in important ways.

States do not have complete freedom in regulating the parties. Over the years, the federal courts have stepped in frequently to protect citizens' voting rights (in cases to be discussed in Chapter 8) and to keep the states from unreasonably limiting access to the ballot by third-party and independent candidates (see Chapter 2). More recently, the courts have even begun to overturn state regulation of party organizational arrangements and practices. In *Tashjian v. Connecticut,* the Supreme Court ruled that the state could not prevent the Republican Party from opening up its primary to independents if it wanted to. In *Eu v. San Francisco County Democratic Central Committee,* the Court unanimously threw out California's statutory requirements that the state chair serve a two-year term, that southern and northern Californians rotate as party chair, and that parties could not endorse candidates in primary elections. In 1994, a federal court judge blocked enforcement of yet another feature of California law which prohibited parties from making endorsements in nonpartisan elections. If the parties choose to challenge the state laws that govern them, it now seems that they could succeed in dismantling much of the regulatory framework that states have imposed on them.[2]

An Organizational Pyramid

Despite the variety in state laws, the party organizations created by the states have a common structure which corresponds to the election districts of the state. The structure can be seen as a pyramid based in the grass roots and stretching up to the statewide organization (Figure 3.1). At the base of the pyramid is usually the smallest voting district of the state—the precinct, ward, or township. Then, in a succession of layers which vary in name and size from state to state, the ward and city committees, county committees, and sometimes even state legislative and congressional districts are piled on

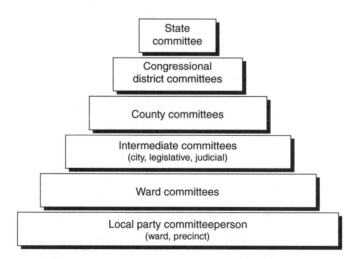

FIGURE 3.1 A typical pyramid of party organization in a state.

top of one other.[3] At the top of this pyramid is the state central committee. The top and the bottom levels of this structure are usually ordained by state laws, but the middle layers may be determined by the parties themselves.

The Elected Committeeman or Committeewoman

The local committeeman and/or committeewoman stands closest to the party's grass roots. These committee leaders are typically chosen at the precinct level. Because there are more than 100,000 precincts in the United States, it would be easy to imagine a vibrant party base made up of at least 200,000 committed men and women. But this exists only in the dreams of party leaders; in reality many of these local committee positions are vacant because nobody wants to serve in them.

When these positions do get filled, it is generally in one of three ways. Most committeemen and committeewomen are chosen at local party caucuses or primary elections, but in a few instances, higher party authorities appoint them. In states that choose them in the primaries, any voter may nominate him- or herself for the job by filing a petition signed by a handful of local voters (see box below). If, as often happens, there are no nominees, the committeeman or woman may be elected by an even smaller handful of write-in votes. In other states, parties hold local caucus meetings in the

---

It Rarely Happens: Competition for County Party Posts

Spirited competition for positions on the county committee is a rare occurrence. Every once in a while, though, there is an organized attempt to take over the local party organization through penetration of its base. These challenges typically involve battles over the ideological direction of the party. The challenges are resolved in favor of the group that most successfully mobilizes its supporters in the low-turnout elections in which party officials are selected.

Such an event occurred in Columbus, Ohio, in 1990, when challenges were mounted for a number of the 133 seats on both the Democratic and Republican county central committees by people identified as Christian conservatives. By seizing these positions they hoped to move the county parties, in their words, more in the direction of preserving "traditional family values." That the challenges came in the May primaries for statewide offices in a year when there was no competition within either party for most offices made the outcome especially dependent upon mobilization efforts on both sides. In the end, the insurgents won only a handful of seats on each committee.

Christian conservatives have been more successful in transforming the ideological posture of the Republican Party in other states. A study by the editorial staff of the magazine *Campaigns and Elections* in Summer 1994 found the "Christian right" to be dominant in eighteen state Republican Party organizations (including such states as California, Florida, Iowa, Minnesota, Oregon, South Carolina, and Texas) and of substantial strength in thirteen others.[4]

wards and precincts open to any voters of the area who declare themselves attached to the party. These party loyalists then elect the committee leaders in the caucuses; they also generally elect delegates to county and/or state conventions. These local committee positions, in short, are not normally in great demand. So the local parties are far from being exclusive clubs; their "front doors" are often open to anyone who cares to find them.

What do these precinct party leaders do? State laws often don't say. In areas where local parties are active, their leaders follow patterns that have been carved out over time. In the past, the fabled local committeemen or "ward heelers" of the American political machine knew the local voters, catered to their needs and problems, introduced the party candidates to them, and promoted the parties' issues— all with the ultimate purpose of turning out a bloc of votes for the party on election day. The main activities of their modern counterparts are similar: registering voters, going door-to-door (called "canvassing") to inform them about candidates, and getting voters to the polls. In the less active local parties, the committeemen and women may do little more than show up at an occasional meeting and campaign for a party candidate or two.

The Local Committees   Several layers of party committees are built on top of the precinct level. Collectively, they often make up the city, town, county, and congressional district committees or they elect the delegates who do. In a few cases, these committees are chosen at county conventions or by the party's candidates for public office. The most important of these is generally the county committee, although in some states the congressional district committees are of comparable importance.

Just as states often regulate the organization of the party, some also regulate its local activities. They may require, for example, that local committees meet within thirty or forty-five days after the primary elections, that they notify the secretary of state or the county clerk of the election of officers within a set time, or that they hold their conventions in certain types of public buildings. State law, then, does not view the political parties simply as private associations. As Leon Epstein has put it, they are public utilities, sometimes subject to a great deal of state direction.[5]

The State Central Committees   The state central committees, too, come in fifty state varieties. In some states, the lawmakers have let the party organizations decide who will serve on their own state committee. Most state legislatures, however, prefer to make that decision themselves. State law often specifies which lower party committees will be represented on the central committee and whether central committee members will be chosen in the party's primaries, by a party convention, or by some other method.

Many state legislatures have prescribed the activities of these state committees in almost painful detail. State law commonly gives party central committees the responsibility for calling and organizing party conventions, for drafting party platforms, for supervising the spending of party campaign funds, and for selecting the party's presidential electors, representatives to the national committee, and at least some of the national convention delegates and alternates.

Other states turn this pattern on its head and give these tasks to the party's statewide convention. In some cases, the convention is even given the power to choose the state central committee. In a few states, the party's state convention actually nominates candidates for some statewide offices—a reminder of the power the party conventions had in the days before the direct primary.

These are the formal organizational structures that state law creates for the state parties. They lead us to three important conclusions. First, the layers of party organization have been set up to correspond to the voting districts in which citizens choose public officials in that state; and the main responsibility of these organizations under state law is to contest elections. State laws, then, see the party organizations as auxiliaries or helpers in the state's task of conducting nominations and elections—tasks that before the turn of the twentieth century belonged almost entirely to the parties alone.

Second, the laws indicate that state legislators are ambivalent about what constitutes a party organization. Many regulations view the parties as cadre organizations run by a small number of party officials. Yet when they specify that local committeemen and women (and other party officials) must be chosen in a primary election, this gives party voters—and potentially, any voters—a vital, quasi-membership role in the party organization. So the party that results is not a private group whose participating members choose its leaders and chart its affairs; it is the semipublic, easily permeable mix of private and public that we have already seen.

Finally, although the use of a pyramid to represent the party organizations makes them seem like a hierarchy in which the lower levels take their orders from the higher levels, they are not. Through much of their history, the state parties were best described as "a system of layers of organization"[6] or as a "stratarchy,"[7] in which each of the levels has some independent power. In fact, power has traditionally flowed from bottom to top in the local and state parties, as opposed to a hierarchy, where power would be centralized at the top.[8] Party organization is a system of party committees close to and growing from the political grass roots. The result is that the party organizations remain decentralized and rooted in local politics even in the face of recent trends toward stronger state and national committees.

PARTY MACHINES, THEN AND NOW

American images of party organizations have been influenced heavily by a single type—the vigor and discipline of the classic urban political machine—and it is useful to judge local party organizations using that standard. Machine politics reached its peak at around the turn of the twentieth century when, by one account, a large majority of American cities were governed by machines.[9] The party machine, accounts tell us, was a durable and autonomous organization that controlled the nominations to elective office. It had the hierarchical structure that today's local parties lack. It relied on material incentives—jobs and favors—to build support among voters. Above all, it controlled the government in a city or county.[10] Its colorful history includes the legendary Tammany Hall in New York, the antics of Chicago's "Big Bill" Thompson (who, among other boasts, threatened to punch the King of England in the nose), and the genial rascality (and mail fraud conviction) of Mayor James Curley of Boston.

Yet for all their power in shaping how we may think of party organizations, the great urban machines were not found in all cities and, like the dinosaurs, they were temporary. The last of the great party machines was Chicago's, and it declined after the death of Mayor Richard J. Daley (the father of the current mayor) in 1976 (see box below). These dinosaurs were brought down by a number of forces. Some, such as the party machines in Pittsburgh and New York, never recovered from election upsets by middle-class reformers. Others, including those in Philadelphia and Gary, Indiana, lost power when new ethnic groups, especially blacks, became the more effective practitioners of the old ethnic politics.[11]

The End of Machine Politics, Chicago Style

The difficulties of the last great party machine signaled the vanishing of that special breed of party organization. In its heyday under the leadership of Mayor Richard J. Daley, the Chicago machine controlled nominations, elections, and the making of public policy in the city. Its dominance was based on control over an estimated 35,000 patronage jobs in government and access to another 10,000 in the private economy. Building from this loyal base by adding families, friends, and relatives, the organization could deliver 350,000 disciplined votes at election time.

With Daley's death in 1976, the machine lost its already-eroding control over Chicago politics and government. Machine candidates were defeated in two successive Democratic primaries, the second of which saw the party polarize along racial lines. It took black Mayor Harold Washington, the narrow victor of the 1983 primary and general election contests, several years to gain even majority support on the Democratic-dominated Board of Aldermen (Chicago's city council). Washington's reelection in 1987 further consolidated his power but over a Democratic Party riven by racial conflict, a government with declining numbers of patronage jobs, and a city with debilitating economic and social problems. It is doubtful that Washington could have overcome these troubles to reconstruct a Democratic Party machine, and his untimely death in 1987 initiated a new round of sharp internecine conflict. When the dust had settled, Chicago had a new mayor, Richard M. Daley, Jr., elected by a substantial majority in 1989 and reelected without serious opposition in subsequent years. Even with all of his electoral strength, there seems to be little chance that the junior Daley can resurrect the Chicago party machine.

There is no simple explanation for the demise of Chicago's heralded machine. Was it the inevitable result of the death of Daley, whose consummate skill had been the only glue binding together antagonistic ethnic, racial, and class groups? Was it just another phase in the unyielding process of ethnic succession, as blacks flexed their muscles in pursuit of their share of political power? Was it the product of a changing political culture in which machine politics was less acceptable and patronage jobs less plentiful? Or was it the simple electoral reaction to a deterioration of city services? As is so often the case, each of these has probably contributed to the decline of machine politics in Chicago.[12]

The Foundations of the Party Machines

Urban machines such as Chicago's based their power on a simple exchange: they offered tangible material benefits in return for citizens' votes for party candidates. Big cities at this time contained large populations of immigrants who arrived with enormous economic needs. First, the newcomers needed jobs, so the most visible of the benefits offered by the party machine were patronage jobs—those awarded on the basis of party loyalty rather than any other qualifications. During the heyday of the machine, thousands of these patronage positions were at the machine's disposal. They had the advantage of assuring that city workers would remain loyal to the machine and would work to keep it successful at election time by delivering not only their own votes but those of their friends, family, and neighbors as well. Local party workers also won voter loyalties by coping with constituents' personal problems—a rebellious child, for example—and their problems with government. The machine and its workers could earn political gratitude by finding social welfare agencies for the troubled or even by providing Christmas baskets or deliveries of coal for the needy.

The machine had favors to offer to local businesses as well. Governments purchase a lot of goods and services from the private sector. If a bank wanted to win the city's deposits, it could expect to compete more effectively for the city's business if it were willing to provide support for the party machine. Insurance agents who hoped to write city policies, lawyers who wanted the city's business, newspapers that printed city notices, even suppliers of soap to city washrooms all could be drawn into the web of the party machine. In addition, city governments make regular decisions on matters that affect individuals' and businesses' economic standing, such as building permits and health inspections. If you were helped by one of these decisions, you could expect the machine to ask for your gratitude in the form of contributions and votes at election time. A political leadership intent on winning support in exchange for these so-called "preferments" can use them ruthlessly and effectively to build its political power.

If these preferments were not enough, machines were capable of creating a "designer electorate" by using force and intimidation to keep less-supportive people from voting. Because the party machines controlled the election process, it was also possible, in a pinch, to change the election rules and even to count the votes in a creative manner. One of the indispensable tools of rival party workers in Indianapolis, for example, was a flashlight—to locate ballots that did not support the dominant party's candidates, and happened to fly out the window at vote-counting headquarters in the dark of night.

An important source of strength for political machines was their ability to appeal to ethnic loyalties. Studies in several nations show that political machines (or organizations similar to them) can flourish in parochial regions where strong loyalties to family, neighborhood, or ethnic group are combined with strong needs for immediate, short-term benefits, provided that there are also competitive elections and mass suffrage. The rise and fall of the American political machine is closely linked to changes in ethnic-group loyalties in our cities. The urban machine was a chief means by which ethnic groups, and especially the Irish, gained a foothold in American politics.[13] It deteriorated as its strongholds became more cosmopolitan, where it could not satisfy the aspirations of competing ethnic groups or where the government bureaucracy was insulated from party control, depriving the party organization of patronage jobs.[14]

The classic urban machine, then, was not just a political party organization but also an "informal government," a social-service agency, and a ladder for upward social and economic mobility. In some ways it looked like the local organization of a European mass-membership party, except that the American machine had little or no concern with ideology. It focused on the immediate needs of its constituents and it ignored the issues and ideologies of the political world beyond. Its world was the city and its politics were almost completely divorced from those that animated national politics.

We think of machine politics as flourishing in the biggest cities, but American party machines took root in other areas too. The conditions that led to the development of machines, especially a large parochially oriented population with short-term economic needs, were also found in small Southern towns and one-company towns. Even some well-to-do suburbs, in defiance of the rule that these organizations take root in poorer areas, have spawned strong machine-style party organizations. In the affluent Long Island suburbs of New York City, for example, a Republican Nassau County political machine developed that controlled local government and politics "with a local party operation that in terms of patronage and party loyalty rivals the machine of the famed Democratic mayor of Chicago, Richard J. Daley."[15]

We cannot be sure how powerful party machines really were even in their heyday. Some evidence from areas of machine strength raises doubts about their functioning. A Chicago study found little evidence that the party machine distributed public services to reward political support in either 1967 or 1977. Instead, services were allotted as the result of historical factors and bureaucratic decision rules.[16] In New Haven, researchers found that a party machine led by Italian politicians distributed summer jobs disproportionately to Italian youths from nonmachine wards who rarely took part in later political work, and not to kids from strong machine areas. This supports Steven Erie's observation (see note 13) that ethnic loyalties often overwhelmed the machine's devotion to its own maintenance and expansion.[17]

These bits of evidence may not reflect what the machines were like at the peak of their strength. Yet there is no doubt that the conditions that helped sustain party machines have been undercut. Most city jobs are now covered by civil service protection, so the number of patronage jobs that can be used to reward the party faithful (as will be discussed more fully in Chapter 5) is greatly reduced. Federal entitlement programs such as welfare and Social Security have taken away another important machine resource. Economic growth since the second World War has boosted many Americans' income levels, ended their dependence on machine favors, and reduced the attractiveness of patronage jobs; the chance to work for the sanitation district just doesn't have the cachet it once did. Higher education levels have increased people's ability to fend for themselves in a complex bureaucratic society.

Do Political Machines Have a Future?

Nevertheless, the conditions that support machine-style parties have not completely disappeared. Major cities still have economically dependent populations, and new immigrant groups have taken the places of the old. Many cities continue to deal with tremendous social-service demands at the same time as they are facing a declining tax base. If party machines thrive by offering help with a confusing government bureaucracy, city governments seem more than happy to oblige by providing the confusing bureaucracy. Even the ethnic strains that figured so prominently in the electoral strength of some machines have not disappeared, although they may now take different forms—for instance, recent immigrants versus long-term residents, whites versus blacks.

Where the demand for their services exists, political organizations will respond, even if they have to work within new and tighter constraints. Even past their peak, political machines were very creative in subverting civil service regulations to create patronage jobs (for example, Mayor Daley hired thousands of long-term "temporary" employees) and in brokering federal benefits for the poor (for example, the summer jobs distributed by the machine in New Haven were provided through a federal employment training program). Local governments continue to have large budgets, provide a wide array of services, and play an active regulatory role, so the opportunity remains to sustain a patron-client form of politics in a supportive political culture.

In short, although political machines in their classic (and often exaggerated) form were clearly part of an earlier time, reports of their death may be premature. Party organizations often learn how to adapt to new realities, and functional equivalents to the old-time machines may well emerge. It is also possible that the machines' disappearance is just another chapter in the battle over ethnic succession, this time between blacks and white ethnics in many cities, and is only a temporary pause in party organizations' centralization of power in American cities.[18]

THE REVITALIZATION OF LOCAL PARTY ORGANIZATIONS

The big city machines set the standard for effective party organizations, but it is a standard rarely achieved. At the other extreme—seldom discussed in the scholarly or popular literature because it offers so little to study—is virtual *dis*organization. In such cases, most of the party positions remain vacant or are held by completely inactive incumbents. A chairman and a handful of loyal party officials may meet occasionally to carry out the most essential affairs of the party. Their main activity occurs shortly before the primary elections, as they plead with members of the party to become candidates or step in themselves as candidates to "fill the party ticket." They are largely without influence or following, for theirs is often a chronic minority party. They meet infrequently, raise little money for election campaigns, and create little or no public attention. This type of organization has probably always been more common than the machine. Most American local party organizations lie between these two extremes.

A comprehensive picture of local organizations was provided by a 1979–1980 study (Table 3.2) which surveyed several thousand county (or the equivalent where there were no counties) leaders.[19] This study found that most county organizations had formal rules or bylaws and were headed by a chair and executive committee who met regularly and were most active during the election season. These party leaders, plus a few associated activists, made decisions in the name of the party, raised funds, sought out and screened candidates (or approved candidates who selected themselves), and got involved in campaigns. Most were volunteers with few resources available for their party work. Virtually none received salaries for their efforts, and only a few had paid staff to assist them or enjoyed such basic organizational support as a regular budget, a year-round office, or even a telephone listing.

When several indicators of organizational strength at the local level were combined in this study, Democratic and Republican organizations did not differ much on average. States, however, differed considerably in the organizational strength of their local parties. Some states in the 1979–1980 study—for example, New Jersey, New York, Pennsylvania, Indiana, and Ohio—had relatively strong local organizations in both parties, while others—such as Louisiana, Georgia, Nebraska, Kentucky, Alabama, and Texas—had relatively weak parties at the county level. In a few states, such as Arizona and Florida, one party was considerably stronger at the local level than the other party. But most often, strong organizations of one party were matched with strong organizations in the other party.[20]

TABLE 3.2 The Organizational Strength of Local Parties, 1979–80 vs. 1992

Attribute	Democrats 1979–80	1992	Republicans 1979–80	1992
Percent with complete/near complete set of officers	90	85	81	65
Percent with year-round office	12	45	14	64
Percent with telephone listing	11	68	16	75
Percent with paid staff				
Full-time	3	22	4	26
Part-time	5	18	6	36
Percent with paid chair	—	2	—	5
Percent with regular volunteer staff	—	80	—	79
Percent with regular annual budget	20	95	31	97
Percent operating a campaign headquarters	55	85	60	65

Note: The 1979–1980 figures are based on responses from a total of 2,021 Democratic and 1,980 Republican organizations to a mail survey; the 1992 figures are based on telephone and mail responses to a survey of 40 Democratic chairs and 39 Republican chairs in 40 counties nationwide. Some of the differences between the figures may be the result of the different timing of the two surveys in the election cycle. The 1992 study reports on the situation during the general election campaign; the 1979–1980 study covers the period before the general election campaign began.

Source: For the 1979–1980 study, Cornelius P. Cotter, James L. Gibson, John F. Bibby, and Robert J. Huckshorn, *Party Organization in American Politics* (New York: Praeger, 1984), p. 43; for the 1992 study, Paul Allen Beck, Russell J. Dalton, and Robert Huckfeldt, *Comparative National Election Project*, United States study.

There is persuasive evidence that the average county organization in 1980 was better organized and more active in political campaigns than it had been two decades earlier and that it has grown more robust since that time. By comparing data on the same counties in 1964 and 1979–1980, these researchers found that local parties had become substantially more involved, on average, in five important campaign activities: literature distribution, arranging campaign events, fund-raising, publicity, and voter registration. These increases continued in subsequent elections. A 1984 repeat survey of a sample of the local organizations studied in 1980 showed that the organizations had become even more vibrant, perhaps as a result of intensive efforts by national and state parties to invigorate local parties.[21] A national survey in 1988 showed even higher levels of activity. Studies over time of Detroit and Los Angeles show similar growth in local party activities.[22]

A study of the county party organizations in forty representative counties across the nation during the 1992 presidential election confirms this trend toward stronger local parties. As shown in Table 3.2, the basic ingredients for a viable party organization (a permanent office, an office during the campaign, a budget, a telephone listing, a staff) were more widespread in 1992 than they had been just a few years before, although the local parties continued to depend heavily on volunteer efforts. The big change seems to have come in the things money can buy, which supports the observation that more money has flowed to local party organizations in recent years. These county organizations were active in the 1992 campaign; only one of the eighty Democratic and Republican organizations sampled failed to perform any campaign activities. A majority of organizations in each party conducted registration drives, transported voters to the polls, ran campaign events, telephoned voters to urge them to support the party ticket, and distributed yard signs and "slate cards" listing the party's candidates.[23]

County party organizations, then, were stronger and more active in the 1990s than they had been just a few decades before.[24] It is harder to determine, because there are so few reliable records before the 1960s, whether the local organizations have regained the levels of vitality that local parties were believed to have achieved a century ago. Even the most active of these organizations is probably no match for a powerful urban machine; on a continuum of organizational strength, the extreme positive end is now empty.[25] But not many of these local parties are completely dead, either. Thus many locales may now have more robust party organizations than ever before. Perhaps these county parties have gained strength to fill (although only partially) a void created by the demise of strong *city* organizations. In an age of candidate-centered campaigns and less party-oriented voters, however, this growing county organizational presence may not matter as much as it would have a few decades ago.[26]

STATE PARTY ORGANIZATION

The state committee sits on top of the pyramid of party organization shown in Figure 3.1. (see p. 58) Yet its location has not been a good indicator of its power through most of party history. Examples of powerful, patronage-rich state party organizations were found in the industrial heartland in the late nineteenth century, where they served as the organizational base for U.S. senators (who were appointed rather than elected prior to 1913), and in Huey Long's Louisiana several decades later. But in most states most of the time, the state committee has not been the site of the party's main organizational authority.[27] Recent years have seen a growing importance of the state organizations, however, in a centralization of activity throughout the party hierarchy.

Traditional Weakness

Traditionally, state party organizations have been federations—and loose ones at that—of semi-independent or autonomous local baronies and baronial county chairmen. Added to this decentralization is a great deal of factional conflict. Parties are divided internally by regions of the state, by rural-urban differences, along ethnic and religious lines, by loyalty to local leaders, and especially by liberal and conservative preferences. Because the leadership of the state party organization is a prize that can be won by only one of them, rather than shared, any consolidation of power at the state level seriously threatens the various factions. In the past, with only the few exceptions mentioned above, this threat was avoided in several ways, often by keeping most of the party's resources out of the hands of the state organization. Power, in other words, was decentralized, collecting in the most viable of the local organizations.

Other forces also weakened the state party organizations. Progressive reforms early in the twentieth century sapped the influence of state parties over nomination and election campaigns for state offices. Since then, candidates have found it increasingly easy to win nominations in primary elections without party organization support and to raise money for their own campaigns and thus run them without party help. Since 1968, the state party's role in the national presidential nominating conventions has been diminished by internal party reforms, especially among the Democrats. Convention delegates are now chosen mainly by voters and almost all come to the convention pledged to a particular candidate for the nomination rather than under the thumb of state party leaders. Continuing extension of civil service protections and unionization contributed to eroding the patronage base for many state parties; in what may have been the final indignity for patronage politics, judicial intervention prevented even the firing of patronage workers when the party controlling government changes. It is little wonder that the state organizations seemed feeble by the 1950s and 1960s.

Increasing Strength in Recent Years

In spite of these obstacles, state parties have become organizationally stronger in recent years, although even the strongest among them does not rival the few powerful state machines of the late 1800s or probably even the typical state party of the early 1900s. In 1960 to 1964, only 50 percent of a sample of state organizations had a permanent state headquarters; two decades later, in 1979–1980, that had increased to 91 percent. The number with a full-time salaried chairman or director grew from 63 percent to 90 percent during the same period, and average staff size in the off-election years increased from 3.5 to 5.9. Thus we are seeing the first real signs of institution-alization of the state parties.

The non-election-year budgets of the state parties were higher in absolute dollars as well, climbing from an average of $188,125 in 1960–1964 to $340,667 in 1979–1980.[28] By the mid–1980s, with the Republican party leading the way, their average expenditures had risen to $424,700 in the off years and more than $1 million in election years, and most of them had paid executive directors. And a decade later most state parties reported receipts of over $3 million to the Federal Election Commission, derived not only from big givers but also from telemarketing and direct mail.[29] In addition, state legislative campaign committees, operating through either the party caucus or the leadership, have come to play an increasingly important role in legislative campaigns.[30]

Campaign Services   The increased strength of the state parties has enabled them to play a more important role in political campaigns. They have devoted their organizational resources mainly to supplying campaign services in the form of training, advertising, polling, and voter-mobilization drives that supplement those of the candidates' own organizations. Coordinated campaigns, emphasizing the sharing of campaign services among a variety of candidates, are also increasingly being run through the state party organizations. These state parties, it appears, have at last learned to make use of modern campaign skills to recapture a role in election campaigns.[31] Their services will certainly win the appreciation and gratitude of the candidates. We do not know yet, however, where that gratitude will lead; will the state parties be able to convert successful candidates' enthusiasm for party services into a willingness to support the party's positions on issues?

Republican Advantage   Data from the 1979–1980 study and a similar 1984 study[32] also show that, unlike the situation at the county level, Republican state organizations were considerably stronger than their Democratic counterparts. The Republicans had more paid leaders, larger and more specialized staffs, and much bigger budgets. This relative advantage in organizational strength enabled the GOP to perform more services for the party and its candidates. For example, twice as many Republican as Democratic state organizations provided public-opinion polling services. The GOP organizational advantage at the state level is nationwide, reflecting to a considerable degree the extensive subsidies the national party has been able to provide to all of the state parties. It is an advantage that persists today.

Allied Groups   State Democratic parties, however, hold an important counterweight. Labor unions, especially teachers' and government employees' unions, work closely with their state Democratic Party organizations to provide money and volunteer help, and other services to party candidates. In states such as Alabama and Indiana, the state teachers' union is so closely connected with the state party that critics might find it difficult to tell where one stops and the other begins. State Republican parties have close ties to allied groups as well. Small business groups, manufacturing associations, pro-life groups and Christian conservative organizations often provide services to Republican candidates.

Groups of a variety of types—not just unions and business associations, but also citizen groups, issue organizations, polling and other political consulting firms, "think tanks," and even informal collections of notable experts and activists—have become more and more closely linked with the state party organizations because of the resources and expertise these groups can provide. For party leaders these groups can be a mixed blessing, of course; labor unions and business groups have their own agendas and they can be as likely to try to push the state party into locally unpopular stands as to help in the effort to elect party candidates. Nevertheless, allied groups play an increasing role in the expanding nexus that surrounds the state party. (For an example of these state party coalitions, see Figure 3.2.)

It is not easy to build a powerful state party organization. It requires having to overcome both the grassroots localism of American politics and the widespread hostility toward strong party discipline. Strong and skillful personal leadership by a governor, a senator, or a state chairman[33] helps. So do political resources—especially money, which is the essential fuel for the modern campaign. It also helps to have a tradition or culture, as well as state regulations embodying it, that accepts the notion of a unified and effective party. Similarly, state law makes a difference. It is no coincidence that central party organization has flourished in the states in which primary elections are least extensive and in which the party organization determines much more directly who the statewide and congressional candidates will be. An environment conducive to strong party organizations is rarely found in the American states. But where it is present (such as in Pennsylvania for both parties; Ohio, Minnesota, and South Dakota for the Republicans; and North Dakota for the Democrats[34]), state organizations have flourished.

National Party Money   By far the most important ingredient in the strengthening of state party organizations, though, has been the party-building efforts of the national parties. With more energetic leadership and more lavish financial resources than ever before, the national party committees since the 1970s have been dedicated to building the organizational effectiveness of the state parties—and local parties too. The full story of these efforts will be told in Chapter 4, but the important point for this chapter is how the state parties have benefited from national party investments. Millions of dollars (since 1980, increasingly in the form of "soft money"[35]) have been channeled from the Democratic and Republican national committees to state party committees to be used in building up organizational capacity and running party campaigns. In the 1997–1998 election cycle alone, the national parties transferred just under $70 million directly to state parties ($35 million for the Democrats, $34 million for the Republicans) and spent another $92 million in joint activities ($49 million by the Republicans, $43 million by the Democrats) to support a variety of "party-building" activities and services. These figures are more than twice the amounts that the national parties infused into the state organizations just six years earlier. State parties, so recently the poor relations of the formal party organizations, have come into money. With these newfound financial resources, the state parties have gained an importance that more closely matches their formal position in the organizational pyramid. Whether their new status has cost them their independence, this time from the national parties, is a question only the future can answer.[36]

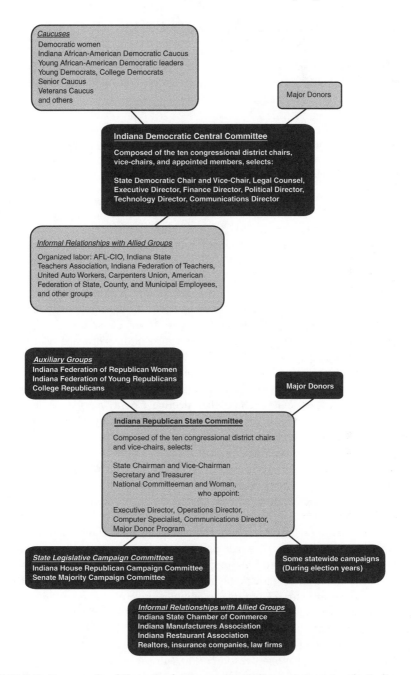

FIGURE 3.2 An example of the web of groups surrounding a state party: the Indiana state party organizations, 2000

Note: Information for this figure comes from the two state party committees (their Web sites are at http://www.indems.org and http://www.indgop.org) and from Brian Vargus, Professor of Political Science at Indiana University-Purdue University at Indianapolis and Director of the Indiana University Public Opinion Laboratory.

PARTY ORGANIZATION IN PERSPECTIVE: TRENDS AND CHANGES

The story of party organizational strength at the state and local levels is complex. Local party organizations are weaker today than they were a hundred years ago when the parties could be described as:

> ... armies drawn up for combat (in which) financial and communications "sinews of war" were provided by an elaborate, well-staffed, and strongly motivated organizational structure. In the field of communications, a partisan press was dominant.... The "drilling" of voters in this period by their party captains was intense.[37]

Although this description did not apply to party organizations throughout the nation even at that time, it might be impossible to find a local party organization that would earn this characterization today.

Since the high point of their strength in the latter part of the nineteenth century, the local parties have been buffeted by numerous forces, only some of which were designed expressly to weaken them. Progressive-movement reforms adopted around the turn of the century undermined party organizations by limiting their control over nominations and general elections as well as over treasured patronage resources. In recent decades, a number of disparate forces—reforms of the presidential nominating process, the welfare state, the almost total demise of the patronage system, national regulation of previously state-controlled party activities, and greater education of the electorate—have threatened further the viability of the local parties.[38]

Yet local parties have shown such staying power in adapting to these changes that we should not exaggerate the extent of their decline. County party organizations seem to have moved to fill at least some of the void created by the absence of the urban machines. It may even be premature to announce the death of the machines, considering the ample rewards local governments still offer to the resourceful political entrepreneur and the continuing dependency of city residents. The local party organizations, in short, are adapting to meet the new challenges posed by a changing environment, demonstrating once again the resilience that has enabled them to survive throughout much of American history.

The state party organizations have followed a different route. Traditionally weak in all but a handful of states, the state parties were little more than vessels that could barely contain vibrant and often warring local organizations. But state party organizations appear to have grown remarkably robust in recent years, becoming more professionalized than ever before. They are providing campaign and organizational services to the local party organizations which in an earlier era would not have dreamed of looking to their state headquarters for help. Recent trends within the states, then, seem to have modified the long-standing decentralization of the party organizations.

In fact the flow of money, resources, and to some degree leadership from the national party to the state party and in turn from the state to the local parties signifies a reversal, at least in part, of the traditional flow of party power. Through most of their lives, the American parties have been highly decentralized, with power and influence lodged at the base of the organizational pyramid. The parties were hollow at the top, depending on the base for whatever influence and resources they had. This extreme decentralization exists no longer, as the result of the death of urban machines and the birth of vigorous state and national party organizations. The nationalization of American society and politics has embraced the political party organizations as well.

Yet for all of this rejuvenated party power, it is clear that the formal statutory party organizations at the state and local level make less of an impact on our politics than they once did. They have been muscled aside by a motley assortment of new and old actors in the electoral process. Membership clubs, candidates and their organizations, ambitious or wealthy individuals, campaign technocrats, donors of political money, issue groups and caucuses, and other allied groups also work the election campaigns. Many of them ally themselves with a party label and, to some extent, with a party organization. Therefore state and local party organizations today are far looser and more difficult to define with precision than the words of the statutes would suggest.[39]

In other words, the party has become a flexible and somewhat undisciplined pool of active groups and individuals. They are recruited to the party for different reasons and they are activated by different candidates, issues, and elections. A hotly contested school-board race will activate one cluster of partisans, and a congressional election will activate another. What we have thought of as the party organization is really a reservoir of organizations and activists from which are drawn the shifting coalitions that speak and act in the name of the party.

In searching for change in American party organization, however, we must also remember what does not change. The American state and local parties remain largely skeletal cadre organizations run by small numbers of activists and involving the great masses of their supporters only at election time. The shift away from the organizational forms described by state law has largely been a shift from a well-defined cadre organization to a looser, more amorphous, but wealthier cadre organization. Yet the American parties are still a long way from becoming mass-membership parties and they are still some distance from achieving the year-round, continuously active tempos of parties elsewhere in the world. By the standards of those parties, American party organization continues to be unusual in that it is so fluid and fast-changing, so lethargic except at election time, and so easily dominated by a handful of activists and elected officials.

Chapter 4
··············
National Organizations: A New Presence at the Summit

South of Capitol Hill, a few blocks from the House and Senate offices, stand the national headquarters buildings of the Democratic and Republican parties. Their upscale quarters demonstrate levels of wealth, independence, and permanence never seen before in the history of the national parties. Their neighborhoods tell even more about the change in their status. They are located closer to Congress than to the White House now, just as the national parties have moved beyond their traditional job as handmaiden to the president and into a new role of party building in the states and localities. The older and more imposing GOP headquarters, purchased in 1970 (the Democrats purchased theirs in 1984), testifies that the Republicans started earlier and have done more to build effective national party organizations.

The change has been remarkable. Only early in the development of party politics, before 1828 when presidential nominations were made by the congressional caucus, were the national parties as important in American politics. Just a few decades ago, the national committees were poor and transient renters—often moving back and forth between New York and Washington and all but disbanding between presidential campaigns. Leading students of the national committees could accurately describe them as "politics without power."[1] For most of their history, in fact, the national parties were no more than nominal titles in a heavily decentralized party system—arenas in which powerful local and state organizations and presidential candidates jockeyed for power. As one noted scholar of American party politics described the old arrangement:

> Decentralization of power is by all odds the most important single characteristic of the American major party; more than anything else this trait distinguishes it from all others. Indeed, once this truth is understood, nearly everything else about American parties is greatly illuminated.... The American major party is, to repeat the definition, a loose confederation of state and local bosses for limited purposes.[2]

There is good reason why the parties have long been decentralized, as Chapter 3 indicated. State and local party organizations pick their own officers, nominate their own candidates, take their own stands on issues, and raise and spend their own funds without much interference from the national party. The state regulation of parties, the thousands of public officials chosen in the states, and their dominance of the local organizations give the parties a powerful state and local focus. All these localizing pressures continue to restrain any shift in power within the party organizations.

Yet there are powerful nationalizing forces in American society which have long since affected most other aspects of American politics. The mass media bring the same reporters, TV images, and commentators into homes in all parts of the country. Government in the American federal system became increasingly centered in Washington beginning in the 1930s. Even the other two sectors of the party have been nationalized in the last few decades. Party voters respond increasingly to national issues, national candidates, and national party symbols and positions; the 1994 congressional elections were the most nationally centered "midterms" in years. And in the party in government, the president and the congressional party leadership have become more than ever the prime spokespersons for their parties.

The party organizations responded more slowly to these nationalizing forces. But since the 1970s there have been striking signs of life in the national committees. Their resources and staffs have grown. They have taken on new roles, new activities, and new influence. They have been able to limit the autonomy of state and local organizations in their one collective function—the selection of delegates to the national conventions. The congressional campaign committees are vital and active.

The changes have led some analysts to note that the national parties have become "federations" rather than "confederations" of the state and local parties. This subtle shift in terminology suggests a greater potential for national authority, just as was seen when the Articles of Confederation were replaced by the Constitution in the early days of the American Republic.[3] There are even some signs of centralization in the major parties. Thus although the state and local pull remains strong, the trend toward an increasing presence for the national party organizations is now clear.

THE NATIONAL COMMITTEES AND NATIONAL OFFICERS

Technically speaking, the nominating convention each party holds during a presidential election year is the party's supreme national authority. The convention's role, however, rarely goes beyond the selection of presidential and vice-presidential candidates and the formulation of party platforms and rules. It does specify the structure and powers of the national committee, but because the convention meets only once every four years, it cannot exercise continuing supervision over the party's national organization.

The Committees

Between conventions, the national committees are the main governing institutions of the two major parties. These are venerable organizations: the Democrats created their national committee in 1848 and the Republicans in 1856. For years, Democrats and Republicans had similar rules for representation on the national committee. Every state (and some territories) was represented equally on both national committees, regardless of its voting population or the extent of its party support. Alaska and California, then, had equal-sized delegations to the national party committees, just as they do in the United States Senate. That system overrepresented the smaller states and also gave roughly equal weight in the national committees to the winning and the losing parts of the party. In practice, this strengthened the Southern and Western segments of each party, which tended to be more conservative.

Since 1972, when the Democrats drastically changed the makeup of their national committee, the parties have structured their committees differently. After a brief flirtation with unequal state representation in the 1950s, the Republicans have retained their traditional confederational structure by giving each of the state and territorial parties three seats on the committee. By contrast, the Democratic National Committee (DNC), now almost four times the size of its Republican counterpart (RNC), gives weight both to population and to party support in representing the states. California, for example, has twenty seats on the committee, and Alaska has four. The Democrats also give national committee seats to groups of elected officials and, through at-large members, to minority constituencies (Table 4.1).

National committee members are selected by the states and, for the Democrats, also by the other constituencies. The state parties differ in how they make their decisions, and in many states the two parties choose their national committee representatives differently. They use four main methods of selection: by state party convention, by the party delegation to the national convention, by the state central committee, and by election in a primary. The choice of method makes a difference. The parties' state organizations can usually control the selection of committee members when they are chosen by the state committee and by the state conventions; party organizations are less effective in influencing choices made by primaries or by national convention delegates. Particularly in states that choose delegates in presidential primaries, a national convention delegation may represent voter support of a momentarily popular candidate more than it represents the leadership of the state party. The classic example occurred in 1972, when a number of Democratic delegations were composed of party newcomers and mavericks pledged to George McGovern. The old-line party leaders in those states had supported other contenders, so they did not even get delegate seats at their party's convention.

The Officers

The national committees select and remove their chairs and other officers. Tradition dictates, however, that immediately after the conventions the parties' presidential candidates can name the national chairs for the duration of the presidential campaign. The committees ratify their choices without question. Because the president's party will continue to respect his (or her) choice of a national party chair, only the "out" party's national committee actually chooses its own national chair. The committees generally have much greater freedom to select other committee officials—vice-chairs, secretaries, and treasurers. Both national committees also elect executive committees, which include these officers and some other members of the committee.

The chairs, together with the national committees' permanent staffs, dominate these organizations. The full committees usually meet only two or three times a year. Cotter's and Hennessy's classic description still applies:

TABLE 4.1 Members of Democratic and
Republican National Committees: 2000

	Number of Members
Democratic National Committee	
Party Chair and Vice-Chair from each state, D.C., Puerto Rico, American Samoa, Guam, Virgin Islands, and Democrats Abroad	112
Other members apportioned to states on the basis of population (at least two per state, with delegations equally divided between men and women)	200
Elected Officials:	
2 U.S. Senators and 2 U.S. House members (the party leader and one other member of each house)	4
Representatives of Democratic Governors Conference	3
Democratic Mayors Conference	3
Democratic County Officials Conference	3
Democratic Legislative Campaign Committee	3
Democratic Municipal Officials Conference	3
Democratic Lieutenant Governors Association	2
Democratic Secretaries of State Association	2
Democratic State Treasurers Association	2
Representatives of Young Democrats	3
National Federation of Democratic Women	3
Representatives of College Democrats	2
Officers of National Committee	13
(National Chair, General Chair, General Cochairs, Vice-Chairs, Treasurer, Secretary, Finance Chair, Deputy Chair)	
Additional at-large members appointed by DNC Chair to implement participation goals for blacks, Hispanics, women, youth, Asians, and Native Americans	up to 75
Approximate Total	433
Republican National Committee	
National Committeeman, National Committeewoman, and State Chair from each state and from D.C., American Samoa, Guam, Puerto Rico, and Virgin Islands	165
Total	165

Note: Two Democratic committee officers also are state committee representatives.

The national committee members have very little collective identity, little patterned interaction, and only rudimentary common values and goals. Except for occasional meetings—largely for show and newsmaking purposes—the national committees may be thought of not so much as groups, but as lists of people who have obtained their national committee memberships through organizational processes wholly separate in each state.[4]

The other officers of the party are not especially influential, and the executive committees meet only a little more often than the full committees. Like the full committees, the executive committees are composed of men and women whose concern is state (and even local) organizational work rather than the building of a strong national party apparatus. Thus by tradition, the national chair, with a permanent staff that he or she has chosen, has in effect been the national party organization.

Shifting Roles with Presidential Control

The national committees' role, and that of their chairs, depends on whether the president is from their party. When their party does not hold the presidency, the national chair and committee can provide some national leadership. They bear the responsibility for binding up wounds, healing internal party squabbles, helping pay debts from the losing campaign, raising new money, and energizing the party organization around the country. The "out" party's national chair may speak for the party and the alternatives it proposes. So the national chair and committees play more influential roles, by default, when their party has less control over the national government.

With a party leader in the White House, on the other hand, the national committee's role is whatever the president wants it to be. Presidents came to dominate their national committees early in this century. Their control reached a new peak in the 1960s and 1970s[5] and has remained strong ever since. Some presidents have turned their national committees into little more than managers of the president's campaigns and builders of the president's political support between campaigns. Other presidents, such as Reagan and Bush, have used their control to build up the national committees to achieve party, not just presidential, goals.

In the president's party, the national chair must be congenial to the president, representative of the president's ideological stance, and willing to be loyal primarily to the president. An example is Bill Clinton's selection of David Wilhelm, his 1992 campaign manager, for the post in 1993. After the Democrats' stunning defeat in 1994 and in preparation for the 1996 campaign, President Clinton tried a different approach—paralleling the one favored by President Reagan a decade earlier—by engineering the selection of a sitting senator, Christopher Dodd of Connecticut, as the party's general chairman and a veteran party official, Don Fowler from South Carolina, as the DNC chair in charge of handling the day-to-day operations of the national committee.

Within the opposition party, the chair will need to get along with or at least be trusted by the various factions or segments of the party. Frequently, he or she is chosen for ideological neutrality or for lack of identification with any of the candidates for the party's next presidential nomination. Experience in the nuts and bolts of party and campaign organization is also desirable. In this respect it is understandable that as the 2000 election cycle began, with the Republicans trying to recapture the White House and the Democrats trying to regain the House and Senate, the chairs in both parties were veteran political operatives. So the qualifications for the job vary depending on the party's electoral circumstances (see box on p. 79).

Joe Andrew and Jim Nicholson: Different Backgrounds, Same Goals

As the 2000 elections began, Joe Andrew and Jim Nicholson faced off as chairs of the Democratic and Republican national committees. Their backgrounds differ markedly, just as those of previous national party chairs have followed a variety of patterns. But as testament to the importance of money in current national party politics, both Andrew and Nicholson have focused especially on moving debt-ridden party organizations into the black with aggressive fund-raising campaigns.

Joe Andrew became the nation's youngest Democratic state chair in Indiana in January, 1995—and promptly got the bill for the party's devastating losses in the 1994 elections. After Andrew's major reorganizing and fund-raising effort, the party raised more money per capita than any other Democratic state party in the U.S.—rare in this Republican State—more money than the state's Republican Party organization. In 1998, for example, the party raised more than $5.8 million in a state with a population of under 6 million—twice what the Republicans had raised. Andrew became DNC chair in 1999 and transferred his fund-raising skills to the national level. A graduate of Yale and Yale Law School, he continues to work as an attorney and to write novels; his first, a spy thriller, has been published internationally.

Jim Nicholson, a generation older than Andrew, grew up on an Iowa tenant farm during the Great Depression. He is a West Point graduate, a Vietnam veteran, and an Army Reservist. With a law degree from the University of Denver, Nicholson practiced law until the late 1970s, when he became a real estate developer. He was elected Republican National Committeeman for Colorado in 1984 and took over as RNC chair in 1997. The party was saddled with a $10 million debt, which he reduced by 95 percent within the year. By the end of 1997, Nicholson had broken all party records for Republican fund-raising in a post–presidential election year; he had another record-breaking fund-raising year in 1998.

THE SUPPORTING CAST OF NATIONAL GROUPS

Clustered around the national committees are a set of more-or-less formal groups which also claim to speak for the national party or for some part of it. Some are creatures of the national committees; others are not. Taken together with the national committee in each party, they come close to constituting that vague entity we call the national party.

Special Constituency Groups

The national party committees sometimes give a formal role in their organization to supportive groups that might not be well represented otherwise. For a long time, both the Democrats and Republicans have had women's divisions associated with their national committees. Both have also had national federations of state and local women's groups: the National Federation of Democratic Women and the National Federation of Republican Women. The importance of these women's divisions has declined markedly in the last thirty years as women have entered regular leadership positions in the parties and served more frequently as convention delegates.

The Young Republican National Federation and the Young Democrats of America also have a long history of representation and support in party councils. These groups are not controlled by the national committees, however, and at times they have taken stands and supported candidates opposed by the senior party organization. The Young Republicans, for instance, remained infatuated with Goldwater conservatism long after the regular leadership of the party had moved to a more centrist position. In the late 1960s and 1970s, their loyalties turned increasingly to the conservatism of Ronald Reagan. The Young Democrats often stood to the left of their senior party organization. In 1969, for instance, their national convention called for repeal of all legal limits on abortion, for liberalization of marijuana laws, for diplomatic recognition of Cuba and Communist China, and for an "immediate and total withdrawal of all American troops in Vietnam." In recent years the Young Democrats have declined, while the Young Republicans have capitalized on the party's enhanced electoral strength to expand their numbers. The strength of the youth groups, then, depends on the fortunes of the party in general.

The Party's Officeholders in the States

State governors have long had an authoritative voice in their national parties. They have the prestige of high office and election victory. Many lead or at least have the support of their state party organizations, and some may run for their party's presidential nomination.

Governors gained a more formal position in the national parties since the 1960s. After the defeat of strongly conservative Republican presidential candidate Barry Goldwater in 1964, moderate Republican governors felt the need of a counterweight to conservatives. They established a full-time Washington office with financial help from the party's national committee; their influence waned, however, after the Republican victory of 1968. Democratic governors began to press for a role in national party affairs in the 1970s, when their party was in opposition. By 1974, they had won modest representation on the national committee. So by the late 1970s and early 1980s, the governors of both parties had Washington offices and staffs. Their organizational influence in the national parties, however, tends to be greatest in the power vacuum created when their party is out of power.

State legislators and local officials in both parties are organized as well, and have formal representation on the Democratic National Committee. It would be hard to argue, though, that they have much influence on either party's national business. A more influential group is the Democratic Leadership Council. Founded in 1985, it brings together elected officials, led by influential members of Congress and governors and some prospective candidates for president. The DLC represents the moderate-to-conservative wing of the party and is attempting to make the party appeal more to Southern and Western voters. It played an important role in Bill Clinton's rise to national prominence leading up to his 1992 nomination for president.

The Congressional Campaign Committees

The most important of all the supporting cast are each party's House and Senate campaign committees (called the "Hill committees" because they used to be housed on Capitol Hill). The House committees were founded in the immediate aftermath of the Civil War; the Senate committees came into being with the beginning of popular election of senators in 1913. The Democratic Congressional Campaign Committee (DCCC), the National Republican Congressional Committee (NRCC), the Democratic Senatorial Campaign Committee (DSCC), and the National Republican Senatorial Committee (NRSC) are organized to promote the reelection of their members and the success of other congressional candidates of their party. They are the campaign organizations of the congressional party in government, much as the national committee serves as the campaign organization of the presidential party.

The congressional campaign committees provide party candidates with an impressively wide range of campaign help, from production facilities for television spots to that most valuable of all resources, money (see box below). They have also

---

Help From the Hill:
Party Committees' Candidate Services

The six Washington party organizations ... train candidates and managers in the latest campaign techniques....

Over the course of the 1996 election cycle, the RNC established campaign management "colleges" and held seminars in forty-one states that served 6,000 Republican candidates and activists....

The Democrats, led by the DNC, held three campaign training sessions in Washington and four in different states that trained approximately 3,000 campaign operatives in general management, research, communications, fund-raising, and field activities....

The two House campaign committees assemble highly detailed issue research packages for candidates involved in some competitive races. These packages present hard facts about issues that are important to local voters and talking points that help candidates discuss these issues in a thematic and interesting manner....

The Hill committees assist selected candidates with campaign communications. The DSCC and the NRCC own state-of-the-art television and radio production facilities and furnish candidates with technical and editorial assistance in producing television and radio ads. The committees have satellite capabilities that enable candidates to beam television communications back to their districts to interact "live" with voters....

All six national party organizations give candidates tips on how to organize fund-raising committees and events. The Republican Hill committees and the DSCC even furnish some candidates with contributor lists, with the proviso that the candidates surrender their own lists to the committee after the election. Sometimes the parties host high-dollar events in Washington or make arrangements for party leaders to attend events held around the country either in person or via satellite television uplink.

Source: Paul S. Herrnson, *Congressional Elections*, 2nd ed. (Washington, DC: CQ Press, 1998), pp. 86–91. Copyright © 1998 by CQ Press. Reprinted by permission.

become increasingly active in channeling contributions from political action committees to the party's candidates. Although controlled by incumbent officeholders, they have been able to resist the pressures to serve only the reelection interests of incumbents and have concentrated considerable resources where they will have the greatest marginal payoff for the congressional party, such as in supporting their party's challengers to incumbents or candidates for open seats.

The new vitality of the congressional campaign committees stems from their increasing ability to raise campaign funds (see the Senate and House columns in Table 4.2). The Republican committees have taken the lead. Together they raised $139 million in the 1996 campaigns and $126 million in 1997–1998. The stunning success of GOP candidates in the 1994 elections was due in part to aggressive fundraising and candidate recruitment by their congressional committees. Some of the

TABLE 4.2 Political Party Net Receipts: 1975–76 to 1997–98 (in millions)

	National	Senate	House	State/Local	Total
Democratic Committees					
1975–1976	$ 13.1	1.0	0.9	0.0	$ 15.0
1977–1978	$ 11.3	0.3	2.8	8.7	$ 23.1
1979–1980	$ 15.1	1.7	2.1	11.7	$ 30.6
1981–1982	$ 16.4	5.6	6.5	10.6	$ 39.1
1983–1984	$ 46.6	8.9	10.4	18.5	$ 84.4
1985–1986	$ 17.2	13.4	12.3	14.1	$ 60.0
1987–1988	$ 52.3	16.3	12.5	44.7	$113.8
1989–1990	$ 14.5	17.5	9.1	44.7	$ 78.5
1991–1992	$ 65.8	25.5	12.8	73.7	$163.3
1993–1994	$ 41.8	26.4	19.4	55.6	$132.8
1995–1996	$108.4	30.8	26.6	93.2	$221.6
1997–1998	$ 64.8	35.6	25.2	63.4	$160.0
Republican Committees					
1975–1976	$ 29.1	12.2	1.8	0.0	$ 43.1
1977–1978	$ 34.2	10.9	14.1	20.9	$ 80.1
1979–1980	$ 76.2	23.3	28.6	33.8	$161.9
1981–1982	$ 83.5	48.9	58.0	24.0	$214.4
1983–1984	$105.9	81.7	58.3	43.1	$289.0
1985–1986	$ 83.8	84.4	39.8	47.2	$255.2
1987–1988	$ 91.0	65.9	34.7	66.0	$251.3
1989–1990	$ 68.7	65.1	33.2	39.3	$202.0
1991–1992	$ 85.4	73.8	35.3	72.8	$264.9
1993–1994	$ 87.4	65.3	26.7	75.0	$244.1
1995–1996	$193.0	64.5	74.2	128.4	$416.5
1997–1998	$104.0	53.4	72.7	89.4	$285.0

Note: Beginning with 1987–1988, total receipts do not include monies transferred among the listed committees.

Source: Federal Election Commission at http://www.fec.gov/press/demhrd98.htm and http://www.fec.gov/press/rephrd98.htm.

funds raised by the committees went directly to candidates, but the larger part went for candidate recruitment and training, research on opponents and issues, media, opinion polling, ads, and other campaign services. The Democrats have followed in a more modest way, raising almost $58 million in 1995–1996 and another $61 million in 1997–1998. In both parties, the Hill committees are much more active and effective than they were in the 1970s. In resources and campaigning skills, they have begun to challenge the importance of their national parties' committees.

TWO PATHS TO POWER

The two national parties have taken very different approaches to filling in the hollow organizational shells from which they came. The Republicans have followed a service path, and the Democrats began on a procedural path. Both have resulted in national party organizations that are stronger than ever before—in an era that was supposed to have been characterized by the "decline of parties."[6]

The key to the national parties' development has been their ability to attract thousands of small contributions through mass mailings to likely party supporters; this has given the parties an independent financial base.[7] The Republicans started this process in the mid–1970s, during the party's lean years. Their new affluence grew most dramatically in 1979–1980, peaked in 1983–1984 and again in 1995–1996, and has leveled off since. The Democratic committees began to follow suit in the midterm elections of 1982, and became even more competitive financially in the mid–1990s.

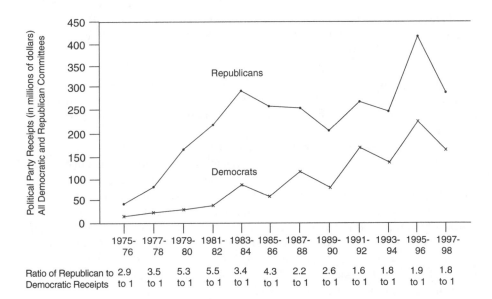

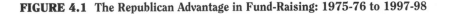

FIGURE 4.1 The Republican Advantage in Fund-Raising: 1975-76 to 1997-98

What began as a three-to-one and even five-to-one financial advantage for the Republicans now has been cut in about half (see Figure 4.1). For both parties, then, the greatest advances in fund-raising and organizational development have come when the party does not hold the presidency. Adversity breeds innovation.[8] With this new financing in hand, the Republicans and later the Democrats have developed strong and active national party organizations, which in turn have worked to support party candidates and state and local organizations throughout the nation. By the mid–1980s, the national parties had become institutionalized as "service" parties.[9]

Beginning in the 1960s, through party action often ratified by state law and court decisions, the Democrats pursued another goal. To represent new party constituencies better, they gave the national parties the authority over the presidential nomination process. Out of deference to its long-standing confederational structure, the GOP chose not to centralize authority. This precedent remains available to the GOP, however, if it ever wants to pursue it.

The Service Party Path

The service party was born when, at some point in the 1960s, a quiet revolution began in the Republican National Committee. The committee's chairman at the time, Ray Bliss, involved the committee more and more in helping state and local parties with the nuts and bolts of party organizational work. Chairman William Brock continued this effort in the late 1970s, turning the national party into an extraordinarily effective service organization for the state and local parties. Bliss and Brock, more than anyone else, revived and strengthened the Republican national party by fashioning a new role for it. Charles Manatt moved the Democratic National Committee onto the same path in the early 1980s.[10]

There were two keys to success in performing the new service role: money and mastery of the new campaign technologies. Using the new ability to generate computer-based mailing lists, the Republicans began a program of direct-mail solicitations that brought in ever higher levels of income (see Table 4.2). By the 1983–1984 election cycle, the Republican National Committee, along with its subsidiary funds and committees, had raised $105.9 million—a record for national committee fund-raising that has been broken only once since then. (Campaign finance is discussed more fully in Chapter 12.) These resources enabled the RNC and its affiliates to provide unparalleled support to candidates and local party organizations.

The Democrats, long mired in debt, began the 1980s badly eclipsed in organizational and service capacity. The good news for the Democrats was that they had dramatically improved their fund-raising capacities (see Table 4.2) and increased their activities in the states and localities. The bad news was that the Republicans were far ahead of them to begin with and were continuing to break new ground. Even so, the Democrats, under the national chairmanship of first Charles Manatt and then Paul Kirk, could see that their only feasible course was to become a service party. The national Democrats made no secret of their effort to imitate the Republican success in raising money and using it to buy services.

By the mid–1980s both parties were providing unprecedented levels of assistance to candidates and state parties. This assistance included a broad array of services— candidate recruitment and training, research, public opinion polling, data processing, computer networking and software development, production of radio and television commercials, direct mailing, expert consultants, and legal services—and millions of dollars to finance campaigns and to build party organizations. Concerned with the weakness of party organizations at the grass roots, Republican efforts have even turned to party-building there. The Republican National Committee, breaking with its tradition of working only with the state parties, lavished money and assistance in 1984 on 650 key counties containing a majority of the nation's voters. What money made possible, a growing professional staff in the national headquarters was able to implement (see Table 4.3). Both national parties have emerged as well-staffed, institutionalized political organizations.

The Democrats' Procedural-Reform Path

Before the national Democrats saw the advantages of a service orientation, they had been intensely engaged in reforming the party's rules for selecting presidential candidates. Beginning with efforts in the 1960s to enforce the loyalty of Southern delegations to the national party ticket and continuing with the nomination process reforms of the McGovern-Fraser Commission and its successors, the Democrats limited the autonomy of the state parties and the authority of state law in determining how delegates were to be selected for the presidential nominating conventions. (This story is told in more detail in Chapter 10.)[11] Key court decisions upheld these actions, further solidifying the newfound authority of the national party.

The immediate intent of the reformers was to make the nomination process more open and democratic. To achieve that goal, the confederate structure of the party, in which each state was sovereign in internal affairs, had to give way. That the reformers were successful in realizing their goals is testimony to the unusual politics of the period, the inattentiveness of state party leaders to the potential threat posed by the reforms,

TABLE 4.3 The Growth of National Party Committee Staff, 1972–96

	1972	1976	1980	1984	1988	1992	1996
Democratic Party Committees							
National Committee	30	30	40	130	160	270	264
House Campaign Committee	5	6	26	45	80	64	64
Senate Campaign Committee	4	5	20	22	50	35	38
Republican Party Committees							
National Committee	30	200	350	600	425	300	271
House Campaign Committee	6	8	40	130	80	89	64
Senate Campaign Committee	4	6	30	90	88	135	150

Note: These numbers fluctuate considerably from month to month and year to year. As a general rule, however, size of the national committees peaks in the presidential election year and is smaller in the interelection period.

Source: 1972–1984: Paul S. Herrnson, *Party Campaigning in the 1980s* (Cambridge, MA: Harvard University Press, 1988), p. 39; 1988: Paul S. Herrnson, "Reemergent National Party Organizations," in L. Sandy Maisel, ed., *The Parties Respond: Changes in the American Party System* (Boulder, CO: Westview Press, 1990), pp. 41–66 at p. 51. 1992: Herrnson, "The Revitalization of National Party Organizations," in Maisel, ed., *The Parties Respond: Changes in American Parties and Campaigns* (Boulder, CO: Westview Press, 1994), pp. 45–68 at p. 54. 1996: Herrnson, "National Party Organizations at the Century's End," in Maisel, ed. *The Parties Respond: Changes in American Parties and Campaigns* (Boulder, CO: Westview Press, 1998), pp. 60–61.

and the vacuum of power at the top of the traditional party organization. Ironically, the GOP, which had no strong desire to alter the rules of its nomination process,[12] was carried along nonetheless by the tide of Democratic Party reform because the bills passed by state legislatures to implement the reforms affected both parties.

In the early 1980s, the Democrats took stock of the reforms and didn't like what they saw. The newly centralized authority in nominating a presidential candidate and the increased grassroots participation in the nominating process had done little to win elections. Further, it had divided the party and alienated much of the Democratic Party in government, many of whom were conspicuously absent from party conventions and conferences in the 1970s. So the national Democrats decided to soft-pedal organizational reforms and move toward the Republican service model. The national committee adopted rules for the 1984 national convention that guaranteed a much greater representation of the party's leaders and officeholders. In addition, in the 1980s the party rushed to broaden the base of its fund-raising and to provide the means and know-how to recruit candidates and revitalize local parties. When the dust from all of this effort settled, the signs of change were everywhere, authority over party rules had been nationalized, and what had been two models for strengthening the national party were rapidly converging into one.[13]

POWER AND AUTHORITY IN THE NATIONAL PARTY

In sum, these dramatic changes in the national parties have helped restore some of the parties' lost roles in nominating and electing candidates. To an important degree, the parties (especially the Republicans) have begun to "muscle in" on the campaign support functions monopolized just a few years ago by political action committees (PACs) and private political consultants. It is unlikely that parties can displace them. But it is certainly possible that the main significance of these competitors to parties will be their service as temporary bridges between the old party, centered at the grass roots, and the new national service party. The buttressing of the national parties also has the potential to alter the relationships within the parties: between the national party and state and local party organizations, the president, and the Congress, as well as among the various segments of the national parties.

The State and Local Connection

Have the greater visibility and power of the national parties led to a centralization of authority within them? The answer is not yet clear. The Democrats seem more likely to become more centralized; they approach the service party role with far more experience than the Republicans have in drafting and enforcing national rules, and a stronger will to assert centralized authority.[14] Moreover, the structure of representation on the DNC can sustain and legitimize centralized authority. The Republicans are more wary of centralization, both by political philosophy and in their structure. Yet because of their vastly superior resources, the national Republicans have penetrated more fully to the state and local level.

Philosophies aside, it certainly seems likely that the national aid to state and local parties and campaigns and the national intervention in their nomination processes will result in some centralization of authority, despite the strains that entails (see box on p. 88). The temptation to guide and direct from above is strong given the expertise and resources of the national parties. The result is likely to be a national imprint on the issues discussed, the kinds of candidates recruited, and the way things are done organizationally in the parties. State and local organizations that resist the national party's suggestions could find themselves on the short end of the national party's money and help. Those who pay the pipers tend to call the tune.[15]

The Presidential Connection

When a party holds the presidency, the president's program and record become the voters. His preferences, whether embodied in the formal measures of the State of the Union address or tossed off more casually at a press conference, impose a policy and a record on his party. He may consult the party chair or other party notables, but it is his decisions, his successes or failures, that form the party record.

Every president in recent memory has kept his national committee on a short leash, but White House dominance of the national party reached its zenith in the presidency of Richard Nixon. The Watergate tapes reveal that Republican Party bodies and officials were so marginal to Nixon's 1972 reelection campaign that they remained ignorant and innocent of the wrongdoing and scandals of the campaign. Democratic presidents, too, have wanted the national committee under their control.

During the 1980s the national committee of the president's party, here the Republican National Committee, really came into its own as an important independent actor in party politics. Federal funding of presidential campaigns, with its strict limits on party spending for presidential politics, freed the national committees from their traditional concentration on presidential elections and allowed them to dedicate their now considerable resources to party-building at the state and local level. At the same time the party committees carved out new roles in raising "soft" money for the presidential campaign and channeling this money to the state and local parties for grassroots mobilization activities (see Chapter 12 on soft money).

In addition, the selection of close advisers to the president as its recent chairs has given the RNC a status it had not enjoyed before, even as presidential influence was being asserted. Designation of President Reagan's longtime friend, Senator Paul Laxalt of Nevada, to the post of general chairman and the appointment of Nevada's party chairman, Frank Fahrenkopf, to the party chairmanship eliminated the tensions between the White House and the national committee that inevitably follow a transition from the leaderless party out of power to a presidential party. The move also brought the party leader into the inner circle of White House advisers. President Clinton's choice of Christopher Dodd as general chair and Donald Fowler as national chair of the DNC in 1995 was similarly designed to integrate the national committee more fully into the presidential reelection effort.

Tension between the State and National Parties

Increased national party activity and authority can produce conflict with the traditionally independent state parties. These two examples illustrate how national
party incursions into areas traditionally left to states have led to tensions
between state and national party leaders.

RNC Favoritism in Contested Primaries

In its efforts to field the strongest party ticket, the RNC under William Brock
adopted a policy of picking one candidate to support in contested state primaries. Occasionally, RNC efforts backfired, such as in 1978 when it supported
the primary opponent of the candidate, Lee Dreyfus, who went on to become
governor of Wisconsin—and no friend of the national party establishment. In
response to criticisms from the state party leaders, the party revised this policy in 1980. Now, before the RNC can support a candidate for nomination, it
must have the approval of the state party chair and the national committee
members from the state.[16]

DNC Efforts to Reduce "Party Bashing"

Recognizing that candidates were undermining their own party by running
against the national Democratic party, in 1986 DNC Chair Paul Kirk asked state
Democratic leaders who wished to participate in a DNC-financed program for
state party-building to sign an agreement that would require them, in the words
of the DNC memorandum,

> to insist that Democratic candidates who benefit from this program do
> not run campaigns against, and instead run with, the national Democra-
> tic Party. This means exerting all of the state party's influence and bring-
> ing to bear all of the pressure it can to ensure that a positive, unified
> Democratic party campaign develops. It also means that the state party
> and state committee shall disagree with and disavow any remarks by a
> candidate or campaign that attack the national party.

Not surprisingly, the Republicans gleefully attacked the Democrats for
attempting to impose an undemocratic loyalty oath, and some state Democratic leaders expressed dismay that the national party was overreacting to a
minor problem.

These cases are the exceptions, however. Candidates for office, often thank-
ful for assistance of any sort, have welcomed the technical and financial
resources offered by the national parties. State and local organizations have usually considered the national efforts at party-building and candidate support to
be more of an opportunity than a threat. Undoubtedly, state and local party
leaders and candidates occasionally resent the intrusion of the sometimes brash
and arrogant national party operatives into their local affairs, but cooperative
relationships have been the norm.

By contrast, in those four long years after presidential defeat, a national party suffers constant jockeying for the right to lead. The defeated presidential candidate, depending on his ties and popularity within the party, may achieve an important voice in the party. Gerald Ford did, but George Bush, Michael Dukakis, and even Robert Dole, a former RNC chair, did not. A strong and vigorous national chair may help to fill the void in national leadership; those with substantial financial and organizational accomplishments, like the RNC's Haley Barbour, are more likely to succeed. Most commonly, however, leadership of the "out" party falls to its leaders in Congress, supported by the resources of its campaign committees. Above all, the congressional party, simply because its legislative responsibilities force it to take policy stands, formulates the party position and challenges the program of the opposition's president.

It seems safe to predict that strengthened national party committees will be able to take a more prominent role in the party out of power, as will their chairs. That was certainly true of the Republicans under William Brock in the late 1970s and Haley Barbour in the 1990s, and the Democrats under Charles Manatt and Paul Kirk during the Reagan years. But the national committees in the president's party may face a more uphill climb. Presidents naturally want the new party power to be at their service. They will certainly want the party committees to mobilize all those members of Congress they recruited, trained, financed, and helped elect, to support the president's program. Also, presidents in their first term will very likely want to draw on the assets of the national party for their reelection campaigns as much as the Federal Election Campaign Act permits. If presidents feared and used the national committees when the committees were weak, they have even more reason to turn to them when the committees are stronger. Even as the national parties continue their party-building, it will be in the service of presidential goals.[17]

The Congressional Connection

Nationalizing forces have overtaken the Congress as well. Congressional campaign committees have become more and more active in recruiting and supporting party candidates. In 1994 and 1996, for example, the two parties' congressional campaign committees initially targeted 160 seats each and later whittled their lists down to about seventy-five—many more races than they normally targeted in the 1980s. This help is more valuable to challengers and candidates for open seats than to incumbents, who are easily able to raise their own campaign resources. In general, however, the committees tend to protect their incumbents when they expect a lean election year and invest in challengers and open seats when a big victory looks likely.

It is tempting to attribute the increased party voting in Congress (see Chapter 13) in part to the campaign funds given by each congressional party's campaign committee. The party leadership has so far refrained from giving out campaign money and services on the basis of a candidate's support for the party's program. But it has not been bashful in reminding members, especially newly elected members, that the party played some role in their election success. The remarkable cohesion of the post–1994 Republican majority in the House surely stems in part from the party leadership's financial and other support for Republicans in the 1994 elections. Constituency pressures will always be paramount in the Congress, but the more senators and representatives can count on campaign support from the congressional party, the more open they will be to party-based appeals.[18] This campaign support may also, to some degree, counterbalance pressures on Congress from PACs and competing centers of party power in Washington—the president and the national party committees.

The Connections within the National Party

There are many opportunities for cooperation among each national party's three main election committees—its national committee and the Senate and House campaign committees—and this cooperation has increased greatly. All three committees benefit, for example, from voter registration and get-out-the-vote drives, and there are often economies of scale to be realized in working together on candidate recruitment and campaigns. The committees are more competitive, however, in raising and spending their money (see box below). They seek financial support from the same contributors (and jealously guard their contributor lists), recruit political talent from the same limited pool, and pursue sometimes incompatible goals. Where resources are as scarce as they are in party organizing, it should not be surprising that different organizations from the same party will struggle over them.[19]

Conflict Among the Party Committees: Ed Rollins and the White House in 1990

Conflict over strategy during the 1990 midterm campaigns pitted Edward Rollins, cochairman of the National Republican Congressional Committee and a well-respected campaign strategist, against the White House and the Republican National Committee. In a memo to Republican House candidates early in the campaign, Rollins advised them to distance themselves from President Bush's recent support for a tax increase (particularly because it violated Bush's 1988 campaign pledge of "no new taxes"). This repudiation of their president's action, urged by Rollins to protect Republican House candidates from electoral retribution, infuriated the White House and led to Rollins's resignation on the eve of the RNC meeting in January, 1991. Rollins was caught in a conflict between two important groups: House candidates, who wanted to win even if that meant deserting their president on a controversial issue, and the national party committee and the White House, who needed to protect the president's authority and national standing. Rollins turned up in 1992, for a short stint at least, as a top campaign advisor to independent candidate Ross Perot, and has remained active in national campaigns.

THE LIMITS OF PARTY ORGANIZATION

Even the new strength in the national party organizations, however, may not be enough to revive the parties in the minds of many Americans. More professional, service-oriented parties may be better at helping candidates in their races for office than in stimulating voter attachments to parties or involving people at the grass roots. The strengthening of parties at the center is a fascinating change, but it may have contributed little to increasing their role in American politics.[20]

Remember that even with these changes, American party organizations remain weak by most standards. In this era of large-scale business, government, universities, and voluntary organizations, the parties cut an unimpressive figure. They lack the top-down control and efficiency, the unified setting of priorities, and the central responsibility we often find in parties in other nations. Rather than provide continuous, goal-related action, most American party organizations are more sporadic; they improvise, and sometimes they disappear from sight. Where the party organizations of other Western democracies have had permanent, highly professional leadership and large party bureaucracies, most American party organizations have generally done without a professional bureaucracy or leadership cadre. Especially at the local level, the business of American party organization is still often in the hands of part-time activists and inexperienced professionals, which is perhaps to say that its business and its organizational relationships require little specialization or high-level professional care. Even at the national level, as Epstein has observed: "The very word 'committee' suggests limited national structure."[21]

It is not surprising that the American party organization's development remains stunted even in these times of unprecedented strength at its national level. There is little in American political values that would welcome an efficient or "businesslike" operation of the parties. These traditional fears of party strength combine with legal limits on the parties and the effects of the separation of powers and the federal structure of our political system. Even recent campaign finance reforms have contributed to the weakness of the party organizations by denying them their traditional position as a major source of campaign funds. By restricting the parties' direct contributions to $5,000 per federal candidate, the statutes now treat parties as just another source of candidate support along with political action committees and individuals, rather than as organizations that are integral to the electoral process.[22]

The very idea of organization implies routine and continuity. Thus an elaborate party organization may be more compatible with a party of unchanging ideology or principle rather than with a party committed to making the adjustments necessary for electoral success in a pragmatic political system. The fundamental character of the American parties is that of flexible, election-oriented organizations involved mainly in supporting candidates for public office and active mainly during campaigns. As such, they have long been led and dominated not by career bureaucrats but by public office seekers and holders. So even though they now boast active and vibrant committees in Washington, the electoral preoccupation of the American parties may have tipped the scales against any genuinely elaborate party organization. They remain candidate-centered organizations in a candidate-centered political world.

Chapter 5
....

The Political Party
of the Activists

*F*ighting the bitter cold on a snowy evening in Iowa, thousands of Democrats and Republicans headed for schools, firehouses, and other locations to begin the process of choosing their party's candidate for president in January, 2000. These were not state party leaders. Many of them were—or would become—party activists, contributing their time and energy to their party on a purely voluntary basis. Even the paid professional party workers who increasingly staff the national and state offices share many of the attributes of these volunteers. They are not quoted in media accounts or mentioned in state laws. Yet their activity and motivations are at the heart of party politics.

As an organization, the political party is designed to unite people in meeting goals. People who become active in the party organization have their own personal goals as well. Individual party leaders and workers have some reasons—seek some payoffs—for devoting their time to the party's activities rather than to their church, their service organization, or their basketball game. So the party has to be able to work toward its organizational goals while at the same time allowing its individual members to achieve theirs. If it fails to do so, its future as a viable party may be short. How it accomplishes this tricky challenge (and whether it does) is determined by the private life of the party—its internal division of labor and allocation of authority, its communication patterns, and the decision-making processes through which it chooses how to mobilize its resources.

INCENTIVES FOR POLITICAL ACTIVITY

The American political parties have never operated primarily in a cash economy. They have rarely bought or hired more than a small proportion of the millions of labor hours they need. Even today, in spite of the increasing professionalization of the national and state party headquarters, very few local party organizations have any paid staff members, and it is a rare local chairman who draws any salary.[1]

The large number of Americans who are active in the parties receive no cash in return for their considerable time and skills. Even the old customs of paying precinct workers on election day or using government employees as the party's workers at election time are vanishing. What, then, induces all these people to lavish their hours and efforts on trying to meet the party's goals?

In their seminal theory, Peter B. Clark and James Q. Wilson identified three different types of reasons why individuals become active in organizations. *Material incentives* are tangible rewards for activity—direct cash payments for work, or an implicit understanding that involvement will be rewarded with some kind of material benefits. *Solidary incentives* are the intangible benefits that people can gain from associating with others, from being part of a group. *Purposive incentives* are intangible rewards of a different kind—based on the sense of satisfaction that comes when people are involved in a worthwhile cause or in activities that promote some issue or principle that matters to them. This typology has been used widely and fruitfully in studying people's motives for becoming and staying involved in party work.[2]

Material Incentives

Historically, the main material inducement to party activity has been the opportunity to share in the "spoils" gained when a party controls the government. These "spoils" have come in the form of patronage and preferments. *Patronage* refers to the appointment of an individual to a government job as a reward for party work. Similarly, the party can provide loyal workers with a base of support if they seek elected office. *Preferments* involve, more generally, granting the favors of government to party supporters. Patronage, access to elected office, and preferments have all played important roles in building and sustaining the American party organizations.[3]

Patronage   Since the beginning of the Republic, but especially since the presidency of Andrew Jackson when federal patronage jobs doubled, Americans have been attracted to party work by the prospect of being rewarded with government jobs. Patronage has been used in other nations as well, but no other party system has relied on patronage as systematically and for as long as has the American system. In the heyday of the political machine, for example, city governments were staffed almost entirely by loyalists of the party in power, all of whom faced the prospect of being thrown out of work if their party were turned out of office.[4]

As the price to be paid for their jobs, patronage appointees traditionally "volunteered" their time, energy, and often even a part of their salary to the party organization. Campaign help was especially expected; American party politics is rich with tales of the entire staff of certain government departments being put to work in support of their boss's reelection. Money, too, has always been an important resource in campaigns, and patronage workers have been called upon to "invest" in the party that gave them their jobs. Even now, when such practices are increasingly frowned upon and sometimes even illegal, government employees can still face compelling pressures to contribute time or money to the party. The line between voluntary and expected support is a fine one, and it is understandable that at least some public employees choose to remain on the safe side of that line by contributing, even if they are not required to do so.

Despite the explosive growth of government to more than 18 million public employees (about 3 million federal, more than 4 million state, and almost 11 million local), the number of patronage jobs available to the parties has declined dramatically.

The main reason is that civil service and merit systems have expanded. The first major step in this process was the establishment of the federal civil service system by the Pendleton Act in 1883, which removed almost 14,000 of the (then) more than 131,000 federal employees from patronage appointment.[5] The number of full-time federal positions filled by political appointees has dwindled over the years to fewer than 10,000 today, many of them high-level policy-making positions.[6] States and cities have followed the same path, but more slowly; large numbers have replaced patronage with appointments made on the basis of competitive exams, at least for employees who are not in policy-making positions.

The Supreme Court has contributed to the dismantling of patronage at the state and local level. In 1976 and 1980 the Court ruled that some county political employees could not be fired simply because of a change of the party in power. The Supreme Court went further in a 1990 Illinois case, determining that politically based hiring and promotion violated the First Amendment freedoms of speech and association. In each case, the Court acknowledged that party affiliation might be a relevant condition in filling policy-making positions but not in filling lower-level offices (see box below).[7]

Even where patronage positions remain, it has become more difficult for parties to use them as incentives for party activity. The available patronage jobs are frequently not very attractive to the kinds of activists the party wants to recruit. The politics of patronage worked best among the disadvantaged, who were willing to accept whatever city or county jobs were offered; most patronage positions do not tempt the educated, "respected," middle-class leadership the parties would like to attract. Further, evidence from a variety of locales shows that the parties achieve only a partial return in party work or contributions from their patronage appointees. And in an age of candidate-centered politics, elected executives are more interested in using patronage to build their own political followings than to strengthen the party organization. As the supply of valuable patronage jobs dwindles, party leaders are probably even more convinced of the old saying that each appointment creates a lot of resentful people who didn't get the job and one ingrate who did.[8]

The Dismantling of Chicago's "Patronage Army"

Unable to defeat a candidate of Chicago's Democratic machine in a race for delegate to the state's 1969 constitutional convention, frustrated reformer Michael Shakman sought judicial relief. He challenged the constitutionality of the city's patronage system in the federal courts. His suit triggered a series of court rulings and subsequent consent decrees between 1972 and 1988 through which the city agreed, though grudgingly, to eliminate political hiring and firing for all but the top policy-making positions and to protect city employees from being forced to do political work or make political contributions. To implement these agreements, the courts required the city to develop stringent plans for compliance and to submit to yearly external audits of its personnel practices. While politics still influences personnel decisions in Chicago government, the large "patronage army" that once was the hallmark of Chicago politics seems to have been dismantled.[9]

Even so, patronage is likely to survive as long as it is attractive to both political leaders and their followers. Mayors, governors, and presidents will continue to reserve top policy-making positions for their loyal supporters. Legislatures at all levels of government will remain reluctant to bring their staff employees under the protection of civil service systems. Civil service rules for governmental employees can be bypassed by hiring politically loyal "temporary" workers outside of the civil service system or by channeling party loyalists into jobs in private firms that depend on government business. Honorary positions on government advisory groups will linger on as coveted rewards for loyal party service. A few big campaign contributors will continue to be named ambassadors to small and peaceful countries. Wherever political leaders retain discretion over personnel appointments, in short, they will find a way to award them to their trusted political supporters. The promise of such awards, in turn, will keep attracting people to political activity—though not the large numbers who once served as the "foot soldiers" of the traditional political machines.

Keep in mind that some thoughtful observers are sorry to lose the practice of patronage, as unsavory as it seems now, that has been central to American political life since early in the nineteenth century. Patronage was a means of keeping party organizations strong, as instruments of democracy; without it, parties can find it more and more difficult to recruit the labor they need. Activists who are recruited by parties in the absence of patronage are likely to have other goals; they may demand more ideological payoffs for their participation, and that would undermine the pragmatic, inclusive approaches that the parties have taken during most of their histories.

The replacement of political appointees by neutral professionals may actually make governmental bureaucracies less responsive to elected political leaders and perhaps even less sympathetic to their clienteles. When government jobs are filled by civil service procedures (and thus protected by those procedures), it becomes almost impossible for reform-minded leaders to replace a stodgy or ineffective bureaucracy with more efficient workers. It is easy to forget that patronage practices were first promoted at the federal level by Andrew Jackson to produce a more democratic and less elitist government, and that career civil service employees today are often criticized as unresponsive to the public they are supposed to serve.[10]

Patronage jobs in government, however, are not the only employment opportunities a party can offer. In recent years, party organizations at the state and national levels have become important employers themselves of paid professional campaign workers. To provide services to their candidates, party organizations need computer specialists, pollsters, media production experts, field directors, researchers, fund-raisers, strategists, Webmasters, direct mail specialists, and other purveyors of new campaign techniques. Many activists are attracted to party work in the hopes of landing these jobs (see box on p. 96).

Elected Office   Some women and men become party activists because they see that as a first step toward running for office. About 40 percent of the county chairpersons interviewed in a 1979–1980 national survey hoped to hold public office, and an earlier study found that one third of all state party chairs became candidates for elective office after serving the party.[11] Involvement in the party, like activity in other community

The New Political Professionals

Professional campaign specialists are an essential part of the workings of modern politics. Here are two such specialists on opposite sides of the political fence:

Celinda Lake, president of Lake Snell Perry & Associates, is a Democratic political strategist. She was responsible for focus group research for the Clinton/Gore campaign in 1992, and served as general consultant to that campaign. Formerly political director for the Women's Campaign Fund, Lake has a special interest in women candidates and in framing issues to women voters. She has done public opinion polling for such candidates as Senators Carol Moseley-Braun, Blanche Lambert Lincoln, and Mary Landrieu and for Governor Gary Locke of Washington State, the first Asian-American governor in the U.S. She also currently polls for *U.S. News & World Report* and for groups including the AFL-CIO, the Sierra Club, and Planned Parenthood.

David B. Hill taught political science at Texas A&M University until he decided to put his public opinion research skills to work in political campaigns. He founded Hill Research Consultants in Texas in 1988. Currently his firm provides a broad array of services to two or three major Republican governor or Senate campaigns in each two-year election cycle, as well as to half a dozen congressional races and a number of referendum campaigns, which often involve education issues. In the 1998 election, for example, his clients included Peter Fitzgerald (Carol Moseley-Braun's Senate opponent) and the re-election campaign of Michigan's governor John Engler. Hill serves as a general consultant with emphasis on polling and focus group analysis. About half of his work is for nonpolitical clients.

organizations, remains an attractive way for aspiring politicians to build a base from which to launch a political career.

A few party organizations enjoy such disciplined control over their primaries that they can and do "give" nominations to public office, especially at the state and local level, to loyal party workers. That degree of control over nomination and election to office, however, is rare today. It is far more common for candidates to see the party as one of the bases, in some areas the most important one, of support for election or reelection. Candidates need advice, know-how, people (staff and volunteers), and money, and the party remains a likely source of all of these. So the lure of party support in a later campaign for elected office may bring some people into party work.

Preferments   Party activity can lead to tangible rewards other than elective or appointive office. Because public officials can exercise at least some discretion in distributing government services and in granting government contracts, the potential for political favoritism exists. Many people become involved in party activity and in making contributions to their party in the hope of attracting these favors. A big giver or "fat cat" might, for example, be hoping to win a government contract to build a new school or library. It is no accident that leaders of the construction industry are so active politically in states and localities that spend millions every year on roads and public buildings.

Preference may take other forms; potential activists may hope for tolerant government regulation or inspection policies, unusually prompt snow and garbage removal, fixed traffic tickets, or admission to a crowded state university. It may also involve the granting of scarce opportunities such as liquor licenses or cable television franchises or the calculated "overlooking" of prostitution or drug trafficking in return for some form of political support. "Preferment," in other words, means receiving special treatment or advantage that flows from the party's holding the decision-making positions in government.

Reformers have promoted a number of safeguards over the years, many of them enacted into law, to limit the discretion available to governments in giving out benefits and buying goods and services from private firms. Examples are competitive and sealed bidding, conflict of interest statutes, privatization, and even affirmative action. Nonetheless, because the potential benefits are so great for both sides, there always seem to be ways to evade even the tightest controls. There is understandable resistance, in the name of both democracy and efficiency, to sacrificing *all* discretion in order to eliminate *political* discretion. The result is that preferments may have taken the place of patronage as the main material incentive for political activity. In the process, though, party leaders have lost an important source of leverage over officeholders, at whose discretion preferments are granted.[12]

Solidary Incentives

Other motivations for party activity are not as easy to measure as a government job or the awarding of a contract. Many people are drawn to party work, however, by the social contact it provides. In an age when some people's closest relationship is with their computer or their television, the face-to-face contact found at a party headquarters or caucus provides a chance to meet like-minded people and feel a part of an active group. Family traditions may lead some young adults to go to party activities looking for social life, just as others may look to a softball league or a religious group. The chance to meet local officials whose photos appear in the newspaper may be a draw. Almost all reported research on the motivations of party activists has found a substantial number who cite the social life of party politics as a valuable reward.[13]

These social satisfactions have psychological roots. "Like the theater, politics is a great nourisher of egos," writes one observer. It attracts men and women "who are hungry for attention, for assurance that somebody loves them, for the soul-stirring music of their own voices."[14] The solidarity of party work can help people feel a part of something larger than themselves—a charismatic leader, an important movement, a moment in history. The party can be a small island of excitement in a sea of routine. For some, party activity provides the lure of power; even a precinct committeewoman can dream of herself as a future state chair or a member of Congress.

Purposive Incentives

To an increasing extent, people are led to party activism by their commitment to particular issues or attitudes about the proper role of government. Someone dedicated to abortion rights, for example, might begin by working for a pro-choice Democratic candidate and then come to see the candidate's party as a vehicle for protecting abortion rights in Congress. A property rights activist may be attracted to the Republican Party by its statements about limited government. Other groups compete for the attention of these activists; the abortion rights supporter, for instance, could also work effectively through organized interests such as the National Abortion and Reproductive Rights Action League and Planned Parenthood. But parties at all levels have seen an influx of issue-driven activists during the last several decades.

A parallel movement has taken place at the national level. One of the early ideological triumphs was the capture of the national Republicans in 1964 by conservatives supporting Senator Barry Goldwater for president. Soon after, liberal ideologues left their mark on the national Democratic Party on behalf of Eugene McCarthy (1968) and George McGovern (1972). Later came the victories of Ronald Reagan in 1980 both within the Republican Party and throughout the nation, and the rise of Christian fundamentalists in the GOP of the 1980s and 1990s. As these examples suggest, it is often the force of an attractive leader that brings ideologically motivated activists into the party. But even in the absence of such a leader, some issues and ideological movements have had enough power to lead activists to switch parties: for example, pro-lifers and Southern conservatives who moved from the Democratic to the Republican Party and who soon made an impact on the issue positions of their new party.[15]

Party activists may also be motivated by a more general sense of civic obligation or a belief in the importance of citizen participation in a democracy. Scholars who have questioned party workers about their motives for service in the party know the familiar answers. They were asked to serve, they say, and they agreed because it was their civic duty. This response is often an honest reflection of deeply ingrained civic values, sometimes derived from local traditions of commitment to political reform and "good government."

Mixed Incentives

No party organization depends on a single incentive, and very few people become party activists for only one reason. Most party organizations rely on a variety of incentives. Activists who hope for an attractive job or some other preferment work together with those motivated by a particular issue or by a sense of civic duty. Both may enjoy the sense of solidarity they derive from social contact with like-minded people. There may be different incentives at different levels of the party organization, with higher-level activists sustained more by purposive incentives and lower-level activists attracted by material or solidary rewards.[16] Alternatively, the mix may differ depending on the type of local community, with more traditional cultures giving rise to parties built around material motives, and reform-oriented cultures attracting purposive activists.

Yet when we look at the two major American parties across communities, the evidence, though limited, shows that issue or ideological incentives—purposive incentives—are now the dominant motive for party activism. Most party workers are attracted by a desire to use the party as a means to achieve policy goals.[17] Although we do not have comparable data on earlier periods, there is reason to believe that this was far less true of party workers a generation or two ago.[18] The energy and passion in party organizations comes increasingly from issue-driven activists.

The incentive that recruits people to party work, of course, may not be the incentive that keeps them there. Several studies suggest that activists who come to the party to fulfill purposive goals—to fight for certain issues—are more likely to remain in the party if they come to value the social contact they get from party activism. The motive that sustains their party work, in short, tends to shift to solidary incentives: friendships, identification with the party itself, and other personal rewards and satisfactions.[19] It may be that committed issue activists simply burn out or that the pragmatic American parties, in their effort to remain flexible enough to win elections, cannot provide the level of ideological dedication needed to sustain party workers whose political lives revolve around a set of issues.

THE PROCESSES OF RECRUITMENT

The simple existence of incentives is not enough to produce a party full of activists. A party, like other organizations, has to recruit the kinds of participants who will be able to work effectively on its behalf. But the parties do not find it easy to recruit. Except at the national level and in some states, where there has been a recent increase in paid positions and exciting professional opportunities, the parties often have no effective means of enlisting new activists. Some local parties can become so inbred that they may not even recognize the need for new blood.

To add to the challenge, state laws often take at least part of the recruitment process out of the party's hands; open party caucuses and the election of party officials in primaries limit the party's control over its personnel. The party organization's limited power over its own recruitment makes a difference. It can lead to the takeover of a local (or even a state) party organization by an intense group of issue activists. At the least, it leaves a party vulnerable to shifts in its direction, as some leaders and activists move on and new, self-recruited personnel take their places.

The Recruitment System

Because party organizations have a chronic need for activists of any kind, they are very likely to accept whatever help is available. The nature of parties' recruitment system, then, is pretty haphazard. Some people, fascinated by public policy or by particular issues, recruit themselves. More often they are persuaded to take part by others. Party leaders and activists may encourage their friends and associates to join them in party work. Over the years, most activists have reported that they first became involved with the party as a result of these informal, personal requests for help.[20]

Events in the larger political world also play an important role in the recruitment of party activists. Some people may be first attracted to party work by a specific candidate or cause and may remain active long after the original reason has disappeared. The nature and direction of the Democratic Party was heavily influenced by the influx of liberals activated by the Vietnam War and the civil rights movement in the 1960s and 1970s. Similarly, the GOP has been energized by religious conservatives, mobilized not only by Barry Goldwater and Ronald Reagan but by fundamentalist ministers such as Pat Robertson. Because this recruitment process often depends on the presence of magnetic personalities and powerful issues, it tends to be episodic rather than continuous. It produces generational differences among party activists in which political outlooks may differ considerably depending on when the individuals became active. More than any other single factor, it defines the ideological direction of the parties.[21]

The result is an extensive, informal recruitment system–a complex of interrelated factors that selects out of the American population a particular group of men and women. Its chief elements are:

- The motives and experiences of the people whom the parties want to recruit.
- The incentives the party can offer for party activity and the value of those incentives.
- The role that state law allows the party to play in recruitment.
- The contacts, opportunities, and events that are the immediate occasions of recruitment.[22]

The components of this system change constantly, and as they do, they affect the number and types of people who become active. That, in turn, makes a difference. A local Democratic Party whose activists come largely from local labor unions will have different concerns and styles from a local Democratic Party dominated by environmental activists, just as a Republican organization run by local business leaders can differ from one dominated by the Religious Right. Recruitment in any form, however, involves a matching of the motives and goals of the individual with the incentives and expectations of the party organization.

How Are Leaders Recruited?

One way to choose leaders is to recruit from within by promoting especially effective party workers to more responsible positions. A study of Detroit showed this system at work in the 1950s: Party leaders had risen exclusively through the avenues of party and public office. One group came up through the precinct positions, another rose through auxiliary organizations (for instance, women's groups, youth organizations, political clubs), and a third and smaller group moved from the race for public office to a career within the party.[23] More recent data suggest, however, that party activists do not invariably inch up the career ladder in the party, position by position. Almost half of a national sample of Democratic and Republican county chairs in 1979–1980, for example, had held no party office before becoming chair.[24] These patterns vary with the nature of the political organization. In party organizations that have relatively open access and easy mobility, careers in the party are developed easily, almost spontaneously. In more disciplined party organizations, party activists must work up the hierarchy in carefully graded steps. Over time, with the decline of the old-style hierarchical organizations, career paths have become more varied.

THE RECRUITS: AMATEURS AND PROFESSIONALS

These various incentives and recruitment processes combine to produce the party cadres—the men and women who do the work of the parties. These activists play a wide range of roles in party affairs, from campaigning on behalf of party candidates and serving as delegates to party-nominating conventions, to staffing the party offices.

Common Characteristics

Who are the party activists? Although they differ in motivations, American party activists have two characteristics in common that set them apart from the general population. First, they tend to come from families with a history of party activity. Study after study indicates that large numbers of party activists had an adult party activist in their immediate family as they were growing up. Second, activists are relatively high in socioeconomic status (SES); they tend to have higher incomes, more years of formal education, and higher-status occupations than does the average American. Lawyers are especially common among the active partisans, just as they are among elected officials.[25] The parties thus attract men and women with the time and financial resources to afford politics, the information and knowledge to understand it, and the skills to be useful in it.[26]

Some local organizations provide exceptions to this general pattern. The patronage-oriented, favor-dispensing machines in the city centers tended to recruit party workers and leaders who were more representative of the populations with which they worked. For many lower-status Americans, the material incentives the machines could provide were probably the crucial reasons for their activism. When patronage and other material incentives dwindled, the social character of these parties changed. A comparison of county committee members from both Pittsburgh parties in 1971, 1976, and 1983 shows that as machine control declined, the education levels of party cadres increased. The mix of incentives that parties can provide, in short, has clear implications for the social composition of the activists it can recruit.[27]

The social characteristics of Democratic activists differ from those of Republicans, consistent with the differing social bases of the parties' voters. Democratic activists are more likely than their Republican counterparts to be black, union members, or Catholic. But differences in education, income, and occupation have declined in recent years. Although they may come from different backgrounds and certainly possess different political views, the leaders of both parties seem to be drawn disproportionately from the higher status groups in American society.[28] This pattern may not be found to the same degree in other nations' party systems because most democracies have a viable socialist party, many of whose activists have been recruited from the ranks of organized labor.

Professionals versus Amateurs

In addition to their social characteristics, activists' goals, expectations, and skills help shape their party organizations. Observers of the American party organizations often classify party activists into two types based not only on their personal characteristics but also on the role they play in the organization and the expectations they have for it. One type of party activist is the *professional*–the traditional party worker whose first loyalty is to the party itself and whose operating style is pragmatic. Its antithesis is the *amateur*–the issue-oriented purist who sees party activity as only one means for achieving important political goals. Professionals and amateurs differ in almost all of the characteristics important for party activists (see Table 5.1).

These polar types are abstractions rather than descriptions of specific individuals. They tend to be purer and more extreme than we are likely to find in reality. Most party workers probably harbor a mixture of professional and amateur orientations. The terms have also become pejorative labels for the opposition in internal party disputes. Nevertheless, the typology has been useful in distinguishing between machine politicians and reformers in city politics, between party regulars and ideological

TABLE 5.1 Professionals and Amateurs: A Typology

	Professionals	Amateurs
Political Style	Pragmatic	Purist
Incentives for activism	Material (patronage, preferments)	Purposive (issues, ideology)
Locus of party loyalty	Party organization	Officeholders, other political groups
Desired orientation of party	To candidates, elections	To issues, ideology
Criterion for selecting party candidates	Electability	Principles
Desired process of party governance	Hierarchical	Democratic
Support of party candidates	Automatic	Conditional on issues, principles
Recruitment path	Through party	Through issue, candidate organizations
SES level	Average to above average	Well above average

insurgents at the party nominating conventions, and even between "old"- and "new"-style party activists (see box below).[29]

A party organization populated by amateurs would seem likely to behave very differently from a party dominated by professionals. Above all, amateur activists are likely to be more issue-oriented and to insist on widespread participation within the organization in order to bring their issue concerns to the party. They tend to be less comfortable with the traditional electoral pragmatism of the parties—that is, with making compromises in their positions in order to win elections. They are drawn into the party, in short, to achieve purposive goals and often disdain material incentives. When they come to dominate party organizations, they often bring a strong push for reform not only in the internal business of the party but also in the larger political system.

Differences that are clear in theory, however, do not always carry over into practice. Amateurs may hold different *attitudes* from professionals on such key matters as the importance of party loyalty and the need for compromise. But there is persuasive evidence that these differences in attitudes do not necessarily carry over into behavior. Among delegates to the 1980 state nominating conventions, amateurs were just as likely as professionals to support candidates who seemed electable rather than those whose ideology they shared.[30] Among county party chairs in 1972, at a time when amateurs were thought to hold the upper hand, at least in the Democratic Party, the amateurs did not differ from professionals in their effort to communicate within the

Don Fowler and Ralph Reed: A Professional and an Experienced "Amateur"

Two major actors in 1990s campaigns give real-life meaning to the terms *professional* and *amateur*.

Don Fowler became a political activist in the 1960s, concerned about the erosion of Democratic Party strength in the South. A moderate, Fowler was a twenty-year veteran of Democratic politics when he was tapped to become cochair of the Democratic National Committee with the challenge of raising money and whipping the party into shape for the 1996 elections—the first after the Republican takeover of the U.S. House and Senate in 1994. Fowler's concern has been to win elections rather than to promote causes. He has worked for candidates with good chances of winning and he maintains ties with the core groups within the Democratic Party.

Ralph Reed, Jr., on the other hand, was a young veteran of Senator Jesse Helms's 1984 reelection campaign when he became director of the Christian Coalition in 1989. Above all, Reed is dedicated to increasing the strength of Christian conservatives in American politics. Reed is pro-life, antipornography, in favor of tax credits for parents to send their children to private schools, and for voluntary prayer in school. Prior to the 1996 presidential race, Reed warned the Republican Party that the Religious Right would not support a pro-choice Republican for president, though he later disavowed that position. He left the Christian Coalition in 1997 to form a consulting firm, Century Strategies, to provide campaign services to pro–family, pro–life, and pro–free enterprise candidates.

party, maintain party morale, or run effective campaigns.[31] It is helpful, in short, not to exaggerate the contrast between professionals and amateurs and the implications of changes in their relative numbers for the parties.

VITALITY OF THE PARTY ORGANIZATION

There are party organizations that succeed impressively in assembling and mobilizing the resources they need to win elections. Chapter 3 offered the classic example: the urban political machine that worked year-round to provide a full range of services in return for voter support at election time. Despite evidence that the local parties have rebounded from their lull in activity during the 1950s and 1960s, party grassroots activity, by any measure, still falls far short of the legendary vitality of the machines.

The problem is not just one of inactivity. It is also very difficult for modern parties to maintain the degree of communication—both within their organization and with party organizations at other levels of government—on which a vital party depends. Although the efforts at centralized party-building and funding have improved the integration among national, state, and local parties, communications remain poor within many organizations, and leaders at each level commonly operate independently of others. A national survey of local party efforts in the 1992 presidential campaign, for example, found that 22 percent of the county party chairs did not communicate with their local counterparts in the presidential campaign organizations, 21 percent had no contact with their state parties, and a majority (61 percent) had no contact with their national parties.[32]

We can trace these major lapses in organizational efficiency to the differing goals of party workers and the processes by which they are recruited. As we have seen, local workers enter and remain in party service for a splendid variety of motives. They pursue different goals and hold different perceptions of political reality and commitments to the party and its leaders.[33] Unable to harness their energies in united pursuit of a common goal, many local parties barely qualify as organizations in the conventional meaning of the term.

That, in turn, makes it difficult for a party to remain competitive. The party's effectiveness in the political marketplace, measured by its vote-getting success, depends crucially on its vitality as an organization. Evidence shows consistently that a well-organized and active local party can win extra votes for its candidates, typically by mobilizing its supporters and getting them to the polls. The margin is not large, but in competitive electoral environments such a small margin may be the critical difference between winning and losing.[34]

It is because organizational effectiveness makes a difference in elections that the search for the strong, vital party organization goes on. This search, however, is hampered by the lack of agreement on what the ideal ought to be. For many, the ideal remains the classic, turn-of-the-century, urban machine. It is an ideal rooted in the methods of campaigning and in the electorate of a past era. Its operations are not acceptable, however, to today's activists and citizens; besides, voters now can be reached by means other than precinct workers. What we need but haven't found is some common conception of party strength and effectiveness for the political realities of the twenty-first century.

Variations in Organizational Strength

We can draw some rough generalizations about the conditions under which strong party organizations develop. First, because of the density of cities and the special needs of urban populations, it is not surprising that party organization has often reached its peak in the nation's metropolitan centers. Differences in political culture also affect the development of party organizations. Persistent party canvassing and the use of patronage are acceptable in some areas but not in others. Even the mix of amateur and professional orientations within the party organization may vary by political culture. The parties of Berkeley, Manhattan, or suburban Minneapolis may contain more amateurs than those of Columbus, Queens, or Chicago.[35] Areas of one-party politics clearly weaken party organizations—not just that of the entrenched minority party but of the majority party as well. Until the 1950s, for example, Republican organizations in the Deep South were largely defunct and their Democratic counterparts were not much stronger. Finally, the statutory regulations of some states are more burdensome than those of others. State laws that make it difficult for the party to remove or replace inactive officials, to use patronage as an inducement for party work, or to decide which candidates will carry its label hamper the development of strong party organizations.[36]

POWER AND DISCIPLINE IN THE PARTY ORGANIZATION

Organization requires discipline—at least enough discipline to coordinate its parts and to implement its decisions. Many Americans, perhaps deriving their picture of the party organization from old movies, have imagined party organizations ruled by authoritarian control—by a boss who controls the party apparatus using a combination of cunning, toughness, and force of will. The boss, in fact, has become something of an American folk hero, feared for his ruthlessness and admired for his rascality. He has been celebrated in the public arts[37] and if he had not existed, it might have been necessary to create him, if only to justify Americans' instinctive distrust of concentrated power (see illustration on p.106).

Very few organizational leaders ruled absolutely by personal magnetism, tactical skill, or the use of sanctions. Even in the era of boss rule, the boss normally shared power with influential underlings, and the terms of that sharing were deeply rooted in the traditions of the organization. Much of the centralization in party machines existed because the party activists in the ranks accepted this hierarchical system of authority as natural and inevitable. If they were active in order to keep patronage jobs, they cared little about what else the party did or did not do.

More recently, however, party activists have come to demand a much louder voice in the affairs of the party. In the 1960s and 1970s, much of the ideological fervor of many amateurs was directed at reforming the party's leadership structure, and very little divides amateurs from professionals more than their attitudes toward openness and representation within the party. The amateurs' commitment to internal party democracy also follows logically from their desire to achieve certain ideological goals; in politics the rules determine the outcome, so if they wanted to change the party's goals, they needed to change its internal rules as well. Thus they had to reform the American parties if they were to reform American society.[38]

THE BOSS IN CARTOON

Source: Walter Appleton Clark, "The Boss," From *Collier's Weekly,* November 10, 1906. Reprinted from Ralph F. Shikes, *The Indignant Eye* (Boston: Beacon Press, 1969), p. 321.

Their success in making parties more participatory is not the only factor that weakens the discipline of the party organization. Discipline also depends on the organization's ability to withhold its incentives. Much of the discipline of the classic machine resulted from the willingness and ability of party leaders to manipulate material rewards. A disobedient or inefficient party worker sacrificed a patronage job or the hope of one. The newer incentives, however, cannot be given or taken away so easily. A local Republican organization is not likely to punish an errant ideologically motivated activist by ending the party's support of school prayer. Even if it did, the activist can find many other organizations that may be even more effective at pursuing that goal, such as religious lobbies or other organized interests.

There are other powerful forces in American politics that have long resisted the creation of centralized, disciplined party organizations. American political culture has been dominated since the beginning by a fear that a few people, responsible to no one, will control the selection of public officials and set the agendas of policy-making in "smoke-filled rooms." Understandably, there has been a long search for means to control party power. The results fall into two major categories: methods that impose controls from outside the parties, and those that try to check the parties from inside.

External Controls

In theory, two-party competition will naturally limit the exercise of both parties' organizational powers; by the very fact of their competition each party has the incentive to check the other.[39] One-party monopoly does not produce this automatic correction—and in fact some of the centers of greater organizational power have emerged in areas that do not have serious two-party competition. The current spread of two-party competitiveness may expose more party organizations to the discipline of the electoral market.

Party reformers have generally preferred legislative controls on party power rather than the unseen hand of competition, but their remedies have often left them disappointed. Primary elections were promoted by reformers as a means of keeping party leaders from appointing and controlling other party officials. Yet where primary elections are held to pick precinct committee members and other party leaders there are rarely contests for these offices and in fact there is frequently no candidate at all. Attempts to regulate the holding of party caucuses and conventions have not always guaranteed access to everyone who would qualify to participate.

The reformers have had a few successes, however. When party caucuses have been required by law to grant access to all qualified partisans, they have opened the party organization sometimes to factional competition and at other times to be reinvigorated by new party activists. Moreover, in all of the states the direct primary has at least forced the parties to face the scrutiny of voters on one key decision: the nomination of candidates for office. Some scholars have argued, in fact, that the introduction of the direct primary into American politics is primarily responsible for the atrophy of local party organizations throughout the country.[40]

Internal Controls

In his sweeping "iron law of oligarchy," Robert Michels declared more than eighty-five years ago that complex organizations will inevitably be oligarchic—ruled by a few—because only a few leaders have the experience, interest, and involvement necessary to manage their affairs. According to Michels, every organization—including political parties—will have an "aristocratic tendency" that divides it into a minority of directors and a majority of people who are directed.[41] To the extent that we believe the myths of the bosses, the smoke-filled rooms, and the deals between oligarchs, we are all disciples of Michels.

Michels' "iron law of oligarchy" has had little relevance, however, to the organizations of the American major parties. The distribution of power within most American party organizations is best described as a stratarchy rather than a hierarchy. It is "the enlargement of the ruling group of an organization, its power stratification, the involvement of large numbers of people in group decision making, and, thus, the diffusion and proliferation of control throughout the structure." Various levels of party organization operate at least semi-independently of other levels. Precinct committee members, district leaders, and county officials freely define their own political roles and nourish their separate bases of party power. Thus, "although authority to speak for the organization may remain in the hands of the top elite nucleus, there is great autonomy in operations at the lower 'strata' or echelons of the hierarchy, and ... control from the top is minimal and formal."[42]

What accounts for stratarchy? What are the internal forces that keep top party leaders from centralizing organizational power in a hierarchy? They include:

- *Participatory expectations.* Large numbers of party activists expect to participate in their party's decision-making processes. Therefore the organization may have to tolerate or even create internal party democracy (or consultation) to lift morale and to unify the party.

- *Lower party levels have some control over higher levels.* The leaders of the lower-level party organizations typically make up the conventions that select higher-level party officials. County chairs who choose state officers are forces to be reckoned with in the state party organizations. Similarly, precinct workers or delegates often form or choose county committees.

- *Internal competition.* Party organizations are rarely monoliths. They are often composed of competing organizations or factions. Differences in goals and political styles produce continuing competition in the selecting of party officials and party activities.

- *Independence of officeholders.* Because they do not need to rely upon the party organization for nomination or election, public officials often create their own power bases within the party which enable them to compete with organizational leaders for control over the party. The most powerful political machines emerged where the leaders of the party organization were also the top elected officials. In Chicago during the 1950s and 1960s, for example, Richard J. Daley was both mayor and chairman of the Cook County Democratic Party.

Diffusion of power marks all but the exceptional party organizations. Top party leaders have to work hard to mobilize support within their own organization; they consult endlessly with middle-level leadership. Even the ward or precinct leader with a small electoral following and a single vote at an important convention must be cultivated. Current American party leaders rarely command, because their commands no longer carry powerful sanctions. They plead, they bargain, they cajole, and they reason, and they even learn to lose gracefully on occasion. They mobilize party power not so much by threats as by appealing to common goals and interests.

One recent development has the potential to counteract these powerful decentralizing forces. Growth in the capabilities of the state, and especially the national, parties through their abundant treasuries and their cadres of skilled professional operatives has converted them into effective organizational forces for the first time in American history (see Chapter 4). With such resources available in the national parties, local party organizations may be tempted to free themselves from their dependence on volunteers and grassroots activity and turn instead to professional campaign organizers and the heavy use of television. The lure of national party money may bring with it more control and direction from the top. It has not happened yet and it may never happen, given the powerful forces that work against centralized authority in the

American parties. Yet it should not come as a complete surprise if these new sources of skilled labor and money were to create new pressures for centralized leadership and discipline within the party organizations.

In a sense, however, these concerns over power, discipline, and control in American party organization seem misplaced. Although earlier generations may have worried about the excesses of party power, we worry about the weakness of party organization. Many reformers have turned their energies from curbing the parties to saving them, and there is even an organization called the Committee for Party Renewal, composed of party activists and scholarly specialists on the parties, dedicated to this goal.

The incentives and rewards available to American party organizations have probably never been equal to their ambitions or their reputations. In that sense the parties have been chronically "underfinanced." They have never been able to recruit the kinds of resources they would need in order to flesh out the party organization that the state statutes create. The thousands of inactive precinct workers and unfilled precinct positions testify to that. The parties, therefore, have had no alternative but to tolerate organizational forms that have permitted them to live within their means and to draw upon activists with diverse motives, backgrounds, and styles. They are, after all, the products of their people.

Part 3
·····················
The Political Party in the Electorate

*I*f there were a Public Opinion Poll Hall of Fame, surely the first question in it would be: Generally speaking, do you usually think of yourself as a Republican, a Democrat, an independent, or what? The question is meant to classify *party identifiers*—people who feel a sense of psychological attachment to a particular party. If you responded that you do usually think of yourself as a Democrat or a Republican, then you are categorized as belonging to the party in the electorate—the second major sector of the American parties. These are the core of the party's support: the people who normally vote for a party's candidates and who are inclined to see politics through a partisan's eyes. They are more apt to vote in the party's primary elections and to volunteer for party candidates than are other citizens. They are, in short, the party organization's and its candidates' closest friends in the public.

Survey researchers have measured Americans' party loyalty since the 1940s. The measure that has dominated research comes from polls conducted by the University of Michigan, now under the auspices of the American National Election Studies (ANES). After asking whether you consider yourself a Republican or a Democrat, the question continues:

> [If Republican or Democrat] Would you call yourself a strong [Republican or Democrat] or a not very strong [Republican or Democrat]? [If independent, no preference, or other party] Do you think of yourself as closer to the Republican Party or to the Democratic Party?

Using these answers, researchers classify people into seven different categories of party identification: strong party identifiers (Democrats or Republicans), weak identifiers (Democrats or Republicans), independent "leaners" (toward the Democrats or Republicans), and pure independents.[1]

Note that this definition is not based on people's actual voting behavior. Strong party identifiers, in particular, do usually vote for their party's candidates. But the essence of a party identification is an attachment to the party itself—a commitment that goes beyond a particular set of candidates. With the large number of elective offices in the United States and the value placed on independence, someone can remain a committed party identifier even while choosing to vote for the opposition party's candidate. In the same sense, we do not define the party electorate in terms of the official act of registering with a party. Almost half the states do not have party registration; in addition, some voters retain their original registration long after their party identification has changed.[2]

The party electorate has an interesting relationship with the party organization and the party in government. Clearly the party cannot survive without the party electorate's support. Yet the party in the electorate is independent of these other party sectors. Party identifiers are not party "members" in any real sense nor do they have any formal role in the party organization. The party organizations and candidates see their identifiers as a separate clientele to be courted at each election but largely ignored between elections. Party identifiers, in turn, rarely feel any obligation to the party organization other than to vote for its candidates if they choose. In these ways, the American parties resemble cadre parties: top-heavy in leaders and activists without any significant mass membership, rather than the mass-membership parties that have been such an important part of the European democratic experience.

Despite its independence, the party in the electorate does give the party organization and candidates a continuing core of electoral support. The parties do not, in other words, have to start from scratch in every campaign. The party in the electorate also largely determines who the party's nominees for office will be, by voting in primaries. It is a reservoir of potential activists for the organization. Its members may donate money to the party or they may work in a specific campaign. They help perpetuate the party by transmitting party loyalties to their children. They give the party an image and a presence in the community and they probably comprise the politically active segment of their community—those who talk about politics, try to persuade friends, and attend political events.

A party in the electorate is more than a group of individuals, however. It is also a set of cognitive images within large numbers of individual voters, a loyalty strong enough to structure the individual's cognitive map of politics. In this sense it is the party in the elector; it acts as a filter through which the individual sees and evaluates candidates and issues. For voters the political party of their cognitions may be far more real and tangible than any observable political activity or organization because they react to what they believe and perceive.

Because the American parties are cadre parties without real membership, it is the party in the electorate that gives the party its mass popular character. When observers speak of the Democrats as the party of the disadvantaged, or of the Republicans as the party of business, the reference is probably at least in part to the party in the electorate. Differences between the major parties in their policy positions and in their public images often spring from differences in the types of people the parties have attracted as identifiers. The interplay between the appeals of the party (its candidates, issues, and traditions) and its loyal supporters—each one shaping and reinforcing the other—comes very close to determining what the parties are.

In their fight to win majorities, parties cannot rely just on their own committed identifiers, of course. They must also attract votes from those with no party attachments and even from some supporters of the other party. Their base, however, is the millions of voters who, by psychologically identifying with that party, comprise its coalition of supporters.

The three chapters in Part 3 explore the variety and importance of these parties in the electorate. Chapter 6 examines them as coalitions of voters, asking what kinds of people identify with each of the two major parties. Chapter 7 looks at the impact of party identification on individuals' political behavior. Chapter 8 focuses on the big differences between the people who vote and those who do not. These differences have an important effect on the parties' choices in mobilizing their faithful and recruiting new supporters.

Chapter 6

The Loyal Electorates

*W*ho are the Democrats? Who are the Republicans? In a political culture that often discredits political parties, many people view them solely as the candidates and office-holders who carry the party label and the activists who run the party organizations—that is, as something set apart from ordinary citizens. But for millions of Americans, the people and groups who loyally support and identify with the party are central to the lives of political parties.

Political parties reside in the electorate, not just in the party headquarters and in Washington. Much of the written history of American parties has recorded their successes and failures in terms of the blocs of voters that support them. Thus the Democrats and Republicans have been described at various times as parties of the North or South, the city or the suburbs, rich or poor, white or black. In this chapter we will examine what kinds of people support the two parties—and the reasons why this makes a difference.

PARTY REALIGNMENTS AND THE AMERICAN PARTY SYSTEMS

Throughout the life of the American party system, the coalitions of voters that define the parties in the electorate seem to have been rearranged every generation or so. If we had survey data with which to measure party identifications since about 1800, we could expect to find long periods of relative stability in the components of each party's coalition punctuated by brief periods of change, or what is called *realignment*.[1] Unfortunately, survey data were not available until the late 1930s. For earlier years, we can only estimate the composition of the parties in the electorate from aggregated voting returns. These voting patterns, showing changes in the levels and the geographical distributions of party support which are then maintained over long periods of time, justify a division of American politics into a series of electoral eras.[2]

Scholars generally agree that the United States has experienced at least five different eras of partisan politics or, as many call them, party systems.[3] Each party system has begun with a realignment of the parties in the electorate (or, for the first party system, an initial alignment), followed by a long period of relative stability in the voter coalitions. In each of these party systems there has been a distinctive pattern of group support for the parties. Each party system can also be distinguished by the kinds of public policies that the government has favored and put into effect.[4] (See Table 6.1 for a summary of each party system.)

The First Party System

The first party system (1801–1828)[5] arose from the conflict between opposing groups within the Washington administration. It was ushered in by the hotly contested 1800 election in which Thomas Jefferson was elected president. For the first time in American history, one of the factions in the nation's capital, with Jefferson and Madison as its leaders, had organized support for its presidential candidate in the country at large. The partisan balance of each electoral era is signified by party control of the presidency and Congress. Beginning in 1801, the party of Jefferson—or the Democratic-Republicans as they came to be called—enjoyed more than two decades of virtually unchallenged dominance in American national politics.

TABLE 6.1 Years of Partisan Control of Congress and the Presidency: 1801–2000

	House		Senate		President	
	D–R	Opp.	D–R	Opp.	D–R	Opp.
First party system						
(1801–1828)	26	2	26	2	28	0
	Dem.	Opp.	Dem.	Opp.	Dem.	Opp.
Second party system						
(1829–1860)	24	8	28	4	24	8
	Dem.	Rep.	Dem.	Rep.	Dem.	Rep.
Third party system						
(1861–1876)	2	14	0	16	0	16
(1877–1896)	14	6	4	16	8	12
Fourth party system						
(1897–1932)	10	26	6	30	8	28
Fifth party system						
(1933–1968?)	32	4	32	4	28	8
Sixth party system?						
(1969–1980)	12	0	12	0	4	8
(1981–2000)	14	6	8	12	8	12
(1969–2000)	26	6	20	12	12	20

Note: Entries for the first party system are Democratic-Republicans and their opposition, first Federalists and then Jacksonians; for the second party system, Democrats and their opposition, first Whigs and then Republicans; for subsequent party systems, Democrats and Republicans.

The Second Party System

The second party system (1829–1860) emerged when the one-party dominance of the earlier years—the Democratic-Republican rule after the demise of the Federalists—proved unable to contain all the issues and conflicts generated by a rapidly changing nation. The Democratic-Republicans split into two factions: one, a populist Western faction under Andrew Jackson which would later grow to become the Democratic Party, and the other, a more elitist and Eastern faction represented by John Quincy Adams which was eventually absorbed into the Whig Party.[6] Controversy over the 1824 presidential election heightened the strains between the factions. In that election, Jackson received the most popular votes in a four-candidate contest but lacked an electoral college majority and was denied the presidency by the House of Representatives.

The development of a new party system to reflect the growth and democratization of the nation seemed inevitable. Its first signs appeared in Jackson's election to the presidency four years later—the first time popular voting played the key role in determining the winner. As this party system matured, the nation experienced its first enduring two-party competition, which the Democrats dominated as the majority party. Their rule was disrupted only twice, both times by the election of Whig war heroes to the presidency. The second party system was class-based, with wealthier voters supporting the Whigs and the less privileged identifying as Democrats.

The Third Party System

The rapid rise of a third party—the abolitionist Republican party—from its birth in 1854 to major party status by 1856, replacing the Whigs in the process, brought about the end of the second party system. The intense conflict of the Civil War ensured that the new third party system (1861–1896) would have the most sharply defined coalitional patterns of any party system before or since. War and Reconstruction divided the nation roughly along geographic lines: the South became a Democratic bastion after white Southerners were permitted to return to the polls in the 1870s, and the North remained a reliable base for Republicans. So sharp was the sectional division that Northern Democratic strength was seen only in the cities controlled by Democratic machines (for example, New York City's Tammany Hall) and areas settled by Southerners (such as Kentucky, Missouri, and the Southern portions of Ohio, Indiana, and Illinois). In the South, the only GOP support came from blacks (whose new right to vote was denied them again as the century drew to a close) and people from mountain areas originally opposed to the Southern states' secession. By 1876, when Southern whites were finally reintegrated into national politics, there was close party competition in presidential voting and in the House of Representatives as these sectional monopolies offset one another.[7]

The Fourth Party System

The imprint of the Civil War shaped Southern politics for the next century, but the Civil War party system soon began to fade elsewhere. Under the weight of farm and rural protest and the economic panic of 1893, the third party system dissolved. It was replaced by a fourth party system (1897–1932) that reflected the great differences between the agrarian and industrial economies and ways of life. This new era pitted the Eastern economic "center," which was heavily Republican, against the Western and Southern "periphery," with the South even more Democratic than before. Beginning with William McKinley's defeat of Democratic populist William Jennings Bryan in 1896, Republicans dominated American national politics. Republican rule was interrupted only by an intraparty split in 1912 which gave Democrats an eight-year turn at leadership.

Just as earlier party systems began to weaken a decade or two after their establishment, the fourth party system showed signs of deterioration in the 1920s, even in the midst of unparalleled Republican successes. The Progressive Party made inroads into major party strength early in the decade, and in 1928 Democratic candidate Al Smith, the first Catholic ever nominated for the presidency, brought Catholic voters into Democratic ranks in the North and drove Protestant Southerners temporarily into voting Republican.

The Fifth Party System

But it took the Great Depression of 1929 and the resulting election of Franklin Delano Roosevelt to produce the fifth, or New Deal, party system. By 1936, the new Democratic majority party had become a grand coalition of the less privileged minorities—industrial workers (especially union members), poor farmers, Catholics, Jews, blacks—plus the South, where the Democratic loyalty imprinted by the Civil War had become all but genetic. This New Deal party system has shaped the parties into modern times.[8]

Does this fifth party system continue today? Even with a wealth of survey evidence, the answer is unclear. There is no doubt that the coalitional patterns that supported the New Deal alignment have eroded. Since the mid–1960s, more Americans have called themselves "independents" when pollsters ask about their party loyalties. So the American electorate is somewhat less partisan now than it was prior to that time. These changes first became apparent in 1968, although the seeds may have been sown in the 1950s (and obscured by the landslide Democratic victory in 1964). They mark an important turning point in the American party system.

A Sixth Party System: Dealignment or Realignment?

Scholars have called this trend a dealignment—a decline in party loyalties, as opposed to a realignment, in which people develop new party loyalties. Some scholars see dealignment (and the higher levels of third-party voting and ticket-splitting that accompany it) as the final stage of a party system. In their view, dealignment is a sign of the aging of the electoral conflicts that established the party system; it is a time when new party coalitions can emerge. The newest members of the electorate were the cutting edge for dealignment in the 1960s—and perhaps in earlier eras as well. Because newer voters don't have the experiences that shaped the partisanship of earlier generations when the party coalitions were being formed, they are more likely to find the major parties irrelevant to their present needs.[9]

What will follow this dealignment? In each previous party system, the dissolution of the old alignment was soon followed by realignment and the emergence of a new party system. Yet a return to party-centered politics is no longer inevitable. The forces that led to the deterioration of the old party loyalties are not necessarily capable of producing the new party loyalties of a realignment. Indeed, Walter Dean Burnham has argued that the American party system may no longer be capable of realignment, especially because it has been weakened by the loss of party control over nominations and the insulation of many state and local elections from national forces by scheduling them in off years.[10] Burnham's view is supported by the fact that the current dealignment, which began in the 1960s, seems to have been the longest in American history.

We can see the rise and fall of Democratic dominance of the fifth party system clearly, thanks to polls taken since 1952 by researchers at the University of Michigan[11] (see Table 6.2). When asked "Generally speaking, do you consider yourself a Democrat or a Republican?" more Americans called themselves Democrats than either Republicans or Independents throughout the 1952–1964 period. This Democratic advantage in party identification held from one presidential election to another; not even a popular president of the minority party, General Dwight D. Eisenhower, could disturb it. (Note that someone who considers him- or herself a Democrat may choose to vote for a Republican candidate but still retain a Democratic Party loyalty.) The Democratic edge began to erode after 1964. Yet Republicans did not immediately benefit. In fact the proportion of Republican identifiers dropped from 1964 through 1980. Even Richard Nixon's landslide victory in the 1972 presidential contest failed to add party loyalists to GOP ranks.

TABLE 6.2 Party Identification: 1952–1996

	1952	1956	1960	1964	1968	1972	1976	1980	1984	1988	1992	1996
Strong Democrats	22%	21%	20%	27%	20%	15%	15%	18%	17%	17%	17%	19%
Weak Democrats	25	23	25	25	25	26	25	23	20	18	18	20
Independents, closer to Democrats	10	6	6	9	10	11	12	11	11	12	14	14
Independents	6	9	10	8	10	13	14	13	11	11	12	8
Independents, closer to Republicans	7	8	7	6	9	10	10	10	12	13	13	11
Weak Republicans	14	14	14	13	14	13	14	14	15	14	15	15
Strong Republicans	13	15	15	11	10	10	9	8	12	14	11	13
Others	4	4	3	2	2	2	1	3	2	2	1	1
	101%	100%	100%	101%	100%	100%	100%	100%	100%	101%	101%	101%
Cases	1793	1762	1928	1571	1556	2707	2864	1614	2236	2033	2478	1714

Note: Based on surveys of the national electorate conducted immediately before each presidential election—in recent years as part of the American National Election Studies (ANES) program. Due to rounding, the percentages do not always add up to exactly 100 percent.

Source: American National Election Studies, Center for Political Studies, University of Michigan; data made available through the Inter-University Consortium for Political and Social Research.

By the 1980s, however, Republican Party identification was on the rise. The most recent readings in the Michigan series, from 1984 through 1996, show levels of Republican identifiers (counting both those who consider themselves "strong" and "weak" Republicans) returning to those of 1960. In contrast to Eisenhower and Nixon, Ronald Reagan in the 1980s seemed to have translated his vote-getting popularity into growth for his party. The Democrats showed a corresponding decline, dropping below the 40 percent level in 1984 for the first time in the entire data series. Perhaps we are now finally experiencing the new realignment following the long period of decline in partisanship. It is easier to see a realignment in the past than to identify one in progress. But the possibility certainly exists, and will get careful consideration later in this chapter.[12]

Who are these Democrats and Republicans in the electorate? From what educational backgrounds, occupations, regions, religions, and social groups do they come, and what interests attract them to one party rather than the other? Each of America's party systems has been dominated by a particular set of issue concerns, which has in turn tended to divide the electorate into distinctive coalitions. Before we can understand the nature of the current coalitions, however, we must ask how and why people develop party identifications.

HOW PEOPLE ACQUIRE PARTY LOYALTIES

People often say that they are Democrats or Republicans because they were brought up that way, just as they may have been raised as a Methodist or a Jew. As children become aware of political parties, they absorb judgments about them and often come to think of themselves as part of their family's partisanship.

Childhood Influences

Party loyalty often develops as early as the elementary grades. Although they do not often consciously indoctrinate their children into party loyalty, parents are the primary teachers of political orientations in the American culture. Their casual conversations and references to political events are enough to convey their party loyalties to their children. These influences can be powerful enough to last into adulthood, even at times when young adults are pulled toward independence (see Table 6.3)[13] This early party identification is usually innocent of information; few children have heard much about political issues or party leaders. It isn't until the middle-school and high-school years that students begin to associate the parties with general economic interests—with business or labor, with the rich or the poor—and thus to have some reasoning to support a party identification. Note the importance of the sequence here: Party loyalty comes first, so it tends to have a long-lasting impact on attitudes toward politics. Only later do people learn about political issues and events, which will then be filtered at least in part through a partisan lens.[14]

Once developed, people's party loyalties are often sustained because friends, associates, and relatives typically share the same partisan loyalties.[15] Some people do leave the parties of their parents. Those whose initial identification is weak are more likely to change. So are people whose mother and father identified with different parties, or

TABLE 6.3 Intergenerational Similarities in Party Identification: 1982

Party of Child as Young Adult (1982)	Party of Parent (1965)		
	Democrat	*Independent*	*Republican*
Democrat	51%	27%	10%
Independent	39	51	46
Republican	10	22	44
	100%	100%	100%
Cases	295	192	211

Note: Democrats and Republicans include strong and weak identifiers. Independents include all respondents answering independent or no preference to the initial party identification question, regardless of whether they later located themselves closer to one of the parties. The young adults had all been high school seniors in 1965 and were aged 34–35 in 1982 when the party identification shown above was measured.

Source: Three Wave Parent-Child Socialization Study. Provided by its principal investigator, M. Kent Jennings.

who live in a social setting where the prevailing party influences differ from their own. But when parents share the same party identification, they are more likely to produce strong party identifiers among their children.[16]

Other agents of political learning tend to support a person's inherited party loyalty or at least do not challenge the family's influence. Schools typically avoid partisan politics; if anything, they are probably more inclined to teach political independence than partisanship. During most of the twentieth century, American churches usually steered clear of partisan conflict even at a time when church-connected political parties existed in Europe. Churches and other religious groups have clearly entered the political fray in American politics, but they are not likely to lead young people away from their parents' partisan influence. The American parties themselves do very little direct socialization; they do not maintain the youth groups, the flourishing university branches (which may have offices, lounges, and eating facilities), the social or recreational activities, or the occupational organizations that some European parties do.

Influences in Adulthood

These influences on children's and teenagers' political learning are more likely to be challenged beginning in young adulthood, when an individual enters the complex world of adult experiences. At this point in the life cycle, adults can test their party loyalties against political reality. They are brought face-to-face with the performance of their favored party and its leaders and they also watch the performance of the "other party." Their adult experiences may reinforce their early-learned loyalties or may undermine them.

> ...there is an inertial element in voting behavior that cannot be ignored, but that inertial element has an experiential basis; it is not something learned at mommy's knee and never questioned thereafter.[17]

The longer people hold a particular party identification, the more intense it tends to become. Older adults are most likely to hold strong party attachments and least likely to change them. Perhaps party identification is more likely to become a habit after decades of political observation and activity. Or partisanship may grow stronger across the life cycle because it is so useful a shortcut for simplifying the political decision-making of older voters.[18]

Nothing threatens the inherited partisan loyalties of large numbers of voters more than a realignment, when the issue bases of partisanship and the party coalitions themselves are being transformed. When a realignment occurs, unless it has been produced entirely by the entrance of previously unaligned groups into partisan politics, it must be that some voters have deserted the partisan tradition of their parents. Evidence from the New Deal realignment of the 1930s as well as from partisan changes in recent years suggests that young adults are highly susceptible to the pressures of the times. Childhood socialization alone is a fragile foundation for adult partisanship and often cracks under the intense challenges of adult experience, especially in response to the powerful forces of a realignment. Older adults may be caught up in the momentum of the moment, but their partisanship, typically reinforced by years of consistent partisan behavior, is much more resistant to change. Thus it is typically young adults who act as the "carriers" of realignment and consequently to whom we should look for early signs of partisan change.[19]

These processes of political socialization tell us how an individual may acquire a party loyalty but not what particular loyalty is acquired. To understand why one party attracts some people but repels others, and why each party assumes a distinctive shape, we must turn in another direction—to the role of social groups and issues.

THE SOCIAL BASES OF PARTY IDENTIFICATION

Political parties have long been seen as representatives of the various social groups in a society. Sectional or regional conflicts, ethnic and religious divisions, disputes between agriculture and industry, and differences in social class and status are common ingredients in the politics of the Western democracies. While the United States may have been spared the intensity of some of these conflicts because of its social diversity and its isolation from the Old World, many of them have been important sources of party cleavage here as well.[20]

Social Status and Class Divisions

Most democratic party systems reflect divisions along social class lines, even if those divisions may have softened over the years.[21] So the search for the social bases of party loyalties should probably begin with social class, or *socioeconomic status* (SES). Socioeconomic status is simply the relative amount of economic and/or social deference the individual can command based on his or her social and economic characteristics. It is best measured objectively by a combination of income, education, and occupation. We can also ask individuals which social class they identify with, to assess their subjective SES.

The footprints of SES conflict are scattered throughout American history. James Madison, one of the most knowing observers of human nature among the Founding

Fathers, wrote in the *Federalist Papers* that economic differences are the most common source of factions.[22] Social and economic status differences underlay the battle between the wealthy, aristocratic Federalists and the less privileged Democratic-Republicans. These differences were even sharper between the Jacksonian Democrats and the Whigs a few decades later. In the 1890s, SES conflicts surfaced again in the presidential contest between Republican William McKinley and William Jennings Bryan. Bryan had converted the Democratic Party into the vehicle for protests by discontented and disadvantaged farmers and tried–unsuccessfully–to join urban workers with them in common cause. Despite his defeat in the general election of 1896, the Democrats twice (1900 and 1908) returned to Bryan as their presidential candidate for the crusade against corporate wealth, Eastern banking interests, and what Bryan liked to call the "plutocracy."

The SES stamp on the parties became even more pronounced in the 1930s. Franklin Roosevelt rebuilt the Democratic Party more firmly than ever as a party of social and economic reform. His New Deal programs—labor legislation, social security, wage and hours laws—strengthened the Democratic Party's image as the party of the have-nots. Even groups such as blacks, long allied with the Republicans as the party of Lincoln, were lured to the Democratic banner; socioeconomic issues were powerful enough to keep both blacks and Southern whites as wary allies in the Roosevelt coalition. Franklin Roosevelt braced the class divisions of industrial society with the programs of the welfare state. Its conflicts and costs heightened the stakes of SES politics.

The relationship between party and SES established in the New Deal party system can still be seen in elections as recently as 1996 (Table 6.4, panels A-C). It is immediately apparent in the data on education and income. Democrats are more likely to have lower income levels and less education than Republicans, and to identify themselves as working rather than middle class (see box on p. 125). Income, of course, is strongly related to an individual's level of education. Income also underlies some of the effects of religion and race on party identification. The tendency for Protestants to be somewhat higher in SES in the United States helps to explain why they are more likely to identify with the Republican Party than Catholics are. And there is an enormous SES difference between whites and blacks.

Yet Table 6.4 shows some interesting differences from the New Deal alignment. Although less-educated respondents are much more Democratic than Republican, those with a college education divide themselves more evenly between the parties. The same is true with regard to occupation. Those with service jobs (which tend to be lower-paying) and blue-collar jobs remain more likely to be Democrats. Professionals, on the other hand, are no longer distinctively Republican. The identification of many professionals with the Democratic Party is reflected in the support Democratic candidates often receive from teachers' unions and trial lawyers' associations.

Further, socioeconomic status has been less important as a basis for party loyalty in the United States than in many other Western democracies[23]—and even at the height of the New Deal, the SES differences between the parties have been less distinct than the parties' rhetoric would suggest. The electorates of both American parties contain a significant number of people from all status groups. As a result, the parties tend not to

TABLE 6.4 Social Characteristics and Party Identification: 1996

| | Democrats | | Independents | | | Republicans | | | |
	Strong	Weak	Closer to Demo.	Closer to Neither	Closer to Rep.	Weak	Strong	Dem. minus Rep.	Cases
A. *Income*	*46*	*63*				*29*	*21*		
Lower 3rd	24%	22	15	10	8	12	9	25	564
Middle 3rd	21%	22	14	8	10	16	9	18	510
Upper 3rd	14%	16	13	7	14	17	19	-6	542
B. *Occupation*									
Service	16%	26	16	9	16	11	6	25	142
Blue collar	16%	21	16	11	12	12	12	13	253
White collar	18%	20	14	8	10	19	12	7	317
Professional	17%	20	14	6	11	17	15	5	414
Farm	6%	18	12	12	0	29	24	-29	17
C. *Education*									
No high sch.	28%	20	12	13	12	10	4	34	225
High sch. grad	21%	22	13	10	10	14	10	19	538
College	16%	18	15	6	11	17	16	1	929
D. *Region*									
South	22%	20	11	8	13	14	12	16	635
Non-south	18%	20	15	9	9	16	13	9	1060
E. *Religion*									
Jews	34%	25	19	9	6	3	3	53	32
Catholics	20%	23	13	8	12	15	9	19	422
Protestants White	18%	20	14	9	10	17	18	3	480
"Born-again" Protestants	12%	14	11	6	13	21	23	-18	392
F. *Race*									
Blacks	44%	22	15	11	4	2	1	63	206
Whites	16%	20	14	8	11	17	14	5	1439
G. *Gender*									
Female	23%	21	15	9	8	14	10	20	939
Male	15%	18	12	8	14	16	16	1	756

Note: Totals add to approximately 100 percent reading across (with slight variations due to rounding). Dem. minus Rep. is party difference calculated by subtracting the percentage of strong and weak Republicans from the percentage of strong and weak Democrats. Negative numbers indicate a Republican advantage in the group.

Source: 1996 American National Election Study, Center for Political Studies, University of Michigan; data made available by the Inter-University Consortium for Political and Social Research.

promote starkly class-based appeals. Their pragmatic, relatively nonideological tone reflects the diversity of their loyalists and their mission as brokers among a variety of social groupings. Because the SES divisions between the Republicans and Democrats are muddy, SES is not the only explanation of differences between the parties.

How to Tell A Democrat from A Republican During the Holiday Season

- Democrats let their kids open all the gifts on Christmas Eve. Republicans make their kids wait until Christmas morning.
- Republican parents have no problem buying their kids toy guns. Democrats refuse to do so. That is why Democratic kids pretend to shoot each other with dolls.
- Democrats get back at Republicans on their Christmas list by giving them fruitcakes. Republicans rewrap them and send them to in-laws.
- Republicans see nothing wrong with letting their children play "Cowboys and Indians." Democrats don't either, as long as the Indians get to win.
- Republicans spend hundreds of dollars and hours of work decorating the yard with outdoor lights. Democrats drive around at night to look at them.
- Republicans first became Republicans when they stopped believing in Santa Claus. Democrats became Democrats because they never stopped believing in Santa Claus.
- Democratic men like to watch football while their wives, girlfriends, or mothers fix holiday meals. Republican men do, too.

Sectional Divisions

Historically, the greatest rival to SES as an explanation for American party differences has been sectionalism. Different sections of the country have often had differing political interests. When these distinct interests have been championed by a political party, they have sometimes united large numbers of otherwise different voters.

The most enduring sectionalism in American party history was the one-party Democratic control of the South. Even before the Civil War, white Southerners shared an interest in slavery and an agriculture geared to export markets. The searing experience of that war and the Reconstruction that followed made the South into the "Solid South" and delivered it to the Democrats for the better part of the next century. The eleven states of the former Confederacy cast all their electoral votes for Democratic presidential candidates in every election from 1880 through 1924, except for Tennessee's defection in 1920. Al Smith's Catholicism frightened four of these states into the Republican column in 1928, but the Roosevelt economic programs brought the South back to the Democratic Party for the four Roosevelt elections. Only the beginnings of the civil rights movement had the power to peel away the South from its traditional party loyalties. Yet, as we saw in Chapter 2, vestiges of this sectional unity have survived into modern times at the state and local level (Table 6.4, panel D),[24] even if not in presidential voting.

Similarly, the party system has periodically reflected the competition between the economically dominant East and the economically dependent South and West. In the first years of the Republic, the fading Federalists held to an ever-narrowing base of Eastern seaport and financial interests, while the Democratic-Republicans expanded westward with the new settlers. Jackson aimed his party appeals at the men of the frontier, and the protest movements that thrust William Jennings Bryan into the 1896 campaign sprang from the agrarian discontent of the Western prairies and the South. Many of the Populists' loudest complaints were directed at Eastern capitalism, Eastern bankers, and Eastern trusts. The geographical distribution of the 1896 presidential vote, with the Democrats winning all but three states in the South and West but losing all Northern and border states east of the Mississippi River, is a striking example of sectional voting.

Sectional divisions are no longer as obvious. As society has nationalized, the isolation and uniformity that maintained sectional interests are breaking down. Sectional loyalties have not completely disappeared, of course. Southern sectionalism reappeared in a new form in the 1960s as states of the Deep South supported Barry Goldwater, the Republican presidential candidate, in 1964, and George Wallace in 1968 on the American Independent ticket. Even the Democratic Party's decision to nominate two Southerners for president and vice president did not prevent about half the Southern states from voting Republican in 1992 and 1996. But the rise of Republican strength in the South and Southwest has generally served to increase rather than dampen two-party competition. In addition, Ross Perot's candidacy in the 1990s never developed a distinctive sectional thrust, marking him as one of the few minor-party presidential candidates not to have drawn upon a sectional base of support.

It is fair to ask whether sectionalism was ever really a major force in its own right. The term *section* may simply indicate a geographic concentration of voters with other interests—economic or ethnic, for example—who identify with a party because of those other interests. Much sectional voting in the past, for instance, reflected conflicts among crop economies in various agricultural sections. The South, of course, has been more than a descriptive category; its political behavior has been truly sectional in the sense of having unified interests and an awareness of its own distinctiveness. But the case for sectional explanations weakens as soon as we look beyond the South.

Religious Divisions

There have always been religious differences between the American party coalitions, just as there are in many other democracies.[25] Since the early days of the New Deal party system, Catholics and Jews were among the most loyal supporters of the Democratic Party (Table 6.4, panel E). Some of the relationship between religion and party loyalty is due to the SES differences among religious groupings. Yet religious conviction and group identification also seem to be involved. Internationalism and concern for social justice, rooted in the religious and ethnic traditions of Judaism, have disposed many Jews toward the Democratic Party as the party of international concern, support for Israel, and social and economic justice.[26] The long-standing ties of Catholics to the Democratic Party reflect the party's greater openness to Catholic participation and political advancement. Most of the national chairmen of the Democratic Party in this century have been Catholics, and the only Catholic presidential nominees of a major party have been Democrats.

The sources of white Protestant ties to the Republicans are less obvious, probably in part because of the enormous diversity of sects and orientations that Protestantism embraces. It may be that the theological individualism of more conservative Protestant denominations disposes Protestants to Republicanism, although it was obscured for decades by the dominance of SES and sectional interests. In recent years, however, the surge in Protestant fervor for the GOP has been led by the political conservatism of white Protestant fundamentalists, triggered by issues such as abortion and school prayer.[27]

Racial Divisions

Decades ago, the Republican Party—the party founded to abolish slavery, the party of Lincoln, the Civil War, and Reconstruction—was associated with racial equality in the minds of both black and white Americans. Between 1930 and 1960, however, the partisan direction of racial politics turned 180 degrees. It is now the Democratic Party, the Kennedy, Johnson, and Clinton administrations, the candidacy of Jesse Jackson, and Democratic Congresses that blacks see as standing for racial equality. As a result, blacks identify as Democrats in overwhelming numbers today, as they have since at least the 1960s, regardless of any other social characteristics (Table 6.4, panel F). There is no closer tie between a social group and a party than that between blacks and the Democrats. Moreover, racial issues have been responsible for transforming party conflict in the South and perhaps in the rest of the nation as well.[28]

Gender Divisions

For more than two decades the votes and stands of adult women have diverged from those of men. Women voted about 6 percent more than men did for Jimmy Carter in 1980. The so-called "gender gap" grew after that. Women's ratings of President Reagan were much lower than men's and also differed from men's on a number of issues, including greater support for social programs and lesser support for defense spending. By the mid–1980s the gender difference had extended to partisanship; women were more supportive of the Democratic Party than men were. This partisan gender gap increased in the 1996 election (Table 6.4, panel G) and there is evidence that it is the product of changing partisanship of men rather than of women.[29]

The Changing Partisan Complexion of Social Groups

Almost seventy years later, the social group patterns of party support that launched the New Deal party system can still be seen in American politics. But these relationships have weakened in recent decades. When we compare the 1996 figures with those from 1960 (Figure 6.1),[30] it is clear that the SES and sectional differences in partisanship that

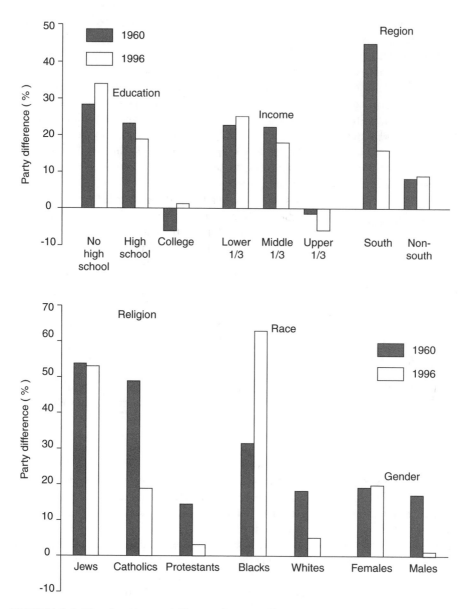

FIGURE 6.1 The changing social bases of partisanship.

Note: Entries are % strong/weak Democrat minus % strong/weak Republican within each group in each year

were so important in the aftermath of the New Deal realignment had narrowed by 1996, especially the contrast between the South and the North. In their place had emerged sharper cleavages along racial, religious, and even gender lines. The New Deal party system still casts its shadow over American politics, but it is no longer as dominant. In fact, a number of researchers argue that the New Deal coalition is now dead.[31]

Yet it would be a mistake to make too much of these group differences. Social groups have never been "delivered" in block to a party or a candidate. Instead the group basis of partisan politics is rooted in the common reactions of individuals to the major issues and candidates of the day. These orientations may be shared by members of particular groups, although the diversity of American society prevents most groups from being very cohesive. It is party differences on these political issues, and the ability of a party to speak for the hopes and interests of particular groups, that result in the partisan distinctiveness of groups in American politics.

Party loyalties do have a lot of staying power, and therefore so do party coalitions. In ordinary times, the group bases of politics are transmitted, perhaps without much reflection, from parents to children. People are slow to reject their inherited party loyalties even when the basis for this loyalty has deteriorated. But these sources of inertia can be overcome. Parties change their positions, especially in realignment periods, and their traditional supporters may forsake them as a result. In recent years, for example, there is ample evidence that changing party images and appealing candidates have influenced many Americans to change their loyalties. It is these individual decisions, not the lockstep march of groups, that have weakened the New Deal Democratic coalition.[32]

THE ISSUE AND IDEOLOGICAL BASES OF PARTY IDENTIFICATION

The party conflicts that appear among various social groups, then, are typically rooted in different views of what kind of society we should have and what the government should do to solve particular problems. Fortunately, we have a huge arsenal of public opinion polls to tell us about the distribution of attitudes on issues within each party. We can also measure the extent to which Democrats differ from Republicans on issues and the kinds of issues on which they differ most strikingly.

Table 6.5 shows the preferences of Democratic identifiers, independents, and Republican identifiers on a range of issues that left their mark on the 1996 presidential campaign. Note the substantial differences between Democrats and Republicans (seen in the "Dem minus Rep" column) on the issues of the welfare state—those involving the government's level of spending for services and its role in providing jobs for the unemployed (panels A and B). These are the issues on which party identification seems most closely related to individuals' views. These could be considered SES issues because they center on questions of equality and the distribution of wealth. Much of the partisan rhetoric and conflict in American politics since the 1930s has focused on SES-based issues, such as jobs, Medicaid, taxes, or what to do with the budget surplus.

Is it their socioeconomic status that causes these Democratic identifiers to prefer more government spending on services? Not necessarily. These views may have status roots for some, but other party identifiers hold views that are not consistent with their socioeconomic status. Some well-to-do people, regardless of their partisan loyalty, may feel sympathy for the economic underdog and thus favor government help to the unemployed; some less-well-off people may be dri-

TABLE 6.5 Issue Positions, Ideological Self-Identification, and Party Identification: 1996

	Democrats		Independents			Republicans			
	Strong	Weak	Closer to Dem.	Closer to Neither	Closer to Rep.	Weak	Strong	Dem. minus Rep.	# Cases
A. Government spending on services									
More	32%	24	18	6	8	9	3	44	544
Same	21%	20	18	10	7	14	9	18	459
Less	7%	13	8	6	16	22	27	-29	456
B. Government role in providing jobs and a good standard of living									
Gov. help	34%	22	17	10	6	8	4	44	401
In between	22%	23	18	7	11	14	5	26	341
Help self	10%	17	10	8	14	18	18	-9	800
C. Government role in improving position of minorities									
Gov. help	38%	20	20	7	6	6	3	49	288
In between	23%	23	13	8	10	15	8	23	363
Help self	12%	18	12	8	14	18	18	-6	897
D. Government spending on defense									
Decrease	25%	23	18	8	9	11	7	30	468
Same	16%	20	15	8	10	17	13	6	488
Increase	16%	15	9	7	14	18	21	-8	516
E. Willingness to use force to solve international problems									
Unwilling	20%	14	13	18	20	7	7	20	55
In between	17%	22	17	11	8	15	11	13	246
Willing	20%	20	13	8	11	16	13	11	1379
F. Abortion									
Own choice	23%	21	16	8	11	13	7	24	704
In between	16%	19	12	8	12	17	16	2	764
Illegal	21%	17	10	10	8	16	18	4	194
G. Ideological self-identification									
Liberal	37%	30	20	4	3	5	1	79	337
Moderate	17%	22	19	12	11	14	6	27	400
Conservative	8%	10	6	5	15	24	31	-46	585

Note: Totals add to approximately 100 percent reading across (with slight variations due to rounding). Dem. minus Rep. is party difference calculated by subtracting the percentage of strong and weak Republicans from the percentage of strong and weak Democrats. Negative numbers indicate a Republican advantage in the group. Individuals who were unable to describe themselves in ideological terms were not included in the data in panel G.

Source: 1996 American National Election Study, Center for Political Studies, University of Michigan; data made available by the Inter-University Consortium for Political and Social Research.

ven by their respect for those who achieve great wealth in the face of great odds and so may oppose government spending on social services. Socioeconomic status is not always a good predictor of people's political attitudes; many other factors make a difference as well.[33]

Party differences are also apparent on non-SES issues, such as civil rights, defense spending, the question of abortion, and the individual's self-described liberalism or conservatism (see Table 6.5, panels C-G). Since the 1960s, for example, party identifiers have been sharply divided in their attitudes toward racial policy. Other non-SES issues have become important in more recent elections. In 1996, defense and foreign policy issues and concerns about abortion separated Democrats from Republicans to a significant degree. Just eight years earlier, however, in 1988, these issues were not related to party identifications; in fact, they cut across party lines, dividing Democrats from Democrats and Republicans from Republicans.[34] When an issue cuts across party lines it can strain the coalitional foundations of a party system. The movement of the abortion issue from crosscutting to reinforcing partisan divisions suggests some important changes in the parties in the electorate. Overall, the party difference between self-identified liberals and conservatives is especially striking.

A SIXTH PARTY SYSTEM?

The parties in the electorate have changed significantly since the 1950s and early 1960s. As we have seen, the Democratic share of the electorate is somewhat smaller than before and the proportion of independents has grown (see Table 6.2). It would seem that young adults are not as likely to inherit their parents' partisanship now as they were in earlier generations. The social group and issue foundations of the New Deal party system have eroded. SES differences continue to separate the Democratic and Republican coalitions, but now they must vie for center stage with powerful social, racial, and foreign policy cleavages.

But what does this change mean? Perhaps a dealignment has undermined the foundations of the New Deal party system without building a new party system in its place. An alternative view, which gained renewed life after the 1994 elections, is that a new, sixth party system has emerged, led by a newly powerful Republican Party. It is possible to find support for both views.

The most convincing evidence for the dealignment scenario is that the New Deal party system has eroded, but the Republican Party has not been able to capitalize fully on the Democrats' losses. In spite of the decline in the percentage of Democratic loyalists since the 1950s, the GOP remains stuck at about the same share of the electorate it had achieved in 1960. At the state and local level, most public officials still come from the Democratic Party. Nationally, Republicans have won the presidency more often in recent decades, but these GOP presidents have invariably had to deal with a Congress in which at least one house was under Democratic control. Republicans finally won a majority in both houses of Congress in 1994 for the first time in forty years—but ironically, this time with a Democrat in the White House.[35]

The argument that there has been a realignment, in contrast, focuses on the successes of Republican presidential candidates, the growth of the GOP in the once one-party Democratic South, and the recent Republican gains in Congress, most notably their stunning victories in 1994. Only Jimmy Carter and Bill Clinton have been able to break the Republican hold on the White House since 1968. Carter barely won in the aftermath of the Watergate scandal[36] and was defeated for reelection, while Clinton won with only 43 percent of the popular vote in 1992, and climbed no higher than

49 percent in 1996. Republican growth in the South, in particular, has been phenomenal. From a beachhead at the presidential level established in the 1950s, the party was soon able to compete with the Democrats in statewide races, and in 1994 there was a GOP majority among the region's U.S. representatives, U.S. senators, and governors for the first time since Reconstruction.[37]

The best evidence as to whether there has been a realignment turns on party identification: the relative size and composition of the parties in the electorate. There was no sign of realignment in the late 1960s and the 1970s; both parties lost supporters (see Table 6.2) and their group and issue coalitions frayed but did not basically change. The 1980s were a different story. With Ronald Reagan's election and GOP capture of the Senate in 1980 followed by victories of Republican presidential candidates in 1984 and 1988, the Republican Party improved its standing throughout the decade, while the Democratic share of the electorate declined. Just as significant for a realignment interpretation was the GOP surge among young voters, who in the 1980s became more Republican than Democratic for the first time in the fifty-year annals of public opinion polling.[38] Perhaps most significant are the changes in party identification among Southerners and among blacks (see Figure 6.1). If we take seriously the definition of realignment as a change in the party coalitions, these changes are too dramatic to dismiss.

Yet in the 1990s the Republican resurgence looked like a sometime thing. On the eve of the 1992 presidential election the percentage of Democratic identifiers had reached its lowest level since 1952, but the surge in GOP party identification seen in the 1980s had stopped, leaving the electorate even less partisan than before. After the 1992 election the regular soundings of *The New York Times*/CBS News poll showed even more Democratic decay with little compensating growth in GOP loyalties. And yet in the 1994 congressional elections the size of the Republican *partisan* victory was unexpectedly large.

After some major missteps by the leaders of the new Republican congressional majority, the Democratic vote rebounded; Democratic congressional candidates made gains in 1996 and 1998, and Democratic Party identification increased a little as well. The share of the electorate that called itself independent dropped a bit. Party watchers could be forgiven for feeling like spectators at a tennis match. This could be more evidence of the electoral volatility that signals a dealignment. Or it could be a temporary blip in the progress of a pro-Republican realignment. The determining factor will probably be the extent to which Democratic and especially Republican party leaders can seize the opportunities for mobilizing voters in the 2000 election and beyond.

As the new millennium begins, then, the American electorate has divided into three groups of roughly similar size: Democrats, Republicans, and independents. Whether this signifies a realigned sixth party system or the continued dealignment of the New Deal system—and this will be in dispute for some time—it is an electorate that has markedly different partisan loyalties from those of a generation or two earlier. Yet it is an electorate still dominated by party loyalists, by the Democratic and Republican parties in the electorate. As long as it contains so many nonpartisans and a near parity between the two party camps, it is also an electorate capable of producing mercurial election results, both within and across elections. And it is fully capable of sustaining third-party and independent candidates for president as well as the divided control of government that has been so characteristic of the American system for the last three decades.

Chapter 7
The Party within the Voter

*P*olitics is a buzzing confusion. Americans cope with more elections, and therefore more occasions on which they need to make large numbers of political choices, than do citizens of any other democracy. On any given day three levels of legislatures—national, state, and local—may be passing laws that affect our lives. It is hard enough for reporters and political activists to keep track of all the action. The challenge is so much greater for less-involved partisans, who spend less time thinking about politics (though their lives are just as affected by political decisions). Their best guide to this confusing political world is their party identification.

This *party identification*—an individual's sense of psychological attachment to a party—in addition to his or her feelings and beliefs about political parties, is a kind of "party within" the voter. It serves as a framework or a lens through which individuals see political reality. We all see the world around us selectively. For someone who considers him- or herself a strong Democrat or a strong Republican, party loyalty is a key to this selectivity. Because a party identification will probably be the individual's most enduring political attachment, it acts as a kind of political gyroscope, stabilizing political outlooks against the buffetings of short-term influences.

With so much attention focused on declining partisanship, it is easy to lose sight of the fact that most Americans continue to consider themselves Republicans or Democrats. More than 30 percent call themselves "strong" partisans (as you saw in Table 6.2 in Chapter 6), and another third express a party identification, though not a strong one. Even among those who at first claim to be independents, more than three fourths confess to some partisan feeling. However we measure partisanship (see box on p. 134), knowing this one fact about people tells us more about their political perceptions and behavior than does any other single piece of information.

THE STABILITY OF PARTY IDENTIFICATIONS

For a large number of Americans, partisanship is a stable anchor in an ever-changing political world. Most Americans, once they have developed such loyalties, tend to keep them, even in the face of major change in the "outside" political world. People who do change their party identification normally change only its intensity (for example, from strong to weak identification) rather than convert to the other party.

The Party Identification Controversy

The most commonly used measure of party identification classifies people into one of seven types of identification: strong Democrat, weak Democrat, independent leaning toward Democrats, "pure" independent, independent leaning toward Republicans, weak Republican, and strong Republican. (There are also a very few people who describe themselves as apolitical or who identify with minor parties.) Is this the best way to classify partisans?

This measure produces a continuum of partisanship. But scholars disagree on where "party identifiers" end and "independents" begin. This decision matters, of course, if we want to draw conclusions about the strength of a particular party or about the likelihood of a realignment. So in most tables in this book, the full seven categories are presented so that readers can draw their own line between partisan and independent. In most of the interpretations here, partisans are defined as strong plus weak party identifiers, and the three categories of independents are combined.

Curiously, however, independent leaners often behave in a more partisan manner than weak partisans do, especially in voting for their party's candidates. Why is that? It could be that the party identification measure is capturing more than a single attitude toward the parties. Your attitude toward Republicans, for example, could be only partly related to your attitude toward Democrats. Or someone could be attracted both to a particular party and to the idea of political independence. If that is true, then a single continuum may not be the best measure of people's partisan feelings.

Scientific controversies over the measurement of key concepts are not uncommon. This particular controversy focuses on refining, not dismissing the idea of party loyalties. Generally speaking, the traditional measure of party identification continues to be regarded as a valid and reliable measure of party loyalty.[1]

Researchers from the University of Michigan convincingly demonstrated the stability of party identifications by interviewing the same set of individuals in three successive surveys, in 1972, 1974, and 1976. They found that almost two thirds of the respondents remained in the same broad category of party identification (44 percent were stable strong/weak Democrats or Republicans, 20 percent stable independents) throughout all three surveys. A third changed from one of the parties to independence. Only 3 percent actually changed parties.[2]

When we compare the consistency of individuals' evaluations of prominent political figures or political issues over two-year periods, we find that individuals' attitudes toward the parties—their party identifications—were more stable than any of these other political orientations (Figure 7.1). This set of surveys was conducted during one of the most turbulent periods in recent history, covering Richard Nixon's landslide victory in 1972, the Watergate scandals that caused Nixon's resignation in 1974, Nixon's subsequent pardon by President Ford, and Ford's own 1976 defeat. It would be hard to find better evidence of the stability of party identification than its consistency during these agitated times.[3]

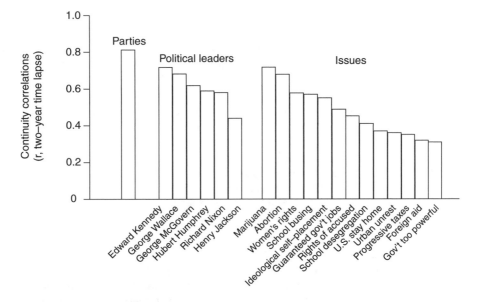

FIGURE 7.1 Consistency in political orientations, 1972–1974–1976.

Note: Entries are the average correlations, across a two-year interval. Complete continuity = 1.0; no continuity = 0.0; complete reversal = −1.0.

PARTY IDENTIFICATION AS A FILTER
FOR POLITICAL VIEWS

Because of their early development (as discussed in Chapter 6) and their stability, partisan loyalties can act as a filter through which voters view the political world. In many cases, individuals will come to hold images of candidates and issues that are heavily colored by the individual's attachment to a party. This may be a perfectly rational thing to do, of course. Party identification can be an information shortcut in a complicated political world. To the extent that people's images of their parties are accurate, these images may well describe the party's candidates as well. Accurately or not, though, voters *project* favorable characteristics and acceptable issue positions onto the candidates of the party they favor and are *persuaded* to support particular candidates or issues because they are associated with their party.[4]

Projection and Persuasion

When a new political candidate begins to get public notice and before most voters know much about him or her, many partisans in the electorate will react to the candidate positively or negatively based solely on party affiliation. Many partisans will project their favorable image of the party onto its new candidate and will be persuaded to support him or her. "The stronger the voter's party bias, the more likely he is to see the candidate of his own party as hero, the candidate of the other party as villain."[5]

Even when a popular nonpolitician like Colin Powell becomes the subject of discussion as a possible candidate, evaluations of that person quickly diverge along partisan lines once the name is associated with a party.

The power of partisanship can be seen even when it competes with other valued loyalties. John F. Kennedy, the Democratic presidential candidate in 1960, was only the second Catholic presidential candidate in American history. Catholics tended to perceive Kennedy more favorably in that election than Protestants did. Catholic Republicans, however, were not as positively disposed toward Kennedy as were Catholic Democrats. Party identification, then, still held its power, even among those with the same religious loyalty. So candidate evaluations say something about the voter doing the evaluating, as well as about the candidate who is evaluated. In politics, too, beauty is in the eyes of the beholder.[6]

Party identification has a selective impact on people's perceptions of candidates, however. People are more likely to project their positive view of the party onto a candidate's political traits than onto such purely personal matters as the candidate's personality, appearance, or social characteristics.[7] Further, this projection is not without limits. Candidates for president who have gone down to defeats of landslide proportions—for example, Barry Goldwater in 1964, George McGovern in 1972, Walter Mondale in 1984—were not evaluated very positively even by their fellow partisans. Yet partisanship remains important even here; as low as the candidate's standing may have sunk, he could count on more sympathy from members of his party than from other voters.

Does an individual's partisanship color his or her feelings about political issues as well as candidate evaluations? That is more difficult to determine; we can ask whether the parties in the electorate respond differently to a new candidate, but there are not many new issues. We have already seen in Chapter 6 that Democratic identifiers differ from Republicans in their stands on several issues. In part, these patterns testify that people are naturally more likely to favor a party that champions their causes. But they also reflect a tendency for partisans to adopt their party's positions on issues, especially when those issues are complicated and remote. To an important degree, voters' policy positions do follow the partisan flag.

Feedback from Political Experiences   *F of C - feedback idea.*

The relationship between partisanship and other political attitudes, then, is not always a one-way street. Just as the individual's party loyalty colors his or her perception of political reality, studies have shown that feelings about candidates and issues can affect the individual's party identification as well. In particular, there is powerful evidence that negative reactions to a president's management of the economy (so-called retrospective evaluations, in that they refer to past actions rather than hopes for the future) can feed back on party loyalties and weaken or change them. In this way, partisanship could act as a kind of "running tally" of party-related evaluations.[8]

The result is a complex two-way process in which party loyalty affects an individual's evaluations of candidates and issues, and those evaluations, in turn, help to shape the way people view the parties. Even if party identification is usually stable enough to withstand the impact of conflicting short-term feelings—for example, disappointment in a party's candidate or the party's stance on an issue—an accumulation of these negative evaluations can shake an individual's partisanship and cut into its ability to lend luster to the party's standard-bearers and stands.

The force of party loyalties in shaping people's views of political reality had diminished in the 1960s and early 1970s. With the decline in partisanship that characterized American politics after the mid–1960s, a smaller share of the electorate wore the partisan lenses that can color political reality. Even among those who considered themselves partisans, there was a moderation in the strength of party loyalties. The impact of partisanship has rebounded, however, and party remains an important source of political orientations.[9]

PARTY IDENTIFICATION AND VOTING

The main significance of the parties in the electorate lies in their patterns of voting. Partisans provide the core support for the candidates of their party. The American electoral system discourages faithful party voting; partisans have to fight their way through long ballots, the culture's traditional emphasis on person over party, and its distrust of strong parties. Nevertheless, partisans support their party with considerable fidelity, which strengthens as the intensity of partisan loyalty grows.

Party Voting

Partisan voting fidelity has been high during the entire period of the American National Election Studies (ANES) surveys, which began in 1952. A majority in each category of partisanship has voted for their party's presidential candidate in every year except for weak Democrats in 1972 and independent Democrats in 1980 (both GOP landslide years). Further, strong partisans have always been more faithful than weak or independent partisans (Table 7.1). Even in the Reagan landslide victory of 1984, almost nine out of ten strong Democrats voted for Reagan's Democratic opponent,

TABLE 7.1 Voting for their Party's Presidential Candidates Among Party Identifiers: 1952–1996

	1952	1956	1960	1964	1968	1972	1976	1980	1984	1988	1992	1996
Strong Democrats	84%	85%	90%	95%	85%	73%	91%	86%	87%	93%	93%	96%
Weak Democrats	62	62	72	82	58	48	74	60	67	70	69	82
Independents closer to Democrats	60	68	88	90	52	60	72	45	79	88	71	76
Independents	—	—	—	—	—	—	—	—	—	—	—	---
Independents closer to Republicans	93	94	87	75	82	86	83	76	92	84	62	68
Weak Republicans	94	93	87	56	82	90	77	86	93	83	60	70
Strong Republicans	98	100	98	90	96	97	96	92	96	98	87	94

Note: The table entries are the percentages of each category of partisans who reported a vote for their party's candidate for president. To find the percentage voting for the opposing party's candidate or some other candidate, subtract the entry from 100 percent. Individuals who did not vote for president are excluded from the table.

Source: American National Election Studies, Center for Political Studies, University of Michigan; data made available by the Inter-University Consortium for Political and Social Research.

Walter Mondale. Strong Republicans have demonstrated the greatest party fidelity in presidential elections (see illustration below). Only twice in forty-five years has their support for the GOP standard-bearer dipped as "low" as 90 percent.

These patterns extend to voting for Congress (Table 7.2). A majority within each group of partisans has voted for their party's congressional candidates in each election, and strong partisans have been the most regular party voters. One key to the Democrats' ability to continue to win congressional majorities in the 1970s and 1980s even as their electoral base was eroding may be that they were more faithful than their GOP counterparts to their party's congressional candidates.

Similar results appear in voting at the state and local level through 1984, which is the last year for which such figures are available (Table 7.3). Straight-ticket voting—voting for one party's candidates only—has declined among all of the partisan groups during these years. But most strong Democrats and strong Republicans remained

The Faithful Republicans

TABLE 7.2 Voting for their Party's Congressional Candidates Among Party Identifiers: 1952–1996

	1952	1956	1960	1964	1968	1972	1976	1980	1984	1988	1992	1996	
Strong Democrats	89%	94%	93%	94%	88%	91%	89%	85%	89%	88%	86%	88%	*86*
Weak Democrats	77	86	86	84	73	80	78	69	70	82	82	71	*71*
Independents closer to Democrats	64	83	84	79	63	80	76	70	78	87	74	69	*70*
Independents	—	—	—	—	—	—	—	—	—	—	—	---	*—*
Independents closer to Republicans	81	83	74	72	81	73	65	68	61	64	65	79	*66*
Weak Republicans	90	88	84	64	78	75	66	74	66	70	63	79	*79*
Strong Republicans	95	95	90	92	91	85	83	77	85	77	82	97	*86*

Note: The table entries are the percentages of each category of partisans who reported a vote for their party's candidate for Congress. To find the percentage voting for the opposing party's candidate or some other candidate, subtract the entry from 100 percent. Individuals who did not vote or did not vote for Congress are excluded from the table.

Source: American National Election Studies, Center for Political Studies, University of Michigan; data made available by the Inter-University Consortium for Political and Social Research.

TABLE 7.3 Straight-Ticket Voting Among Party Identifiers: 1952–1984

	1952	1956	1960	1964	1968	1972	1976	1980	1984
Strong Democrats	86%	84	87	80	72	66		62	69
Weak Democrats	69	72	74	53	43	38	—	39	46
Independents closer to Democrats	56	58	56	37	32	28	—	23	38
Independents	56	43	65	53	24	28	—	21	25
Independents closer to Republicans	65	56	51	33	43	30	—	28	33
Weak Republicans	72	69	68	44	49	40	—	35	41
Strong Republicans	85	83	79	71	74	60	—	61	59

Note: The table entries are the percentages of each category of partisans who reported voting a straight ticket in state and local elections. To find the percentage splitting their tickets, subtract the entry from 100 percent. Individuals who did not vote or did not vote in state and local elections are excluded from the table. The question was not asked in 1976, 1988, 1992, or 1996.

Source: American National Election Studies, Center for Political Studies, University of Michigan; data made available by the Inter-University Consortium for Political and Social Research.

straight-ticket voters. In fact, in these races rates of straight-ticket voting steadily increased with strength of partisanship.[10] The higher level of party voting among independent partisans than among weak partisans, which appeared as a curious anomaly in presidential and congressional voting, is absent at the state and local level.[11]

Voting patterns such as these are the product of the push of an enduring partisan loyalty and the pull of the candidates and issues particular to each year. Typically this push and pull are reinforcing; they incline the voter in the same direction. On the occasions when they conflict, however, the short-term force of candidates and issues may lead the partisan to defect from his or her party. In fact, the most powerful influence in leading voters to defect from their party loyalty is a highly visible candidate, most often an incumbent, from the opposing party.[12]

Like reeds in a pond that bend as the wind blows, though, the likelihood that voters will temporarily desert their party's candidate depends upon the degree to which their partisan roots are firmly anchored and on the strength and direction of that election's special characteristics. In a year during which short-term forces are running in a Republican direction, for example, many Democrats will defect to vote for GOP candidates, but the strong identifiers will remain most steadfast. Of course, the longer these short-term forces pull in the same direction, the greater is the chance that the defectors may turn into converts as voters change their partisanship to bring it into line with their vote.[13]

A Party-in-the-Electorate-Based Typology of Elections

Elections can be classified into three types depending on the degree to which party identifiers vote for their party's presidential candidate:

> The *maintaining* election, in which the party attachments of the recent past prevail without any great change. In these elections, the candidate from the largest party in the electorate wins.

> The *deviating* election, in which the basic distribution of party loyalties is not changed, but short-term candidate or issue forces cause the defeat of the majority party.

> The *realigning* election, in which a new coalition of party loyalists emerges and governs the outcome. These elections typically produce a new majority party.

Since 1952 deviating elections have become common at the presidential level. The majority Democratic Party won the presidency in a maintaining election in only five of the twelve elections beginning with 1952. In the other years Republicans were victorious, and they earned their victories by inducing considerable defection among Democrats. In three of these contests, in fact, the GOP candidate won by the landslide proportions of more than 15 percent of the popular vote.

No other period of American history can match the past four decades in terms of the success of the minority party at the presidential level. Whether this era represents a new brand of American politics without strong party alignments (or without party playing much of a role in presidential politics), the prolonged unraveling of the New Deal party system, or the advent of realignment, of course, is the subject of considerable debate. However this debate is resolved, it is clear that in recent American elections party identification has not been as consistent a force as we might have expected.

One reason why partisanship has had less influence on voting choices is that since the mid–1960s there have simply been fewer partisans and especially fewer strong partisans. But this is not the whole story. Partisan fidelity in voting has also varied within both parties. Except for Ronald Reagan's landslide reelection in 1984, weak Republicans' support of their party's presidential candidates in recent years has not returned to the levels achieved in the 1950s. The same is true of their Republican congressional voting, at least in presidential years—even in 1984 (see Tables 7.1 and 7.2). Strong Republicans have generally been faithful in presidential races, however, and have recently returned to fidelity in congressional elections. And partisan voting among Democrats in presidential election years has dipped occasionally but is higher now than in the 1950s.[14]

The most recent congressional midterm elections provide more evidence of this bumpy ride. Republican partisanship was especially strong in 1994 and 1998. Unlike their typical behavior since the 1960s, more Republicans than Democrats supported their party's candidates for the House of Representatives. The figures for strong and weak Republicans were 93 percent and 79 percent in 1994, and 95 percent and 77 percent in 1998, according to the University of Michigan's ANES survey; Democrats' support of Democratic congressional candidates was 5 to 10 percent lower. In both years Republicans also won a clear majority of the support of independents, but it was probably that extra boost in loyalty from their own partisans that gave them control of Congress for the first time in forty years. In mirror image, Democratic voting fidelity dropped in the 1990s.

Party versus Candidates and Issues

Scholars of voting behavior find that three main factors influence individuals' voting decisions: their party identification, the candidates' characteristics, and the issues in the race. A great deal of research has tried to determine the relative impact of each of these three. Analyses of elections through the 1970s showed that the relative influence of party identification had declined, just as would be expected because of the decreasing number of partisans and their weakening party voting. Since that time there is evidence of revived party influence.[15]

It is difficult to separate the effects of party from those of candidate images and issues, however, because the three factors are so strongly interrelated. Conclusions about relative importance often depend upon how well each of the factors is measured and what one is willing to assume about the causal priority of one over the other. The classic accounts of the dominant role of party identification in the 1950s assumed that party was causally prior to candidates and issues, influencing them but not in turn influenced by them. These early studies lacked adequate measures to determine how close the voter felt to the candidates on the issues.[16] With new measures of issue closeness and an allowance for reciprocal influences of issue, candidate, and party orientations, some recent research finds that elections since the 1970s have been dominated by short-run forces: the impact of the issues and candidates in a particular election.[17]

This does not mean, however, that party was unimportant in earlier years or that it is unimportant now. When we take a longer-term perspective and examine changing orientations across a four-year period among the same voters, party identification has continuing importance in structuring the immediate context of the electoral decision.[18] If we want to explain the general trends of American electoral politics, then, party identification plays a prominent role.

Party Identification and Political Activity

Another important effect of party identification is that individuals who consider them-selves Democrats and Republicans have high rates of involvement in political life. It is the strongest partisans who are the most likely to vote, to pay attention to politics, and to take part in political activities.

Over the years, strong partisans have consistently expressed more interest in pol-itics, and especially in election campaigns, than other citizens do. The 1996 ANES survey shows, for example, that strong Democrats and strong Republicans were more likely than weak identifiers or independents to be attentive to politics and highly inter-ested in the campaign (Table 7.4). Strong partisans were also more inclined than weak partisans or independents to follow reports about politics and the campaign on tele-vision and in newspapers.

The strongest partisans are also the most active in other ways. A total of 86 and 96 percent, respectively, of the strong Democrats and Republicans reported having voted in 1996—much higher than the turnout levels among other partisans or inde-pendents.[19] They were also more likely than other citizens to try to persuade other people to vote a certain way, to wear campaign buttons, display bumper stickers, or use yard signs, to attend political meetings or rallies, and to contribute money to a candidate or party. The combatants of American electoral politics, in short, come dis-proportionately from the ranks of the strong Democrats and strong Republicans.

TABLE 7.4 Political Involvement of Partisans and Independents: 1996

| | Democrats | | Independents | | | Republicans | |
| | | | Closer to... | | | | |
	Strong	Weak	Dem	Neither	Rep	Weak	Strong
Very much interested in politics	44%	15	19	14	21	23	52
Follow public affairs most of time	33%	14	19	12	25	16	42
Great deal of attention to campaign via TV	25%	9	12	9	13	12	31
Read about campaign in newspapers	68%	50	55	49	56	56	71
Voted	86%	69	70	55	76	80	96
Tried to persuade people to vote certain way	30%	20	20	22	35	27	54
Displayed button, bumper sticker, sign	12%	8	4	5	14	7	20
Attended rally or meeting	6%	5	2	3	8	5	13
Contributed money to:							
Candidate	7%	4	2	2	7	6	11
Party	7%	4	4	2	4	6	16

Source: 1996 American National Election Study, Center for Political Studies, University of Michigan; data made available by the Inter-University Consortium for Political and Social Research.

PARTY IDENTIFICATION AND PARTY PERCEPTIONS

Strong party identifiers tend to see the parties in sharper relief than do weak identifiers and independents. They are considerably more likely to find differences between the Democrats and Republicans in general (Table 7.5) and on specific policy issues. They hold more strongly differentiated evaluations of the two parties and their candidates, as well as of the parties' abilities to govern for the benefit of the nation. Strong partisans are more inclined than weaker partisans and independents to contend that their party's president has performed his job well and that a president of the opposing party has performed poorly.[20] In the mind of the strong partisan, in sum, the political parties are clearly defined and highly polarized along the important dimensions of politics.

These data do not prove that party identification alone results in greater activity or sharper party images. Involvement in political affairs has diverse roots. Higher socioeconomic status (SES) and the greater political sophistication and easier entry into politics that it often brings contribute a lot to involvement. The relatively greater involvement of partisans (and in most years, of Republicans), in fact, comes in part from their generally higher SES levels as well as from their more ideological commitment to politics.[21] Nonetheless, party identification has a major impact on people's political activity.

PARTISANSHIP AND PEROT

One of the biggest stories of the 1992 presidential election was the unprecedented showing of independent candidate H. Ross Perot. Unlike most independents, Perot flourished rather than faded as the campaign came to an end. He finished with almost 20 million votes, 19 percent of those cast. Poll results from late spring of 1992 suggested that he might have done even better if he had not temporarily withdrawn from the contest during the summer of 1992.

Electoral conditions were especially ripe for a strong independent or third-party candidate in 1992. Partisan loyalties, including the percentages of weak and strong

TABLE 7.5 Differences Between the Parties as Perceived by Partisans and Independents: 1996

Perceived differences between Democratic and Republican Parties	
Strong Democrats	81%
Weak Democrats	59
Independents closer to Democrats	52
Independents	47
Independents closer to Republicans	63
Weak Republicans	67
Strong Republicans	87

Source: 1996 American National Election Study, Center for Political Studies, University of Michigan; data made available by the Inter-University Consortium for Political and Social Research.

party identifiers, were weaker than ever. Coupled with the dissatisfaction many voters felt with their incumbent president, there was ample opportunity for a candidate who could appeal to both independents and disgruntled Democrats and Republicans.

Perot seemed to be such a candidate. In the end, however, his appeal was not strong enough or widespread enough to construct a winning coalition from among such a diverse set of voters.[22] Very little of Perot's support came from strong party identifiers. He drew his votes mainly from independents, independent "leaners," and weak Republicans (Table 7.6), as had third-party candidates John Anderson (in 1980) and George Wallace (in 1968) before him.[23] Based on the ANES estimates, a majority of Perot's total vote came from self-identified independents. The same was true of Perot's third-party candidacy in 1996. Thus partisanship and the continued loyalty of partisans to their party's standard-bearer were able to overcome even the well-financed Perot challenge.

THE MYTH OF THE INDEPENDENT *talk about this*

It is intriguing that party loyalties govern so much political behavior in a culture that so warmly celebrates the independent voter. There is clearly a disjuncture between the American myth of the high-minded independent—the well-informed citizen who is moved by issues and candidates, not parties—and the reality of widespread partisanship. The problem is with the myth.

Attitudinal Independents

One definition of independents refers to those Americans who tell poll-takers that they do not identify with a political party. In that, of course, they resemble the myth. It is also true, according to survey research, that they split their tickets more frequently and wait longer in the campaign to make their voting decisions. But they fall short of the mythical picture of the independent in most other respects. They are less well informed than party identifiers are, less concerned about specific elections, and less active politically. They are also less likely to vote in any given election. In 1996, for instance, independents stayed home from the polls at a higher rate than did party identifiers.

TABLE 7.6 Votes for Ross Perot Among Party Identifiers and Independents: 1992 and 1996

Voted for Perot	1992	1996
Strong Democrats	4%	2%
Weak Democrats	18	6
Independents closer to Democrats	23	15
Independents	37	18
Independents closer to Republicans	27	11
Weak Republicans	25	10
Strong Republicans	11	1

Source: 1992 and 1996 American National Election Studies, Center for Political Studies, University of Michigan; data made available by the Inter-University Consortium for Political and Social Research.

But there is an important distinction to be drawn between independents who say they feel closer to one of the two parties (independent "leaners") and those who do not ("pure" independents). The independent leaners often turn out to be more politically involved (see Table 7.4) and sometimes even more partisan in voting (especially for president) than weak partisans (see Tables 7.1 and 7.2). It is only in comparison to strong partisans that these partisan-oriented independents fall short. By contrast, the pure independents typically have the most dismal record, with relatively low levels of political interest and information, turnout, and education.[24] It is the pure independents who are the least involved and least informed of all American citizens (see Table 7.4).[25]

Behavioral Independents

We can also define independents in terms of their behavior. In his last work, the unparalleled researcher V. O. Key explored the idea of political independence. The picture of the American voter that was emerging from the electoral studies of the time, Key thought, was not a pretty one; it was one of an electorate whose voting decision was determined by deeply ingrained attitudes and loyalties—an electorate that had not grasped the major political issues.[26]

Key's search for electoral "rationality" centered on party switchers—the voters who switched their party vote in a consecutive pair of presidential elections—rather than on the self-styled independents. Key's switchers came much closer to the flattering myth of the independent than did the self-described independents. He found the switchers to express at least as much political interest as did the stand-patters (those who voted for the same party in both elections). Above all, the switchers showed an issue-related rationality that well fitted the mythical picture of the independent. They agreed on policy issues with the stand-patters toward whose party they had shifted, and they disagreed with the policies of the party from which they had defected.

It is the attitudinal independents, however—those who call themselves independents or voice no party preference—who are the subject of the most research, especially as their numbers have increased in recent years (see Table 6.2 in Chapter 6). The contemporary view is that they are, and always have been, a diverse group containing many of the least involved and least informed voters but also including some who come close to matching the mythological independent. The myth that they are a uniformly sophisticated and involved group of voters operating above the party fray has withered under the glare of survey research.

THE LOYAL ELECTORATES AND CHANGING PARTY POLITICS

The leaders of the party organizations scarcely know the men and women of the parties' loyal electorates. They know them largely in the same way that political scientists do—in some abstract, aggregate profile. They know that members of the party in the electorate see the issues and candidates through party-tinted glasses. They know that the party electorate is more likely to vote the party ticket and that it is easier to recruit into activity for the party or for a candidate. Party strategists know, in other words, that the party electorate is a hard core of party supporters. In a general way they see, as do political scientists, that party identification is a commitment that is often strong enough to guide other beliefs and behavior.

Toward a Candidate-Centered Electoral Politics

As we have seen, however, the size of this hard core is changing, and with it changes critical elements of American politics. For a century after the establishment of the current two-party system, the Democratic and Republican parties in the electorate had a great stabilizing influence on party politics. Because large numbers of people had party identifications, because they rarely changed them, and because those identifications strongly governed their voting decisions, patterns of voting support for the two parties were remarkably stable. In election after election, many people voted straight party tickets. The patterns of party support were also stable geographically.[27]

The events of recent years have jolted this long-term stability to the point that a different style of party politics seems to have emerged. Compared with the early 1960s, the two parties have relatively smaller shares of the electorate. The loyalty of the remaining Democratic and Republican partisans to the candidates of their party has waxed and waned. The consequence is that across the nation some contend that electoral politics has become less party-centered and more candidate-centered.[28]

The possibility of realignment remains; changes in the proportion of party loyalists and partisan fidelity are probably natural as one party system dies and another takes its place. But for the present—a present that has now lasted for at least two decades–the parties in the electorate have more competition from other elements of American electoral politics. One important result is that elections now turn more than ever on short-run forces: candidates, issues, and the particular events of the immediate campaign. This has important effects for the party organizations and their campaign strategies (see box on p. 147) as well as for the role of the parties in government.

The Continuing Significance of Party

Yet the importance of the party in the electorate must not be underestimated. Most Americans—a clear majority if we count only strong and weak identifiers, and almost all Americans if leaners are included as well—still claim some degree of loyalty to either the Democratic or the Republican Party. Many Americans are faithful to these loyalties in voting for candidates for office. Voters may stray from the party fold here and there; the very abundance of elected offices encourages such defections. But voters continue to perceive candidates, issues, and elections in partisan terms and often vote accordingly. Although challenged by strong antiparty forces since the mid–1960s, the party within the voter continues to influence electoral choices, and the parties in the electorate remain major players in American elections.

The 1994 midterm elections were the most party-oriented contests in some time; the GOP was able to overcome the localism that protected incumbents by appealing to national issues, especially dissatisfaction with the Democratic president. The new

Republican majority in the Congress, rallying around its "Contract with America," demonstrated the power of a cohesive party. Four years later, party voting remained high among Republicans but declined among Democrats. The 1994 vote shows that under the right conditions it is still possible to have a party-dominated election in contemporary U.S. politics. But ironically, that partisan interlude may well be just a piece of the broader picture of electoral instability of recent years.

Party Electorates and Campaign Strategies

The nature of these loyal party electorates shapes the strategies of American political campaigns. The cardinal rule of campaigning is to reinforce and activate your own partisans while making candidate and issue appeals to independents and partisans of the other party.

How this rule applies depends upon the relative sizes of the party electorates. The job of the majority party is to mobilize its loyalists by appealing to the party's core issues. Democrats since the 1930s, for example, have continually stressed the economic issues that gave them their majority status. The minority party's job is to divert attention from these issues by choosing candidates who transcend partisan politics (Ronald Reagan, for example, whose attractive personality had wide appeal) or by raising issues that crosscut the party coalitions (such as the GOP emphasis on symbols of patriotism and traditional morality). When the minority party tries to debate the majority party's core issues, it risks a defeat of historic proportions, as the Republicans learned in 1964 with candidate Barry Goldwater.

Campaign strategies also vary with the size and loyalty of the party electorates. Appeals to party loyalty are effective in a party-committed electorate, but can undermine candidate support in an electorate with weak party attachments. Just as Republican Ronald Reagan frequently mentioned his Democratic roots as a means of expanding his voter base, Bill Clinton was willing to desert traditional party issues in order to stem the erosion of the Democratic electoral party. In general, a less party-identified electorate inclines party candidates to craft their own unique electoral appeals, occasionally even running against the party, and, as the Perot showing illustrates, opens up the electoral system to candidates from outside the major-party mainstream.

Chapter 8

The Active Electorate

*T*he size and nature of the Democratic and Republican parties in the electorate are vitally important to the parties' success. More fundamentally, however, parties are shaped by a political system's answers to these questions: Who will be allowed to vote? What proportion of those people actually show up at the polls? And how well do those voters represent the adult population as a whole in their social characteristics and their views on political issues? These questions have been answered differently at different times in American history, and the answers still vary today.

We have seen that the American parties grew and changed in response to—and in part stimulated—the expansion of the right to vote. As the electorate was expanded to include lower-status people and then women and minorities, the parties were forced to change their organizations and appeals. Parties that failed to adjust to the new electorates—the early Federalists, for example—have become extinct. Others, such as European socialist and labor parties, have gained prominence by fighting to secure the suffrage for lower-status voters and then using these voters' support to win political power. The nature of the parties depends on the nature of the electorate.

Even more, the fate of the parties depends on the active electorate—the types of people who actually go to the polls. Those who vote are rarely a representative sample of all adult citizens; some groups in society are more likely to exercise their right to vote than others are. Because groups have different profiles of support for the parties, as Chapter 6 showed, the composition of the active electorate affects the balance of party power. The remarkably low voter turnout in American elections heightens the impact of these group differences in party support.

THE LOW TURNOUT IN AMERICAN ELECTIONS

It is extremely significant for American elections that so small a percentage of the eligible adult population actually shows up at the polls. Only 49 percent of the eligible electorate cast a ballot for president in 1996. The only other presidential contests since 1824 in which turnout fell below 50 percent were the first two elections of the 1920s, before many women had become accustomed to their new right to vote. Even fewer people vote in midterm elections; in 1998, only 34 percent of the eligible voters cast a ballot for the top office on the ballot (see Figure 8.1).[1]

As low as they may seem, these figures hide even lower turnout rates in many states. In the 1996 presidential contest, for example, only 38 percent of the voting-age population cast a ballot in Nevada in comparison to almost 72 percent in Maine.

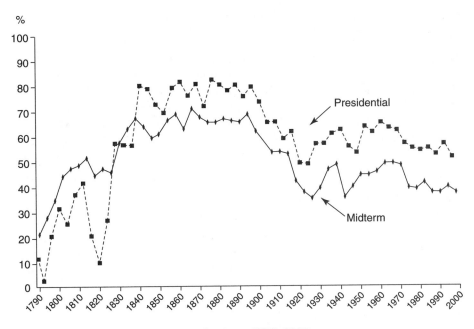

FIGURE 8.1 Turnout in American elections: 1790–1998.
Note: These are the percentages voting for president and for the office with the highest vote in midterm elections. Because the base is the total of eligible votes, which is somewhat less than the voting-age population, these turnout rates are somewhat higher than are commonly reported.

The figures also ignore roll-off, or voting for the most important office on the ballot but not for lesser offices; turnout in the 1996 congressional elections, for example, was about 4 percent less than presidential turnout. An even smaller percentage votes in local elections and party primaries.

These low turnouts have long generated serious debate. Some observers ask: How healthy can our democracy be when fewer than half of its citizens bother to vote?[2] Others wonder whether democracy would be helped or harmed by encouraging the participation of less-involved, and presumably less-informed, citizens. Nevertheless, at other times and in other places, democracies have enjoyed much broader participation. Voting turnout in the United States reached an all-time high toward the end of the nineteenth century.[3] In more recent times, turnout in congressional elections peaked at 55 percent in 1958, and presidential turnout was as high as 73 percent in 1960. It is even more startling to note that voter turnouts in the U.S. lag so far behind other nations. In no other democratic nation in the world does such a small share of the electorate take part in choosing the most important government officials.[4]

There are several reasons for low voter participation in the United States. The size of the active electorate is affected by state laws (and the way they are applied in practice), economic and social influences, and the political conditions present in any given election. Forces within the individual make a difference as well: individual values, motivation levels, and sense of civic responsibility.

CHANGING LEGAL DEFINITIONS OF THE ELECTORATE

The Constitution leaves it to the states to decide on the qualifications for voters. The result is that even for national elections there is no uniform national electorate in the United States. Since the Civil War, however, the national government has been given the authority, most often through constitutional amendments, to keep states from imposing particularly objectionable restrictions on voting. Thus state and national authorities have both had a hand in expanding and occasionally even contracting the right to vote during the last two centuries.

National Protections for the Right to Vote

White males were given the vote earlier in the United States than in any other democracy. In the early 1800s, the states themselves gradually repealed the property, income, and taxpaying qualifications for voting by which they had so severely restricted male suffrage.[5] By 1860 no states required property-holding and only four required substantial taxpaying as a condition for voting. About a century later, the Supreme Court and then the Twenty-fourth Amendment finally ended even the small poll tax as a requirement for voting.[6]

Complete women's suffrage did not come until the twentieth century, and it required federal action. By the mid-1870s, women had begun to press state governments for the right to vote; in 1890, with its admission to the Union, Wyoming became the first state to grant full voting rights to women. The push for women's suffrage then bogged down, especially in the Eastern states, and women shifted their hopes to the United States Constitution. The Nineteenth Amendment, forbidding states to deny the vote on grounds of gender, was finally ratified in 1920.

The right to vote for black Americans has a more checkered history. Some New England states granted blacks the suffrage before the Civil War. The Fifteenth Amendment was adopted after that war, stating that the right to vote could not be abridged on account of race. As the federal government turned its attention to other matters, however, Southern states effectively restricted the franchise for blacks through poll taxes, literacy tests, and outright intimidation. By the early 1900s, black turnout in the South was negligible. It remained that way in most Southern states until the 1960s, when the federal government began to enforce the Fifteenth Amendment and new voting rights laws on the reluctant states.

Lowering the voting age to eighteen has been the most recent change in the legal definition of the electorate. In the 1960s, only a handful of states allowed people under the age of twenty-one to vote. In 1970, Congress passed a law lowering the minimum voting age to eighteen in both state and federal elections. Less than half a year later, the Supreme Court decided that the act was constitutional as it applied to federal elections but unconstitutional for state and local elections.[7] Congress then passed a constitutional amendment lowering the age to 18 for all elections, and it was quickly ratified by the states in 1971.

The national government has taken further steps to expand the electorate. Congress banned literacy, understanding, and "character" tests for registration and waived residence requirements for voting in presidential elections. The recent "motor voter" law (see box below) requires the states to offer citizens the opportunity to register to vote when they apply for driver's licenses, by mail, and through agencies that disburse federal benefits. The Supreme Court has enlarged its own powers in this area, citing the Fourteenth Amendment's equal protection clause ("no state shall make or enforce any law which shall ... deny to any person within its jurisdiction the equal protection of the laws") to keep states from discriminating against blacks in defining their electorate. Presumably, this same clause would similarly protect the voting rights of other social groups.[8]

Between the constitutional territory of the states and that of the nation there is a tiny no-man's-land, the District of Columbia. For almost all of American history, the citizens of the district remained voteless, even in their own local affairs. Since the passage of the Twenty-third Amendment in 1961, however, the District of Columbia has had three votes in the electoral college. Its citizens also elect a nonvoting delegate to Congress and a series of local officials.

The "Motor Voter" Law Controversy

The continuing controversy over the National Voter Registration Act (the so-called "motor voter" law), passed in 1993, highlights some of the issues involved in trying to make it easier for citizens to vote. Many states refused to implement the new law. They protested the costs of yet another unfunded mandate imposed on them by the national government. State leaders, as well as Republicans in Congress, were concerned that easier access to voting would result in fraudulent registration. Many objected to letting new voters register at welfare offices and to limits on the state's ability to strike people from the registration rolls for failing to vote. In early 1995 the Justice Department announced it was prosecuting states—among them California, Illinois, and Pennsylvania—that had refused to comply with the new law.

Clearly this is a partisan issue; it is not surprising that a bill passed by a Democratic Congress and signed by a Democratic president would run into fierce opposition two years later, after Republicans took control of Congress and many statehouses. Many Republicans feared that the new law would make it easier to register likely Democrats than likely Republicans. But beyond the partisan implications, this is another round in the long-running dispute between those who would make voting as cost-free as possible to stimulate greater participation and those who, in the Progressive tradition, are concerned with guarding the electoral process against vote fraud.[9]

Early experience with the "motor voter" law supports both sides of this debate. After the new law took effect in 1995, voter registration surged in many areas of the nation—perhaps the biggest increases ever recorded. On the other hand, there have been anecdotal accounts of fraudulent registration as well, including the enrollment of aliens as voters along the U.S.-Mexican border and in large cities such as Chicago and New York. The early registration surges did not seem to favor either the Democrats or the Republicans. Nor, ironically, did the jump in registration lead to increased voter turnout in elections.

LEGAL-INSTITUTIONAL BARRIERS TO VOTING

These constitutional amendments have limited states' discretion in determining who can vote. So have the political pressures for universal adult suffrage as well as increased supervision by Congress and the Supreme Court. Over the years, then, the various states have converged on legal definitions of the suffrage that are fairly similar.

Citizenship

Since the 1920s all states have required that voters be citizens of the United States. As surprising as it may now seem, prior to 1894 at least twelve states permitted noncitizens to vote,[10] although some required that the individual had begun to seek American citizenship. The requirement of citizenship remains the biggest legal barrier to voting; there are millions of adults living in the United States—most of them concentrated in California, Florida, Texas, and New York—who are not eligible to vote until they qualify as citizens.

Residence

For most of American history, states could require citizens to live in a state and locality for a certain period of time before being allowed to vote there. Most states had three-layer residence requirements: a minimum period of time in the state, a shorter time in the county, and an even shorter period in the local voting district. Southern states had the longest residence requirements (which kept migrant farmworkers from voting), but other states also had long waits for eligibility. As recently as 1970, the median residence requirement among the states was one year in the state, three months in the county, and one month in the voting district.

States began to lower their residence requirements in the 1950s and 1960s as society became more mobile; many states set up even lower requirements for newcomers wishing to vote in presidential elections. In 1970, Congress settled the latter issue by establishing a national requirement of thirty days' residence within a state for voting in presidential elections. Shortly after, the Supreme Court struck down Tennessee's one-year residence requirement for state and local elections, indicating a strong preference for a thirty-day limit.[11] Since then, almost half of the states have dropped residence requirements altogether, and most of the rest have fixed them at one month.

Despite these changes, residency requirements are still a barrier to voting. The United States is a nation of movers. About 16 percent of the population moved within the United States between 1997 and 1998, with about 5 percent moving to a different county and 2 percent to a different state.[12] One study shows that those who have recently moved are far less likely to vote; with the impact of mobility removed, this study estimates that turnout would be about 9 percent higher.[13]

Registration

One of the most effective barriers to voting is the requirement in most states that citizens must take the initiative to register in order to vote in an election. This Progressive reform was implemented in most states toward the end of the nineteenth century to limit illegal voting in the teeming cities. Before then, prospective voters only had to show up on election day or be listed on the government's voting roll to be able to cast a ballot, which is also the practice today in most European democracies. These registration requirements cut into the high turnout levels of the late nineteenth century by increasing the motivation needed to vote and reducing the fraudulent padding of voter rolls.[14]

States differ in their registration requirements and thus in the burden they place on citizens. The relevant provisions involve the closing date for registration (which ranges from none to thirty days before the election), the frequency with which registration rolls are purged (a few states remove voters from the rolls after missing one election, but most do it only after four years of nonvoting), and the accessibility of registrars.[15]

Although registration requirements have been liberalized, they still impose a formidable cost on the exercise of the right to vote. The higher these costs, the more citizens will choose not to participate in elections. Studies have consistently estimated that turnout in presidential elections would be considerably higher if all states allowed election day registration, set regular as well as evening and Saturday hours for registering, and did not purge for nonvoting. The greatest gains would be realized by eliminating the closing date, which would let citizens cast a ballot even if they did not get interested enough to take part until the last, most exciting days of the campaign.[16]

THE SPECIAL CASE OF VOTING RIGHTS FOR AMERICAN BLACKS

Nowhere have legal-institutional barriers to voting been more effective than in denying suffrage to Southern blacks. Black males were enfranchised nationwide after the defeat of the Confederacy, by the constitutional amendments extending to blacks the rights of citizenship. But when Union occupation troops withdrew from the South as the Reconstruction came to an end, Southern states set about systematically to remove blacks from the active electorate. By the beginning of the twentieth century, they had succeeded.

Systematic Denial of the Right to Vote

The disenfranchisement of Southern black voters is a story of blatant manipulation of the electoral system in order to control political outcomes. It was accomplished by a variety of laws, capricious election administration, and outright intimidation and violence when these subtler methods were not effective. By these means blacks were kept away from the polls in the former Confederacy and some neighboring states for almost a century.

Southern states employed an arsenal of weapons to restrict the black vote. Residence requirements were most stringent in the South. Most states in that region required payment of a poll tax in order to vote—just one or two dollars, but often demanded well before an election, with the stipulation that the taxpayer keep a receipt and present it at the voting booth. Many states also required passage of a literacy test, often of both reading ability and understanding (frequently as judged by a hostile reg-istrar). These laws were intentionally directed at the poor and uneducated black pop-ulation. They created huge barriers to voting.

If the law was not enough to discourage blacks from voting, other devices were available. Blacks hoping to register traditionally found themselves blocked by endless delays, unavailable or antagonistic registrars, technicalities, and double standards (see box below). Those who persevered were often faced with economic reprisal (the loss of a job or a home) and physical violence. It is not surprising, given this unremittingly hostile environment, that only 5 percent of voting-age blacks were registered in the eleven Southern states as late as 1940.[17]

The Long Struggle for Voting Rights

For years after the end of Reconstruction, the states and the Supreme Court played a game of constitutional "hide and seek." The states would devise a way to disenfran-chise blacks, the Court would strike it down as unconstitutional, and the states would find another. States were sometimes careful not to disenfranchise poorer whites along with blacks; one method was the "grandfather clause," which automatically registered all men whose ancestors had been eligible to vote before the Civil War.

The "white primary" is a good example of the ingenuity shown by Southern states determined to avoid black registration. Faced with the threat of black voting in the Democratic primary, some states simply declared the party a private club open only to whites. This practice appeared at a time when the Republican Party was weak to nonexistent in Southern states, so the candidate who won the Democratic primary was assured of winning the general election. The white primary finally expired, but only after twenty-one years of litigation and five cases before the Supreme Court.[18]

Barriers to Black Registration in the South

In their account of the civil rights movement in the South, Pat Watters and Reese Cleghorn describe how blacks were prevented from registering by simple but effective administrative practices:

> Slowdowns were common. Separate tables would be assigned whites and Negroes. If a line of Negroes were waiting for the Negro table, a white might go ahead of them, use the empty white table, and leave. In Annis-ton, Alabama, a report said the white table was larger, and Negroes were not allowed in the room when a white was using it. Another variation was to seat four Negroes at a table, and make three wait until the slowest had finished, while others waited outside in line. These methods were partic-ularly effective when coupled with the one or two day a month registra-tion periods.... In one north Florida county, the registrar didn't bother with any of these refinements, and didn't close his office when Negro applicants appeared. He simply sat with his legs stretched out across the doorway. Negroes didn't break through them.[19]

Court action was not nearly as effective against the more informal hurdles faced by blacks trying to vote. Increasingly, then, legislative and administrative remedies were tried. The federal Voting Rights Act of 1965 made a frontal assault on these forms of discrimination. The act and its 1982 extension involved the national government directly in local registration practices. It authorized the U.S. Justice Department to seek injunctions against anyone who prevented blacks from voting. When the Justice Department could convince a federal court that a "pattern or practice" of discrimination existed in a district, the court could send federal registrars there to register voters. It could also supervise voting procedures in states and counties where less than 50 percent of potential voters had gone to the polls in the most recent presidential election. And it put local registrars under greater regulation and control.[20]

The Growth of Black Registration in the South

This unprecedented federal intervention in state electoral practices, combined with the civil rights movement's efforts to mobilize black voters, has enabled the black electorate to grow enormously in the South. Black registration increased from 5 percent of the black voting-age population in 1940 to 29 percent in 1960, and then surged dramatically to 64.5 percent in the 1992 election—a level close to that of white Southerners. Black registration levels continue to vary among the Southern states, however. These variations reflect differences in the size and socioeconomic characteristics of states' black populations, the states' political traditions, and the barriers they continue to raise to black participation (Table 8.1).[21]

TABLE 8.1 Black and White Voter Registration in the South: 1960 and 1996

	1960			1996		
State	Whites	Blacks	Whites minus Blacks	Whites	Blacks	Whites minus Blacks
Alabama	63.6%	13.7%	+49.9%	75.8%	69.2%	+6.6%
Arkansas	60.9	38.0	+22.9	64.5	65.5	-1.0
Florida	69.3	39.4	+29.9	63.7	53.1	+10.6
Georgia	56.8	29.3	+27.5	67.8	64.6	+3.2
Louisiana	76.9	31.1	+45.8	74.5	71.9	+2.6
Mississippi	63.9	5.2	+58.7	75.0	67.4	+7.6
North Carolina	92.1	39.1	+53.0	70.4	65.5	+4.9
South Carolina	57.1	13.7	+43.4	69.7	64.3	+5.4
Tennessee	73.0	59.1	+13.9	66.3	65.7	+.6
Texas	42.5	35.5	+7.0	62.7	63.2	-.5
Virginia	46.1	23.1	+23.0	68.4	64.0	+4.4
Total	61.1	29.1	+32.0	67.0	64.7	+2.3

Note: Table entries are the percentage of each group in that year who are registered to vote.

Source: For 1960 figures, *U.S. Bureau of the Census, Statistical Abstract of the United States, 99th edition* (Washington, DC: U.S. Government Printing Office, 1980), p. 514; for 1996 figures, *U.S. Bureau of the Census, Current Population Survey*, P20–504, Table 2.

From Voting Rights to Representation

Even though they are no longer systematically excluded from the electorate, blacks have continued to find it difficult to gain an effective political voice in many areas of the South. In the debate over extending the 1965 Voting Rights Act in 1981 and 1982, the major issue was the effort by some states and localities to dilute the impact of black votes or to limit the opportunities for blacks to choose black officeholders. The most common such devices were shifts to at-large local elections, legislative redistricting to divide black voters among a number of districts, and the annexation of white suburbs to offset black majorities in the cities or towns. These changes must now be approved by the Justice Department, which, since 1982, has broader authority to reject them.

Attention has now shifted from registration and voting to the representation of black voters in the legislative districts drawn up after the 1990 census. Under pressure from the Bush administration's Justice Department to create more minority districts in the South and through legislative alliances of black and Hispanic Democrats with white Republicans, a number of Southern states redrew legislative district lines so as to concentrate black voters in "majority-minority" districts. The effect has been to increase the number of black seats. Because the Democratic vote is concentrated in these majority-minority districts, however, Republican prospects are improved in neighboring districts.

The Supreme Court has questioned the constitutionality of the most flagrantly gerrymandered of these majority-minority districts. In a case challenging a congressional district in Georgia represented by a black Democrat, a slim majority of the Court found gerrymandering that violated the equal protection clause of the Fourteenth Amendment because race was the "predominant" factor in the redistricting.[22] This controversy is sure to continue in redistricting plans drawn up after the 2000 census.

POLITICAL INFLUENCES ON TURNOUT

Many political factors also draw voters to the polls or drive them away. These include the amount of competition between the parties, the attractiveness of candidates in a race, the importance of the contest, and the grassroots efforts of political groups. Variations in these factors lead to differential levels of voter turnout.

Differences in Interest Levels among Elections

American voters face more frequent elections than almost any other population in the democratic world. Within four years, they will be called to the polls for national, state, and local elections to select scores of legislative and executive offices (and judges in many states). Most of these elections are preceded by primaries. In some areas voters will have to deal with initiatives, referenda, and even an occasional recall election. Americans pay dearly, in the currency of numerous and frequent voting decisions, for the right to keep government on a short electoral leash.

Voter participation varies a great deal depending on the type of election. It is generally highest in presidential elections and lowest in local races. General elections normally attract far more voters than primaries. Initiatives and referenda, the Progressives' devices for allowing voters to decide issues directly, bring out fewer voters than ordinary elections. At times, an emotionally charged referendum can elicit substantial turnout, but the absence of a personal clash in these questions tends to reduce their allure, and they are often complicated enough to confuse many would-be voters.[23]

It is understandable why the more intense general election campaigns for the presidency and governorships entice more voters to participate. The personalities and issues involved are more highly publicized. Because party fortunes are involved, people's party loyalties are aroused, in contrast with the situation of many nonpartisan local elections. Yet on occasion a highly personalized mayor's or school board race can make even a presidential contest look dull.[24]

Competition

Political competition brings voters to the polls. Turnout is higher in areas where the parties and candidates regularly compete on a fairly even basis—for example, in the states in Table 2.2 (in Chapter 2) that fall into the two-party range.[25] Voting participation increases in elections that have hotly contested races.[26] This holds true regardless of the type of office, the nature of the electorate, and the district's historical voting trends. Closely fought contests generate excitement and give voters more assurance that their vote will make a difference.

Changes in party competition, historically brought about by realignment, have affected turnout levels. National politics was fiercely competitive in the two decades before 1900; control of government turned on razor-thin margins of victory. The realignment of 1896 brought an abrupt end to this close competition: in the South, the Populist movement was absorbed into the Democratic Party, and outside the South, the Democrats' appeal declined. After the realignment participation in presidential elections dropped markedly—from almost 80 percent of the voting-age population in prior elections to about 65 percent in the early 1900s. Some scholars argue that the realignment caused the decline. Even the realignment of the 1930s failed to restore the competition and high voter turnouts of that earlier era.[27]

Alternatively, this drop in turnout may have been due to legal and institutional factors. At around the time of the 1896 realignment, such devices as poll taxes and literacy tests began to increase the "cost" of voting, as did the introduction of the secret ballot and tightened registration requirements.[28] More evidence would be needed to resolve this controversy. But it is likely that the decline in party competition produced by that realignment had at least some role in reducing turnout.

The Representativeness of the Party System

Turnout tends to be much higher in European multiparty systems, where each sizable group in the society is often represented by its own party. The broad, coalitional nature of the two major American parties may make it more difficult for citizens to feel that a party gives voice to their individual interests and needs. One price the United States may pay for its two-party system, then, is lower turnout.[29] The particular types of conflicts that shape the party system—whether social, economic, religious, or racial—can also affect voter involvement. Those citizens who feel that they have a big stake in the prevailing political conflicts are clearly more likely to see a reason to vote.[30]

Organized Efforts to Mobilize Voters

One of the most important findings about voter turnout is that people go to the polls when somebody encourages them to do so. As we saw in Chapter 5, this voter mobilization has long been the goal of the party organizations' grassroots efforts. (Sometimes parties or campaigns may try to *demobilize* voters; see box below) In a nation with low voter turnouts, bringing additional voters to the polls has been a very attractive strategy, not only for the parties but for other groups as well.[31]

American history is filled with examples of group efforts to increase turnout. The civil rights movement helped to achieve dramatic gains in voter registration and election day turnout. More recently, the excitement produced by candidacies such as Jesse Jackson's for president and black contenders for other offices have produced more voter participation.[32] The expanded influence of Christian conservatives in the Republican Party stems from the efforts of Christian conservative groups to develop a base of loyal followers and mobilize them in elections. Not all such efforts have been as effective. Mobilizing groups of people for a common cause is a very difficult task. Some groups, however, have been able to expand their political influence substantially.

TURNOUT: THE PERSONAL EQUATION

If we view the voting decision as a calculated balancing of costs and benefits, it may seem surprising that so many people do make the effort to vote. Individuals pay some costs for the privilege of voting, not in cash but in time, energy, and attention. On the other side of the equation, the benefits of voting may seem elusive; the impact of a single vote is likely to be small.[33] Individuals differ in the ways they estimate these costs and benefits of voting.

Party *Demobilization* in New Jersey

Voters can be mobilized with a variety of strategies, such as a phone call or personal visit from a local leader or friend, the whipping up of enthusiasm at a rally or in church, or a mailed appeal to action. Parties and other organizations sometimes find it in their interest to *demobilize* voters as well, by actively discouraging their desire to participate. For a century, for example, a wide variety of devices were used to demobilize black voters in the South and Hispanics in the Southwest. In recent years, well-advertised efforts to challenge voters' credentials in some states have dampened turnout.

In one example, charges were made of Republican efforts to depress black turnout in the 1993 New Jersey gubernatorial election. The allegations arose when GOP strategist Ed Rollins told reporters that Republicans gave "walking-around money" to black ministers and Democratic precinct workers to persuade them to drop their usual voter-mobilization efforts in black neighborhoods. These comments created a firestorm of controversy, leading to a retraction by Rollins, denials of wrongdoing by Republican leaders, and a subsequent state and federal investigation. The investigation found no evidence to support the allegations.

Socioeconomic Status

People participate in elections when they have the resources to do so. The biggest difference between voters and nonvoters is their socioeconomic status (SES); lower-status Americans are much less likely to vote.[34] This sounds so self-evident that we would expect to see it in other democracies as well. Interestingly, however, the relationship between status and voting is muted in many other democratic nations. In these nations, the disadvantages of low SES seem to be overcome by the efforts of parties and other groups to mobilize lower-SES citizens to vote.[35]

The most careful study of voting attributes the relationship between status and turnout almost solely to education level. The impact of income and occupational differences is minimal once education is taken into account (Table 8.2, panel A). According to this study:

> Education ... does three things. First, it increases cognitive skills, which facilitates learning about politics. Schooling increases one's capacity for understanding and working with complex, abstract, and intangible subjects such as politics. This heightens one's ability to pay attention to politics, to understand politics, and to gather the information necessary for making political choices.... Second, better educated people are likely to get more gratification from political participation. They are more likely to have a strong sense of citizen duty, to feel moral pressure to participate, and to receive expressive benefits from voting. Finally, schooling imparts experience with a variety of bureaucratic relationships: learning requirements, filling out forms, and meeting deadlines. This experience helps one overcome the procedural hurdles required first to register and then to vote.[36]

Youth

After socioeconomic explanations, the next most powerful personal factor in accounting for differences between voters and nonvoters is youth. For a long time, younger Americans have voted at rates well below the average (see Table 8.2, panel B). This is largely due to the high "start-up" costs younger people must pay: the difficulties of settling into a community, registering for the first time, and establishing the habit of voting, all at a time when other, more personal interests dominate their lives.[37] The lowering of the national voting age to eighteen and the entry of the unusually large "baby boom" generation into the electorate increased the impact of young people's low turnout rates on American politics.

Gender and Race

For many decades after their enfranchisement in 1920, women voted less frequently than men. Women's increasing education levels, however, and changes in women's roles in society have eliminated this gender difference (see Table 8.2, panel C). Traditionally, too, blacks have been less likely to vote than whites; this gap still persists, though it is no longer as large (see Table 8.2, panel D). These racial differences in voting are due almost entirely to the differences in education and occupational status, on average, between whites and blacks.[38]

TABLE 8.2 Personal Characteristics and Voter Turnout: 1996

| | Percentage Voting | |
	ANES Survey	US Census Survey
A. Education		
No high school degree	57%	32%
High school graduate	69	49
Attended college	85	66
B. Age		
Under 35	64	39
35 or more	81	62
C. Gender		
Females	75	56
Males	78	53
D. Race		
Blacks	68	51
Whites	78	56
E. Interested in politics		
Very much	95	—
Somewhat	78	—
Not much	53	—
F. Party identification		
Strong Democrat	86	—
Weak Democrat	69	—
Independent closer to Democrats	70	—
Independent closer to neither	55	—
Independent closer to Republicans	76	—
Weak Republican	80	—
Strong Republican	96	—

Note: Table entries are the percentages of each group who reported having voted in the 1996 presidential election. The Census survey does not ask attitudinal questions so it provides no data on partisanship or interest.

Source: The ANES data are from the *1996 American National Election Study*, Center for Political Studies, University of Michigan; data made available by the Inter-University Consortium for Political and Social Research. The US Census data are from the *U.S. Bureau of the Census's Current Population Survey*, P20–504, Voting and Registration in the Election of November 1996 (Washington, DC: U.S. Government Printing Office, 1997).

Social Connectedness

People who have a lot of social ties—those who belong to a variety of organizations and are closely connected with friends and family—are much more likely to participate in elections than others are. Social interaction itself increases the likelihood of involvement in politics. Members of organizations have much higher voting rates than nonmembers; this adds weight to the conclusion that organizations play an important role in mobilizing voters. Voting is also more common among people who are well integrated into the community through home ownership, longtime residence, church attendance, or a job outside the home. Even marriage or the loss of a spouse affects the likelihood that an individual will vote.[39]

Personal Costs of Voting

There are several reasons why the occasion to vote may seem like a threat. For some adults whose political cues are mixed—for example, who have Democratic relatives and a Republican spouse—voting can be stressful. Less-educated citizens may find the length and complexity of the ballot intimidating. Some people refuse to register because the registration rolls are used to choose citizens for jury duty, which they may want to avoid. Or there may be less pressing reasons to avoid voting (see box on p. 162).

Political Attitudes

Certain attitudes toward politics affect individuals' motivation to vote. Those who find politics more interesting (see Table 8.2, panel E) and who have stronger party loyalties (see Table 8.2, panel F) are more involved in elections. In addition, study after study has shown that a cluster of so-called "civic attitudes" predisposes individuals to vote. The most important of these are perceptions that government is responsive to citizens (or what is termed *external political efficacy*) and can be trusted to do what is right (*trust in government*), and a sense of responsibility to take part in elections (*citizen duty*).[40]

THE PUZZLE OF DECLINING VOTER TURNOUT

Since the 1960s, turnout in American elections has declined substantially. Voting in presidential elections has fallen by almost 25 percentage points from its postwar peak in 1960 (73 percent) to the 1996 figure of 49 percent. Turnout in midterm elections suffered a similar free fall, from a postwar high of 57 percent in 1966 to 34 percent in 1998.

Explaining the Decline

Why should this change have occurred in the face of powerful forces that should have propelled turnout upward instead? Southern blacks have voted in increasing numbers since 1960. Southern whites, stimulated in part by the presence of blacks at the polls, increased their turnout levels as well. Earlier generations of women who were unaccustomed to voting have been succeeded by generations comfortable with an active political role. The costs of voting have been greatly reduced as the result of liberalized residence and registration rules and big increases in educational levels. Yet in spite of all of these trends, turnout has declined, at least outside the South.[41]

One main reason is that the political attitudes that support participation—especially the belief that government is responsive to its citizens (external political efficacy)—have declined since 1960. Variations over time in the strength of partisanship have also played a role. These two attitudes contributed separately to the turnout declines from 1960 through 1996, with partisanship accounting for more of the change than efficacy, as can be seen in Table 8.3 (p. 163). Their combined effects were even stronger.[42]

Excuses for Nonvoting

The advertisement below appeared as a full page in the *New York Times* the day before the 1977 local elections (Monday, November 7, 1977). It carried no title or heading, nor did it need one. Barney's is a clothing store in New York City.

THE NEW YORK TIMES, MONDAY, NOVEMBER 7, 1977

I only vote for President.
The polls are too far away.
I don't want to be called for jury duty.
I had to work late.
I was too tired when I got home.
It's raining.
I didn't know I had to register.
I have a headache.
I hate making decisions.
Whenever I vote, they lose.
I forgot.
Tuesday's my bowling night.
I hate waiting on lines.
The voting booth gives me claustrophobia.
I didn't know where to vote.
My company doesn't give me off.
I was out of town.
There's no one to watch the kids.
I broke my glasses.
The polls were closed when I got there.
I hate crowds.
The Knicks were playing.
I'm moving anyway.
My car broke down.
Everyone knows who's gonna win.
I had a doctor's appointment.
When was the election?
I already voted in the primaries.
I had to study for a test.
It was my vacation day.
My vote won't make the difference.

A collection of the classics from Barney's.

Polls will be open tomorrow from 6:00 AM to 9:00 PM

Source: Courtesy of Barney's, New York.

TABLE 8.3 Voting Participation Among Categories of Partisan Strength and External Political Efficacy: 1996

External Political Efficacy	Strong Partisans	Weak Partisans	Independents Closer to Party	Independents	Total
High	92%	61	86	43	86
Medium	93%	80	75	51	80
Low	82%	61	65	46	67
Total	90%	74	73	49	76

Note: Table entries are the percentage of each combined efficacy-partisan group from the ANES survey who were recorded in the official records as having voted in the presidential election.

Source: 1996 American National Election Study, Center for Political Studies, University of Michigan; data made available through the Inter-University Consortium for Political and Social Research.

Other forces have taken their toll on voting turnout as well. Since 1960 the American electorate has become more mobile, less inclined to attend religious services on a regular basis, and less likely to be married. These indicate a drop in social "connectedness"—a weakening of the ties binding Americans to the social networks that stimulate participation. This has also been a time of reduced electoral mobilization. After the 1960s, labor-intensive campaigning and social-movement activism declined. With this slackening of effort to arouse the electorate, voters had less motivation to go to the polls.[43]

Could Voter Participation Revive?

The decline in turnout seemed to have come to a halt in the 1992 and 1994 elections. Although participation was still low by most standards, it reached its highest levels in a decade for midterm contests and in two decades in presidential contests. These two elections proved to be a "blip"; low turnouts returned in 1996 and 1998. Yet the reasons for these brief improvements in voter turnout suggest that the long-term turnout decline could be interrupted again.

The surge in presidential turnout in 1992 is best explained by the compelling political forces operating in that year. It was the closest election since 1976; public opinion polls showed a tight race through the entire fall campaign. Most states were won by only a small plurality. It was also a genuine three-candidate contest packed with dramatic events, in which independent candidate Ross Perot posed a serious challenge to the major-party standard-bearers. As a result, interest in the election was considerably higher than the 1964–1988 average, and that buoyed turnout. Perot succeeded in attracting into the active electorate many disaffected Americans who were looking for an alternative to the two traditional parties.[44]

Similarly, greater voter participation in the 1994 congressional elections can be traced to the political situation in that election. The GOP seemed to have its best prospects in decades to capture the Congress and to gain more governorships and state legislative seats. Media attention focused on the "Contract with America," a statement of conservative principles signed by most Republican congressional candidates in an effort to nationalize the campaign. It was an effective strategy; otherwise, the localism typical of midterm elections would probably have advantaged incumbent Democrats.

The result was an unprecedented mobilization of Republican voters. GOP House candidates drew almost 9 million more votes than four years before, and Democrats lost nearly 1 million votes in comparison with 1990 totals. Such one-sided mobilization is a rare occurrence; it last appeared in the 1934 election during the realignment that created the New Deal party system.

The 1992 and 1994 campaigns were a hard act to follow. In fact, 1996 and 1998 were business as usual: low turnouts, low political interest. The 2000 elections began with such media draws as Donald Trump, Jesse Ventura, and the ever-present Ross Perot considering runs for president, but settled fairly quickly into more predictable patterns. But the lesson of the early 1990s is that when a presidential race is up for grabs, when the candidates are entertaining, and when congressional elections turn on an identifiable set of divisive themes, political interest should increase and carry voting turnout along with it. Without the stimulation of an interesting contest or the active mobilization of partisans, turnout levels are unlikely to recover.

CONSEQUENCES FOR THE POLITICAL PARTIES

The American parties operate within an electorate that is not representative of the full adult population nor of all those eligible to vote. This electorate constantly shifts in size and composition. The parties' strategies, especially in contesting elections, must take account of these facts.

Long-Range Consequences

In the long run, the parties have been profoundly affected by the addition of new groups to the electorate. In recent decades, the American parties have absorbed two major new voting groups: blacks and young adults between the ages of eighteen and twenty-one. Another such change is occurring now, prompted by a flood of Hispanic and Asian immigrants in recent years, the amnesty for illegal aliens in the 1986 immigration reform law, and recent incentives for immigrants to become citizens quickly.

These newly enfranchised groups have reshaped the parties. Blacks have flowed into the Democratic Party—three quarters of blacks identify as Democrats and in each presidential election since 1964 more than 80 percent have voted Democratic. On the other hand, this influx of black support seems to have triggered a counter-movement of whites away from the Democrats, particularly in the South.[45] The enfranchisement of young voters has had more mixed partisan impact. The new young voters were more likely to be Democrats than Republicans in the 1970s. That trend reversed in 1984 and 1988, and then re-reversed in the early 1990s. On balance the youngest voters have tended to be more attuned to the short-term forces of a particular election than to the parties' more fundamental appeals.[46]

Long-term shifts in the distribution of the electorate have also affected the parties. For instance, the parties of eleven states—all of them in the South and West—saw their state populations grow by more than 15 percent between 1990 and 1999 due to population growth and migration. The aging of the population has enlarged the group of elderly voters in each successive presidential election. As these groups expand, their distinctive interests carry greater weight in the electorate. If the parties hope to thrive, they must adapt to these changes.

The size and nature of the nonvoting population is a vital element of the parties' environment. More than 70 million adults are not registered to vote. Because the nonvoters tend to have lower socioeconomic status, they have long been suspected to harbor more Democratic than Republican supporters. That is why proposals to permit voter registration at the polls, to make illegal aliens eligible for citizenship, or to make it easier to register (as did the "motor voter" law) are often assumed to benefit the Democrats. Yet increases in registration seem to be due to group efforts rather than to broad-scale invitations; a good example is the dramatic gains in Republican registration in the Sunbelt in the 1990s, when Democratic registration was hardly increasing at all.[47]

The most basic of all the consequences of voting and nonvoting concerns the distribution of political influence in the American political system. Citizens who fail to register or vote deny themselves a potent voice in American politics. The implications of that loss are all the more serious when the nonvoters differ markedly from the voters. The lesser turnout among low-status Americans probably limits the attention elected officials pay to their needs. To some degree, then, the marginalization of the disadvantaged in American society may be attributable to their failure to participate in the electoral process.[48]

This observation must be tempered by the finding of careful studies that nonvoters, despite their social backgrounds, tend not to have very different views on the issues from those of voters.[49] Yet we do not have a clear answer to the fundamental question of what nonvoters' political views and goals might be if they were mobilized into political involvement.

Short-Range Consequences

In addition to the long-range consequences of changes in the eligible electorate, the political parties must deal with short-range changes in turnout from election to election. Because increases or decreases in turnout are not likely to benefit all parties and candidates equally—because nonvoters as a group have different political characteristics from voters—these changes too have potent political consequences. Adding to or reducing turnout becomes a focus of party strategy. Democratic and Republican efforts to attract Perot voters show how much political strategists appreciate the consequences of mobilization and demobilization.

The conventional wisdom is that big turnouts favor the Democrats. There is reason to believe it. Most nonvoters come from groups ordinarily disposed to the Democratic Party. Thus Democrats are thought to benefit more than Republicans from effective registration or get-out-the-vote campaigns. This explains why organized labor spends so much money and manpower on registration campaigns. It suggests why Republicans tend to prefer that gubernatorial elections be held in non–presidential election years—because the smaller electorate may be more favorable to Republican candidates. It even explains the corollary belief that rainy weather is Republican weather.

The conventional wisdom, however, is not subtle enough. Because people who are more interested and involved in politics are more likely to vote, increases in turnout tend to come from the less-involved segment of the electorate. People who are less politically involved are often more responsive to the momentary appeal of a dramatic issue or a popular candidate, whether Democratic or Republican. In fact, Republican presidential candidates have won most of the large-turnout elections in the last five decades.[50]

Party strategists often nourish the hope—fragile though it may be—that they can affect turnout selectively and thus can bring potentially favorable voters to the polls and discourage unfavorable voters from participating. In primary elections, strategists may hope to minimize the turnout by selective campaigning, because in general, the smaller the turnout, the more of it will come from the party's most loyal electorate. In general elections, strategists may aim their efforts at areas of known party strength to maximize that turnout. It is an interesting challenge for people planning a congressional career that they will face different electorates in alternate elections: the larger turnout of the presidential election followed by the smaller turnout of the midterm election two years later.

THE BROADER ISSUES

This chapter began by citing one of the most striking facts about current American politics: that even in the most high-profile elections, more than half of the potential voters stay home. The case for democracy often rests on the argument that the best decisions are made when the responsibility for decision-making is most widely shared. Full participation in democratic self-governance, then, would seem to be a valuable ideal. Yet American politics falls far short of that ideal—a finding that is all the more bitter when we see that voting turnouts are higher in most other democracies.

If widespread nonvoting is an insult to the democratic spirit, it also raises questions about the effectiveness with which the political parties—the groups most directly concerned with contesting elections—are able to involve the whole electorate. The parties are the organizations that developed to mobilize the new democratic masses. It is their great strength that they can recruit large and diverse groups of people into politics, in contrast to organized interests of other kinds. As the instruments of democratic politics, it would seem that the parties ought to maximize political participation.

Yet their record is clearly mixed. Granted, the parties have at times competed actively for the support of new voters. But the parties do not always seem to relish the challenge of attracting new voting groups, especially those of low status. Long experience with political power has made them (especially the parties in government) sympathetic to the comfortable status quo. The party in government, which helps to make the rules as to who can vote, has won office with the support of the electorate as it now exists; it is understandable that the parties do not welcome the uncertainties that a radical expansion of the electorate would bring.

In short, the active electorate in the United States is not as diverse as the nation's population. The result is to reduce the amount of political conflict and the range of political interests to which the parties must respond. That, in turn, makes it easier for the parties to be moderate and pragmatic. It may well be that the American parties can be moderate and nondoctrinaire because they have an electorate that agrees on the fundamental questions. It is probably also true that these pragmatic parties, in a two-party system, do not jump at the chance to appeal to the lower-status, alienated, dissident individuals who are not a part of that moderate consensus. In a predominantly middle-class society, that may be another price we pay for a two-party system.

Some devotees of democracy may be happy to pay that price. They fear that the sudden influx of new and uninformed voters would dilute the quality of the voting result. They recall that the German Nazi Party in the 1920s and 1930s, which rejected the norms of civility and tolerance for minority opinion on which democracy rests, was supported by less-informed and involved citizens. Democracy, then, may seem to be threatened by the mobilization of large numbers of new voters. Most other Western democracies seem to have avoided these problems even though their electorates are more inclusive. Yet fears remain that a major expansion of the American electorate could threaten political stability. Thus we are left with a troubling challenge. Is it necessary to choose between greater stability and greater participation? Or is there a way to reconcile concerns about political instability with the democratic value of engaging as many of the people as possible?

Part 4
··················
The Political Parties in the Electoral Process

Campaigns and elections are the times when party activity is most visible to the public. The television ads, yard signs, media coverage of interviews with voters, and headlines of candidates' charges and countercharges bring all three sectors of the American parties to public attention. The need to unite around the party nominees and, once the candidates are selected, to coordinate their efforts in the general election campaign are powerful reasons for the three parts of the parties to combine and to reconcile their differences, at least temporarily.

Elections unite the American parties in another important way. However briefly, the focus on elections helps to overcome the parties' decentralization. The choice of a presidential candidate and the subsequent campaign bind the state and local parties into a fleeting coalition with the national party. A statewide election similarly focuses the energies of local party organizations and their leaders within the state. The infusion of soft money into the party organizations now provides funding that can support campaign activity on behalf of the party *ticket* generally.

Other electoral forces also help to unite the party in search of victories. Candidates' chances of winning affect not only their own ability to attract money and other resources but also that of their party organization. Their victory is crucial to party activists' issue agendas as well as to the patronage opportunities that can bring more activists into the party organization. In order to win, candidates and their party organizations must mobilize large numbers of voters; their campaign events are designed to be visible enough to alert even some of the least enthusiastic party identifiers. The party's candidates help to personify and simplify the difficult choices that voters make. American political campaigns have always been more candidate-centered than most, but the party organizations play important roles in mobilizing support across the party ticket, and party identifiers in the electorate are obviously a key target of their efforts.

All this cooperative activity does not come easily, however. Almost every aspect of the electoral process, and especially the nomination process, provokes struggles among the various parts of the party to satisfy their particular needs. The party organizations, thanks to the direct primary, cannot control the selection of their candidates; thus there will inevitably be times when the party in the electorate selects candidates that the party organization is not thrilled to support. When party organizations work to raise money, their efforts will compete with those of the party's candidates. It is the candidates who choose which campaign issues they will emphasize, whether or not these issues are the top priorities of party activists. These candidates will organize their own campaigns, recruit their own workers, hire their own campaign advisers, and raise their own funds; they control the campaigns, then, in the name of the whole party. If it is true that the party in government controls the central, most visible activities of the party (at the expense of a frustrated party organization), can the party organizations reasonably achieve the goals set by their activists?

At the same time that the party competes internally for control over its election strategies, parties also compete on the larger electoral stage with interest groups, PACs, and other political organizations. Groups such as single-issue organizations, labor unions, religious organizations, reform groups, and corporations increasingly take part in campaigns in order to achieve their political goals. Some of these groups play aggressive roles in helping candidates win nomination and election, raising money, and trying to influence public opinion.

The outcomes of this struggle are strongly influenced by a variety of political institutions. One such institution, the direct primary, touches every attempt the parties make to control the nomination of candidates. It is the primary that so often demonstrates the greater strength of candidate organizations and interest groups than that of the party organization. Primaries are the most obvious example of the ways in which political institutions affect the nature of American party politics, but we will see many other examples as well in the coming chapters.

The chapters in this section explore the relationships among the party organization, the party electorate, and the party in government (which will be examined in more detail in Part 5) as they take part in campaigns. Chapters 9 and 10 focus on the first of the two key points at which parties are involved in the electoral process: the nomination of candidates. The first of these chapters looks at the nomination process in general, and the second, at the fascinating and peculiar practices through which the parties select their presidential candidates. The second point of party involvement is the contesting of the general election, which is the topic of Chapter 11.

Chapter 12 discusses the key resource for campaigners: money. Campaign money has come to play an increasingly important and controversial role in American electoral politics. The inexorable quest for dollars to run campaigns gave rise to extensive reform efforts in the 1970s and has prompted more recent debate about the effects of these reforms. In exploring the role of money in elections, we can see the extent to which financial capabilities and constraints influence what parties do in the electoral process and what they are unable to do.

Chapter 9
The Naming of the Party Candidates

*P*rimaries are an American invention. In a primary election (more formally known as a *direct primary*), the party electorate chooses which candidates will run for office under its party label. Then, in a later *general* election, all voters make the final choice between the two parties' nominees for each office. To American voters, neck-deep in primaries during an election season, this may seem the "normal" way for parties to nominate candidates. It is not; in the rest of the democratic world, the party's candidates are selected by party leaders, activists, or elected officials, not by voters.

These different nomination procedures explain a great deal about the differences between American party politics and those of other democracies. The direct primary has forced the American parties to develop a different set of strategies in making nominations, contesting elections, and attempting to hold their successful candidates accountable while serving in office.

No state has been untouched by the irresistible advance of the direct primary in the twentieth century. The great majority of states employ it in all nominations, and the rest use it in most. It dominates the presidential nomination process (see Chapter 10). Even though it is only the first of the two steps in electing public officials, it does the major screening of candidates by reducing the choice to two in most constituencies. Especially in areas of one-party domination, the real choice is made in the primary. In the eyes of many voters, the party's nominees *are* the party; their images, positions on issues, and visibility form the party's public image. Their quality and ability also determine, to a considerable extent, the party's chance for victory in the general election.

HOW THE NOMINATION PROCESS EVOLVED

The direct primary was born with the twentieth century. Prior to that, for the first 110 years of the Republic, the party caucus and then the party convention dominated the nomination of candidates for public office. Each gave way successively under the criticism that it permitted, if not encouraged, the making of nominations by self-chosen and often irresponsible party elites. Finally, early in the twentieth century, the primary triumphed on the belief that the greatest possible number of party members ought to take part in the nomination of the party's candidates. In the 1970s, when most states began to use primaries to select party candidates for president, the triumph of the primary was complete.

Nominations by Caucus

Once they had evolved beyond legislative coalitions, the parties emerged largely as groups to nominate candidates for public office. In the early years of the Republic, local caucuses (or meetings) were held to select candidates for local offices. Frequently, caucuses of like-minded partisans in Congress met to nominate presidential and vice-presidential candidates. Similar caucuses in state legislatures nominated candidates for governor and other statewide offices. Whatever their form, the caucuses were informal; the participants were self-selected. There was no procedure for ensuring even that all the major figures of the party would take part.

Nominations by Convention

The spread of democratic values made these elite caucuses an inviting target. Followers of Andrew Jackson attacked what they called "King Caucus" as an aristocratic device that thwarted popular wishes. In 1832, the Jacksonian Democrats met in a national convention—the first for a major party—and nominated Andrew Jackson for president. The conventions were the primary means of nominating candidates for the rest of the nineteenth century. These nominating conventions were composed of delegates chosen by state and especially local party leaders, often at their own lower-level conventions.

These large and chaotic conventions looked more broadly representative than the caucuses but often were not. The selection of delegates and the management of the conventions were guided by the heavy hands of the party leaders. Party insurgents, unhappy with what they considered "bossism," attacked the convention system with fervor and cunning. The Progressive movement led the drive against conventions, and their journalistic allies, the muckrakers, furnished the often shocking details of democracy denied.[1]

Nominations by Direct Primaries

The cure offered by the Progressives—the direct primary—reflected their core beliefs. The best way to cure the ills of democracy, they felt, was to prescribe larger doses of democracy. Appropriately, it was one of progressivism's high priests, Robert M. La Follette, who wrote the nation's first statewide primary law in Wisconsin in 1902 (see box on p. 173). Some Southern states had adopted primaries at the local level in the years after the Civil War, often to introduce some competition into a prevailing system of one-party politics. In the first two decades of the twentieth century all but four states turned to primaries for at least some of their statewide nominations.

The direct primary took root at a time when one party or the other dominated the politics of many states—the most pervasive one-party rule in American history. In such states the dominant party's nominations are crucially important. It might be possible to tolerate the poor choices made by conventions when voters have a real choice in the general election, but when the nomination of one party was equivalent to election, those shortcomings were harder to accept. The convention could choose the most dismal party hack without fear of challenge from the other party. Thus the Progressives, who fought economic monopoly with antitrust legislation, used the direct primary as their major weapon in battling political monopoly.

La Follette and the Primary

No one has captured the rhetoric and fervor of the movement for the direct primary as well as its leader, Robert M. La Follette, governor and then U.S. senator from Wisconsin. Writing in his autobiography, in the chapter "Struggle with the Bosses," La Follette reports his speech in February 1897 at the University of Chicago. Here are some excerpts from its conclusion:

> Put aside the caucus and convention. They have been and will continue to be prostituted to the service of corrupt organizations. They answer no purpose further than to give respectable form to political robbery. Abolish the caucus and the convention. Go back to the first principles of democracy; go back to the people. Substitute for both the caucus and the convention a primary election ... where the citizen may cast his vote directly to nominate the candidate of the party with which he affiliates.... The nomination of the party will not be the result of "compromise" or impulse, or evil design ... but the candidates of the majority, honestly and fairly nominated.

Source: Robert M. La Follette, *La Follette's Autobiography* (Madison: R. M. La Follette, 1913), pp. 197–198.

Although the primary was designed to democratize the nominating process, many of its supporters saw it as a way to cripple the political party itself. For them, the best way to weaken party and "boss" rule was to strike at the party organization's chief activity—the nomination of candidates. Primaries wrested control from party leaders over the choice of the party's candidates and vested that power instead in a broad party electorate. Taking this principle to its logical extreme, some states such as Wisconsin adopted so permissive a definition of the party electorate that it included any voters who chose to vote in the party's primary on election day.

Regardless of the motives of those who supported the primary laws, there is little doubt that primaries undermined the power of party organizations. Not only did they greatly limit party leaders' influence on nominations, but they also opened up the possibility that public officeholders without any loyalty to the party organization or its principles could penetrate its top leadership. Largely because of the existence of primaries, party leaders have less control over who will receive the party nomination in the United States than in any other democratic political system. When primaries were used to select party organization leaders, the parties risked losing control even over their own internal affairs.

THE PRESENT MIX OF PRIMARY AND CONVENTION

The use of conventions for nominating candidates has faded in the face of the primary's democratic appeal. Decline has not meant death, however; conventions are still used to nominate candidates in a few states and most conspicuously in the contest for the presidency.[2] Because states have the legal authority to devise their own nominating practices, the result is a mosaic of primary and convention methods for choosing candidates for state offices.

All fifty states now use primaries in some fashion to nominate statewide officials, and thirty-eight of them (plus the District of Columbia) use this method exclusively.[3] In Alabama and Virginia, the party may choose to hold a convention instead of a primary, but only in Virginia is the convention option currently used (see box below).

The remaining states use some combination of convention and primary. Iowa requires a convention when no candidate wins at least 35 percent of the primary vote. Three states (Indiana, Michigan, and South Dakota) use primaries for the top statewide offices but choose other nominees through conventions. Five (Colorado, New Mexico, New York, North Dakota, and Utah) hold conventions to screen candidates for the primary ballot. A convention is held in Connecticut, but any candidate who has received at least 15 percent of the convention vote can challenge the endorsed candidate in a primary. If there is no challenge, no primary is held.[4] These differing choices again demonstrate that despite the national parties' growing strength, party power is still decentralized.

The Last State-Convention Nominating System: Virginia and "Ollie" North in 1994

In recent years, Virginia has stood alone among the states in nominating some major statewide candidates by convention. Under Virginia law, parties nominate their candidates by primaries in federal elections if they had used primaries the last time for that office, unless the incumbent chooses a different method.

In 1994, the Virginia GOP used a convention to choose its nominee for the Senate seat held by Democrat Charles Robb. The convention was composed of more than 14,000 Republicans who had paid a $45 fee to serve as delegates. The state's counties each received a share of the votes.

The candidates were James Miller, former budget director in the Reagan Administration, and Oliver North. North had been convicted on three felony counts for his role as a Reagan White House aide in a scandal involving the sale of arms to Iran, with the proceeds used to ship weapons to one side of a civil war in Nicaragua. (North's conviction was later overturned.) Because of his dramatic performance before the congressional committee investigating this scandal, and his passionate defense of core conservative values, North had emerged as a hero to Christian conservatives, who flocked to his cause at the convention. He had become one of the most visible and polarizing figures in American politics.

North won the party's nomination with 55 percent of the vote. In a tight general election contest with the equally controversial Democratic incumbent, North lost narrowly. The devotion of his followers, so critical in winning him the nomination at the convention, was not enough to give him a plurality in the much larger November electorate. Similarly, polls suggested that it would not have won him the GOP nomination if the party had used a primary rather than a convention.

VARIETIES OF THE DIRECT PRIMARY

States also vary in the criteria they use to determine who can vote in their primaries. There are three basic forms. In the states with so-called "closed" primaries, only voters who have publicly declared their affiliation with a party are able to participate. In states with "open" primaries, voters can decide in the privacy of the voting booth which party's primary they will select. A few states with "blanket" primaries allow voters to choose from among all the candidates for office, Democratic and Republican; they do not restrict voters to the nomination contests of a single party.[5]

The Closed Primary

Most states hold closed primaries in which voters must publicly declare their affiliation with a party before they can vote in that party's primary. Typically voters have to specify their party affiliation when they register in advance of the election. Then at the primary election they are given the primary ballot of only their own party. Voters may change their party affiliation on the registration rolls, but most states require that this be done sometime ahead of the date of the primary. Only a few states permit voters to change their party registration at the polls.

In the other closed-primary states, voters simply declare their party preference at the polling place and are given their declared party's ballot. What if they choose to vote in the primary of a party different from their own? In some states, their declaration can be challenged by one of the party observers at the polls; if so, the voter may be required to take an oath of party loyalty. Some states require voters to affirm that they have voted for the candidates of the party in the past; others ask challenged voters to declare themselves sympathetic at the moment to the candidates and principles of the party; and some ask nothing at all. These latter provisions make it possible for independents and even the other party's identifiers to vote in a party's primary.

The Open Primary

Citizens of many states can vote in the primary of their choice without ever disclosing which party ballot they have selected.[6] They receive either a consolidated ballot or ballots for every party and they select the party of their choice in the privacy of the voting booth. They cannot, however, vote in more than one party's primary in a given election.

The Blanket Primary

A blanket primary (used in Alaska, California, Louisiana, and Washington in 2000) gives voters even greater freedom. Not only do they not need to disclose their party affiliation but they can vote in more than one party's primary; that is, they may choose a Democrat for one office and a Republican for another. Louisiana's version of the blanket primary, sometimes called the unitary primary, goes even further. Any candidate who wins a majority of votes in the primary is elected to the office immediately. If no candidate wins an outright majority, then the general election serves as a runoff between the top two vote-getters, regardless of party (see box on p. 176).

David Duke and the Louisiana Blanket Primary

Louisiana's blanket primary system demonstrates a party's dilemma when the primary rules do not let it control its own nominations. The leading Democratic candidate for U.S. Senate in 1990 was the incumbent, Sen. J. Bennett Johnston. On the Republican side, State Senator Ben Bagert had been endorsed by prominent GOP leaders, including President Bush, and had received a lot of party money. Also filing as a Republican was former Ku Klux Klan leader and American Nazi Party member David Duke. Duke had campaigned successfully for a state legislative seat in 1989, to the embarrassment of Republican leaders.

Public opinion polls on the eve of the election showed Johnston in the lead and Duke running second. To win the election outright, Johnston would need a majority of the primary votes. It looked as though Duke might receive enough votes to force Johnston into a runoff. Republican leaders blanched at national media coverage featuring a former American Nazi as the leading Republican candidate. At the last moment, Bagert withdrew and, along with major GOP leaders, reluctantly threw his support to Johnston. The incumbent won the race with 54 percent of the vote. Duke received 44 percent, and more than half of the white vote.

There have been several well-publicized elections like this one, in which a state or local party has been put in the position of choosing to support the *other* party's candidate in the general election. The reason is inherent in the nature of a primary; voters can choose any of the available candidates, and at times they may select a candidate who embarrasses the party. Yet whoever wins the primary is the party's candidate, whether the party leaders like it or not.

Primary Types and the Role of Parties

These varieties of primaries represent different answers to a long-standing debate: Is democracy better served by competition between disciplined parties or by a system in which the parties have relatively little power? Open and blanket primaries reflect the belief that parties and rigid party loyalties are harmful to a democracy. The closed primary, in contrast, suggests that it is valuable to give loyal party followers the right to choose the party's candidates.

Party organizations clearly prefer the closed primary in which voters must register by party before the primary. It pays greater respect to the party's own right to choose its candidates. Prior party registration also gives the parties a bonus—published lists of their partisans. Further, the closed primary reduces the biggest dangers of open and blanket primaries, at least from the perspective of party leaders: crossing over and raiding. Both terms refer to people who vote in the primary of a party they do not generally support. They differ in the voter's intent. Voters *cross over* in order to take part in a more exciting race or vote for a more appealing candidate in the other party. *Raiding* is a conscious effort to weaken the other party by voting for its least attractive candidates.

Studies of primary contests in Wisconsin—cradle of the open primary—and other open primary states show that crossing over is common, especially by independents.

Partisans rarely cross over in gubernatorial primaries, because that would keep them from having a voice in other party contests. But because only one office is at stake in a presidential primary, both independents and partisans often cross over; in the 2000 presidential race, for example, more Democrats and independents voted in some Republican primaries than Republicans did. Not surprisingly, the candidate preferences of crossover voters may differ a great deal from those of regular party voters.[7]

As for organized raiding, there is little evidence to suggest that it is more than a worrisome myth. It is a party's greatest fear, of course, that its opponents will make mischief by voting in its primaries for the least attractive candidates. Careful studies of open primaries have uncovered little basis for these fears. Voters cross over to vote their real preferences rather than to weaken the party in whose primary they are participating.[8]

PRIMARIES: RULES OF THE GAME

The states also vary in the ease with which candidates can get their names on the primary ballot and in the support required to win the nomination.

Candidate Access to the Primary Ballot

In most states, a candidate can get on the primary ballot by filing a petition. State election laws specify how many signatures the petition has to contain, citing either a specific number or a percentage of the vote for the office in the last election. States vary a lot in the difficulty of this step. New York, with its complicated law that favors party insiders, has by far the most stringent requirements for filing (see box on p. 178). In some other states a candidate needs only to appear before the clerk of elections and pay a small fee. A few states even put candidates on the ballot if public opinion polls show them to have party support.

These simple rules have consequences for the parties. The easier it is for candidates to get on the ballot, the more likely it becomes that dissident or even crackpot candidates will enter a race and engage the party organization's candidates in costly primary battles. Sometimes such candidates even win. In states with easy ballot access, citizens can be treated to grudge campaigns in which people file to oppose the sheriff who arrested them, for instance, or who simply enjoy the thought of wreaking havoc in a primary.[9]

Runoff Primaries

What if the leading candidate in a primary gets less than a majority of the votes? In most states' primaries, a plurality is enough. Nine states, however—all from the South and its border states—hold a runoff between the top two candidates if one candidate does not win at least 50 percent. This Southern institution was developed in the long period of one-party Democratic rule of the South; when there were no Republican candidates, winning the Democratic Party's nomination was the same as winning the general election, and intense Democratic factionalism often produced three, four, or five serious candidates for a single office.

Jump How High?
Getting on the Ballot in New York

Five weeks before the New York primary in the 2000 presidential race, a state judge threw Sen. John McCain off the primary ballot in much of the state. McCain was one of the two leading contenders for the Republican nomination. The state's Republican establishment, which supported Texas Governor George W. Bush for the nomination, had initiated the action, reportedly in order to help the New York governor, who hoped to become Bush's running mate.

Under the New York ballot access rules, passed by the state legislature at the request of the state party, candidates have to circulate petitions in each of the state's thirty-one congressional districts under very restrictive rules. This system, described as "tortuous," is the toughest in the nation. It is especially hostile to candidates who do not have the state party's support; those who do can rely on the party's volunteers to conduct the separate petition drives in each district.

A McCain lawyer said in reaction to the state judge's decision: "It demonstrates the absurdity of the election law when a candidate such as John McCain, who is a leading candidate in the race, can't get on the ballot in more than a third of the election districts."

Democrats on the State Board of Elections had tried to keep McCain on the ballot in order to set up a more divisive Republican primary. McCain's campaign made good use of the controversy, citing it to portray himself as an outsider running against a corrupt political system. He was later added to the ballot after a successful appeal to a federal judge, who, to the state party's chagrin, invalidated some requirements for circulating nominating petitions.

Source: New York Times stories by Clifford J. Levy: "McCain Off Ballot in Much of Upstate New York," January 28, 2000, p. A1; "McCain on Ballot Across New York as Pataki Gives In," February 4, 2000, p. A1; "Judge Adds McCain to New York Ballot and Rejects Rules," February 5, 2000, p. A1.

In recent years, the Southern runoff primary has become very controversial. Citing instances in which black candidates who received a plurality in the first primary in the South have lost to whites in the runoff, some have charged that runoffs discriminate against minority groups, in violation of the Constitution and the federal Voting Rights Acts. Others have countered that it is the voters, not the runoff, who produce this result, and that in fact the runoff helps to force Southern parties to build biracial coalitions. The debate is far from being resolved.[10]

THE THREAT OF THE DIRECT PRIMARY

The Progressives designed the direct primary to break the party organization's monopoly control of nominations, and in important respects it did. In doing so, it compromised parties' effectiveness in elections more generally.

The Problem of Unattractive Party Nominees

Party leaders fear that in a primary a candidate could win the party's nomination who, because of his or her background or issue stands, has no chance of gaining much party support in the general election. Every election year seems to bring forth a few nominees, usually for low-level offices, whose only electoral advantage is that they have a famous name. (The number of John Kennedys who hold office in Massachusetts, for example, is remarkable.) Or a candidate can ride strong feelings on a hot-button issue to the nomination, though the voters in the general election may be more temperate. Imagine the discomfort of party leaders, for instance, when the controversial Oliver North won the 1994 GOP nomination for senator in Virginia over a far more electable conservative (see box on p. 174). In another classic case, some Democratic party leaders in southern California even felt the need to disown their own candidate when a former officer of the Ku Klux Klan captured the Democratic nomination for Congress in a multicandidate primary race.

The Problem of Divisiveness

In addition, primaries can create conflict that may open up old party wounds:

> A genuine primary is a fight within the family of the party and, like any family fight, is apt to be more bitter and leave more enduring wounds than battles with the November enemy. In primaries, ambitions spurt from nowhere; unknown men carve their mark; old men are sent relentlessly to their political graves; bosses and leaders may be humiliated or unseated. At ward, county, or state level, all primaries are fought with spurious family folksiness and sharp knives.[11]

The resulting damage can be difficult to mend.

It is easier to measure the effects of primary divisiveness on the party in the short term, at the next general election, than over the long run. First, the activists who campaigned for the losing candidate in the primaries may choose not to work for their party's nominee—though the excitement of the primary may bring in new activists to take their places.[12] Second, the losing candidate's supporters may be so disgruntled that they sit out the general election rather than vote for the candidate who won their party's primary. Because this is a public fight, the wounds the candidates inflict on one another and on their followers often seem slower to heal.[13]

The Problem of Candidate Recruitment

The direct primary has also complicated the party's task in recruiting candidates. Candidate recruitment has never been an easy job. It is a real challenge to find candidates for offices the party has little hope of winning. And in races that are more winnable, the party must struggle to keep its preferred candidates from facing serious competitors in their own party.

Primaries have made these problems worse. Consider the situation of one-party areas. If an ambitious candidate has the opportunity to challenge the party favorite in the dominant party's primary, he or she is less likely to consider running for office under the minority party's label. This makes it harder for the minority party to recruit good candidates, and thus helps to perpetuate one-party politics.[14] Further, because they cannot control access to their own primaries or guarantee the outcome, parties have less to offer to candidates they are trying to recruit.[15]

The biggest problem is that in races a party is not likely to win, it is often unable to find a willing candidate, and the office goes to the other party's nominee by default.[16] Uncontested elections for statewide office have become less frequent in recent years.[17] But they are regular occurrences in races for the state legislature and other less visible offices in many states.[18]

The damage primaries can do to the minority party is an unintended result of this Progressive reform. The Progressives were intent on destroying the party monopoly in nominations, but it was certainly not their aim to make general elections less competitive. A modern-day version of a Progressive reform—the movement to limit the number of terms public officials can serve—could have a similar unintended effect. By preventing one officeholder from staying in office decade after decade, term limits may produce more competition—but probably only in the year when the term limit has been reached, and then only in the majority party's primary in a one-party area. In the other years, competition may be reduced as attractive candidates sit back and wait until the officeholder's term limit has been reached.

Other Problems

As if these problems were not enough of a burden, the direct primary often causes party organizations many other inconveniences as well:

- Primaries greatly escalate the costs of politics. Supporting candidates in a contested primary is almost always more expensive than holding a convention. Spending in the primaries, moreover, leaves less money for the party to commit in the general election.

- Primaries deny the party a powerful means of enforcing party loyalty on its officeholders. If the party cannot control or prevent the reelection of a maverick officeholder, it really has no effective sanction for enforcing loyalty.

- Primaries permit the nomination of candidates hostile to the party organization and leadership, opposed to the party's platforms, or out of step with the public image that party leaders want to project—and sometimes all of the above.

- Primaries create the real possibility that the party's candidates in the general election will be an unbalanced ticket if primary voters select all or most of the candidates from a particular group or region.

THE PARTY ORGANIZATION FIGHTS BACK

Parties recognize the distinct threats that primary elections pose, but they are also aware that a direct attempt to abolish primaries is futile. (Note that the parties were not able to keep primary laws from passing initially, at a time when they were probably stronger than they are now.) Thus, in the tradition of "joining 'em if you can't beat 'em," the parties have developed a range of strategies for dealing with the primary. Some local parties lack the will or the strength to try to affect primary outcomes, but others have succeeded in dominating the primaries completely.

Party Influence on Candidate Entry

The surest way to control a primary is to make sure that the party's preferred candidate has no competition. To do that, the party must act as early as possible. In some party organizations, a powerful party leader or committee has the job of making preprimary decisions for the party. If their sources of information are good, they will know who intends to run and who is merely considering the race. They may arbitrate among prospective candidates or coax an unwilling but attractive candidate into the primary. If they command a strong and winning organization, they may have ways to induce less-preferred candidates to withdraw from consideration. They may be able to offer a patronage position or a chance to run in the future. On the negative side, they may threaten to block a candidate's access to campaign money. Such control of nominations by the party organization is difficult to achieve, though it is the norm in most of the world's other democracies.

Some state parties have replaced this informal process of candidate selection with representative, publicized party conventions. Ten states have formalized them; but in several of those cases, candidates who are not endorsed by the party meeting can still get their names on the primary ballot if they choose or if they file petitions that request it. State law in Utah even directs the parties to nominate two candidates for each office. Other states have attempted by law, however, to keep such preprimary endorsement meetings from occurring.

In some states, party-endorsing bodies act informally and extralegally—that is, without the laws of the state taking notice of them. This form of endorsement has proved less effective, however, because it is not communicated on the ballot. Only the most attentive voters, as a result, are likely to know that the party is supporting a particular candidate, and they are the ones least in need of the guidance provided by an official party endorsement.[19]

Party Support for Preferred Candidates

If the party is unable to prevent a challenge to its preferred candidates, then it must fall back on more conventional approaches. It may urge party activists to help the anointed candidates circulate nominating petitions and leave the other candidates to their own devices. It may make party workers, money, and expertise available to the chosen candidates. It may publish ads announcing the party's endorsees or print handy reference cards that forgetful voters can take right into the polling booth. On the day of the primary, the party organization may help to get the party's voters to the polls. This is more likely to happen in areas where the political culture is favorable to the party; in other areas voter sensitivity to party intervention (or "bossism") may dictate that the candidates appear untouched by party hands.

Party efforts to influence primary elections vary from state to state and within states, and descriptions of local party efforts are hard to come by. It is probably safe to say that the most common nominating activity is the recruiting of candidates. Efforts to dissuade would-be nominees are less common. The situation is complicated by the fact that in most parts of the country, parties are only one of a number of groups seeking out and supporting men and women to run for office. Local business, professional, farm, and labor groups, civic associations, ethnic, racial, and religious organizations, and other interest groups and officeholders may be active in recruiting candidates. Some party organizations, however, are indeed able to control candidate recruitment; generally, these are the parties that also intervene in the primary itself.

CANDIDATES AND VOTERS IN THE PRIMARIES

Two factors help to make primaries more "manageable" for the parties: often only one candidate files for each office in a primary, and the vast majority of voters do not vote in them. One or both of these factors may be of the party's making; the absence of competing candidates, for example, may reflect the skill of the party's preprimary persuading and dissuading. No matter why they occur, however, the result is that nomination politics can be more easily controlled by aggressive party organization.

The Candidates

In every part of the United States, large numbers of primary candidates win nomination without a contest. Probably the most important determinant of the extent of competition in a primary is the party's prospects for victory in the general election; candidates are not inclined to fight for the right to face almost certain defeat. The ease of getting on the ballot seems to make a difference in the number of candidates who run. Primary contests are also less likely when an incumbent is running and where parties have made preprimary endorsements.[20]

The power of incumbency to discourage competition is another of the ironies of the primary. In an election where voters cannot rely on the party label to guide their choices, name recognition and media coverage are important influences. Incumbents, of course, are more likely to have these resources than are challengers. To dislodge an incumbent, a challenger will often need large amounts of campaign money. Few challengers have access to large quantities of campaign contributions. By weakening party control of nominations through the direct primary, then, Progressive reformers may have unintentionally strengthened the hold of incumbents on their positions.

The Voters

If competition is scarce in the primaries, so are voters. There is one primary conclusion about the participation of the American electorate in primaries: Most do not vote. Even a study of gubernatorial primaries (in 1960–1986) that identified a relatively high incidence of contested races found modest turnout levels. In all of the contested races in that period, only 30 percent of voting-age adults voted.[21] Turnout in races for less important offices is even lower.

How can we explain such low turnout? One reason is that there is no competition in so many primary races. Turnout is found to be lower in the minority party's primary, in primaries held separately from the state's presidential primary, and in elections where independents and the other party's identifiers are not allowed to vote.[22] And it certainly doesn't help that no one is elected in a primary; a race for the nomination lacks the drama inherent in a general election that is followed by victorious candidates taking office.

Because it is such a small sample of the eligible voters, the primary electorate possesses some distinctive characteristics. A substantial part of it is composed of party loyalists and activists, which makes it more likely to respond to party endorsements and appeals on behalf of certain candidates. Primary voters, as would be expected, have higher levels of education and political interest. They are often assumed to hold more extreme ideological positions than those of other party voters. While early studies of Wisconsin's open primary found little support for that assumption, more recent research (coming largely from presidential primaries, which will be considered later) suggests that it is accurate.[23] Even if the ideological positions of primary voters turn out not to be distinctive, the intensity of their ideological commitment may be.

In addition, primary voters often make unexpected choices. Because all the candidates come from the same party, partisan loyalties cannot guide decisions. The primary campaign is brief, the candidates are often not well known, and the issues, if any, may be unclear. The presence of an incumbent in the race may be the only continuing, stabilizing element. Thus the voter's choice in a primary is not as well structured or predictable as that in a general election. Many voting decisions are made right in the polling booth, where a famous name or a candidate's location on the ballot can make a difference. It is small wonder that parties are rarely confident of primary results, and public opinion pollsters prefer not to forecast them.

Southern primaries in earlier years were the one great exception to the rule that turnouts are low in primaries. From the end of Reconstruction to the years right after World War II, the South was securely and overwhelmingly a one-party Democratic area. Winning the Democratic nomination was tantamount to winning the office itself. Therefore, candidate competition centered in the Democratic primary, and turnout in primary elections was relatively high—often even higher than in the general elections.

As the Republican Party has become stronger and more competitive in the South, however, the Democratic primaries have lost their special standing. The general election has become more significant. The result is that participation has declined in primaries, even at a time when the mobilization of blacks into Democratic Party politics should have increased competition within the party. Republican primaries are attracting more voters now, because their candidates' prospects in the general election have greatly improved. But the GOP increase has not been large enough to compensate for the drop in Democratic turnout. The result is that turnout in Southern primaries has become less and less distinctive.[24]

THE DIRECT PRIMARY IN RETROSPECT

Americans have had nearly a century of experience with the direct primary. On balance, how has it affected us? Has the primary democratized nominations by taking them out of the hands of party oligarchs and giving them to voters? Has it weakened the party organizations overall? In short, have the Progressives' intentions been realized?

The Impact on Democratization

The hope that primaries would result in more democratic elections has been dashed by the low levels of candidate competition and voter participation. If voters are to have meaningful alternatives, then there must be more than one candidate for an office. And if the results are to be meaningful, people must go to the polls. By its very nature, however, the primary tends to reduce participation. Would-be candidates are discouraged by the cost of an additional race, the difficulty of getting on the primary ballot, and the need to differentiate themselves from other candidates of the same party. The large number of primaries and the frequent lack of party cues reduce the quantity and quality of voter participation. If widespread competition for office and extensive mass participation in the nominating process were goals of the primary's architects, then their hopes have not been realized.

Nor has the direct primary fully replaced party leaders in making nominations. There are still vestiges of the caucus-convention system, most visibly in presidential nomination politics, though they are more open than they used to be. Moreover, parties can influence the competition in primaries. They may control the money, symbols, and organization essential for primary victory. Their loyalists may be a significant share of the primary's voters. If only 30 or 40 percent of registered voters go to the polls, 15 or 20 percent will be enough to nominate a candidate. Parties count on the fact that a large part of that group is likely to be loyalists who respond to the party leaders' cues or endorsements. Thus strong party organizations—those able to mobilize voters, money, and manpower—can still make a big difference in primary outcomes.

Yet trying to influence primary outcomes is extremely costly and time-consuming, even for strong parties. The Jacksonian tradition of electing every public official down to the local coroner has confronted the parties with numerous contests. The time and expense of supporting a number of candidates forces many organizations to be selective in their primary interventions. Parties sometimes stand aside because playing a role in a primary would threaten their internal harmony. They may be paralyzed by the fear that their activity in the primary will open new wounds or heat up old resentments, or run the risk of offending the possible winner.

The primary, in short, has left its mark. In competitive districts, especially when an incumbent has stepped down, voters often do play the kind of role the reformers envisioned. In all districts, the primaries set tangible limits. It is no longer easy, even for a viable party organization, to whisk just any "warm body" through the nomination process. The direct primary gives party dissidents a chance to take their case to the party's voters, and thus creates a potential veto over the party's nomination preferences.

The Impact on the Parties

V. O. Key argued that the primary encourages one-party politics by drawing the voters and the attractive, prestigious candidates to the primary of the dominant party. Little by little, the majority party becomes the only viable instrument of political influence, and the minority party atrophies.[25] However persuasive this argument may once have been, however, it is of questionable validity today. There has been a decline in one-party politics in recent years, so it does not seem likely that primaries push us in the direction of one-partyism. Even in areas that remain dominated by one party, the internal competition that the primary promotes can keep officeholders responsive to their constituents.[26]

It is more likely that the direct primary has had a more general effect, weakening dominant as well as minority parties. Even though some state party organizations have kept some control over their primaries by making preprimary endorsements or holding conventions to nominate some candidates, the bottom line is this: when the party organization cannot choose who will carry the party label into the general election, the party has been deprived of one of its key resources.[27]

The primary has also changed the distribution of power within the party. It clearly enhances the power of the party's candidates and the party in government at the expense of the party organization. Because candidates (especially incumbents) can defy the party organization and still win its nomination, the idea of party "discipline" loses its credibility. This sets the United States apart from many other democracies, in which the party organization has a lot of power over the party in government. Just as the direct primary undercuts the ability of the party organization to recruit candidates who share its goals and accept its discipline, it prevents the organization from disciplining partisans who already are in office.

The goal of the Progressives was to shift the power of nomination from the party organization to citizen control by the party in the electorate. Instead, they made possible a shift of power from the leaders of the party organization to the leaders of the party in government. The effect of the primary, then, was to multiply the party oligarchies rather than to democratize them.

Another irony in this long line of unintended effects of the direct primary is the expanded power of the media. Television image-building has come to substitute for the kind of labor-intensive door-to-door campaigning that strong party organizations traditionally supplied. That is especially true of primary campaigns, where party labels do not guide voter choice. Campaigning has come to cost a great deal more as a result (see Chapter 12). It would be sad news for Progressive reformers if, in their quest to free the electoral process of control by party bosses, the result was to vest that control in the hands of an even more unresponsive group of bosses—media consultants and the special interests who finance political campaigns.[28] Surely the last thing these reformers wanted was to promote primary elections in which the candidates were incumbents and challengers backed by wealthy special interests.

A Force for Decentralization

Finally, the direct primary has reinforced the decentralization of power in the American parties. As long as the candidates or incumbents can appeal to a majority of local primary voters, they are free from the control of a state or national party or its leaders. If the advocates of the direct primary wanted to aim beyond the nomination process and strike the parties themselves, they found their target. In many important ways, it has made the American political parties what they are today.

Is the Primary Worth the Cost?

How party candidates should be nominated has been a controversial matter since political parties first appeared in the United States in the early 1800s. It raises the fundamental question of what a political party is. Are parties only alliances of officeholders—the party in government? That seemed to be the prevailing definition in those early years, when public officials selected their prospective colleagues in party caucuses. Should the definition be expanded to incorporate the party's activists and leaders? The change from a caucus to a convention system of nominations, where the party organization played its greatest role, reflects such a change in the definition of party.

Alternatively, should the term "party" be extended, well beyond the limits accepted by most other democracies, to include the party's supporters in the electorate? If so, which supporters should be included: only those willing to register formally as party loyalists or anyone who decides to vote for a party candidate in a primary election? Even though political scientists continue to debate this question, the American answer to it has evolved over the years toward the most inclusive definition of party. In fact, in states with an open or blanket primary—and in practice, in closed primary states where there is no formal party registration—the "party" has become so permeable that its boundaries are hard to locate (see box below).

The choice of a nomination system is one more arena for the continuing debate over the distribution of power within the parties and, more generally, within American politics. The Progressives and their current counterparts were not just expressing a theory of candidate selection. They used party reform as a weapon with which to wrest control of the party and ultimately of government from party organization regulars, just as the Jacksonians used the convention system to overturn control by the congressional party leaders. Because the nomination process helps to define voters' choices, those who control this process have great influence over the political agenda and, in turn, over who gets what in the political system. The stakes in this debate, as a result, are extremely high.

Who Decides Who Votes?

California voters approved an initiative in 1996 that would let them vote for candidates of more than one party in the primary election. Called a "blanket primary," this plan let voters who were not affiliated with a party help choose that party's candidates. Proponents said it would boost voter participation in the primary — and it did — and encourage the choice of more moderate candidates. Party leaders saw it differently; the state's Democratic and Republican parties and two minor parties sued to overturn the law. They claimed that by opening up the primary, the plan kept the party's loyal supporters from choosing candidates who best represented their views. That, they said, violated the First Amendment's guarantee of freedom of association. The state's lawyers countered that a primary "belongs to the voters," not to the parties. A U.S. Circuit Court of Appeals agreed. But in June, 2000, the U.S. Supreme Court (in the case of *California Democratic Party v. Jones*) sided with the parties. The result was to give the right to decide who votes in a primary, at least in California, back to the party organization.

Chapter 10

Choosing the Presidential Nominees

*T*he most dramatic use of primaries in American politics is to nominate candidates for president. When delegates arrive at the parties' national conventions every four years—at which presidential candidates are nominated—the delegates' candidate choices have already been prescribed by the voters in their states' nominating events. The great majority of states use primary elections for this purpose; a few others hold participatory caucuses instead.

The states have taken a long route to the present heavy reliance on primaries in presidential nominations. After Wisconsin adopted the first presidential primary in 1905, other states rushed to follow suit. Within little more than a decade, a majority of states had begun to use this Progressive tool for reforming the nominating system.

The early enthusiasm for primaries soon waned. Advocates may have lost faith in the effectiveness of primaries; opponents probably worked hard to get rid of them and restore party leaders' control over nominations. Whatever the cause, only fourteen states were still using primaries in 1936 to select delegates to the parties' national conventions. That number had hardly changed by by 1968.[1]

In that year, however, in the furor over the Democratic Party's presidential nomination, the primary movement was given new life. Reform rules led states to adopt presidential primaries. By the 1980s, a decisive majority of convention delegates were selected in primary elections. Even in states that retained the caucus-convention system, the rules were changed to increase participation greatly. Yet even in this reformed system, the parties retain influence, and the conventions, though their presidential choices may be predetermined, still have some important functions.

The presidential nominating system differs, then, from the process by which candidates for almost every other major office are selected in American politics. It is a process that commands more media coverage than almost any other political event and tells us a lot about recent changes in American political life.

FIRST STEPS TOWARD THE NOMINATIONS

American voters may sometimes suspect that the next presidential campaign begins the morning after the last one ended. Each campaign's purpose is the same as it has been for a century and a half: to win the support of most delegates to the party's nominating convention. (The process is shown in the box below) But little else about the campaigns has remained the same.

The Post-1968 Reforms

For years the state parties had the power to decide how they would choose their delegates to the national conventions that select the parties' presidential candidates. Party leaders dominated the process and often even selected the state's delegates. In most states, the selection was done through a series of party-controlled caucuses, or meetings, beginning at the local level and culminating in statewide party conventions. Even in many states that held primaries, voters were invited only into a "beauty contest" among the presidential candidates; the delegates who went to the national convention to choose a presidential candidate were selected elsewhere. That state party power was restricted beginning in 1968. The reasons and the results are part of a fascinating and dramatic story in which the national Democratic Party took control of the delegate selection process away from the state parties.

The 1968 Democratic convention was a riotous event. Insurgent forces within the party protested that the nomination of Hubert Humphrey betrayed the wishes of Democratic voters in the primaries. To try to make peace with their critics, the national party leaders agreed to change the methods by which convention delegates were selected. A commission chaired by Senator George McGovern of South Dakota and Representative Donald Fraser of Minnesota recommended, and the Democratic National Committee and the 1972 Democratic convention later approved, major changes for the 1972 nominating process. One of the striking elements of this story is the remarkable ease with which Democratic Party leaders accepted rule changes that greatly reduced their influence on the awarding of the party's greatest prize, the presidential nomination.[2]

Nominating Candidates for President

Step 1: Voters cast a ballot in their states for the candidate they want their party to nominate for president. Most states hold primary elections for this purpose; a few use participatory caucuses and state conventions.

Timing: between late January and early summer of each presidential election year.

Step 2: Delegates representing the chosen candidate(s) are sent by each state's party voters to that party's national convention.

Timing: By tradition, the party that does not currently hold the presidency has its convention in July; the other party's is held in August.

Step 3: The two major parties' conventions ratify the choice of presidential candidate made in the nominating season (Step 1), and that candidate's choice of a vice-presidential nominee, and adopt a party platform.

Step 4: The two candidates chosen in this process run against one another in the general election.

Timing: the first Tuesday after the first Monday in November.

In attempting to comply with the complicated new rules imposed by the national Democratic Party, many states substituted primary elections for their traditional caucus-convention systems, The few caucuses that remained were hemmed in by strict party rules requiring delegates to be selected in timely, open, and well-publicized meetings. Techniques formerly used by state party organizations to control the caucuses were outlawed. In the process, not only were the delegate selection rules radically changed, but also the principle was established that the national parties, rather than the states or the state parties, determine the rules of presidential nomination.[3]

Once the reform genie was let out of the bottle, it proved difficult to contain. The Democrats have tinkered with their presidential nomination process in advance of almost every election since 1972. First they used national party leverage to make the process more open and more representative of women, blacks, and young people. (The quotas that were first used to accomplish that goal produced bitter debate, however, and were eliminated.) More recently, the Democrats have "fine-tuned" the rules so that voter support for candidates is more faithfully represented in delegate counts and so that uncommitted elected and party officials can be guaranteed a place at the convention. Ever since 1992, candidates in primaries or caucuses who win at least 15 percent of the vote are guaranteed a share of the state's delegates proportional to their vote total.

The result has been a stunning transformation in the process by which the Democrats select their presidential nominees. Many state legislatures responded to the new Democratic requirements by changing state election laws for both parties. When states decided to run a primary for one party, for example, they typically did it for both. Thus the Republicans became the unwilling beneficiaries of the Democratic reforms.

Republicans have maintained their tradition of giving state parties wide latitude in developing their own rules, however, which has kept the national party out of issues of rules reform. As a result, many Republican state parties have retained statewide winner-take-all primaries. Republicans have not followed the Democrats' lead in formally setting aside seats for party and public officials or developing affirmative action programs for women or minorities.

The Presidential Primaries

Presidential primaries are now used in more than four fifths of the states, including most of the largest.[4] The proportion of delegates selected in primaries has reached a high plateau in the Republican Party and continues to climb for the Democrats (see Table 10.1). Because the decision to use primaries or caucuses is made by states and state parties, though, these numbers fluctuate from one presidential election to the next.

In the primaries, the popular vote determines how the state's delegates are apportioned among the presidential candidates. In earlier years, primary voters in some states were permitted to select only the convention delegates themselves, without any assurance as to which presidential candidates these delegates supported. Now, however, the names of the presidential candidates normally appear on the ballots, and the candidates or their agents in the states usually select the members of their own delegate slates. This all but guarantees that the popular vote for candidates will be faithfully translated into delegates committed to the respective candidates at the national

TABLE 10.1 The Use of Presidential Primaries: 1968–2000

	Democrats		Republicans	
Year	No. of states	Percent of delegate votes	No. of states	Percent of delegate votes
1968	17	37.5	16	34.3
1972	23	60.5	22	52.7
1976	29	72.6	28	67.9
1980	35	71.8	34	76.0
1984	25	62.1	30	71.0
1988	34	66.6	35	76.9
1992	36	69.6	39	79.1
1996	36	62.8	43	88.3
2000	38	77.8	44	89.3

Note: Includes all convention constituencies (fifty states plus D.C., American Samoa, Guam, Puerto Rico, Virgin Islands, and Democrats abroad). Excludes states with nonbinding preference ("beauty contest") primaries in which delegates were chosen by caucus/convention methods. Delegate percentages exclude Democratic superdelegates.

Source: William Crotty and John S. Jackson III, *Presidential Primaries and Nominations* (Washington, DC: CQ Press, 1985), p. 63, for 1968–1984; and *Congressional Quarterly Weekly Report* convention issues for 1988 and 1992. Data for 1996 are based on calculations from figures reported in *Congressional Quarterly Weekly Report*, August 19, 1995, p. 2485, and January 13, 1996, pp. 98–99. Data for 2000 come from the Democratic and Republican National Committees: http://www.dems2000.com/files/2000AllocationTable.pdf and http://www.rnc.org/election2000/dates2000.htm.

convention, even though there are no laws requiring delegates to support the popular vote winner in their state.[5]

Most primary states use some form of closed primary. In fact, Democratic Party reform commissions have tried several times to ban open primaries, which allow non-Democrats to have a voice in the selection of party candidates. The open primary has survived these assaults, however. After a notable struggle, the national party allowed Wisconsin to return to its cherished open primary in 1988, and the other states that hold open primaries need no longer fear a veto by the national party.[6]

In fact, in the 2000 nominating season, even the closed primaries did not look very closed. In the rush to move their presidential primaries to the early weeks of the nominating season, as we will see later, several states separated their presidential primary from the remainder of their primary elections. This also helped state parties protect their favorites for lower-level offices from the crossover voters attracted by presidential contests. In the most notable case, California held two simultaneous presidential primaries in 2000: a unified ballot for president, in which any voter could select a candidate of any party, and a separate balloting, in which only self-identified Republicans' votes would be counted, to elect presidential convention delegates and candidates for other offices.

The Party Caucuses

States that have not adopted presidential primaries use a longer process that begins with local caucuses. Unlike primaries, these meetings involve face-to-face interaction among participants, often take several hours to complete, and usually conduct their voting in the open. People gather in local schools and other public buildings to choose delegates to conventions held at higher levels. In Iowa, for example, the much-publicized caucuses are only the first of four steps used to choose delegates to the state convention, where the final delegate slate for the national convention is determined.[7] Most other caucus states also use a multilayered process like Iowa's.

For years, the selection of delegates in the caucus states took place outside the glare of media coverage. The events of 1976, however, changed all that. A virtually unknown Democratic governor, Jimmy Carter, made himself a serious presidential candidate by conducting a strenuous campaign in Iowa that brought him both media attention and about 30 percent of the state's Democratic delegates.

As a result, the caucus states will probably never be invisible again, and party officials in them will find it harder to control their outcomes or keep their delegations uncommitted. A classic case occurred in 1986, when Michigan GOP leaders scheduled their precinct caucuses two years before the 1988 state convention in order to boost the influence of their brand of moderate Republicanism in national nomination politics. Their efforts backfired when supporters of Pat Robertson, a leader of the Christian Right, flooded the local caucuses and threw the state's nomination process into turmoil for the next two years. In the 2000 Iowa precinct caucuses, supporters of the candidates favored by the state party organizations—Democrat Al Gore and Republican George W. Bush—had to fight hard to defeat the backers of competitors such as Democrat Bill Bradley and Republican Steve Forbes (see box on p. 192).

THE POLITICS OF DELEGATE SELECTION

To a presidential candidate, the marathon of primaries and caucuses is do-or-die; there has been no time in recent history when a candidate who did poorly in the nominating season has been resurrected by his party's national convention. Every presidential nomination in both parties since 1956 has been won on the first ballot of the convention, and since 1968 that first-ballot nominee has always been the winner of the most delegates in the primaries and caucuses. Just as they are crucial, however, the events of the nominating season are unpredictable; front-runners slip, and surprises occur regularly.

Candidate Strategies

It takes years to prepare for a presidential race. Almost all serious candidates enter the contest at least a year before the presidential election and begin raising money much earlier than that. They must make endless strategic choices as to which states to contest and how much effort and money to put into each one. Even when these hard choices are made, they will probably need to be reconsidered many times; "conventional wisdom" in a presidential race can change from week to week.

The most important factor to be weighed in making these strategic choices is the nature of the opposition. Front-runners, for example, normally need to demonstrate overwhelming support in the early delegate selection events. Otherwise, their supporters' and contributors' confidence may be so badly undermined as to derail their hopes for the nomination. George W. Bush entered the nomination season in

Athens in Missouri Valley:
The 2000 Iowa Caucuses

"He bit his lip as he rose, his hands fumbling on the table and the butterflies careering around his stomach, but then Kris Cunard looked around at his neighbors' faces and just let the words tumble out.

'Steve Forbes is unapologetic in his pro-life positions,' said Mr. Cunard, an insurance salesman. 'I have to vote my conscience, and to me that's the most important thing.

'It's a matter of life and death,' Mr. Cunard added firmly, and then he slumped back in his seat and allowed himself a relieved smile for having done his part.

The Republican caucus here in Missouri Valley, a town of 2,800 people in the far west of Iowa, 130 miles west of Des Moines, was one of the 2,100 caucuses held all around Iowa tonight. It can be criticized for all the reasons people denigrate the Iowa caucuses: scarcely anybody turned up, those who did did not represent the electorate, and the votes are little more than a meaningless straw poll.

Yet for Mr. Cunard and 105 other people who turned out for two hours on a freezing night at the Missouri Valley High School … it was a deadly serious venture, one in which they invested passion, indignation, and occasional bits of information as they dreamed aloud of a country without sin, abortion, or the Internal Revenue Service.

It would be a stretch to offer Iowa as an American answer to Athenian democracy, and Pericles certainly did not show up tonight in Missouri Valley. It would be pretty easy to mock the citizens of Missouri Valley, which has ten churches, six police officers and three stoplights, for engaging in debates that were at times dizzying in their impracticality, and some speakers were clearly more impassioned than informed.

But others had an impressive understanding of their candidates' tax policies and other positions, and the meetings at Missouri Valley High were far more civil than most political discussion shows on television. The participants invested far more effort into the Iowa caucuses than voters in other states do to their contests, and the lengthy discussions of candidates and issues reflected just the kind of citizen participation that Americans often bemoan as lacking today."

Source: Nicholas D. Kristof, "Shy Neighbors Debate and Look for Meaning on a Night of Voting," *New York Times,* January 26, 2000, p. A16, reprinted by permission.

January 2000 with more campaign money than any other candidate had raised in American political history and the widespread expectation that he would coast to the Republican nomination. After he lost the very first primary, in New Hampshire, to Arizona Senator John McCain, his advisers were forced to rethink his approach to the race. In turn, McCain's success after New Hampshire shows how a candidate with less initial support can improve his or her chances for the nomination simply by exceeding expectations in an early and heavily reported contest.

Money and organization also are critical to a candidate's chances. A very few presidential candidates—Bush is the most notable example—have been able to raise enough money to resist the lure of federal matching funds for their campaigns (see Chapter 12). The others must follow the rules that can give them access to those matching funds. First, they must build nationwide campaign organizations in order to qualify for the federal money, and then they must decide how to allocate their personnel and funds. Public funding will not cover (or permit) full-blown campaigns in every state. The early primaries and caucuses necessarily attract the greatest candidate spending, but candidates must then set priorities; legal restrictions on the federal funds prevent candidates from raising money quickly from a few sources,

All these decisions must take into account the rules of the process as set down by the parties and the states. A candidate who expects to do especially well among independents will need to concentrate resources in states with open primaries, in which independents and other partisans can vote, as John McCain did in 2000 (see box below). These rules of the game, complicated as they are, differ from party to party. Because Democrats require a "fair reflection" of candidate strength in the selection of delegates, a candidate with significant support will not be shut out in any state. Because the Republican Party permits winner-take-all primaries, however, and many state Republican parties hold them, it is still possible for a Republican candidate to win 49 percent of the votes and come away without a single delegate.[8]

The Critical Importance of Timing

The strongest imperative is the need to win early. Victories in the early primaries and caucuses bring coverage in the media and name recognition in the public. They create credibility for the campaign and make it easier to raise money. Victors in the early events become increasingly hard to overtake. In short, early wins create momentum; they bring the support and resources that increase the likelihood of later victories.

A Tale of Two Primaries

In politics, as in everything else, the rules affect the results. Consider the rules that governed primary elections in the race for the 2000 Republican presidential nomination. Michigan's Republican contest is an *open primary*, in which voters do not have to declare a party affiliation to take a Republican ballot. In fact, in an exit poll conducted by Voter News Service, only 47 percent of the voters in the Republican primary were Republicans! Texas Governor George W. Bush got the votes of Republicans by a margin of more than two to one, but Arizona Senator John McCain received enough independent and Democratic votes to win the primary.

New York held a *closed primary* two weeks later. Here, 72 percent of the Republican primary voters were Republicans, according to the exit poll, and almost all of the others called themselves independents. Eighty-four percent of the Bush voters said they were Republicans; 34 percent of the McCain voters were independents. Bush won the primary and clinched the nomination that day.

Source: R. W. Apple, Jr., "On a Rocky Road, the Race Tightens," *New York Times,* February 23, 2000, p. A1 (on Michigan) and *http://www.nytimes.com/library/pol* (on New York).

The attention attracted to the early delegate selection events has not been lost on the states themselves. Several states in recent years have moved their primaries forward to the early weeks of the campaign in order to benefit from this attention, not to mention the campaign spending that comes with it. There was such a stampede among states to occupy an early position in the 2000 electoral calendar that party contests were more front-loaded than ever before. Between late January and March 14, thirty-four states held their primaries or caucuses in at least one party, including California, Florida, New York, and Texas; and 75 percent of the delegates had been selected by the end of March (see box below).

Party Interests versus Candidates' Interests

The party organizations have interests at stake in the selection of delegates too, and their interests can clash with those of the aspiring presidential nominees. State and local parties want a presidential candidate who will be best able to bring voters to the

---

Front-Loading the Nomination Process

Before Californians were able to express their preferences in the 1996 presidential primaries, the race for the parties' nominations was effectively over. Why were the voters in the nation's biggest state not consulted? Because their primary was held in late March, and by the end of March primaries had already been held in states containing almost two thirds of the parties' national convention delegates.

Even by the early 1990s, state parties had learned that their influence over the presidential nominations would be diluted if they held their primaries or caucuses too late in the process. By 1996, then, many of the largest states had moved up their primary and caucus dates markedly. California, in fact, had moved up its traditional June primary to March 26. The "front-loading" of the nomination process was well under way.

Front-loading was even more prominent in 2000. By the end of March 7— a day on which an avalanche of sixteen states held primaries or caucuses—almost 40 percent of the Democratic convention delegates and 45 percent of the Republicans had been selected. (One of those March 7 primaries was California's, which had determined not to be left behind again.) The Democratic and Republican nominees had been effectively decided—Al Gore and George W. Bush, respectively—and it was a full eight months to the general election.

This front-loading of the calendar has had important implications for the nomination process. It increased the importance of early money. That meant candidates had to start raising serious money even earlier than in past years. Bush, for example, had raised $68 million before the first caucuses were held and spent all but about $20 million of it by the end of February, 2000. With a majority of the delegates selected in only about seven weeks, there was no time for a long-shot candidate to get enough bounce from an early primary or caucus to raise the money needed to compete in California or New York. Further, in such a short time the cost of a strategic miscalculation, such as John McCain's attacks on Christian conservative leaders, could be exceedingly high.

polls to support party candidates for state and local offices; a weak presidential candidate may hurt their chances. Party leaders also generally prefer early agreement on a presidential candidate; a hotly contested race often heightens conflict within local and state parties, which can weaken the party effort in the general election.[9]

Historically, the state parties protected their interests by selecting delegates uncommitted to any candidate and mobilizing those delegates as a bloc in convention decisions. The bargaining power of such a delegation enhanced the state party's influence at the convention. The parties' ability to engineer the selection of an uncommitted delegation has been stymied by the new system. In most primary states, it is the candidates who set up their delegate slates, whose primary loyalty in turn is to the candidate. In the caucuses, delegates committed to a candidate simply have a greater appeal to the voters and party activists. Moreover, for delegates to remain uncommitted while one of the contenders for the nomination is locking up a majority of the convention votes is to lose all influence over the outcome. In a process dominated by the candidates, refusing to take sides carries major risk.

Party leaders, then, have a more difficult time protecting the party's interests in a nominating process that increasingly reflects popular sentiments. For the Republicans, this has been one of the considerations in allowing state parties to maintain winner-take-all elections and other practices of the prereform era. The Democrats responded to this need in 1984 by setting aside delegate slots at the national convention for elected and party officials. These "superdelegates"—all Democratic members of Congress and governors, current and former presidents and vice presidents, and all members and former chairs of the Democratic National Committee—were intended to be a large, uncommitted bloc totaling nearly 20 percent of all delegates. The early closure of the nomination race in recent years, however, has denied them an independent role in the nomination process.[10]

CITIZEN PARTICIPATION AND CHOICE IN PRESIDENTIAL NOMINATIONS

The move to primaries has greatly increased citizen participation in the process of nominating a president. What determines the level of voter participation, and what guides the voters' choices in these contests?

Differences in Turnout

Turnout varies a great deal from state to state and across different years in any one state.[11] The first caucuses (Iowa) and the first primary (New Hampshire) usually have relatively high participation rates because of the interest those early contests attract. More generally, turnout tends to be higher in states with a better-educated citizenry, higher percentages of registered voters, and a tradition of two-party competition—the same states that enjoy higher general election turnout. The nature of the contest matters too. Voters are most likely to participate in early races that are closely fought, where the candidates spend more money and the excitement is high.[12] In general, participation varies with the expected closeness of the contest and the level of voter interest in the race.[13]

Representativeness of Voters

Yet turnout is lower in primary than in general elections. Are primary voters, then, atypical of other citizens? It is true that primary voters are better educated, better off, and older than nonvoters, but so are general election voters. Compared with party identifiers—an appropriate comparison, because primaries are the means by which the party electorate chooses its nominees—there are few important differences. Primary voters are slightly older, better educated, more affluent, better integrated into their communities, and less likely to be black or Hispanic. Their positions on key policy issues, however, are similar to those of other party identifiers.[14] On empirical grounds, then, it is hard to sustain the argument made by some critics of the party reforms that primary voters are less representative of the party than are other groups of voters.

Bases of Voter Choice

Another criticism of the primaries is that voters do not make very well-informed choices. Primary voters have been found to pay less attention to the campaign and to have less knowledge about the candidates than do voters in the general election. Especially in the early contests, voters are influenced by candidate momentum, as bandwagons form for candidates who have won by a large margin or even just exceeded reporters' expectations. Candidates' personal characteristics make a difference, while ideology and issues often play only minor roles in primary voters' choices. The result, so this argument goes, is a series of contests decided mainly on the basis of short-run and insubstantial considerations.[15]

Most analysts believe that this indictment of the primaries goes too far. They feel that voters respond with some rationality to the challenge of having to choose among several candidates in a short campaign without the powerful guidance provided by party labels. Primary voters react to what Samuel Popkin has referred to as "low-information signaling" based on candidates' chances of winning, personal and demographic characteristics, and whatever inferences can be drawn about their policy positions.[16]

Larry Bartels's sophisticated modeling of primary voting[17] suggests that candidate momentum can be a rational basis for sorting through a pack of candidates about whom voters have fairly little information. Primary voters are more influenced by strategic considerations, such as which of the acceptable candidates is most likely to win, when there is no well-known front-runner.[18] Even then, candidates who benefit from the momentum are often quickly subjected to more searching evaluations. Other candidates who are better known, such as incumbent presidents or vice presidents, are less likely to be affected by the ups and downs of the campaign unless their chances of winning drop substantially.

In sum, even though primary voters often base their decisions on less information than do general election voters, their choices are not necessarily irrational. In contests that pit a party's candidates against one another, issue differences among candidates are likely to be minor. It should not be surprising, then, that other factors, including candidates' characteristics and issue priorities, as opposed to issue positions, would become important.

Further, it is reasonable for someone trying to make the most effective use of his or her vote to take into account a candidate's chances of winning the nomination and the presidency. A concern with electability does not necessarily indicate irrationality or ignorance. Thus the bases for voter decisions in primaries may not differ much from those in caucuses or in general elections.[19] In fact, questions raised about the quality of voter decision-making in primaries could be just as easily raised about the judgment of the party leaders who selected candidates under the earlier caucus-convention system.

PRIMARY VERSUS PARTY SELECTION

What other differences do we find in the nominating process when delegates to the national conventions are chosen by primaries, rather than by party-run methods of selection? Do the delegates chosen in a primary behave any differently from those chosen through party processes?

Prior to the reforms, two patterns of candidate selection could be seen. In states that held presidential primaries, a more open and candidate-centered politics worked to the advantage of well-known candidates and people who challenged the party organization. In the other states, the party organization controlled delegate selection and could choose both delegates and presidential nominees on the basis of their acceptability to the party's leaders and activists. Some candidates, such as John F. Kennedy in 1960, won the nomination by mixing victories in both types of states; others, such as Hubert Humphrey, who won the 1968 Democratic nomination in a brokered convention without entering a primary, were the product of a party-controlled process.

Since the reforms, the politics of choosing delegates has become more similar in all states, whether they use primary elections or caucuses and conventions. Candidates are forced to run more nationalized campaigns, media coverage has become national in scope, and delegate selection is more open. The result is a more homogeneous nomination politics. As a consequence, the results of the primaries and the caucuses do not differ as much.

Nevertheless, the primaries maintain their special role and appeal. Because of their openness to the voters, their results confer great legitimacy on the winners. Primary victories may be just as important to candidates for their symbolic value, then, as for the delegates they award. The primaries give candidates an opportunity to show their public support, to raise campaign funds, and to demonstrate their stamina and ability to adapt to stressful situations. Candidates' performance in the primary contests may not be valid indicators of their behavior in the White House, but they do give voters a measure of the candidates' (and their advisers') grace under pressure.

THE FINAL ACT:
THE NATIONAL PARTY CONVENTIONS

For several days every four years, the Democrats and Republicans assemble as national parties to make decisions on a national scale. The conventions draw together for collective action the different parts of the party: the party organization, the party in the electorate, and the party in government. Now, however, when their traditional purpose of selecting the party's nominee for president has been preempted by the primaries and caucuses, what functions do the conventions have left?

Origins and Development of the Party Conventions

The national party conventions are venerable institutions. They first emerged as the means through which the state parties and their leaders could wrest control of the presidential selection process from congressional leaders. In 1832, the Democratic-Republicans, soon to become the Democratic Party, became the first major party to hold a convention.[20] Because the nomination of Andrew Jackson was a foregone conclusion, the convention's main purpose was to enable state political leaders to secure the vice-presidential nomination for Martin Van Buren over Henry Clay, the favorite of the congressional caucus. By the time the Republican Party emerged in 1854, the convention had become the accepted means through which a major party's candidates for president and vice president were to be selected; the GOP held its first convention in 1856.

Every four years since their birth, then, America's two major parties have held national party conventions to nominate their candidates for president. Even though this core function has been undermined by the nationalization of politics and the use of the direct primary, the conventions remain visible party institutions.[21]

The Structure of the Convention

The conventions are creatures of the parties themselves. They are subject to no congressional or state regulation, and even the federal courts have been reluctant to intervene in their operation. Responsibility for them falls to the national party committees and their staffs, although an incumbent president strongly influences the planning for his (or, someday, her) party's convention.

Months before the convention, its major committees begin their work (see box below). What these committees decide can be overruled by the convention itself, which acts as the ultimate arbiter of its own structure and procedures. As a result, some of the most famous battles on the floor of the convention have involved disputes over committee recommendations.

Key Committees of the National Party Conventions

Over the years there have been four important committees of the national conventions:

Credentials considers the qualifications of delegates and alternates. Once the scene of some of the fiercest battles over delegate seating, it has become less important in recent years as delegate contests are resolved through regularized state procedures approved by the national parties.

Permanent Organization selects the officials of the convention, including the chairperson, secretary, and sergeant at arms.

Rules sets the rules of the convention, including the length and number of nomination speeches. It is often the scene for a struggle over the procedures for future conventions.

Platform (or Resolutions) drafts the party's platform for action by the convention. As intraparty struggles leading into the convention have focused more on issues, it has emerged in recent years as the most important of the committees.

The Business of the Conventions

The convention warms up with the keynote address by a party "star," tries to maintain momentum and suspense as it considers the platform, and reaches a dramatic peak in the nomination of the presidential and vice-presidential candidates. This general format has remained basically the same convention after convention.

The Platform   Aside from the nomination, approving the platform is the convention's chief business. The platform committees begin public hearings long before the convention opens, so that a draft can be ready for the convention. The finished platform is then presented to the convention for its approval. That approval is not always forthcoming; platforms have caused some spirited convention battles because many of the delegates care deeply about this single statement of the party's beliefs. In 1980, Democrats held a seventeen-hour debate over economic policy that was the last gasp of Senator Ted Kennedy's ill-fated challenge to President Carter. In more recent conventions, struggles over the abortion issue have taken place or have loomed large as threats to convention goodwill.[22]

Party platforms are like foreign films: referred to, but rarely seen. Even party leaders often ignore them; Republican Senate Majority Leader Robert Dole admitted during his 1996 presidential campaign that he had not read his party's platform. Rather than a statement of continuing party philosophy, the platform is really an expression of the policy preferences of majorities that can be assembled around each of its planks. The platform is also a campaign document intended to position the party favorably for the general election in the fall.

Even though platforms are an attempt to satisfy various party constituencies, they do define the major differences between the parties. In recent years, the Democratic and Republican platforms have disagreed on a number of issues, most notably abortion, taxes, collective bargaining rights, gun control, racial policy, deficit spending, and American involvement in the world. (See Chapter 15 for specification of some of their differences.) The party platform is important, its leading scholar says, "because it summarizes, crystallizes, and presents to the voters the character of the party coalition."[23]

Finally, platforms are shaped by the fact that they are drafted and approved in conventions mainly concerned with picking a presidential candidate. Because the party's presidential nominee generally controls the convention, the platform has ordinarily been a reflection of his views—or at least of the bargains he has been willing to strike for other gains or to preserve party harmony.[24]

Selecting the Presidential Candidate   The vote on the party's nominee for president begins with nominations made by delegates, shorter seconding speeches, and boisterous floor demonstrations by the candidate's supporters. As lively as they are, these events are sedate compared with the tumultuous conventions of earlier years. The presence of media coverage encourages party leaders to aim for a carefully crafted picture of the party's strength and vision; this tends to deprive conventions of much of the drama, the sense of carnival, that was so much a part of their tradition.

Once the nominee (or, in rare cases, the nominees) has been presented, the secretary calls the roll of the states (and other voting units), asking each delegation to report its vote. The result in recent times has taken only one ballot—far from the days when, in 1924, the Democrats plodded through 103 ballots in sultry New York's Madison Square Garden before John W. Davis won the majority needed for the nomination. Yet a convention that requires more than one ballot to choose the presidential nominee is still a possibility—perhaps especially for the Democrats because of their adoption of proportional representation in the primaries and caucuses.

In previous years, when a convention had more than one candidate for the nomination and the first ballot did not produce a majority, intense negotiations would follow. The leading candidates would need to keep the competition from chipping away their supporters, to protect their image as potential winners. New support for frontrunners would come most easily from the delegates preferring minor candidates. It is difficult to envision how these negotiations could work in conventions today; because the delegates are tied to candidates rather than to state party leaders, it is unclear who could play the traditional role of broker. The leading candidates might choose to negotiate among themselves for the nomination. Another possibility is that the uncommitted "superdelegates" would broker a majority for one candidate.[25]

Selecting the Vice-Presidential Nominee   The day after the naming of the presidential nominee, the secretary calls the roll again to select the vice-presidential candidate. This process too is largely ceremonial; presidential nominees almost always choose their own running mates and conventions routinely ratify their choice. This method of selecting vice-presidential candidates has drawn criticism—not so much because they are handpicked by the presidential nominee as because the decision is so often made by a tired candidate and advisers and then sprung at the last minute on convention delegates. George Bush's nomination of Indiana Senator Dan Quayle in 1988 was criticized on these grounds. But without any viable procedure to replace it, this choice and the responsibility for a poor selection will remain in the hands of the party's presidential nominee.

Launching the Presidential Campaign   The final business of the conventions is to present their party's presidential choice to both assembled delegates and the American voters. The speeches on candidates' behalf at the convention and their own acceptance speeches are the opening shots of the fall campaign. Coming out of their conventions, nominees generally receive a boost in popular support (a "convention bounce"). For the presidential candidates at least, then, the convention's most important role is as a campaign event.

THE DELEGATES

Convention delegates are among the most visible of the party's activists. They help to shape the public's image of the two parties. Who the delegates are says a great deal about what the parties are.

Apportioning Delegate Slots among the States

It is the parties that determine how many delegates each state can send to the convention. The parties make these choices differently. The Republicans allocate delegates more equally among the states; the Democrats tend to weigh the size of the state's population and its record of support for Democratic candidates more heavily.

These formulas affect the voting strength of the various groups within the party coalitions. The GOP's decision to represent the states more equally has advantaged its conservative wing. By giving relatively more weight to the larger states with stronger Democratic voting traditions, in contrast, the Democrats have favored the more liberal interests in their party. Even if these delegate allocation formulas have only marginal effects on the balance of forces within the parties, many a nomination has been won—and lost—at the margin.

The Representativeness of the Delegates

The delegates to the Democratic and Republican conventions have never been a cross section of American citizens or even of their party's rank and file. Whites, males, the well educated, and the affluent have long populated the convention halls. Reflecting their different coalitional bases, since the 1930s Democratic delegations have had more Catholics, Jews, and trade unionists, whereas the Republican conventions have drawn more Protestants and business entrepreneurs.

Demographic Characteristics   In recent decades the delegates of both parties, but especially the Democrats, have become more representative of other citizens in some ways. The Democrats used affirmative action plans after 1968 to increase the presence of women, blacks, and for a brief time, young people; since 1980 they have required that half the delegates be women. The percentage of female delegates at Republican conventions has increased during this period as well, but without party mandates. The Democratic National Committee has urged its state organizations to recruit more low- and moderate-income delegates, but the low political involvement levels of these groups and the high price of attending a convention pose powerful barriers to their participation. Thus the conventions remain meetings of the affluent and well educated (see Table 10.2).[26]

Political Experience   Although it might seem as though delegates would be a self-perpetuating group making return appearances year after year, that was not an accurate description even before the 1970s reforms; even then, a comfortable majority of delegates were attending each party convention for the first time. With the move to primaries, the percentage of newcomers increased after 1968—to about 80 percent—before declining steadily through 1988. The increased representation of Democratic "superdelegates" brought the total of newcomers to less than a majority in 1992.

Yet, for all of this infusion of new blood, conventions remain the province of party activists and leaders. In 1992, for example, 69 percent of a random sample of Democratic delegates reported that they "worked year after year" for the party, 45 percent held party office, and 24 percent held elected office. Comparable Republican figures may be even higher, as they were in previous years.[27] In spite of the high turnover, then, these national party meetings still bring together the activists of the state and local party organizations and the leaders of the party in government.

Issue and Ideological Representativeness   Convention delegates are clearly more involved in politics, more aware of issues, and more ideologically extreme than are party voters more generally. Democratic delegates are more liberal than Democratic

TABLE 10.2 The Representativeness of 1996 Democratic and Republican
Convention Delegates

	Dem. Delegates	Dem. Registered Voters	All Registered Voters	Rep. Registered Voters	Rep. Delegates
Gender					
Female	57%	58%	52%	51%	39%
Race					
Black	21%	23%	11%	1%	2%
White	67	69	81	95	92
Hispanic	6	6	4	2	2
Age					
18–29	4%	15%	16%	15%	2%
60+	24	30	25	25	31
Education					
Didn't finish HS	<.5%	21%	16%	10%	0%
HS graduate	8	35	34	32	7
Some college	20	19	21	22	20
College grad	27	15	19	24	37
Postgraduate	45	10	11	12	36
Household Income					
Under $12,000	1%	14%	12%	11%	<.5%
$12–20,000	1	15	12	9	1
$20–30,000	6	21	18	16	4
$30–50,000	18	21	25	25	14
$50–75,000	25	20	21	22	24
Over $75,000	46	10	13	18	56

Source: Data on convention delegates were collected by the *Washington Post* during June, July, and August, 1996. Data for party identifiers and all registered voters come from exit polls conducted by Voter Research & Surveys, which is funded by CNN and the three major networks. See Mario A. Brossard, "Delegates Leaning More Liberal Than Their Leader or the Rank and File," *Washington Post*, August 25, 1996, p. M4 (for the Democrats) and Brossard, "Delegates, Party Voters Sometimes at Odds; Polling Finds Many in Both Groups Disappointed with Dole Campaign," *Washington Post*, August 11, 1996, p. M8 (for the Republicans).

voters and much more liberal than the average voter; Republican delegates tend to be further to the right than either their party voters or voters generally. As Table 10.3 shows, 1996 Democratic delegates were closer to Democratic voters on the issue of banning assault weapons and more similar to all voters in their preference for reducing defense spending, than Republican delegates were. On the other hand, Republican delegates closely resembled Republican voters on several issues, including the balanced budget amendment, the death penalty, and welfare reform.

The degree to which delegates are found to hold more extreme views than party voters bears on a long-standing debate about the nominating process. Democratic reformers had charged that the old caucus-convention system did not represent the views of regular party supporters. Their critics, in turn, have claimed that

TABLE 10.3 Delegates, Voters, and Issues: 1996

	Dem. Delegates	Dem. Registered Voters	All Registered Voters	Rep. Registered Voters	Rep. Delegates
A constitutional amendment to require a balanced federal budget	32%	77%	82%	87%	88%
The death penalty for people convicted of murder	48	67	76	88	88
Cut off public assistance payments a poor person can get after a maximum of 5 years	38	67	73	81	88
Ban the sale of most assault weapons	93	78	73	67	47
Impose a 5-year freeze on legal immigration	15	57	59	65	29
Reduce spending on social programs	20	44	55	71	84
Reduce spending on defense and the military	65	47	44	29	11
Amend the U.S. Constitution to allow organized prayer in public schools	19	66	66	73	50
Oppose affirmative action programs giving preference to women, blacks, and other minorities	14	34	52	66	83
Bar illegal immigrants from public schools, hospitals, and other state-run social services	16	36	48	61	65

Note: Figures are the percentage of each group who agreed with the statement.

Source: Data on convention delegates were collected by the *Washington Post* during June, July, and August, 1996. Data for party identifiers and all registered voters come from exit polls conducted by Voter Research & Surveys, which is funded by CNN and the three major networks. See Mario A. Brossard, "Delegates Leaning More Liberal Than Their Leader or the Rank and File," *Washington Post,* August 25, 1996, p. M4 (for the Democrats) and Brossard, "Delegates, Party Voters Sometimes at Odds; Polling Finds Many in Both Groups Disappointed with Dole Campaign," *Washington Post,* August 11, 1996, p. M8 (for the Republicans).

the delegates selected under the reformed rules are ideologically out of step with ordinary party voters and the general electorate.

The reality is that the reforms have not made the conventions more representative of the views of party identifiers. Prior to 1972, it was the Republican conventions whose delegates appeared to be more ideologically out of step with party voters, and even more compared with the general voting public.[28] The Democratic reforms first seemed to reverse that pattern. Democratic delegates in 1972 were more ideologically distant than Republican delegates from their party identifiers, and even farther away from the public. The reforms seemed to have made Democratic conventions less rather than more representative.[29] Later Democratic conventions were better reflections of the views of Democratic identifiers. The infusion of "superdelegates" since 1984 seems to have reduced the ideological gap between Democratic delegates and party voters even more.[30]

The real effect of the reforms has been to link the selection of delegates more closely to candidate preferences. Thus, when an ideologically committed candidate does well in the primaries and caucuses, more ideologically oriented activists become convention delegates. At those times, conventions may be less representative of the party in the electorate. On the other hand, they may offer clearer choices to voters.

Amateurs or Professionals?   The reforms were also expected to result in delegates with a different approach to politics. Using the terms described in Chapter 5, some convention delegates can be described as amateurs, others as professionals. Amateurs are more attracted by issues, more insistent on internal party democracy, less willing to compromise, and less committed to the prime importance of winning elections. Professionals, in contrast, are more likely to have a long-term commitment to the party and to be more willing to compromise on issues in the interest of winning the general election.

One study confirmed that the Democratic Party's reforms had, as intended, reduced the presence of party professionals between the 1968 and the 1972 conventions.[31] As we have seen, however, the party later moved to reverse this trend, particularly by adding "superdelegates." Research indicates that even after the reforms, convention delegates have remained strongly committed to their parties and to enduring party goals.[32] For both professionals and amateurs, involvement in this highly public party pageant may encourage commitment to the party's aims.

Who Controls the Delegates?   It would not matter how representative delegates are if they act as pawns of powerful party leaders. In fact, for most of the history of party conventions, that is exactly how the state delegations would have been described. Anecdotes referred to the commanding presence of top state party leaders and some big-city mayors, especially at Democratic conventions.

Now, however, strong party leaders no longer control the convention by dominating their state delegations. When the Democrats eliminated their long-standing unit rule in 1968, through which a majority of a state delegation could throw all of its votes to one candidate, they removed a powerful instrument of leadership control. In addition, by opening up the delegate selection process after 1968, both parties also made it difficult for elected leaders to claim delegate seats without committing early to a presidential candidate, which they were reluctant to do. Democratic elected leaders were much less likely to become convention delegates after 1968, until they gained delegate slots as "superdelegates" beginning in 1984.

Perhaps the most powerful restriction on control of conventions by a few state leaders, though, is the fact that so many delegates in both parties now come to the conventions already committed to a candidate and unavailable for "delivery" by party leaders. If anyone controls the modern conventions, then, it is the party's prospective nominee for president, not leaders of the state parties.

CONVENTIONS IN THE NEW NOMINATING PROCESS

We have seen that although much of their pageantry is age-old, the conventions are very different now from the way they were even a generation ago. Among the other important changes, interests and ideology have assumed greater power in the nominating conventions, and the role of the media has changed.

New Centers of Power

Because candidates must mobilize grassroots constituencies in order to win primaries and caucuses, and many of these constituencies are concerned with particular policies, the reforms made issues and ideological orientations all the more important in convention politics. Many delegates arrive at the convention committed not only to a candidate but also to a cause. The ideological pressures exerted by Christian conservatives at Republican conventions in the 1990s are a good illustration. Ideological factions and their preferred goals, then, have become new centers of power in the postreform convention.

Changing Media Coverage

Media coverage of conventions has significantly changed as well, and in turn conventions have been reshaped and rescheduled to meet the media's needs. The result, as Byron Shafer has put it, is a "bifurcated politics" in which the convention is one thing to delegates in the meeting hall and quite another to the millions catching a glimpse of it on television.[33]

Live gavel-to-gavel televising of the meetings beginning in the 1950s turned them into political spectaculars intended as much for a national television audience as for the delegates. Party officials gave key roles to telegenic partisans, quickened the pace of proceedings, and moved the most serious business into prime-time hours. Reporters swarmed through the convention halls, covering the strategic moves of major candidates, the actions of powerful figures in the party, and the complaints of individual delegates. Even the formerly secret work of platform committee came to be done in the public eye.

For the party, television coverage offered a priceless opportunity to reach voters and party workers and to launch its presidential campaign with maximum impact. For television news the convention became a major story, like a natural disaster or the Olympics, through which it could demonstrate its skill and provide a public service. Thus the media spotlight shifted the emphasis of the convention—not completely but perceptibly—from the conduct of party business to the stimulation of wider political audiences.

Interestingly, however, just as media attention to it increased, the convention began to lose its audience appeal. Because postreform nominations were settled before the convention began, the drama and suspense of the conventions waned. In search of color and excitement to hold an audience, media people became actors in the event themselves, ready to fan the flames of conflict or to turn rumors into full-fledged stories. When audiences continued to decline, the major networks reduced their coverage to broadcast only the most significant events (see Figure 10.1). Although convention

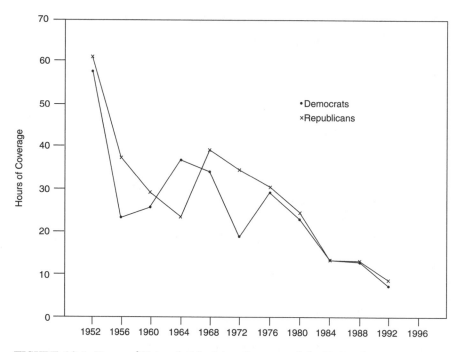

FIGURE 10.1 Hours of Network Television Coverage of the National Party Conventions, 1952–1992

Note: Figures are the number of hours of televised party conventions on the major networks (ABC, CBS, NBC).

Source: Harold W. Stanley and Richard G. Niemi, *Vital Statistics on American Politics* (Washington, DC: Congressional Quarterly Press, 1994), Table 2–13, p. 75; figures for 1996 are not available.

"junkies" still can turn to C-SPAN or CNN for comprehensive coverage, the major networks' desertion of the convention signifies a change in public attention.[34]

Media coverage, of course, is a two-edged sword; it does not always produce the results the parties want. Television's capacity to dramatize and personalize can make a convention come to life for its audience, as it did in covering the struggles in the convention hall and streets of Chicago in 1968 that led to the nomination reforms. But the media tend to underplay the more essential processes of negotiation and compromise, which do not make for good ratings. Television cameras encourage some participants to use the convention as a podium to advance their own causes even if they risk undermining the party's interests. The public visibility given to defeated candidate Patrick Buchanan at the 1992 Republican conclave, for example, was thought by some to have threatened the general election chances of the party's nominee.

Conventions in Future Party Politics

The conventions, in short, have lost much of their deliberative character and independence in fulfilling their original purpose—selecting the presidential nominees. Genuinely brokered conventions and last-minute compromise candidates seem to belong to the past. Even if a convention were to have a choice to make among presidential candidates, the resulting negotiation would be more open, involving the majority of delegates as well as prominent party leaders.

Despite their declining significance, however, the national conventions are living symbols of the national parties. They provide a unique occasion for rediscovering common traditions and interests and for celebrating the party's heroes and achievements. Conventions encourage state and local party candidates, energize party workers, and launch presidential campaigns. They may not win Emmy awards for compelling viewing but they frequently remind party activists and even some party identifiers why the party matters to them.

THE CASE FOR CHANGE

The reforms of the presidential nominating system are variations on an old theme in American politics: efforts by reformers to break up concentrations of party power. As with all other reforms, however, they have had a number of unintended effects.

Pros and Cons of the Current System

The drawbacks of the reformed system are serious. Candidates must invest such an enormous amount of time, energy, and money before the presidential campaign has even begun that the ultimate winner can arrive at the party convention personally and financially exhausted. The marathon of primaries and caucuses puts a premium on campaign strategy and candidate images rather than on other aspects of presidential leadership. The results of a few early contests in states not very representative of the nation have a truly disproportionate effect on the national outcome.[35] Primaries can create internal divisions in state party organizations that may not heal in time for the general election. The low turnouts in primaries and caucuses can increase the influence of well-organized groups on the ideological extremes: the right wing of the Republican Party and the left wing of the Democrats. All of these problems increase the risk that a party will choose an ineffective nominee.

Yet there is no going back to the old system. As the reformers charged, it was often controlled by state and local party leaders who seemed increasingly out of touch with the electorate. In the nonprimary states, it kept party voters and even many party activists out of the crucial first step in picking a president. It violated the desire for a more open, democratic politics. And it did not help presidential candidates learn how to prepare themselves for the most powerful leadership position in the world.[36] By comparison, the system of primaries and a weaker convention seems more secure in public opinion.[37]

Possible Reforms

There have been recent efforts to reform the reforms again. One proposal is to create regional contests in which the states in a given region would all schedule their primaries on the same day. The aim is to bring more coherence to the welter of state contests by limiting the number of dates on which they could be held and reducing the enormous strain on the candidates.

For a time in the late 1980s and 1990s one regional primary existed; most Southern states chose to hold their primaries early in March on a date referred to as Super Tuesday. The aim of these states was not to benefit the candidates, it was to draw greater attention to Southern concerns in the nominating process and to encourage the nomination of moderate candidates acceptable to the South. By 1996, New England states also scheduled their primaries on this date. In 2000, six Southern and Southwestern states attempted another Southern primary, but the front-loading of other states' events reduced its impact.

A variant of a regional primary system was proposed in 2000 by a Republican Party committee. Under this plan, four multistate primaries would be held during a four-month period. The smallest states would vote in the first primary in order to give less well-known candidates a chance to build support. Because the largest states with the most delegates would vote last, the nomination would not be locked up too early. Understandably, though, those large states were not anxious to risk taking a back seat in the selection of a presidential candidate.

Another option might be to hold a national primary in which all the states' delegate selection events were held on the same day. This, however, would serve the interests of neither the parties nor the states. States would lose their chance of becoming pivotal players in nomination contests. The parties would completely lose control over presidential selection, throwing the contest for the presidency wide open to any candidate who could mobilize a national constituency. A national primary could be accomplished only by ending the long tradition of state and party control over the presidential nomination process—and for all of the reforms we have seen in recent decades, there is little chance that will happen.

Chapter 11

Parties and the Campaign for Election

*I*f a 1970s-era candidate for Congress or governor were to appear in the middle of a current campaign for the same office, he or she would feel like Rip Van Winkle. The world of campaign politics has changed radically since that time, and continues to transform itself. Especially in statewide and national races, but even in many local contests, campaigns are dominated by professional managers, pollsters, media specialists, direct mail experts, Web page designers, and fund-raisers. These consultants have replaced the state and local party organizations as the main planners and managers of campaigns.

It would be easy to assume as a result that the traditional grassroots party organization has become technologically obsolete—that it has been superseded by newer, more efficient, and more powerful campaign techniques. But the party organizations are highly adaptable. Throughout their history, the Democratic and Republican parties have responded to change; that in part accounts for their long life. Instead of relegating the parties to the sidelines, then, we need to examine their current role in political campaigns.

The impact of changing technologies also brings up a fundamental fact of political campaigning: campaigns operate within a broader context, determined by a number of forces beyond the campaigners' immediate control. Before we can understand the changes in campaigning, we need to take a look at the context. We have already discussed much of it—parties' organizational strength, political activists, party loyalties, voter turnout, and the rules governing party nominations. We will later examine other aspects of it, including campaign finance rules and the role of the party in government. In this chapter we will begin with the legal context of campaigns: the regulation of the electoral process itself. We cannot hope to understand the electoral game without examining the rules.

THE ELECTORAL INSTITUTIONS

The rules, in politics as well as everything else, are never neutral. Each rule of the electoral game—for example, how votes must be cast or when elections must be held—not only puts limits on a campaign's choices but also affects the different parties and candidates differently. Some rules, as we will see, are likely to benefit certain types of candidates, parties, or party systems; other rules would have had different effects. Over the years, reformers have worked hard to alter the rules in order to weaken the parties, just as the parties have tried to tinker with the rules to gain strength. The net effect is that American election laws have been shaped even more by the Progressives and their descendants than by the parties.

The Secret Ballot

American elections did not always use secret ballots. Until the late nineteenth century in many areas, voters simply told the election officials which candidates they preferred. Gradually, during the nineteenth century, this "oral vote" was replaced by ballots printed by the parties or candidates. The voter brought the ballot of a particular candidate or party to the polling place and deposited it in the ballot box. The ballots of different parties were different in appearance, so observers could often tell how an individual had voted. That was not accidental; if party leaders in urban machines had done a voter a favor in exchange for a vote, they wanted to be sure they had gotten their money's worth. This type of ballot also discouraged ticket-splitting.

The secret ballot, called the Australian ballot after the country where it originated, was introduced as a way of discouraging vote-buying. The reform quickly swept the nation in the 1890s. By the beginning of the twentieth century, its success was virtually complete; only South Carolina waited until 1950 to adopt it. Because the ballot is administered and paid for by the government (meaning, of course, the taxpayer), this reform involved the government in running elections, and that opened the door to government regulation of the parties. It has also enabled voters to split their tickets easily by voting for candidates from different parties for different offices.[1]

The Format of the Ballot

The *format* of this secret ballot varies from state to state, however, which makes a difference in the role of the parties. Some states use a party-column ballot, in which the candidates of each party are grouped together so that voters can perceive them as a party ticket (see the sample ballots in Figure 11.1). Several other states have adopted an office-block ballot form, which groups the candidates according to the office they seek. Nonpartisan elections in cities and towns use the office-block ballot but without listing the candidates' party affiliations.

This simple decision about ballot format affects election outcomes. The use of a party-column ballot encourages straight-ticket voting (i.e., voting for all of a party's candidates for the offices being filled). States can also increase the likelihood of a straight-ticket vote by providing a single lever on voting machines, or a single box on the ballot, by which an individual can cast a vote for the entire party ticket. About twenty states offer this time-saving technique for casting a party-line vote; generally, these are states that use the party-column ballot.[2]

Other aspects of the ballot format can affect a candidate's chance of winning. It is a curious fact that some voters are more likely to select the first name on a list of candidates than they are to select the names listed later.[3] Therefore some states randomly assign the order in which candidates' names appear on the ballot or even rotate the order

Party–Column Ballot

	Democratic Party ◯	Republican Party ◯
Offices		
Congressional Ticket United States Senator	☐ Zonker Harris	☐ Dick Tracy
State Ticket Governor	☐ Barbara Ann Boopstein	☐ Michael J. Doonesbury
State Treasurer	☐ Annie Mudge	☐ Daddy Warbucks
County Ticket Animal Control Officer	☐ Woodstock	☐ Garfield

Office–Block Ballot

Congressional Ticket
For United States Senator:
 (Vote for ONE)

   ☐ Zonker Harris, Democrat
   ☐ Dick Tracy, Republican
   ☐ _____

State Ticket
For Governor:
 (Vote for ONE)

   ☐ Barbara Ann Boopstein, Democrat
   ☐ Michael J. Doonesbury, Republican
   ☐ Duke, Reform
   ☐ _____

State Ticket
For State Treasurer:
 (Vote for ONE)

   ☐ Annie Mudge, Democrat
   ☐ Daddy Warbucks, Republican
   ☐ _____

County Ticket
For Animal Control Officer:
 (Vote for ONE)

   ☐ Woodstock, Democrat
   ☐ Garfield, Republican
   ☐ _____

FIGURE 11.1 Examples of the party-column and office-block ballots.

among groups of ballots; in other states, incumbents' names appear first. The decision to list incumbents first increases their already substantial electoral advantages. The order of the candidates' names probably matters most in primaries and other nonpartisan contests, when voters can find no information about the candidates on the ballot itself.

A related decision must be made in general elections: Which party should be listed first? States often give the preferred position to the majority party and almost always give more prominence to the major parties than to minor parties. On the other hand, the election rules in almost every state allow voters to write in the names of people not listed on the ballot. Write-in candidates hardly ever win, but rules permitting their existence give independent candidates at least a small avenue into the election process.[4]

Another important "rule" is that American voters traditionally face a long ballot. Americans elect large numbers of state and local officials who would be appointed in other democracies. In one amazing example, San Francisco voters in 1990 faced a ballot containing seventeen initiatives and constitutional amendments, eleven bond measures, eleven local propositions, and an array of statewide elected offices—everything but a partridge in a pear tree. The ballot guide provided to voters by the California Secretary of State was more than 200 pages long.

Voters would have to gather a great deal of information about candidates and ballot measures in order to cast a meaningful vote in such an election. Many citizens consider this an invitation to stay away from the polls. Those who do vote may find that the cost is too high to gather the necessary information, and selectively abstain. This partial voting, called roll-off, is most often seen on minor offices, and referenda, where as many as 20 or 30 percent of the voters abstain.[5] The voter fatigue caused by the long ballot leads people to use various shortcuts to make their choices; party identification, of course, is one.

Single-Member Districts

American officeholders are elected from single-member constituencies by plurality election. In other words, only one person per constituency is elected to a city council, a state legislature, or mayor's office; and the candidate who wins the most votes (the plurality) is elected. Multimember districts are rare.[6]

These rules have important consequences for the American parties. As discussed in Chapter 2, single-member districts and plurality elections discourage minor political parties (and candidates). A third party that wins 10 or 20 percent of the vote under these rules will not win any races. In contrast, in several European democracies that use proportional representation, such a party can win legislative seats and cabinet positions. Plurality rules affect the major parties as well. A party that is ideologically distinctive takes the risk that it may not be able to win a plurality and thus might not elect any candidates. The rules, then, encourage parties to broaden their appeal in order to win.

Further, plurality elections deprive the party of one means of influence over its candidates. In electoral systems with multimember districts using proportional representation rules, the voters cast a ballot for a list of party candidates rather than for individual candidates. The parties then divide the seats according to the percentage of the votes they polled, as was described in Chapter 2.[7] In drawing up their list and determining what position on it each candidate will have, the parties directly affect the chances of election for each of their candidates. In short, the prevailing single-member plurality rules for American elections help to reinforce the two-party system of broadly based parties as well as the independence of candidates and officeholders from their parties.

Election Calendars

Even a feature so seemingly innocuous as when elections are held can have important consequences for the candidates and the parties. Since 1845, federal elections have almost always been held on the first Tuesday after the first Monday in November of the even-numbered years. To save money, many statewide and local elections have traditionally been held at the same time.

Scheduling elections for various offices at the same time on the same ballot links the electoral fates of their candidates. A voter's decision on one contest can affect his or her other choices on the same ballot. This is termed a *coattail* effect: the ability of candidates at the top of the ticket to carry into office "on their coattails" other candidates on the same party ticket.[8] As a result, candidates for lesser offices have an incentive to want the strongest possible candidates at the top of the party ticket to ensure that those coattails are long and sturdy.

Parties often prefer to enhance this linkage because it fosters party cohesion. Progressive reformers, not surprisingly, worked to weaken it, using devices such as office block ballots and nonpartisan elections. Some incumbents and other candidates have also found it preferable to insulate their campaigns from the powerful and distracting forces present in federal contests. Most states now elect governors and other top state officials in the second year after a presidential election, at the same time as the midterm congressional contests. Most local elections are scheduled at some other time when no federal offices are on the ballot. This practice of insulating elected officials from one another limits the possibilities for coattail effects and has also worked to reduce the cohesiveness of the party in government.[9]

Election Districts

Candidates' strategies are also affected by the size and composition of the district they hope will elect them. Small, compact districts encourage a level of face-to-face campaigning that simply is not possible in a large, sprawling constituency where voters may be reachable only through the mass media. The partisan composition of a district influences in a different way what the parties and candidates do. By setting the initial odds of victory or defeat, it determines the quality of the candidates who are attracted to the race and, often, the amount of effort that candidates and parties will feel the need to expend. Districts with lopsided majorities in favor of one party discourage activity by minority-party candidates; districts that are well balanced between the parties can prompt spirited campaigns by both candidates and parties.

In a broader sense, the peculiar American institution of the electoral college produces another kind of electoral district effect. Since the 1830s, victory in the presidential race has required winning a majority of the state electoral votes rather than getting the most popular votes across the nation. Presidential candidates develop their strategies accordingly. Candidates normally concentrate their attention on the states with the largest number of electoral votes and the greatest interparty competition, which are generally the largest and most diverse states. They typically write off the less populous states and those they are unlikely to win regardless of their efforts.[10]

That can make a difference in the issues they choose to address and the groups to which they appeal.

POLITICAL CONSEQUENCES OF ELECTORAL LAW

Most important, the "rules" of American elections have tended to focus attention on the candidates rather than on the parties. The American electoral process has few institutions, such as parliamentary-cabinet government or proportional representation, which can encourage the voter to see elections as contests between parties for control of government. Rather, features such as the office-block ballot and even single-member districts (in the absence of a parliamentary system) focus voters' choice on a series of contests between individual candidates. Nonpartisan elections for local offices have reduced the parties' visibility in elections even further, and the separate scheduling of contests at different levels of government makes it difficult for the parties to coordinate their campaigns and their programmatic emphases.

Who Benefits?

Clearly, then, the rules are not neutral in their impact; they are always likely to advantage some candidates and parties over others. For example, if office-block ballots encourage voter fatigue (roll-off) among less educated voters,[11] then the Democratic Party may lose a disproportionate number of votes. If the state makes it relatively easy to vote absentee, that can benefit any local party well-organized enough to distribute absentee ballots to its supporters. Ballot formats that simplify the process of voting a straight ticket work to the advantage of the majority party in the constituency.

Legislative Redistricting

One obvious way in which parties and officeholders try to change the rules to benefit themselves has been through the drawing of constituency lines. Every ten years, after the national census, state legislatures and other governmental bodies must redraw the boundaries of congressional and state legislative districts in order to take into account changes in population size and distribution. How these opportunities have been turned to political advantage is a continuing story of the creativity and resourcefulness of American politicians.

Partisan Redistricting through Malapportionment and Gerrymandering   There have been two traditional methods for turning redistricting opportunities into political gains. The first and most obvious has been simply to ignore population changes. Many states used this tactic for most of the twentieth century by refusing to shift legislative districts, and thus political power, from the shrinking rural and small-town populations to the growing cities. By the 1960s many state legislatures and the U.S. House of Representatives better represented the largely rural America of 1900 than the urban nation it had become. Such *malapportionment* worked to the disadvantage of Republicans in the South and Democrats elsewhere—and of the needs of cities everywhere. In a series of decisions in the early 1960s, however, the United States Supreme Court ended these inequities by requiring that legislative districts be of equal population size. As the courts have applied the "one person, one vote" rule to all types of legislatures, they have closed off this way to exploit the rules of the electoral game.[12]

It is still possible, however, to *gerrymander*—to draw district lines in a way that maximizes one party's strength and disadvantages the other party. That can be done by dividing and thereby diluting pockets of the other party's strength to prevent it from winning office. Alternatively, if the other party's strength is too great to be diluted, then a gerrymander can be accomplished by consolidating that party's voters into a few districts and forcing it to win elections by large, wasteful majorities. The party in power when it is time to redistrict is probably always tempted to gerrymander; whether it succeeds often depends on the actions of the federal government. (see box below).

Federal Involvement in Redistricting   Even after federal courts had worked their way through a series of cases to give meaning to the prescription of one person, one vote, they still resisted entering the "political thicket" of gerrymandering. No matter how insistently the courts enforced the idea of "precise mathematical equality" among

---

Gerrymandering Then and Now

Gerrymandering is the nickname given to the artful drawing of legislative district lines by the party in power so as to give it a greater share of legislative seats than its share of votes:

> The term is derived from the name of Governor Gerry, of Massachusetts, who, in 1811, signed a bill readjusting districts so as to favor the Democrats and weaken the Federalists, although the last named party polled nearly two-thirds of the votes cast. A fancied resemblance of a map of the districts thus treated led [Gilbert] Stuart, the painter, to add a few lines with his pencil, and say to Mr. Russell, editor of the *Boston Centinel,* "That will do for a salamander." Russell glanced at it: "Salamander?" said he, "Call it a Gerrymander!" The epithet took at once and became a Federalist warcry, the map caricature being published as a campaign document.[13]

Because redistricting is an inherently political process, gerrymandering is practiced whenever the states set out to redraw their legislative district lines to take into account the new distribution of population as determined by the census. Even within the strict requirement of equal population sizes, legislators who draw those district lines, now guided by computer programs designed to maximize whatever goal they seek, show impressive creativity. In the 1990s, for example, new districts were created which rival Gerry's original "salamander" in their bizarre shapes. For example, in describing North Carolina's 160-mile-long twelfth Congressional District, it is joked that a car driving down Interstate 85 with its doors open would strike every eligible voter; and Louisiana's originally drawn fourth Congressional District was labeled the "mark of Zorro" because it cut a Z-shaped swath from the top nearly to the bottom of the state to find enough black voters for a black-majority district.

legislative districts, they rarely rejected plans for equal-sized districts on the ground that the lines were drawn to favor one party.[14]

That began to change in the early 1980s with the passage of extensions of the Voting Rights Act. The aim of the legislation was to protect the voting rights of minorities, who had suffered from decades of disenfranchisement and discrimination. The act required a number of states, including all Southern states, to get prior approval of any changes in their election laws—from redistricting plans to voting laws—by officials of the U.S. Department of Justice. Justice rejected nine state redistricting plans after the 1980 census.[15]

Federal involvement in the reapportionment process took a new turn in the 1990s. The 1982 Voting Rights Act mandated the states to go one step further and construct legislative districts so as to maximize the opportunities for black and Hispanic candidates to win office. Republicans in many states joined with black Democrats, with the encouragement of the Bush administration Justice Department, to create new districts with clear black and Hispanic majorities. For minorities, these new *majority-minority districts* promised greater representation in Congress and state legislatures. For Republicans, there was the promise of more victories as well. By concentrating Democratic-leaning black and Hispanic voters into a few majority-minority districts, Republicans might have a better chance to win the newly constructed adjacent districts, which were now less Democratic.

The plan worked, at least initially; American legislatures gained more minority group members than ever before, and the Republicans made significant inroads in previously Democratic strongholds, especially in the South.[16] Yet there is reason to ask whether minority groups benefit from an increase in black and Hispanic representatives that comes at the cost of decreasing Democratic legislative strength.

The debate may be moot, however. The Supreme Court has recently taken a dim view of using race as the "predominant factor" in drawing congressional districts. It has required the states to redraw existing district lines and has upheld the resulting drop in the number of majority-minority districts. Whether this signals a wholesale judicial assault on racial gerrymandering or merely a judicial fine-tuning of the most blatant gerrymanders remains to be seen.[17]

Do Parties Still Gain from Gerrymandering?   When the majority party redraws the district lines, either to favor its candidates generally or to protect incumbent officeholders of both parties, the assumption is that the tactic is effective. That may not always be the case. Although a notorious gerrymander in California in the early 1980s provided great advantage for the Democrats, an equally notorious redistricting to benefit the Republicans in Indiana had a short-lived effect; the state's congressional delegation, with a bare Democratic majority in 1981, had an even greater Democratic majority ten years later! Researchers found that by the 1980s and 1990s, with the exception of the creation of majority-minority districts, effects of redistricting seemed to be minimal, especially after the first few years.[18]

The apparent erosion of the party advantage from controlling redistricting may result from the scrutiny the courts and the Justice Department have been giving to reapportionment plans. Their involvement seems to have stimulated more challenges and thereby more public attention to possible gerrymanders. When courts have become involved in redistricting, they have been more willing to draw district lines across counties and other political divisions, and thus across the lines of local party organization. The result is to make it harder in yet another way for party organizations to maintain a role in electoral politics.

CAMPAIGN STRATEGY

These "rules" of American elections structure the environment of political campaigns. They are, however, among the only certainties in modern political campaigning. Although a great deal has been written about campaign politics,[19] the overarching rule is that the rules keep changing. Most American campaigns lurch from one improvisation to another, from one immediate crisis to the next. They are frequently underorganized, underplanned, underfinanced, and understaffed; consequently they often play by ear with a surprising lack of information. If the great majority of voters had strong party loyalties, of course, this would not be the case; the majority party would turn out its voters and win. But as attractive as that may sound (at least to candidates of the majority party), the life of a campaigner is much more unpredictable.

In designing a campaign strategy, the most critical variables are the nature of the district and the electorate, the type of office being sought, the candidate's skills and background, the availability of money and other resources, and the party organizations and other organized groups in the constituency. The most important early task of campaign strategists is to evaluate the opportunities and the hazards embedded in each of these factors and to determine which ought to be exploited and which need to be downplayed.

Once a campaign's strategists have identified its likely strengths and weaknesses, they must choose how to spend each unit of their scarce time, energy, money, and other resources in order to achieve the greatest possible return in terms of votes. If the candidate's party is in the majority in a district where party voting is common, the campaign can spend most of its resources on appeals to party voters and get-out-the-vote drives. If that is not the case, how can they most effectively attract independents without losing their base of party identifiers? Can they afford television and radio ads, and if so, do the audiences of various stations coincide well enough with the election district to make this spending cost-effective? Is theirs a district in which money can be raised successfully through direct mail appeals, or do donors insist on meeting the candidate face to face?[20]

The two most important factors conditioning the campaign's decisions are incumbency and the competitiveness of the race. Incumbents, even in years when hostility toward the government is high, have enormous advantages in running for reelection. Congressional incumbents, as we have seen, probably have a greater chance of being mugged in Washington, D. C., than of losing their next race.[21] Incumbents of any office, of course, are greatly advantaged by having put together a successful campaign for that office at least once before. Part of that campaign organization is likely to remain in place between elections, some of it perhaps employed as members of the incumbent's office staff. Incumbents tend to have greater name recognition, more success in attracting media coverage, and greater appeal to campaign contributors than do most of their potential competitors.

The result is that challengers—candidates who run against incumbents—face a predictable spiral. Especially if they have not won any political office before, challengers do not start with an experienced organization, proven fund-raising skills, or the other incumbent advantages. In the days when party organizations dominated campaigns, this might not have been a problem. Now it is. One obvious answer might be to purchase an experienced campaign organization by hiring political consultants. But most challengers do not have the money to do that. Thus the cycle begins: the challenger lacks an existing organization and enough money to attract the interest of well-known consultants, so he or she cannot reach many voters; and without these two vital resources, a challenger is not likely to raise enough money to be able to afford either one.

Candidates for open seats (those where no incumbent is running) often have the means to break out of this spiral, especially when the office they seek is prominent. Those who choose to run for the most visible offices—governorships, Congress and the presidency, major city offices—typically start with considerable name recognition, which increases because of the attention given to the race. They are in a position to raise enough money for extensive media campaigns. Their major challenge will be to spend their money most effectively and to succeed in defining themselves to the voters before their opponents get the opportunity to define them.

The great majority of campaigns in the United States, however, are far less visible. Candidates whose names are hardly household words and whose campaign resources are modest must run far less ambitious campaigns. The means they use to reach voters will depend in part on the prevailing political practices of their constituency; in some areas, state legislative candidates rely on yard signs and door-to-door campaigning to make their names known, while in others, full-scale media assaults planned by professional consultants are expected of any serious candidate.

CAMPAIGNING IN THE NEW MILLENNIUM

Within less than a generation, changes amounting to a revolution have altered much of American political campaigning. In particular, campaigns have found effective ways to apply advances in polling, media use, and computer technology. With the new technologies have come the new campaign professionals: specialists in an ever widening range of political skills whose services are available to candidates who can afford the price.

The New Professional Consultants

Professional campaign consultants come from a variety of backgrounds. Some have been involved in party or other political work since they were old enough to pick up a phone. Others received their training in public relations and continue to work for corporations and other groups as well as political campaigns. Several of the best-known pollsters got their start in university graduate programs or in the small number of professional campaign management institutes. Not only have they prospered in American politics, they have also exported their campaign expertise to the rest of the democratic world.[22]

Campaign consultants come in all sizes and shapes. Some are general consultants, similar to the general contractors who oversee the construction of a building; others concentrate on the minutiae of mailing lists or Web page design. Some are experts in the development of media messages, others in how and where to place media ads. Some can provide organizational skills and sometimes even lists of local party people and possible volunteer workers; they can organize rallies, coffee parties, phone banks, and handshaking tours of shopping centers. Some provide lawyers and accountants to steer the campaign away from legal shoals and to handle the reporting of campaign finances to state and federal regulators. Some are publicists who write speeches and press releases, some sample public opinion, and some are skilled in raising money.

As a sign that it is a developing profession rather than just a collection of talented talkers, the consulting business has become more specialized and has even begun to police itself through a national association. The growth of its influence has been dramatic. There is no better testimony to the takeover of so many campaigns by professional consultants, displacing the candidate loyalists who made these decisions in earlier years, than the fact that the names of some of these campaign professionals—for example, James Carville, Alex Castellanos, Geoff Garin, David Garth, Peter Hart, Mary Matalin, Joe Napolitan, Ralph Reed, Ed Rollins, Lance Tarrance, Bob Teeter—have become as familiar as some of the candidates for office, at least in political circles.[23]

Professional consultants typically work for several different campaigns during the same election cycle. It is not uncommon for a consulting firm to handle a collection of Senate, House, and gubernatorial races in a given election year, though many of these firms like to stabilize their business by taking nonpolitical clients as well. As "hired guns" they work independently of the party organizations. Yet they almost always work with clients from only one of the parties—some consultants restrict themselves even further to one wing or ideological grouping within the party—and they normally maintain a cooperative relationship with that party's leaders and organization. In fact, national party committees often play an important matchmaking role in bringing together consultants and candidates.

The New Sources of Information

Computers   Experienced candidates develop a picture of their constituency in their minds. They know what kinds of people support them and how they believe they can trigger that support again. This picture comes from years of contact with constituents. In past years, this "theory" of the campaign would have guided the candidate's strategy—even if the candidate's beliefs were inaccurate or the constituency had changed.

Computer technology now provides a much more sophisticated check on the candidate's beliefs. Computers enable campaigners to process a massive amount of information about the constituency in an incredibly short time. Computerized records can produce a much faster and more accurate answer to questions about voter behavior in recent elections than even the most experienced party workers can.

The first sophisticated use of computers in campaigns occurred when the managers of John F. Kennedy's presidential campaign commissioned a simulation of the

1960 electorate as an aid to campaign planning.[24] Since then, computer technology has made possible an incredible array of organized detail. A local party can computerize reports from canvassers so that they can quickly compile lists of voters to contact on election day. Fund-raisers can merge mailing lists from groups, publications, and even businesses whose customers may be predisposed to favor their candidate, and then produce targeted mailings within hours. "Oppo" researchers can search computerized records to locate statements made by the opposing candidate on any conceivable campaign issue.

Polls   No new avenue to political knowledge has been more fully exploited than the public opinion poll.[25] Candidates poll before deciding whether to run for an office, to probe for weaknesses in the opposition and assess voters' views of the candidate. When the campaign begins, polls are used to determine what political issues are uppermost in voters' minds. Early polls can also trace the development of the candidate's public image to see whether the campaign's first steps are reducing the candidate's "negatives" and enhancing his or her "positives."

Consultants use polls to decide whether the campaign should emphasize party loyalties or whether the candidate would be better advised to ignore an unpopular party or candidate at the top of the ticket. Close to the end of the race, tracking polls can follow the reactions of small samples of voters each day in order to measure immediate responses to a campaign event or a new ad or appeal. In fact polls have become so ubiquitous in campaigns, even in local elections, that stealth volleys of attack ads have been disguised as polls (see box below).

Not all candidates have access to poll data, of course. The expense of sophisticated polling puts it beyond the reach of many candidates, although recent technical support efforts by the parties' national committees and congressional campaign committees (reviewed in Chapter 4) have made some poll data available even to low-budget campaigns. The difficulty runs deeper, however. American political campaigns, despite popular impressions to the contrary, have rarely been run on a solid base of

---

Controversial New Campaign Techniques: Push Polling

In the early weeks of the 2000 presidential primaries, a big media story was the report that the campaign of Republican candidate George W. Bush was found to have conducted "push polls" among registered voters. Push polling, which began to spread widely during the 1990s, is not polling at all, but a form of telemarketing disguised as a poll. In it, callers ask questions that contain misleading information for the purpose of pushing voters away from the campaign's opponent. (An example—*not* used by the Bush campaign—might be: "Does John Doe's support for gay rights and AIDS research make you less likely to vote for him?").

Push polling has been condemned by the American Association for Public Opinion Research, but candidates are apparently more ambivalent about its use.

information. Thousands of party organizations have never kept even basic voting data by precincts, wards, cities, and counties. Thus such a shift to the "new knowledge" involves a basic commitment to gathering knowledge as well as a willingness to bear the costs of acquiring it.

The New Techniques of Persuasion

Campaigns are exercises in mass persuasion. Each candidate seeks to define him- or herself to the voters as a trustworthy and qualified representative. Because of the large size of most election districts, the predominant means of persuasion are the mass media: television, radio, newspapers, and the Internet. Even old-style communications are pursued with the media in mind: a candidate takes the time to address a rally or meeting largely in the hope that it will produce a brief report on the local TV news. (To nurture that hope, the campaign staff has probably prepared news releases and accompanying photo opportunities for the local media.) Early in the campaign, candidates fight to buy choice TV time and billboard space for the concluding weeks of the campaign. As the campaign progresses, the candidates' faces, names, and slogans blossom on billboards, newspaper ads, radio and TV spot announcements, and even on yard signs, brochures, shopping bags, and potholders.

Television   Television is the medium of choice for most campaigns as long as its audience is reasonably well matched to the candidate's constituency. Time on TV often consumes the majority of the campaign's funds. In the early and inexpensive days of television, candidates bought large chunks of time for entire speeches that were carried nation- or statewide. Now, however, campaign messages are compressed into thirty- or sixty-second spot ads that can be run frequently or targeted to a particular audience (see cartoon on p. 222). The writing, producing, and placing of these spots (after the pro football game? before the evening news?) has become a central focus of campaigns, as have the fund-raising activities needed to pay for them. Thus what was a long, stem-winder of a speech by the candidate in a sweaty hall fifty or sixty years ago is now a few carefully crafted visual images and a very simple text put together by professionals.[26]

Because of the high cost of network television, candidates and consultants look for alternatives. The cost of advertising on cable television stations is often lower than on the networks and may also be more efficient for local campaigns whose constituencies are too small to warrant buying time in major media markets. Many cable stations have more specialized "niche" audiences than do the major networks; this permits campaigns to target their messages (called narrowcasting). In addition, it makes good sense for campaigns to maximize their exposure on the "free media" of television newscasts and newspaper columns. When newscasts provide coverage of a candidate, the information may seem more credible and "objective" than if it is conveyed through the campaign's own spot ads.

Some candidates do a masterful job of attracting free media coverage that transmits the images they want voters to see. John McCain, for example—who began a run for the Republican presidential nomination in 2000 in relative obscurity—gained flattering media coverage by remaining almost constantly available to reporters aboard

The Medium of Choice

his "Straight-Talk Express" campaign bus. Unaccustomed to such a refreshing degree of candor, television and print reporters transmitted positive images of McCain's personal history and political stances that probably helped the candidate vault over the other lesser-known Republican candidates and become the chief alternative to the front-runner, Texas Governor George W. Bush.

To obtain media coverage, campaigns need to provide material that the media want. In particular, the campaign's information and its visuals must meet the media's definition of what constitutes "news."[27] If "news" is that which is different from the norm, dramatic, and controversial, then a candidate is not likely to earn media coverage with yet another rendition of a standard stump speech. Candidates who depend on free media will be driven to stage campaign events that make for good television, such as meetings with well-known or very telegenic people, visits to natural disasters or other tragedies, or dramatic confrontations.

Direct Mail   Ironically, in the midst of all this high-tech effort, computers have brought the postal service back to the center of the campaign. Computers can produce personalized, targeted letters by the millions. They are effective both for campaigning and for fund-raising; the well-written letter seeking money is also an appeal for the candidate seeking the funds. Direct mail appeals raise the emotional temperature of a campaign. Reporter E. J. Dionne quotes a prominent direct mail specialist: "The one thing direct mail letters are not is dispassionate. 'You've got to have a devil,' said

Mr. (Roger) Craver. 'If you don't have a devil, you're in trouble.' … 'You need a letter filled with ideas and passion.… It does not beat around the bush, it is not academic, it is not objective.' "[28] The direct mail campaign is an effort to build a list of reliable contributors and supporters who can be counted on to respond whenever the campaign calls. Some veteran campaigners have "called" for long periods of time, using their contributor list as a base for moving on to higher office.

Internet and E-Mail   The newest means of campaign persuasion is the Internet, which began to be marshaled by candidates and consultants in 1996. By now every major campaign has a Web site, as do many local races. Some of these sites are elaborate and professionally designed; others make use of the skills of Web-savvy teenagers. Internet technology permits the combination of Web pages and electronic mail to create interactive Web sites; campaigns can then communicate with visitors to their site via e-mail.

In the 2000 elections the Republican National Committee worked to develop a computerized version of a phone tree in which a core group of Republican supporters each created an e-mail distribution list to send campaign information to other supporters, who in turn spread the information more widely and, of course, almost simultaneously. Campaigns can also load their spot ads on-line and distribute them nationally through the Internet without the cost of buying TV time. Because not all voters have ready access to the Internet, however, on-line campaigning is more likely to benefit candidates who seek the voters most likely to be "wired": young, highly educated, more affluent people.

Traditional campaign techniques are by no means obsolete. Shaking constituents' hands at factory gates is still a common campaign activity, even when the television cameras do not show up. Candidates still seek endorsements from local groups, meet with newspaper editors, and look for gimmicks with which to penetrate the consciousness of busy citizens. The old ways, in short, are very much alive. The new campaign technologies have simply layered on a set of tools that are highly sophisticated and that demand expert knowledge and substantial amounts of money.

The Old Standby: Negative Campaigning

Attacks on the opponent have also gone high-tech. Negative campaigning is nothing new in American politics, of course; politicians since the earliest days of the Republic have been the focus of vicious attacks. Concern about negative campaigns has increased recently, however, because they can be spread much more quickly and widely by the new media; rumors about a candidate's personal life that were once circulated mainly within political circles can now be accessed on the Internet in Honolulu and Fairbanks. It has become a staple of political consulting that when a candidate is falling behind in the polls, one of the surest ways to recover is to "go negative" and launch attacks on his or her opponent.

Does negative campaigning work? The findings are mixed. Some researchers find that negative ads are particularly memorable and that a negative campaign drives down turnout because it increases voter cynicism. Others find no difference in effectiveness and no evidence of turnout decline. One of the biggest challenges in tracing the impact of negative ads is the difficulty of defining "negative"; what one person considers irrelevant mudslinging is helpful, "comparative" information to another.[29] (See box below)

THE NEW CAMPAIGNING FOR THE PRESIDENCY

Nowhere are the techniques and technicians of the new campaigning more visible than in presidential election campaigns. The campaign for the presidency is in many ways the generic American political campaign writ large. Yet many of the usual campaign problems are heightened by the nature of the presidential office and constituency. The vast expanse of the country, the variety of local conditions, and the candidate's isolation from the grass roots make it difficult for the campaign to assess how it is doing. To solve this problem, modern presidential candidates make extensive use of professional pollsters and other consultants, whereas their earlier counterparts relied more heavily on the reports of local politicians. Campaigning across a huge country also places heavy demands on the candidates. Their packed schedules and their need to address the concerns of varied audiences (all within the clear view of a media corps that follows them almost continuously) put exceptional physical and mental strains on a candidate.

A Classic in Negative Advertising: The Willie Horton Commercial

One of the most infamous negative ads is the thirty-second "Willie Horton" commercial that was aired nationally for twenty-eight days on cable television during the 1988 presidential race. In comparing the positions of presidential candidates George Bush and Michael Dukakis on crime, it linked Dukakis to a controversial prison-furlough program adopted while he was governor. The ad stated, "Bush supports the death penalty for first-degree murderers.... Dukakis not only opposes the death penalty, he allowed first-degree murderers to have weekend passes from prison. One was Willie Horton, who murdered a boy in a robbery, stabbing him nineteen times.... Despite a life sentence, Horton received ten weekend passes from prison. (He) fled, kidnapped a young couple, stabbing the man and repeatedly raping his girlfriend." As the narrator recounted these details, a glaring Willie Horton was pictured and the words *kidnapping, stabbing,* and *raping* were flashed on the screen. The conclusion left no doubt about what message was to be drawn from the ad: "Weekend prison passes. Dukakis on crime."

The Willie Horton ad was devastatingly effective. Even though it was not produced by the Bush campaign and was later denounced by Bush and his campaign manager, it worked to Bush's benefit in the presidential race. The ad was produced, it turned out, by advertising consultants long associated with the Republican party and was paid for by an independent conservative political action committee. The PAC claimed that it had the tacit approval of the Bush campaign organization and had offered Bush campaign leaders the opportunity to veto the ad.

Given these difficulties, it is not surprising that presidential campaigns are run largely through the mass media, especially television. With a media-based campaign, presidential candidates can communicate efficiently with a national audience, reaching more potential voters than they could ever hope for with any series of local campaign appearances. Nonetheless, these local appearances remain important for the free media coverage they generate. Presidential candidates also transmit their message through paid media advertising, especially on television. Of course, such extensive usage of the media by presidential candidates is made possible by sums of money that few other candidates can command, but, ironically, it is made necessary by the limits on campaign spending that go along with public funding of the presidential campaigns.[30]

DO CAMPAIGNS MAKE A DIFFERENCE?

The barrage of words and pictures in an election season is staggering, but is anyone paying attention? Do the television spots, the fliers, the poll data, and the money actually sway many votes?

Selective Exposure

The impact of any campaign is limited by the nature of the voter. We know that American voters pay selective attention to campaigns just as they do to most other events. They tend to surround themselves with friends, literature, and even personal experiences (such as rallies and meetings) that support their perceptions and loyalties. They usually perceive events through a filter of stable, long-term orientations, the most stable of which for most voters is party identification. A great deal of American campaigning, then, has the effect of activating and reinforcing the voter's existing political inclinations, as it always has. In fact, much of the effort of a campaign is directed at getting people out to vote, not just influencing their voting decision.[31]

The Dominance of Short-Term Impressions

Yet in an environment of changing partisan loyalties and large numbers of independents, the potential of the campaign for shaping voter perceptions of the candidates may be higher than it has ever been. When long-term voter commitments to party come into question, short-term impressions can predominate, especially where there is no incumbent candidate in the race. Some recent campaigns have produced big swings in public support for candidates right up to election day. In the information-rich environment of current campaigns, there are more opportunities for candidates and campaign appeals to break through the filter of a voter's predispositions.

The Impact of Television

When the traditional intermediaries (local party and group leaders) play a reduced role as cue-givers for voters, television can have a greater influence on their decisions. As Austin Ranney has observed, candidates recognize that in the modern:

world of mass constituencies and of voters who would rather stay home and watch television than attend a political rally in some auditorium, appearing on television is the closest candidates can get to all but a handful of their constituents and provides by far the most cost-effective campaigning device they have. Moreover,... while eye-to-eye contact and a warm handshake between politician and voter may be best, having the politician's voice and face appear in living color on the tube a few feet away from the constituent in his own living room is surely second best.[32]

Television is now the predominant source of political information in the United States. By the early 1960s, television had replaced newspapers as Americans' most important and credible source of political news; TV has been the leading news source ever since.[33] Television has supplanted the parties as well in providing campaign information. Only 22 percent of a national sample reported being personally contacted on behalf of a presidential candidate during the 1992 campaigns, and only 39 percent said they had received materials supporting a candidate through the mail. By contrast, 94 percent of the respondents paid at least some attention to television news about the campaign.[34]

Yet questions remain about the impact of television on political attitudes and behavior. There is ample evidence that the media do not directly determine political preferences, largely because the media provide fairly balanced coverage of political candidates.[35] Rather, media influence is more subtle. By the kinds of issues and events they emphasize, the media affect what people consider important in a campaign; this process is called agenda-setting. This agenda in turn "primes" viewers and readers to look for some qualities in candidates rather than others.[36] Moreover, the simple presence of a variety of viewpoints in the media can provide people with alternatives to the cocoon of homogeneous political views in which many voters would otherwise find themselves.

The Impact of Campaigning

It might be assumed that campaigns make a difference in voters' choices because campaigning rivets so many people's attention. Reporters and other observers focus heavily on the strategies, the surprises, and the drama of the competition. The image of the "horse race" appears frequently in media coverage.[37] The ending of the race is inherently riveting as well: some candidates are chosen to serve in government, and others are sent home. With such a capacity to engage people's attention, the campaign would also seem likely to affect their voting decisions.

On the other hand, election results can usually be predicted successfully from conditions that existed before the campaign began: the distribution of party loyalties, economic conditions, incumbents' poll ratings. Some analysts argue, then, that what happens in between—the events of the campaign itself—apparently has little bearing on the outcome. Instead, they say, campaigns simply provide voters with information about these precampaign conditions so that they will move to this largely preordained outcome.[38]

It is difficult to choose between these arguments because it is hard to specify the effects of particular campaign activities, not to mention the campaign's collective effect. How greatly was a voter affected by a particular candidate's television ads relative to an interest group's endorsement of the candidate or the voter's preexisting party identification? Researchers frequently examine impact by comparing the views of those who are heavily exposed to a stimulus with the views of those who are lightly exposed or not exposed at all. But it is not easy to measure the exposure of an individual to a particular campaign ad or set of ads—and it would be challenging to find the rare individual who is not exposed to TV at all.

Early studies of campaign effects found that traditional grassroots precinct work by party activists produced a small but meaningful boost in the expected party vote. Precinct work, they reported, probably had more influence in local elections than in presidential races because there were fewer alternative sources of information in the local contests.[39] These early studies also showed that personal contacts activated voters more often than mailed propaganda did, and door-to-door canvassing had more influence than telephone calls.[40] Other researchers found that precinct canvassing in a presidential campaign increased turnout but had little effect on voter choice.[41] More recent studies indicated that in areas where parties were active, the vote share for that party was enhanced by 2 to 3 percent—a small amount overall but a critical margin in a close race.[42]

We know even less about the effects of newer campaign techniques such as computerized direct mail messages, which target individual citizens in the privacy of their homes, and various types of television ads. The rapid increase in their use suggests that candidates and consultants think they are effective. In the intense competition of campaigns, candidates cannot wait until the researchers' empirical evidence has been carefully analyzed before they make a decision on how to spend their scarce campaign funds. Instead they must rely on a cruder but more practical measure: Is their opponent using this technique? Did other candidates who used it win or lose?

THE PARTY ORGANIZATION'S ROLE IN MODERN CAMPAIGNING

Nothing assures the party organizations a place in the campaign. They must compete constantly for a role in it, just as they fought without much success to control the nominations after the direct primary was introduced. Their competitors are the candidates themselves, the personal campaign organizations they create, the professional consultants, and those who provide the money. Although the realities of American politics usually force candidates to run under a party label, nothing forces them to let the party organization control or even participate in their campaigns.

In a few places, as we have seen, the party organization still retains the traditional assets that made it valuable to candidates and their campaigns. Where it still commands armies of local workers, it can provide the candidate with an effective force that costs very little in either money or issue commitment. These traditional organizational efforts occur chiefly in a declining number of one-party urban areas in which parties control primaries and voters habitually vote the party ticket in the general election. Canvassing and turning out the vote are still relevant there. Further, the urban candidate is much more likely to have been nominated by the party organization through its control of the primary and thus to be its creature in the general election campaign.

The Resurgent Party Role

Elsewhere, parties have been able to retain an important campaign role by adapting to new realities. In place of traditional grassroots contacts by party volunteers, they have adopted the newer campaign techniques and hired at least some paid campaigners. From primarily in-kind contributions, they have turned increasingly to a cash economy, paying for the activities they perform with funds from generous state and national organizations. As professional campaign specialists have become more important, the parties have often served as their placement offices, matching them up with needy campaigns and even sustaining them during the lean years between campaigns. But by its very nature this new kind of party effort, which relies less on face-to-face contacts, may not signify a more effective grassroots party.[43]

Nevertheless, party organizational involvement in campaigns has expanded. The large sums of money that have flowed to the national parties have enabled them to stimulate greater activity in the state and local parties as well as to assist candidates directly in their own campaigns.[44] With their newfound wealth and the services it can buy, the national parties have become significant players in political campaigns at all levels. And the recent infusion of millions of dollars of "soft money" into state and local parties, as well as their own increasing fund-raising capabilities, has enabled them to expand their campaign roles even more.[45]

The Continuing Struggle for Control

In their struggle for control of the campaign, the candidate's interests and those of the party organization never completely converge. The candidate, unless he or she has been dragooned to fill a ticket in a lost cause, takes the candidacy seriously. Even the longest shot among candidates expects to win; the degree of ego involvement in the campaign almost demands it. The party, on the other hand, wants to be selective in its use of campaign resources. It would prefer to spend as few scarce resources as possible on the inefficient parts of the campaign—the races it regards as hopeless. In addition, the party organization wants to activate party loyalty, but candidates may not find that to be helpful to their own prospects. The organization may want to promote a program, help a presidential or gubernatorial candidate, or win control of a legislature, but these may not be the goals and interests of individual candidates.

When parties organize campaigns on behalf of an entire ticket, there are many clear advantages. The party organization can distribute campaign literature for a number of candidates at the same time and mount voter registration drives. It can coordinate the main election-day activities: setting up a headquarters, providing poll-watchers to oversee the voting, offering cars to get people to the polls, checking voter lists to alert nonvoters late in the day. But that very efficiency necessarily limits a candidate's independence. Although the party organization may prefer to raise money in order to prevent competition for contributors' dollars, a candidate may well believe he or she can raise more individually. Although the party may prefer billboards that celebrate the full party ticket, some candidates on that ticket may prefer to go it alone.

In this struggle for control of campaigning, the party organizations have historically been disadvantaged by the nature of American elections. The sheer number of offices to be contested has forced the parties to surrender control by default. Electoral institutions, from the direct primary to the office-block ballot, have been on the side of the candidates. Now recent revolutions in the ways of campaigning threaten to make it harder for parties. New sources of political information and persuasion are available to the candidate, as are the sources of money to pay for them. They enable candidates to run campaigns and communicate with voters without the party's help. Even if the parties have more to offer candidates than they did just a few years ago, many candidates can do quite well on their own.

The result is to intensify the competition between party organizations and the parties in government over the control of campaigns. This control is critical; whoever controls the selection of candidates and the running of campaigns controls the parties. Years ago, party activists were satisfied with victory itself; their goals were to hold public office and control the preferments that flowed from it. The new activists, however, seek much more than mere victory: they seek candidates and officials who will pursue specific issues and policy options after victory. Thus, to achieve their own goals, the workers of the party organization need to assert greater control over the party's candidates and officeholders at the very time when it seems harder to do so.

The new campaigning works against the party and the party organization in another way: it reinforces the development of personalism in politics. It is the candidate, not the party, who is "sold" on TV and the other media. The new campaign techniques foster a tie between voter and candidate in which party loyalty is not as important. By controlling their own campaigns, candidates are free to pursue their own relationships with their constituents and their alliances with other, nonparty groups. The failures of the party organizations also enhance the competitive positions of other groups that want to play electoral politics and influence public policy. The new campaign techniques, then, threaten to displace the party within the voter as well as the party organization in the campaign.

Chapter 12
....
Financing
the Campaigns

*M*oney has always been a vital part of political campaigns. Consider the example of one big spender: George Washington, long before his service as president began. When Washington ran for the Virginia House of Burgesses in 1757:

> he provided his friends with the "customary means of winning votes": namely 28 gallons of rum, 50 gallons of rum punch, 34 gallons of wine, 46 gallons of beer, and 2 gallons of cider royal. Even in those days this was considered a large campaign expenditure, because there were only 391 voters in his district for an average outlay of more than a quart and a half per person.[1]

But money has never been more important in elections than it is today. In past years, the party organization contributed the volunteer labor to a campaign, and the candidate raised the money. As the parties' volunteer manpower has diminished and campaigns have come to depend more on paid professionals and television, money has become increasingly crucial in marshaling the resources necessary for serious campaigns. Candidates cannot compete without a big campaign budget, especially for state and national office.

Until the campaign finance reforms of the 1970s, much of the collecting and spending of campaign money took place in secret. Candidates were not required to disclose their funding practices, and contributors were often reluctant to be identified publicly. The few laws governing campaign contributions were full of loopholes and were regularly ignored. Large amounts of money could be raised and spent for many state and local contests without any public accounting at all.

As a result of the 1970s reforms, we now have a flood of data about campaign spending and contributions.[2] The Federal Election Commission (FEC) produces mountains of reports on the contributions and spending in U.S. House, Senate, and presidential campaigns. Yet the mind-boggling complexity of campaign finance makes it difficult to fathom even with—or perhaps because of—all these data. The tremendous volume of reports requires a great deal of effort to summarize and interpret. Regulation varies from state to state and from the state to the federal level. And it is constantly under assault by candidates and contributors who are adept at finding loopholes through which they can pursue their aims.

Amid all this change, the basic questions remain the same. How much money is spent on campaigns and who spends it? Who contributes the money? What difference have the efforts to reform campaign finance made? What is the party's role in funding campaigns?

HOW BIG HAS THE MONEY BECOME?

Total campaign spending at all levels, including both nominations and general elections, would seem to have exploded since 1960. The most authoritative source on campaign funding, Herbert Alexander and his colleagues, estimates total campaign expenditures at $4.2 *billion* in 1996, a twenty-four-fold increase over 1960 (see Table 12.1)[3] Growth in actual expenditures was especially dramatic in 1968 and 1972 and again in the 1980s.

Yet when we adjust for inflation, which has reduced the purchasing power of the dollar during this time, the increase is not as impressive (see the adjusted columns of Table 12.1). Campaign spending actually decreased from 1972 to 1976, the temporary result of reforms of the process, before surging in the next election. By the early 1990s, even with the well-funded candidacy of Ross Perot, the rise in spending had been halted. In 1996 the pattern turned upward again.

TABLE 12.1 Total Campaign Expenditures for all Offices in Presidential Years: 1960–1996

Year	Expenditures (in millions)		Percentage change since previous election	
	Actual	Inflation-Adjusted	Actual	Inflation-Adjusted
1960	$175	$175	–	–
1964	200	191	+14.3%	+9.1%
1968	300	256	+50.0	+34.0
1972	425	301	+41.7	+18.0
1976	540	281	+27.1	–6.7
1980	1,200	432	+122.2	+53.7
1984	1,800	513	+50.0	+19.0
1988	2,700	677	+50.0	+32.0
1992	3,220	681	+19.3	+.6
1996	4,177	790	+29.7	+16.0

Note: Estimates are for two-year cycles ending in the presidential election years. Inflation-adjusted figures are computed by deflating the actual expenditures by changes in the price level as measured by the Consumer Price Index using 1960 as the base year.

Sources: For campaign expenditures, John C. Green, ed., *Financing the 1996 Election* (Armonk, NY: M.E. Sharpe, 1999), p. 13. CPI deflator is based on Table No.775 in U.S. Bureau of the Census, *Statistical Abstract of the United States: 1999* (Washington, DC: U.S. Government Printing Office, 1999), p. 493.

Presidential Campaigns

The most expensive campaigns for public office in the United States are those for the presidency (Table 12.2). The size of these campaign budgets varies depending on the amount of competition in the primaries and the willingness of the candidates to refuse federal funding (and its accompanying fund-raising limits) and raise all their campaign money themselves. Texas Governor George W. Bush decided to do just that in the 2000 nomination race, and had pulled in almost $80 million in contributions before even half of the primaries were over.

Congressional Campaigns

Individual House and Senate races are run on much more meager budgets, though their collective cost has surpassed that of the presidential race in recent years (Table 12.3).[4] The total spending is higher in House contests simply because there are many more House races in a given year than there are Senate races. The actual spending figures have generally increased during the past thirty years. When we examine the figures adjusted for inflation, however, the picture is different. Now we find that the purchasing power of House expenditures actually declined more often than it increased, and Senate spending went up only a little more often than it went down. In real dollars, then, campaign spending in congressional races has not changed markedly from one election to the next. Only in the hotly contested 1978 and 1992 elections

TABLE 12.2 Total Spending by Candidates, Parties, and Groups in Presidential General Elections: 1960–1996

Year	Expenditures (in millions) Actual	Expenditures (in millions) Inflation-Adjusted	Percentage change since previous election Actual	Percentage change since previous election Inflation-Adjusted
1960	$30.0	$30.0	–	–
1964	60.0	57.3	+100.0%	+91.0%
1968	100.0	85.2	+66.7	+48.7
1972	138.0	97.8	+38.0	+14.8
1976	160.0	83.3	+15.9	−14.8
1980	275.0	99.1	+71.9	+19.0
1984	325.0	92.6	+18.2	−6.6
1988	500.0	125.4	+53.8	+35.4
1992	550.0	116.3	+10.0	−7.3
1996	700.0	132.4	+27.3	+13.8

Note: Estimates are for two-year cycles ending in the presidential election years. Inflation-adjusted figures are computed by deflating the actual expenditures by changes in the price level as measured by the Consumer Price Index (yearly averages) using 1960 as the base year.

Source: John C. Green, ed., *Financing the1996 Election* (Armonk, NY: M.E. Sharpe, 1999), Table 2.5, p. 19, for actual spending. The CPI deflator is the same as that listed for Table 12.1.

TABLE 12.3 Total Spending by Candidates in Congressional Campaigns, 1971–1972 to 1997–1998

	Expenditures (in millions)				Percentage change since previous election			
	Actual		Inflation-Adjusted		Actual		Inflation-Adjusted	
Year	House	Senate	House	Senate	House	Senate	House	Senate
1971–1972	$46.5	$30.7	$46.5	$30.7	–	–	–	–
1973–1974	53.5	34.7	45.4	29.4	+15.1	+13.0	−2.4	−4.2
1975–1976	71.5	44.0	52.5	32.3	+33.6	+26.8	+15.6	+9.9
1977–1978	109.7	85.2	70.3	54.6	+53.4	+93.6	+33.9	+69.0
1979–1980	136.0	102.9	69.1	52.3	+24.0	+20.8	−1.7	−4.2
1981–1982	204.0	138.4	88.3	59.9	+50.0	+34.5	+27.8	+14.5
1983–1984	203.6	170.5	81.8	68.5	−.2	+23.2	−7.4	+14.4
1985–1986	239.3	211.6	91.4	80.8	+17.5	+24.1	+11.7	+18.0
1987–1988	256.5	201.2	90.8	71.2	+7.2	−4.9	−.7	−11.9
1989–1990	265.8	180.4	85.2	57.8	+3.6	−10.3	−6.2	−18.8
1991–1992	406.7	271.6	121.3	81.0	+53.0	+50.6	+42.4	+40.1
1993–1994	406.2	319.0	114.7	90.0	−.1	+17.5	−5.4	+11.1
1995–1996	477.8	287.5	127.5	76.7	+17.6	−9.9	+11.2	−14.8
1997–1998	452.5	287.8	113.6	72.2	−5.3	0	−10.9	−5.9

Note: Estimates are for two-year cycles ending in the presidential and midterm election years. Inflation-adjusted figures are computed by deflating the actual expenditures by changes in the price level as measured by the Consumer Price Index (yearly averages) using 1972 as the base year.

Source: John C. Green, ed., *Financing the1996 Election* (Armonk, NY: M.E. Sharpe, 1999), Table 2.7, p. 23 for actual spending through 1995-1996; FEC Wec page release http://www.fec.gov/press/canye98.htm for 1997-1998. CPI deflator is the same as that listed for Table 12.1.

were major increases recorded. More substantial growth in campaign costs has taken place at the state and local level.[5]

Yet all these figures, state and federal, tell only part of the story. Although the increase in total campaign spending has outstripped increases in the cost of most other items in the economy, it still doesn't match the amounts some large corporations spend each year to advertise soap and cigarettes (see box on p. 234). Given the value of learning about the candidates for leadership positions in a democracy relative to the value of learning about the attributes of soaps and cigarette brands, it may be that the amounts spent on campaigns are a real bargain.

WHO SPENDS THE CAMPAIGN MONEY?

In most other democracies it is the parties that do the campaign spending. In the American system most campaign money is spent by the candidates' own campaign organizations. But parties and other groups, especially political action committees (PACs),

Campaign Spending: Too Much or Too Little?

What will $4.2 billion buy in the United States?

- About four fifths of the tobacco advertising run in 1998
- A year's advertising for General Motors plus Proctor & Gamble
- Eight percent of the amount spent yearly on gambling
- About twice the amount Americans paid for basketball sneakers in 1998
- Two B-2 bombers
- All the political campaigns run at all levels of government by and for all candidates in 1996

Sources: http://www.cdc.gov/tobacco/adv-pro.htm (on tobacco advertising); http://www.mind-advertising.com/us/us_advs.htm (on GM and Proctor & Gamble); *CQ Weekly*, October 23, 1999, p. 2496 (on gambling); http://sportlink.furfly.net/press_room/1998releases/afa98-3.html (on basketball sneakers); http://www.dote.osd.mil/reports/FY98/airforce/98b2.html (on the B-2 bomber).

have roles in campaign funding as well. To understand the flow of money in American campaigns, we must disentangle the various actors who disburse it.

Presidential Campaigns

Becoming a party's nominee for president requires a great deal of money. In the 1996 presidential race, a grand total of $700 million was spent in the primaries and general election, including $282.5 million prior to the parties' nominating conventions (see Table 12.4). Of that total, Robert Dole's campaign spent more than $42 million simply for the right to run as the Republican nominee in that year, and President Bill Clinton, with only nominal opposition for the nomination, spent $38 million. Even candidates who lost the nomination race by a mile parted with millions of dollars for the privilege. Steve Forbes, a wealthy businessman, spent $4 million on the 1996 Iowa caucuses alone and almost $42 million in the nomination contest before he withdrew in mid-March; nearly $38 million of that total came from Forbes's personal fortune. He won only 70 convention delegates, at a "cost" of about $600,000 a delegate. Forbes spent another $41 million by the end of January in the 2000 race, with similar results.

The price goes up in the general election, but the candidates get their money from other sources. Since the campaign finance reforms of the 1970s, all major party candidates have accepted federal funds to run their general election campaigns. (The story of these reforms—and the many loopholes that have weakened them—will be told later in this chapter.) To get the federal money, candidates must agree to raise no other funds (with the exception of money they need to pay the lawyers and accountants required to fill out the FEC forms). Thus in 1996 the Clinton and Dole general election campaigns

TABLE 12.4 Costs of Nominating and Electing a President: 1996

	Amount (in millions)
I. Prenomination	
Spending by major party candidates	$228.6
RNC spending on Dole nomination campaign	14.0
DNC spending on Clinton nomination campaign	17.0
Compliance costs	10.0
Independent expenditures	.7
Communication costs	1.1
Spending by minor-party candidates	11.7
Prenomination Total	$282.5
II. Conventions	
Republicans' expenditures	$31.0
Democrats' expenditures	34.0
Conventions Total	$65.0
III. General Election	
Spending by major-party candidates	$125.2
Parties' coordinated expenditures	18.4
Parties' soft money, issue advertising	68.0
Independent expenditures	.7
Communication costs	1.6
Expenditures by labor, corporations, and associations	20.0
Nonparty organizations	25.0
Spending by minor parties	27.6
Compliance costs	13.6
General Election Total	$300.1
Miscellaneous Expenses	$ 52.4
Grand Total	*$700.0*

Source: John C. Green, ed., *Financing the 1996 Election* (Armonk, NY: M.E. Sharpe, 1999), Table 2.3, p. 17.

were able to spend $61.8 million each plus the money needed for accountants and lawyers (listed as "compliance costs" in Table 12.4).

As Table 12.4 indicates, then, more of the total spending is done by the candidates' own campaigns in the nomination race than in the general election. The implications are important. The candidates' campaigns are (largely) under their own control; spending by other groups in the election is not and thus may emphasize themes or appeals that the candidate would prefer to avoid. Most of the remaining spending is "friendly fire" laid down by the parties' committees. But other spenders can affect voter perceptions of candidates in the general election.

Who are the other spenders listed in Table 12.4? The major party organizations spent a great deal on their national conventions and also spent money themselves in the general election on advertising, consultants, and other services to support their party's candidate, both in coordinated expenditures and in soft money. (We will look more closely at these types of spending later.) Individuals and PACs (and now party organizations) are permitted to spend as much as they choose on behalf of or in opposition to a candidate; under the law, this spending must be done without the knowledge or cooperation of any candidate or party. These *independent expenditures* vary a lot from election to election.[6]

Communication costs involve spending by organizations to urge their workers or members to vote for a particular candidate; labor unions account for most of them. Additional expenditures by labor unions, corporations, and membership associations in "nonpartisan" voter mobilization—mainly in programs to register voters and get them to the polls on election day—totaled a substantial $20 million in 1996, again most of it spent by labor unions.[7]

Congressional Campaigns

Candidates for Congress in 1996 spent a total of $764 million in the primaries and general elections (see Table 12.3). In campaigning for the midterm elections of 1998, the candidates' spending total dipped to $740 million. The candidates themselves are normally the biggest spenders in the congressional contests. Since it is the candidates who control the money, our attention should be primarily focused on them.[8]

One of the cardinal rules of modern campaign finance is that incumbent officeholders vastly outspend their challengers in campaigns for Congress. In the 1991–1992 electoral cycle, the spending edge for incumbents was almost 1.8 to 1; in 1997–1998, it increased to 2.4 to 1. But the partisan beneficiaries of this rule have changed. Until 1994, most congressional incumbents in most election years were Democrats, so Democrats were normally able to outspend Republicans in congressional elections. In 1992, for example, Democratic candidates outspent Republicans by 1.25 to 1. But the electoral tides were running Republican in 1994; Republican candidates were able to increase their spending by almost 25 percent overall, which put them ahead of the Democrats ($371 million to $359 million), and the Republican Party won majorities in both the House and the Senate for the first time since 1954. The Republicans' new status as the majority party gave them an even greater financial advantage going into the 1996 House and Senate elections, and again in 1998.

Looking beneath these totals, we see a great deal of variation in individual campaigns. A typical Senate candidate now spends several million dollars in the general election; the average general election spending in 1998 Senate contests was $3.6 million. Except in the case of token challengers, a serious Senate campaign will cost not less than a million dollars, even in a small state. Record spending in Senate races increases by the decade. North Carolina's Senator Jesse Helms spent $13.4 million to set a spending record in the 1980s; in 1994, Republicans Oliver North and Michael Huffington, the losing Senate candidates in Virginia and California, respectively, spent $20.6 million and $28 million in their efforts to beat Democratic incumbents. In 2000, former investment banker Jon Corzine set a new record by spending more than $33 million *in the primary election alone* to defeat a prominent New Jersey Democrat for nomination to the U.S. Senate. The average 1998 House general election campaign, by contrast, cost less than $493,000–up from an average of $481,000 in 1996. But a growing number of

House candidates are running million-dollar campaigns; in 1998, according to the FEC, the leaders were then-Speaker Newt Gingrich ($7.6 million), Phil Maloof of New Mexico ($5.4 million), and Christopher Gabrieli of Massachusetts ($5.3 million).

The candidates are not the only important spenders in congressional campaigns. The parties invest money in races for Congress in addition to the sums they give directly to the candidates. Their House and Senate campaign committees, national committees, and state and local committees spent almost $53.6 million on behalf of candidates of their parties in 1995–1996; Republican committees considerably outspent the Democrats. Corporations, labor unions, and other organizations also invest money directly in campaign activities. The money is intended to encourage their members to oppose or support particular candidates and to convince voters to go to the polls.[9]

State and Local Campaigns

We know much less about spending practices in the thousands of campaigns for state and local office, mainly because there is no central reporting agency comparable to the FEC. The range in these races is tremendous. Many state and local candidates win after spending a few hundred dollars. On the other hand, candidates for mayor in a large city are likely to spend millions. In Dallas in the late 1980s, a mayoralty candidate spent more than $1 million to win a job that pays $50 per week.

Campaigns for governor of the larger states often cost as much as or more than races for the U.S. Senate; California typically sets the records. Successful contests for the state legislature in large states now sometimes require more than $100,000, and spending in these contests seems to be growing more rapidly than for any other office. Again, the most expensive contests are usually found in California. By 1990, the average expenditure per seat in the lower house of the California legislature had surpassed $512,000,[10] and some particularly competitive contests drove that cost up far more.

WHAT IS THE IMPACT OF CAMPAIGN SPENDING?

Money does not buy victory—but it certainly doesn't hurt, either. In the general election for president, both sides have enough money to reach voters with their messages, so the candidate with the largest war chest does not gain an overwhelming advantage. Money matters more in the nomination race for president, especially in buying the early visibility that is so vital to an underdog. Nevertheless, a big budget did not make Steve Forbes a front-runner, and once a candidate has qualified for federal matching funds, the advantage money can confer narrows considerably.

The best evidence we have about the impact of campaign spending refers to congressional races. Researchers conclude that in these elections, money makes a real difference. The more challengers can spend when they run against incumbents, the better their chances of victory become. The same is not always true for incumbents. Gary Jacobson found that the more incumbents spend, the worse they do in the race. It is not that incumbent spending turns voters away, but rather that incumbents tend to spend a lot when they face serious competition. A big budget for an incumbent, then, signals that he or she has (or expects) an unusually strong challenger.

Other researchers have challenged this conclusion. They argue that when incumbents spend more, they do get a return in terms of votes. The dispute turns on thorny questions about the proper way to estimate the impact of spending, but it does establish two points. First, House incumbents rarely face a serious challenge for re-election. Second, when they do have a strong opponent, incumbents may not be able to survive the challenge by pouring more money into their reelection effort.[11]

These findings have important implications for current efforts to reform campaign spending. If both incumbents and challengers have a better chance of winning as their campaign spending increases, then reforms that limit campaign spending will not advantage either one. But if challengers get more votes when they spend more, while incumbents' chances decline or are unaffected by increased spending, then putting a ceiling on campaign spending would benefit incumbents. It seems likely that challengers need to spend more than their incumbent opponents just in order to compensate for all the advantages incumbents have in campaigns: greater name recognition, more media coverage, greater experience, and so on. Most members of Congress have assumed, following Jacobson, that spending limits would in fact favor incumbents. Therefore, in congressional debates about campaign finance reform, members of the majority party are more likely to support proposals to cap spending in congressional races.

Some kinds of spending may not always benefit the candidates it is designed to support. Perhaps the best example is independent spending, the funds that individuals, groups, or parties are permitted to spend without limit in federal campaigns as long as they do not coordinate their plans with a candidate's campaign. In recent years, most independent spending has favored Republican candidates in both presidential and congressional races. Yet the spending, because it must be made independently of the candidates' campaign plans and strategies, may not communicate the message the campaign would prefer. A group called Americans for Job Security, for instance, spent $2 million to defeat Democratic House member Frank Pallone in 1998—twice Pallone's entire campaign budget—but flooded the airwaves with so much negative advertising that Pallone's opponent felt it may have helped the incumbent win re-election.[12]

Similarly, the communications costs incurred by labor unions overwhelmingly support Democrats yet their effectiveness is unclear. Labor support can be the kiss of death in some areas, especially when opponents make it a campaign issue. It is just as difficult to measure the effects of "nonpartisan" voter registration and get-out-the-vote drives. They are nonpartisan on the surface, but the unions, corporations, and associations that mount them usually do so in the confidence that they are mobilizing voters strongly in favor of one party or ideological preference.

SOURCES OF FUNDS IN FEDERAL CAMPAIGNS

Where does the money come from? Candidates raise their campaign funds from five main sources: individual contributors, political action committees, political parties, the candidates' own resources, and public funds. There are no other sources from which candidates can raise significant amounts of money. Campaign finance reform, then, cannot do much more than mandate a different mix among these five or try to eliminate one or more of these sources altogether (Table 12.5).

TABLE 12.5 Sources of Campaign Funds for Presidential and Congressional Candidates (in millions)

	Presidential, 1995–1996					
	Democrats		*Republicans*		*Total*	
	Nomination	*General*	*Nomination*	*General*	*Nomination*	*General*
Individuals	$31.3	0	$93.1	0	$126.5	$4.3
Candidates	0	0	44.0	0	52.3	0
PACs	0	0	0	0	0	0
Party	0	6.7	0	11.6	0	18.3
Public Funds	14.0	61.8	41.6	61.8	56.0	152.7
Other	.8	0	8.4	0	9.2	0
TOTAL	$46.2	$68.5	$187.0	$73.4	$244.0	$175.3

	Congressional, 1997–1998						
	Democrats		*Republicans*		*Total*		*Grand Total*
	House	*Senate*	*House*	*Senate*	*House*	*Senate*	
Individuals	$115.3	$81.3	$138.0	$85.2	$256.0	$166.8	$422.8
Candidates							
Contributions	1.6	.5	3.7	.9	5.4	1.4	6.7
Loans	27.3	19.5	19.6	32.7	48.2	52.3	100.4
PACs	77.7	20.7	80.9	27.3	158.7	48.1	206.8
Party	1.5	.3	2.1	.5	3.6	.8	4.5
Party Coordinated	4.6	9.3	6.3	9.3	10.9	18.7	29.6
Public Funding	0	0	0	0	0	0	0
Other	.4	.2	.9	0	1.4	.2	1.6
TOTAL	$228.4	$131.8	$251.5	$155.9	$484.2	$288.3	$772.4

Note: The figures are for the two-year cycles ending in the presidential and midterm election years. Candidate loans are personal loans by the candidate to her or his campaign. The total columns include funds for Democratic, Republican, and other candidates.

Source: For the presidential nomination campaign, FEC data from http://www.fec.gov/pres96/presmstr.htm#receipts; for Congress, http://www.fec.gov/press/allsum98.htm

Individual Contributors

It is one of the best kept secrets in American politics that individual contributors still dominate campaign finance. Although public funding has greatly reduced the role of the individual donor in presidential general elections, individuals still fund most of the nomination races, both by their contributions and through the federal matching funds they generate. Individuals also donate the largest portion of congressional campaign funds. In 1997–1998 individuals accounted for 52 percent of the contributions to House candidates and 58 percent of all of the money given to Senate candidates. Data on state elections are more scarce, but it is likely that individual contributors also provide the majority of funds for state campaigns.[13]

There has been a big change, however, in the nature of the individual contributor. Prior to the campaign finance reforms of 1974, congressional and presidential candidates were allowed to solicit large sums of money from individual givers. The contributions of W. Clement Stone and Richard Mellon Scaife (see the box below) were notable examples. Well-supported fears that these "fat cats" were getting something in return for their money—in the form of government largesse ranging from tax breaks to plum federal posts—led Congress to set a maximum of $1,000 on donations to any single candidate for federal office. "Fat cats" could no longer expect to have the influence on candidates that they had exercised for so long.

Since the reforms, congressional campaigns have been financed not by a handful of large contributors but by large numbers of people making small contributions. Small contributors also dominate the nomination phase of the presidential campaigns. Even these small contributors, though, comprise a very unrepresentative slice of the American electorate. Generally speaking, they are older, more involved in politics, more conservative,

Pioneers in Political Fund-Raising

Mark Hanna, an Ohio industrialist, was one of the most prodigious fund-raisers in American history. Hanna personally funded the nomination campaign of William McKinley in 1896 and then raised most of the reputed $6 to 7 million (the equivalent of almost $100 million in current dollars) spent in McKinley's successful general election campaign. Hanna extracted campaign contributions from American corporations with an accountant's precision. "Banks, for instance, were assessed one quarter of one percent of their capital; Standard Oil contributed about a quarter of a million dollars, and the large insurance companies slightly less. If a company sent in a check Hanna believed to be too small, it was returned; if a company paid too much, a refund was sent out." Hanna's accomplishments outraged enough reformers to result in two federal laws: a prohibition of corporate contributions in 1907 and a campaign fund disclosure law in 1910.

The era of the big contributors ended with the greatest feat of fund raising in the twentieth century: the collection of more than $60 million for the reelection campaign of President Richard Nixon in 1972. Two individuals—Chicago insurance magnate W. Clement Stone and Richard Mellon Scaife, heir to the Mellon fortune—donated $3 million between them. Some of this money was illegally diverted to finance the Watergate break-in and related activities. These breaches of law, as well as the unprecedented level of Nixon's fund-raising, stimulated reforms of campaign fund-raising that ended more than a century's reliance on large contributors.

In that same presidential election, attention was first drawn to the pioneer of computerized direct mail fund-raising. Richard Viguerie used contributor lists from two failed presidential candidates—Barry Goldwater and George Wallace—to build a computerized list of millions of donors to conservative causes and candidates. For a fee (averaging 50 percent of the proceeds) and access to his client's own contributor list, Viguerie devoted his fund-raising talents to conservative candidates and causes. Despite its high initial cost, computerized direct mail has become the principal means of raising campaign funds as a result of the 1970s campaign finance reforms.[14]

and more affluent than the average American.[15] Still, they resemble the typical American voter far more closely than did the storied fat cats of a generation ago.

Over the years, parties and candidates have devised innumerable ways to separate prospective contributors from their money. Personal visits, phone calls, and conversations with the candidate or campaign workers are the preferred form of soliciting larger contributions. Group events—a gala dinner or a briefing from a top adviser—also help to bring in large sums. Increasingly, however, political money is raised by mail, especially from small contributors, with the use of computerized mailing lists and the technology for personalizing letters. Mailing lists of dependable donors, in fact, have become one of the most treasured resources in modern campaign politics.

Prior to 1994, individual donors had typically been more generous to Democratic congressional candidates than to Republicans. In the 1993–1994 election cycle, however—consistent with the findings reported earlier about fund-raising more generally—Republican candidates raised 21 percent more from individual contributors than did their opponents. By 1997–1998 the Republican edge was 14 percent. As long as they remain in the majority in the House and Senate, Republicans may be able to maintain this edge for some time.

The Soft Money Loophole

When Congress provided federal funding for presidential general elections, beginning in the early 1970s, in another effort to limit the "fat cats," the spending ceilings in the bill led candidates to put most of their scarce resources into media advertising. The presidential campaigns spent much less on the traditional paraphernalia of campaign buttons, leaflets, and bumper stickers. Local and state parties objected that they were hit hard by the reform; these traditional activities were vital in drumming up enthusiasm among party loyalists. So as a means of strengthening the state and local parties, the new law in 1979 exempted *soft money* from federal regulation; that is, the money raised and spent by state and local parties for volunteer, voter registration, and get-out-the-vote activities—even if those activities were conducted in support of a presidential or congressional campaign.

The law was interpreted to allow unlimited contributions not only to be donated to state and local parties but also to pass through the national party committees on their way to the state parties. This soft money has become a way for individuals, corporations, and labor unions to avoid the contribution limits set by the 1970s reforms. Even though individuals can give no more than $1,000 each to a federal candidate per election, individuals can provide unlimited amounts of money to the parties as soft money which can then be channeled into spending on presidential and congressional races. The result has been to give big individual contributors a way to reenter federal campaigns.

Tremendous sums of money have flowed through the soft-money conduit in recent years (see box on p. 242). In 1996, for example, $262 million in soft money was raised by the major natoinal party committees. State parties do not have to report soft money repeipts to the FEC. Most of this total was generated by the efforts of the Democratic National Committee ($101.9 million) and the Republican National Committee ($113.1 million). The Democrats' fund-raising practices, in fact, proved to be a major controversy

The New Fat Cats:
Soft-Money Donors in the 2000s

Both political parties raise hundreds of millions of dollars in soft-money contributions from a few wealthy individuals, corporations, or organizations. The top ten soft money donors in 2000 (as of July 1) included eight corporations and two labor unions. The Democrats' biggest contributors were the Communications Workers of America ($1.6 million) and the American Federation of State County and Municipal Employees, which is a public employees' union ($1.9 million). The other eight big givers provided most of their money to Republican candidates. They were AT&T ($2.2 million), Philip Morris ($1.3 million to both parties), Microsoft ($1.3 million), Freddie Mac ($1.2 million), SBC Communications ($1.1 million), Citigroup ($1.1 million), UPS ($1 million) and Verizon Communications ($1 million).[16]

in the campaign. A substantial portion of this money came from individuals who had pledged at least $100,000 apiece, but large contributions were also made by corporations, PACs, and labor unions.[17]

Political Action Committees

Political action committees (PACs) are political committees other than party committees that raise and spend money to influence election outcomes. The great majority of PACs have been created by a sponsoring parent organization; that is, they are PACs of corporations, labor unions, and membership associations. Some, however, have no sponsoring organization and thus are called *nonconnected* PACs; these are most likely to be ideological PACs of the right or the left. The PACs spend their money in several different ways. Some, especially the ideological PACs, may use it in independent expenditures, as we have seen. Most often, however, PACs contribute the money directly to candidates.

Only 608 PACs were operating in national elections in 1974; but by the beginning of 2000 that number had climbed to 3835. The greatest growth over time has come in the number of corporate and nonconnected PACs. Corporate PACs climbed from 15 percent of the 1974 total to 40 percent by 2000, and nonconnected PACs grew from 0 to 25 percent during this same period; the number of labor and association PACs increased as well.[18]

A number of factors account for that growth. Most important was the reform legislation of the post-Watergate years. The Federal Election Campaign Act of 1974, in its zeal to limit the big individual spenders of American politics, put the limit on individual contributions far below that for PACs. Thus campaigns found it more efficient to raise money from PACs than from contacts with individual donors. The new law also explicitly permitted corporations doing business with government to have PACs, which clarified a previous law that had barred direct or indirect contributions to federal election campaigns by government contractors. Federal court decisions and the

FEC confirmed the legality of PACs and the right of sponsoring organizations to pay their administrative and overhead expenses. Their political funds, though, must be collected and kept separately in what federal statutes call a *separate segregated fund*; under federal law, the sponsoring corporation or labor union may not use its regular assets and revenues for political expenditures.

Although PACs are often portrayed as bullies with checkbooks, they are not the primary sources of campaign money. Because of public funding, PACs do not contribute directly to presidential general election campaigns. They can contribute to candidates for the presidential nominations, but these contributions have tended to be modest in recent years ($2.5 million in 1995–1996). PACs can also make independent expenditures for or against presidential candidates. This independent spending totaled only $800,000 in the 1995–1996 electoral cycle.

The bulk of PAC contributions instead go to congressional candidates. PACs gave a total of $206.8 million to House and Senate candidates in 1997–1998 (Table 12.5), a slight increase over the prior election cycle. Of the 1997–1998 total, the largest amounts came from corporate PACs (34 percent) and PACs of trade associations (29 percent). Nonconnected PACs added 13 percent, and labor PACs gave 21 percent. Even these large numbers, however, accounted for only a quarter of all the money received by congressional candidates in 1997–1998 (26.7 percent).

So PACs, though they are an important source of campaign contributions, are not the big spenders that they may seem. Further, there is no single, monolithic PAC "interest"; these PAC totals are the collective contributions of several thousand different PACs representing a number of diverse and sometimes even competing interests. Although corporate PACs are the largest PAC givers, donating almost twice as much to Republicans as to Democrats, there are both business and labor PACs among the biggest PAC spenders (see Table 12.6). Further, because labor PACs concentrate almost all of their money on Democratic candidates, they help to compensate for the Republican edge in corporate contributions. Other types of PACs give to candidates from both parties.

Most PAC money is intended to gain access for the giver rather than to achieve a partisan or ideological aim. The result is that most PAC contributions go to incumbents; there is little advantage, after all, in getting access to a likely loser. PAC money, like individual donations, therefore flows to the party with the most incumbents, and since the 1994 elections, that has been the Republicans.

Candidates pursue the PACs at least as seriously as they pursue individual contributors. Both parties' congressional and senatorial campaign committees put their candidates in touch with PACs likely to be sympathetic to their causes, and the parties are increasingly active in channeling PAC money directly to candidates. Candidates and their campaign managers also seek PAC help directly, assisted by the directories and information services that list PACs by their issue positions, the size of their resources, and their previous contributions. Incumbent Congress members invite PACs or the lobbyists of their parent organizations to fund-raising parties in Washington at which a check earns the PAC people hors d'oeuvres, drinks, and, they hope, legislative gratitude. PACs take the initiative as well. Unlike most individual contributors, they are in the business of making political contributions and they don't necessarily wait to be asked.[19]

TABLE 12.6 The Top-Ten List of the Biggest PACs (In Contributions
to Federal Candidates, 1997–1998)

		Contributions to federal candidates		
Rank	PAC	Democrats	Republicans	Total
1.	Realtors PAC	$1 million	$1.5 million	$2.5 million
2.	Association of Trial Lawyers of America PAC	2.1	.3	2.4
3.	American Federation of State, County & Municipal Employees*	2.3	<.1	2.4
4.	American Medical Association PAC	.7	1.7	2.3
5.	Democratic Republican Independent Voter Education Committee	(na)	(na)	2.2
6.	National Automobile Dealers Association PAC	.6	1.5	2.1
7.	United Auto Workers Voluntary Community Action Program*	1.9	<.1	1.9
8.	International Brotherhood of Electrical Workers PAC*	1.8	<.1	1.9
9.	National Education Association PAC*	1.8	<.1	1.9
10.	National Association of Home Builders Guild PAC	.5	1.3	1.8

Note: *Labor union PACs. Totals do not always add up to 100% due to rounding error.

Source: http://www.opensecrets.org. Opensecrets is a nonprofit group that tracks PAC spending and lobbying. Its data are from FEC reports.

What do PACs buy with their donations to congressional campaigns? Certainly their contributions do help them get access to lawmakers. What elected officials will fail to listen to representatives of interests that have provided money for their political campaigns? It is harder to determine, however, how hard they listen and whether the PAC's concerns will influence their legislative behavior. There is not much evidence that PAC contributions affect the recipients' roll call votes.[20] But legislators who receive PAC money do seem to become more active in congressional committees on behalf of issues of concern to their PAC donors.[21]

There are many reasons why PAC money rarely "buys" votes. A single PAC can give no more than $5,000 to a member of Congress in each election or $10,000 for the primary and general election together; in fact, the great majority of PACs give much less. That puts most PACs in the ranks of "small" contributors. PACs give most of their money to incumbents, who normally have a relatively easy time raising other campaign funds. PAC contributions also flow mainly to legislators who have already demonstrated their support of the PAC's issues rather than to legislators who are not yet convinced. As a result, PAC contributions are not as politically potent as they might otherwise be.

Some PACs seem unable to pursue the most effective strategies for influencing legislators because their local members, who provide most of these PACs' money, want to support local incumbents even when these incumbents are not helpful to the national PAC.[22] Finally, PACs have a great deal of competition—from party leaders, constituents, and other PACs—for the ear and the vote of a legislator. They are most likely to succeed in this competition when they represent powerful constituency interests and do not encounter party opposition or when their issue is of little concern to anyone else.

Political Parties

With so much political money flowing, it is easy to lose sight of the party role in campaign finance. Yet the parties are important players in raising and spending campaign money. They invest considerable resources in party activities during the nomination phase and in running the parties' conventions. They also, as we have seen, channel their increasingly rich flow of soft money into supporting the general party ticket in campaigns.

The parties' direct contributions are only a tiny portion of the candidates' campaign budgets. More substantial are the two parties' *coordinated expenditures*—the funds they spend on behalf of their candidates, typically for services such as polls, television and radio ads, fund-raising, and consultants' fees. The limit for coordinated expenditures by national party organizations in the 2000 House campaigns was $33,780 per election (with the primary and general elections counted as separate contests). In Senate campaigns it varied with the state's population size: from $135,120 in Delaware to $3.3 million in California. Counting direct contributions by party's national committee, the relevant congressional campaign committee, and the state party, plus two elections' worth of coordinated spending, then, each party could spend almost $100,000 in a House race and much more in a Senate race. Coordinated spending is particularly useful to the party not only because it allows the party organizations greater opportunities to contribute, but also because party committees have more control over how the money is spent than they do in making direct contributions to candidates.

Even these coordinated expenditures, however, amounted to only about 4 percent of the candidates' total spending in 1997–1998. These figures suggest how much more money the parties will have to raise and spend before they can reestablish a major role for themselves in American elections or achieve the position in financing and running campaigns that parties assume in the other democracies of the world. That the party money now comes mainly from party committees in Congress as vehicles of the party in government, rather than the party organizations, also makes an important point about the party presence in American campaigns: that the power lies with the elected officials, not with party leaders and activists.

The Candidates Themselves

Candidates have always spent their personal wealth on their campaigns, but that has been especially true in recent years. The prime example is Ross Perot, whose personal fortune underwrote his presidential campaign in 1992; FEC reports show that he invested more than $63 million of his own money. (He accepted taxpayer funding in 1996.) In 1997–1998, congressional candidates bankrolled their campaigns to the tune of $6.7 million plus $100.4 million in loans, representing 14 percent of all their campaign money (Table 12.5). The averages can be greatly inflated by a few wealthy candidates, however. In 1993–1994 congressional fund-raising, for example, just one candidate, Michael Huffington of California, accounted for almost a quarter of the total personal contributions and loans.

Public Funding

Finally, public funding is available for presidential campaigns if the candidate wishes to accept it—and thus, of course, to accept the spending limits that come along with it. Congress voted in the early 1970s to let taxpayers designate a dollar (now $3) of their tax payments to match small contributions to candidates for their party's presidential nomination and to foot the total bill for the major-party nominees in the general election campaign, mainly as a means of limiting campaign corruption. In 1996, public matching funds in the nomination race and the general election campaign totaled $208.7 million, which is 50 percent of all candidate spending in the nomination contests and general election (see Table 12.5), and 30 percent of the total costs of those campaigns. Congress has chosen not to extend public funding to its own races.

SOURCES OF FUNDS
AT THE STATE AND LOCAL LEVEL

Evidence suggests that national patterns generally prevail in state and local campaigns as well. Individual contributors are the most important source of campaign funds, followed by PAC contributions and then, at greater distance, by party and personal funds. A minority of states and even some cities (for example, New York City) provide public funding, but it generally defrays only a small portion of the campaign costs and often goes to parties rather than candidates.[23]

There are a few interesting differences, however, between federal and state or local campaign finance. One is that individual contributions are relatively more important in local campaigns because parties and PACs play a lesser role at this level. There are, as always, exceptions; in Oregon, Pennsylvania, and Washington, PACs have provided at least a third of the campaign funds for legislative candidates compared to 13 percent in Wisconsin and 12 percent in Missouri.[24] In addition, legislative leaders and legislative caucuses in an increasing number of states are supplying campaign funds to their party's state legislative candidates. Because many states do not limit campaign contributions in state legislative contests, such donations can play a significant role in a candidate's campaign.[25]

REFORM OF THE CAMPAIGN FINANCE RULES

For years, campaign finance laws in the United States were a jerry-built structure of halfhearted and not very well integrated federal and state statutes. Periodically reformers tried to strengthen legal controls over the raising and spending of campaign money. A new episode of reform was under way in the early 1970s when the Watergate scandals broke over the country. The result in 1974 was the most extensive federal legislation on the subject in the history of the Republic.

The Supreme Court, acting in 1976, invalidated some of these 1974 reforms. Congress then moved to revise the law and in the late 1970s to amend it again. The resulting legislation has two main parts: it limits campaign contributions and spending, and it sets up a system of public funding for presidential campaigns.[26]

Limitations on Contributions

The law limits the amounts of money an individual, a PAC, and a party organization can give to a candidate in each federal election (primary or general) or for the year (see Table 12.7). These limits apply only to federal campaigns—those for president and Congress. Corporations and labor unions are not allowed to contribute directly but they may set up political action committees and pay their overhead and administrative costs. These limits have gone a long way toward reducing the role of "fat cats" in campaigns. Now big contributors can give unlimited amounts only if they spend independently on behalf of a candidate or if they give soft money to a party organization.

Spending Limits

Spending by presidential candidates was also limited by the 1970s reform. Those who accept federal money in the race for their party's nomination must also accept spending limits in each of the fifty states. These limits are set according to the state's voting-age population and ranged in 1996 from a high of $11.3 million in California to a low of $618,000 in the smallest states. In the general election campaign, presidential candidates who accept federal subsidies can spend no more than the law permits.

Congress tried to limit spending in House and Senate campaigns as well, but the Supreme Court would not agree. A coalition of strange bedfellows, including conservative New York Senator James Buckley, liberal Democratic Senator Eugene McCarthy, and the New York Civil Liberties Union, attacked the campaign reform law, arguing that its restrictions on campaign spending infringed on the rights to free speech and political activity. The Court agreed. In a 1976 decision it ruled that Congress could limit campaign spending but only as a condition for accepting public subsidies of campaigns.[27] So Congress could apply spending limits to its own campaigns only as part of a plan for subsidizing them. That would mean subsidizing their challengers' campaigns as well. For congressional incumbents, who are normally quite capable of outraising their challengers, that was not an attractive prospect.

TABLE 12.7 Limits on Campaign Contributions Under Federal Law

	Limit on Contributions		
	Individual	*Political Action Committee*	*Party Committee*
To candidate or candidate committee per election	$1,000	$5,000*	$5,000*
To national party committee per year	$20,000	$15,000	no limit
To any nonparty committee (PAC) per year	$5,000	$5,000	$5,000
Total contributions per year	$25,000	no limit	no limit

Note: *If the political action committee or the party committee qualifies as a "multicandidate committee" under federal law by making contributions to five or more federal candidates, the limit is $5,000. Otherwise the PAC is treated as an individual with a limit of $1,000. Party committees can contribute up to $17,500 to Senate candidates.

Source: Adapted from Federal Election Commission, *Campaign Guide* (June, 1985).

Public Disclosure

A vital part of the reform was the requirement that contributions and spending be disclosed publicly. The principle was that if voters had access to information about the sources of candidates' cash, they could punish greedy or corrupt campaigners with their ballots. All donations to a federal candidate must now go through and be accounted for by a single campaign committee; before the reforms candidates could avoid full public disclosure by using a complex array of committees. Each candidate must file quarterly reports on his or her finances and then supplement them with reports ten days before the election and thirty days after it. All contributors of $200 or more must be identified by name, address, occupation, and name of employer.

Earlier legislation had tried and failed to achieve this goal. Required reports were sketchy at best and missing at worst. The new legislation improved the quality of reporting, however, by creating the Federal Election Commission to collect the data and to make them available. Some members of Congress still try to undercut the disclosure of campaign finance data by regularly threatening to reduce the FEC's funding. But the commission's public files, available on the Internet as well as on paper, have provided a wealth of campaign finance information for scholars and journalists.

Public Funding of Presidential Campaigns

Although Congress has not yet been willing to fund its own challengers from the public treasury, since 1976 it has provided public support for presidential candidates. To get the money, a candidate for a party's presidential nomination must first raise $5,000 in contributions of $250 or less in each of twenty states as a way of demonstrating broad public support. After that, public funds match every individual contribution up to $250. In addition, each of the major parties received $13.5 million in 2000 to help pay for its national nominating convention. Once a candidate has received the Democratic or Republican nomination, he or she will receive money for the general election campaign from tax funds. The figure rises every year with increases in the consumer price index; it reached $67.6 million in 2000.

Minor parties fare less well. They receive only a fraction of that total and then only after the election if they have received at least 5 percent of the vote. Once they have reached that milestone, however, they have qualified to receive their payment before the election in the next presidential year. Because Ross Perot won 8 percent of the vote as the Reform Party's presidential candidate in 1996, the party's candidate in 2000 was guaranteed to receive $12.6 million in advance of that campaign. That clearly enhanced the attractiveness of the Reform Party's nomination. No other minor party has received public funding, however. This makes it difficult for parties to reach major-party status and, because of the need to pay cash for many campaign expenses, adds to the difficulty of financing even a modest campaign.

The Consequences of Reform

The reforms achieved most of the goals they were intended to reach. They have slowed the growth of campaign spending in presidential races. Between 1960 and 1972, presidential campaign expenditures had shot up by 225 percent; from 1972 to 1996, real spending increased by only 36 percent, and in three of the seven elections spending actually declined. The reforms also removed the veil of secrecy that had shrouded campaign finance, and opened the process to public scrutiny.

Like all reforms, however, the campaign finance reforms of the 1970s have had some unintended and not always desirable effects. First, as "fat cats" have become less important in congressional campaigns, alternative sources of money—PACs and wealthy candidates—have become more valuable and plentiful, though not necessarily any less worrisome. Observers have found many other flaws in the reforms. Presidential candidates complain that the limits on spending in the presidential primaries and caucuses are too low. Low ceilings in the early state contests make it difficult for lesser-known candidates to compete. When they spend up to the ceilings in these states, candidates often reach their overall spending ceiling before the last primaries and caucuses occur—though the nomination races have been decided so early in recent elections that the impact has not been felt.

The regulations have also introduced new sources of inequality into campaign finance. Independent expenditures were stimulated by the reforms. Because Republican candidates tend to be favored by the groups that do independent spending—at first individuals and ideological PACs and more recently corporate and trade association PACs and the parties themselves—this reform's impact has padded the existing Republican advantage, at least in congressional campaign spending.

Independent spending is a classic challenge for a democratic system. On one hand, the Supreme Court finds it to be clearly protected by free speech rights. On the other, it can easily promote irresponsible campaign attacks. By definition, independent spending campaigns are not supposed to be coordinated with any candidate's campaign; therefore they are free to make whatever charges they wish, and the candidate they favor cannot be held responsible.

Voters were subjected to a virtual independent spending war in 1996. The first volley was fired by the AFL-CIO, which spent around $22 million in ads urging the defeat of Republican House candidates. The U.S. Chamber of Commerce organized a smaller campaign in reaction. The debate, featuring claims about "big labor bosses" and "Gingrich clones," was not edifying. It was augmented by large amounts of so-called "issue advocacy" ads, in which parties or other groups can spend unlimited sums of money (including soft money) on issue-based advertising as long as the phrases "vote for," "vote against," "elect" or "defeat" are not included.

Because of the reforms, campaigns rely much less now on the loosely coordinated efforts of local campaign organizations and volunteers, and much more on paid professionals, including lawyers and accountants as well as consultants of all kinds. The reforms have made the "little" contributor more valuable to candidates than ever. Because "little" contributors take more skill and effort to pursue, the experts at computerized direct mail fund-raising have also seen their stock rise as a result of the financing changes. Direct mail advertising seems to be most effective when it makes dramatic and even inflammatory appeals—a prospect some thoughtful observers of politics find disturbing. The increase in small contributions has made campaign financing a broader-based process but not yet an equitable one.

The reforms, in short, have clearly not affected all candidates and parties in the same way. Federal matching funds in the primaries, for example, have erased the usual Republican advantage in spending (at least for GOP candidates who accept the matching funds) and helped less-well-known presidential candidates raise money. Yet at the same time, contribution limits and the rise of PACs have probably increased the edge of the already-advantaged incumbents in congressional races.

Effects on the Parties   Have the reforms strengthened or weakened the party's influence, especially in comparison with that of interest groups and individual contributors, on the party in government? In some ways, the party organizations seem to have been victims of the reforms. Their direct contributions to presidential and congressional candidates have been limited, making the parties no more privileged in the campaign process than PACs or any other player. The public funding of presidential campaigns goes to the candidates themselves, not to the parties as it does in most other democracies. That creates more distance between the party organization and the presidential campaign.

Yet some aspects of the reforms have elevated the parties' role. There are higher ceilings on contributions made to parties than to PACs or candidates; that gives the parties an edge in fund-raising, and in fact both national parties are raising money more successfully now than ever before. The limits on individual contributions make party funds even more attractive to congressional candidates. Most important, the parties have found several creative ways to get around the $5,000 limit on their contributions to candidates; these include providing valuable services, acting as conduits for individual contributions to candidates (so-called bundling), channeling soft money to the state parties, making coordinated expenditures for the party ticket as a whole, and investing in long-term state and local party-building.

Thus the national party committees now play a much more important role in political campaigns than ever before. That increases the opportunity for more centralized direction for the American parties and their candidates. The state and local parties, energized by the new funding directed their way from the national parties and by their own successes in fund-raising, are becoming more actively involved in campaigns as well and especially in the labor-intensive grassroots work that was the staple of party organizations in an earlier era. Money was not the vital resource that the traditional party organizations brought to political campaigns, so their current financial contributions are a newfound source of influence. But the conclusion of this story about the effects of campaign finance reform on the parties has not yet been written. It is quite possible that the parties' role in campaigns ultimately depends more on their own initiative than on changes in the campaign finance laws.[28]

State Regulation and Financing

Even more complicated than this tangled federal reform is the fabric of fifty different state regulations. The states have long set at least some limits to campaign activity, usually in response to egregious violations of fair campaign practices. All states prohibit bribery and vote buying; some outlaw such practices as buying a voter a drink on election day. Most states also require that expenditures be made through an authorized campaign treasurer or committee and that contributions and spending be reported.

The Watergate scandals spurred a new round of campaign finance legislation in the states after 1972. Public disclosure has been instituted in several states. Many have put some restrictions on campaign contributions. As of 1998, thirty-five states limited campaign contributions by individuals; all but seven either prohibited or limited contributions from corporations and all but ten had such a prohibition or limit on union contributions; and thirty-six put limits on PAC giving. The Supreme Court in 2000 upheld states' power to limit the size of individuals' contributions to state campaigns. Some states have even limited contributions from the candidates themselves—a step the Supreme Court would not let Congress take in federal elections–and twenty-eight states put limits on party contributions.

A growing number of states, now nearly half, have ventured into public funding for state elections. In ten of these states the payments go to the political parties, which in turn can spend the money on behalf of candidates. Another ten give the funding directly to the candidates, and in three states public funding goes to both the parties and the candidates. The level of the funding provided is not large, however, and is not typically accompanied by limits on campaign spending.[29]

Continuing Efforts at Reform

The unintended effects of the 1970s reforms—and some of the intended effects as well—continue to create pressures for new reforms. Concern about the effects of PACs has led to proposals to put lower limits on PAC contributions, limit the amount congressional candidates could accept from PACs, or even eliminate PACs altogether. Some reformers hope to restrict the amount of money a candidate can raise from outside his or her state. Others keep looking for a way to reduce independent spending without running afoul of the Supreme Court's interpretation of the First Amendment. And after the cascade of soft money on the 1996 elections, limiting or banning soft money has topped many reformers' wish lists, including the major campaign finance bills authored by Senators Russell Feingold (D-WI) and John McCain (R-AZ).

Many observers expected that the experience with these reforms would result in a move toward public funding of congressional campaigns. It has not for several reasons. Proponents worried that voters would see subsidies as an improper use of tax monies or as a congressional raid on the Treasury for its own advantage. Some members of Congress grumbled that by instituting public funding, they would be subsidizing their own opponents. Research suggests that challengers who spend more are significantly better able to give an incumbent a close race, so public funding of congressional campaigns would seem likely to stimulate competition.

Any additional reforms of the campaign finance system would be likely to face very imposing hurdles. The Supreme Court, in *Buckley* and more recent cases, has stated very clearly that a limit on independent expenditures or on the spending of candidates who do not have public funding would restrict their free speech rights. That certainly makes it difficult to cap the costs of campaigning. A second hurdle is that campaign finance has partisan implications; it is almost inevitable that any reform proposal will help one party's candidates more than the other party's and will thus generate party conflict. Major reform at the national level, then, is unlikely unless one party controls both Houses of Congress and the presidency.

Even if one-party control occurs, incumbents are understandably wary of changing the rules under which they were elected, especially if the rules changes might benefit challengers too. Unless a major scandal causes enough public outrage to put pressure on Congress, the chance for major changes in the current campaign finance laws seems slim.[30]

MONEY, PARTIES, AND POWER IN AMERICAN POLITICS

The study of money in politics raises important questions about power and who holds it. Prevailing patterns of political finance help meet the needs of current elected officials—not surprisingly given that they make the campaign finance laws—and permit them to maintain their independence from the party organizations. So long as candidates can continue to finance their own campaigns, they block the organizations' control of access to public office. One reason why Congress members and state legislators are reluctant to change the present patterns of campaign finance is that they are satisfied with the independence these patterns bring. The 1970s reforms did leave the parties a potentially expandable role, and they have expanded it with enthusiasm. But it is much less than would be necessary to establish strong and disciplined parties with power over their candidates and officeholders.

More generally, the results of the reforms remind us that money will always have an important effect on the selection of government officials. Campaign finance reforms may be designed to limit and channel it, but they have tended to resemble sandcastles in the face of big waves. The most foolproof restrictions become challenges for the resourceful campaigner and contributor to overcome. Reformers are often able to alter the flow of money at least temporarily, though sometimes in ways they did not anticipate or approve. But they will never be able to eliminate it.

CAMPAIGN FINANCE: A REFLECTION OF THE AMERICAN WAY

The American way of campaign finance reflects the American way of politics. High campaign costs reflect the vastness of the country, the many elective offices on many levels of government, the localism of American politics, and the increasing length of our campaigns for office. The domination of spending by candidates reflects our candidate-dominated campaigns and, more generally, the dominance of the party in government within the American parties. The importance of media in American campaigns reflects the importance of media in our lives as well as the sheer size of our constituencies.

Campaign finance in Britain offers a dramatic contrast. The British election campaign runs for only about three weeks, during which paid television and radio political advertising is banned; British campaigners instead get free time on the government run network BBC. The average constituency in the House of Commons has less than one fifth as many people as the average American congressional district. So smaller sums of money are spent, generally under the control of the party organizations. British campaigns are organized around their national party leaders, but there is considerable integration between the local parliamentary candidate and the leader, rather than the largely separate campaigns of American congressional and presidential candidates.

Aided by institutions such as the direct primary and the office-block ballot and supported by their ability to recruit the campaign resources they need, the American parties in government thus largely escape the control of party organizations. Two of each party's national organizations, the congressional campaign committees, are under the thumb of elected officeholders rather than party professionals. Even the national committees receive powerful direction from the party's president and presidential candidates, and much of their soft-money resources are raised in conjunction with the presidential campaign. In many states and localities, the officeholders also dominate, and legislative leaders are important sources of campaign funds in many of the states.

What price does the American political system pay for this? Certainly there is the price of a loss of cohesion as a party in government—for example, in the loss of a unified presence as party representatives in American legislatures. The impact also weakens the party organization not only relative to the party in government but also internally in terms of its ability to achieve the goals of its activists. There is no clearer demonstration of the competition between the party in government and the party organization than the struggle between them over the control of campaign funds. As the costs of campaigning rise, the future is with the sector of the party with access to cash resources. So far, the advantage is clearly with the candidates and officeholders.

Part 5
....

The Party in Government

*A*merica's first political parties began as factions in the government.[1] The party in government has dominated the American parties ever since. Even today we find that the legislative parties and the party in the executive structure partisan political conflict and profoundly shape our images of the Republican and Democratic parties.

These parties in government, however, are far from being a unified force. Unlike their counterparts in parliamentary systems, the American parties in government are notoriously loose coalitions. Each legislative party member represents a different constituency and pays more attention to the constituency than to his or her party leaders. The design of the federal government, with a Congress elected separately from a president, fractures the party in government and prevents it from setting the government on a coherent policy path. As a prominent scholar has written:

> it remains true that ... the parties are unable to hold their lines on a controversial public issue when the pressure is on.... (This) constitutes the most important single fact concerning the American parties.... What kind of party is it that, having won control of government, is unable to govern?[2]

For decades reformers have dreamed of an alternative. The best-known alternative is the idea of party government, or party responsibility. As expressed by a group of political scientists decades ago, this view suggests that American democracy would be strengthened if the parties were to offer clearer and fuller statements of their proposed policies, nominate candidates pledged to support those policies, and then see to it that their winning candidates enacted those programs while in office.[3] The parties, then, would serve as means through which the voters could choose between alternative policies and be assured that the winning alternative would be put into effect.

If party government were to exist in the United States, the role of the parties would be greatly changed. Parties would become the initiators of public policy. They would give voters a means to register their choices not only among candidates but also on competing policy alternatives. Parties would be the main representative link, then, between American citizens and the uses of government power. As the policy component of the parties' working lives increased, so would the parties' power increase. The result, reformers hoped, would be to strengthen voters' ability to hold their government accountable.

The idea has significant drawbacks. Because of the separation of powers throughout the American system, Republicans can hold a majority in the Congress while a Democrat sits in the White House, or one party can dominate the House while the other controls the Senate. In fact, in recent years divided control of government has been the norm, not the exception. Within the parties as well, each of the different sectors has its own goals and motives. Party activists may be dedicated to certain policy goals but they may also be motivated by personal rewards or the thrill of victory. Party voters may desire certain policies but they also respond to personalities, traditional party loyalties, or the power of incumbency. Candidates and elected officials seek to put policies into effect but also to earn recognition, the perks of power, and other intangible rewards.

The key point here is that none of the three sectors of the parties is committed wholly to winning office for the purpose of enacting party policies into law. Even if they were, there would still be the question of *which* of the party's sectors would dominate: Would the party's program be determined by the party organization, by its candidates and elected officials, or by the party electorate? And if the party in government were to set the party's policies, what would lead the legislative party to agree on goals with its colleagues in the executive? In short, agreement on a coherent policy program, not to mention enforcement of it, is difficult if not impossible in the American setting.

Several European parties come closer to the ideal of responsible parties. In Britain, for example, the parliamentary government fosters the kind of legislative party unity—the sharply drawn party lines—that the advocates of responsible parties have in mind. Giving the House of Commons the power to select the chief executive of the government, the prime minister, from its own ranks and making the prime minister dependent on holding a legislative majority to continue in office creates powerful incentives for party government. The party in government then tries to carry out a program that was adopted with the help of party leaders, activists, and members at party conferences.

Although the example of European parties is interesting as a point of comparison, change in the American parties cannot follow the same path. It must respond to the uniquely American set of governmental rules, including federalism and separation of powers. And to an interesting degree, it has. In recent years, both parties have become more oriented toward policy goals and toward using government authority to achieve them. The days when party activists contested elections mainly because of the spoils at stake, such as jobs and contracts, are largely past. As more and more citizens are attracted to the party organizations for reasons of policy, pressure builds for at least some degree of party responsibility.

The American parties do not dominate the government, but they are critical to its functioning. Party lines are the chief lines of conflict in American legislatures, both state and federal. The party winning the presidency normally succeeds in carrying out much of its party platform.[4] The staffing of top executive offices and the appointment of judges are affected by partisan considerations. Thus government policies change depending on the composition of the party in government.

The chapters in this next part address these questions of party influence in government. Chapters 13 and 14 examine the role of the parties in the organization and operation of the three branches of government: the impact of internalized party loyalties and external party influences on public officials. Chapter 15 looks at the general question of party government, its desirability and its feasibility in the American political setting. It also examines the reasons for and the effects of the development of a more policy-oriented perspective within the parties.

Chapter 13
Party and Partisans in the Legislature

*P*arty power in American legislatures is both fundamental and elusive. On one hand, Congress and state legislatures are organized by party, and legislative party leaders have a full array of incentives with which to hold their members' loyalty. On the other, legislators' voting often crosses party lines and violates party platforms, sometimes even on big issues. It is this curious combination of dominance and dependence that has intrigued observers and reformers of the legislative party for so long.

The character of the American legislative party has been deeply affected by the American separation of powers. In a parliamentary regime, such as that of Great Britain, a majority party in the legislature must unite in support of its leaders in the government. When those leaders cannot muster a majority in parliament, either the governing cabinet must be reshuffled or the legislature must be dissolved and its members sent home to face a new election. This creates powerful pressures for unity within the legislative party.

American legislators do not face these pressures. They suffer no great penalty if they vote against the majority of their party and its leadership on bills. They can reject the proposals of a president or governor of their own party without causing a crisis. The party role in American legislatures is not as institutionalized as it is in parliaments. It may be that Congress and state legislatures would run more smoothly if there were higher levels of party cohesion. But they can run without it as well–and they have had a great deal of experience doing so.

PARTY ORGANIZATION
AND PARTY POWER IN LEGISLATURES

Almost all members of Congress and state legislators are elected as candidates of a political party.[1] The ways in which they organize and behave as a legislative party, however, differ enormously. In some states the legislative party scarcely exists; in others it dominates the legislative process through an almost daily regimen of party caucuses. Parties in most state legislatures and in Congress fall in between these extremes.

Party Organization in Congress

Organizing the Congress   Both parties in both houses of Congress meet prior to the beginning of each congressional session. These party meetings (called *caucuses* by the Democrats and *conferences* by the Republicans) nominate candidates for Speaker of the House or president pro tempore of the Senate and set up procedures for appointing party members to congressional committees. Thus these party meetings do the initial work of organizing the House and Senate. They select the leadership of the party (the leaders, whips, policy committees) and structure the chamber itself (the presiding officer and the committees). (The party leadership positions are described in the box below)

In this fashion the organization of the two parties and the organization of the House and Senate are woven into what appears to be a single fabric. This organizational system is dominated by the majority party, which was the Democratic party for most of the time since World War II and has been the Republicans since 1995. The majority party chooses the Speaker of the House. The vice president of the United States is the formal presiding officer of the Senate, but it is the majority party that manages floor action–to the degree that floor action is managed in that highly democratic institution. The majority party chooses the chairs of all the standing committees in both houses. It hires (and fires) the staff of these committees and of the chambers (see box on p. 261). A majority of each committee's members come from the majority party, and by a margin similar to the majority's margin in the House. The majority party, in short, controls the action in both the committees and on the floor.

Party Leadership Positions in the House and Senate

Each party creates its own leadership structure in each house of Congress; the individual leaders are elected by the entire party membership of the chamber. At the top of the hierarchy is the party leader (called the *majority* or *minority leader*, depending on whether the party controls the chamber). In the House of Representatives, the *Speaker* ranks above the majority leader as the true leader of the majority party.

These party leaders have assistants, called *whips* and *assistant whips*, who are responsible for mobilizing party members to vote the way the party leadership wants.

Each congressional party also has several specialized leadership positions. There is a *caucus* or *conference chair* to head the meeting of all party members. Other chairs are selected for the *Steering Committee* (among all but the Senate Republicans, where it is called the Committee on Committees), which assigns party members to committees; the *Policy Committee,* which advises on legislative action and policy priorities; the *Campaign Committee,* which provides campaign support to the party's congressional candidates; and any other committees the legislative party may create.

The Spoils of Victory:
The GOP Purge of the House Committee Staff

In 1994 Republicans gained majority control of the House of Representatives for the first time in forty years. That gave them the power to choose the leaders of the House, determine its rules, and select the staff for both the chamber and its committees. Congressional staff members do not have the job-security protections that most other government employees enjoy. With the ruthless efficiency of the old-time patronage system, then, the new Republican majority summarily dismissed large numbers of the existing mostly Democratic congressional staffers and replaced them with Republicans. The immediate response of the fired staff members was a combination of panic and determination; resumes flew out over official Washington like a paper blizzard. But the longer-term result was that the House Republican leadership ensured that its staff would be sympathetic to the Republican policies the voters were thought to have endorsed in the 1994 elections.

Party Leadership and Party Coordination   The party leadership positions in Congress carry considerable authority, but because their occupants are chosen by the votes of all members of the legislative party, their power is in effect delegated to them by the party caucus.[2] Leaders, then, serve subject to the approval of their legislative party. Some party leaders have wielded more power than others, in part due to their personal characteristics and to the willingness of the party rank and file to accept strong leadership.

Years ago, power in the House of Representatives was highly centralized in the hands of the Speaker. Powerful Speaker Joe Cannon, in the first decade of the 1900s, chaired the Rules Committee, the "traffic cop" through which he could control the flow of legislation to the floor. He appointed committees and their chairs, putting his lieutenants in the key positions, and generally had the resources and sanctions necessary for enforcing party discipline. But House members revolted against "Czar" Cannon in 1911, and later Speakers could not command such a powerful institutional position. Instead they had to operate in a far more decentralized House in which party discipline could be maintained only through skillful bargaining and strong personal loyalties. Successful Speakers during this era, such as Sam Rayburn and Tip O'Neill, were consummate brokers rather than czars.[3]

Party coordination has increased more recently, however, especially in the House. The Republicans took a first tentative step in this direction in the late 1960s by giving rank-and-file party members more opportunity to influence party policy through the party conference. In the 1970s, under the prodding of its reform-minded Democratic Study Group,[4] the Democrats took more dramatic steps toward the same goal by strengthening both the party caucus and the party leadership.

The most visible of these Democratic reforms was that the party caucus assumed the power to challenge and even oust committee chairs by secret ballot. During the preceding six decades the most senior member of the majority party on a committee automatically became that committee's chair–the famed *seniority rule*. Soon after the Democratic caucus changed that rule, some chairs were in fact challenged in the caucus, and a few were actually stripped of their committee positions and replaced by the caucus's choice, who was not always the second most senior party member.[5] The reform, designed to give rank-and-file Democratic members more committee rights and to offer party leaders more power relative to the formerly all-powerful committee chairs, fundamentally changed the structure of authority within the Democratic-run House.[6] It took power away from the aged and sometimes autocratic committee chairs and enhanced the position of the party caucus.

The power to assign members to committees was vested in the new Steering and Policy Committee chaired by the Speaker. The Speaker was also allowed to choose, subject to caucus approval, the chair and other Democratic members of the Rules Committee. The whip system was made more responsive to party leaders as well. These Democratic party reforms provided the levers for a more forceful Democratic leadership.

Policy Leadership   The reforms, then, gave the legislative party in the House, with its strengthened leadership, an opportunity to use its new power on behalf of policy goals. It is usually the party leadership, not the caucus, that sets and implements party policy. This is especially true in the large and unwieldy House of Representatives. The floor leaders and other powerful party figures consult widely throughout the party, but the final codification of party policy, the sensing of a will or consensus, rests primarily on the leaders' judgment.[7]

In order for the legislative party to become an instrument of policy, however, most individual party members in the House would have to be willing to use the party caucus for collective party purposes, and party leaders would have to be willing and able to play an active coordinating role.[8] As both parties in the House became more ideologically homogeneous during the 1970s and 1980s, the chances of accomplishing the former were increased. With changes in the Southern electorate, fewer conservative Democrats were being elected to Congress and their strongholds of committee power were fading. Democratic House members, then, were more cohesively liberal than had been the case in earlier decades.

During the same period congressional Republicans, energized especially by the conservative policy leadership coming from the White House under Ronald Reagan, became more ideologically unified as well. When parties are ideologically cohesive, it is easier for the caucus to develop a party position on legislation and to pressure straggling party members to come into line. Speaker Jim Wright, during his brief tenure as party leader in the late 1980s, took advantage of these opportunities to become one of the most assertive Democratic leaders in decades. His successor, Thomas Foley, was not as inclined to aggressive partisanship; Foley returned to a more collegial style before being defeated for reelection in the Republican surge of 1994.[9]

Ironically, given that the Democrats in the House had been the instigator of stronger legislative party leadership during the 1970s and 1980s, it was a Republican who brought party leadership to its recent pinnacle of power. The Republican minority had been bystanders to the Democratic procedural reforms of the 1970s and 1980s.

But the 1994 election produced landmark changes. Republicans won a majority of House seats that year, after a campaign centered on their "Contract with America," a set of pledges of comprehensive policy change made most visible by the party's leader in the House, Rep. Newt Gingrich.

With a Democrat in the White House and a slender majority in the House, the GOP members realized that their only hope of realizing the goals of their contract and of the spending cuts needed to produce a balanced budget lay in unshakable party discipline and strong party leadership. They elected Gingrich as their Speaker. They ceded to him the power to select committee and subcommittee chairs committed to bringing the desired legislation to the floor. They permitted him to challenge the autonomy of committee chairs on substantive legislation in order to promote the GOP agenda. The result was a level of party discipline with which "Czar" Cannon would probably have felt very comfortable (see Table 13.1).

Gingrich became the strongest Speaker in modern times. His party colleagues in the House were willing to give him more authority than usual in pursuing the Republican agenda, and Gingrich was more willing than usual to exercise authority over the party rank and file. Yet after three hard-driving years and a serious ethics investigation, Gingrich faced a palace coup by some party insiders, and later stepped down in 1998 (see box on p. 265). Even the strongest party leaders must cope with limits to their power.

And even a party leader with the authority of Gingrich typically finds it easier to organize the two Houses of Congress than to mobilize party colleagues for coordinated action on public policy. Each legislative party has a policy committee created to serve as a broadly based instrument of party policy-making. But these committees are often collections of the assorted blocs and wings of the party rather than unified instruments for action. Nor have the party caucuses or conferences always served to unite the party on behalf of policies. They do meet to discuss important issues, but only occasionally do they "bind" their members, or insist that members commit themselves to vote the party's position on a bill.

Further, the party policies that are created by party leaders in this process are *legislative* party policies to a greater extent than they are "party policy" more broadly. They rarely flow from the party's national platform; instead, they are a more ad hoc reflection of the legislative party's needs and constraints and in particular the demands of legislative constituencies and the need to support or oppose a president. They represent a negotiated compromise among the goals of the party members who hold committee power, the party leaders themselves, the rank and file of the legislative party, and (in one party) the president. Legislative party policy, in short, is normally developed as much to serve the individual reelection needs of each party member as to implement any coherent party philosophy.[10]

Parties in the State Legislatures

In contrast with the increasing power of party leadership in Congress, the pattern of legislative party leadership in the states has been more variable. In some state legislatures, daily caucuses, binding party discipline, and autocratic party leadership make for a party every bit as potent as the Republicans in the 1995 U.S. House. In others,

TABLE 13.1 Party Cohesion on the Republican Contract with America, 1995

Provisions of House Republican Contract with America	Republicans For	Republicans Against	Democrats For	Democrats Against
A. Commitments to enact				
1. End of congressional exemptions from workplace laws	218	0	171	0
2. Cuts in committee budgets/staffs	224	0	191	12
B. Commitments to vote on				
1. Balanced-budget amendment	228	2	72	129
Line-item veto	223	4	71	129
2. Anticrime measures	220	9	18	182
3. Welfare reform	225	5	9	193
4. Protection for families/children				
Parental consent for children participating in surveys	225	0	192	7
Increased penalties for sex crimes against children	225	0	191	0
Stronger enforcement of child-support laws	228	0	204	0
5. Tax cuts	219	11	27	176
6. Various national security provisions (prohibit U.S. troops under UN command; reduce U.S. funds for UN peacekeeping; change defense funding priorities)	223	4	18	176
7. Repeal of 1993 tax increase on social security benefits (part of tax cuts in #5 above)	219	11	27	176
8. Reductions in federal regulations	219	8	58	132
9. Changes in liability laws				
Limits on punitive damages in product liability	220	6	45	154
Restrictions on investor suits	226	0	99	98
Institution of "loser pay" rules in certain lawsuits	216	11	16	181
10. Congressional term limits	189	40	38	163

Note: The Contract with America was publicized by the House Republicans during the 1994 congressional campaign. Under its provisions, if they became the majority party in the House, the Republicans promised to enact some procedural changes in Congress (listed under A above) and to bring ten bills (listed under B above) to a vote on the House floor in the first hundred days of the congressional session. The latest vote taken was on April 4, 1995—well within the hundred-day limit. All of the bills were passed by the House, but some of them were defeated or modified in the Republican-controlled Senate, and still others were vetoed by the Democratic president.

Source: Various issues of the *Congressional Quarterly Weekly Report* for the different votes. CQ's "Contract Score Card" was used to identify the various bills and their content.

especially the traditionally one-party states, party organization is weaker than it was in Congress before the reforms of the 1970s.

Even the state legislative parties with a full apparatus of party organization often fail to make it operate effectively. The party caucuses in Congress at least maintain cohesion in their first decision: they always agree on candidates for the presiding officers. State legislative parties sometimes find themselves too divided by factionalism

The Downfall of a Powerful Party Leader

Newt Gingrich was credited with engineering the 1994 Republican takeover of the House and in his first months as Speaker his party colleagues granted him unprecedented authority. Later in 1995, however, Gingrich's aura of invincibility began to break down. When a standoff between President Clinton and the House Republicans led to a shutdown of the government, Gingrich and his colleagues got the blame. The Speaker was dogged by charges of ethics violations and declining popularity ratings. House Republicans were frustrated by the vagaries of his leadership style. An aborted effort to oust Gingrich from the Speaker's chair in 1997 had quiet help from some House party leaders. Then, when the Republicans lost a net of five House seats in the 1998 election–which was only the second time since the Civil War that the party not in control of the White House lost seats in a midterm election–there were widespread demands among the House Republicans for new leadership. Gingrich resigned three days later, leaving many to wonder whether he had been better suited to be the leader of a contentious minority than of the day-to-day demands of a majority.

For an excellent summary of Gingrich's tenure as Speaker, see "Gingrich Weakened by Ethics Case," *CQ Almanac 1997* (Washington, DC: CQ Press, 1998), pp. 1.11–1.15.

or ambition even to organize the legislature. In some states with fairly weak legislative parties, such as California, legislative leaders have occasionally been elected by coalitions that cross party lines. A recent example was the dramatic running battle over the position of Speaker in the California Assembly, in which longtime Speaker Willie Brown first won with the vote of a Republican defector and then engineered the election of a Republican maverick. Party discipline in selecting legislative leaders often breaks down under the pressure of electoral realignment as well. In Florida in the late 1980s, for example, conservative Democrats joined with a growing minority of Republicans to choose the leadership of the state senate.

More typically, however, the party leaders chosen by state legislators have great power over the day-to-day workings of the legislature. They do not usually have to defer to steering or policy committees, whose chairs they appoint, and they normally have great influence on party caucuses. In many state legislatures the party leaders also control resources that are vital to their legislative colleagues. Unlike members of Congress, most state legislators have few personal staff members to assist them; the labor that a party leader can provide to help perform the tasks of legislative life can be very valuable. Campaign funds are also in short supply at this level; party leaders can draw on their legislative leadership funds to help out.[11] Where a state legislator depends on the party leadership for needed resources, he or she has a greater incentive to listen when a leader calls for party discipline. As state legislatures become more professionalized, however, with larger staffs, their members may be better able to resist centralized party control.

Party leaders' influence is often exercised in part through the party caucus. Malcolm Jewell and David Olson reported that in the 1980s the majority caucuses in two states actually bound their members on budget bills. In twenty-eight states, the caucuses in one or both parties played at least some role in policy-making by meeting frequently to discuss legislation, polling their members, and deciding what bills to push on the floor. On the other hand, party caucuses in eleven states mainly provided information to legislators and made no effort to gauge party opinion or build consensus.[12]

In sum, although the parties' legislative organizations look pretty similar across the states–their party leadership positions are fairly uniform–they differ in their behavior. The power of state party leaders varies substantially, even between the two Houses of the same state legislature. So does the influence and effectiveness of the party caucus.[13]

PARTY IMPACT AND INFLUENCE

How do legislative parties use their power? Do they try to shape themselves into a unified force–and if so, do they succeed–or do they organize just to distribute the goodies of legislative service, such as offices and staff?

Influence in Congress

At first glance, once they have organized both Houses the parties seem to have little impact on the legislative behavior of their members. Representatives and senators can normally vote without fear against their party's platform, majority, or leadership or against major bills proposed by their party's president. The Republicans who opposed Republican President Bush's tax increases in the late 1980s and the Democratic leaders who organized opposition to Democratic President Clinton's North American Free Trade Agreement (NAFTA) in the early 1990s–and were not penalized by their parties for doing so–demonstrate that traditionally members of Congress have not been burdened by much party discipline.

During the last century there has been just one deviation from party loyalty that has been consistently punished in Congress: a member's support of the other party's presidential candidate in the general election. In 1965 the House Democratic caucus stripped committee seniority from two Southern Democrats who had supported the Republican presidential candidate, Barry Goldwater, the year before. In 1968 the same fate befell Representative John Rarick, a Democrat from Louisiana, for supporting George Wallace.

Yet even here the penalty was no greater than the loss of seniority or committee assignments. In 1983, the Democratic caucus removed Representative Phil Gramm from his seat on the prestigious House Budget Committee. Caucus members felt that Gramm, a conservative Democrat from Texas, had betrayed his party by leaking the details of secret Democratic party meetings on the Reagan budget to Republicans. Some of his Southern Democratic colleagues who had merely voted for the Reagan budget were not disciplined in any way. In 1995, Newt Gingrich, the new Republican Speaker, made veiled threats to remove some GOP committee chairs from their positions when they stood in the way of action on the party's Contract with America. In the end, however, the chairs became more compliant and Gingrich backed down.

The party organizations in Congress rely on carrots much more than these fairly weak sticks to increase party cohesiveness. Party leaders can offer desirable committee assignments, help in passing a member's bills, or even provide additional office space in order to cultivate party support. Through their control of floor activities party leaders can set the agenda in a way to maximize party unity on important matters.[14] They can also provide political help, for example by giving speeches and raising money to boost the member's reelection effort. And if they are of the president's party, they can convey the president's enthusiasm for a particular action.

The most powerful rival of the party leaders' persuasive abilities is constituency pressure. Constituents have one important advantage over party leaders in influencing members of Congress: it is constituents, not party leaders, who vote on their reelection. When party and constituency conflict, responsiveness to the folks back home usually outweighs calls for party unity. It did not help the cause of party discipline when Phil Gramm, after having been punished by the Democratic Party in the House, resigned his seat, went back to Texas, and was reelected by his constituents to the House–and later the Senate–as a Republican. Legislative party leaders cannot keep a party maverick from being renominated and reelected, and that inevitably limits their influence on party legislators.

In past years efforts to build party discipline were also undercut by the committee system and the seniority rule. Independent committees can provide a set of influences that directly oppose any influences the parties might exert. The seniority rule for gaining power in and attaining the chairmanship of a committee puts a premium on getting reelected rather than on party loyalty within Congress.[15] Thus the House Democrats' efforts to reform seniority and the committee system in the 1970s were nothing less than struggles for the control of Congress.

The House Democrats succeeded in their reform efforts because they were willing to punish committee chairs–by relieving them of their positions–if they too flagrantly ignored their responsibility to the party and its congressional caucus. As a committee chair's independent power was curbed, one barrier to the influence of party organization was lowered. When the Republicans took over the House in 1995, they continued this practice of deviating from strict seniority rules in choosing committee chairs and thus chose committee leaders who were sympathetic with the party's policy agenda and leadership (see box on p. 268).

Influence in the State Legislatures

What kinds of inducements do state legislative party leaders have to influence other legislators? In some states, even former Speaker Gingrich would be envious. Party leadership posts and powerful committee positions go much more frequently to legislators loyal to the party. Party leaders, the party caucus, or a party's governor may expect legislators to support the party's stands. Lapses in party loyalty may result in penalties that would be inconceivable in Congress. Errant legislators may lose influence or a position of power. In a state with numerous patronage jobs they may find that the applicants they sponsor are not selected as often. In the next election they may not receive campaign funds from the state or local party, or may even find that the party is supporting someone else in the primary. In states like these it is not surprising that legislators have looked to party leaders for cues and direction much more frequently than members of Congress have.[16]

Party Versus Committee Leaders in the Gingrich House

After their stunning takeover of the House of Representatives in the 1994 elections, House Republicans made almost as stunning a change in the chamber's leadership structure. They set aside the long tradition of committee autonomy in the shaping of legislation and instead centralized power in their Speaker, Newt Gingrich. The committee chairs, the chief losers in this extraordinary usurpation of committee power, agreed to it for several reasons: personal loyalty to the leader credited with the Republican victory, commitment to the party's policy agenda, and even fear for their political careers if they resisted. It was a giant step in the expansion of party power in the House that had been initiated by the Democratic reforms of the 1970s. As Speaker Gingrich's personal and political weaknesses became more apparent during the three years that followed, however, his authority no longer went unquestioned, and he resigned his post after the 1998 elections. His successor, Dennis Hastert of Illinois, voiced his commitment to the "regular order," permitting committee chairs to take the lead on most legislation, though Hastert is more willing to assert his authority than pre-Gingrich Republican leaders. The most long-lasting effect of the Gingrich reforms seems to be the six-year term limit on committee chairs, which remains in effect. The normal pressures for committee autonomy, then, did not disappear; instead they were briefly overwhelmed by partisan zeal.[17]

Conditions of Party Power in Legislatures

Clearly, then, parties in some of the competitive, two-party state legislatures have advanced the art of discipline far beyond its normal state in the Congress. The reasons for their success tell us a lot about the building of party power in legislatures. Among the most important factors that produce strong legislative parties in the states and in Congress are the following.

Absence of Competing Centers of Power   The more the legislature's committees become independent units in which influence comes from seniority or some other criterion than party loyalty, the less they owe to parties and their priorities. In Congress, the committees were traditionally autonomous centers of legislative power, centrifugal forces countering the centripetal tendencies of party. Committees are the screens that sift through the great mass of legislative proposals for those relatively few nuggets of legislative gold. Much of the real business of Congress goes on in them. Thus they became centers of power alternative to that of the parties.

In the typical state, on the other hand, because the legislature is less attractive as a career, legislators accumulate less seniority,[18] and seniority is used far less often as a criterion for allocating positions of power. State parties are freer to appoint their party loyalists to powerful legislative positions; the committees and other legislative agencies of the states generally operate as instruments of party power. In this way,

Congress since 1995 may be coming to resemble the patterns of power in many state legislatures or the Congress of the late nineteenth and early twentieth centuries.

Availability of Patronage and Preferences   Patronage and other forms of governmental preference still exist in some states to a far greater extent than they do in the national government. Especially in the hands of a vigorous and determined governor or state legislative leader, these rewards may be potent inducements to legislative party discipline. Legislators who are loyal to their party's needs can be amply rewarded with political appointments for their constituents and supporters, and legislators who ignore their party's pleas may find themselves ignored. In Congress, by contrast, about the only material inducements to party discipline are projects in the member's home district that can be given priority or held back by the intercession of a party leader or even a president.

Strong Influences from the Party Organization   State and local party organizations exert greater influence on state legislators than does the party's national committee over members of Congress. In the states the party organization and the legislative party are far more likely to be allies. State party leaders may be able to deny mavericks the ability to advance within the party. They may be able to convince local parties to oppose the renomination of candidates who are disloyal to the party, although the spread of primaries limits that possibility. Moreover, it is not rare in the states–as it is in Washington, where serving in Congress is a full-time job–for state and local party leaders also to be legislative leaders.

The state and local parties also figure prominently in the lives of state legislative candidates as a result of the campaign money the parties provide. State legislative campaigns are more likely to depend on the party organization for financial support than are congressional campaigns for several reasons. First, the few states that provide public funding for campaigns are as likely to channel that money through the parties as to give it directly to candidates. Second, many states place no ceilings on party contributions to campaigns, unlike the situation at the congressional level, so parties can make substantial investments if they wish. Third, although more states now have significant legislative campaign committees, many candidates are still forced to look to the state parties themselves for campaign money and services–and the state parties are better prepared to respond now than they have been in past years.

Greater Political Homogeneity   Greater party unity in some state legislatures also reflects the greater homogeneity of state parties. There is a narrower spectrum of interests and ideologies in any given state party than in that same party at the national level. Thus there are a smaller range of differences and disagreements and fewer sources of internal conflict. The political culture of the state is also more homogeneous and, in some cases, more tolerant of party discipline over legislators than the national constituency is. Legislative party strength has traditionally flourished, for example, in the Northeastern part of the country (such as in Rhode Island, Connecticut, Pennsylvania, and New Jersey), where we find greater party organizational strength, more patronage, weak primaries, and a political culture that seems to be more accepting of centralized political control.

Lesser Legislative Professionalism   Over the years Congress has evolved into a highly professionalized legislative body. Each member controls a sizable and well-paid personal staff and a considerable budget which are employed to meet personal legislative and reelection needs. Congress now meets almost continuously, and the office has become a full-time job with high pay (an annual salary of $141,300 in 2000) and good benefits.

The state legislatures have become much more professional in recent years, but very few provide ordinary members with levels of support that even approach those in the Congress. State legislators are fortunate to have as much as a private office and personal secretary. Staff and budget resources are typically minimal (only a minority of state legislatures provide any personal staff at all) and sometimes they are under the control of the party leadership rather than the individual member. Many state legislatures remain part-time groups meeting for only part of the year and providing such low levels of pay that most members must hold other jobs and live only temporarily in the capital. As a result of these restrictions, state legislators in most of the states are much less able to operate independently of their party leaders than members of Congress are.[19]

PARTY COHESION IN LEGISLATIVE VOTING

Party influence in legislatures is broader than the efforts of the organized legislative party to achieve party discipline. Party influence may also operate within the legislator as a set of internalized loyalties and frameworks for organizing his or her legislative decisions. To discuss party only in the organizational sense of leaders and caucuses, then, is to miss the richness and complexity of the party's role.

Party is only one of a number of claimants for the vote of a legislator on any given issue. In addition to a legislator's constituents, there are demands from the more ideological party workers back home. Nor can the wishes of the president or a governor be easily dismissed. There are pressures as well from interest groups, financial contributors, friends and associates in the legislature, and the legislator's own experiences and beliefs. All or most of these pressures point in the same direction on many issues. When they do not, party loyalty understandably gives way.

We can gauge the influence of party, relative to these many other voting cues, by looking at how legislators vote on bills. Their roll-call votes on legislation are not the only important dimension of legislative behavior. Yet the public nature of the roll-call vote makes it a good test of the ability of the party to maintain discipline among its members.

Levels of Party Discipline

How much discipline do the American parties generate in legislative voting? The answer depends to a great extent on how we define *discipline*.

Party Voting   One classic measure of party voting discipline in legislatures has been the party vote–any nonunanimous legislative roll call in which 90 percent or more of the members of one party vote yes and 90 percent or more of the other party vote no. By such a strict test, party discipline appears regularly in the British House of Commons but rarely in American legislatures. Julius Turner found that from 1921 through 1948 only 17 percent of the roll calls in the House of Representatives met this standard of party discipline.[20] In the 1950s and 1960s the proportion dropped steadily to about 2 or 3 percent.[21] During approximately the same period in the British House of Commons, the percentage of party votes averaged very close to 100 percent.

Although the "90 percent versus 90 percent" standard discriminates well between British and American party cohesion, it is too stringent a standard for comparisons within the American experience. Only three of the seventeen provisions of the House Republicans' Contract with America, for example, had 90 percent or more of the Republicans voting yes against 90 percent or more of the Democrats voting no.

Scholars of the American legislatures, therefore, have opted for a less-demanding criterion: the percentage of instances in which the majority of one party opposed a majority of the other. By this measure the 1990s produced the highest levels of congressional party voting in years. In the Senate a majority of Democrats opposed a majority of Republicans in 63 percent of all contested Senate votes in 1999. Four years earlier the figure was 69 percent–the highest recorded in the Senate since these measurements started in 1954. Party voting has at times been even more prevalent in the House. From its twentieth-century low in 1969–1970 it has climbed steadily to levels not seen since the partisan divisions over New Deal legislation in the 1930s (Figure 13.1). In the rancorous 1995 session, party voting reached a fifty-year high of 73 percent in the House. Those levels could not be sustained after 1995 but remained much higher than those of two decades ago.[22]

What has caused the changes over time in levels of party voting? In the nineteenth century, congressional party voting was substantial (although still far below those of the British Parliament). This was a time when there was party competition in most congressional districts, party leaders exercised considerable legislative authority, and Congress was far less professional. After 1900, following what Nelson W. Polsby has termed the "institutionalization" of Congress and what Walter Dean Burnham has seen as a "disaggregation" of party,[23] party voting dropped dramatically. The New Deal realignment of the 1930s increased the cohesiveness of the legislative parties, but since the early 1900s the level of party voting has not matched those recorded in the nineteenth century or that of the most party-oriented states.

Focusing on the ebbs and flows of party voting over a shorter time span, Samuel Patterson and Gregory Caldeira reported that, at least during the 1949 to 1984 period, party voting peaked when Democrats controlled both the White House and the Congress and when the two parties' platforms diverged most clearly. These are times when party polarization is most obvious. Large and homogeneous majorities in the House also enhanced party voting, while the Senate was found to respond mainly to presidential leadership, both pro and con.[24]

Systematic information on levels of party voting in all state legislatures is not available for recent years. Studies of selected states in the 1950s and 1960s, however, supplemented by occasional measurements since then tell a familiar story: there is a great deal of variation in the extent to which state legislative parties vote as cohesive units. In some states, especially those with strong party organizations, competitive

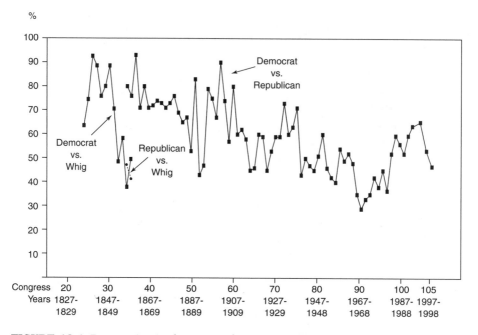

FIGURE 13.1 Party voting in the House of Representatives: 1835–1999.
Note: Entries are the percentage of roll-call votes on which a majority of one party opposed a majority of the other party for both sessions combined.
Source: For 24th through 36th Congresses, Thomas B. Alexander, *Sectional Stress and Party Strength* (Nashville, TN: Vanderbilt University Press, 1967). For 37th through 93rd Congresses, Jerome B. Chubb and Santa A. Traugott, "Partisan Cleavage and Cohesion in the House of Representatives, 1861–1974," *Journal of Interdisciplinary History* 7 (1977), 382–383. For the 94th through 103rd (1993–1994) Congresses, *Congressional Quarterly Weekly Report*, December 31, 1994, p. 3658. For the 104th and 105th Congresses, *CQ Almanac* 1995, p. C8; 1996, p. C8; 1997, p. C7; 1998, p. B6; for 1999, *CQ Weekly*, December 11, 1999, p. 2972.

politics, and ideological divisions between the parties, party is the dominant force in legislative voting. In other states–and probably most of them–party voting seems to be no more prominent than in the modern Congress.[25]

Party Cohesion   We can go beyond the incidence of party votes to ask how unified or cohesive the legislative parties are. The results show some interesting changes in both parties. In the 1960s and 1970s, the congressional Democrats were less cohesive than the Republicans; conservative Southern Democrats often crossed the aisle at this time to vote with Republicans, and the more decentralized party leadership tolerated the defections. Once Ronald Reagan was elected president, however, the congressional Democrats developed even greater unity than the Republicans throughout the 1980s; the gap grew wider after 1985 (Figure 13.2). Party cohesion continued to increase during the Clinton presidency but now especially among the Republicans once they took control of Congress in 1995.

David Rohde has argued that the increasing cohesiveness in the Democratic Party is due in part to greater ideological homogeneity. The Voting Rights Act, bringing

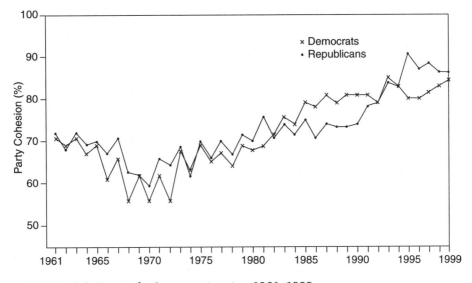

FIGURE 13.2 Party cohesion on party votes, 1961–1999

Note: Entries are the average percentages of members voting in agreement with a majority of their party on party votes. Party votes are votes in which a majority of one party voted against a majority of the other party. Figures for the House and Senate are combined.

Source: CQ Weekly, December 11, 1999, p. 2993.

Southern blacks into the electorate, changed the composition of the Southern congressional delegation; combined with the spread of two-party competition, these forces narrowed the policy differences between Northern and Southern Democrats. The old "conservative coalition" of Northern Republicans and Southern Democrats grew weaker, leaving the Democratic Party more cohesive than it has been in decades. As a result, there are clearer differences to be seen between the policy preferences of Democrats and those of Republicans. In addition, the organizational reforms discussed earlier in the chapter, which reduced the power of committee chairs and strengthened the power of party leaders, made it easier for the Democratic leadership to unify its party and to fend off Republican appeals to more conservative Democrats.[26]

Levels of Cohesion

Cohesive voting among members of a legislative party is greater on some issues than on others. Studies in Congress and the state legislatures find that three kinds of legislative concerns are most likely to stimulate high levels of party discipline: those touching the interests of the legislative party as a group, those involving support of or opposition to an executive program, and those concerning the issues that tend to divide the party electorates.

Party-Oriented Cohesion   The interests of the legislative parties as parties often spur the greatest party unity. Among the clearest examples are the basic votes to organize the legislative chamber. In Congress, for example, it is safe to predict 100 percent party cohesion on the vote to elect the Speaker of the House. In 1999 when the 106th Congress began, Republican Dennis Hastert, who succeeded Gingrich, got all of the Republican votes and not a single Democratic vote. Cohesion also tends to be extremely high on issues affecting party strength. In a 1985 vote on whether to award a congressional seat to Democrat Frank McCloskey or Republican Richard McIntyre after a disputed Indiana election, for instance, House Democrats voted 236 to 10 to seat McCloskey and Republicans voted 180 to 0 for McIntyre.

Discipline runs high in the state legislatures over issues such as patronage (and merit-system reform); laws regulating parties, elections, and campaigning; the seating of challenged members of the legislature; and the creation or alteration of legislative districts. Whatever form these issues take, they all touch the basic interests of the party as a political organization: its activists, its organizational structure, its system of rewards, its electorate, or its competitiveness.

Executive-Oriented Cohesion Legislators of a party may also rally around the party's executive or unite against the executive of the other party. The reaction may not be as marked as it would be in a parliamentary system because American presidents freely court the support of the other party. But the partisan reaction is clear. Figure 13.3 traces the support that each legislative party has given to the president on issues he has clearly designated a part of his program. From 1966 through 1999, Republicans supported Republican presidents and Democrats supported Democratic presidents on a majority of votes; the only exception occurred among Senate Democrats in 1968 as Lyndon Johnson's presidency was eroding. Conversely, support from the opposition party for a president's program almost always fell below 50 percent. Consider, for example, the beginning of the Clinton presidency. Democrats' support for their president was never higher, and Republicans' support was relatively low (with the exception of the Senate Republicans in 1997). The increased partisanship in Congress during the last two decades is apparent in these figures.[27]

This executive-oriented cohesion in Congress, which appears in the state legislatures as well, reflects a number of realities of American politics. It may result from the executive's control of political sanctions–patronage in some states, personal support in fund-raising and campaigning, or support of programs for the legislator's constituency. It reflects the fact that the executive increasingly symbolizes the party and its performance. Legislators of the president's party or the governor's party know that they threaten their party and their own political future if they make the party's executive look ineffective. Of course, it may also result from the coincidence of preferences and constituencies between the congressional party and its president.

Nonetheless, there are occasions when loyalty to the chief executive of a legislator's party gives way to other pressures and demands. Although the legislative party's disloyalty to its president can be a major embarrassment to the president and a source of tension between the White House and Capitol Hill, it does not carry the threat of a new election or a new leader (see box on p. 276) as it does in a parliamentary system.

Issue-Oriented Cohesion Legislative parties have long been most cohesive on the issues of the welfare state–the debate over the role of government that has dominated

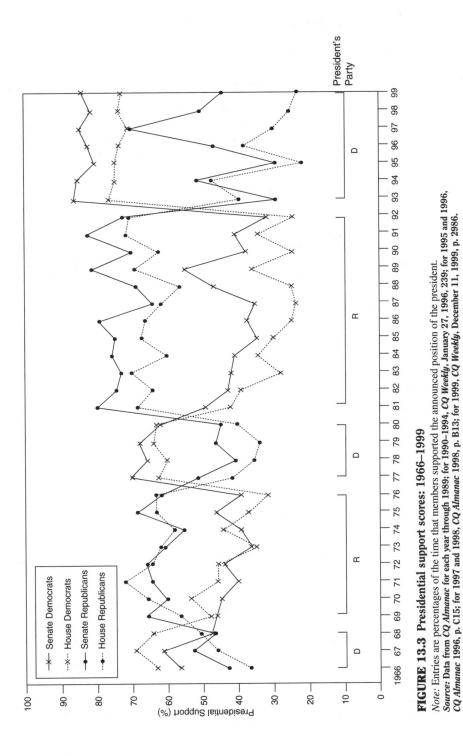

FIGURE 13.3 Presidential support scores: 1966–1999

Note: Entries are percentages of the time that members supported the announced position of the president.
Source: Data from *CQ Almanac* for each year through 1989; for 1990–1994, *CQ Weekly,* January 27, 1996, 239; for 1995 and 1996, *CQ Almanac* 1996, p. C15; for 1997 and 1998, *CQ Almanac* 1998, p. B13; for 1999, *CQ Weekly,* December 11, 1999, p. 2986.

Partisans' Support of Their President

Two congressional votes help to illustrate how differing circumstances can produce different levels of loyalty to a president by the members of his party. The congressional party usually gives overwhelming support to its president on issues involving the president's authority to commit American troops abroad. In 1993, congressional Republicans called for a pullout of American forces from Haiti less than a month after President Clinton had sent them there. House Democrats voted 223 to 32 against the pullout proposal; Republicans were 173 to 1 in favor. Senate Democrats had voted unanimously against an earlier effort to tie the president's hands which Republicans favored 34 to 10.

In contrast partisans sometimes desert their president on issues where they face powerful constituency pressures. President Clinton pushed hard in the spring of 2000 for the establishment of permanent normal trade relations with the People's Republic of China. Big business supported the bill, but labor unions and many local industries worried about the impact of an increase in Chinese imports. The president got his way in the House of Representatives, but only because he won the support of almost three fourths of the Republican representatives. On an issue that Clinton had identified as vital to his legacy, almost two thirds of his Democratic House colleagues, lobbied heavily by organized labor and other interests, voted no.

party conflict since the 1930s. In the states these issues include social security, welfare, and insurance programs; unemployment compensation; labor-management relations; laws governing workers' wages and hours; and aid to agriculture and other sectors of the economy. In Congress a similar set of issues–social welfare, government management of the economy, and agricultural assistance–have stimulated the most partisan voting over the years.[28]

The Constituency Basis of Cohesion

The cohesiveness of the legislative parties depends mainly on the extent to which the parties represent the fundamental divisions in interests and values within the electorate. Party cohesion is greatest where the two parties are highly competitive. One-partyism in a legislature invites the disintegrating squabbles of factions and regional or personal cliques within the dominant party. The South, therefore, has traditionally been the region of the least cohesive legislative parties. Representatives from the one-party South were also those most responsible for undermining the cohesion of the Democratic majority in Congress during much of the post–World War II period.

Party cohesion, furthermore, has typically reached its high point in the legislatures of urban, industrialized states. In these states, the parties tend to divide the voters along the urban-rural and SES lines that have most differentiated the parties since the New Deal. Each party has a relatively homogeneous constituency: one urban and lower-income, the other suburban and rural and higher-income. The backgrounds and lifestyles of each party's legislators usually reflect those of their constituents; thus the differences in their values and experiences reinforce the party differences in constituencies. The result is an issue-oriented politics that reflects those divisions. In these state legislatures, for instance, an attempt to change the eligibility requirements for unemployment compensation will pit one cohesive party against another, with the legislators' prolabor or promanagement stands reinforced by their roots in their home districts and by their own lives and values.

In historical perspective, the bases of party cohesion vary with changes in the nature of the party system, as described in Chapter 6. As realignments have transformed the party systems over the course of American history, the issues that dominate party conflict have changed, and with them, the bases of legislative party cohesion. At the time of the Civil War, the questions of slavery and Reconstruction generated the greatest party conflict and intraparty cohesion. These issues were displaced by conflicts between agrarian and industrial interests in the realignment of 1896.

The questions of social welfare and government management of the economy have come to produce the greatest party voting since the 1930s because they capture best the differences between the Democratic and Republican parties during the New Deal party system. If a new party system emerges, then we would expect a new set of issues to define interparty conflict; perhaps these might include abortion, school prayer, or environmental protection. The parties, in short, may well not divide cleanly on every issue that comes before the legislature. Rather, they will be most distinctive on policy matters closest to the electoral divisions that underlie the current party system.[29]

As Figure 13.1 shows, party voting in the U.S. House has generally peaked during party realignments. These realignments focus attention on national rather than local issues; thus they overcome the inherent localism of Congress. They also tend to produce an increase in membership turnover and a bigger legislative majority party. In doing so, realignments promote party unity on the issues most central to the new party system and thereby permit a degree of party discipline that is rare in the American political system. This newly "responsible" majority party is then in a position to enact the major policy changes that we have come to associate with realignments.[30]

In the same sense, party voting and cohesion tend to decline as the prevailing party system ages and dealignment sets in.[31] Low levels of party voting in the 1960s and 1970s, then, may have reflected the fading of the New Deal party system and, as a result of electoral dealignment, the increased insulation of incumbents from partisan tides. By that logic it would seem that the enhanced levels of party voting since the early 1980s could be another signal that the long-awaited realignment is on its way. The dramatic Republican victory in the 1994 elections followed a campaign in which national forces were dominant. There was an unusually high turnover in legislative seats. The new congressional majority voted cohesively and appeared to be committed to a set of policy goals. The result was a Congress even more sharply divided along party lines. But as Chapter 6 indicated, more recent events warn that there is still a lot of room for argument as to whether the constituency bases of party cohesion have changed enough to justify the term "realignment."

Constituency pressures, the principal basis of party cohesion in the states and Congress, can also inhibit that cohesion. On some legislative issues, the representative must bend to constituency wishes in opposition to the party position, acting as an instructed delegate, if he or she wishes to be reelected. Party leaders rarely demand the member's loyalty in this situation. A study of the relationship between constituency opinion and the representative's vote in the 1958 U.S. House of Representatives found that representatives did not stray far from constituents' preferences on civil rights issues, for example, especially in the South where constituency pressures were intense.[32] As long as the American parties cannot protect legislators from such constituency pressures, it stands to reason that party cohesion will suffer.

Other Bases of Cohesion

Constituency pressures explain a lot of party cohesion but not all of it. The party organizations themselves affect party unity. Times when party leadership in Congress was more centralized–the period from 1881 to 1911, and again in recent years–have been associated with higher levels of party voting. The weakening of the party leadership in between helps to account for the lower levels of party voting during most of the twentieth century. Daily caucuses, party representatives roaming the legislative corridors, and the party pressures of a vigorous governor or powerful party leader enhance cohesion in some of the states today. Yet even when that leadership is strong, it is more likely to be concerned with the smooth operation of the legislature than with the passage of a particular party policy so it is often inclined to settle for compromise solutions rather than complete policy victories.

Party regularity may also be related to the competitiveness of the legislator's constituency. Legislators from unsafe, marginal districts with highly competitive parties are more likely to defect from their party in the legislature than are those from the safer districts. Many of these marginal districts may have characteristics different from those of the parties' usual constituencies. Alternatively, they may be marginal because of the organizational strength of the opposing party or the appeal of its candidates, which in turn forces the legislator to be more than usually sensitive to the constituency.

LEGISLATIVE PARTIES AND PARTY GOVERNMENT

In short, the view that the legislative parties had given away their policy-making role to powerful committees and individual members–or had been forced to do so by organizational patterns unfriendly to party power–was probably always an exaggeration. As the importance of the congressional parties grows, we now see parties as working at the very center of the legislative process. Some even view them as "legislative leviathans" that dominate the business of the Congress in order to benefit their individual members.[33]

This view fits the evidence presented in this chapter. Even though party cohesion in American legislatures falls far short of the standards of some parliamentary parties, party remains the most powerful determinant of legislative roll-call voting and serves as an important force throughout the legislative process. Party affiliation goes further to explain the legislative behavior of state legislators and Congress members than any other single factor in the legislator's environment. Legislators seem normally disposed to support the leadership of their party unless some particularly pressing consideration intervenes.[34]

Yet, despite their importance, the fact remains that most American legislative parties achieve only modest levels of cohesion. The coalitions that produce important legislation often cross party lines. For several decades, in fact, a conservative coalition of Southern Democrats and Northern Republicans rivaled the Democratic Party as a source of legislative organization in Congress. Interest groups, powerful governors, local political leaders, and committee chairs all compete with the legislative party for the ability to organize legislative majorities. In this system of fragmented legislative power and constituency pressure, the legislative party often finds itself in conflict with other voices in the party and outside it.

This is another instance in which the fragmenting institutions of American government have left their mark. With the separation of powers, there is no institutionalized need for party cohesion as there is in the parliamentary systems.[35] It is possible for government in the United States to act, even to govern, without disciplined party support in the legislature. In fact, at those times when one party controls both houses of Congress and the other controls the presidency–or when there is divided party control in a state government–the possibility of reaching agreement on policy would become even more remote if each party were highly unified on behalf of its own party program.

Even at times when American legislative parties have been very cohesive, there is no guarantee that party-dominated government will result. The culprit here is the very nature of the American parties: the party in government has only limited ties to the various parts of the party organization. The legislative parties in Congress and the state legislatures are not controlled by–or always even in contact with–the party's national, state, or local party committees. American legislative parties find it easy to remain independent of the party organization and its commitments to particular policies. When the legislative parties are able to muster some degree of discipline, it is usually on behalf of a set of proposals that originated in the executive or within the legislative party itself.[36]

When the legislative party behaves in a disciplined way, then, it is only rarely accepting the discipline of the party organization or fulfilling pledges that the party organization has previously made. It is politically self-sufficient as a legislative party. To a considerable extent it controls its own rewards. It also tries to control its own political future by setting up party campaign committees, particularly in Congress, to boost the election chances of its members. So long as the members of the legislative party can protect their own renomination and reelection, they can keep the rest of the party at arm's length. Because what we call "the party" is divided geographically along the lines of the American federal system, functionally by the separation of powers, and politically by the diversity of goals and commitments its members bring to it, there really is no unified political party that could establish some control over and responsibility for the actions of its legislative party.

This is not to say that the legislative parties are free agents. They are linked with their party organizations by common concerns and loyalties. In many state legislatures and in Congress the parties differ enough in their concerns and in their supporting constituencies that we find clear differences among cohesive parties. These differences may or may not show up in party platforms and they may or may not be reinforced by the party organizations. Legislative parties may even set them aside in the short run on particular issues. But they exist and they are the main unifying force in a political party that often finds it difficult to articulate a clear and specific set of goals for all its activists and adherents.

Chapter 14

The Party in the Executive and Judiciary

*A*merican presidents, governors, and even judges are almost inevitably drawn into party politics. This partisan involvement appeared soon after the Republic began, in the battles within George Washington's administration between supporters of Alexander Hamilton and Thomas Jefferson, and in the difficult transition from the Federalists to the Democratic-Republicans after the 1800 election.

The framers of the American Constitution gave the president a degree of independence from the legislative branch of government that is unparalleled among modern-day democracies. But it was not until the emergence of the presidency as a popularly elected office in the early 1800s that it became possible for the president to be a party leader in his own right at the national level, just as many governors had long been in their states. Today it is hard for a president or a governor to avoid the dominant leadership role of her or his political party.

The framers also designed an independent federal judiciary with lifetime appointments and a clear separation from the legislative branch in the hope that it would be above the daily battles of partisan politics. But at least since the historic confrontation between Chief Justice John Marshall and the new Jefferson administration in 1803, the federal judiciary has been unable to remain completely aloof from partisan politics.[1] We can see evidence of party considerations in the judiciary today in the conflicts over nominations of federal judges.

The forces for popular democracy enabled party politics to penetrate deeply into the executive and the judiciary to a degree that was almost without peer among Western democracies. The belief that democracy is best guaranteed by popular election of leaders led to the long ballot, on which judges, state administrative officials, and even local surveyors and coroners were elected. That in turn opened the door to party influence in those elections. At the same time, the spoils system justified the use of party ties in choosing appointees to administrative office. Even later reforms intended to insulate judges and bureaucrats from partisan pressures have not overcome these tendencies.

Thus parties affect the recruitment and selection of these public officials. Do parties also influence the way these officials exercise their powers? We have seen that the parties have had success in mobilizing American legislatures. Have they had equal success with the executive and judicial branches? In their policy decisions, does it make any difference whether executives and judges are selected by the Democrats or by the Republicans? Do the parties try to affect the selection of these officials only in order to meet their internal needs for rewards and incentives, or do they do so as well to promote party programs?

THE EXECUTIVE AS A PARTY LEADER

The twentieth century was a century of political leadership of mass publics in democracies and as well as in dictatorships. In the democracies electorates expanded to include virtually all adults. At the same time the new mass media brought political leaders closer than ever to citizens. In the United States these changes culminated in the personal leadership of the presidency. Wilson, Roosevelt, Kennedy, Reagan—to millions of American citizens these names signify both executive power and a personal tie. The post-Watergate reaction against the "imperial presidency" stalled the trend only temporarily. Even nations with parliamentary systems have been energized by the growth of personal leadership and their election campaigns increasingly center on the potential prime ministers.[2]

A major ingredient of executive leadership in the United States has been the leadership of a mass political party. When Andrew Jackson combined his quest for the presidency with leadership of a party, he began a revolution in both the American presidency and the American political party. The presidency ceased to be the repository of elitist good sense and conservatism that Hamilton hoped it would be and became an agent of mass political leadership. Thus it was the president rather than the Congress who was seen as the voice of the people.

The chief executive now incorporated both of the chief agents of popular democracy: a popularly elected leader and a mass party. The power of the office was reinforced by the power of the party. Presidents, governors, and mayors are rarely formal party leaders; others hold those responsibilities. Rather, the chief executive's role as party leader is a subtle combination of several overlapping partisan roles.

Party Leader as Representative of the Whole Constituency

One of the unique features of the American system is that the president and the Congress represent different constituencies. The national constituency the president represents is not the same as the sum of the congressional constituencies. Congressional constituencies are local and particularistic and in the Senate they collectively overrepresent the rural areas of the country. The president's constituency, in contrast, overrepresents the large, urban, industrial states on which the electoral college places such a premium. It is a constituency that often leads its incumbent to support greater governmental responsibility for solving national problems than the congressional party is likely to do. Further, because his is the only truly national constituency, the presidential candidate is the only candidate of the national party.

Similarly, American governors represent the entire state, in contrast to the local ties of the state legislators. Other public officials may also have statewide constituencies; the constitutions of some states have made the state treasurer, attorney general, state insurance commissioner, and even state supreme court justices into elected officials. Unlike these lesser-known officials, though, the governor embodies the party on the statewide level, just as most mayors do at the local level. Like the president, he or she is recognized by voters as the executive and must develop a policy record and a concern for the problems of the whole state.

Party Leader as Organizational Leader

American executives may also choose to be concerned with the organizational affairs of their political party. Some presidents may try to cultivate an image of being "above" partisan politics.[3] But most realize that they symbolize their party for millions of Americans and they take their partisan leadership role seriously. Ronald Reagan, for example, championed his party's cause more actively than almost any president since Franklin Roosevelt. Bill Clinton has remained an active Democratic fund-raiser while president, not only in Senate and House races but in contests for governor as well.[4]

The president's major influence on the party organization rests in his control of the national party committee. Its chair must be acceptable to him and usually is selected by him. The president is also free to shape the committee's role, even if only to turn it into his personal campaign organization. However, the national committee and state party organizations no longer play a role in appointments to the president's immediate White House staff.[5] Whereas earlier presidents often included their national party's chairman in their cabinet and relied on him or her for advice on the intricacies of party politics, presidents now appoint cabinet members and White House staff members to help them govern and to protect their own political positions rather than to serve the political needs of the party organization.

In particular, presidents' relationships with state and local party organizations have weakened. Presidents are less inclined now to do the kind of "party-building"—strengthening state parties and their leadership—that presidents routinely did early in the twentieth century. Although President Reagan campaigned unusually hard for Republican candidates, for example, the Republican National Committee's extensive party-building efforts were largely independent of the White House.

Party Leader as Electoral Leader

Executives, by their political successes or failures, affect the election chances of other candidates of their party. A good example was Ronald Reagan's win in 1980 and landslide reelection in 1984, which were accompanied by higher than normal levels of success for other Republican candidates. The Republicans captured control of the Senate in 1980 for the first time since the 1952 election. Republican House candidates also received a higher percentage of the votes cast in the two presidential election years than in the preceding and following midterm elections, when Reagan was not on the ballot.

Coattail Effects   This link between presidential success and party victories is traditionally explained by the metaphor of coattails. Presidents ran "at the top of the ticket," the explanation goes, and the rest of the party ticket came into office clinging to their sturdy coattails. (Nineteenth-century dress coats did have tails.) Coattail effects seemed especially prominent in the nineteenth century when, in a time when the parties printed their own ballots, it was difficult to split the ticket in voting for candidates from different parties.

Researchers continue to find coattail effects in congressional elections, but these effects have declined since World War II.[6] Incumbent Congress members are better able now to insulate themselves from outside election forces, including presidential popularity, by increasing attentiveness to their districts and because their campaign resources are normally so much greater than those of their challengers.

We can see the limits of the coattail effect in recent presidential-year elections. In 1988, even though Republican George Bush defeated Michael Dukakis by 54 to 46 percent in the popular vote and the Republican House candidates received a 1 percent gain in votes, the party actually lost two seats in the House of Representatives. Vote gains in congressional elections do not translate perfectly into gains in House seats; this moderates the effect of coattails. Bush's successor, Bill Clinton, seemed to have even shorter coattails. In Clinton's 1992 victory in a three-candidate presidential race, Democratic House candidates ran well ahead of their presidential candidate. When he won reelection in 1996 with an improvement of 6 percent in his vote share, Democrats gained nine seats in the House but lost two in the Senate, and Clinton was not able to restore Democratic control in either house of Congress.

Nevertheless, presidents do develop coattails in particular races even now. At times, presidential coattails have extended beyond House elections to contests for the state legislature and even to some Senate elections, in spite of the high visibility of most Senate candidates.[7] From 1944 through 1984, when a president ran strongly in a state the president's party typically did better in state legislative contests on the same ballot. This coattail effect in state legislative races was not as strong as it could be in races for Congress. Even so, many states decided to move their state legislative elections to years when the presidency was not on the ballot, to insulate state elections from presidential politics.

Coattails Even without the Coat   In fact presidential leadership is so prominent in voters' eyes that a president can influence election results for other contests even if he is not on the ballot. In midterm congressional elections, voters' expressed intentions to vote for candidates of the president's party varies during the campaign in tandem with their levels of approval of the way the president is handling his job. And since the late 1930s there has been a strong relationship between voters' approval of the president and the midterm gains or losses of his party in congressional races. In the 1994 midterm election, drops in President Clinton's approval rating coincided with big Democratic losses in the House and Senate. Clinton's public approval was on the upswing in time for the 1998 congressional elections—ironically, in that he was just a few weeks away from being impeached by the House, and in part because of public discomfort with the unremitting pursuit of impeachment by the Republican congressional majority.[8]

Further, the absence of a president's coattails may help explain the intriguing tendency of the president's party to lose House seats in midterm elections. Since 1856, the presidential party's share of seats in the House of Representatives has been reduced in the next midterm election with only two exceptions: the midterm contests of 1934 at the beginning of the New Deal realignment, and 1998 (see the discussion in Chapter 13). Just as a popular presidential candidate can boost the chances of his party's candidates in the presidential year, his absence from the ticket may deprive them of this advantage at midterm.[9]

A Broader Perspective on Electoral Influence   In sum, there are several important ways in which a president is the electoral leader of his party. Presidential coattails vary in strength but they indicate that at least some voters seem to be influenced by the president's performance when they cast ballots for other offices. The candidates for these other offices—both the president's partisans and their opponents—recognize this relationship and must take it into account as they plan and conduct their campaigns.[10]

The weakening of presidential coattails and of the impact of presidential popularity certainly dilutes his power as party leader and his influence in Congress. Yet even if the president's popularity accounts for only small percentage shifts in the congressional vote, these small shifts can make a big difference in party strength in Congress. From 1952 to 1970, each shift of 1 percent in the popular vote added or subtracted about eight seats in the House of Representatives.[11] Although House seats have become less responsive to popular vote changes since then, the balance between conservative and liberal forces and the less-than-perfect levels of party cohesion allow even a small change in seats to have a big impact on legislation.

In the years between elections, as well, popular support is a valuable resource for the chief executive in getting Congress to go along with his programs. In the first year of the Reagan administration, for example, President Reagan's popularity in the country was one reason for his considerable success on the Hill, just as President Clinton's unpopularity made it harder for him to steer health care reform through a Democratic Congress. Members of Congress apparently assume that being linked with the proposals of an unpopular president will hurt them electorally—and with good reason. There is evidence that citizens who disapprove of the president's performance vote in larger numbers in midterm elections than those who approve, and that their disapproval leads them to vote for the other party and its candidates.[12]

People's evaluations of a president or governor also seem to affect the way they view the parties. Executive programs are seen as party programs, and the successes and failures of executives are party successes and failures. For a public that views politics chiefly in personal terms, a president, a governor, or even a big-city mayor personifies the party. In addition, a popular president's fund-raising capabilities are a great advantage to his party's candidates, especially the ones he favors. This gives the president important leverage over party office seekers.

Limits on Electoral Leadership

The ties between chief executives and their party have real limits, however. Some presidents and governors lack the desire to lead a party or they do not think it proper for an executive to do so. They may feel that they gain a political advantage by appearing bipartisan. Even those who want to be party leaders may find that the pressures to be a president, governor, or mayor of "all of the people" limit their ability to behave as a partisan.

Chief executives may also lead only part of a party. Governors from one-party states, for example, often represent only a party faction. Executives may share leadership of the party with other partisans. Presidents who are not especially secure in national party affairs may find the more experienced leaders of the congressional party asserting major leadership in the national party. Governors may compete with senators, who represent as broad a constituency, and other representatives of their party for leadership of the state party. These legislators and state party leaders may fear that the governor will use party control for his or her own political ambitions.

The Executive-Centered Party

Nonetheless, the president heads and occasionally even unifies the national party. In addition to his dominance of the national committee and the rest of the national organization, he often exerts enough mastery of the legislative party to speak for the party in government. Most important from a public standpoint, for millions of American voters he is the symbol of the party, its programs, and its performance. Within the state and local parties, the governors and many mayors have the same unifying role and they, too, have their leverage on legislative parties and organizations.[13]

Therefore it is no exaggeration to speak of the American parties as executive-centered coalitions. No other leader can compete with the executive in representing the party to the public, in commanding a broad array of tools of influence, or in enjoying as much legitimacy as the center of party leadership. Even in the party out of power, opposition to the other party's executive and planning for the next campaign assault on that office provide the major unifying focus. In the meantime the "headless" quality of the party out of power is an indicator of its reduced status.

This central role of the executive would certainly surprise anyone whose knowledge of American politics is limited to a reading of the Constitution. The writers of the Constitution gave the presidency a paltry grant of power—not enough to hold his own in struggles with the Congress. Faced with this shortage of formal powers, presidents have learned to rely heavily on other sources of power, one of which is their party leadership. They generally put the leverage they derive from their position as party leader into efforts to maximize support for their programs and their own political futures rather than into work to strengthen the party organization.

PARTY LEADERSHIP AND LEGISLATIVE RELATIONS

Presidents must share policy-making power with Congress in fields other than national defense and foreign policy—and even in those fields, where presidents have primacy, they must deal with congressional challenges. To influence the making of policy they must influence the actions of the legislature. In order to do that presidents and other chief executives rely frequently on party ties.

The Problems of Divided Control of Government

This reliance is complicated by the possibility—a frequent possibility in modern American politics—that the president's party will be in the minority in Congress. Between 1968 and 2000, for example, the president's party has controlled both houses of Congress for only six years: four under President Carter and two under President Clinton. During the same period almost all of the states have also experienced divided party control of the legislature and the governorship. At such times presidents and governors find it risky to rely heavily on partisan appeals. Because of the closeness of the party division in many legislatures and the unreliability of some legislators of their own party, they must also curry favor of some legislators of the opposing party. Thus American chief executives must walk a fine line, making partisan appeals to legislators of their own party and nonpartisan or bipartisan appeals to those in the opposition.

Tools of Executive Influence

In trying to get Congress to pursue their objectives presidents rely on a variety of resources. They make constant use of their prestige and persuasiveness and their command of the media. Explicitly or not, they also use their identification with the party, whatever lingering patronage or preferments they can command (a judicial appointment here, a government project there), and their ability to influence coming elections. Members of the president's party know that if they make him look bad, to some extent they also make themselves and their party look bad. That produces a tendency to rally around the president on important votes despite their own legislative preferences. When their president has exercised his veto of congressional bills, for example, members of his party are sometimes even willing to reverse their original support for the bill by voting to uphold his veto (see Table 14.1).

In fact members of Congress who benefited in the past from presidential coattails are more likely to support the president's program than those who did not. Legislators, then, seem to anticipate and also to react to the fact that the president heads the party ticket when he runs, and his performance becomes the party's record when he does not. The president's standing figures prominently in legislators' hopes and fears of a change in their party's success and, by extension, their own success. Only the president has the political visibility required to capitalize on favorable political conditions for the party or with an incautious misstep to turn the public mood against the party. President Clinton, for example, has done both.

Legislative Support for Executives

Even so, Congress is often stubbornly resistant to presidential leadership. Recent presidents have often been unable to gain congressional approval of their proposals even when their party controls the Congress. President Carter had only about a 75 percent success rate with a Democratic Congress, and President Clinton scored only about 10 percent higher during his first two years in office, when the Democrats held majorities in Congress. Presidents get much less support when Congress is in the hands of the opposing party, as the battles between President Clinton and the Republican Congress in 1995 demonstrate.

There are occasions—the early Nixon years and the early Reagan years are examples—when especially effective presidential leadership is able to get even a Congress controlled by the other party to go along with what he wants. President Reagan was greatly helped, of course, by the fact that his party had won a majority in the Senate (see Figure 14.1, p. 288).[14] But American presidents have never been able to gain as much support in Congress as prime ministers naturally enjoy in parliamentary systems.

Moreover, presidential success rates have dropped a bit in recent decades. In addition to the challenge of divided government, changes in congressional elections have also been a factor here. Weaker and more variable presidential coattails have an effect,

TABLE 14.1 Pre and Post–Veto Support of President by his Party on Selected Votes, 1973–1998

	Percent of President's Party Supporting President's Position	
	Original Passage	Vote on Veto Override
President Nixon		
Vocational Rehabilitation, Senate, 1973	5	76
Water-Sewer Program, House, 1973	31	87
Cambodia Bombing Halt, House, 1973	66	72
President Ford		
Public-Works Employment, Senate, 1976	44	68
Aid to Day-Care Centers, Senate, 1976	47	70
Hatch Act Revisions, House, 1976	65	84
President Carter		
Weapons Procurement Authorization, House, 1978	26	69
Public-Works Appropriations, House, 1978	18	48
Oil Import-Fee Abolition, Senate, 1980	12	22
President Reagan		
Standby Petroleum Allocation Act, Senate, 1982	13	62
Supplemental Appropriations, House, 1982	27	56
South African Sanctions, Senate, 1986	27	40
President Bush		
FS-X Development Restrictions, Senate, 1989	56	73
Most-Favored-Nation Status for China, House, 1992	8	32
Family Leave, Senate, 1992	65	67
President Clinton		
Military Construction Appropriations, House, 1996 (Line item veto)	3	27

Source: For presidents Nixon through Reagan: selections from Randall B. Ripley, *Congress, Process and Policy* (New York: Norton, 1988), p. 189. For Presidents Bush and Clinton, various issues of the *Congressional Quarterly Weekly Report* (now *CQ Weekly*).

as does the high reelection rate of incumbents. The practice of cultivating the constituency by attending closely to its interests and providing more services to individual constituents helps to insulate members of Congress from the heavy hand of the president's electoral impact.[15] In consequence, presidents are led to place less emphasis on their role as party leaders and more on other components of their influence.

Governors, on the other hand, are often able to exercise much greater and more direct party organizational power over the legislators of their party. Many state legislatures do not use seniority rules, so some governors can take an active part in selecting committee chairs and party floor leaders when the legislative session begins. Some governors lead powerful state party organizations; legislators who cross them may

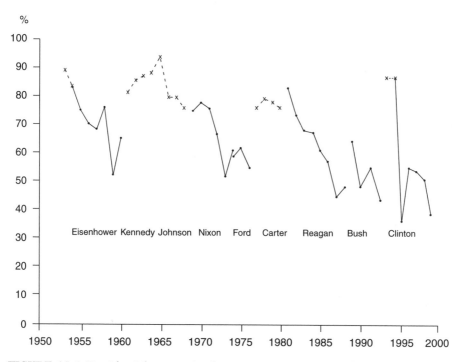

FIGURE 14.1 Presidential success in the U.S. Congress, 1953–1999.

Note: The entry for each year is the percentage of time members of both the House and the Senate voted in support of the announced position of the president. Years in which the president's party controlled both houses of Congress are indicated by an "x" and connected by dotted lines. Years in which the opposition party controlled at least one house of Congress are indicated by a "." and connected by solid lines.
Source: *Congressional Quarterly Weekly Report,* **December 31, 1994, 3654 and, for 1995–1999, other end-of-the-year *CQ Weekly* issues.**

risk undermining their legislative career as well as their future ambitions. In short, the average governor has far greater control over party rewards and incentives than a president does. On the other hand, governors are less visible and salient than presidents, so their coattails and prestige—their symbolic role—are likely to be less potent than those of presidents.

PARTY POWER AND ADMINISTRATIVE POLICY

The rest of the executive branch stands in the president's shadow but exercises a great deal of power. Bureaucrats—those who work in cabinet-level departments and other federal agencies in the executive branch—are charged by the Constitution with carrying out the laws Congress passes. In spite of a burst of deregulation in the 1980s and 1990s, government agencies still regulate vast areas of the economy—food safety, prescription drugs, insurance, radio and TV, and pollution, for example—under congressional mandates that require a lot of interpretation.[16] The bureaucrats who implement these laws therefore must make important decisions on public policy; they shape policy by applying it. We need to ask, then, whether presidents, governors, and mayors are able to hold these administrators responsible for implementing a party program—or any program at all.

Limits on Executive Leadership

Perhaps the biggest problem executives face in enforcing party discipline on their subordinates is the same problem faced by legislative party leaders: constituency pressure. Just as legislators identify with the needs of their constituents, administrators often identify with the needs of the groups and individuals their agencies deal with. Top-level administrators know that their best political protection is the support of their client groups. The Department of Labor, for instance, depends heavily on the support of labor unions, and the Environmental Protection Agency works very closely with environmental groups and the industries it regulates. Party loyalties do not compete very well with the power of these constituencies; in the executive as well as the legislative branch, the party has less to give and less to take away than the constituency does.[17]

Many other factors limit an executive's ability to unify an administration and hold it accountable for achieving a party's programmatic goals; several of these limits stem from Progressive reforms enacted decades ago:

- The legislature may place administrative positions outside executive control by specifying that their appointments last longer than the chief executive's term (such as for the governors of the Federal Reserve System, which acts as the nation's central bank), by limiting the executive's power to remove them, or by placing policy-makers under a merit system.

- Legislatures can take special steps to prevent partisan control of an administrative agency—for example, by requiring that its leadership include members of more than one political party. (The Federal Election Commission board, for instance, must include three Democrats and three Republicans.)

- Top administrators in many states are elected. Thus voters may choose a Republican for governor and a Democrat for state treasurer, for example, to work together in an uncomfortable alliance. Even if both officials are of the same party, their offices are often politically and constitutionally independent.

- Most American executives are term-limited; presidents can run for only two terms, and most governors can serve only one or two consecutive terms. As these officeholders approach the end of their terms, their authority over other officeholders diminishes.

- Finally, executives must often share power with others. The practice of senatorial courtesy gives the U.S. Senate a say in presidential appointees. In forming a cabinet, as well, presidents cannot ignore the preferences of groups within the party that contributed to the president's victory.

Tools of Executive Influence

It is probably not as difficult to hold high-level administrators such as cabinet members responsible to a party program as it is to affect other administrators, however. People appointed to these top-level jobs have often been politically active, and they are likely to have a commitment to the party's goals and programs. President Clinton's cabinet (see box below) shows that party remains a reservoir of talent, even a recruiter

Partisan Democratic Backgrounds of the Clinton Cabinet

Most of the members of President Bill Clinton's cabinet in early 2000 had at least some experience in Democratic party politics as elected officeholders and candidates for office, appointees to political positions in previous Democratic administrations, or campaign strategists. Here are their former party roles:

Madeleine Albright (State): Member of President Carter's National Security Council and White House staff; Chief Legislative Assistant to former Democratic Senator Ed Muskie

Bruce Babbitt (Interior): Democratic Attorney General and Governor of Arizona

William Cohen (Defense): Republican Senator from Maine

Andrew Cuomo (Housing and Urban Development): Campaign manager for Mario Cuomo, former Democratic governor of New York

William M. Daley (Commerce): Host Committee for the 1996 Democratic National Convention and key adviser to his brother, Democratic Chicago Mayor Richard M. Daley

Dan Glickman (Agriculture): Democratic U.S. Representative from Kansas

Alexis Herman (Labor): Longtime Democratic operative, former Democratic National Committee chief of staff

Janet Reno (Justice): Democratic State Attorney, Dade County (Miami), Florida

Bill Richardson (Energy): Democratic U.S. Representative from New Mexico

Richard W. Riley (Education): Democratic member of the South Carolina legislature; Democratic Governor of South Carolina

Donna E. Shalala (Health and Human Services): Assistant Secretary of Housing and Urban Development under Democratic President Carter

Rodney Slater (Transportation): Served in the administration of then-Governor Clinton; Federal Highway Administration head under Clinton

Lawrence Summers (Treasury): Deputy Secretary of the Treasury under Clinton; Harvard Professor

Togo D. West, Jr. (Veterans Affairs): Secretary of the Army, Carter administration's General Counsel for the Navy

of talent, for modern administrations. Presidents are no longer as explicitly partisan as they once were in making cabinet appointments; they no longer use these positions as rewards for loyal party service. Instead they look for individuals with experience in the areas of policy they will administer.[18] Nevertheless, most presidential appointees have been active partisans whose values and political careers have been shaped to a significant degree by their party.

Just below this administrative level, however, officeholders are less likely to have party and governmental experience. These officials are most often chosen for their administrative skills and experience and only secondarily for their political credentials. The role of the party organization in their selection may extend only to verifying that they are politically acceptable (that is, inoffensive) in their home states. Yet they continue to come largely from the party of the president, and the party link can produce a commitment to a common outlook.[19]

Administrations with an ideological mission, such as the Reagan administration, have worked hard to ensure this common political outlook. They try to fill executive positions with ideological sympathizers, not just fellow partisans, and to charge them with the mission of carrying out the president's policies. In such cases, tension is likely to develop between the party loyalists and the ideologues in the administration's top leadership. Appointing ideological sympathizers can produce a cohesive administration but it can weaken the party's impact and undermine the president's influence with fellow partisans in the Congress.

In all these ways it is a formidable problem to establish political control over the executive bureaucracy, especially at the national level. Modern presidents can make only about 3,500 political appointments—fewer appointive positions than some governors have—to try to gain control of an executive branch employing several million civilian employees. Many of the president's men and women are novices with little time to "learn the ropes" and little prospect of gaining the necessary support of career bureaucrats. As Hugh Heclo has shown, together they comprise "a government of strangers": a set of executives whose limited familiarity and interaction with one another prevent them from acting as an effective team and who are therefore likely to be overwhelmed by a huge, fragmented, and more or less permanent bureaucracy.[20]

Not surprisingly, then, recent presidents, and especially Republican presidents, have relied more and more on their immediate White House staff and the Office of Management and Budget in trying to mobilize the executive branch on behalf of their policy goals.[21] Even though party can be an important instrument for controlling the administrative bureaucracy, serving as both a recruitment channel for executive talent and a common bond between the executive and top bureaucrats, it is often inadequate for accomplishing the difficult task of executive leadership.

Changing Political Outlooks in the Federal Bureaucracy

Yet in its own way the federal bureaucracy (and many of the state bureaucracies as well) is responsive to partisan forces. As the federal government expanded in the 1930s, President Roosevelt drew people into the career bureaucracy who were committed to his programs. These dedicated New Dealers became a bulwark against later efforts to weaken these programs, especially as they were promoted during the years to more and more senior positions in their agencies.

By 1970, Joel Aberbach and Bert Rockman found that nearly a majority of these career bureaucrats said they normally voted Democratic and only 17 percent usually voted Republican. In federal social service agencies, even the administrators who were not Democrats said that they favored liberal policies. Republican President Richard Nixon, in office at that time, thus faced a federal bureaucracy that had little sympathy for his conservative agenda. His administration spent a lot of time trying to control the bureaucracy by appointing White House loyalists to top bureaucratic positions.[22]

By 1992, however, the bureaucratic environment had changed. When Aberbach and Rockman returned to interview career administrators in comparable positions, they found slight Republican pluralities, although the career executives were still much more Democratic and liberal than the Reagan and Bush political appointees. As older civil servants retired, a new generation less committed to New Deal and Great Society programs had been recruited into senior executive positions. Changes in civil service laws, further, allowed positions formerly reserved for career employees to be filled by political appointees who could be carefully screened by the White House. The bureaucracy was no longer as unsympathetic to Republican initiatives. But the inherent difficulties of controlling even a sympathetic bureaucracy remained.[23]

In sum, executives use their party leadership role mainly for the tasks of governing and meeting their public responsibilities. For most, the goals and interests of their party organization are only secondary. Many governors do use some patronage appointments purely for party goals, and presidents may use some cabinet appointments to recognize various groups within the party, but they do so at a cost to the executive's own administrative goals. Ultimately, chief executives build party cohesion mainly in order to promote their own programs and their own reelection. It is the goals of the office, not of the party, that they pursue.

THE SHADOW OF PARTY IN THE JUDICIARY

Courts and judges are affected by party politics as well. Many American judges are political men and women who took office after careers that involved them in some aspect of partisan politics. Even though reformers have tried to insulate the judicial system from politics and especially from party politics, the selection of judges continues to be shaped by partisanship in elections and through appointments. Because of the nature of the judiciary, however, the influence can be subtle.

Judicial Voting along Party Lines

Hints of party influence appear when we examine the voting in American appellate courts. Several studies show that in cases such as those involving workers' compensation, judges split into partisan blocs. A study of state courts found that Democratic judges, for example, tended to decide more often for the defendant in criminal cases, for the government in tax cases, for the regulatory agency in cases involving the regulation of business, and for the claimants in workers' compensation, unemployment compensation, and auto accident cases.[24] In recent redistricting cases, U.S. District Court judges have tended to uphold plans enacted by their party more than those enacted by the opposing party.[25] There is clearly much less party cohesion in judges' decision-making than there is in legislatures. It appears only in certain types of cases, yet it appears; Democratic judges render different decisions from their Republican colleagues.

A small amount of this party influence may reflect efforts by party officials, at least at the state and local level, to influence judges' decisions in particular cases. Occasionally a judge may continue to be deeply immersed in partisan politics even after going on the bench, although explicit partisan activity now violates judicial norms. In a few counties, the local district or county judge slates candidates behind the scenes and arbitrates among the conflicting ambitions of party candidates. A judge who is closely tied to the local party may provide a reservoir of patronage for the party organization: guardianships, receiverships in bankruptcy, and clerkships that can be given to party loyalists who are attorneys.[26]

The Influence of Party in and on the Judge

A much better explanation of the impact of party on judges' behavior, however, is simply that judges, like other well-educated people, bring partisan frames of reference to their work. Just as the two parties reflect different sets of values, so do their identifiers, including those who become judges. Two judges might vote together on the issue of regulating business because of the values they share about the proper role of government in the economy. Those same values led them years earlier to join the same party or were developed out of experience in the same party. In other words, it is not usually the external pressure provided by a party organization or leader, but rather the party *in* the judge that leads judges with similar partisan backgrounds to the same decisions.

Parties have an opportunity in many states to influence the selection of judges. That gives them a means to further party goals by encouraging the appointment or election of judges who believe in the values for which the party stands. It also permits them to further the careers of lawyers who have served the party loyally. To what extent do the parties or partisan forces influence the process by which judges are chosen?

Partisan Considerations in Judicial Selection

Those who appoint judges to their posts are well aware of the link between a judge's values and his or her party affiliation. They need to be. There are cases in which judges have options, and the choices they make may reflect in part their own experiences and beliefs. Thus the selection of judges has traditionally taken the values and attitudes of the candidates into account. For example, as President Theodore Roosevelt, considering a Supreme Court nomination, wrote to Senator Henry Lodge in inquiring about a certain Judge Oliver Wendell Holmes of the Massachusetts Supreme Court (later to become a distinguished U.S. Supreme Court justice):

> In the ordinary and low sense which we attach to the words "partisan" and "politician," a judge of the Supreme Court should be neither. But in the higher sense, in the proper sense, he is not in my judgment fitted for the position unless he is a party man, a constructive statesman, constantly keeping in mind his adherence to the

principles and policies under which this nation has been built up and in accordance with which it must go on.

Now I should like to know that Judge Holmes was in entire sympathy with our views, that is, with your views and mine ... before I would feel justified in appointing him.[27]

Selection of Federal Judges   Congress, like President Roosevelt, also examines judges' values and beliefs in reviewing presidential nominations for federal judgeships. There were major Senate battles over the confirmation of two Supreme Court nominees, Robert Bork and Clarence Thomas, during the Reagan and Bush administrations; both nominees were known to be outspoken conservatives. Even party platforms have sometimes called for the appointment of judges with certain ideological characteristics. For the last two decades, for instance, Republican platforms have pledged the selection of judges who believe in the sanctity of all human life—in other words, who are antiabortion.

Whether or not a president or a governor should consider such questions, prospective judges' political party and ideology serve as important indicators of their attitudes and thus, potentially, their decisions in some kinds of cases. That is a major reason why every American president during the twentieth century has made at least 80 percent of his judicial appointments from within his own party (see Table 14.2), and the average is higher than 90 percent.

TABLE 14.2 Partisan Appointments to Federal District and Appellate Courts: Presidents Cleveland to Clinton

	Percentage from the President's Party
Cleveland	97.3
Harrison	87.9
McKinley	95.7
T. Roosevelt	95.8
Taft	82.2
Wilson	98.6
Harding	97.7
Coolidge	94.1
Hoover	85.7
F. Roosevelt	96.4
Truman	93.1
Eisenhower	95.1
Kennedy	90.9
Johnson	94.5
Nixon	92.8
Ford	81.2
Carter	88.8
Reagan	92.7
Bush	88.6
Clinton	88.5

Source: Harold W. Stanley and Richard G. Niemi, *Vital Statistics on American Politics 1999–2000* (Washington, DC: CQ Press, 2000), Table 7.6, p. 278.

Recent presidents have differed in the extent to which ideological and party considerations have affected their judicial appointments. The Reagan and Bush administrations took special care to screen candidates for their dedication to conservative principles. The tradition of allowing the presidential party's senators to select candidates for district and appellate judgeships was modified; senators were asked to submit three names for consideration, and the administration made the final choice.[28] As a result, Reagan and Bush appointees were even more ideologically distinctive (as well as more likely to have been active in party politics) than the average among recent presidents.

By contrast, the Clinton administration has given a larger role to his party's senators and other leaders in suggesting judicial nominees and has been less concerned with ideological screening. Clinton has also appointed a somewhat lower percentage of federal judges from his own party than most of his predecessors did and has been less inclined to choose judges with records of party activity.[29]

Selection of State Court Judges   State court judges are selected in a very different manner from federal court judges. States use five different methods of selection: gubernatorial appointment, legislative election, partisan election, nonpartisan election, and the merit or "Missouri" plan in which judges are first selected (usually by the governor) from a list compiled by a nonpartisan screening committee and then must run in a retention election within several years of their appointment. Also in contrast to federal courts, lawyers play a more decisive role in screening judgeship candidates for state courts; in states using the Missouri plan, lawyers are often the major influence on the ultimate choices.

The states are divided fairly evenly among the different selection methods. Governors appoint the judges in seven states, and in another four the legislature chooses them. Partisanship intrudes directly into the selection process in nine states: candidates for at least some of their judgeships must run for office in partisan elections. The partisanship can be more apparent than real, however; at times both parties will endorse the same candidate, who is often the choice of the state bar association.

Most states have made serious efforts to take partisanship out of the process of selecting judges. Thirteen states, following the Progressive tradition, elect judges on a nonpartisan ballot. (In some of these states it is common for each party to endorse its own slate of candidates publicly, so the nonpartisanship is a facade.) Merit selection by the Missouri plan is an increasingly popular alternative; seventeen states used this method in 1998.[30]

Regardless of the selection process, partisanship is certainly present in most state court systems. No matter what selection procedure is used, for example, the division of votes in multijudge panels often shows evidence of party lines. Further, even in states where voters elect the judges, there is a good chance that many of these judges will have first been appointed—by a partisan official—to their posts. Judicial terms tend to be long ones. Those who are elected to them are typically middle-aged or older. When an elected judge leaves the bench because of death or illness, the governor normally fills the vacancy until the next election. The appointee, with the advantage of even a brief period of incumbency, then usually wins a full term at the next election. Of course the high probability of reelection can free appointed judges from partisan pressures. But these pressures are so often already internalized in the judge's values and preferences that a long-term judgeship merely allows them to flourish.[31]

The selection process is one reason why there is such a substantial tie between partisanship and the judiciary in the United States. Another major reason is that in the American system there is no special training process for judges—no examination to take, no advanced degree in "judgeship." Any lawyer can be a judge if he or she can win election or appointment to the job. By contrast, in many continental European countries someone prepares for the career of judging through study and apprenticeship and then becomes a judge by special civil service examination. Under those circumstances party organizations will find it much harder to affect the selection of judges. But even so, those who become judges will still have political preferences, many of which will have been shaped by their earlier partisan experiences.

THE PARTY WITHIN THE EXECUTIVE AND THE JUDGE

It is interesting, then, that party influence on political executives and judges shows some clear similarities. In both cases the main avenue of party influence is indirect; it stems from the fact that executives and judges are people who hold commitments and values, and those values tend to differ according to the individual's partisanship and loyalties. The parties do not have the means to enforce party discipline in the executive or judicial branches through patronage or the threat of removal. So party influence depends mainly on the presence of party values or ideological commitments *within* the men and women who hold administrative or judicial office.

Efforts have been made—the use of the merit system to appoint officials, for instance—to wring partisan considerations out of the selection process. But there is no way to eliminate individuals' views and values—and thus their partisanship—from their selection as administrators or as judges. In fact in a nation where the courts play an important policy-making role, it may be naïve to think that the administrative agency or the bench can be purged of party influence—or that it should be.

Chapter 15

The Quest for Party Government

Political parties are among the many interesting paradoxes of American politics. On one hand, parties are everywhere. They pervade the political process. Even where there is no obvious influence of party organization or leaders, party considerations can weigh heavily in the decisions made by voters, activists, bureaucrats, and even judges. Yet compared with many European democracies the American parties are weak. They find it difficult to mobilize elected officials behind a unified set of party policies. They have very limited ability to control any officials, elected or appointed. In short, they find it hard to govern.[1]

This fundamental problem has attracted a great deal of critical attention. To some critics the problem is much broader than the parties themselves. The challenge is the fragmentation of American politics: the principles of separation of powers and federalism which do such a good job of hobbling governmental initiatives and of blurring political alternatives. These critics, bolstered by an early report constructed by some of the leading academic experts on political parties,[2] have argued for a system of more "responsible" parties. A governing party in this system would translate a coherent political philosophy into government action and would then be held responsible for the results; this, they argue, would improve the American version of democracy.

Others see a more limited problem which they lay right at the parties' doorstep. When Ross Perot charged in the 1990s that both the Democrats and the Republicans were wedded to the status quo, he was singing an old tune. For decades the parties have been assailed as being too much alike in their platforms, too centrist, and not clear and specific enough on major issues.[3] Conservative Republican activists in the 1964 presidential campaign pleaded for a platform that would be "a choice, not an echo" of the Democrats. In his third-party candidacy in 1968, George Wallace spoke for the view that there was "not a dime's worth of difference" between the major parties. John McCain campaigned in the 2000 Republican primaries on the charge that both parties were tied to the demands of the moneyed special interests.

These two sets of critics have different perspectives but at heart they make the same point. The scholars who favor party government and the ideologically oriented activists of the left and right both want the parties to present clearer and more specific platforms. They want each party to develop a greater commitment to a coherent set of principles and they want the winning party to put its principles to work in public policy. And to a certain extent their complaints have been answered. Both parties have

297

become more ideologically distinctive in the last two decades. The Democratic Party is more uniformly liberal now, after many Southern conservatives moved away from their traditional Democratic allegiance and into the Republican Party, and the Republicans have followed a more clearly conservative path. Are they now more like "responsible" parties? What is the role of policy and ideology within the American parties?

THE DEBATE OVER RESPONSIBLE PARTY GOVERNMENT

The idea of *party government*, or *responsible parties*, offers an alternative vision of a democratic political system. It is a vision that contrasts sharply with the traditional American commitment to limited government and the equally traditional American hostility to powerful political parties.

The Case for Responsible Party Government

Most proponents of party government believe that we need a strong and decisive government—and in particular a strong executive—to solve American social and economic problems. Our political institutions, they feel, may have been well suited to the limited, gingerly governing of the early years of American history but they do not serve us well today, when we depend on more vigorous government action. Decentralized political parties containing diverse interests only make the problem worse. So the idea of party government described below is an effort to make the American political system resemble more closely the plan of a parliamentary government, in which party politics and government are bound into a more integrated whole.

Those who argue for party government do not always agree on the purposes that they feel a strong, decisive government should serve, however. Many conservatives, once suspicious of a powerful central government, grew to like it better when conservative Presidents Reagan and Bush used their power to try to make Congress reduce domestic spending and eliminate liberal programs. In the same sense liberals who were frustrated by the separation of powers developed renewed enthusiasm for the principle when Congress proved capable of checking President Reagan's initiatives. It is much easier to like party government, apparently, when your party is in charge.

In any case, proponents of party government feel that a more unified central government, ironically, would give individuals a bigger voice in politics. Current American politics is so complicated and confusing, they argue, that individuals rarely have the time or the information to play an active role. It is hard for citizens even to find out what their elected representatives are doing. Individuals vote without knowing what the candidates stand for, so they drift from one meaningless decision to another.[4] Candidate-centered politics and divided government make it even harder for citizens to control their government in any meaningful way. With citizens hamstrung by their lack of knowledge, it becomes easy for well-financed minorities—corporate and union powers, single-issue groups—to step in and influence the decisions made by public officials.

What Is Party Government (Responsible Parties)?   The best way to deal with this problem, the party government advocates say, is to restructure the American parties.

In turn, the parties would play the primary organizing role in government and would in the process reinvigorate the other institutions of popular democracy. The process of party government would work like this:

- Each party would draw up a reasonably clear and specific statement of the principles and programs it favors. It would pledge to carry out those programs if the party won.

- The parties would nominate candidates loyal to the party program and willing to enact it into public policy if elected.

- Each party would run a campaign that clarifies the programmatic differences between the two parties, so that voters would grasp these differences and vote largely on that basis.

- Once elected, the party would hold its officeholders responsible for carrying out the party program. It could discipline them if they failed to do so. Voters could then determine whether they approved of the results and decide whether to keep or throw out the governing party at the next election.

The primary focus of a responsible party, then, is the set of policies it has pledged to put into effect. Winning elections would not be an end in itself, nor would it center on the right to distribute patronage or preferments. Nominations and elections would become no more—and no less—than a means to achieve certain public policy goals[5] (see box below).

For this to happen, all the elected branches of government would have to be controlled by the same party at a particular time. The party, then, would bind the divided

The Responsible Party, Mid-1990s Style

House Republican candidates sounded very much like a responsible party when they issued a "Contract with America" prior to the 1994 congressional elections. In this statement they pledged that if the voters would give them a House majority, they would change the way Congress worked and would guarantee a vote on each of ten pieces of legislation, all embodying conservative principles, within the first hundred days of the next Congress. The statement concluded: "If we break this contract, throw us out. We mean it."

They did get a majority of House seats in 1994. Once in office, the new Republican leadership used its iron control of the House agenda to vote on each of those bills before their self-imposed deadline expired. Levels of voting cohesion on these pieces of legislation were higher than they had been in decades. That, however, is when party government stalled. The Senate Republican majority had not committed itself to the Contract with America and it did not feel bound to consider these bills promptly or to pass them when they came up. The House Republicans' efforts were further stymied by a Democratic president, who had the power to veto any legislation that made it through both houses. If responsible party government is to develop under the American rules of government, then, it is not enough for partisans who control a single house of Congress to be dedicated to a set of clear and consistent party principles.

institutions of government into a working whole. The result would be to give citizens a set of clear choices that could simplify their job of voting coherently.

What qualifies the party to play this crucial role? In the words of a prominent party scholar, it is because:

> …the parties have claims on the loyalties of the American people superior to the claims of any other forms of political organization…. Moreover, party government is good democratic doctrine because the parties are the special form of political organization adapted to the mobilization of majorities. How else can the majority get organized? If democracy means anything at all it means that the majority has the right to organize for the purpose of taking over the government.[6]

Only the parties, their supporters believe, are stable and visible enough to take on this kind of responsibility. Thus parties would hold a privileged position in politics compared with interest groups, their major rivals as intermediaries between citizens and government.[7]

The Case against Party Government

The advocates of party government are persuasive, but a sizable number of American political scientists and political leaders remain unconvinced. Their concerns about party government and responsibility take two forms. One is the argument that party government would not produce desirable results. The other is that it simply would not work in the American context.[8]

First, these skeptics fear that the nature of party government—its dedication to providing clear alternatives on major issues—would stimulate a more intense and dogmatic politics. Compromise would become more rare. Legislators, they say, would be bound to a fixed party position; they would no longer be free to represent their own constituents and to negotiate mutually acceptable solutions. That in turn would weaken the deliberative character of American legislatures.

Critics of party government also fear that a system that makes parties the primary avenue of political representation could undercut or destroy the rich variety of interest groups and other nonparty organizations. Without these alternative means of representing the nation's diversity, the two major parties might be seriously overloaded. Minor parties would be likely to pop up, which would further fragment the American system. In short, they fear what European critics have called *partyocracy*—the domination of politics and legislatures by a number of doctrinaire, unyielding political parties, none of them strong enough to govern yet none willing to let others govern.

The second major argument against responsible parties is that the idea could not take root in the United States because it is not compatible with American political culture. In particular, they argue that institutions such as federalism and the separation of powers, which were intended to divide constitutional authority among various levels and branches of government, would not permit party government to develop.[9] The separation of powers, for example, allows voters to give control of the executive branch to one party and the legislative branch to the other. Elections for Congress take place on a different schedule from presidential elections, so they can insulate themselves to some extent from presidential coattails. Federalism permits different parties to dominate in different states. It would be difficult to unite branches of government that the Constitution has separated.

In addition, the direct primary makes it impossible for parties to insist that their nominees be loyal to the party program. Changes in campaigning and campaign finance have freed candidates and officeholders even more from the party organization. The parties, then, find it harder to establish and promote a unified party "team" in elections. Even legislators who often buck their party's executive or its platform are able to keep their jobs as long as their constituents keep voting for them.

Critics of the responsible parties model have also argued that:

- American voters are not issue-oriented enough to be willing to see politics only through ideological lenses.
- The diversity of interests in American society is too great to be contained within just two platforms.
- The parties themselves are too decentralized to be able to take a single, national position on an issue and then enforce it on all their officeholders.
- Americans have distrusted parties too much—as seen by their frequent efforts to reduce party influence in politics—to be willing to make institutional changes that would increase party power.

The idea of a responsible, governing party, in other words, seems to the critics to ask too much of the voters, the parties themselves, and the institutions of American government.

Ways of Achieving Greater Cohesion

One way to create responsible parties is through institutional change. Instead of the separation of powers, many political systems have institutional arrangements that promote party cohesion. A parliamentary system—such as Britain's, for example—would give the party a powerful incentive to remain unified in the legislature, and to a lesser extent in the electorate and the party organization, if it intends to stay in office. To adopt this system in the United States would require a constitutional amendment. That is unlikely, to say the least. But short of a formal move toward responsible parties, it may be possible to make the parties more cohesive. The challenge would be to unite the party organization with the party in the electorate and the party in government in active and responsible support of a party program.

This could be accomplished, at least in part, if the party organizations had the power to discipline their activists, their candidates, and their elected officials. We have seen that the direct primary makes it almost impossible for a party organization to insist that its balky partisans in office toe the party line by controlling their ability to be renominated to their positions. But powerful party leaders might be able to discipline officeholders by granting or taking away the rewards they control, such as patronage and other preferences. The value of these rewards is shrinking, however, as is the tolerance for party control in most parts of the United States. Even so, the growing resources of the national party organization could be used to encourage some degree of party discipline among its officeholders.

Finally, a party could grow into a more cohesive unit if its various parts were to come to agree on a basic party program or at least on a set of shared interests. The party's leaders, activists, and identifiers would then have achieved a unity that would be maintained by their own commitment to those goals. It would be the most agreeable kind of party discipline because it would be self-enforced; the more distasteful forms of external discipline would not be necessary.

This latter alternative is the only feasible one in modern American politics. The chance for party government, then, rests on the possibility of a more ideological politics developing in the United States. If each party were to commit itself to an ideological program, then a system of responsible parties might be more within reach. Is there any chance of that happening?

IDEOLOGICAL PARTIES IN THE UNITED STATES?

Throughout their long histories, the American political parties have been remarkably free of ideology. Even the Republican Party, born out of the impassioned abolitionist movement of the 1850s, soon moved away from its ideological roots as slavery ended and it tried to hold together a national constituency as a majority party.

There are several reasons why the American parties are pragmatic rather than ideological. Most important, there are only two of them to divide up a tremendous array of interests in American politics. In a system with several parties, a party can cater to one particular ideological niche in the voting public and still hope to survive. In a diverse two-party system, such specialized appeals can be made only by minor parties—or by a major party with a death wish. With so many different interests and people to represent, the American parties are justly called "catch–all" parties.[10] It has also been argued that Americans are unusually free of the kinds of deep-seated animosities that fuel an ideological politics in other democracies[11]—though this may surprise observers of American presidential campaigns.

The Nature of Party Differences

To say that the parties are pragmatic, however, is not to say that they take similar stands on issues. The Democrats and Republicans clearly differ in their principles and in their stands on specific policies. These differences appear in the platforms they adopt every four years at their national nominating conventions (see box on pp. 303–305), in their candidates' speeches, and in the policies they pursue when they win.[12] These differences grow out of the realigning periods that have shaped the different American party systems (see Chapter 6).

Even these clear differences on major issues do not add up to the kinds of sharply articulated, all-encompassing political philosophies that are found in genuinely ideological parties—old-style Communist or European Socialist parties or the Muslim fundamentalist parties that have arisen in Middle Eastern nations. Nor do the American parties insist that their elected officials and identifiers obey these principles faithfully. They permit—and the localism of American politics encourages—their leaders and followers to be drawn into the party for whatever reasons they choose, without having to pass any kind of ideological "litmus test" to enter.

What the Democrats and Republicans Stand for: The 1996 Party Platforms

Party platforms are not binding on their candidates or their followers and they sometimes mask more than they reveal. Nonetheless they do express the sentiments of the national party conventions about what the parties stand for at a particular time. The following excerpts from the 1996 platforms highlight some of the most important differences between the parties. For more detail, the full text of the platforms can be found at *http://www.democrats.org/hq/resources/ platform/index.html* (for the Democrats), and *Congressional Quarterly Weekly Report,* August 17, 1996, pp. 2317–2339 (for the Republicans).

Abortion

> **Democrats:** "The Democratic Party stands behind the right of every woman to choose, consistent with *Roe v. Wade,* and regardless of ability to pay."
>
> **Republicans:** "The unborn child has a fundamental individual right to life which cannot be infringed.... We oppose using public revenues for abortion and will not fund organizations which advocate it."

Civil Rights

> **Democrats:** "We continue to lead the fight to end discrimination on the basis of race, gender, religion, age, ethnicity, disability, and sexual orientation.... When it comes to affirmative action, we should mend it, not end it."
>
> **Republicans:** "... we oppose discrimination based on sex, race, age, creed, or national origin.... We reject the distortion of those laws to cover sexual preference.... Because we believe rights inhere in individuals, not in groups, we will attain our nation's goal of equal rights without quotas or other forms of preferential treatment."

Crime

> **Democrats:** "The best way to fight crime is to prevent it. That is why we fought for drug-education and gang-prevention programs in our schools."
>
> **Republicans:** "... we believe in tough law enforcement, especially against juvenile crime and the drug traffic, with stiff penalties, no loopholes, and judges who respect the rights of law-abiding Americans."

Defense

> **Democrats:** "The Administration has undertaken the most successful restructuring of our military forces in history. Even as the size of our forces has decreased, their capabilities, readiness and qualitative edge have increased.... The Democratic party supports efforts to sign a Comprehensive Test Ban Treaty this year...."
>
> **Republicans:** "We must reverse the decline in what our nation spends for defense. In just three and a half years, an amateur approach to military matters and dramatic reductions in defense spending under the Clinton administration have had a serious negative impact on the readiness and

(box continued)

the capabilities of our armed forces.... The Clinton administration's proposed Comprehensive Test Ban Treaty (CTBT) is inconsistent with American security interests."

Education

Democrats: "We should expand public school choice, but we should not take American tax dollars from public schools and give them to private schools."

Republicans: "We ... urge state legislators to ensure quality education for all through programs of parental choice among public, private, and religious schools."

Environment

Democrats: "The Republican Congress ... tried to make taxpayers pick up the tab for toxic wastes, and let polluters who caused the problem and can afford to fix it off the hook.... We believe that America should insist that toxic waste cleanup is paid for by those responsible for it in the first place."

Republicans: "Achieve progress, as much as possible, through incentives rather than compulsion.... Many States have enacted environmental education and 'voluntary self-audit' laws to encourage people to find and correct pollution.... Republicans consider private property rights the cornerstone of environmental progress."

Foreign Trade

Democrats: "As we work to open new markets, we must negotiate to guarantee that all trade agreements include standards to protect children, workers, public safety, and the environment."

Republicans: "Republicans are for vigorous enforcement of the trade agreements we already have on the books, unlike the Clinton administration that uses United States trade policy as a bargaining chip and as a vehicle for pursuing a host of other social agenda items."

Guns

Democrats: "Four years ago ... convicted felons could walk into any gun shop and buy a handgun. ... as long as Bill Clinton and Al Gore are in the White House, any attempt to repeal the Brady Bill or assault weapons ban will be met with a veto."

Republicans: "We defend the constitutional right to keep and bear arms."

Health Care

Democrats: "The Democratic party is proud that we held the line against the Republicans' ... Medicare and Medicaid cuts that would risk the health care of millions of Americans, from infants to seniors."

Republicans: "... we are determined to restructure Medicaid, the federal-state program of health care for the poor. Rife with fraud, poorly administered, with no incentives for patient or provider savings, Medicaid has mushroomed into the nation's biggest welfare program.... We must find better ways to ensure quality health care for the poor."

(box continued)

Immigration

Democrats: "We deplore those who use the need to stop illegal immigration as a pretext for discrimination. And we applaud the wisdom of Republicans like Mayor Giuliani and Senator Domenici who oppose the mean-spirited and short-sighted effort of Republicans in Congress to bar the children of illegal immigrants from schools...."

Republicans: "Illegal immigration has reached crisis proportions.... Illegal aliens should not receive public benefits other than emergency aid, and those who become parents while illegally in the United States should not be qualified to claim benefits for their offspring."

Labor

Democrats: "We beat back efforts to undermine workers' rights to form and join unions and to dismantle the enforcement powers of the National Labor Relations Board.... We believe in equal pay for equal work and pay equity...."

Republicans: "Congressional Republicans have already launched a fight against the union bosses' ban on flex time and comp-time in private industry."

Taxes

Democrats: "Americans cannot afford to return to the era of something-for-nothing tax cuts and smoke-and-mirrors accounting that produced a decade of exploding deficits."

Republicans: "Bill Clinton has demonstrated that he fails to understand the role excessive tax burdens play on the economy and family incomes...."

Welfare

Democrats: "Over the past four years, President Clinton has dramatically transformed the welfare system. ... and welfare is becoming what it should be: a second chance, not a way of life."

Republicans: "The Clinton administration's 'Reinventing Government' program to reform the welfare state bureaucracy has failed.... The key to welfare reform is restoring personal responsibility and encouraging two-parent households."

If they were to become responsible parties in a form of party government, however, some kind or degree of ideology would be necessary. Clear differences on issues are not enough. There must be some set of basic commitments or values that can connect different issues into a single logical structure—some means by which voters and leaders are able to distill the large number of policy issues into one or a few major dimensions—so that voters can easily understand and predict the party's stands, and so that the party's supporting coalition remains constant from one issue to the next. There must be some standard by which issues that crosscut the party coalitions can be relegated to the Siberia of the party's agenda.

The Rise of Ideological Parties

In spite of the forces that fragment them, both major parties have become more concerned with issues in the last few decades, more cohesive, and as a result, a little more like ideological parties. A major contributor was the issue of civil rights. As issues of racial justice emerged as an important focus of national policy debate, white Southerners deserted the Democratic Party in increasing numbers and took with them their more conservative views on a variety of other issues as well. This has eroded the Democrats' strength in elections but it has also lowered the biggest barrier to unity within the Democratic Party along more or less ideological lines.[13] As a result, the Democratic congressional party votes more cohesively now than it has in decades. The Republicans have also become more united on key party principles. The liberal Northeastern wing of the Republican Party, which thrived for many years, no longer exists; the party is dominantly conservative in its principles.

Together with these shifts, purposive or issue-based values have become a more important force in bringing people into party activity. As Chapter 5 suggested, political ideas and even ideologies have become more prominent as incentives for party work than patronage and material rewards, which have been waning on their own accord. At the same time more ideologically oriented leaders have been selected in both parties and have gained a platform to pursue a more ideologically driven agenda.

A prime example was the election and reelection of Ronald Reagan in the 1980s. Reagan, a candidate strongly identified with the conservative wing of the Republican Party, demonstrated the appeal of a simple vision based on one major principle: less government involvement in social welfare programs. The clarity of his message appealed even to voters who were not persuaded by its content. His principled assault on the role of government as it had developed since the New Deal gave a more ideological tone to American politics than it had witnessed in decades and led the way to the Republican congressional majority in the mid-1990s.

These signs of greater ideological concern are found mainly among party leaders and activists, however. What about party voters? Are they bored or alienated by the programmatic concerns of many party activists? Or is it true, as many ideologically motivated people have claimed, that very many voters and other citizens are truly dedicated to ideological principles and have turned away from the major parties because the Democrats and Republicans are not willing or able to provide clearly defined ideological alternatives?

IDEOLOGY IN THE AMERICAN ELECTORATE

Popular and media commentary certainly makes it seem as though the American public is ideologically oriented. Reports of election results often use the terms "liberal" and "conservative" to describe particular candidates and pieces of legislation. It has been common to explain the Republican electoral successes since 1980 and the emergence of more moderate Democratic leaders as a response to what is regarded as a more conservative mood among American voters.[14]

How Ideological Is the American Public?

Careful study of American political attitudes since the 1950s, however, raises serious doubt that most voters can be described as "ideological." Researchers find that only a small minority of the public—never more than a quarter of the electorate and often less—refer to identifiable liberal or conservative principles when they discuss their political views. Americans are much more likely to evaluate candidates and parties based on the personal characteristics of the candidates, the interests of groups they identify with, or a particular issue that energizes them. An individual's responses to different aspects of one issue area—civil rights, for example—may be reasonably consistent, as an ideological perspective would produce. But when we compare an individual's attitudes toward several different issues, such as welfare and foreign policy or economic policy and civil rights, we find much less consistency.[15]

When asked by a poll-taker whether they consider themselves liberals, moderates, or conservatives, most Americans will respond using those terms. In a 1999 CBS News/*New York Times* national survey, for example, 56 percent of the respondents called themselves either liberals or conservatives, and another 38 percent thought of themselves as moderates. But this tells us nothing about the beliefs that underlie these common terms. In particular, the idea of a "moderate" ideology is puzzling; it is probably another way of saying that the individual does not feel comfortable with the consistent choices that an ideology would demand.

Moreover, different people define "liberal" or "conservative" in different ways. The label they choose for themselves may have little to do with the positions they take on specific issues or with their party choice. In this same survey, for instance, only 55 percent of the Republicans called themselves conservatives and 54 percent of Democrats said they were liberals. Interviewers for one of the first major studies of public opinion reported respondents who defined "liberal" as meaning "generous" (in the sense that Democrats were liberal with price supports whereas Republicans were "stingier"), and "liberalist" as meaning someone who liked both parties.[16]

Even today there is little evidence that many of those who call themselves liberals or conservatives are ideologues at heart. Although Ronald Reagan campaigned for president as a principled conservative, for example, many voters supported him in spite of his conservative policy positions rather than because of them. In both 1980 and 1984, the voting public on balance preferred the policy stands of Reagan's opponent. Reagan benefited instead from *retrospective evaluations* of presidential performance—voters' judgments as to whether the most recent presidency had turned out well. Negative appraisals of the Carter presidency led voters to choose Reagan in 1980, and favorable evaluations of his performance in office promoted his reelection in 1984.

In the cases of George Bush and Bill Clinton, as well, voters tended to choose a president based on their satisfaction or dissatisfaction with the administration's performance in the recent past. Bush capitalized on his association with the popular Reagan administration in 1988. Voters chose Clinton in 1992 in part out of dissatisfaction with Bush's record on the economy and kept Clinton in 1996 when the economy improved. These were results-oriented retrospective evaluations, not ideological judgments.[17]

Ideological thinking, in short, has not been common enough within the American public to provide a dependable foundation for responsible parties. For most Americans, politics revolves around concrete problems and pragmatic efforts to solve them. So parties and candidates try to stitch winning coalitions together by appealing to a wide range of qualities—the personal characteristics of candidates, group interests, single issues, hostility toward the party in power—but rarely through ideological appeals.

Responsible party government may not require an ideologically oriented public. Even in nations that have ideological party systems, the political thinking of the average citizen is not typically as highly structured as that of political activists and leaders; it is the institutional arrangements and the leaders' perspectives that sustain party government.[18] In American politics, however, none of these supports for responsible party government is especially strong or stable.

The Dilemma of Ideology

In recent years, then, an interesting gulf has opened up within the parties. Leaders, activists, and some voters seem to be increasingly concerned with programmatic questions, and both parties appear to be more united around consistent positions: the Democrats more liberal, and the Republicans more conservative. Yet most voters remain more interested in pragmatic questions. Ideological concerns, then, are distributed unevenly in a number of ways:

Differences by Social Class   An individual's level of education is closely related to his or her affinity for ideological thinking. The abstractions and the verbal content of ideologies come more easily to people with higher levels of formal education. Because education levels are closely related to income and job status, ideological concerns are most often found among the affluent, well-educated, upper-middle-class elite in American politics—the people most likely to become party activists.

Differences between Activists and Voters   The ideological gulf between party activists and party voters is deepened by the related tendency for activists to take more extreme positions than party voters on many issues. Careful scholarly studies of party leaders and delegates to the two national parties' nominating conventions have consistently found Democratic activists on the left of the liberal-conservative continuum and Republican activists on the right, with both parties' voters much closer to the center (see Chapter 10). In fact, at times one party's activists are more distant from their own party's supporters on this continuum than are the other party's activists (see Figure 15.1).[19]

The party's candidates and officeholders often find themselves caught in between: closer to the left or right than the party's voters but not as extreme as its activists. That can put candidates in a difficult position. On one hand, it can provoke conflict between candidates and party activists. On the other, it can lead a candidate to a difficult choice: to be candid with voters about his or her more extreme views or to be honest and risk losing the next election. It is no wonder that party candidates often prefer to remain ambiguous when asked about issues in their campaigns and resist the push toward clearer, more ideological commitments within the parties.[20]

Do you support or oppose:
    (a) Reducing or spending on social programs?

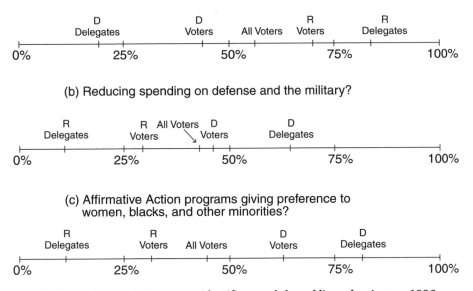

FIGURE 15.1 Party activists, party identifiers, and the public on key issues, 1996.
Source: The data can be found in Chapter 10, Table 10.5. "Delegates" are delegates to the parties' national presidential conventions.

Differences among the Party's Three Parts   These differences between more ideological activists and more flexible candidates can aggravate the tensions among the party organization, the party in government, and the party's voters. The ideologues in both parties erupt periodically into dissatisfaction with the moderation of the party in government. In 1976, even so conservative a "moderate" as President Gerald Ford found himself rejected by many of the organization Republicans in favor of the more conservative Ronald Reagan. Conservative Republicans were never comfortable with President Bush's pragmatic approach to policy-making and many of them bitterly opposed the possible candidacy of "Rockefeller Republican" Colin Powell for the presidency in 1996, even though polls showed him to be the most electable of all their candidates. In the same way, liberal Democrats have often objected to the more centrist policies of Democratic President Clinton.[21]

Regional Differences   The spread of ideology within each party varies as well by state and region—differences that are often on display at a party's national convention. States differ in their economies, their populations, and their political culture.[22] These differences lead them to different issue orientations and to different levels of cohesion in the parties' stands. State Republican parties in the mountain West, for instance, would not be mistaken for their counterparts in New England in the stances nor in the degree of unity they can muster with regard to property rights and environmental issues. A parliamentary system would impose on these different state parties a need to unite; a system of separated powers does not.

Striking the Right Ideological Balance

Thus the problem of ideology is not whether the American parties can become genuinely ideological parties. They cannot. The problem is whether they can contain the increasing ideological commitment of their activists without letting it tear them apart. The prospect of factionalism and conflict is never very far from the parties' door. A further challenge that ideology poses is that the more ideologically oriented activists may become so inflexible that they can no longer accept the party's pragmatic approach to winning elections. Many Republican and Democratic convention delegates in recent years seemed prepared to nominate candidates without much concern for their electability. They were more attracted to defeat with principle than to victory with compromise. If a party's ideological goals ever become more important than its desire to elect candidates, then the parties—and American politics—will be greatly changed.

PARTY RESPONSIBILITY AMERICAN-STYLE

The responsible party model is an ideal. Even the British Parliament, so often used as the model by proponents of party government, has not yet developed the cohesion and the binding party discipline that a "pure" responsible party government would require.[23] The parties in some American state legislatures can be very disciplined, but normally in support of a program drawn up by the governor or the legislative party leaders, not by the party organization. In such a system, party responsibility is left up to the voters in the next election, who can reward or punish their legislators' decisions[24]—and then it is the legislators, not the party as a whole, who are being held responsible for the legislative program. This weak form of party responsibility simply reflects an agreement based on common interests rather than a party organization able to hold its elected officials to a coherent set of principles.

Occasionally, however, the American parties may approach the ideal of responsible party government. Under what conditions is this more likely to occur?

Presidential-Centered Responsibility

At times, strong presidential leadership can produce a fairly cohesive program that becomes a party program. Especially when the president's party controls both houses of Congress, that program can be translated into law. Some presidents—Ronald Reagan and Lyndon Johnson are good examples—have been able to push successfully for the enactment of large parts of the party platform on which they ran for office. In addition, strong, party-oriented presidents can draw attention to party differences and act as reference points for voters' approval or disapproval. But the result is that presidential performance, not a party program, guides voters' decision-making. So although this presidential government offers some features of a responsible party system, it does not necessarily produce the kinds of unified parties and clear ideological alternatives that the reformers demand.

Crisis-Stimulated Responsibility

At critical times in American history, the parties have divided in ways that were, if not truly ideological, at least determinedly programmatic. In the 1936 presidential election, for example, the Democrats and the Republicans offered dramatically different solutions to the nation's devastation by the Great Depression. The burdens of that economic collapse may have focused voter attention to an unusual degree on the possible remedies that public policy could provide. This, combined with a campaign centered on the pros and cons of the Roosevelt program for social and economic change, may well have produced something close to a mandate in the election for both the president and Congress. When strong presidential leadership is combined with crisis conditions, then, perhaps a degree of responsible party government can be achieved, at least for relatively short periods of time.

Realignment and Responsibility

It is during party realignments, however, that the American political system seems to have approached the requirements for party government most closely. During realignment periods, the party coalitions have tended to become more sharply defined along a single line of political cleavage, and party leaders, activists, and voters seem to reach their highest levels of agreement with one another and their greatest differences with the other party.[25] Realignments typically produce a unified federal government with the same party controlling both houses of Congress and the presidency and a judiciary that, through the president's appointment power, comes to reflect the new majority. On only five occasions in American history has one party enjoyed control of Congress and the presidency continuously for more than a decade, and each time this control was first established during a realignment.

Such party control does not guarantee that the policy-making branches of the government will cooperate with one another. But cooperation is certainly more likely when a president is dealing with a majority of his own party in Congress—especially if its members feel they owe their positions to their party label, as often is the case during a realignment—than when Congress is controlled by the opposition. Moreover, during realignments party cohesion in the Congress is especially high. Therefore it is not surprising that major bursts of comprehensive policy change have typically followed realignments.[26] These wholesale realignments of the party system, and the atmosphere of crisis and the strong presidential leadership that have accompanied them, have brought the United States as close to responsible party government as we have ever been able to achieve.

Even during realignments, however, the American version of party government is a pale imitation of its European counterparts. In previous U.S. realignments, party commitment to a set of shared ideological principles has still fallen short of the level that would be necessary for truly responsible parties. The realignment of the 1930s, for example, produced a majority Democratic Party by linking a liberal Northern wing, attracted to the party because it represented the hopes of disadvantaged groups and championed the developing welfare state, and a conservative Southern wing that often opposed both of these goals. Franklin D. Roosevelt had a congressional majority large enough to achieve many of his policy goals as president, but throughout his long career in the White House he faced persistent opposition within his own party.

In short, even when they are most unified around a single political agenda during a realignment, the American parties are broad coalitions of differing interests and goals. They have never been sufficiently united in a set of common principles to be able to overcome the institutional forces—federalism and the separation of powers—that tend to disunite and decentralize them.

BARRIERS TO RESPONSIBLE PARTIES: DIVIDED GOVERNMENT

The enduring barriers to responsible party government in the United States would be quite sufficient in themselves to sink its chances. But that goal has seemed especially distant in recent years because of the prevalence of *divided government*: the situation in which a president or governor faces at least one house of the legislature controlled by the other party. In most of the years since 1950, control of the federal government has been shared by the two parties rather than vested in a single party (see Table 15.1). In state governments as well, one-party control has declined steadily during this period, from about 75 percent of state governments to fewer than 50 percent.[27]

Divided control of the national government appeared much less frequently in earlier times. There have been only twelve presidential elections since Andrew Jackson's in which voters gave the presidency to one party and at least one house of Congress to the other party. A majority of these elections came after 1950. Most of the earlier instances were very close elections, some in which the margin of victory was razor-thin. There were other, more frequent cases in which divided government came about because the president's party lost control of at least one house of Congress in a midterm election.

Divided government in recent decades, in contrast, has typically resulted from the weakening grip of partisanship on voters' behavior. At the national level, many voters have been willing to split their votes between Republican presidential candidates and Democratic candidates for Congress, most of them incumbents seeking reelection. In the 1990s, voters chose a Democratic presidential candidate and Republicans for the House and Senate, a number of whom were not incumbents—but the end result was a federal government just as divided. Widespread ticket-splitting, resulting in divided control of government, has also been evident in the states.[28] And the pattern of midterm losses by the president's party has continued, with the sole exception of the 1998 congressional races.

Divided government makes responsible party government impossible. By giving control of different branches of government to opposing parties, it requires agreement between the parties for successful policy-making—or what James Sundquist has labeled "coalition government."[29] Negotiation and bargaining are necessary ingredients for government action in any democratic system, especially the American one. But when opposing parties are the prime actors in such a process, voters are hard-pressed to hold any party responsible (see box on p. 314). Many observers ascribe the federal government's failure to address a number of major

TABLE 15.1 Party Control of Government at the National Level, 1951–2000

Year	Party in control of the: President	House	Senate	Divided Government
1951–1952	D	D	D	*(✓)*
1953–1954	R	R	R	✓
1955–1956	R	D	D	X
1957–1958	R	D	D	X
1959–1960	R	D	D	X
1961–1962	D	D	D	✓
1963–1964	D	D	D	✓
1965–1966	D	D	D	✓
1967–1968	D	D	D	✓
1969–1970	R	D	D	X
1971–1972	R	D	D	X
1973–1974	R	D	D	X
1975–1976	R	D	D	X
1977–1978	D	D	D	✓
1979–1980	D	D	D	✓
1981–1982	R	D	R	X
1983–1984	R	D	R	X
1985–1986	R	D	R	X
1987–1988	R	D	D	X
1989–1990	R	D	D	X
1991–1992	R	D	D	X
1993–1994	D	D	D	✓
1995–1996	D	R	R	X
1997–1998	D	R	R	X
1999–2000	D	R	R	X

9 of 27

10 of 28 times.

Note: D = Democratic control; R = Republican control; X = president, House, and Senate controlled by different parties.

2000 – 2002   R   R   R/D   ✓

issues, from health care concerns to energy supplies, to the division of authority and the consequent bickering between Republicans and Democrats that has become a familiar feature of our time.[30]

Some even feel that divided government undermines the democratic process itself. When both parties share governing power, they say, the voters are deprived of their most effective instrument for controlling government: the ability to determine which party is responsible for unsatisfactory policies and to throw that party out and replace it with the opposition. The jury is still out on some aspects of divided government; some argue that the American national government has learned to cope with shared party power, and a few researchers even contend that American voters make an effort to divide federal power between the Democrats and the Republicans as an alternative to putting their trust in either one.[31] Clearly, though, this American version of "coalition government" produces a politics just the opposite of what the responsible party model promises.

The Challenge of Policy-Making Under Divided Government

With House Republicans committed to their Contract with America in 1995 and a Republican majority in the Senate, the stage seemed set for greater party responsibility. But as the separation of powers permits, Democrats controlled the White House. Neither party could determine federal policy on its own. The result was intense partisan conflict across a wide range of major issues.

The start of the 1996 fiscal year came—and went—without resolution of the battle between the parties over budget priorities. The conflict became so severe that the federal government was shut down twice and a large number of its workers furloughed—even the Washington monument was closed to visitors—because Congress and the president could not agree on a budget. Ultimately the two parties compromised their radically different approaches, and a budget was adopted after half the fiscal year was over. But this compromise could not take place without an elaborate partisan dance in which both parties' leaders did their best to avoid blame for the shutdown while still maintaining the support of their more hard-line activists. Just a decade earlier, during the Reagan administration, the two parties' pursuit of competing principles led to a huge increase in the national debt. Divided government does not necessarily produce political paralysis, but when it is combined with increasingly ideological parties, the chances of deadlock increase.

THE CONTINUING SEARCH FOR RESPONSIBLE PARTY GOVERNMENT

With all these barriers to overcome, responsible party government seems even more distant now than it was a half-century ago. Yet it continues to appeal to many different kinds of observers and participants. Party scholars, a number of political leaders and activists, and other citizens still press for greater difference between the parties, more ideological parties, and governments that can be more easily held responsible for their policy decisions.[32]

In some important ways the parties have responded to these appeals. The national party committees never have been stronger than they are today or more active in coordinating the activities of the state and local parties. The various national committees also play a larger role in financing both federal and nonfederal campaigns than they ever did before. The parties in the electorate, and especially the congressional parties, are more cohesive philosophically than they have been in decades. Moreover, throughout the American system, but especially in Washington and in the party platforms, the level of party conflict over basic principles of public policy is very high.

Yet political candidates remain pretty much on their own in gaining their party's nomination and running in the general election. Candidates still have the responsibility of raising most of their campaign money. Voters have become even more responsive to individual candidate appeals than they used to be. All these forces give candidates greater independence from their parties than the increase in party resources can counteract. And no amount of party money can buy an exception to the rules of federalism and the separation of powers.

For the immediate future, barring a wholesale partisan realignment of traditional proportions,[33] it seems likely that the American parties will not be able to go beyond the modest governing role that has characterized them during most of the twentieth century. Neither the American parties nor the voters can meet the demands that the classic model of party responsibility would impose on them. The three parts of the party will continue to be linked by a fairly loose commitment to a set of issue positions. That commitment, reinforced occasionally by a strong president or a passionately partisan congressional leadership, may produce enough cohesion for a modest degree of responsibility. But the party organizations have not been able to achieve the central role, of drawing up a party program and enforcing it on candidates and officeholders, which the reformers so valued. The question remains whether this level of party responsibility is enough to sustain American democracy through the pressing demands of the new century.

Chapter 16

The Place of Parties
in American Politics

T he American parties have faced great change in recent decades. By the 1970s they appeared to be in decline on a number of fronts, and the decay in their performance was often blamed for the drop in public confidence that we continue to see today. Because their troubles had started a decade or two earlier in response to long-term changes in American society, it was easy to assume that the decline was permanent. By the time their decay had become the central theme of books and articles about the parties, however, there were clear signs of party resurgence. This revival has not restored parties to the position they once enjoyed in American politics. But it signals that they will remain an important part of the American political landscape.

To look at as to how these trends have changed the parties, let us return to a prominent theme of this book. Political parties influence the world around them in important ways but they are also powerfully shaped by that world. This central truth is easy to forget. The Progressives held the parties responsible for many of society's ills; later reformers who favor responsible parties also see the parties as the cause of major failures in government. But to reform the parties these groups found it necessary to effect changes in the parties' environment.

To conclude this look at the American parties, then, it is vital to focus on the interaction between parties and the various elements of their environment. Did the party decline noted in the 1960s and 1970s result from changes in the party organization, or did both of these changes result from broader forces? In summing up, we can draw on an analysis of party change in relation to what else has changed in their environment and can take advantage of the possible comparisons across different periods of their development and with other democratic systems.

PARTIES AND THEIR ENVIRONMENT

Political parties have a variety of means to affect their environment. Party organizations and the parties in government decide how candidates will be nominated and who will have the opportunity to elect them. Through their own performance and the messages they offer, parties influence public attitudes about the Democrats and the Republicans and about politics more generally. The parties mobilize citizens, converting resources such as money and loyalties into various forms of influence. They play a major role in the process that links citizens' beliefs, demands, and fears on the one hand and public policies on the other.

Yet the impact of their environment on the parties is probably even more powerful. Three types of factors have been especially influential in helping to shape the American parties as well as those in other Western democracies. They include the ways in which the electorate is defined, the nation's basic governmental institutions and rules, and the forces that mold the broader society (Table 16.1).[1]

The Nature of the Electorate

As an environmental influence the nature of the electorate is made up of many things. At the most basic level the nation's constitution and laws determine who will have the right to vote. Beyond that, social conditions affect the numbers and types of people who exercise that right: their education, affluence, and age distribution, for instance. Information channels and other forces help shape the voters' attitudes and expectations, their levels of concern about political questions, and their political information and understanding. The fault lines that divide the electorate into opposing groups and thereby define the party system are critical influences as well.

TABLE 16.1 Major Types of Environmental Influences on the American Parties

Influences	Examples
1. Nature of the electorate	Spread of the franchise, citizens' political interest and knowledge, social characteristics of the electorate, lines of political division
2. Political institutions and rules	
(a) Institutions	Federalism, separation of powers, nature of the presidency, judicial review, single-member districts
(b) Electoral processes	The direct primary, office block ballots, non-partisan elections
(c) Statutory regulation	Legislation on campaign finance, structure of party organization, merit system
3. Social forces	
(a) National events and conditions	State of the economy, war, current national problems
(b) Other political intermediaries	Types of other organized interests, nature and importance of television and other media, independent consultants
(c) Political culture	Attitudes toward parties, politics, and politicians

The American electorate has changed over time; these changes trace the rise of mass popular democracy. In general the nature of the electorate has moved from a limited to a broader adult suffrage; from lesser to greater political awareness among citizens; from minimal to more wide-ranging expectations of participation in a democracy. This process, which began soon after the Republic was born, continues to evolve. In recent decades, for example, the extension of voting rights to Southern blacks helped to reshape the party system in the South.

Only one trend in the American electorate appears to have moved in the opposite direction: rates of voter turnout. The drop in turnout since 1960 may be temporary or it may signal a fundamental, long-term change in the electorate. If it does, we may be seeing a withdrawal of the less affluent from an increasingly middle-class American politics.

The nature of the electorate affects the parties in several important ways. It influences the distribution of party loyalties and the extent to which people rely on the parties for their political information. It affects the way candidates campaign: the kinds of appeals they make and the groups to whom they appeal. It probably helps to determine what kinds of people are most likely to be regarded as potential leaders. Thus the nature of electoral politics depends to a great extent on the nature of the electorate—a force that the parties can help to shape, especially early in their lives, but mostly have to accept as it is.

Political Institutions and Rules

The second cluster of environmental influences on the parties includes the main institutions and "rules" of government. Most important here is the basic framework of political institutions: whether the government is federal or unitary, whether it is parliamentary or has separated powers, and how its positions of power are structured. Then there are the laws that regulate nominations and elections, the parties and their activities, from those prescribing the party's organizational arrangements to those regulating campaign spending. We have discussed, for example, the effects of the separation of powers, the direct primary, and the use of plurality elections in single-member districts on the development of party organizations.

The American parties have been subjected to more regulation than have parties anywhere else. The direct primary constrains their selection of candidates to a degree unknown in other democracies, and American state laws defining the party organizations have no parallel in the democratic world. The effect of this regulation—and in most cases its intention—is to put limits on the party organization; an unintended consequence is to boost the party in government. The trend lives on, for example in efforts to revise states' primary rules as a means of gaining more public control over the nominating process.

Although these institutional influences such as the direct primary, the separation of powers, and the extensive legal regulation of the parties have undergone nips and tucks over time, the American and British electoral systems have remained fairly stable during the last century. That has not been true of many other democracies. France during this time has launched five entirely separate republics, each one intended to be a break with, even a repudiation of, its predecessor. Similarly many other European countries have tinkered with various election systems, whereas Britain and the United States have stayed with plurality elections in single-member constituencies.[2] With the important exception of the direct primary, then, changes in the institutional aspects of the parties' environment have probably been less profound during the last century than have changes in the electorate, such as rising educational levels and the expansion of the franchise.

Societal Forces

A third set of environmental influences refers to events and trends in the larger society that affect politics at a particular time. The wild rise in the stock market, the relocation of U.S. industries to Mexico and other nations, the threat of terrorism here and abroad can become policy issues on the nation's agenda. Thus they help to determine the demands and goals that individuals try to achieve through the parties. Although they are often beyond the parties' influence, they affect the parties' behavior and their electoral coalitions.

Other societal forces include the number and character of organized interests in the society, the types and behavior of the media, and other means of representing interests. If individuals find other, more effective ways to pursue their political goals than through the parties, they will use them. If a congressional staff member is better able to track down a Social Security check, or an interest group is more forthright and effective in opposing abortion or gay rights, why work through a party? The nature of the parties at any given time, then, depends in part on the available alternatives to parties and the competition among them.

All these elements of their environment have contributed to the unique character of the American parties. But the most extensive and systematic changes have probably involved the nature of the electorate. Thus as we summarize the dramatic changes that have occurred in the parties' structure, supporting coalitions, and strength during the last four decades, we will pay special attention to their relationship to changes in the electorate.

PARTY DECAY IN THE 1960S AND 1970S

A fundamental and unique feature of the American parties is that the three party sectors are bound together only loosely. The party organization has never been able to involve large numbers of party identifiers in its structure and activities, nor has it been successful in asserting its leadership of the campaigns or the policy-making of the party in government. The party decline that was becoming apparent in the 1960s, then, affected the three sectors very differently.

The Parties in the Electorate

American voters' loyalty to their parties weakened substantially in the late 1960s and 1970s. Increasing numbers of adults began to think of themselves as independents rather than party identifiers. Those who remained attached to a party no longer relied on that identification as much as they once did; voters were less and less willing to delegate their choices in elections to a party's judgment. The parties, then, found themselves with smaller numbers of less loyal identifiers.

One concrete example was a surge in ticket-splitting. Beginning in the late 1960s, the percentage of Americans who reported voting for a presidential candidate of one party and a House candidate of the other began to grow. That percentage had doubled by 1972, and similar increases occurred in ticket-splitting between Senate and House races and in state and local elections. By 1968, almost half of the respondents in national surveys said they had voted for more than one party's candidates in state or local elections, and by 1974 that figure topped out at 61 percent. At the aggregate level, the number of congressional districts selecting a presidential candidate of one party and a congressional candidate of the other party exceeded 30 percent for the first time in history in 1964 and had reached 44 percent early in the next decade.[3]

In place of party identification and as education levels increased, some voters became more responsive to the increasingly issue-oriented candidacies of the time period. The campaigns of Barry Goldwater in 1964, Eugene McCarthy and George Wallace in 1968, and George McGovern in 1972 prompted greater awareness of political issues in parts of the electorate. For other voters, the most effective appeals were those of a candidate's personality and media image. The handsome faces, ready smiles, and graceful lifestyles that television screens so fully convey attracted some of the support that party symbols once commanded.

Voters became more inclined, then, to respond to candidates as individuals rather than as members of a particular political party. Independent candidates for president—McCarthy in 1976, John Anderson in 1980—and for governor gained greater success than in previous years as the result of this decline in party voting. Because candidates and issues change far more frequently than parties, the result was a less stable and predictable pattern of voting.

The Party Organizations

The last of the great party machines were fading in the 1960s and 1970s. The famous Daley machine in Chicago was ripped apart in a series of tumultuous struggles after Richard J. Daley's death in 1976 and then stripped of its patronage base. Party organizations could no longer depend on the patronage and preferments that once were so vital in recruiting party activists. Instead people were being drawn into party activism because of their commitment to particular issues. These were better-educated people and they demanded greater participation in the party's decisions. Some of these new activists thought compromise was a dirty word; they rejected the idea that winning elections was more important than a dedication to certain principles. If their party did not satisfy their ideological goals, they stood ready to leave it for other groups—particular candidates' campaigns and single-issue organizations—that would meet their needs with more enthusiasm.

Other aspects of the party organization were under fire as well. As the use of the direct primary spread, the party organization gave up its control over nominations to whoever chose to vote in its primary. By the time a primary season had ended the party's presidential nominee had been determined, so the party's presidential nominating convention no longer had much of a deliberative role. As grassroots activists came to expect a bigger say within the party organization, its own internal decision-making was no longer under its control. This was particularly true of the Democrats who, in 1972 and 1976, nominated presidential candidates who were well outside the organizational mainstream of their own party.

In addition to their declining influence over nominations, by the 1960s and 1970s the party organizations had lost their central role in election campaigns. Candidates now built their own campaign organizations, raised their own campaign money, and made their own decisions on how to spend it. The campaign assets they once received from their local party organizations and activists—public opinion data, strategic advice, fund-raising, willing helpers—could now be obtained directly from pollsters, the media, public relations experts, issue-oriented activists, or campaign consulting firms that were, in effect, "rent-a-party" agencies.

In fact, in comparison with these independent consultants, the campaign skills that local party organizations could offer their candidates were fairly primitive. The national parties began to develop expertise in newer campaign technologies during the 1970s and shared their resources with state and local parties. But the consultants and the other nonparty providers of campaign expertise had already established a beachhead. The state and local party organizations, in particular, saw their influence on candidates wane.

The party organizations in the 1970s remained much more decentralized than did life and politics in the United States. Voters were looking more and more to national political leaders and symbols, but the party organizations still tended to be collections of state and local fiefdoms. Even in the face of the new vigor in their national committees—stronger organizations and more central authority—the real power in the parties seemed likely to remain at the local level.

The Party in Government

Elected officials came to depend more than ever on direct appeals to voters in the 1960s and 1970s. That was not surprising; they had been freed from reliance on the party organization by the direct primary, by their direct access to the media, and by the money they could raise and the volunteers they could attract independent of the party's efforts. Because of split-ticket voting, candidates didn't even need to rely on party identification. Through personal style, personal appeals, and personal funds they developed a "personal vote" independent of party.[4]

It became harder than ever before to unseat an incumbent, especially in Congress. The cycle perpetuated itself; because there was not as much chance of beating an elected official, serious challengers did not appear as frequently. When they did, party organizations were not vigorous enough to provide challengers with the campaign resources they so desperately needed. Holding public office became more of a profession—a lifetime career—even at the state and local level, where political professionals had formerly been rare.

As incumbents became more secure electorally—even though many did not feel that way—the congressional parties enjoyed greater freedom from the party organizations. Even the legislative party's leaders found it harder to marshal their troops on behalf of the legislative party's bills or the programs of the party's president. Party-line voting in Congress fell to an all-time low in the late 1960s and early 1970s. But it was a perverse kind of freedom. Protected from the demands of party activists and party organizations, legislators were thus more exposed to other pressures, mainly from constituents and organized interests.

When the legislative party lacks cohesion and strength, the executive party rushes into the vacuum. Presidents and governors exercised greater power and leadership. More than other elected officials, they came increasingly to personify the party and its programs to the voters. The parties, then, could be viewed as executive-centered coalitions during the late 1960s and 1970s. This was especially true of national politics and in particular of the ability of presidents to dominate their national party organizations. Presidents did not depend on their party organizations for much; in fact, with the help of federal campaign money after 1974, presidential candidates were able to run their campaigns free of obligation to the party organization at any level. Ironically, though, just as the dominance of the parties by chief executives became clear, divided government became the norm. That undercut executives' power by permitting the opposition party to block their leadership.

Shifting Power Centers in the Tripartite Party

These changes produced a major shift of power within the parties. Power flowed from the decentralized party organization to the individual members of the party in government, especially the executives. The changes also accentuated a shift in influence away from the parties and toward rival political intermediaries, especially organized interests and the mass media.

At the core of these changes was the increasing isolation of the party organization not only within the parties but also in American politics more generally. The organizations had enjoyed their days of glory but they ultimately failed to retain the unquestioned loyalty of many party voters. Isolated from the electorate and without its broad-based support or participation, party organizations and their leaders became even more vulnerable to suspicions that they were run by irresponsible oligarchies. The myth of the smoke-filled room clung to life. Visions of "boss rule" were as much alive at party conventions in the 1960s and 1970s—particularly the 1968 and 1972 Democratic conventions—as they were in the early 1900s. But ironically, the resources party organizations had in the early 1900s, which could have justified at least some charges of boss rule at that time, were largely eroded by the 1960s and 1970s.

The result was a peculiar kind of political party. It seems reasonable that the vital core of any party would be a vibrant party organization. The party organization, after all, is the only sector of the party whose interests go beyond the winning of individual elections. It is the party organization that sustains the party when its candidates lose their races. It is the organization that links the party's officeholders and office seekers and can call them to collective action of the type that political parties were created to achieve. Without it party candidates become individual entrepreneurs seeking individual goals in a political system that requires collective decisions. The decline of the party organizations was clearly a major force in the decline of the parties more generally.[5]

PARTY RENEWAL

This marked decline was not the end of the story, however. The American parties responded to these challenges in the 1980s and 1990s, just as they adapted to changing circumstances at other times in the past. The steady decay of the parties was stopped and even reversed. But some of the changes that took place in the 1960s and 1970s have left their imprint even now. In some ways, then, the parties have had to adjust to a new role in American politics.

Toward a Realignment of the American Electorate

Changes in the party coalitions in recent years have rekindled expectations of a party realignment. The symptoms that normally precede a realignment began to be present in the early 1960s, especially within the electorate: low levels of voter turnout, the weakened impact of party loyalties on people's voting, more ticket-splitting, greater support for third-party or independent candidates, less predictable elections, and divided government.[6]

When Republicans won both the presidency and the Senate in 1980 and gained control of the House in 1994—the first time since 1954 that there was a Republican majority in both Houses of Congress—some concluded that the long-awaited realignment had finally happened. There is no doubt that one condition of a realignment has been fulfilled in that the party coalitions have clearly changed; black Americans are now steadfastly Democratic, white Southerners have moved disproportionately into the Republican Party's ranks, and religious conservatives are now a vital force within the GOP. The decline of Democratic strength in the South has been especially striking (see Figure 16.1). Important parts of the Democratic New Deal coalition have deserted the party. The proportion of Republican identifiers has come closer to matching that of Democrats, at least at times, than it had in fifty years. And as we have seen, the proportion of Americans expressing a party loyalty has rebounded from its low point in the 1970s.

Yet if this is a realignment, it is an unusual one. Elections continued to be volatile in the 1990s. Republican House candidates looked like powerhouses in 1994 but like desperate survivors in 1998. The proportion of the public calling themselves independents remains high. New parties and independent candidacies have aroused a lot of public interest and attracted a notable percentage of the vote in 1992 and 1996. Public opinion polls do not show any signs of great public enthusiasm for the major parties or their conventions, or, for that matter, many other aspects of American politics. If the party system is no longer in dealignment, then any realignment is at best incomplete.

Even a full-fledged realignment of the party coalitions might not restore the parties to their previous dominance of American politics. In a world of primaries, realignment would not give back the party organizations' power to nominate and elect candidates. Lasting change in the parties' coalitions could not guarantee an end to the more candidate-centered electoral world that has resulted. Even a complete realignment would not guarantee that Americans would become straight-ticket voters again.

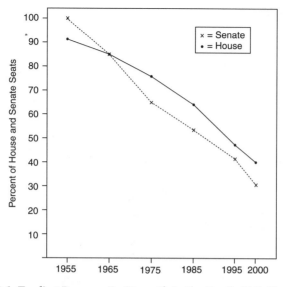

FIGURE 16.1 Eroding Democratic Strength in the South: U.S. House and Senate Seats, 1955–2000

Note: Data points are the percentage of Senators and House members from the thirteen Southern states who are Democrats.

Source: Data for 1955–1995 from *Congressional Quarterly Weekly Report*, November 12, 1994: 3231. Data for 2000 calculated from Harold W. Stanley and Richard G. Niemi, *Vital Statistics on American Politics 1999–2000* (Washington, DC: CQ Press, 2000), Tables 5.10 and 5.11, pp. 213–238.

A party realignment under current American electoral rules and environmental conditions would not necessarily renew the strength of the parties in the electorate.[7]

Yet whether or not they led to a realignment, the events of the 1960s and 1970s produced an irreversible "sea change" in American party loyalties. Large numbers of voters now rely on sources other than the parties—the media, single-issue groups, increasingly diverse primary groups—for their information about politics. In earlier times these sources may have helped to reinforce partisan views and loyalties; now they often do not.[8] This range and variety of sources encourages people to create their political commitments as they would a patchwork quilt: an issue from this group, a candidate from that party. A party loyalty, in contrast, demands that they buy a whole collection of commitments. It asks them to divide the political world into two simple categories: ours and theirs. This all-or-nothing choice may be increasingly unattractive as the average education level of voters rises.[9]

The Rise of More Cohesive Parties in Government

If voters' commitment to the parties has not rebounded to full vitality, the opposite has occurred among the parties in government. By the 1970s, the long decline in party cohesion in Congress had stopped, and the organizational seeds had been sown for greater party strength. By the 1980s, the congressional parties had emerged as more cohesive and their leadership stronger and more assertive than they had been since the early part of the century. As historically one-party areas (such as the South) gained two-party competition, the party coalitions in Congress began to diverge much more clearly from one another. Both congressional parties were now more homogeneous, which made it easier for them to offer distinctive alternatives on major issues. The House Republicans' Contract with America in 1995 and the House Democrats' response to it offer a classic example. Similarly, in a number of states legislative parties were becoming more unified and taking clearer positions on issues.

Party impact on the executive branch increased as well. The Reagan administration came into office in 1981 as the most ideologically committed in decades. Reagan's leadership placed conservative principles at the top of the GOP's agenda and solidified the hold of his brand of conservatives on the party. The Democrats, though more internally diverse than the Republicans, became more unified in response. By the mid–1990s there was intense partisan warfare in Washington between a programmatically committed Republican majority in Congress and an activist Clinton White House. Though clearer party lines were drawn, however, responsible party government did not result; divided party control at the federal level saw to that. Nor did these battles seem to produce a more party-oriented electorate. Instead voters' immediate response seemed to be a sense of disgust directed at both parties.

The New "Service" Parties

The renaissance of parties can be seen most fully in the party organizations. The parties responded to changes in the electorate and the resulting candidate-centered politics by retooling their national organizations as providers of services to the party's candidates. With bigger budgets and professional staffs skilled in applying the latest campaign technologies, they have become more active in recruiting candidates for office. They have distributed their resources not only to candidates but also to state and local parties; these resources, including valuable soft money, enable the party organizations to step up their role in campaigns, at least in comparison with the recent past. The infusion of resources is both timely and necessary; as two-party competition spreads, state and local parties need to become more effective just to keep up with the competition.

The new service party, however, is a very different type of party from the grassroots organizations of earlier years. Because its primary role is to support candidates, it is not very visible to voters. Nor is its impact on candidates assured. In the big-spending world of campaign finance, the party organizations do not bring enough money to the table to be able to dominate political campaigning—or at times even to be heard very clearly. The service party is one of many forces trying to win the attention of candidates. To succeed it must compete with independent campaign consultants, interest groups, and others. As service parties, then, the party organizations are no longer as distinctive as they used to be, in the sense of providing campaign resources that no other group could deliver.[10]

The party organizations, in short, are more vigorous now than they have been in years. But instead of building on their old sources of strength, they have adapted to new conditions and taken on a new form: that of the service party. These service parties live in a political world in which they compete increasingly with other transmitters of political symbols and information: media, organized interests and PACs, candidates' organizations, social movements. They vie with these groups to provide campaign money for candidates, to influence elected officials, and to get citizens registered and mobilized to vote on election day.[11]

THE FUTURE OF PARTY POLITICS IN AMERICA

How will the parties continue to change? Predictions are especially risky about institutions that are so profoundly influenced by their environments. Nonetheless, some trends in party development and features of recent party politics are so persistent that they seem destined to give shape to the future.

A Changing Intermediary Role

Parties are the only political organizations whose names go on the ballot alongside those of candidates. A candidate for U.S. Senate is identified in the polling booth not as a Sierra Club member nor as a pro-lifer—and usually not even as an incumbent—but rather as a Democrat or Republican. Parties developed in part out of voters' need for a guide, a shortcut, to the confusing choices that elections require. The willingness of large numbers of voters to respond to that party label is what has made it so valuable. When the party label is able to produce stable and enduring loyalties to the party and to dominate voting decisions, then it is clear that political parties serve as key intermediaries between citizens and the wider political world.

The value of the party label in elections is probably greatest when a mass electorate has just begun to develop and has serious need for information. As the electorate matures, its needs change. One explanation for American voters' decreased reliance on party loyalties is that voters are better educated and better informed now than they were sixty or eighty years ago. This may better prepare them to sift through a broader range of political messages without the need for party labels as a guide.

Current voters also have a great deal of exposure to information through the mass media, which tend to emphasize candidates' personal characteristics and styles rather than their party. Most current voters have grown up with media that feed them great visuals but fairly small snippets of content. Many have grown accustomed to thinking of politics in terms of the personalities and personal images that the mass media carry so effectively. It is not that media coverage ignores political parties; the media that activists and elected officials rely on continue to refer frequently to the parties in their domestic political coverage.[12] But more popular media—and especially the entertainment media that also affect people's views about politics—are more likely to be party-free.

Citizens also have larger numbers of political organizations now to help them reach their goals. Early in the twentieth century someone concerned about environmental quality would probably have had to pursue his or her goals through a political party; not many groups focused specifically on resource conservation, much less pollution control. Now, however, in tandem with the growing reach of government into most aspects of private life, a huge array of organized interests has developed that permit individuals to establish a "designer link" with the political system. If someone prefers to discriminate among the causes he or she will support and to see politics entirely through the perspective of gun rights, or gay rights, several groups exist to make that possible. There is no need to compromise or to support a coalition of other groups' needs and a range of candidate styles, as a party loyalty would require.

So it is not that Americans no longer need cues or labels to help them make sense of politics. Rather it is that voters rely more on organized interests or the media and less on the shorthand of the party label. They are exposed, then, to a less partisan vision of politics. The parties' traditional dominance has been eroded by competition from other powerful intermediaries.[13] It may be that the diversity of goals in the electorate and the intensity of feelings about them cannot easily be handled even by two pragmatic, broad-based political parties—much less more ideological ones—unless the voters realign along newly distinctive lines of cleavage.

Domination by the Party in Government

In their glory days at the beginning of the twentieth century the American parties may have been dominated by their party organizations, but no longer. Now the parties are ruled by their candidates and officeholders—by the party in government. More and more it is the members of the party in government who run the campaigns, control the party's image, and govern in office without much pressure from their party organizations.

A party dominated by its officeholders and office seekers differs in several basic ways from a party led by its organization (Table 16.2). Where the party in government dominates, almost by definition, the party's focus is electoral because the party's

TABLE 16.2 Characteristics of Alternative Types of Political Party Structures

Party Organization Dominates	*Party in Government Dominates*
1. Party voters can become members of the party organization	1. Little or no opportunity for formal party membership
2. Party organization controls nomination of candidates and much of the election campaign	2. Party organization has little control over candidates' nominations and campaigns
3. Relatively high degree of unity in legislative party	3. Relatively low degree of unity in legislative party
4. Three party sectors are highly integrated	4. Low degree of integration of three sectors
5. Unified behind goals of the party organization's activists	5. Unified (if at all) by goals and programs of the executive party
6. Activities are mainly electoral, but programmatic as well	6. Activities almost exclusively electoral

officeholders are primarily concerned with winning elections. Elected officials work to control the resources necessary for election victory. Once they win, they govern so as to create a record of accomplishment in office and to increase their chances of reelection.

Alternatively, when a party is dominated by its organizational sector it is the party organization that speaks for the party, chooses its candidates, and maintains some degree of leverage over its legislators. The result is that the issue commitments or ideologies of the organization's activists have much greater influence on the party as a whole than in a party dominated by its candidates and officeholders. Perhaps the best examples of party organizational dominance were the early working-class parties of the European parliamentary democracies, although even they, too, have come under more control by their officeholders in recent years.[14]

These two types of parties differ in their ability to create strong links among the party organization, the party in government, and the party electorate. In the party dominated by its organization, ties of loyalty and party discipline bind the three sectors closely together. Much of the party's electorate becomes part of the organization through membership in it. Candidates are tied closely to the party organization because they are indebted to it for their nomination and for its campaign help. In the classic urban party machines, the party organization and its candidates were united in their dedication to winning elections and their commitment to the pragmatism that demanded. In the responsible party model these two sectors could be held together by loyalty to the same principles or by the organization's ability to discipline elected officials by denying them renomination.

In the party controlled by the party in government, by contrast, the focus is on whatever is needed to win. Alliances can be made and broken depending on their contribution to that goal. The dominant party in government is free to form alliances with interest groups or other organizations rather than to work with its own party organization. In fact it is free to ally with members of the opposition party if that will enhance its chances of winning; we have seen how Southern Democrats, for example, frequently allied with Republicans in Congress in the 1950s and 1960s in a "conservative coalition."[15]

In addition, its candidates and elected officials tend to make contact with party voters without relying on the party organization—and for good reason, since the organization typically has few resources to offer its candidates. This was particularly true of the American parties in the 1950s and 1960s. Thus the party organizations were ignored by many candidates during the campaign and had little influence on them afterward. The congressional parties, for instance, set up their own campaign committees in Congress from which they derived their party resources, so they were able to ignore the national party organizations.

The differences between these two types of parties affect the character of a democratic system. A party that is dominated by its candidates and public officials is not likely to provide the continuity needed to maintain public accountability. On the other hand, where the party organization dominates, the party can be something more than the sum total of the candidates who run on its label. It can be strong enough to exert policy leadership, perhaps even approaching the model of the responsible party. It can provide leadership in the recruitment of public officials and offer a stable cue to millions of voters. That in turn can bolster officeholders' responsibility to their constituents. The collection of a party's candidates and elected officials are not likely to have the incentive to join together in this way; only the party organization has the necessary commitment to all the party's goals, and to the party itself.

What causes some parties to be dominated by their party organizations and others to be led by their elected officials and candidates? Several environmental factors seem to make a difference:

- The institutions of government play an important role. As many scholars have noted, a parliamentary system demands that the parties be disciplined and unified; a system of separated powers does not. In practice nations with parliamentary forms of government are more likely to have organization-dominated parties.

- American electoral law (primaries and the regulation of campaign finance, for example) favors the party in government, giving it easy access to nomination and great freedom from the party organization in waging campaigns.

- State governments have seriously hindered the state party organizations, making it difficult for them to develop large memberships and requiring them to use unwieldy organizational forms and to remain open to penetration by outsiders. This reformist urge, which has been so antiorganization in its goals, has all but ignored the party in government.

Once one part of the party comes to dominate, moreover, it can usually perpetuate its control through the laws and customs that govern party practices. The development of sophisticated new campaign techniques offers a good example. In a number of democratic nations that have parliamentary systems, party organizations have used their power to push legislation that limits candidates' independent access to these campaign technologies—for instance, by mandating that free television time goes to the party organizations to be doled out to their candidates, rather than to the candidates directly. The party organization, then, administers the new campaign tools, which buttresses its central role. In the United States, however, the dominant party in government has no reason to reduce its power by passing laws that turn over control of these new technologies to the party organizations; therefore the television time and other valuable tools remain available directly to candidates and officeholders.[16]

Other forces in the American political environment have reinforced dominance of the party in government. Many aspects of the Progressive reforms were intended to weaken the party organizations. The result, however unintended, was to give a decided advantage to the party in government. Even the increasing role of organized interests and the media further undercuts the party organizations. Under such an assault, what is remarkable is not that the party organizations' role has eroded but that they have survived at all.

The Need for Strong Parties

Democracy is unthinkable without parties. But political life in the United States without the dominance of two major parties is no longer unthinkable. Much of American local politics has been nonpartisan for some time. At the state and national levels, divided government, independent candidates, and third (and fourth and fifth) parties have become familiar parts of the political landscape.

The consequences of a multiparty system or a more fragmented political system would be profound.[17] Much more disturbing, however, would be a politics in which parties played a much smaller role. It is no exaggeration to suggest that the quality of American democracy would be weakened. Among the many links between citizens and government in American society, only the parties have the incentive to create majorities in order to win a wide range of elections over a long period. That in turn gives the parties—to a greater extent than interest groups, PACs, or even elected officials—good reason to pay attention to those citizens who are not activists or big campaign contributors. Walter Dean Burnham writes,

> Political parties, with all their well-known human and structural shortcomings, are the only devices thus far invented by the wit of Western man which with some effectiveness can generate countervailing collective power on behalf of the many individually powerless against the relatively few who are individually—or organizationally—powerful.[18]

It is the parties that mobilize sheer numbers against the organized minorities who hold other political resources. The parties do so in the one political arena where sheer numbers count most heavily: elections. Because of that, parties traditionally have been the means by which newly enfranchised but otherwise powerless groups gained a foothold in American life. The old-style urban machines, for example, provided the tool by which recent immigrants won control of their cities from older, largely white, Anglo-Saxon Protestant elites.

In other periods of American history as well, the party has been the form of political organization most available to those citizens who lack the resources to make a real impact on public decisions—on who gets what from American politics—using other means. In a less party-driven, more fluid politics where bargaining takes place among many more types of political organizations and millions more uncommitted voters, the well-organized minorities with critical resources such as money, insider knowledge, and technological expertise would probably have an even greater advantage than they would otherwise. We can see from research on nonpartisan elections, for instance, that the elimination of the party symbol and of the party as an organizer in these elections has probably helped wealthier and higher-status groups of both the right and the left to dominate these elections.[19]

It could be argued that the development of more ideological parties might have the same effect to a limited degree. To the extent that an ideological perspective is more likely to be found among the better educated and activist citizens, the parties might become focused on issues that were even less important and less comprehensible to the less involved, more poorly educated voters. That may be one reason why the participation declines of the last few decades have been somewhat greater among lower-status and less-educated Americans: they may feel less represented by a politics in which the parties are no longer dominant.[20]

Finally, weakened parties would rob the political system of an effective vehicle for creating governing coalitions. Without at least moderately strong parties it becomes harder to mobilize majorities that can come together in support of policies. Individual candidates, freed from lasting party loyalties, would have to re-create majorities for every new legislative proposal. The result could be political immobility in which legislatures splinter into conflicting and intransigent groups. This can undermine public confidence in democratic politics. Laws and policies would continue to be made. But they would be made by shifting coalitions made up of interest groups, campaign contributors, bureaucrats, and elected officials acting as free agents. These coalitions would be less permanent and less identifiable to the public—and therefore, much harder to hold accountable—than the parties have been, and can be.

It is important not to exaggerate the parties' traditional contributions to democratic politics. Although no democracies so far have survived without parties, it is possible for a mature political system to develop workable alternatives to stable, two-party politics. But in a diverse nation the challenge is whether any of the alternatives could pull together the pieces of a fragmented politics and separated political institutions as effectively as the parties have done. It is risky, to say the least, to move toward a politics without parties whose hazards would not be known until it was too late for them to avoided.[21]

CONCLUSION: THE PARTY DILEMMA

The American parties face a range of difficult problems. The American electorate is more and more varied. The breakdown of traditional group ties encourages greater individualism. Voters respond with more differentiated loyalties. The great majority of voters maintain an identification with a political party but they also respond to candidates and issues, stylistic matters and ideologies. The result is a more diverse, complicated politics that no single set of loyalties and no single set of political organizations can easily contain.

The parties cannot be all things to all citizens. It is difficult for them to represent the narrow interests of each self-oriented citizen effectively while trying to build a majority coalition. They cannot be pure in their ideology and still make the compromises that are necessary for coalition-building and governing. They find it hard to offer policy alternatives in elections without engaging in the partisan conflict and competition that many Americans find so distasteful. They cannot unite their officeholders and office seekers in common cause while giving candidates full electoral independence and freedom. They cannot depend on unwavering party loyalty in an electorate that wants to choose candidates individually.

These conflicting expectations are not likely to be resolved. The American parties will continue to need to adapt to them while facing attack from a rich assortment of critics. The parties' distinctive character has sustained them longer than any other tool of democratic governance. For the sake of accountability in governance, even the most independent-minded citizens have a stake in sustaining vigorous party politics in the United States.

Party Politics
on the Internet

*T*he two major parties and a variety of minor parties maintain Web pages. These can provide a fascinating glimpse into the world of each party's politics, and can serve as the basis for some interesting assignments.

http://www.democrats.org
This is the official Web site of the Democratic National Committee. It contains party news, information about Republican candidates (as seen through DNC eyes), and radio actualities. Poll questions are posted on the site along with the results of previous questions. Visitors can find out how to contact state Democratic parties, enroll in campaign training seminars, and register to vote. Job and internship opportunities at the DNC are listed, and the party's most recent platform is included.

http://www.rnc.org
The Republican National Committee's official Web site provides news about national politics, the RNC, and a range of party activities. Information about Democratic candidates is posted here, and although the party's most recent platform is not accessible through the site, material is included about party stands on a range of issues. There is also a listing of allied groups, such as the College Republican National Committee. Links enable the visitor to contact state Republican organizations.

http://www.reformparty.org
This is the site of the dominant branch of the Reform Party, founded in the mid-1990s by Ross Perot. The party's platform is posted here, along with membership information, ways to contact local party groups, and interactive opportunities.

http://www.americanreform.org
The American Reform Party is an anti-Perot group that split off from the main body of the Reform Party in 1997. The site contains a history of the organization, position papers, a party platform, and links to state groups.

http://www.dsausa.org/dsa.html
The Democratic Socialists of America's site provides a statement of the party's principles and links to information about socialism.

http://www.greens.org/na.html
The Green Parties of North America list their platform, which emphasizes environmental issues, peace, and social justice, on this Web site. The site includes a series of party publications, its elected officials and candidates, local affiliates, and email lists.

http://www.lcr.org
The Log Cabin Republicans are the largest national gay and lesbian Republican organization. Their site includes legislative information, material about party conventions and Republican candidates, and a newsletter.

http://www.lp.org
The Libertarian Party's home page begins with a quiz: "Are You a Libertarian?" You'll also find a statement of the party's principles, its history and activities, and a list of state chapters.

http://www.natural-law.org
The Natural Law Party says it wants to "bring the light of science into politics." The site includes the party platform, news and party events, a listing of state activities, and party publications.

http://www.newparty.org
The New Party is a progressive, grassroots party concerned mainly with local elections in a variety of cities. The site features materials about the party's principles, its chapters, candidates, the party's governance, and links to media articles about the party's activities.

http://www.pww.org
This is the home page of the Communist Party USA. Posted here are party position papers, locations of regional offices, and a list of party-related newspapers and journals.

http://www.southernparty.org
Founded in 1998, the Southern Party argues for the sovereignty and perhaps eventually the independence of the Southern states. The site features position papers, press releases, and a listing of state parties.

http://www.uhurumovement.org
The Web site of the African People's Socialist Party, a black socialist revolutionary movement, contains news from the party's perspective, its platform, and a list of publications.

http://www.USTaxpayers.org
also reachable at   http://www.Constitutionparty.com
Formerly the U.S. Taxpayers Party, the Constitution Party favors limited government. Its site offers press releases, a list of party events, its platform, and a list of its state party organizations.

http://www.workers.org
A socialist party organization, the Workers World Party has a forty-year history in the United States. Its site contains news of issues that the organization finds interesting, events, and a listing of local parties.

Here are some other Internet sites through which you can get information about political parties, elections, and voting:

http://www.fec.gov
This is the Federal Election Commission's Web site. In addition to information about the commission itself, it provides access to current and past campaign finance data in federal (presidential and congressional) races, as well as a variety of reports about those data.

http://www.govote.com
This site has a wealth of information on the 2000 elections. It posts other political news and permits visitors to track legislation in Congress, learn how to register to vote, see poll results, and take part in discussion groups about a variety of issues. It contains links to federal and state government offices.

http://www.opensecrets.org
The Center for Responsive Politics, a nonpartisan research group, maintains this site to provide information on money in politics. Its databases include presidential and congressional races, political action committees, soft money, lobbyists, and news links of various kinds.

http://www.umich.edu/~nes/
The National Election Studies, based at the University of Michigan, have been conducted since 1952 to provide information on public opinion, political participation, and voting behavior. Students can view and download survey data from current and earlier studies and find research reports.

http://www.vote-smart.org
Project Vote Smart provides information on federal and state candidates, including biographical data, interest-group ratings, and candidates' responses to questions about their issue priorities. It offers data on campaign finance, tracks legislation in Congress, and tells site visitors how to register to vote.

http://www.washingtonpost.com
Major national newspapers such as the *Washington Post* can be read on the Internet. The Post is notable for the excellence of its political coverage.

You can also find an enormous list of politics-related Web sites at the *New York Times* on the Web: http://www.nytimes.com/library/politics/polpoints.html

SAMPLE ASSIGNMENTS USING THESE WEB SITES:

- Pick two political issues that interest you. Use the Democratic and Republican parties' Web sites to determine where they stand on these issues. How clear are their stands and how much difference do you find between them? Do they offer you a clear choice?

- Compare the positions of the two major parties with those of two minor parties. How easy is it to find out where the minor parties stand on these issues that interest you? How different are their stands from those of the Democrats and Republicans? What would be the advantages and disadvantages for American politics if these alternatives were more widely publicized?

- What can you learn from these sites about the parties' organizations? At what levels of government do the major parties have organizations? Where do the minor parties have chapters or branches, other than at the national level?

- What kinds of activities do the Democrats and Republicans sponsor? To what extent do minor parties offer similar activities to their sympathizers?

- Does a party's Web site show evidence that the party offers material rewards for activists, or solidary or purposive rewards (see Chapter 5)? Which type of rewards seems to be most common?

- Which do the Democrats' and Republicans' home pages stress most: their candidates' experience and personal qualities, or the party's issue stands?

- Do the two major parties seem to be targeting particular groups in the population, such as women, Hispanics, or others? Which ones? Do the Democrats and Republicans target the same groups, or different groups?

- What kinds of news stories do various parties feature on their home pages? Why do you think they chose these stories? If the same news item is posted on more than one party's site, is it treated differently or explained differently by the two parties?

- Using the American National Election Studies Web site, familiarize yourself with the results of survey questions on citizens' feelings about the parties. When you read a survey question, predict what you expect the responses to be. Compare your prediction with the actual data. Have the responses changed over time?

- Use the American National Election Studies Web site to create cross-tabulations: How do Democratic and Republican identifiers compare in their views on various issues? Are there big differences among strong identifiers, weak identifiers, and independent leaners? Which group expresses the greatest interest in politics? Would you have expected this finding?

- Using the Opensecrets site, check out the information on soft money (see Chapter 12). Which party would you expect to raise the most soft money? Compare your prediction with the actual data. How do the parties spend their money?

- What interest groups would you expect to give Democrats in Congress high ratings? Republicans? Go to the VoteSmart site and test your guesses against their findings.

- Using the *Washington Post's* Web site, read articles, columns, and editorials about political issues. Are the major parties mentioned? If so, what aspects of the parties' activities are emphasized? Are political candidates mentioned more frequently than parties are, or the reverse? Do you find any mention of minor parties?

End Notes

PART 1

1. This is the title of Harold Lasswell's pioneering book, *Politics: Who Gets What, When, How* (New York: McGraw-Hill, 1936).
2. E. E. Schattschneider, *Party Government* (New York: Rinehart, 1942), p. 1.
3. Discussion of the important role of parties in the development of new democracies can be found in David Apter, *The Politics of Modernization* (Chicago: University of Chicago Press, 1965), Chap. 6; and Joseph LaPalombara and Myron Weiner, *Political Parties and Political Development* (Princeton, NJ: Princeton University Press, 1966).
4. Austin Ranney provides an excellent account of these antiparty attitudes and reforms in *Curing the Mischiefs of Faction* (Berkeley: University of California Press, 1975).

CHAPTER 1

1. These definitions are taken from: John H. Aldrich, *Why Parties? The Origin and Trans- formation of Party Politics in America* (Chicago: University of Chicago Press, 1995) pp. 283–284; Edmund Burke, "Thoughts on the Cause of the Present Discontents" (1770), in *The Works of Edmund Burke* (Boston: Little, Brown, 1839), vol. I, pp. 425–426; William Nisbet Chambers, "Party Development and the American Mainstream," in Chambers and Walter Dean Burnham, eds., *The American Party Systems* (New York: Oxford University Press, 1967), p. 5; Anthony Downs, *An Economy Theory of Democracy* (New York: Harper and Row, 1957), p. 24; Leon Epstein, *Political Parties in Western Democracies* (New Brunswick, NJ: Transaction Books, 1980; originally published in 1967), p. 9; and V. O. Key, *Politics, Parties, and Pressure Groups* (New York: Crowell, 1958), pp. 180–182. For an extended discussion of key issues in defining political parties, see Giovanni Sartori, *Par- ties and Party Systems* (New York: Cambridge University Press, 1976), pp. 3–38; Leon Epstein, *Political Parties in Western Democracies*; Gerald Pomper, *Passions and Interests: Political Party Concepts of American Democracy* (Lawrence: University of Kansas Press, 1992); and Joseph Schlesinger, *Political Parties and the Winning of Office* (Ann Arbor: Uni- versity of Michigan Press, 1991), pp. 5–10.
2. This treatment does not exhaust the various notions of political parties. Gerald Pomper iden- tifies at least eight different party models–governing caucus, ideological community, cause advocate, social movement, bureaucratic organization, urban machine, rational team of office seekers, and personal faction–by differentiating between a mass versus elite focus, collective versus coalitional goals, and instrumental versus expressive modes of operation. His approach recognizes the cacophony of party images in the American political tradition. See Pomper, *Passions and Interests*.
3. This account of the Mountaineer Party's misfortune draws upon a report in *Ballot Access News,* August 23, 1994.
4. John Aldrich views parties as enduring organizations through which teams of ambitious politicians combine to solve collective action problems in achieving their goals. Although he appreciates that voters may be a valuable component of a party and were so from the

1830s to about 1960, he does not see a mass base as fundamental for an organization to constitute a political party. See his Why Parties?, especially Chap. 1.

5. This tripartite conception of the political parties is attributed to V. O. Key, Jr., who used it to organize his classic political parties textbook, *Politics, Parties, and Pressure Groups.* Key attributed the concept of party-in-the-electorate to Ralph M. Goldman, *Party Chairmen and Party Factions, 1789–1900* (Chicago: University of Chicago Ph.D. dissertation, 1951), Chap. 17.

6. This point is emphasized by a number of critics of the tripartite approach. See especially Denise L. Baer and David A. Bositis, *Elite Cadres and Party Coalitions: Representing the Public in Party Politics* (Westport, CT: Greenwood Press, 1988), pp. 21–50; and Pomper, *Passions and Interests,* pp. 3–5.

7. The failure to recognize that political parties do not single-mindedly seek only to win office but also are motivated by the benefits that can be derived from control of office has led to some confusion about the electoral goals of parties. For clarification, see Joseph A. Schlesinger, "The Primary Goals of Political Parties: A Clarification of Positive Theory," *American Political Science Review* 69 (1975): 840–849.

8. On the party as a series of task-oriented nuclei, see Joseph A. Schlesinger, "Political Party Organization," in James G. March, ed., *Handbook of Organizations* (Chicago: Rand McNally, 1965), pp. 764–801; and "The New American Political Party," *American Political Science Review* 79 (1985): pp. 1152–1169.

9. Theodore Lowi has brought together a number of descriptions of party functions in his article "Toward Functionalism in Political Science: The Case of Innovation in Party Systems," *American Political Science Review* 57 (1963): 570–583. See also A. James Reichley, *The Life of the Parties: A History of American Political Parties* (New York: Free Press, 1992), pp. 1–2 and 414–415.

10. John Aldrich sees parties as organizations that are created by rational politicians to solve their most challenging collective action problems: (a) to organize political officeholders into an enduring and cohesive group in support of key policy principles; (b) to forge durable majorities; and (c) to mobilize voters in elections and political activity on behalf of their cause. See Aldrich, *Why Parties?* especially Chaps. 2 and 9.

11. There are many histories of the development of American political parties. Most devote virtually all their pages to the candidates and platforms of the parties; few discuss the parties themselves. The most notable ones that do are William N. Chambers, *Political Parties in a New Nation* (New York: Oxford University Press, 1963); Chambers and Burnham, *The American Party Systems;* Everett C. Ladd, Jr., *American Political Parties* (New York: Norton, 1970); Reichley, *The Life of the Parties;* and John H. Aldrich, *Why Parties?*

12. See *The Federalist* (New York: Mentor Books, 1961), p. 77, for the quoted material. What is referred to as *The Federalist* is the collection of eighty-five essays written to justify the new Constitution that was undergoing ratification in the states and published as letters to the editor in New York newspapers in 1787 and 1788 under the pseudonym of Publius. Their authors were Alexander Hamilton, James Madison, and John Jay; Madison was clearly the author of essay number 10. Partly because of the powerful justification for it fashioned by Hamilton, Jay, and Madison, the new Constitution was adopted and has served the nation ever since.

13. See John H. Aldrich and Ruth W. Grant, "The Antifederalists, the First Congress, and the First Parties," *Journal of Politics* 55 (1993): 295–326; Aldrich, *Why Parties?* Chap. 3; Chambers, *Political Parties in a New Nation;* Joseph Charles, *The Origins of the American Party System* (New York: Harper & Row, 1961); John F. Hoadley, *Origins of Ameri-*

can Political Parties 1789–1803 (Lexington: University of Kentucky Press, 1986); and Reichley, *The Life of the Parties,* Chaps. 3 and 4.

14. For a detailed account of the extension of the suffrage focusing on the separate actions of the states, see Chilton Williamson, *American Suffrage: From Property to Democracy* (Princeton, NJ: Princeton University Press, 1960).

15. For a more complete account, see Neal R. Peirce and Lawrence D. Longley, *The People's President: The Electoral College in American History and the Direct Vote Alternative* (New Haven, CT: Yale University Press, 1981).

16. Both Aldrich, in *Why Parties?* Chap. 4, and Reichley, in *The Life of the Parties,* Chap. 5, provide excellent descriptions of how mass parties first appeared in the decades after the 1820s. Martin Van Buren, leader of the Albany, New York, Regency machine and the eighth president of the United States, is credited as being the lead architect in the creation of the first of the mass parties, the Democratic Party, which itself was a direct descendent of the Democratic-Republican party.

17. For a more complete account of parties during their golden age, see Reichley, *The Life of the Parties,* Chaps. 6–11.

18. A spirited account of the development of American parties and party organizations into their golden age from a disapproving normative perspective is found in Moisei Ostrogorski, *Democracy and the Organization of Political Parties, Volume II: The United States* (Garden City, NY: Anchor Books, Doubleday and Company, 1964; originally published in 1902).

19. On the various episodes of party reform in American history and their effects, see Austin Ranney, *Curing the Mischiefs of Faction* (Berkeley, CA: University of California Press, 1975). A good account of the Progressive movement may be found in Richard Hofstadter, *The Age of Reform* (New York: Vintage Books, 1955). On the issue of "party decline," see Martin P. Wattenberg, *The Decline of American Political Parties, 1952–1996* (Cambridge, MA: Harvard University Press, 1998); and James W. Ceaser, "Political Parties—Declining, Stabilizing, or Resurging?" in Anthony King, ed., *The New American Political System,* 2nd ed. (Washington, DC: American Enterprise Institute, 1990), pp. 87–137.

20. So extensive is government regulation of political parties that Leon Epstein was moved to characterize them as public utilities rather than as the private associations they were during the nineteenth century. See his *Political Parties in the American Mold* (Madison, WI: University of Wisconsin Press, 1986), pp. 155–199.

21. The best discussions of the concept of political culture remain Gabriel Almond and Sidney Verba, *The Civic Culture* (Princeton, NJ: Princeton University Press, 1963); and Lucian W. Pye and Sidney Verba, *Political Culture and Political Development* (Princeton, NJ: Princeton University Press, 1965). For an interesting application of the political culture concept to American state and local politics, see Daniel Elazar, *American Federalism: A View from the States* (New York: Crowell, 1972), Chap. 4.

22. Some of the most interesting results of this survey conducted by the National Election Studies at the University of Michigan can be found in The NES Guide to Public Opinion and Electoral Behavior, located on the Internet at:
http://www.umich.edu/~nes/nesguide/toptable/tab2b_2.htm

CHAPTER 2

1. For comprehensive studies of other party systems, see, *inter alia,* Kenneth Janda, *Political Parties: A Cross-National Survey* (New York: Free Press, 1980); and Arend Lijphart, *Electoral Systems and Party Systems: A Study of Twenty-Seven Democracies, 1945–1990* (New York: Oxford University Press, 1994).

340   *End Notes*

2. For a sophisticated critique of the traditional classification and analysis of party systems, see Giovanni Sartori, *Parties and Party Systems* (New York: Cambridge University Press, 1976).

3. Other relevant records in presidential elections are the greatest electoral college vote— Ronald Reagan in 1984, with 525 votes—and the greatest percentage of the two-party popular vote—Calvin Coolidge in 1924, with 65.2 percent.

4. Historical studies of competition for the House of Representatives show that the high and increasing level of competitiveness through the mid–1890s was replaced by a steady decrease in competitiveness for the next 90 years. See James C. Garand and Donald A. Gross, "Changes in the Vote Margins for Congressional Candidates: A Specification of Historical Trends," *American Political Science Review* 78 (1984): 17–30; and Donald A. Gross and James C. Garand, "The Vanishing Marginals, 1824–1980," *Journal of Politics* 46 (1984): 224–237.

5. The original measurements were presented for 1946–1963 by Austin Ranney, "Parties in State Politics," in Herbert Jacob and Kenneth Vines, eds., *Politics in the American States* (Boston: Little, Brown, 1965), p. 65. For an alternative index based on state legislative races, see Thomas M. Holbrook and Emily Van Dunk, "Electoral Competition in the American States,"*American Political Science Review* 87 (1993): 955–962.

6. Harvey J. Tucker, "Interparty Competition in the American States," *American Politics Quarterly* 10 (1982): 93–116; and Patrick J. Kenney and Tom W. Rice, "Party Composition in the American States: Clarifying Concepts and Explaining Changes in Partisanship since the 1950s," *Political Behavior* 7 (1985): 335–351.

7. These were the results of a study relating the Ranney index for the 1970–1980 period to various characteristics of the states. See Samuel C. Patterson and Gregory A. Caldeira, "The Etiology of Partisan Competition," *American Political Science Review* 78 (1984): 691–707.

8. The figures on incumbency success rates through 1992 are drawn from Paul R. Abramson, John H. Aldrich, and David W. Rohde, *Change and Continuity in the 1992 Elections* (Washington, DC: Congressional Quarterly Press, 1994), pp. 255–280 and especially Tables 9.1 and 9.6. Data for 1994–1998 come from the *Congressional Quarterly Weekly Report* postelection figures. On the influence of incumbency in general, see, *inter alia,* Garand and Gross, "Changes in the Vote Margins for Congressional Candidates"; Gross and Garand, "The Vanishing Marginals, 1824–1980"; David R. Mayhew, "Congressional Elections: The Case of the Vanishing Marginals," *Polity* 6 (1974): 295–317; Gary C. Jacobson, *The Politics of Congressional Elections,* 4th ed. (New York: Longman 1997), Chap. 3; and Stephen Ansolabehere, James M. Snyder, Jr., and Charles Stewart, III, "Old Voters, New Voters, and the Personal Vote: Using Redistricting to Measure the Incumbency Advantage," *American Journal of Political Science* 44 (2000): 17–34. On incumbency in state legislative elections, see Malcolm Jewell and David Breaux, "The Effect of Incumbency on State Legislative Elections," *Legislative Studies Quarterly* 13 (1988): 495–514.

9. Gary C. Jacobson, "The Marginals Never Vanished: Incumbency and Competition in Elections to the U.S. House of Representatives, 1952–82," *American Journal of Political Science* 31 (1987): 126–141. On how redistricting and scandals make incumbents vulnerable, also see Monica Bauer and John R. Hibbing, "Which Incumbents Lose in House Elections: A Response to Jacobson's 'The Marginals Never Vanished,'" *American Journal of Political Science* 31 (1987): 262–271.

10. The original development of this "law" is found in Maurice Duverger, *Political Parties* (New York: Wiley, 1954); for an even earlier illustration of the institutional explanation, see E. E. Schattschneider, *Party Government* (New York: Rinehart, 1942). For more recent evidence of the influence of electoral institutions on the size of the party system, see Arend Lijphart, "The Political Consequences of Electoral Laws, 1945–85," *American Political Science Review* 84 (1990): 481–496; Douglas Rae, *The Political Consequences of Elec-*

toral Laws (New Haven, CT: Yale University Press, 1967); William Riker, "The Two-Party System and Duverger's Law," *American Political Science Review* 76 (1982): 753–766; and Lijphart, *Electoral Systems and Party Systems.*

11. In the past, many states have had multimember districts for one or both houses of the state legislature. As late as 1955, 58 percent of all state legislative districts were multimember compared to 10 percent by the 1980s. See Theodore J. Lowi, "Towards a More Responsible Three Party System," *PS* 16 (1983): 699–706. On competition in multimember districts, see Richard Niemi, Simon Jackman, and Laura Winsley, "Candidates and Competitiveness in Multimember Districts," *Legislative Studies Quarterly* 16 (1991): 91–109.

12. This statement requires some qualification to be wholly accurate. The presidency goes to the party whose candidate has won a majority of the electoral votes; a state's electoral votes have almost always gone to the candidate who has won a *plurality* of the votes in the state. Gubernatorial victors in most states are the simple plurality winners; some Southern states, however, require the winner to attain a majority of the votes and provide for a runoff between the top two vote-getters if no candidate receives a majority in the first round. On these runoff elections, see Charles S. Bullock, III, and Loch K. Johnson, *Runoff Elections in the United States,* (Knoxville: University of Tennessee Press, 1991).

13. Leon Epstein, *Political Parties in the American Mold* (Madison: University of Wisconsin Press, 1986), pp. 129–132.

14. See, for example, V. O. Key, Jr., *Politics, Parties and Pressure Groups,* 5th ed. (New York: Crowell, 1964), pp. 229ff.; and Seymour Martin Lipset, Martin A. Trow, and James S. Coleman, *Union Democracy* (New York: Free Press, 1956), especially Part III.

15. Louis Hartz, *The Liberal Tradition in America* (New York: Harcourt, Brace, and World, 1955).

16. The clearest statements of this view are found in Oliver P. Williams and Charles Adrian, "The Insulation of Local Politics under the Nonpartisan Ballot," *American Political Science Review* 53 (1959): 1052–1063; and Willis D. Hawley, *Nonpartisan Elections and the Case for Party Politics* (New York: Wiley, 1973).

17. Susan Welch and Timothy Bledsoe, "The Partisan Consequences of Nonpartisan Elections and the Changing Nature of Urban Politics," *American Journal of Political Science* 30 (1986): 128–139.

18. A list of these third-party and independent governors through 1992 is provided by J. David Gillespie, *Politics at the Periphery* (Columbia: University of South Carolina Press, 1993), Appendix 5, pp. 302–305. More recent information can be found in election statistics on the Federal Election Commission's Web site (http://www.fec.gov).

19. The literature on American third parties is rich and varied. The best general treatments of third parties may be found in Daniel A. Mazmanian, *Third Parties in Presidential Elections* (Washington, DC: Brookings Institution, 1974); Steven J. Rosenstone, Roy L. Behr, and Edward H. Lazarus, *Third Parties in America,* 2nd ed. (Princeton: Princeton University Press, 1996); Paul S. Herrnson and John C. Green, *Multiparty Politics in America* (New York: Rowman & Littlefield, 1997); and Gillespie, *Politics at the Periphery.*

20. For more on the Libertarian Party, see Gillespie, *Politics at the Periphery,* pp. 174–178; and especially Joseph M. Hazlett II, *The Libertarian Party* (Jefferson, NC: McFarland and Company, 1992).

21. Evidence of the effects of voter skepticism about their chances is the fact that almost all third-party presidential candidates in this century have received less support on election day than they had exhibited in public-opinion polls prior to the election. See Rosenstone, Behr, and Lazarus, *Third Parties in America,* p. 41. The Perot candidacy in 1992 and 1996 continued this pattern.

22. Ibid., p. 162.

23. On the attitudes and preferences of Perot voters, see Paul R. Abramson, John H. Aldrich, and David W. Rohde, *Change and Continuity in the 1992 Elections* (Washington, DC: CQ Press, 1994). For the argument that Perot voters were less drawn to him than repulsed by the major-party candidates, see Herbert B. Asher, "The Perot Campaign," in Herbert Weisberg, ed., *Democracy's Feast: The 1992 U.S. Elections* (Chatham, NJ: Chatham House, 1994), Chap. 6.
24. Federal Election Commission figures show that the Perot organization invested almost $73 million in the 1992 campaign (June 28, 1994, report). Richard L. Berke reported in *The New York Times* (October 27, 1992, p. A11) that as much as $46 million of this money may have been spent on television.
25. This claim is made by David Gillespie, as quoted in *The Washington Post National Weekly Edition,* September 19–25, 1994, p. 13.
26. Third parties and independents have compiled a checkered record of success in ballot-access cases. State laws requiring filing fees and petitions signed by large numbers of voters before such candidates are allowed on the ballot have been overruled in some cases but upheld in others. On balance, the courts have made access to the ballot for third parties and independents easier in recent years. But this action has been taken on a piecemeal basis that requires petitioners to raise the challenge in each state and has left in place many curbs on access to the ballot as reasonable state efforts to avoid voter confusion and frustration when faced with a long ballot. See Clifton McCleskey, "Parties at the Bar: Equal Protection, Freedom of Association, and the Rights of Political Organization," *Journal of Politics* 46 (1984): 346–368; John Moeller, "The Federal Courts' Involvement in the Reform of Political Parties," *Western Political Quarterly* 40 (1987): 717–734; and Lee Epstein and Charles D. Hadley, "On the Treatment of Political Parties in the U.S. Supreme Court, 1900–1986," *Journal of Politics* 52 (1990): 413–432. For regular reports on access to the ballot by minor parties and independents, see Richard Winger's *Ballot Access News,* on the Internet at http://www.ballot-access.org.
27. The case was *Williams v. Rhodes*, 393 U.S. 23 (1968).
28. This account of Anderson's efforts to gain access to the ballot draws upon Jack W. Germond and Jules Witcover, *Blue Smoke and Mirrors: How Reagan Won and Why Carter Lost the Election of 1980* (New York: Viking, 1981), pp. 236–237. The Supreme Court case was *Anderson v. Celebrezze* 460 U.S. 780 (1983).
29. For an account of how New York election laws permitting multiple nominations and multiple ballot placement foster minor parties, see Howard A. Scarrow, *Parties, Elections, and Representation in the State of New York* (New York: New York University Press, 1983).
30. There are signs that this space increased in the 1990s, although it remains small. Christian Collet and Jerrold R. Hansen, writing in *Vox Pop,* the Newsletter of Political Organizations and Parties (volume 14, issue 2, p. 2), describe an upturn in independent and third-party voting in the 1990s in statewide, state legislative, and U.S. House contests.

CHAPTER 3

1. The results of this study are reported in Timothy Conlan, Ann Martino, and Robert Dilger, "State Parties in the 1980s," *Intergovernmental Perspective* 10 (1984): 6–13, 23; and *The Transformation in American Politics* (Washington, DC: Advisory Commission on Intergovernmental Relations, 1986), pp. 95–162.
2. The case citations are *Tashjian v. Republican Party of Connecticut,* 479 U.S. 1024 (1986); and *Eu* (Secretary of State of California) *v. San Francisco County Democratic Central Committee et al.,* 103 L. Ed. 2nd 271 (1989). The injunction against enforcement of the

endorsements law was issued on August 5, 1994, in *California Democratic Party v. Lungren,* no. C94–1703–WHO, Northern District. For a review of earlier federal court decisions in this area, see Clifton McCleskey, "Parties at the Bar: Equal Protection, Freedom of Association, and the Rights of Political Organizations," *Journal of Politics* 46 (1984): 346–368. On deregulation of parties in California, see Roy Christman and Barbara Norrander, "A Reflection on Political Party Deregulation Via the Courts: The Case of California," *Journal of Law and Politics* 6 (1990): 723–742.

3. Within the same state, the various intermediate committees may cover geographical areas of varying sizes and thus may occupy different positions in the organizational pyramid. Congressional districts, for example, may be smaller than a city or larger than a county, depending on the density of population.

4. The results of this survey are reported on p. 22 of John F. Persinos, "Has the Christian Right Taken Over the Republican Party?" *Campaigns and Elections,* September 1994, pp. 20–24.

5. Leon Epstein, *Political Parties in the American Mold* (Madison: University of Wisconsin Press, 1986), pp. 155–199.

6. V. O. Key, Jr., *Politics, Parties and Pressure Groups* (New York: Crowell, 1964), p. 316.

7. Samuel J. Eldersveld, *Political Parties: A Behavioral Analysis* (Chicago: Rand McNally, 1964).

8. The organization of American political parties leads one to question whether Michels' "iron law of oligarchy" —that organizations are inevitably controlled from the top—is really an iron law after all. See Robert Michels, *Political Parties* (Glencoe, IL: Free Press, 1949; originally published in 1915); and Eldersveld, *Political Parties.*

9. These estimates on the number of machines governing American cities at various times during their heyday come from M. Craig Brown and Charles N. Halaby, "Machine Politics in America, 1870–1945," *Journal of Interdisciplinary History* 17 (1987): 587–612.

10. These are the characteristics David Mayhew uses to define traditional party organizations, which when they hold overall control of a city or county at the local level are synonymous with machines. See Mayhew's *Placing Parties in American Politics* (Princeton, NJ: Princeton University Press, 1986), pp. 19–21. This book provides excellent descriptions of traditional party organizations in a variety of states through the 1960s.

11. For an interesting comparison of reform movements in three cities, see Kenneth Finegold, *Experts and Politicians: Reform Challenges to Machine Politics in New York, Cleveland, and Chicago* (Princeton, NJ: Princeton University Press, 1995).

12. The colorful politics of Chicago has stimulated a rich literature, probably the richest on the subject of party politics in any American city. An early study of the Chicago machine is Harold Foote Gosnell's classic *Machine Politics: Chicago Style* (Chicago: University of Chicago Press, 1939). Good studies of the Daley years are Edward C. Banfield, *Political Influence* (New York: The Free Press, 1961); Milton Rakove, *Don't Make No Waves, Don't Back No Losers* (Bloomington, IN: Indiana University Press, 1975); and Thomas M. Guterbok, *Machine Politics in Transition: Party and Community in Chicago* (Chicago: University of Chicago Press, 1980). For perspectives on the post-Daley years and their roots in earlier times, see Paul Kleppner, *Chicago Divided: The Making of a Black Mayor* (DeKalb, IL: Northern Illinois University Press, 1985); William J. Grimshaw, *Bitter Fruit: Black Politics and the Chicago Machine* (Chicago: University of Chicago Press, 1992); and Kenneth Finegold, *Experts and Politicians.*

13. Steven P. Erie makes a persuasive argument that the great urban machines were principally organizations of, by, and for the Irish, who proved unwilling to accommodate other ethnic groups. See his *Rainbow's End: Irish-Americans and the Dilemmas of Urban Machine Politics, 1840–1985* (Berkeley: University of California Press, 1988). The mobi-

lization of ethnics, including the non-Irish, however, required the right kind of political leadership. On how such an ethnic group coalition was built by the Tammany Hall political machine in New York, see Martin Shefter, The Electoral Foundations of the Political Machine: New York City, 1884–1897," in Joel H. Silbey, Allan G. Bogue, and William H. Flanagan, eds., *The History of American Electoral Behavior* (Princeton, NJ: Princeton University Press, 1978), pp. 263–298.

14. For an insightful discussion of the conditions for machine politics here and abroad, see James C. Scott, "Corruption, Machine Politics, and Political Change," *American Political Science Review* 63 (1969): 1142–1158. On the importance for party development of an autonomous bureaucracy insulated from being used for patronage by a political party in its quest for votes, see the rich comparisons among Britain, Germany, Italy, France, and the United States by Martin Shefter, *Political Parties and the State* (Princeton, NJ: Princeton University Press, 1994), Chap. 2. A useful perspective on the development of American machines also is provided by Amy Bridges, *A City in the Republic: Antebellum New York and the Origins of Machine Politics* (New York: Cambridge University Press, 1984).

15. On the Nassau County machine, see Anne Freedman, *Patronage: An American Tradition* (Chicago: Nelson-Hall, 1994), Chap. 5. One of its leaders, U.S. Senator Alphonse D'Amato, remains a powerful figure in New York politics.

16. Kenneth R. Mladenka, "The Urban Bureaucracy and the Chicago Political Machine: Who Gets What and the Limits to Political Control," *American Political Science Review* 74 (1980): 991–998.

17. Michael Johnston, "Patrons and Clients, Jobs and Machines: A Case Study in the Uses of Patronage," *American Political Science Review* 73 (1979): 385–398.

18. A few thoughtful scholars have resisted the stampede to sound the death knell for political machines. See Raymond Wolfinger's "Why Political Machines Have Not Withered Away and Other Revisionist Thoughts," *Journal of Politics* 34 (1972): 365–398. Others have also questioned whether the replacement of the machines by more bureaucratic and less centralized government has been beneficial for American cities. See Theodore Lowi, "Machine Politics—Old and New," *Public Interest,* Fall 1967, pp. 83–92.

19. The results of this survey are reported in James L. Gibson, Cornelius P. Cotter, John F. Bibby, and Robert J. Huckshorn, "Whither the Local Parties?" *American Journal of Political Science* 29 (1985): 139–160; and Cornelius P. Cotter, James L. Gibson, John F. Bibby, and Robert J. Huckshorn, *Party Organization in American Politics* (New York: Praeger, 1984).

20. Cotter et al., *Party Organization in American Politics,* pp. 49–53. The states with strong and weak local organizations, respectively, are virtually the same ones cited in Mayhew's survey of party strength in the late 1960s. See Mayhew, *Placing Parties in American Politics.*

21. James L. Gibson, John P. Frendreis, and Laura L. Vertz, "Party Dynamics in the 1980s: Change in County Party Organizational Strength, 1980–1984," *American Journal of Political Science* 33 (1989): 67–90.

22. See Cotter et al., *Party Organization in American Politics,* p. 54, for the 1964–1980 comparison. The 1964 figures come from Paul Allen Beck, "Environment and Party," *American Political Science Review* 68 (1974): 1229–1244. The 1988 figures are from a study conducted by John Kessel and William Jacoby and are reported in Charles E. Smith, Jr., "Changes in Party Organizational Strength and Activity 1979–1988," The Ohio State University, unpublished manuscript, 1989. On Detroit and Los Angeles, see Samuel J. Eldersveld, "The Party Activist in Detroit and Los Angeles: A Longitudinal View, 1956–1980," in William J. Crotty, ed., *Political Parties in Local Areas* (Knoxville: University of Tennessee Press, 1986), pp. 89–119.

23. This study of local party organizations was conducted by Paul Allen Beck, Russell J. Dalton, Audrey Haynes, and Robert Huckfeldt as a part of the American component in the Cross-National Election Project. The forty counties were selected to represent, with probabilities proportionate to size, the locales of voters in the 1992 election. Democratic and Republican county chairs or their equivalents were contacted by phone or by mail in all forty counties, and information on their organization and its activities was collected from all but one respondent. For early reports on the results of this study, see Beck, Dalton, Haynes, and Huckfeldt, "Local Party Organizations and Presidential Politics," in Birol Yesilada, ed., *Comparative Political Parties and Party Elites* (Ann Arbor: University of Michigan Press, 1999), pp. 55–79; and "Presidential Campaigning at the Grass Roots," *Journal of Politics* (1997): 1264–1275.

24. Increased levels of local party activity in 1992 also are reported in a study of the party role in legislative campaigns in eight states. See John Frendreis, Alan R. Gitelson, Gregory Flemming, and Anne Layzell, "Local Political Parties and the 1992 Campaign for the State Legislatures," paper presented at the 1993 Annual Meeting of the American Political Science Association.

25. For excellent descriptions of these traditional organizations before they suffered their recent declines, see Mayhew, *Placing Parties in American Politics*.

26. These notes of caution, among others, are sounded by John J. Coleman in "The Resurgence of Party Organization? A Dissent from the New Orthodoxy," in Daniel M. Shea and John C. Green, eds. *The State of the Parties: The Changing Role of Contemporary American Parties* (Lanham, MD: Rowman and Littlefield, 1994), pp. 282–298.

27. A. James Reichley cites Illinois, Michigan, Ohio, Pennsylvania, and Wisconsin as states with powerful state organizations near the turn of the twentieth century. They had been fueled by the federal patronage allocated by the states' U.S. senators, one of whom typically served as their leader, since the time of the Grant presidency. Probably the most powerful state organization ever, though, was that built by Governor (then Senator) Huey Long in the 1920s and 1930s using state government powers and patronage. See Reichley's *The Life of the Parties* (New York: Free Press, 1992), pp. 144–160 and 268–272.

28. These estimates come from Robert J. Huckshorn and John F. Bibby, "State Parties in an Era of Political Change," in Joel L. Fleishman, ed., *The Future of American Political Parties* (Englewood Cliffs, NJ: Prentice-Hall, 1982), pp. 70–100; and James L. Gibson, Cornelius P. Cotter, John F. Bibby, and Robert J. Huckshorn, "Assessing Party Organization Strength," *American Journal of Political Science* 27 (1983): 193–222.

29. Figures for the mid–1980s come from a survey conducted by the Brookings Institution and reported in Reichley, *The Life of the Parties,* p. 388. Data for 1995–1996 can be found on the Federal Election Commission's Web site.

30. For an account of these legislative campaign committees, see Anthony Gierzynski, *Legislative Party Campaign Committees in the American States* (Lexington, KY: University of Kentucky Press, 1992).

31. See John F. Bibby, "State Party Organizations: Coping and Adapting," in L. Sandy Maisel, ed., *The Parties Respond* (Boulder, CO: Westview, 1994), pp. 21–44.

32. The 1979–1980 study is Cotter et al., *Party Organizations in American Politics.* The 1984 study is Advisory Commission on Intergovernmental Relations, *The Transformation in American Politics.*

33. For an account of how one of the pioneers of effective state party organization operated, see John H. Kessel, "Ray Bliss and the Development of the Ohio Republican Party During the 1950s," in John C. Green, ed., *Politics, Professionalism, and Power* (Lanham, MD: University Press of America, 1994), pp. 48–61.

34. These were identified as the strongest state organizations in 1979–1980 by Cotter et al., *Party Organizations in American Politics,* pp. 28–29.
35. "Soft money" refers to campaign contributions raised by the national parties and presidential candidates that would be illegal under federal law if they remained at the national level but become legal when they are directly funneled to the state parties for use in nonfederal elections and for generic party activities. For more on soft money, see Chapter 12.
36. On the role of the national parties in state-party building, see Bibby, "State Party Organizations: Coping and Adapting," especially pp. 36–43. Funding figures for 1997–1998 come from the Federal Election Commission Web page, at: http://www.fec.gov/press/ptyye98.htm.
37. Walter Dean Burnham, *Critical Elections and the Mainsprings of American Politics* (New York: Norton, 1970), p. 72.
38. For an intensive examination of how factors such as these undermined Democratic organizations in three different locales, see Alan Ware, *The Breakdown of the Democratic Party Organization 1940–80* (Oxford, England: Oxford University Press, 1985).
39. This notion of the state and local parties fits Mildred Schwartz's conceptualization of the party as a network of interactions in *The Party Network: The Robust Organization of Illinois Republicans* (Madison: University of Wisconsin Press, 1990). She found that the most central actors within the modern Illinois Republican Party were financial contributors, interest groups, advisors, state senators and representatives, county chairs, and the governor—not solely the occupants of the formal party organization.

CHAPTER 4

1. Cornelius P. Cotter and Bernard C. Hennessy, *Politics without Power: The National Party Committees* (New York: Atherton, 1964). For a comprehensive history of the national committees, see Ralph M. Goldman, *The National Party Chairmen and Committees* (Armonk, NY: M. E. Sharpe, 1990).
2. E. E. Schattschneider, *Party Government* (New York: Rinehart, 1942), pp. 129, 132–133.
3. Leon D. Epstein, *Political Parties in the American Mold* (Madison: University of Wisconsin Press, 1986), pp. 200–238; and Gary D. Wekkin, "National-State Party Relations: The Democrats' New Federal Structure," *Political Science Quarterly* 99 (1984): 45–72.
4. Cotter and Hennessy, *Politics without Power,* p. 39.
5. James W. Ceaser, "Political Parties—Declining, Stabilizing, or Resurging," in Anthony King, ed., *The New American Political System* (Washington, DC: American Enterprise Institute, 1990), pp. 87–137 at pp. 114–117. For a more general treatment of how American parties have become more tightly linked to the president as they have become more nationalized, see Sidney M. Milkis, *The President and the Parties: The Transformation of the American Party System Since the New Deal* (New York: Oxford University Press, 1993).
6. For illustrations of these antithetical views of party strength, compare David Broder's *The Party's Over* (New York: Harper and Row, 1972), an early chronicle of the decline of parties thesis, with *The Party Goes On* by Xandra Kayden and Eddie Mahe, Jr. (New York: Basic Books, 1985) or Larry J. Sabato, *The Party's Just Begun* (Glenview, IL: Scott Foresman/Little, Brown, 1988).
7. Their ability to raise substantial sums of money directly through individual donations has contributed to the national parties' increased power by freeing them from their previous dependence on assessments upon the state parties, another characteristic of a confederated structure, and from the resultant state party influence. For a description of this earlier system, see Cotter and Hennessy, *Politics without Power,* pp. 180–182. For more on

modern party finance, see Frank J. Sorauf and Scott A. Wilson, "Political Parties and Campaign Finance: Adaptation and Accommodation Toward a Changing Role," in L. Sandy Maisel, ed., *The Parties Respond: Changes in American Parties and Campaigns,* 2nd ed. (Boulder, CO: Westview Press, 1994), pp. 235–53; and David B. Magleby and Candice J. Nelson, *The Money Chase* (Washington, DC: Brookings, 1990).

8. John H. Kessel, "Organizational Development of National Party Committees: Some Generalizations and Supporting Evidence," *Vox Pop: Newsletter of Political Organizations and Parties,* vol. 7, no. 3, p. 1.

9. F. Christopher Arterton calls them "service vendor" parties, while Paul Herrnson refers to them as "broker" parties. See Arterton's "Political Money and Party Strength," in Joel Fleishman, ed., *The Future of American Political Parties* (Englewood Cliffs, NJ: Prentice-Hall, 1982), pp. 101–139; and Herrnson, "National Party Organizations and Congressional Campaigning: National Parties as Brokers," paper presented at the 1986 Annual Meeting of the Midwest Political Science Association, Chicago.

10. Excellent accounts of the roles of Brock and especially Bliss in party building at the national level are contained in various chapters of John C. Green, ed., *Politics, Professionalism, and Power: Modern Party Organization and the Legacy of Ray C. Bliss* (Lanham, MD: University Press of American, 1994). On the role of Manatt and the others, see A. James Reichley, *The Life of the Parties* (New York: Free Press, 1992), pp. 353–381.

11. On Democratic Party reform, see Austin Ranney, *Curing the Mischiefs of Faction: Party Reform in America* (Berkeley: University of California Press, 1975); William J. Crotty, *Decisions for the Democrats: Reforming the Party Structure* (Baltimore, MD: Johns Hopkins University Press, 1978); and Byron E. Shafer, *The Quiet Revolution: The Struggle for the Democratic Party and the Shaping of Post-Reform Politics* (New York: Russell Sage Foundation, 1983).

12. A reform committee, the Rule 29 Committee, was mandated by the 1972 Republican National Convention, but its recommendations for RNC review of state party "positive action" programs were rejected by the RNC and later by the 1976 convention. In general, the GOP has been far more protective of states' rights for the parties than have the Democrats. See John F. Bibby, "Party Renewal in the Republican National Party," in Gerald M. Pomper, ed., *Party Renewal in America* (New York: Praeger, 1981), pp. 102–115.

13. Comprehensive recent accounts of the increased strength of the national parties include A. James Reichley, *The Life of the Political Parties* (New York: Free Press, 1992), pp. 353–381; and Paul S. Herrnson, "The Revitalization of National Party Organizations," in Maisel, *The Parties Respond,* pp. 45–68.

14. For a good description of the traditional relationships of state party leadership and the national parties, see Robert J. Huckshorn, *Party Leadership in the States* (Amherst: University of Massachusetts Press, 1976), Chap. 8.

15. See Epstein, *Political Parties in the American Mold,* p. 237; and Xandra Kayden, "The Nationalization of the Party System," in Michael J. Malbin, ed., *Parties, Interest Groups, and the Campaign Finance Laws* (Washington, DC: American Enterprise Institute, 1980), pp. 257–282.

16. This incident and the policy change it induced are described in Kayden and Mahe, *The Party Goes On,* pp. 78–79.

17. Party-presidential relations during the Reagan years are discussed in A. James Reichley, "The Rise of National Parties," in John E. Chubb and Paul E. Peterson, eds., *The New Direction in American Politics* (Washington, DC: Brookings Institution, 1985), pp. 175–200. The traditional relationship between the president and his party's national committee is discussed in Cotter and Hennessy, *Politics without Power,* pp. 81–94.

18. The national committees may also exert considerable influence over the management of a campaign, particularly for nonincumbents, who are most in need of their assistance, through their power to withhold services and funds. See Paul S. Herrnson, *Party Campaigning in the 1980s* (Cambridge, MA: Harvard University Press, 1988), p. 59.

19. Herrnson, *Party Campaigning in the 1980s,* pp. 41–42.

20. This observation is made by Reichley, *The Life of the Party,* pp. 377–381. It echoes a challenge to the presumption that local parties are now more effective by John J. Coleman, "The Resurgence of Party Organization? A Dissent from the New Orthodoxy," in Daniel M. Shea and John C. Green, eds., *The State of the Parties* (Lanham, MD.: Rowman and Littlefield, 1994), pp. 311–328.

21. Epstein, *Political Parties in the American Mold,* p. 200.

22. This point is made by Ceaser in "Political Parties—Declining, Stabilizing, or Resurging?" p. 120.

CHAPTER 5

1. A 1992 national survey of county party organizations conducted by Paul Allen Beck, Russell J. Dalton, Audrey Haynes, and Robert Huckfeldt found that only 24 percent of the county organizations had paid staff and fewer than 4 percent had paid chairs. This is higher than in 1980, when a national survey put these figures at 10 percent and 2 percent, respectively, but it still shows how reliant the local parties are on volunteers. See Cornelius P. Cotter, James L. Gibson, John F. Bibby, and Robert J. Huckshorn, *Party Organizations in American Politics* (New York: Praeger, 1984), pp. 42–43, for a report on the 1980 study.

2. See Peter B. Clark and James Q. Wilson, "Incentive Systems: A Theory of Organizations," *Administrative Science Quarterly* 6 (1961): 129–166, for the original development of this theory; and James Q. Wilson, *The Amateur Democrat* (Chicago: University of Chicago Press, 1960) and *Political Organizations* (New York: Basic Books, 1973), Chap. 6, for the application of this typology to political organizations.

3. For a lively account of the use of patronage and preferments, see Martin and Susan Tolchin, *To the Victor* (New York: Random House, 1971).

4. Insightful treatments of the development of patronage practices in the United States and attempts to reform them can be found in A. James Reichley, *The Life of the Parties* (New York: Free Press, 1992), pp. 55–56, 67–68, 88–92, and 202–220; Martin Shefter, *Political Parties and the State* (Princeton, NJ: Princeton University Press, 1994); and Anne Freedman, *Patronage: An American Tradition* (Chicago: Nelson-Hall, 1994). Shefter contends that the conditions for patronage were especially ripe in nineteenth-century United States. Lacking the tradition of a strong professional bureaucracy, patronage was used freely by parties in power, especially in American cities, to recruit new voters into their ranks. By contrast, patronage practices never became embedded in those European nations where professional bureaucracies were already established or where, as in the case of the European socialists, the lack of access to government forced parties to appeal to constituents along ideological rather than material lines.

5. These figures are cited in Stephen Skowronek's study of the reform of the federal bureaucracy. See his *Building a New American State* (New York: Cambridge University Press, 1982), p. 69.

6. All are listed in a publication unofficially known as the "Plum Book" (its official title is *U.S. Government Policy and Supporting Positions*), compiled alternately by the House Committee on Government Reform and Oversight and the Senate Committee on Governmental Affairs.

7. The 1976 case is *Elrod v. Burns,* 427 U.S. 347; the 1980 case is *Branti v. Finkel,* 445 U.S. 507; and the 1990 case is *Rutan v. Republican Party of Illinois,* 111 L. Ed. 2d 52.

8. On the problems of using patronage, see Frank J. Sorauf, "State Patronage in a Rural County," *American Political Science Review* 50 (1956): 1046–1056; W. Robert Gump, "The Functions of Patronage in American Party Politics: An Empirical Reappraisal," *Midwest Journal of Political Science* 15 (1971): 87–107; and Michael Johnston, "Patrons and Clients, Jobs and Machines: A Case Study of the Uses of Patronage," *American Political Science Review* 73 (1979): 385–398.

9. For a full account of the Shakman decrees and their effect, see Freedman, *Patronage: An American Tradition,* Chap. 2. The term *patronage army* is hers.

10. The case for patronage, grounded essentially on its utility for democratic control of the bureaucracy, has been articulated over the years in *The Washington Monthly* and in the dissenting opinions to the Supreme Court's *Elrod, Branti,* and *Rutan* decisions. The case against patronage is well put in Freedman, *Patronage: An American Tradition,* Chap. 5.

11. For the 1979–1980 results, see Cotter, et al., *Party Organizations in American Politics,* p. 42; the figures on state chairs are for 1962–1972 and come from Robert J. Huckshorn, *Party Leadership in the States* (Amherst: University of Massachusetts Press, 1976), p. 37.

12. This point is made by A. James Reichley in *The Life of the Parties,* p. 313.

13. A 1980 collaborative study of local parties in five cities, based on interviews with precinct and ward committee members, found that social incentives figured prominently among the motivations for activity. See the chapters by Richard W. Murray and Kent L. Tedin on Houston (p. 51), Anne H. Hopkins on Nashville (p. 74), Samuel J. Eldersveld on Detroit and Los Angeles (pp. 104–105), and William Crotty on Chicago (p. 174) in William Crotty, ed., *Political Parties in Local Areas* (Knoxville: University of Tennessee Press, 1986). For a general treatment of solidary incentives, especially in political club life, see Wilson, *The Amateur Democrat.* The importance of solidary incentives is illustrated well in George V. Higgins' novel, *Victories* (New York: Holt, 1991).

14. John Fischer, "Please Don't Bite the Politicians," *Harper's* (November 1960), p. 16. The classic treatment of the psychological roots of political behavior is Harold Lasswell's *Psychopathology and Politics* (Chicago: University of Chicago, 1931).

15. A 1988 study of county leaders of the Bush campaign organization found that 32 percent of them had switched to the GOP from the Democratic Party, typically to align their ideological convictions with their party; see John A. Clark, John M. Bruce, John H. Kessel, and William Jacoby, "I'd Rather Switch than Fight: Lifelong Democrats and Converts to Republicanism among Campaign Activists," *American Journal of Political Science* 35 (1991): 577–597. Studies of conversions among Democratic and Republican state party convention delegates in 1980 and 1984 corroborate the strong ideological bases of party-switching. See Mary Grisez Kweit, "Ideological Congruence of Party Switchers and Non-switchers: The Case of Party Activists," *American Journal of Political Science* 30 (1986): 184–196; and Dorothy Davidson Nesbit, "Changing Partisanship among Southern Party Activists," *Journal of Politics* 50 (1988): 322–334.

16. Samuel Eldersveld, *Political Parties: A Behavioral Analysis* (Chicago: Rand McNally, 1964), p. 278 and Chap. 11.

17. See Dwaine Marvick, "Party Organizational Personnel and Electoral Democracy in Los Angeles, 1963–1972," in William Crotty, ed., *The Party Symbol: Readings on Political Parties* (San Francisco: Freeman, 1980), pp. 63–86; Barbara C. Burrell, "Local Political Party Committees, Task Performance and Organizational Vitality," *Western Political Quarterly* 39 (1986): 48–66; and the various city studies contained in Crotty, *Political Parties in Local Areas.*

18. The fact that Eldersveld finds little change between 1956 and 1980 in the incentives for party activity (except the expected declines in party loyalty) in Detroit and Los Angeles, though, should rein in sweeping generalizations about motivational change. It is possible that what may distinguish modern from traditional party workers is the direction of their ideology, not its intensity. See Samuel J. Eldersveld, "The Party Activist in Detroit and Los Angeles: A Longitudinal View, 1956–1980," in Crotty, *Political Parties in Local Areas,* Chap. 4.

19. Among others, see M. Margaret Conway and Frank B. Feigert, "Motivation, Incentive Systems, and the Political Party Organization," *American Political Science Review* 62 (1968): 1159–1173.

20. Lewis Bowman and G. R. Boynton, "Recruitment Patterns among Local Party Officials," *American Political Science Review* 60 (1966): 667–676; Samuel J. Eldersveld, *Political Parties in American Society* (New York: Basic Books, 1982), p. 175; Henry E. Brady, Kay Lehman Schlozman, and Sidney Verba, "Prospecting for Participants: Rational Expectations and the Recruitment of Political Activists," *American Political Science Review* 93 (1999): 153–168.

21. Paul Allen Beck and M. Kent Jennings found that strong conservatives were the most active participants in the 1956, 1960, and 1964 campaigns but that strong liberals matched their activism in 1968 and then surpassed it from 1972 through 1980. See their "Political Periods and Political Participation," *American Political Science Review* 73 (1979): 737–750, and "Updating Political Periods and Political Participation," *American Political Science Review* 78 (1984): 198–201. Steven E. Finkel and Gregory Trevor, "Reassessing Ideological Bias in Campaign Participation," *Political Behavior* 8 (1986): 374–390, attribute the hyperactivity of strong liberals in 1984 to the competitiveness of the Democratic primaries that year.

22. For similar theories of recruitment, see Bowman and Boynton, "Recruitment Patterns"; and C. Richard Hofstetter, "Organizational Activists: The Bases of Participation in Amateur and Professional Groups," *American Politics Quarterly* 1 (1973): 244–276.

23. Eldersveld, *Political Parties,* pp. 142–143.

24. Cotter et al., *Party Organizations in American Politics,* p. 42.

25. On the prominence of lawyers in American politics, see Heinz Eulau and John D. Sprague, *Lawyers in Politics* (Indianapolis: Bobbs-Merrill, 1964).

26. The relatively high status of party activists is documented in Sidney Verba and Norman H. Nie, *Participation in America* (New York: Harper Row, 1972), Chap. 8, for campaign activists; in Crotty, *Political Parties in Local Areas,* pp. 45, 72, 94–95, and 162–163, and Cotter, et al., *Party Organizations in American Politics,* p. 42, for local leaders; in Ronald Rapoport, Alan I. Abramowitz, and John McGlennon, *The Life of the Parties* (Lexington: The University of Kentucky Press, 1986), Chap. 3, for state convention delegates; and in Warren E. Miller and M. Kent Jennings, *Parties in Transition* (New York: Russell Sage Foundation, 1986), pp. 67–85, for national convention delegates.

27. Michael Margolis and Raymond E. Owen, "From Organization to Personalism: A Note on the Transmogrification of the Local Political Party," *Polity* 18 (1985): 313–328.

28. These assertions are supported by a variety of data. See Martin Plissner and Warren J. Mitofsky, "The Making of the Delegates, 1968–1988," *Public Opinion* 11 (September/October 1988): 45–47, on characteristics of delegates to the national nominating conventions through 1988; data from *The Washington Post* survey of convention delegates in 1996 (see Chapter 10) show that the Democrats remained highly atypical of the rank and file of their party and more like Republicans in both income and education. See Cotter, et al., *Party Organizations in American Politics,* p. 42.

29. This distinction between amateurs and professionals is developed in Clark and Wilson, "Incentive Systems"; Wilson, *The Amateur Democrat;* Aaron Wildavsky, "The Goldwater Phenomenon: Purists, Politicians, and the Two-Party System," *The Review of Politics* 27 (1965): 386–413; and John W. Soule and James W. Clarke, "Amateurs and Professionals: A Study of Delegates to the 1968 Democratic National Convention," *American Political Science Review* 64 (1970): 888–898.

30. Walter J. Stone and Alan I. Abramowitz, "Winning May Not Be Everything But It's More Than We Thought: Presidential Party Activists in 1980," *American Political Science Review* 77 (1983): 945–956.

31. Michael A. Maggiotto and Ronald E. Weber, "The Impact of Organizational Incentives on County Party Chairpersons," *American Politics Quarterly* 14 (1986): 201–218.

32. The 1992 national survey of county party organizations was conducted by Paul Allen Beck, Russell J. Dalton, Audrey Haynes, and Robert Huckfeldt. These data are from the study's codebook.

33. On traditional differences among organizational activists, see Robert H. Salisbury, "The Urban Party Organization Member," *Public Opinion Quarterly* 29 (1965–1966): 562, 564; Lewis Bowman and G. R. Boynton, "Activities and Role Definitions of Grass Roots Party Officials," *Journal of Politics* 28 (1966): 132–134; Eldersveld, *Political Parties,* p. 348; and Burrell, "Local Political Party Committees."

34. On the effects of party effort, see Gerald H. Kramer, "The Effects of Precinct-Level Canvassing on Voter Behavior," *Public Opinion Quarterly* 34 (1970–1971): 560–572; William J. Crotty, "Party Effort and Its Impact on the Vote," *American Political Science Review* 65 (1971): 439–450; David E. Price and Michael Lupfer, "Volunteers for Gore: The Impact of a Precinct-Level Canvass in Three Tennessee Cities," *Journal of Politics* 35 (1973): 410–438; and John P. Frendreis, James L. Gibson, and Laura L. Vertz, "The Electoral Relevance of Local Party Organizations," *American Political Science Review* 84 (1990): 225–235.

35. See Daniel Elazar, *American Federalism: A View from the States* (New York: Crowell, 1972), Chap. 4, for the distribution of individualistic, moralistic, and traditionalistic political cultures throughout the nation.

36. V. O. Key, Jr., *American State Politics* (New York: Knopf, 1956), Chap. 6.

37. The most notable fictionalized accounts of real-life "bosses" are to be found in Edwin O'Connor, The Last Hurrah (Boston: Little, Brown, 1956); and Robert Penn Warren, All the King's Men (New York: Harcourt, Brace, 1946). See also William L. Riordon, Plunkitt of Tammany Hall (New York: Dutton, 1963; first published in 1906).

38. Wilson, The Amateur Democrat, Chap. 5. These reform orientations are sometimes rooted as much in the deprivations of being out of power as in principled opposition to the concentration of power in a political machine. For some evidence of this in a Chicago reform club, see David L. Protess and Alan R. Gitelson, "Political Stability, Reform Clubs, and the Amateur Democrat," in William Crotty, ed., The Party Symbol (San Francisco: Freeman, 1980), pp. 87–100.

39. This theory is elaborated in Anthony Downs, An Economic Theory of Democracy (New York: Harper & Row, 1965).

40. Key, American State Politics; and Walter Dean Burnham, Critical Elections and the Mainsprings of American Politics (New York: Norton, 1970), p. 75.

41. Robert Michels, Political Parties (Glencoe, IL: Free Press, 1949; originally published in 1915), p. 32.

42. The quotations in this paragraph come from Eldersveld, *Political Parties,* pp. 99–100.

PART 3

1. The concept of party identification and the most familiar measure of it were introduced in Angus Campbell, Philip E. Converse, Warren E. Miller, and Donald E. Stokes, *The American Voter* (New York: Wiley, 1960), Chap. 6.

2. For an examination of some alternatives in identifying party adherents, see Everett C. Ladd and Charles D. Hadley, "Party Definition and Party Differentiation," *Public Opinion Quarterly* 37 (1973): 21–34; and Steven E. Finkel and Howard A. Scarrow, "Party Identification and Party Enrollment: The Difference and the Consequence," *Journal of Politics* 47 (1985): 620–642.

CHAPTER 6

1. The most common definition of a *realignment,* and the one adopted here, involves changes in the party coalitions or parties in the electorate. For elaborations of this conceptualization, see V. O. Key, Jr., "A Theory of Critical Elections," *Journal of Politics* 17 (1955): 3–18; Walter Dean Burnham, *Critical Elections and the Mainsprings of American Politics* (New York: Norton, 1970); and James L. Sundquist, *Dynamics of the Party System* (Washington, DC: Brookings Institution, 1973). For one alternative view of what constitutes a realignment, see Jerome M. Clubb, William H. Flanigan, and Nancy H. Zingale, *Partisan Realignment: Voters, Parties, and Government in American History* (Beverly Hills, CA: Sage, 1980). Another view is that realignment is elite rather than mass based—the product of the changing party loyalties of American industrial and business interests. See Thomas Ferguson, *Golden Rule: The Investment Theory of Party Competition and the Logic of Money-driven Political Systems* (Chicago: University of Chicago Press, 1995).

2. Aggregate elections returns have some drawbacks as measures of a realignment. They are affected by short-term forces (for example, candidate appeal, issues, and levels of turnout) as well as long-term party loyalties. They reflect geographical divisions more clearly than SES-based divisions. It is helpful, then, to examine aggregate election results together with other data in defining realignment periods.

3. Not all scholars are persuaded that the notion of periodic party realignments captures the essence of American electoral change, especially in recent years. These doubts are expressed in the essays by Joel Silbey, Everett Carll Ladd, Byron Shafer, and Samuel T. McSeveney in Byron E. Shafer, ed., *The End of Realignment? Interpreting American Electoral Eras* (Madison: University of Wisconsin Press, 1991). See also Allan J. Lichtman, "The End of Realignment Theory—Toward a New Research Program for American Political History," *Historical Methods* 15 (1982): 170–188; and, for a view that the important changes are subnational rather than national in scope, Peter F. Nardulli, "The Concept of a Critical Realignment, Electoral Behavior, and Political Change," *American Political Science Review* 89 (1995): 10–22.

4. For similar classifications of American political history from the realignment perspective, see Burnham, *Critical Elections;* William Nisbet Chambers and Walter Dean Burnham, eds., *The American Party Systems* (New York: Oxford University Press, 1967); Clubb, Flanigan, and Zingale, *Partisan Realignment;* Charles Sellers, "The Equilibrium Cycle in Two-Party Politics," *Public Opinion Quarterly* 30 (1965): 16–38; and Sundquist, *Dynamics of the Party System.*

5. Because the realignments that transform one party system into another take place during a period of time rather than occurring sharply, the exact beginning and end of a party system cannot be reduced to a single year. For convenience, though, the beginning of each party system must be located at a particular time—the year in which the new majority party coalition

first took office (having been elected at the end of the previous year) to begin the period of undisputed control of government which began each of the first five party systems.

6. In the two-party competition that has characterized the American party system since its inception, these coalitions are never simple or predictable on issue grounds. What gave the Democrats their dominance was the unification of their Western, populist supporters with the New York political organization run by Martin Van Buren, who was attracted to the party because of interstate rivalries and the promise of political patronage. Such odd alliances have been a hallmark of the American two-party system.

7. From the end of the Civil War in 1865 through 1876, Democratic voting strength in the South was held in check by the occupation Union army and various Reconstruction policies and laws. Thus in presenting party control figures that reflect the true party balance during the third party system, it is necessary to differentiate between 1861–1876 and the more representative 1877–1896 period.

8. Comprehensive treatments of the different party systems may be found in Paul Goodman, "The First Party System," in Chambers and Burnham, *The American Party Systems*, pp. 59–89; Richard McCormick, *The Second American Party System: Party Formation in the Jacksonian Era* (Chapel Hill: University of North Carolina Press, 1966); and, for the party systems since the 1850s, Sundquist, *Dynamics of the Party System.* Especially valuable (because they are used to explain why parties emerge and change) accounts of the development of the first three party systems may be found in John H. Aldrich, *Why Parties? The Origin and Transformation of Party Politics in America* (Chicago: University of Chicago Press, 1995), Chaps. 3–5.

9. See Paul Allen Beck, "The Electoral Cycle and Patterns of American Politics," *British Journal of Political Science* 9 (1979): 129–156. This view of recent nonpartisanship as largely a result of neutrality toward the parties rather than rejection of them is developed in Martin P. Wattenberg, *The Decline of American Political Parties, 1952–92* (Cambridge: Harvard University Press, 1994). For evidence that Americans have also become more negative toward the parties, see Stephen C. Craig, "The Decline of Partisanship in the United States: A Reexamination of the Neutrality Hypothesis," *Political Behavior* 7 (1985): 57–78.

10. Burnham, *Critical Elections,* Chaps. 4 and 5.

11. The seminal work on party identification is based on survey data from the 1952 and 1956 elections. See Angus Campbell, Philip E. Converse, Warren E. Miller, and Donald E. Stokes, *The American Voter* (New York: Wiley, 1960). Since this first large-scale presidential-year survey in 1952, scholars at the University of Michigan have continued to conduct surveys of the American electorate in presidential and midterm election years, most recently under National Science Foundation auspices as the American National Election Studies (ANES).

12. This description of the changes in partisanship since 1952 is justified regardless of whether partisans are defined as strong identifiers, strong plus weak identifiers, or all respondents who indicate some kind of preference for one of the parties.

13. Paul Allen Beck and M. Kent Jennings, "Family Traditions, Political Periods, and the Development of Partisan Orientations," *Journal of Politics* 53 (1991): 742–763.

14. Fred I. Greenstein, *Children and Politics* (New Haven: Yale University Press, 1965). See also Robert D. Hess and Judith V. Torney, *The Development of Political Attitudes in Children* (Chicago: Aldine, 1967), especially pp. 80–81.

15. For recent evidence on the partisan homogeneity of social networks, see Robert Huckfeldt and John Sprague, *Citizens, Politics, and Social Communication* (New York: Cambridge University Press, 1995), especially Chap. 7; and Robert Huckfeldt and Paul Allen Beck,

"Contexts, Intermediaries, and Political Behavior," in Lawrence C. Dodd and Calvin Jill-son, eds., *The Dynamics of American Politics: Approaches and Limitations* (Boulder, CO: Westview Press, 1994), pp. 252–276.

16. Arthur S. Goldberg, "Social Determinism and Rationality As Bases of Party Identification," *American Political Science Review* 63 (1969): 5–25.

17. Morris P. Fiorina, *Retrospective Voting in American National Elections* (New Haven: Yale University Press, 1981), p. 102. For an application of retrospective voting theory to recent elections, see Paul R. Abramson, John H. Aldrich, and David W. Rohde, *Change and Continuity in the 1992 Elections* (Washington, DC: Congressional Quarterly Press, 1995), especially Chap. 7. For an analysis of the role contemporary issues may play in disrupting the transmission of partisanship from parents to children, see Robert C. Luskin, John P. McIver, and Edward G. Carmines, "Issues and the Transmission of Partisanship," *American Journal of Political Science* 33 (1989): 440–458; and Richard G. Niemi and M. Kent Jennings, "Issues and Inheritance in the Formation of Party Identification," *American Journal of Political Science* 35 (1991): 970–988.

18. See William Claggett, "Partisan Acquisition vs. Partisan Intensity: Life-Cycle, Generational, and Period Effects," *American Journal of Political Science* 25 (1981): 193–214. On how much partisanship strengthens as the voter ages, see Philip E. Converse, *The Dynamics of Party Support* (Beverly Hills, CA: Sage, 1976); Paul R. Abramson, "Developing Party Identification: A Further Examination of Life-Cycle, Generational, and Period Effects," *American Journal of Political Science* 23 (1979): 78–96; and W. Phillips Shively, "The Development of Party Identification among Adults," *American Political Science Review* 73 (1979): 1039–1054.

19. For the view that realignments are attributable to mobilization of the young and other new voters, see Kristi Andersen, *The Creation of a Democratic Majority 1928–1936* (Chicago: University of Chicago Press, 1979); Paul Allen Beck, "A Socialization Theory of Partisan Realignment," in Richard G. Niemi, ed., *The Politics of Future Citizens* (San Francisco: Jossey-Bass, 1974), pp. 199–219; and James E. Campbell, "Sources of the New Deal Realignment: The Contributions of Conversion and Mobilization to Partisan Change," *Western Political Quarterly* 38 (1985): 357–376. For an alternative view, emphasizing partisan conversions among older voters, see Robert S. Erikson and Kent L. Tedin, "The 1928–1936 Partisan Realignment: The Case for the Conversion Hypothesis," *American Political Science Review* 75 (1981): 951–963. The role of the young in contemporary partisan change is discussed in Helmut Norpoth and Jerrold G. Rusk, "Partisan Dealignment in the American Electorate: Itemizing the Deductions Since 1964," *American Political Science Review* 76 (1982): 522–537; and Warren E. Miller, "Generational Changes and Party Identification," *Political Behavior* 14 (1992): 333–352.

20. For a comprehensive treatment of these various cleavages, see Seymour Martin Lipset and Stein Rokkan, "Cleavage Structures, Party Systems, and Voting Alignments," in Seymour Martin Lipset and Stein Rokkan, eds., *Party Systems and Voter Alignments* (New York: Free Press, 1967), pp. 1–67.

21. The classic statement of the role of social class in the elections of the Western democracies appears in Seymour Martin Lipset, *Political Man* (New York: Doubleday, 1960), especially Chap. 7. Also see Richard Hamilton, *Class and Politics in the United States* (New York: Wiley, 1972).

22. See Madison's *Federalist* 10: "The most common and durable source of factions has been the various and unequal distribution of property."

23. See Robert A. Alford, *Party and Society* (Chicago: Rand McNally, 1963); and Russell J. Dalton, Scott C. Flanagan, and Paul Allen Beck, eds., *Electoral Change in Advanced Industrial Democracies* (Princeton, NJ: Princeton University Press, 1984). For an appraisal of class voting in the Western world during the past century from the perspective of work-

ing-class support for a left-wing party, see Adam Przeworski and John Sprague, *Paper Stones: A History of Electoral Socialism* (Chicago: University of Chicago Press, 1986).

24. So powerful have these Southern ties to the Democratic Party been that some voters, termed *split-level partisans,* have retained their Democratic loyalties in state and local politics even after rejecting them for the purpose of national politics. For more on this phenomenon, see Charles D. Hadley, "Dual Partisan Identification in the South," *Journal of Politics* 47 (1985): 254–268; and Richard G. Niemi, Stephen Wright, and Lynda W. Powell, "Multiple Party Identifiers and the Measurement of Party Identification," *Journal of Politics* 49 (1987): 1093–1104.

25. Richard Rose and Derek Urwin have shown that religion rivals social class as a basis for partisan loyalties in the Western democracies. See their "Social Cohesion, Political Parties and Strains in Regimes," *Comparative Political Studies* 2 (1967): 7–67.

26. Lawrence Fuchs, *The Political Behavior of the American Jews* (Glencoe, IL: Free Press, 1956). For a somewhat more recent treatment, see Milton Himmelfarb, "The Case of Jewish Liberalism," in Seymour Martin Lipset, ed., *Emerging Coalitions in American Politics* (San Francisco: Institute for Contemporary Studies, 1978), pp. 297–305.

27. See Ted G. Jelen, *The Political Mobilization of Religious Belief* (Westport, CT: Praeger, 1991); David C. Leege and Lyman A. Kellstedt, eds., *Rediscovering the Religious Factor in American Politics* (Armonk, NY: M. E. Sharpe, 1993); and Kenneth D. Wald, *Religion and Politics in the United States* (New York: St. Martin's Press, 1987).

28. On black political behavior, see Patricia Gurin, Shirley Hatchett, and James S. Jackson, *Hope and Independence: Blacks' Response to Electoral and Party Politics* (New York: Russell Sage Foundation, 1989); and Katherine Tate, *From Protest to Politics* (Cambridge, MA: Harvard University Press, 1994).

29. Karen M. Kaufman and John R. Petrocik, "The Changing Politics of American Men: Understanding the Sources of the Gender Gap," *American Journal of Political Science* 43 (1999): 864–887. See also Paul R. Abramson, John H. Aldrich, and David W. Rohde, *Change and Continuity in the 1992 Elections* (Washington, DC: Congressional Quarterly Press, 1995), pp. 136–137. On the gender gap in 1992, see Elizabeth Adell Cook and Clyde Wilcox, "Women Voters in the 'Year of the Woman,'" in Herbert F. Weisberg, ed., *Democracy's Feast* (Chatham, NJ: Chatham House, 1995), 195–219.

30. Data from 1960 are more appropriate for this comparison than data from 1964, when the Democratic landslide victory produced a temporary surge in Democratic partisanship across most of the social groups. The 1960 figures are taken from Warren E. Miller and Santa A. Traugott, *American National Election Studies Sourcebook, 1952–1986* (Cambridge, MA: Harvard University Press, 1989).

31. On social group changes in the party coalitions, see John R. Petrocik, *Party Coalitions* (Chicago: University of Chicago Press, 1981); Robert Axelrod, "Presidential Election Coalitions in 1984," *American Political Science Review* 80 (1986): 281–290; and Harold W. Stanley and Richard G. Niemi, "The Demise of the New Deal Coalition: Partisanship and Group Support, 1952–1992," in Weisberg, *Democracy's Feast,* pp. 220–240. Stanley and Niemi, in particular, feel that the New Deal coalition has eroded so much that it is no longer visible.

32. For demonstrations of how attitudinal and behavioral deviance from one's partisanship can undermine it, see Fiorina, *Retrospective Voting in American National Elections;* and Benjamin I. Page and Calvin C. Jones, "Reciprocal Effects of Policy Preferences, Party Loyalties and the Vote," *American Political Science Review* 73 (1979): 1071–1089.

33. On this point, see David O. Sears, Richard R. Lau, Tom R. Tyler, and Harris M. Allen, Jr., "Self-Interest vs. Symbolic Politics in Policy Attitudes and Presidential Voting," *American Political Science Review* 74 (1980): 670–684. For an alternative view, see Paul Sniderman and Thomas Piazza, *The Scar of Race* (Cambridge, MA: Harvard University Press, 1993).

34. For a discussion of the crosscutting nature of some of these issues, see Warren E. Miller and Teresa E. Levitin, *Leadership and Change: The New Politics and the American Electorate* (Cambridge, MA: Winthrop, 1976).

35. For more on the case for dealignment, see Paul Allen Beck, "Incomplete Realignment: The Reagan Legacy for Parties and Elections," in Charles O. Jones, ed., *The Reagan Legacy* (Chatham, NJ: Chatham House, 1988); Walter Dean Burnham, *The Current Crisis in American Politics* (New York: Oxford University Press, 1982); and Wattenberg, *The Decline of American Political Parties.*

36. The Watergate affair began in 1972 with the arrest of burglars with ties to the Nixon reelection campaign for breaking into the offices of the Democratic National Committee and culminated with the resignation of President Nixon in the face of sure impeachment by the House of Representatives for trying to cover up his role. The unpopularity of the subsequent pardon of Nixon by his former vice president and successor Gerald Ford played a key role in the 1976 presidential campaign and may have cost Ford the presidency.

37. For more on the case for realignment, see John Aldrich, *Why Parties: The Origin and Transformation of Party Politics in America* (Chicago: University of Chicago Press, 1995), Chap. 8; Earl Black and Merle Black, *Politics and Society in the South* (Cambridge, MA: Harvard University Press, 1987); and Edward G. Carmines and James A. Stimson, *Issue Evolution* (Princeton, NJ: Princeton University Press, 1989).

38. On the party loyalties of the young, see Helmut Norpoth, "Under Way and Here to Stay: Party Realignment in the 1980s?" *Public Opinion Quarterly* 51 (1987): 376–391; and Warren E. Miller, "Party Identification, Realignment, and Party Voting: Back to Basics," *American Political Science Review* 85 (1991): 557–570.

CHAPTER 7

1. See John R. Petrocik, "An Analysis of the Intransitivities in the Index of Party Identification," Political Methodology 1 (1974): 31–47; Ralph W. Bastedo and Milton Lodge, "The Meaning of Party Labels," Political Behavior 2 (1980): 287–308; and Herbert F. Weisberg, "A Multidimensional Conceptualization of Party Identification," Political Behavior 2 (1980): 33–60.

2. See Paul Allen Beck, "The Dealignment Era in America," in Russell J. Dalton, Scott C. Flanagan, and Paul Allen Beck, eds., Electoral Change in Advanced Industrial Democracies (Princeton, NJ: Princeton University Press, 1984), pp. 244–246.

3. Philip E. Converse and Gregory B. Markus, "Plus ça change...: The New CPS Election Study Panel," American Political Science Review 73 (1979): 32–49. Even greater stability in partisanship, as expected because of the shorter time period, was found from January to November during the 1980 presidential campaign. See Donald Philip Green and Bradley Palmquist, "Of Artifacts and Partisan Instability," American Journal of Political Science 34 (1990): 872–902, and "How Stable is Party Identification?" Political Behavior 16 (1994): 437–66.

4. On the political impact of the psychological processes of projection and persuasion, see Bernard R. Berelson, Paul F. Lazarsfeld, and William N. McPhee, Voting (Chicago: University of Chicago Press, 1954), pp. 215–233; and Benjamin I. Page and Richard A. Brody, "Policy Voting and the Electoral Process: The Vietnam War Issue," American Political Science Review 66 (1972): 979–995.

5. Donald E. Stokes, "Some Dynamic Elements of Contests for the Presidency," American Political Science Review 60 (1966): 23.

6. On the importance of party as a shortcut in candidate evaluations, see Pamela J. Conover and Stanley Feldman, "Candidate Perceptions in an Ambiguous World: Campaigns, Cues, and Inference Processes," *American Journal of Political Science* 33 (1989): 912–940; and

Wendy M. Rahn, "The Role of Partisan Stereotypes in Information Processing about Political Candidates," *American Journal of Political Science* 37 (1993): 472–496.

7. Roberta A. Sigel, "Effects of Partisanship on the Perception of Political Candidates," *Public Opinion Quarterly* 28 (1964): 483–496.

8. See Morris Fiorina, *Retrospective Voting in American National Elections* (New Haven, CT: Yale University Press, 1981); Benjamin I. Page and Calvin C. Jones, "Reciprocal Effects of Policy Preferences, Party Loyalties and the Vote," *American Political Science Review* 73 (1979): 1071–1089; and Michael B. MacKuen, Robert S. Erikson, and James A. Stimson, "Macropartisanship," *American Political Science Review* 83 (1989): 1125–1142.

9. See Arthur H. Miller, "Partisan Cognitions in Transition," in Richard R. Lau and David O. Sears, eds., *Political Cognition* (Hillsdale, NJ: Erlbaum, 1986), Chap. 9, in contrast with Larry M. Bartels, "Partisanship and Voting Behavior, 1952–1996," *American Journal of Political Science* 44 (2000): 35–50.

10. An examination of patterns across the ballot in voting for five state executive offices in Ohio found party identification to be the principal predictor of straight-ticket voting. See Paul Allen Beck, Lawrence Baum, Aage R. Clausen, and Charles E. Smith, Jr., "Patterns and Sources of Ticket Splitting in Subpresidential Voting," *American Political Science Review* 86 (1992): 916–928.

11. The unexpectedly greater partisan voting of the independent identifiers compared to the weak partisans, and similar "intransitivities" in the relationship between partisanship and political involvement shown later, are commonly cited as evidence of the weakness of the party-identification measure. This anomaly may appear because independents asked to indicate which party is closer will name the one for which they intend to vote that year. A truer indication of their partisan strength, instead, is found in their straight-ticket voting patterns. For a persuasive case that the independent leaners are really partisans, see Bruce E. Keith, David B. Magleby, Candice J. Nelson, Elizabeth Orr, Mark Westlye, and Raymond E. Wolfinger, *The Myth of the Independent Voter* (Berkeley, CA: University of California Press, 1992).

12. Beck, Baum, Clausen, and Smith, "Patterns and Sources of Ticket Splitting in Subpresidential Voting."

13. Philip E. Converse, "The Concept of a Normal Vote," in Angus Campbell, Philip E. Converse, Warren E. Miller, and Donald E. Stokes, eds., *Elections and the Political Order* (New York: Wiley, 1966), pp. 9–39.

14. *Split-ticket voting,* defined as supporting candidates from different parties on the same ballot, has also been higher since the mid–1960s than it was in the 1950s for both president-House and Senate-House combinations. See Martin P. Wattenberg, *The Decline of American Political Parties: 1952–1992* (Cambridge, MA: Harvard University Press, 1994), Chaps. 9 and 10.

15. See Norman H. Nie, Sidney Verba, and John R. Petrocik, *The Changing American Voter* (Cambridge, MA: Harvard University Press, 1976), Chaps. 10, 16, and 20 (especially pp. 373–378); Frederick Hartwig, William R. Jenkins, and Earl M. Temchin, "Variability in Electoral Behavior: The 1960, 1968, and 1976 Elections," *American Journal of Political Science* 24 (1980): 353–358; and Bartels, "Partisanship and Voting Behavior."

16. For the classic view, see Angus Campbell, Philip E. Converse, Warren E. Miller, and Donald E. Stokes, *The American Voter* (New York: Wiley, 1960); and Arthur S. Goldberg, "Discerning a Causal Pattern among Data on Voting Behavior," *American Political Science Review* 60 (1966): 913–922.

17. Page and Jones, "Reciprocal Effects of Policy Preferences, Party Loyalties and the Vote."

18. Gregory B. Markus and Philip E. Converse, "A Dynamic Simultaneous Equation Model of Electoral Choice," *American Political Science Review* 73 (1979): 1055–1070.

19. Overall turnout in 1996 among citizens of voting age was estimated at 51 percent. Reported turnout levels in the 1996 ANES survey are considerably higher for reasons specified in Chapter 8.

20. These differences are documented in Paul R. Abramson, John H. Aldrich, and David W. Rohde, *Change and Continuity in the 1996 Elections* (Washington, DC: CQ Press, 1998), Chap. 8, especially Table 8.5 and Figure 8.1.

21. On similar Republican hyperactivity in the 1960s, see Verba and Nie, *Participation in America,* (New York: Harper & Row, 1972), Chap. 12. The varying relationships between ideology and campaign activity over a longer period are examined in Paul Allen Beck and M. Kent Jennings, "Political Periods and Political Participation," *American Political Science Review* 73 (1979): 737–750.

22. Although it is easy to picture independents as providing a ready constituency for a new party or independent candidacy, the truth is that their heterogeneity on issues and in other sources of political orientation makes them an unlikely electoral coalition. On their heterogeneity, see Keith, Magleby, Nelson, Orr, Westlye, and Wolfinger, *The Myth of the Independent Voter.*

23. For comparisons of the support for Wallace, Anderson, and Perot among white party identifiers, see Paul R. Abramson, John H. Aldrich, and David W. Rohde, *Change and Continuity in the 1992 Elections,* (Washington, DC: CQ Press, 1995) Table 8.9, p. 245. For more on the Perot candidacy, see Herb Asher, "The Perot Campaign," in Herbert F. Weisberg, ed., *Democracy's Feast* (Chatham, NJ: Chatham House, 1995), Chap. 6.

24. See Petrocik, "An Analysis of Intransitivities in the Index of Party Identification," pp. 31–47; and Keith, Magleby, Nelson, Orr, Westlye, and Wolfinger, *The Myth of the Independent Voter.*

25. See Keith, Magleby, Nelson, Orr, Westlye, and Wolfinger, *The Myth of the Independent Voter.* The myth of the independent as the highly informed, sophisticated voter (in contrast to the slavish partisan) is effectively laid to rest for the 1952 and 1956 elections by Campbell, Converse, Miller, and Stokes, in *The American Voter.*

26. V. O. Key, Jr. (with the assistance of Milton C. Cummings), *The Responsible Electorate* (Cambridge, MA: Harvard University Press, 1966).

27. V. O. Key and Frank Munger characterized the century-long stable voting patterns of Indiana counties as "standing decisions" to support a particular party. See their "Social Determinism and Electoral Decision," in Eugene Burdick and Arthur J. Brodbeck, eds., *American Voting Behavior* (Glencoe, IL: Free Press, 1959), pp. 281–299.

28. See Martin P. Wattenberg, *The Rise of Candidate-Centered Politics: Presidential Elections of the 1980s* (Cambridge, MA: Harvard University Press, 1991); and Morris P. Fiorina, "The Electorate at the Polls in the 1990s," in L. Sandy Maisel, ed., *The Parties Respond* (Boulder, CO: Westview, 1994), pp. 123–142.

CHAPTER 8

1. Because of the difficulties in estimating American turnout, most "official" turnout figures *underestimate* it. The figures cited here follow the method of Walter Dean Burnham, which carefully corrects for this underestimation; consequently they will be higher than the widely reported turnout figures. Their denominator is based on the adult population of voting age minus the number of aliens restricted from voting by state law, which since 1924 has included all aliens. The numerator of the turnout fraction is the number of voters who cast a vote for president or for the office with the highest vote in midterm elections. Estimated turnout would be slightly higher if there was a reliable way to include in the numerator blank or spoiled ballots, write-in votes for the office with the highest vote total, and

voters who did not vote for that office, and to exclude from the denominator citizens who are ineligible under the laws of the various states because they are institutionalized in prisons or mental hospitals. For a discussion of the pitfalls in estimating turnout, see Walter Dean Burnham, "The Turnout Problem," in A. James Reichley, ed., *Elections American Style* (Washington, DC: Brookings Institution, 1987), pp. 97–133, especially footnote 1.

2. On the normative problems nonvoting may pose for democracy, see Benjamin Barber, *Strong Democracy: Participatory Politics for a New Age* (Berkeley: University of California Press, 1994). For an empirical examination of some of these normative issues which discounts the threat to democracy posed by nonvoters, see Stephen Earl Bennett and David Resnick, "The Implications of Nonvoting for Democracy in the United States," *American Journal of Political Science* 34 (1990): 771–802.

3. The classic examination of turnout over the course of American history is Walter Dean Burnham, "The Changing Shape of the American Political Universe," *American Political Science Review* 59 (1965): 7–28.

4. Data on turnout in other democracies are presented and analyzed in G. Bingham Powell, Jr., "American Voter Turnout in Comparative Perspective," *American Political Science Review* 80 (1986): 17–44. Also see Burnham, "The Turnout Problem," p. 107. Only Switzerland has had lower national turnout levels than the United States, but national elections are less important than local contests there.

5. On the early development of the American electorate, see Chilton Williamson, *American Suffrage: From Property to Democracy* (Princeton, NJ: Princeton University Press, 1960).

6. The Supreme Court case overturning the poll tax was *Harper v. Virginia State Board of Elections,* 383 U.S. 633 (1966).

7. *Oregon v. Mitchell,* 400 U.S. 112 (1970).

8. The legal and constitutional issues involved in defining the electorate through the 1960s are covered in Richard Claude, *The Supreme Court and the Electoral Process* (Baltimore, MD: The John Hopkins University Press, 1970).

9. Stephen Knack, "Does 'Motor Voter' Work? Evidence from State-Level Data," *Journal of Politics* 57 (1995): 796–811.

10. Paul Kleppner, *Continuity and Change in Electoral Politics, 1893–1928* (Westport, CT: Greenwood Press, 1987), pp. 165–166.

11. The landmark Supreme Court cases dealing with residency requirements are *Dunn v. Blumstein,* 405 U.S. 330 (1972); and *Burns v. Fortson,* 410 U.S. 686 (1973).

12. U.S. Bureau of the Census, Table A.1, Annual Geographical Mobility Rates, By Type of Movement: 1947–1998, found at http://www.census.gov/population/socdemo/migration/tab-a-1.txt.

13. Peverill Squire, Raymond E. Wolfinger, and David P. Glass, "Residential Mobility and Voter Turnout," *American Political Science Review* 81 (1987): 45–65.

14. See Philip E. Converse, "Change in the American Electorate," in Angus Campbell and Philip E. Converse, eds., *The Human Meaning of Social Change* (New York: Russell Sage Foundation, 1972), pp. 263–337; Walter Dean Burnham, "Theory and Voting Research: Some Reflections on Converse's 'Change in the American Electorate,'" *American Political Science Review* 68 (1974): 1002–1023; and Frances Fox Piven and Richard A. Cloward, *Why Americans Don't Vote* (New York: Pantheon Books, 1988).

15. A state-by-state list of registration requirements is reported each year in *The Book of the States* (Lexington, KY: The Council of State Governments).

16. The most recent estimates—that turnout would be 7.8 percent without the most burdensome requirements—are provided by Ruy A. Teixiera, *The Disappearing American Voter* (Washington, DC: Brookings Institution, 1992), Chap. 4. For similar estimates from earlier years,

see Raymond E. Wolfinger and Steven J. Rosenstone, *Who Votes?* (New Haven, CT: Yale University Press, 1982), pp. 61–78; and Glenn E. Mitchell and Christopher Wlezien, "The Impact of Legal Constraints on Voter Registration, Turnout, and the Composition of the American Electorate," *Political Behavior* 17 (1995): 179–202.

17. The story of black disenfranchisement in the South is well told by V. O. Key, Jr., in *Southern Politics in State and Nation* (New York: Knopf, 1949). See also J. Morgan Kousser, *The Shaping of Southern Politics* (New Haven: Yale University Press, 1974); and Donald R. Matthews and James W. Prothro, *Negroes and the New Southern Politics* (New York: Harcourt, Brace and World, 1966).

18. The white primary was finally overturned by the Supreme Court in *Smith v. Allwright,* 321 U.S. 649 (1944). Not only is this a landmark case in the area of black voting rights, but it is also significant in establishing that political parties, in spite of their right to handle their own affairs under the freedom of association guaranteed in the Bill of Rights, are not free to violate constitutional prohibitions on discrimination.

19. Pat Watters and Reese Cleghorn, *Climbing Jacob's Ladder* (New York: Harcourt Brace Jovanovich, 1967), pp. 122–123.

20. For a review of the impact of the Voting Rights Act of 1965 and its extensions, see Chandler Davidson and Bernard Grofman, eds., *Quiet Revolution in the South* (Princeton, NJ: Princeton University Press, 1994). On black turnout in the South generally, see Harold W. Stanley, *Voter Mobilization and the Politics of Race* (New York: Praeger, 1987).

21. See Matthews and Prothro, *Negroes and the New Southern Politics;* H. Douglas Price, *The Negro and Southern Politics* (New York: New York University Press, 1957); David Campbell and Joe R. Feagin, "Black Politics in the South: A Descriptive Analysis," *Journal of Politics* 37 (1975): 129–162; and Lester M. Salamon and Stephen Van Evera, "Fear, Apathy, and Participation," *American Political Science Review* 67 (1973): 1288–1306.

22. The case is *Miller v. Johnson,* decided on June 29, 1995. On the impact of majority-minority districts, see Charles Cameron, David Epstein, and Sharyn O'Halloran, "Do Majority-Minority Districts Maximize Substantive Black Representation in Congress?" *American Political Science Review* 90 (1996): 794–812; and David Lublin, "Racial Redistricting and African-American Representation," *American Political Science Review* 93 (1999): 183–186.

23. The falloff in voting for issues is especially pronounced among lower-socioeconomic-status voters. For an extensive review of voting on ballot propositions, see David B. Magleby, *Direct Legislation: Voting on Ballot Propositions in the United States* (Baltimore, MD: The Johns Hopkins University Press, 1984); and Thomas E. Cronin, *Direct Democracy* (Cambridge, MA: Harvard University Press, 1989).

24. For systematic explanation of variations in turnout across the election calendar and for different combinations of contests, see Richard W. Boyd, "Election Calendars and Voter Turnout," *American Politics Quarterly* 14 (1986): 89–104, and "The Effects of Primaries and Statewide Races on Voter Turnout," *Journal of Politics* 51 (1989): 730–739.

25. Jae-On Kim, John R. Petrocik, and Stephen N. Enokson, "Voter Turnout among the American States: Systemic and Individual Components," *American Political Science Review* 69 (1975): 107–123.

26. See Steven J. Rosenstone and John Mark Hansen, *Mobilization, Participation, and Democracy in America* (New York: Macmillan, 1993), pp. 177–188; Gregory A. Caldeira and Samuel C. Patterson, "Contextual Influences on Participation in U.S. State Legislative Contests," *Legislative Studies Quarterly* 3 (1982): 359–381; Samuel C. Patterson and Gregory A. Caldeira, "Getting Out the Vote: Participation in Gubernatorial Elections," *American Political Science Review* 77 (1983): 675–689; and Gregory A. Caldeira, Samuel C. Patterson, and Gregory A. Markko, "The Mobilization of Voters in Congressional Elections," *Journal of Politics* 47 (1985): 490–509.

27. Walter Dean Burnham makes this point in "The Changing Shape of the American Political Universe" and "Theory and Voting Research: Some Reflections on Converse's 'Change in the American Electorate,'" *American Political Science Review* 68 (1974): 1002–1023. Also see Paul Kleppner, *Who Voted?* (New York: Praeger, 1982).

28. The challenge to Burnham is raised primarily by Converse, "Change in the American Electorate"; and Jerrold G. Rusk, "The American Electoral Universe: Speculation and Evidence," *American Political Science Review* 68 (1974): 1028–1049. The colloquy between Burnham and his critics is continued in this 1974 issue of the *American Political Science Review;* see also later works by Burnham, especially *The Current Crisis in American Politics* (New York: Oxford University Press, 1982), pp. 121–165.

29. At least this is the conclusion reached by scholars who have attempted to explain why American turnout levels are so much lower than those in other democratic nations. See Sidney Verba, Norman H. Nie, and Jae-on Kim, *Participation and Political Equality* (Cambridge, UK: Cambridge University Press, 1978) and Powell, "American Voter Turnout in Comparative Perspective."

30. Of course, this is why turnout may change as the result of a realignment. For an insightful discussion of how the nature of political conflict affects participation, see E. E. Schattschneider, *The Semi-Sovereign People* (New York: Holt, Rinehart, and Winston, 1960).

31. The importance of political mobilization, often neglected in research on American turnout, is the main theme of Rosenstone and Hansen, *Mobilization, Participation, and Democracy in America.*

32. On the mobilization of black voters, see Rosenstone and Hansen, *Mobilization, Participation, and Democracy in America,* pp. 188–196 and 219–224; Lawrence Bobo and Franklin D. Gilliam, Jr., "Race, Sociopolitical Participation, and Black Empowerment," *American Political Science Review* 84 (1990): 377–394; Frederick C. Harris, "Something Within: Religion as a Mobilizer of African-American Political Activism," *Journal of Politics* 56 (1994): 42–68; and Katherine Tate, "Black Political Participation in the 1984 and 1988 Presidential Elections," *American Political Science Review* 85 (1991): 1159–1176. In "Mass Mobilization or Governmental Intervention: The Growth of Black Registration in the South," *Journal of Politics* 57 (1995): 425–442, Richard Timpone shows that significant black mobilization in the South was attributable to both organizational mobilization efforts and federal intervention under the Voting Rights Act of 1965.

33. From the perspective of strict rationality, some theorists have argued, it is paradoxical that people do vote in a large electorate. For a careful review of these arguments and a theory of why it may be rational to vote under these conditions nonetheless, see John H. Aldrich, "Rational Choice and Turnout," *American Journal of Political Science* 37 (1993): 246–278.

34. Sidney Verba and Norman H. Nie, *Participation in America* (New York: Harper and Row, 1972), pp. 125–137. See also Teixiera, *The Disappearing American Voter,* Chap. 3.

35. Verba, Nie, and Kim, *Participation and Political Equality.*

36. Wolfinger and Rosenstone, *Who Votes?* pp. 35–36.

37. Verba and Nie, *Participation in America,* pp. 145–147. Of course, chronological age indexes the varying political experiences of different generations in addition to stage of the life cycle, but scholars have found little evidence that generation exerts an independent impact on turnout. On this point, see Rosenstone and Hansen, *Mobilization, Participation, and Democracy in America,* pp. 136–141.

38. Bobo and Gilliam, "Race, Sociopolitical Participation, and Black Empowerment."

39. Verba and Nie, *Participation in America,* Chap. 11, examines the effects of organizational membership. See Laura Stoker and M. Kent Jennings, "Life-Cycle Transitions and Political Participation: The Case of Marriage," *American Political Science Review* 89 (1995):

421–436, for the salutary impact of getting married; and Rosenstone and Wolfinger, *Who Votes?* on the detrimental effects of losing a spouse among the elderly.

40. See Rosenstone and Hansen, *Mobilization, Participation, and Democracy in America,* pp. 141–156; and Verba and Nie, *Participation in America,* pp. 133–136.

41. See Richard A. Brody, "The Puzzle of Participation in America," in Anthony King, ed., *The New American Political System* (Washington, DC: American Enterprise Institute, 1978), pp. 287–324.

42. The emphasis on efficacy and partisanship appears in Paul R. Abramson and John H. Aldrich, "The Decline of Electoral Participation in America," *American Political Science Review* 76 (1982): 502–521; and Paul R. Abramson, John H. Aldrich, and David W. Rohde, *Change and Continuity in the 1992 Election* (Washington, DC: CQ Press, 1995), pp. 114–120.

43. Studies by Teixeira, *The Disappearing American Voter,* Chap. 1, and Rosenstone and Hansen, *Mobilization, Participation, and Democracy in America,* Chap. 7, echo the emphasis on efficacy but attribute the greatest additional effects to declines in social connectedness (both studies) and electoral mobilization (Rosenstone and Hansen). For a general account of the deterioration of social connectedness in the United States, see Robert D. Putnam, "Bowling Alone: America's Declining Social Capital," *Journal of Democracy* 6 (1995): 65–78.

44. See Stephen M. Nichols and Paul Allen Beck, "Reversing the Decline: Voter Turnout in the 1992 Election," in Herbert F. Weisberg, ed., *Democracy's Feast* (Chatham, NJ: Chatham House, 1995), Chap. 2.

45. On this point, see Edward G. Carmines and James A. Stimson, *Issue Evolution* (Princeton, NJ: Princeton University Press, 1989).

46. The youngest voters were key actors in the last clear-cut realignment, casting heavily Democratic first votes during the New Deal realignment of the 1930s. The frequent switches in their recent party support are thus more likely to indicate a dealignment than a realignment.

47. *Congressional Quarterly Weekly Report,* January 13, 1996, pp. 97–100.

48. On this point, see Verba and Nie, *Participation in America,* Part III; and Bennett and Resnick, "The Implications of Nonvoting for Democracy in the United States."

49. Wolfinger and Rosenstone, *Who Votes?* Chap. 6; and Teixeira, *The Disappearing American Voter,* Chap. 3.

50. See James DeNardo, "Turnout and the Vote: The Joke's on the Democrats," *American Political Science Review* 74 (1980): 406–420; the exchange between DeNardo and Harvey J. Tucker and Arnold Vedlitz, "Does Heavy Turnout Help Democrats in Presidential Elections?" *American Political Science Review* 80 (1986): 1291–1304; and Teixeira, *The Disappearing American Voter.* Recent research also indicates that increasing registration and voting do not necessarily favor Democrats; see Jack H. Nagel and John E. McNulty, "Partisan Effects of Voter Turnout in Senatorial and Gubernatorial Elections," *American Political Science Review* 90 (1996): 780–793.

CHAPTER 9

1. For the story of the convention system and the early years of the direct primary, see Charles E. Merriam and Louise Overacker, *Primary Elections* (Chicago: University of Chicago Press, 1928). For a discussion of the early spread of the direct primary, see V. O. Key, Jr., *American State Politics: An Introduction* (New York: Knopf, 1956), pp. 87–97.

2. The methods for selecting delegates to the national nominating conventions also vary across the states, and, as we shall see, they are not always the same as the methods employed for choosing party nominees for statewide office.

3. Some states allow third parties to nominate their candidates through conventions.
4. *The Book of the States 1998–99* (Lexington, KY: The Council of State Governments, 1998), pp. 159–160. For a general discussion of the various methods, see Malcolm E. Jewell and David M. Olson, *Political Parties and Elections in American States* (Chicago: Dorsey, 1988), pp. 94–97.
5. Experts disagree on where to draw the line between a "closed" and an "open" primary. For an account of variations within these broad categories, see Craig L. Carr and Gary L. Scott, "The Logic of State Primary Classification Schemes," *American Politics Quarterly* 12 (1984): 465–476; and Steven E. Finkel and Howard A. Scarrow, "Party Identification and Party Enrollment: The Difference and the Consequence," *Journal of Politics* 47 (1985): 620–652.
6. A 1986 Supreme Court decision (*Tashjian v. Republican Party of Connecticut,* 106 S.Ct. 783 and 1257) upheld the Connecticut party's attempts to override the state's closed-primary law. This decision affirms the authority of the party, rather than the state, to control its own nomination process and may clear the way for other state parties to regulate participation in their primaries as they wish. Most state parties would prefer a closed primary to an open one, however.
7. See David Adamany, "Cross-over Voting and the Democratic Party's Reform Rules," *American Political Science Review* 70 (1976): 536–541. Also see Ronald D. Hedlund and Meredith W. Watts, "The Wisconsin Open Primary: 1968 to 1984," *American Politics Quarterly* 14 (1986): 55–74; and Gary D. Wekkin, "The Conceptualization and Measurement of Crossover Voting," *Western Political Quarterly* 41 (1988): 105–114.
8. Alan Abramowitz, John McGlennon, and Ronald Rapoport, "A Note on Strategic Voting in a Primary Election," *Journal of Politics* 43 (1981): 899–904; and Gary D. Wekkin, "Why Crossover Voters Are Not 'Mischievous' Voters," *American Politics Quarterly* 19 (1991): 229–247.
9. Access to the major-party ballot has become easier as a result of court action in recent decades. In key early cases, the United States Supreme Court invalidated a Texas law requiring candidates to pay both a flat fee for candidacy and a share of the cost of the election (up to $9,000) and overturned the California scale of filing fees because they did not provide an alternative means of access to the ballot (such as a petition) for candidates unable to pay. The cases were *Bullock v. Carter,* 405 U.S. 134 (1972); and *Lubin v. Panish,* 415 U.S. 709 (1974). The monthly newsletter *Ballot Access News* chronicles continuing efforts to regulate ballot access, especially for third parties and independents.
10. That blacks are disadvantaged by runoff primaries is challenged by Charles S. Bullock, III, and A. Brock Smith in "Black Success in Local Runoff Elections," *Journal of Politics* 52 (1990): 1205–1220. For more on the discriminatory impact of runoff primaries, see Harold Stanley, "The Runoff: The Case for Retention," *PS* 18 (1985): 231–236; and Charles S. Bullock, III, and Loch K. Johnson, *Runoff Elections in the United States* (Knoxville: University of Tennessee Press, 1991). For the argument that blacks are not necessarily advantaged by maximizing the number of offices they can win, see Carol Swain, *Black Faces, Black Interests* (Cambridge, MA: Harvard University Press, 1993).
11. Theodore H. White, *The Making of the President 1960* (New York: Atheneum, 1961), p. 78.
12. See Emmett H. Buehl, Jr., "Divisive Primaries and Participation in Fall Presidential Campaigns," *American Politics Quarterly* 14 (1986): 376–390; Walter J. Stone, "The Carryover Effect in Presidential Elections," *American Political Science Review* 80 (1986): 271–280; and Martin P. Wattenberg, "The Republican Presidential Advantage in the Age of Party Disunity," in Gary W. Cox and Samuel Kernell, eds., *The Politics of Divided Government* (Boulder, CO: Westview, 1991), Chap. 3.

13. The most recent and comprehensive studies have found that divisive primaries depress general election support for most offices except for the House of Representatives. See Patrick J. Kenney, "Sorting Out the Effects of Primary Divisiveness in Congressional and Senatorial Elections," *Western Political Quarterly* 41 (1988): 765–777; Patrick J. Kenney and Tom W. Rice, "Presidential Prenomination Preferences and Candidate Evaluations," *American Political Science Review* 82 (1988): 1309–1319; and James I. Lengle, Diana Owen, and Molly W. Sonner, "Divisive Nominating Mechanisms and Democratic Party Electoral Prospects," *Journal of Politics* 57 (1995): 370–383. Lonna Rae Atkeson finds, however, that divisive primaries have only modest effects on general election results; see "Divisive Primaries and General Election Outcomes: Another Look at Presidential Campaigns," *American Journal of Political Science* 42 (1998): 256–271.

14. See V. O. Key, *American State Politics: An Introduction*, Chap. 6.

15. The party's role in recruiting candidates for office varies with how much control it has over the primary, which in turn is affected by the type of primary. For example, one study found that parties were more active in recruiting and endorsing legislative candidates and in scaring off challengers in closed primary than in open primary states. See Richard J. Tobin and Edward Keynes, "Institutional Differences in the Recruitment Process: A Four-State Study," *American Journal of Political Science* 19 (1975): 667–682.

16. Followers of Lyndon LaRouche have cleverly taken advantage of these situations by filing as the only candidates for minority party nomination in one-party areas. If the major-party candidate subsequently stumbled on the way to what seemed to be sure victory, this put LaRouche's candidates in position to win the office.

17. In a survey of gubernatorial primaries in forty-nine states from 1960 to 1986, Malcolm Jewell and David Olson found that the major parties had contests for the gubernatorial nominations 74 percent of the time overall. See their *Political Parties and Elections in American States*, pp. 104–106.

18. About a third of all state legislative races have been uncontested in recent years. On the phenomenon of uncontested races, as well as candidate recruitment more generally, see L. Sandy Maisel, Linda L. Fowler, Ruth S. Jones, and Walter J. Stone, "Nomination Politics: The Roles of Institutional, Contextual, and Personal Variables," in L. Sandy Maisel, ed., *The Parties Respond* (Boulder, CO: Westview, 1994), pp. 148–152.

19. See Jewell and Olson, *Political Parties and Elections in American States*, pp. 94–104; and Maisel, Fowler, Jones, and Stone, "Nomination Politics," pp. 155–156.

20. On the factors that promote or suppress competition in the primaries, see Tom W. Rice, "Gubernatorial and Senatorial Primary Elections: Determinants of Competition," *American Politics Quarterly* 13 (1985): 427–446; Harvey L. Schantz, "Contested and Uncontested Primaries for the U.S. House," *Legislative Studies Quarterly* 4 (1980): 545–562; and Jewell and Olson, *Political Parties and Elections in American States*, pp. 104–118.

21. Jewell and Olson, *Political Parties and Elections in American States*, p. 110.

22. Malcolm E. Jewell, "Northern State Gubernatorial Primary Elections: Explaining Voting Turnout," *American Politics Quarterly* 12 (1984): 101–116; and Patrick J. Kenney, "Explaining Turnout in Gubernatorial Primaries," *American Politics Quarterly* 11 (1983): 315–326.

23. The early studies are Austin Ranney and Leon D. Epstein, "The Two Electorates: Voters and Non-Voters in a Wisconsin Primary," *Journal of Politics* 28 (1966): 598–616; and Austin Ranney, "The Representativeness of Primary Electorates," *American Journal of Political Science* 12 (1968): 224–238. Similar results appear for turnout in more recent Senate primaries; see Patrick J. Kenney, "Explaining Primary Turnout: The Senatorial Case," *Legislative Studies Quarterly* 11 (1986): 65–74. On different results in presidential primaries, see John G. Geer, "Assessing the Representativeness of Electorates in Presidential Primaries," *American Journal of Political Science* 32 (1988): 929–945.

24. Jewell and Olson, *Political Parties and Elections in American States*, pp. 112–113.

25. Key, *American State Politics*, p. 195.

26. See John G. Geer and Mark E. Shere, "Party Competition and the Prisoner's Dilemma: An Argument for the Direct Primary," *Journal of Politics* 54 (1992): 741–761.

27. On the relationships among party, mechanism of nomination, and primary competition, see Andrew D. McNitt, "The Effect of Preprimary Endorsement on Competition for Nominations: An Examination of Different Nominating Systems," *Journal of Politics* 42 (1980): 257–266.

28. A study of gubernatorial nominations in 1982 suggests this by showing that more money was spent on campaigns and the spending was more related to the outcome in the contests in states where party organizations did not make preprimary endorsements. Sarah M. Morehouse, "Money versus Party Effort: Nominating for Governor," *American Journal of Political Science* 34 (1990): 706–724.

CHAPTER 10

1. After the movement to primaries for nominations of state officials had begun in 1902, it seemed only natural to involve voters in the selection of presidential candidates as well. But the national conventions remained in place, and even where presidential primaries were adopted, they only supplemented rather than displaced the traditional convention system.

2. For an excellent account of this episode, a rare event of political leaders willingly giving up power, see Byron E. Shafer, *Quiet Revolution* (New York: Russell Sage Foundation, 1983). Other useful sources on the reform of the presidential nomination process are James W. Ceaser, *Presidential Selection* (Princeton, NJ: Princeton University Press, 1979); William J. Crotty, *Party Reform* (New York: Longman, 1983); Nelson W. Polsby, *The Consequences of Party Reform* (Oxford: Oxford University Press, 1983); and Austin Ranney, *Curing the Mischiefs of Faction: Party Reform in America* (Berkeley, CA: University of California Press, 1975).

3. In a case involving the Wisconsin open primary, the Supreme Court upheld the power of the national party to refuse to seat delegates chosen under a state law which violated its rules. See *Democratic Party of the United States v. La Follette,* 450 U.S. 107 (1981).

4. The parties in a few states have held both primaries and caucuses. Texas Democrats select some delegates through primaries and some through caucuses. In recent years the Democrats in four other states have held preference primaries called "beauty contests" because their results have no bearing on delegate selection, which is done through the caucus-convention system.

5. On the shift to candidate-oriented delegate loyalties, see Byron E. Shafer, *Bifurcated Politics: Evolution and Reform in the National Party Convention* (Cambridge, MA: Harvard University Press, 1988), pp. 181–184.

6. For an account of the struggle between the Wisconsin Democrats and the national party over open primaries, see Gary D. Wekkin, *Democrats versus Democrats* (Columbia: University of Missouri Press, 1983).

7. On the Iowa caucuses, which have received more media coverage than any other caucus and most primaries, see Peverill Squire, ed., *The Iowa Caucuses and the Presidential Nominating Process* (Boulder, CO: Westview, 1989).

8. For a discussion of these various strategic considerations, see John H. Aldrich, *Before the Convention* (Chicago: University of Chicago Press, 1980). For a more recent account, emphasizing the strategic trade-off between winning delegates and gaining momentum through media coverage, see Paul-Henri Gurian, "Candidate Behavior in Presidential Nomination Campaigns: A Dynamic Model," *Journal of Politics* 55 (1993): 115–139; and

Paul-Henri Gurian and Audrey A. Haynes, "Campaign Strategy in Presidential Primaries," *American Journal of Political Science* 37 (1993): 335–341.

9. Studies of the effect of primary divisiveness on the presidential races are cited in footnotes 12 and 13 of Chapter 9.

10. Differences between "superdelegates" and regular delegates are examined in Richard Herrera, "Are 'Superdelegates' Super?" *Political Behavior* 16 (1994): 79–92; and Priscilla L. Southwell, "The 1984 Democratic Nomination Process: The Significance of Unpledged Superdelegates," *American Politics Quarterly* 14 (1986): 75–88.

11. Turnout rates in nomination contests are very difficult to estimate. The turnout rate cannot be counted as a percentage of the voters registered with that party because many states do not have party registration. Should it be based on the potential general election electorate for that party? That number surely is affected by who the nominee is. Is it the total voting-age population? Party turnout from that base depends upon how much competition there is in each party's primary or caucus. The best estimate of turnout under these circumstances, although hardly ideal, is a comparison of two different calculations—the one based on general election voters for that party, the other on the voting-age population.

12. See Jack Moran and Mark Fenster, "Voter Turnout in Presidential Primaries: A Diachronic Analysis," *American Politics Quarterly* 10 (1982): 453–476; Patrick J. Kenney and Tom W. Rice, "Voter Turnout in Presidential Primaries: A Cross-Sectional Examination," *Political Behavior* 7 (1985): 101–112; and Barbara Norrander and Gregg W. Smith, "Type of Contest, Candidate Strategy, and Turnout in Presidential Primaries," *American Politics Quarterly* 13 (1985): 28–50.

13. See Barbara Norrander, "Selective Participation: Presidential Voters as a Subset of General Election Voters," *American Politics Quarterly* 14 (1986): 35–54.

14. Evidence on the representatives of primary electorates may be found in Larry M. Bartels, *Presidential Primaries and the Dynamics of Public Choice* (Princeton, NJ: Princeton University Press, 1988), pp. 140–148; John G. Geer, "The Representativeness of Presidential Primary Electorates," *American Journal of Political Science* 32 (1988): 929–945; and Barbara Norrander, "Ideological Representativeness of Primary Voters," *American Journal of Political Science* 33 (1989): 570–587.

15. The most severe indictment of the primaries on these grounds appears in Scott Keeter and Cliff Zukin, *Uninformed Choice* (New York: Praeger, 1983). On the limited influence of ideology and issues, see John G. Geer, *Nominating Presidents: An Evaluation of Voters and Primaries* (New York: Greenwood Press, 1989) and Barbara Norrander, "Correlates of Vote Choice in the 1980 Presidential Primaries," *Journal of Politics* 48 (1986): 156–166. Also see J. David Gopoian, "Issue Preferences and Candidate Choice in the 1980 Presidential Primaries," *American Journal of Political Science* 26 (1982): 523–546.

16. Samuel L. Popkin, *The Reasoning Voter* (Chicago: University of Chicago Press, 1991), especially Chaps. 6–8.

17. Bartels, *Presidential Primaries and the Dynamics of Public Choice.*

18. For a persuasive analysis of strategic voting in primaries, in which voters temper their "sincere" preferences with calculations of their candidate's viability, see Paul R. Abramson, John H. Aldrich, Phil Paolino, and David W. Rohde, "'Sophisticated' Voting in the 1988 Presidential Primaries," *American Political Science Review* 86 (1992): 55–69.

19. A similar blend of preferences and strategic calculations has been found to influence the decisions of participants in the Iowa caucuses and convention. See Walter J. Stone, Ronald B. Rapoport, and Alan I. Abramowitz, "Candidate Support in Presidential Nomination Campaigns: The Case of Iowa in 1984," *Journal of Politics* 54 (1992): 1074–1097.

20. Credit for the idea of a national party convention goes to a long-forgotten minor party, the Anti-Masons, who brought together their supporters in a Baltimore meeting in 1831 to

nominate a candidate for president. But it is the major parties that have made the convention a familiar institution of American politics.

21. The best account of the evolution of the national party conventions is Byron E. Shafer, *Bifurcated Politics*. Shafer contends that the central role of the conventions—nominating a president—was eroding with the nationalization of American politics prior to the post–1968 reforms. On pre–1960 conventions, see Paul T. David, Ralph M. Goldman, and Richard C. Bain, *The Politics of the National Party Conventions* (Washington, DC: Brookings Institution, 1960).

22. Party platforms first appeared in the 1840s, and all of them through 1976 are available in one volume: Donald B. Johnson, *National Party Platforms, 1840–1976* (Urbana: University of Illinois Press, 1978). For summaries of more recent platforms, see postconvention issues of the *Congressional Quarterly Weekly Report* (more recently known as *CQ Weekly*).

23. Gerald Pomper, *Elections in America* (New York: Dodd, Mead, 1968), p. 201.

24. The candidates, especially the winning candidate, play a more important role in platform development now than ever before. See L. Sandy Maisel, "The Platform-Writing Process: Candidate-Centered Platforms in 1992," *Political Science Quarterly* 108 (1993–1994): 671–699. On the sometimes conflicting goals of candidates and issue-oriented delegates, see Byron E. Shafer, *Bifurcated Politics*, Chaps. 4 and 6.

25. In *Bifurcated Politics* (pp. 333–337) Shafer discusses the possibility, in a "deviant" year, of the nomination decision returning to the convention.

26. On the representativeness of convention delegates, see Howard L. Reiter, *Selecting the President* (Philadelphia: University of Pennsylvania Press, 1985), Chap. 4.

27. Information on the party activities and offices of delegates to the 1992 Democratic convention is provided by *The New York Times* from the *Times*/CBS News Democratic Delegate Poll conducted with a random sample of delegates between June 18 and July 2, 1992. Information on Republican delegates comes from a survey conducted by CBS News.

28. The classic account of this relationship, in which delegates to the 1956 conventions are compared to Democratic and Republican identifiers from a national survey, is found in Herbert McClosky, Paul Hoffman, and Rosemary O'Hara, "Issue Conflict and Consensus among Party Leaders and Followers," *American Political Science Review* 54 (1960): 406–427. For a replication and extension with similar results, see David Nexon, "Asymmetry in the Political System: Occasional Activists in the Republican and Democratic Parties, 1956–1964," *American Political Science Review* 65 (1971): 716–730.

29. These were the findings and the conclusion of Jeane Kirkpatrick, *The New Presidential Elite* (New York: Russell Sage Foundation and Twentieth Century Fund, 1976).

30. For comparisons of post–1972 convention delegates with their respective party rank and files, see John S. Jackson III, Barbara L. Brown, and David Bositis, "Herbert McClosky and Friends Revisited: 1980 Democratic and Republican Party Elites Compared to the Mass Public," *American Politics Quarterly* 10 (1982): 158–180; Warren E. Miller and M. Kent Jennings, *Parties in Transition* (New York: Russell Sage Foundation, 1986), Chaps. 7–9; Denise L. Baer and David A. Bositis, *Elite Cadres and Party Coalitions* (New York: Greenwood Press, 1988), Chap. 8; and Shafer, *Bifurcated Politics*, pp. 100–107.

31. See John W. Soule and Wilma E. McGrath, "A Comparative Study of Presidential Nomination Conventions: The Democrats 1968 and 1972," *American Journal of Political Science* 19 (1975): 501–517. The seminal study is John W. Soule and James W. Clarke, "Amateurs and Professionals: A Study of Delegates to the 1968 Democratic National Convention," *American Political Science Review* 64 (1970): 888–898.

32. For studies of amateurs and professionals among convention delegates, see Denis G. Sullivan, Jeffrey L. Pressman, Benjamin I. Page, and John J. Lyons, *The Politics of Representation: The Democratic Convention 1972* (New York: St. Martin's, 1974); Kirkpatrick,

The New Presidential Elite; Thomas H. Roback, "Motivations for Activism among Republican National Convention Delegates," *Journal of Politics* 42 (1980): 181–201; and Denise Baer and David Bositis, *Elite Cadres and Party Coalitions*, Chap. 7.

33. Byron E. Shafer, *Bifurcated Politics*, Chap. 8.

34. See the figures cited in Shafer, *Bifurcated Politics,* Chap. 8, especially p. 280.

35. Iowa and New Hampshire, whose citizens comprise only 2.9 percent of the U.S. population, receive a disproportionate share of the media coverage in the nomination process. On media coverage of these states in 1984, see William C. Adams, "As New Hampshire Goes…," in Gary R. Orren and Nelson W. Polsby, eds., *Media and Momentum* (Chatham, NJ: Chatham House, 1987), pp. 42–59.

36. A good statement of the case against the 1970s party reforms may be found in Polsby, *Consequences of Party Reform.* The case for party reforms is best articulated in William J. Crotty, *Decision for the Democrats* (Baltimore: The Johns Hopkins University Press, 1978).

37. See Michael W. Traugott and Margaret Petrella, "Public Evaluations of the Presidential Nomination Process," *Political Behavior* 11 (1989): 335–352.

CHAPTER 11

1. Jerrold G. Rusk found that the introduction of the Australian ballot was accompanied by an increase in split-ticket voting. See his article, "The Effect of the Australian Ballot Reform on Split Ticket Voting: 1876–1908," *American Political Science Review* 64 (1970): 1220–1238.

2. The best account of the effects of ballot form on voting remains Angus Campbell, Philip E. Converse, Warren E. Miller, and Donald E. Stokes, *The American Voter* (New York: Wiley, 1960), Chap. 11. For an inventory of ballot provisions in the various states, see *The Transformation in American Politics: Implications for American Federalism* (Washington, DC: Advisory Commission on Intergovernmental Affairs, 1986).

3. Delbert A. Taebel, "The Effect of Ballot Position on Electoral Success," *American Journal of Political Science* 19 (1975): 519–526.

4. Provisions for write-ins allow access to the ballot by candidates who have not been nominated by any of the parties. As was shown in Chapter 2, the states have typically protected the parties by making it difficult for such candidates to earn a position on the ballot. Moreover, a majority of states have so-called sore-loser laws that prevent candidates who have lost in the contest for their party's nomination from qualifying for the general election ballot as an independent.

5. The introduction of the secret ballot increased roll-off by requiring that voters actually mark their choices for each office or, where it was permitted, consciously cast a straight-ticket vote. See Walter Dean Burnham, "The Changing Shape of the American Political Universe," *American Political Science Review* 59 (1965): 7–28. This effect can be limited by ballot forms that encourage straight-ticket voting. See Rusk, "The Effect of the Australian Ballot Reform on Split Ticket Voting," p. 1237; and Jack L. Walker, "Ballot Forms and Voter Fatigue: An Analysis of the Office Block and Party Column Ballots," *Midwest Journal of Political Science* 10 (1966): 448–463. A recent study has also shown that roll-off is decreased by electronic voting machines that use a blinking light to call voters' attention to their failure to vote the entire ballot. See Stephen M. Nichols and Gregory A. Strizek, "Electronic Voting Machines and Ballot Roll-off," *American Politics Quarterly* 23 (1995): 300–318.

6. For a good survey of the effects of various types of districts, see Howard D. Hamilton, "Legislative Constituencies: Single-Member Districts, Multi-Member Districts, and Floterial Districts," *Western Political Quarterly* 20 (1967): 321–340.

7. On some of the complexities of proportional representation, see Douglas W. Rae, *The Political Consequences of Electoral Law* (New Haven, CT: Yale University Press, 1967);

and Arend Lijphart, *Electoral Systems and Party Systems: A Study of Twenty-Seven Democracies, 1945–1990* (New York: Oxford University Press, 1994).

8. The classic study of presidential coattails is Warren E. Miller, "Presidential Coattails: A Study in Political Myth and Methodology," *Public Opinion Quarterly* 19 (1955–56): 353–368.

9. Walter Dean Burnham, *Critical Elections and the Mainsprings of American Politics* (New York: Norton, 1970), p. 94; and V. O. Key, Jr., *American State Politics: An Introduction* (New York: Knopf, 1967), pp. 41–49 and 52–84.

10. For an analysis of the relative importance of states in presidential elections due to the electoral college, see George Rabinowitz and Stuart Elaine MacDonald, "The Power of the States in U.S. Presidential Elections," *American Political Science Review* 80 (1986): 65–87. See also Claude S. Colantoni, Terrence J. Levesque, and Peter C. Ordeshook, "Campaign Resource Allocation under the Electoral College," *American Political Science Review* 69 (1975): 141–154; and Larry M. Bartels, "Resource Allocation in Presidential Campaigns," *Journal of Politics* 47 (1985): 928–936.

11. Walker, "Ballot Forms and Voter Fatigue," makes the latter point.

12. The landmark Supreme Court cases striking down as unconstitutional malapportioned congressional and state legislative districts are *Baker v. Carr,* 369 U.S. 186 (1962); *Reynolds v. Sims,* 377 U.S. 533 (1964); and *Wesberry v. Sanders,* 376 U.S. 1. In fact, in *Karcher v. Daggett* (462 U.S. 725 [1983]), the Supreme Court struck down a New Jersey plan because by creating districts that differed in population size by seven tenths of one percent from the average, it violated the constitutional requirements of "precise mathematical equality."

13. The original quotation comes from Charles Ledyard Norton in his 1890 book, *Political Americanisms;* quoted in William Safire, *Safire's Political Dictionary* (New York: Random House, 1978), pp. 254–255.

14. For example, the Supreme Court refrained from invalidating the notoriously gerrymandered Indiana (*Davis v. Bandamer,* 478 U.S. 109 [1986]) and California redistricting plans (*Badham v. Eu,* 488 U.S. 1024 [1989]). Some years before, however, in *Gomillion v. Lightfoot,* 364 U.S. 339 (1960), the Court had struck down an Alabama gerrymander in which the municipal boundaries of a city were redrawn to exclude blacks.

15. On the Voting Rights Act and Justice Department involvement in preclearance of electoral laws, see Chandler Davidson and Bernard Grofman, eds., *Quiet Revolution in the South* (Princeton, NJ: Princeton University Press, 1994), especially Chap. 1.

16. For systematic empirical evidence showing partisan gains from the creation of more minority districts, see Kimball Brace, Bernard Grofman, and Lisa Handley, "Does Redistricting Aimed to Help Blacks Necessarily Help Republicans," *Journal of Politics* 49 (1987): 169–185; and Kevin A. Hill, "Does the Creation of Majority Black Districts Aid Republicans? An Analysis of the 1992 Congressional Elections in Eight Southern States," *Journal of Politics* 57 (1995): 384–401.

17. In its 1993 decision on the North Carolina districting plan (*Shaw v. Reno,* 113 S Ct 2816), the Supreme Court seemed to be disturbed by the bizarre shape of the district. In its 1995 decision on the Georgia districting plan (*Miller v. Johnson,* 115 S Ct 2475), the Court took issue with political boundaries drawn with racially based representation in mind to create a majority-minority district of rather conventional shape. A subsequent redistricting plan drawn up by a panel of federal judges eliminated two of Georgia's three majority-minority districts for the 1996 elections.

18. On the effects of redistricting, see Amihai Glazer, Bernard Grofman, and Marc Robbins, "Partisan and Incumbency Effects of 1970s Congressional Redistricting," *American Journal of Political Science* 31 (1987): 680–707; Richard Born, "Partisan Intentions and Election Day Realities in the Congressional Redistricting Process," *American Political Science Review* 79 (1985): 305–319; and Richard G. Niemi and Laura R. Winsley, "The Persis-

tence of Partisan Redistricting Effects in Congressional Elections in the 1970s and 1980s," *Journal of Politics* 54 (1992): 565–572. For somewhat contrary evidence of more than minimal effects in 1972 and 1982 but not in 1992, see Richard G. Niemi and Alan I. Abramowitz, "Partisan Redistricting and the 1992 Congressional Elections," *Journal of Politics* 56 (1994): 811–817. On California, see Bruce E. Cain, "Assessing the Partisan Effects of Redistricting," *American Political Science Review* 79 (1985): 320–334; on Indiana, see John D. Cranor, Gary L. Crawley, and Raymond H. Scheele, "The Anatomy of a Gerrymander," *American Journal of Political Science* 33 (1989): 222–239. Finally, a comprehensive study covering all state lower-house redistricting from 1968–1988 found significant partisan advantages even while affirming that redistricting fostered greater responsiveness; see Andrew Gelman and Gary King, "Enhancing Democracy through Legislative Redistricting," *American Political Science Review* 88 (1994): 541–559.

19. See Paul S. Herrnson, *Congressional Elections: Campaigning at Home and in Washington* (Washington, DC: CQ Press, 1998); Marjorie Randon Hershey, *Running for Office: The Political Education of Campaigners* (Chatham, NJ: Chatham House, 1984); John H. Kessel, *Presidential Campaign Politics* (Chicago: Dorsey, 1988); Lucius J. Barker and Ronald W. Walters, *Jesse Jackson's 1984 Presidential Campaign: Challenge and Change in American Politics* (Champaign: University of Illinois Press, 1979); Sidney Blumenthal, *Pledging Allegiance: The Last Campaign of the Cold War* (New York: HarperCollins, 1990); L. Sandy Maisel, *From Obscurity to Oblivion: Running in the Congressional Primary* (Knoxville: University of Tennessee Press, 1986); David R. Runkel, *Campaign for President: The Managers Look at '88* (Dover, MA: Auburn House, 1989); Jack W. Germond and Jules Witcover, *Mad as Hell: Revolt at the Ballot Box, 1992* (New York: Warner Books, 1993); Mary Matalin and James Carville, *All's Fair: Love, War, and Running for President* (New York: Random House, 1994); and the best-selling novel *Primary Colors* (New York: Random House, 1996), written by an anonymous author who later identified himself as Joe Klein.

20. For an examination of how presidential candidates allocated one scarce resource, campaign visits, among various constituency groups, see Darrell M. West, "Constituencies and Travel Allocations in the 1980 Presidential Campaign," *American Journal of Political Science* 27 (1983): 515–529.

21. On congressional elections, see Herrnson, *Congressional Elections*, and Gary C. Jacobson, *The Politics of Congressional Elections* 4th ed. (New York: Longman, 1997).

22. For a colorful account of American campaign professionals in other foreign nations, see John M. Russonello, "The Making of the President ... in the Philippines, Venezuela, France ...," *Public Opinion* 9 (1986): 10–12.

23. Among the many books on the subject, see especially Sidney Blumenthal, *The Permanent Campaign* (New York: Simon and Schuster, 1980); and Larry J. Sabato, *The Rise of Political Consultants* (New York: Basic, 1981); as well as the magazine *Campaigns and Elections*.

24. Described in Ithiel de Sola Pool, Robert P. Abelson, and Samuel Popkin, *Candidates, Issues, and Strategies* (Cambridge, MA: MIT Press, 1964). A fictionalized version can be found in Eugene Burdick, *The 480* (New York: McGraw-Hill, 1964).

25. Although soundings of public opinion have been a staple of political campaigns from the beginning, the first use of a more or less "scientific" public opinion poll on behalf of a candidate appears to have been in advance of the 1936 presidential election. Campaign strategists for President Franklin Roosevelt, hiding the poll's true sponsor, mailed out more than 100,000 straw ballots and used the returns to help position Roosevelt for the presidential contest. See Edwin Amenta, Kathleen Dunleavy, and Mary Bernstein, "Stolen Thunder? Huey Long's 'Share Our Wealth,' Political Mediation and the Second New

Deal," *American Sociological Review* 59 (1994): 678–702, especially 687–691. For an interesting study of the use of private polls in the 1960 presidential campaign, see Lawrence R. Jacobs and Robert Y. Shapiro, "Issues, Candidate Image, and Priming: The Use of Private Polls in Kennedy's 1960 Presidential Campaign," *American Political Science Review* 88 (1994): 527–540.

26. On the use of television advertising in modern campaigns, see Kathleen Hall Jamieson, *Packaging the Presidency: A History and Criticism of Presidential Campaign Advertising* (New York: Oxford University Press, 1996); Montague Kern, *Thirty-Second Politics: Political Advertising in the Eighties* (New York: Praeger, 1989); and Darrell West, *Air Wars: Television Advertising in Election Campaigns, 1952–92* (Washington, DC: CQ Press, 1993).

27. For a discussion of the routines of media coverage, see Doris A. Graber, *Mass Media and American Politics,* 5th ed. (Washington, DC: CQ Press, 1977), Chap 4.

28. E. J. Dionne, Jr., in the *New York Times,* September 7, 1980.

29. For an examination of how negative advertising by single-issue groups defeated four of six targeted Senate incumbents in 1980, see Marjorie Hershey's *Running for Office.* On negative campaigning generally, see Kathleen Hall Jamieson, *Dirty Politics: Deception, Distraction, and Democracy* (New York: Oxford University Press, 1992). One study of negative campaigning suggests that its major effect is to demobilize voters, especially supporters of the target of the ads; see Stephen Ansolabehere, Shanto Iyengar, Adam Simon, and Nicholas Valentine, "Does Attack Advertising Demobilize the Electorate?" *American Political Science Review* 88 (1994): 829–838: and Stephen Ansolabehere and Shanto Iyengar, *Going Negative: How Campaign Adversing Shrinks and Polarizes the Electorate* (New York: Free Press, 1995). These findings are evaluated in a symposium in the *American Political Science Review* 93 (1999): 851–909.

30. Thoughtful reflections on how television is used in presidential campaigns are contained in Mathew D. McCubbins, ed., *Under the Watchful Eye* (Washington, DC: CQ Press, 1992), and Thomas E. Patterson, *Out of Order* (New York: Knopf, 1993).

31. The classic studies of the mobilizing effects of a political campaign were conducted in the 1940s before the appearance of television. See Paul Lazarsfeld, Bernard Berelson, and Hazel Gaudet, *The People's Choice* (New York: Columbia University Press, 1948); and Bernard Berelson, Paul Lazarsfeld, and William McPhee, *Voting* (Chicago: University of Chicago Press, 1954). Evidence that most voters continue to be found in highly homogeneous political environments and consequently are more likely to be mobilized than persuaded may be found in Robert Huckfeldt and John Sprague, "Networks in Context: The Social Flow of Political Information," *American Political Science Review* 81 (1987): 1197–1216; and Paul Allen Beck, "Voters' Intermediation Environments in the 1988 Presidential Contest," *Public Opinion Quarterly* 55 (1991).

32. Austin Ranney, *Channels of Power: The Impact of Television on American Politics* (New York: Basic Books, 1983), p. 90.

33. See Harold W. Stanley and Richard G. Niemi, *Vital Statistics on American Politics 1999–2000* (Washington, DC: CQ Press, 2000), Table 4.5, p. 173.

34. These were the responses of a national sample of the American electorate interviewed after the 1992 campaign in a study directed by Paul Allen Beck, Russell J. Dalton, and Robert Huckfeldt.

35. Various studies of media content have demonstrated that the media do not systematically favor either candidate in presidential elections. Content analyses of ABC, CBS, and NBC evening news by the Center for Media and Public Affairs during the 1996 presidential campaign found that positive assessments of all three candidates were about half of all media assessments, ranging from Clinton's 44 percent to Dole's 51 percent. See Stanley and Niemi, *Vital Statis-*

tics on American Politics, Table 4.12, pp. 188–189. Similar findings for earlier years are reported in Doris A. Graber, *Mass Media and American Politics* (Washington, DC: CQ Press, 1989); C. Richard Hofstetter, *Bias in the News* (Columbus: Ohio State University Press, 1976); Thomas Patterson, *The Mass Media Election* (New York: Praeger, 1980); and Michael J. Robinson and Margaret A. Sheehan, *Over the Wire and On TV: CBS and UPI in Campaign '80* (New York: Russell Sage Foundation, 1983). For the first time in the sixty years that records have been kept, a majority of newspapers even failed to endorse a candidate for president in 1988—and 70 percent remained uncommitted in 1996. See Stanley and Niemi, *Vital Statistics on American Politics,* Table 4.15, pp. 192–193.

36. For evidence on the agenda-setting effects of the media, see Donald Shaw and Maxwell E. McCombs, *The Emergence of American Political Issues: The Agenda-Setting Function of the Press* (St. Paul, MN: West, 1977); Lutz Erbring, Edie Goldenberg, and Arthur Miller, "Front-Page News and Real-World Cues: A New Look at Agenda-Setting by the Media," *American Journal of Political Science* 24 (1980): 16–49; and Shanto Iyengar and Donald Kinder, *News That Matters* (Chicago: University of Chicago Press, 1987). For evidence on priming, also see Iyengar and Kinder, *News That Matters.*

37. Media scholars for years have depicted the media as covering elections as if they were strategic games or horse races. The most recent case for this is made by Thomas E. Patterson, *Out of Order,* pp. 53–133. In the 1996 election, for example, a content analysis of the evening network news conducted by the Center for Media and Public Affairs showed that 33 percent of all news coverage of the presidential campaign focused on the "horse race." This figure is reported in Stanley and Niemi, *Vital Statistics on American Politics,* Table 4.8, p. 179.

38. Andrew Gelman and Gary King, "Party Competition and Media Messages in U.S. Presidential Elections," in L. Sandy Maisel, ed., *The Parties Respond* (Boulder, CO: Westview), pp. 255–295; and Thomas M. Holbrook, "Campaigns, National Conditions, and U.S. Presidential Elections," *American Journal of Political Science* 38 (1994): 973–998.

39. Phillips Cutright and Peter H. Rossi, "Grass Roots Politicians and the Vote," *American Sociological Review* 23 (1958): 171–179; Daniel Katz and Samuel J. Eldersveld, "The Impact of Local Party Activity upon the Electorate," *Public Opinion Quarterly* 25 (1961): 1–24; and Raymond E. Wolfinger, "The Influence of Precinct Work on Voting Behavior," *Public Opinion Quarterly* 27 (1963): 387–398.

40. Samuel J. Eldersveld, "Experimental Propaganda Techniques and Voting Behavior," *American Political Science Review* 50 (1956): 154–165; and John C. Blydenburg, "A Controlled Experiment to Measure the Effects of Personal Contact Campaigning," *Midwest Journal of Political Science* 15 (1971): 365–381.

41. Gerald H. Kramer, "The Effects of Precinct-Level Canvassing on Voter Behavior," *Public Opinion Quarterly* 34 (1970): 560–572; and William J. Crotty, "Party Effort and Its Impact on the Vote," *American Political Science Review* 65 (1971): 439–450.

42. John P. Frendreis, James L. Gibson, and Laura L. Vertz, "The Electoral Relevance of Local Party Organizations," *American Political Science Review* 84 (1990): 225–235.

43. Such skepticism, for example, is expressed by A. James Reichley in *The Life of the Parties* (New York: The Free Press, 1992), pp. 377–381.

44. An excellent account of these developments is provided by Paul S. Herrnson, *Party Campaigning in the 1980s* (Cambridge, MA: Harvard University Press, 1988). See also Paul Allen Beck, Russell J. Dalton, Audrey Haynes, and Robert Huckfeldt, "Party Effort at the Grass Roots," paper delivered at the Annual Meeting of the Midwest Political Science Association, Chicago, 1994.

45. Soft money refers to contributions to the national parties that would be illegal under federal law if they stayed at the national level. Acting under the aegis of a 1979 amendment

to the federal campaign-finance laws, the parties have been able to make these contributions legal by passing them on to the states for party-building and voter mobilization activities. See Frank J. Sorauf, *Inside Campaign Finance* (New Haven, CT: Yale University Press, 1992), pp. 146–152.

CHAPTER 12

1. George Thayer, *Who Shakes the Money Tree?* (New York: Simon and Schuster, 1973), p. 25.
2. An excellent study of modern campaign finance is Frank J. Sorauf *Inside Campaign Finance: Myths and Realities* (New Haven, CT: Yale University Press, 1992). The standard accounts of campaign finance before modern times are Louise Overacker, *Money in Elections* (New York: Macmillan, 1932) and *Presidential Campaign Funds* (Boston: Boston University Press, 1944); and Alexander Heard, *The Costs of Democracy* (Chapel Hill: The University of North Carolina Press, 1960). Estimates of presidential campaign spending as early as 1860 may be found in Erik W. Austin, *Political Facts of the United States since 1789* (New York: Columbia University Press, 1987), Table 3.9.
3. Studies by Herbert Alexander and colleagues are: *Financing the 1960 Election* (Princeton, NJ: Citizens' Research Foundation, 1962); *Financing the 1964 Election* (Princeton, NJ: Citizens' Research Foundation, 1966); *Financing the 1968 Election* (Lexington, MA: Heath, 1971); *Financing the 1972 Election* (Lexington, MA: Heath, 1976); *Financing the 1976 Election* (Washington, DC: Congressional Quarterly, Inc., 1979); *Financing the 1980 Election* (Lexington, MA: Heath, 1983); (with Brian A. Haggerty) *Financing the 1984 Election* (Lexington, MA: Heath, 1987); (with Monica Bauer) *Financing the 1988 Election* (Boulder, CO: Westview Press, 1991); (with Anthony Corrado) *Financing the 1992 Election* (Armonk, NY: M.E. Sharpe, 1995), and John C. Green, ed., *Financing the 1996 Election* (Armonk, NY: M.E. Sharpe, 1999).
4. This table omits some of the spending on congressional elections. While most of the money spent by parties' congressional campaign committees goes directly to the candidates and is therefore reflected in their totals, these committees also make so-called coordinated expenditures for a number of campaigns. In addition, much smaller amounts are spent independently by political action committees or individuals for or against particular candidates and on communication expenditures.
5. The state and local totals can be estimated fairly precisely (except for the spending mentioned in note 4 above) by subtracting the presidential expenditures in Table 12.2 and the congressional expenditures in Table 12.3 from the overall totals in Table 12.1.
6. The Willie Horton commercials discussed in Chapter 11 are examples of independent expenditures. They were paid for by a politcal action committee that was, technically speaking, independent of the Buch campaign and the Republican Party and did not count against the Bush campaign expenditure limit. Constitutional protection for such independent expenditures was provided by the United States Supreme Court in *Buckley v. Valeo*, 424 U.S. 1 (1976).
7. For more on 1996 presidential campaign finance, see Anthony Corrado, "Financing the 1996 Elections," in Gerald M. Pomper, et al., eds., *The Election of 1996* (Chatham, NJ: Chatham House, 1997), pp. 135–171, and Green, *Financing the 1996 Election*. Specific spending figures cited in the text come from Green and from FEC reports.
8. Just because money is spent "by" the campaign does not mean that it is spent "on" the campaign itself. Campaigns have a number of expenses beyond those meant to persuade voters to support their candidate. On this point, see Stephen Ansolabehere and Alan Gerber, "The Mismeasure of Campaign Spending: Evidence from the 1990 U.S. House Elections," *Journal of Politics* 56 (1994): 1106–1118.

9. The spending figures come from the FEC; see http://www.fec.gov/press/ptyye1.htm. For more on recent congressional campaign spending, see Green, *Financing the 1996 Election*; and Paul S. Herrnson, *Congressional Elections: Campaigning at Home and in Washington*, 2nd ed. (Washington, DC: CQ Press, 1998).

10. The figures for the Dallas race are reported in the *New York Times,* April 4, 1987; for the 1990 California gubernatorial race, in the *New York Times,* October 14, 1990; and for the California house races, in Frank J. Sorauf, *Inside Campaign Finance,* p. 36.

11. These differing conclusions are well represented in an exchange in the *American Journal of Political Science.* See Donald Philip Green and Jonathan S. Krasno, "Salvation for the Spendthrift Incumbent: Reestimating the Effects of Campaign Spending in House Elections," 32 (1988): 884–907; Gary C. Jacobson, "The Effects of Campaign Spending in House Elections: New Evidence for Old Arguments," 34 (1990): 334–362; and Donald Philip Green and Jonathan S. Krasno, "Rebuttal to Jacobson's 'New Evidence for Old Arguments,'" 34 (1990): 363–372.

12. See Philip D. Duncan, "Incumbent in the Cross Hairs," *Campaigns & Elections* (1999), on the Internet at http://www.camelect.com.

13. For a discussion of campaign spending in the states, see Ruth S. Jones, "State Election Campaign Financing: 1980," in Michael J. Malbin, ed., *Money and Politics in the United States* (Chatham, NJ: Chatham House, 1984), pp. 172–213; and Frank J. Sorauf, *Money in American Elections* (Glenview, IL: Scott, Foresman, 1988), Chap. 9.

14. On Hanna, see Thayer, *Who Shakes the Money Tree?,* pp. 48–52; the quotation is taken from pp. 49–50. For a discussion of campaign finance in the 1972 election, see Thayer, *Who Shakes the Money Tree?,* pp. 108–16; and Michael J. Malbin, "Looking Back at the Future of Campaign Finance Reform," in Malbin, *Money and Politics in the United States*, pp. 245–47. The discussion of Richard Viguerie is based on Nick Kotz, "King Midas of 'The New Right'," *The Atlantic* 242 (1978): 52–61.

15. Ruth S. Jones and Warren E. Miller, "Financing Campaigns: Macro Level Information and Micro Level Response," *Western Political Quarterly* 38 (1985), 187–210.

16. The contribution figures come from the files of the Federal Election Commission as reported in http://www.opensecrets.org.

17. On soft-money contributions in the 1996 campaign, see Corrado, "Financing the 1996 Elections."

18. The figures are for the number of PACs registered at the federal level and come from the end-of-year reports of the Federal Election Commission, typically dated in early January.

19. For a more extensive discussion of the role of PACs in campaign financing, see Sorauf, *Inside Campaign Finance,* Chap. 4. See also Larry J. Sabato, *PAC Power: Inside the World of Political Action Committees* (New York: Norton, 1984).

20. The conclusion that PAC contributions do not influence voting is reached by, among others, Janet M. Grenzke, "Shopping in the Congressional Supermarket: The Currency Is Complex," *American Journal of Political Science* 33 (1989): 1–24; and John R. Wright, "PACs, Contributions, and Roll Calls: An Organizational Perspective," *American Political Science Review* 79 (1985): 400–414. A good summary of the studies on the effects of campaign contributions may be found in Sorauf, *Inside Campaign Finance,* Chap. 6.

21. On access, see Laura I. Langbein, "Money and Access: Some Empirical Evidence," *Journal of Politics* 48 (1986): 1052–1064. On committee involvement, see Richard L. Hall and Frank W. Wayman, "Buying Time: Moneyed Interests and the Mobilization of Bias in Congressional Committees," *American Political Science Review* 84 (1990): 797–820.

22. Wright, "PACs, Contributions, and Roll Calls."

23. On the state experience with public funding, see Ruth S. Jones, "State Public Campaign Finance: Implications for Partisan Politics," *American Journal of Political Science* 25 (1981):

342–361; and Jack L. Noragon, "Political Finance and Political Reform: The Experience with State Income Tax Checkoffs," *American Political Science Review* 75 (1981): 667–687.

24. The figures come from William E. Cassie, Joel A. Thompson, and Malcolm E. Jewell, "The Pattern of PAC Contributions in Legislative Elections: An Eleven State Analysis," paper delivered at the Annual Meeting of the American Political Science Association, Chicago, 1992.

25. For a general review of state campaign financing, see Malcolm E. Jewell and David M. Olson, *Political Parties and Elections in American States* (Chicago: Dorsey, 1988), pp. 154–173. On the regulation of PAC contributions in the states, see Arnold Fleischmann and David C. Nice, "States and PACs: The Legacy of Established Decision Rules," *Political Behavior* 10 (1988): 349–363. On legislative caucus and leadership funds in the states, see Anthony Gierzynski, *Legislative Party Campaign Committees in the American States* (Lexington: University of Kentucky Press, 1992).

26. Good accounts of federal campaign finance reform legislation may be found in Sorauf, *Inside Campaign Finance,* Chap. 7; and Robert E. Mutch, *Campaigns, Congress, and the Courts* (New York: Praeger, 1988).

27. *Buckley v. Valeo,* 424 U.S. 1 (1976).

28. Particularly useful treatments of the effects of campaign finance reforms on the parties can be found in F. Christopher Arterton, "Political Money and Party Strength," in Joel L. Fleishman, ed., *The Future of American Political Parties* (Englewood Cliffs, NJ: Prentice-Hall, 1982), pp. 101–139; and Sorauf, *Inside Campaign Finance,* Chap. 7.

29. The data on state campaign finance provisions are drawn from Harold W. Stanley and Richard G. Niemi, *Vital Statistics on American Politics, 1999–2000* (Washington, D C: CQ Press, 2000), Tables 2.2 and 2.3, pp. 84 –87.

30. Some of the most interesting proposals for campaign finance reform include reduced broadcast and postal rates for candidates, free broadcast time for parties to be used by their candidates, and exemptions from spending limits for some part of the contributions from the candidate's home state. They were key recommendations in a 1990 report of the Campaign Finance Reform Panel established by Democratic and Republican party leaders of the U.S. Senate. This report and subsequent proposals by party leaders have not led to any changes in campaign finance laws so far. For additional proposals for reform, see Green, *Financing the 1996 Campaign.*

PART 5

1. See John F. Hoadley, "The Emergence of Political Parties in Congress, 1789–1803," *American Political Science Review* 74 (1980): 757–779.

2. E. E. Schattschneider, *Party Government* (New York: Rinehart, 1942), pp. 131–132.

3. See the report of the Committee on Responsible Parties of the American Political Science Association, *Toward a More Responsible Two-Party System* (New York: Rinehart, 1950). The report also appears as a supplement to the September 1950 issue of the *American Political Science Review.*

4. Ian Budge and Richard I. Hofferbert, "Mandates and Policy Outputs: U.S. Party Platforms and Federal Expenditures," *American Political Science Review* 84 (1990): 111–131. See also the discussion of this approach by Budge, Hofferbert, and others in "Party Platforms, Mandates, and Government Spending," *American Political Science Review* 87 (1993): 744–750.

CHAPTER 13

1. The Nebraska legislature is chosen in nonpartisan elections, although the partisan affiliations of its members are usually no secret. Of the 7,376 legislators in the remaining states and the 535 members of Congress, only eighteen were neither Democrats nor Republi-

cans in 1998–1999, according to the *Book of the States* (Lexington, KY: Council of State Governments, 1998–1999).

2. The view of leadership power as authority *delegated* to leaders by the party caucus is one of the cornerstones of the principal-agent conceptualization of Congress. In this view, the majority party is the principal, and its power to make policy is delegated to agents such as the leadership, the committees, the president, and even the bureaucracy. The effectiveness of the majority party lies less in how much authority is delegated, for delegation is necessary in modern governments, and more in how well delegation helps the congressional party to carry out its policy goals. For a clear articulation of this view and a compelling argument that the congressional party has delegated much better than is commonly supposed when it comes to the appropriations process, see D. Roderick Kiewiet and Mathew D. McCubbins, *The Logic of Delegation: Congressional Parties and the Appropriations Process* (Chicago: University of Chicago Press, 1991).

3. See Joseph Cooper and David W. Brady, "Institutional Context and Leadership Style: The House from Cannon to Rayburn," *American Political Science Review* 75 (1981): 411–425.

4. On the Democratic Study Group, see Arthur G. Stevens, Arthur H. Miller, and Thomas E. Mann, "Mobilization of Liberal Strength in the House, 1955–1970: The Democratic Study Group," *American Political Science Review* 68 (1974): 667–681. For more on the reforms, see Leroy N. Rieselbach, *Congressional Reform: The Changing Modern Congress* (Washington, DC: CQ Press, 1994).

5. For a list of the cases between 1947 and 1988 when the Congress violated seniority in allocating committee positions, see Gary W. Cox and Mathew W. McCubbins, *Legislative Leviathan: Party Government in the House* (Berkeley and Los Angeles: University of California Press, 1993), pp. 279–282. Once a few committee chairs had been stripped of their positions in 1975, the surviving chairs tended to become more solicitous of their committee and party colleagues. One study finds that the reforms increased party loyalty in roll-call voting among House Democrats who chaired committees or subcommittees or who were next in line to be a chair. See Sara Brandes Crook and John R. Hibbing, "Congressional Reform and Party Discipline: The Effects of Changes in the Seniority System on Party Loyalty in the U.S. House of Representatives," *British Journal of Political Science* 15 (1985): 207–226.

6. On this point, see Steven S. Smith, "New Patterns of Decisionmaking in Congress," in John E. Chubb and Paul E. Peterson, eds., *The New Direction in American Politics* (Washington, DC: Brookings, 1985), pp. 203–233.

7. There is a rich literature on party leadership in Congress. Among the best works are Ralph K. Huitt, "Democratic Party Leadership in the Senate," *American Political Science Review* 55 (1961): 333–344; Charles O. Jones, *The Minority Party in Congress* (Boston: Little, Brown, 1970); Robert L. Peabody, *Leadership in Congress* (Boston: Little, Brown, 1976); Barbara Sinclair, *Majority Leadership in the U.S. House* (Baltimore: John Hopkins University Press, 1983); David W. Rohde, *Parties and Leaders in the Postreform House* (Chicago: University of Chicago Press, 1991)*;* and Barbara Sinclair, "The Emergence of Strong Leadership in the 1980s House of Representatives," *Journal of Politics* 54 (1992): 657–684.

8. This account of how the reforms provided the conditions under which more ideologically homogeneous congressional parties would support stronger leadership and in turn be more cohesive draws heavily from Rohde, *Parties and Leaders in the Postreform House.* Also see Barbara Sinclair, *Legislators, Leaders, and Lawmaking: The U.S. House of Representatives in the Postreform Era* (Baltimore, MD: Johns Hopkins University Press, 1995).

9. On Wright, see Rohde, *Party and Leaders in the Postreform House,* pp. 105–118; and Barbara Sinclair, "House Majority Party Leadership in the Late 1980s," in Lawrence C. Dodd

and Bruce I. Oppenheimer, eds., *Congress Reconsidered* (Washington, DC: CQ Press, 1989), pp. 307–330. On the transition in styles from Wright to Foley, see Rohde, *Party Leaders in the Postreform House,* pp. 184–189.

10. That the activity of Congress is organized around the election needs of its members is a view powerfully articulated in David R. Mayhew, *Congress: The Electoral Connection* (New Haven, CT: Yale University Press, 1974).

11. On the activities of legislative leadership campaign committees, see Anthony Gierzynski, *Legislative Party Campaign Committees in the American States* (Lexington, KY: University of Kentucky Press, 1992); and Daniel M. Shea, *Transforming Democracy: Legislative Campaign Committees and Political Parties* (Albany, NY: State University of New York Press, 1995).

12. Malcolm E. Jewell and David M. Olson, *Political Parties and Elections in American States* (Chicago: Dorsey, 1988), pp. 235–244.

13. For more on parties and party leadership in state legislatures, see Keith E. Hamm and Robert Harmel, "Legislative Party Development and the Speaker System: The Case of the Texas House," *Journal of Politics* 55 (1993): 1140–1151; and Malcolm E. Jewell and Marcia Lynn Whicker, *Legislative Leadership in the American States* (Ann Arbor, MI: University of Michigan Press, 1994).

14. See Barbara Sinclair, "Majority Party Leadership Strategies for Coping with the New U.S. House," *Legislative Studies Quarterly* 6 (1981): 391–414. On the favors leaders can bestow, see Roger Davidson, "Senate Leaders: Janitors for an Untidy Chamber?" In Dodd and Oppenheimer, eds., *Congress Reconsidered*, pp. 225–252. On leaders' control of the floor through the Rules Committee and other devices, see Steven Smith, *Call to Order: Floor Politics in the House and the Senate* (Washington, DC: Brookings Institution, 1989).

15. The rise of seniority as a principle for allocating committee positions in the House of Representatives can be traced to the period around the turn of the twentieth century, when House members became more likely to spend a long career in the chamber, and especially to the weakening of the Speaker after 1911. See Nelson W. Polsby, Miriam Gallaher, and Barry Spencer Rundquist, "The Growth of the Seniority System in the U.S. House of Representatives," *American Political Science Review* 68 (1969): 787–807.

16. Eric M. Uslaner and Ronald E. Weber, *Patterns of Decision Making in State Legislatures* (New York: Praeger, 1977).

17. This discussion draws upon Jackie Koszczuk, "Gingrich Puts More Power Into Speaker's Hands," *Congressional Quarterly Weekly Report,* 53 (October 7, 1995): 3049–3053, and on updated analysis by Leroy Rieselbach.

18. Membership turnover in state legislatures varies considerably across the states. From one session to the next in 1990 and 1992, upper-house turnover ranged from a low of 4 percent in Maryland and Pennsylvania to a high of 70 percent in Alaska; average turnover was 29 percent. Lower-house turnover varied between a low of 2 percent in Alabama to a high of 58 percent in Alaska during the same period, with an average of 31 percent.

19. Party influence in the states should not be exaggerated, however. In one survey, state legislators were asked who made the most significant legislative decisions. A majority cited the party leadership in sixty-seven of ninety-nine legislative chambers, and the party caucus was important in fifty chambers, but committees were significant in eighty-seven. Of course, party leaders may have an indirect influence here, because the party leadership selects the committee chairs in many states. See Wayne L. Francis, "Leadership, Party Caucuses, and Committees in the U.S. State Legislatures," *Legislative Studies Quarterly* 10 (1985): 243–257.

20. Julius Turner, *Party and Constituency: Pressures on Congress,* rev. ed. by Edward V. Schneier (Baltimore, MD: The Johns Hopkins University Press, 1970), pp. 16–17.

21. The corresponding number of uncontested or "universalistic" votes, in which 90 percent of Congress votes the same way, conversely, increased steadily from the late 1940s to 1980. See Melissa P. Collie, "Universalism and the Parties in the U.S. House of Representatives," *American Journal of Political Science* 32 (1988): 865–883.

22. To even out this "session effect," the data in Figure 13.1 are averaged across the two sessions of each Congress. The downturn in party voting in the even years, when House members stand for reelection, is seen as early as the 1830s.

23. Institutionalization is the term Polsby uses to characterize the development of a professionalized Congress with greater specialization of party and committee roles, established norms, deference to congressional experience, and greater longevity in office; see Nelson W. Polsby, "The Institutionalization of the United States House of Representatives," *American Political Science Review* 62 (1968): 144–168. By disaggregation, Burnham means a decline in the party-based linkage among candidates for various offices. Walter Dean Burnham, *Critical Elections and the Mainsprings of American Politics* (New York: Norton, 1970), pp. 91–134.

24. Samuel C. Patterson and Gregory A. Caldeira, "Party Voting in the United States Congress," *British Journal of Political Science* 18 (1988): 111–131.

25. On party voting in state legislatures, see Jewell and Olson, *Political Parties and Elections,* pp. 246–249. Data on party voting and cohesion in selected state legislatures from 1959 to 1974 are provided by Malcolm E. Jewell and Samuel C. Patterson, *The Legislative Process in the United States* (New York: Random House, 1977), pp. 384–385. For data on South Carolina, see Cole Blease Graham, Jr., and Kenny J. Whitby, "Party-Based Voting in a Southern State Legislature," *American Politics Quarterly* 17 (1989): 181–193.

26. Rohde, *Parties and Leaders in the Postreform House,* especially Chap. 3. On changes in the South, also see Franklin D. Gilliam, Jr., and Kenny Whitby, "A Longitudinal Analysis of Competing Explanations for the Transformation of Southern Politics," *Journal of Politics* 53 (1991): 504–518, and M. V. Hood III, Quentin Kidd, and Irwin L. Morris, "Of Byrd[s] and Bumpers: Using Democratic Senators to Analyze Political Change in the South, 1960–1995," *American Journal of Political Science* 43 (1999): 465–487.

27. For more on variations in presidential support in Congress, see Jon R. Bond and Richard Fleisher, *The President in the Legislative Arena* (Chicago: University of Chicago Press, 1990); Mark A. Peterson, *Legislating Together: The White House and Capitol Hill from Eisenhower to Reagan* (Cambridge, MA: Harvard University Press, 1990); and Cary R. Covington, J. Mark Wrighton, and Rhonda Kinney, "A 'Presidency-Augmented' Model of Presidential Success on House Roll Call Votes," *American Journal of Political Science* 39 (November, 1995): 1001–1024.

28. See Aage Clausen, *How Congressmen Decide* (New York: St. Martin's, 1973); and James M. Snyder, Jr., and Tim Groseclose, "Estimating Party Influence in Congressional Roll-Call Voting," *American Journal of Political Science* 44 (2000): 187–205. Political ideology also provides a powerful explanation of legislators' votes; some scholars have argued that it can account for most voting behavior in Congress. See Keith T. Poole, "Recent Developments in Analytical Models of Voting in the U.S. Congress," *Legislative Studies Quarterly* 13 (1988): 117–133; and Jerrold Schneider, *Ideological Coalitions in Congress* (Westport, CT: Greenwood Press, 1979).

29. This theme underlies such diverse historical studies of party voting in the House of Representatives as Jerome M. Clubb and Santa A. Traugott, "Partisan Cleavage and Cohesion in the House of Representatives, 1861–1974," *Journal of Interdisciplinary History* 7 (1977): 374–401; David W. Brady and Philip Althoff, "Party Voting in the U.S. House of Representatives, 1890–1910: Elements of a Responsible Party System," *Journal of Politics* 36 (1974): 752–775; and Barbara Sinclair, "Party Realignment and the Transforma-

tion of the Political Agenda: The House of Representatives, 1925–1938," *American Political Science Review* 71 (1977): 940–953.

30. David W. Brady, "A Reevaluation of Realignments in American Politics: Evidence from the House of Representatives," *American Political Science Review* 79 (1985): 28–49; and *Critical Elections and Congressional Policy Making* (Stanford, CA: Stanford University Press, 1988).

31. Paul Allen Beck, "The Electoral Cycle and Patterns of American Politics," *British Journal of Political Science* 9 (1979): 129–156.

32. Warren E. Miller and Donald E. Stokes, "Constituency Influence in Congress," *American Political Science Review* 57 (1963): 45–57.

33. Cox and McCubbins, *Legislative Leviathan,* see the majority party as the prime actor in the House of Representatives. Other key works are Kiewiet and McCubbins, *The Logic of Delegation;* Rohde, *Parties and Leaders in the Postreform House;* and Sinclair, *Legislators, Leaders, and Lawmaking.*

34. U.S. Representative David E. Price offers a valuable insider's perspective on the role of party in Congress; see Price, *The Congressional Experience* (Boulder, CO: Westview, 1992).

35. Studies of legislative party voting in Britain and Canada suggest the parliamentary form is the main reason for the greater party discipline there than in the United States. On Britain, see Austin Ranney, "Candidate Selection and Party Cohesion in Britain and the U.S.," in William J. Crotty, ed., *Approaches to the Study of Party Organization* (Boston: Allyn and Bacon, 1968), pp. 139–168; and Gary Cox, *The Efficient Secret* (New York: Cambridge University Press, 1987). On Canada, see Leon D. Epstein, "A Comparative Study of Canadian Parties," *American Political Science Review* 58 (1964): 46–59; and Allan Kornberg, "Caucus and Cohesion in Canadian Parliamentary Parties," *American Political Science Review* 60 (1966): 83–92.

36. Even the *Contract with America* was created only by House Republicans, especially party leaders Newt Gingrich and Dick Armey, and not by the Republican Party organization, the Republican National Convention, or even Republican senators.

CHAPTER 14

1. In the landmark *Marbury* case, Federalist Chief Justice Marshall refrained from ordering the new Jefferson administration to deliver a commission to Marbury that had been approved by the previous Federalist administration. In so doing, though, he claimed for the Supreme Court the power to judge congressional actions as to their constitutionality and used this power to rule that Congress had (wrongly) authorized the Supreme Court to exercise powers denied to it by the Constitution. This case is regarded as the key precedent for the Court's power of judicial review. See *Marbury v. Madison* 1 Cranch 137 (1803).

2. See Clive Bean and Anthony Mughan, "Leadership Effects in Parliamentary Elections in Australia and Britain," *American Political Science Review* 83 (1989): 1165–1180.

3. Dwight D. Eisenhower was long considered one such president, but Fred I. Greenstein finds persuasive evidence that President Eisenhower's public avoidance of partisan politics masked, in his characteristic "hidden hand" fashion, an abiding sense of partisanship and a commitment to strengthening the Republican party. See his "Eisenhower as an Activist President: A Look at New Evidence," *Political Science Quarterly* 94 (1979–1980): 575–599, as well as his *The Hidden-Hand Presidency: Eisenhower as Leader* (New York: Basic Books, 1982). Also see Cornelius P. Cotter, "Eisenhower as Party Leader," *Political Science Quarterly* 98 (1983): 255–283.

4. Franklin Roosevelt is considered the consummate party leader as president in the twentieth century. For a comprehensive study of him in this role, see Sean J. Savage, *Roosevelt:*

The Party Leader, 1932–1945 (Lexington: University Press of Kentucky, 1991). On the legacy Roosevelt left and how subsequent presidents have tried to use it, see Sidney M. Milkis, *The President and the Parties* (New York: Oxford University Press, 1993).

5. Roger G. Brown, "Party and Bureaucracy: From Kennedy to Reagan," *Political Science Quarterly* 97 (1982): 279–294.

6. On presidential coattails in U.S. House elections, see Randall L. Calvert and John A. Ferejohn, "Coattail Voting in Recent Presidential Elections," *American Political Science Review* 77 (1983): 407–419; John A. Ferejohn and Randall L. Calvert, "Presidential Coattails in Historical Perspective," *American Journal of Political Science* 28 (1984): 127–146; Richard Born, "Reassessing the Decline of Presidential Coattails: U.S. House Elections from 1952–80," *Journal of Politics* 46 (1984): 60–79; and James E. Campbell, "Predicting Seat Gains from Presidential Coattails," *American Journal of Political Science* 30 (1986): 164–183.

7. See James E. Campbell, "Presidential Coattails and Midterm Losses in State Legislative Elections," *American Political Science Review* 80 (1986): 45–63; and James E. Campbell and Joe A. Sumners, "Presidential Coattails in Senate Elections," *American Political Science Review* 84 (1990): 512–524. The first Campbell study finds evidence of gubernatorial coattails as well.

8. This view that midterm congressional contests are in part a referendum on presidential performance was initially offered by Edward R. Tufte, "Determinants of the Outcomes of Midterm Congressional Elections," *American Political Science Review* 69 (1975): 812–826; and *Political Control of the Economy* (Princeton, NJ: Princeton University Press, 1978), Chap. 5. Even more persuasive evidence of the relationship between presidential approval and midterm congressional outcomes may be found in Robin F. Marra and Charles W. Ostrom, Jr., "Explaining Seat Change in the U.S. House of Representatives, 1950–86," *American Journal of Political Science* 33 (1989): 541–569.

9. Angus Campbell attributed this phenomenon to the absence in midterm elections of the short-term forces that had favored the president two years earlier. This in turn led to declines in turnout among those without strong partisan loyalties. See his "Surge and Decline: A Study of Electoral Change," in Angus Campbell, Philip E. Converse, Warren E. Miller, and Donald E. Stokes, eds., *Elections and the Political Order* (New York: Wiley, 1966), pp. 40–62.

10. An attractive "strategic politicians" explanation for this relationship has been offered by Gary Jacobson. Rather than voters explicitly linking presidents to legislators, the Jacobson thesis is that presidential popularity and other factors impinging upon the standing of the party determine the quality of candidates (especially challengers) in the president's party which, in turn, affects outcomes in the fall election. See his "Strategic Politicians and the Dynamics of U.S. House Elections, 1946–86," *American Political Science Review* 83 (1989): 773–793.

11. This translation of votes into seats, called the "swing ratio," is calculated by Edward R. Tufte in "The Relationship between Seats and Votes in Two-Party Systems," *American Political Science Review* 67 (1973): 540–554. The swing ratio declined sharply to a low of 0.71 in 1966–1970 and may have stayed around that level since, which means that only 0.71 percent of 435 seats (or three seats) changed hands for each 1 percent vote change.

12. Samuel Kernell, "Presidential Popularity and Negative Voting: An Alternative Explanation of the Midterm Congressional Decline of the President's Party," *American Political Science Review* 71 (1977): 44–66. The negative voting thesis, though, has been challenged by Richard Born, who concludes that it is the return of presidential defectors to their home party and not negative voting that accounts for the presidential party's loss of seats at midterm. See his "Surge and Decline, Negative Voting, and the Midterm Loss Phenomenon: A Simultaneous Choice Analysis," *American Journal of Political Science* 34 (1990): 615–645.

13. On the role of the governor in party leadership, see Alan Rosenthal, *Governors and Legislatures: Contending Powers* (Washington, DC: CQ Press, 1990).

14. In addition to the data in Figure 14.1, see George C. Edwards III, "Measuring Presidential Success in Congress: Alternative Approaches," *Journal of Politics* 47 (1985): 667–685.

15. See Bruce Cain, John Ferejohn, and Morris Fiorina, *The Personal Vote: Constituency Service and Electoral Independence* (Cambridge, MA: Harvard University Press, 1987).

16. In *The End of Liberalism: The Second Republic of the United States* (New York: Norton, 1979), Theodore J. Lowi criticized Congress for delegating so much authority to the executive branch bureacracy that they have compromised the democratic nature of the American political system. In their *The Logic of Delegation: Congressional Parties and the Appropriations Process* (Chicago: University of Chicago Press, 1991), D. Roderick Kiewiet and Mathew D. McCubbins have defended these large grants of discretion by congressional "principals" to bureaucratic "agents" as reasonable and controllable exercises of majority party power. Whether bureaucratic discretion is too large or about right, there is no question that it is considerable in the American system—or, for that matter, any modern government.

17. In his *Building a New American State* (Cambridge, U.K.: Cambridge University Press, 1982), Stephen Skowronek shows how a federal regime dominated by political parties (through Congress and patronage) and the courts turned into government by a professional bureaucracy around the turn of the twentieth century. This change has made the executive branch bureaucracy less responsive to the political parties per se but probably more responsive to the president.

18. Hugh Heclo, "Issue Networks and the Executive Establishment," in Anthony King, ed., *The New American Political System* (Washington, DC: American Enterprise Institute, 1979), pp. 87–124.

19. Dean E. Mann, *The Assistant Secretaries* (Washington, DC: Brookings Institution, 1965); and Brown, "Party and Bureaucracy."

20. Hugh Heclo, *A Government of Strangers: Executive Politics in Washington* (Washington, DC: Brookings Institution, 1977).

21. See Terry M. Moe, "The Politicized Presidency," in John E. Chubb and Paul E. Peterson, eds., *The New Direction in American Politics* (Washington, DC: Brookings Institution, 1985), pp. 235–271.

22. Joel Aberbach and Bert A. Rockman, "Clashing Beliefs Within the Executive Branch: The Nixon Administration Bureaucracy," *American Political Science Review* 70 (1976): 456–468.

23. Joel D. Aberbach and Bert A. Rockman, "The Political Views of U.S. Senior Federal Executives, 1970–1992," *Journal of Politics* 57 (1995): 838–852. For a similar report through 1987, see Joel D. Aberbach and Bert A. Rockman with Robert M. Copeland, "From Nixon's *Problem* to Reagan's *Achievement*: The Federal Executive Reexamined," in Larry Berman, ed., *Looking Back on the Reagan Presidency* (Baltimore, MD: Johns Hopkins University Press, 1990), pp. 175–194.

24. See Sidney Ulmer, "The Political Party Variable on the Michigan Supreme Court," *Journal of Public Law* 11 (1962): 352–362; Stuart Nagel, "Political Party Affiliation and Judges' Decisions," *American Political Science Review* 55 (1961): 843–850; Glendon A. Schubert, *Quantitative Analysis of Judicial Behavior* (Glencoe, IL: Free Press, 1959), pp. 129–142; and David W. Adamany, "The Party Variable in Judges' Voting: Conceptual Notes and a Case Study," *American Political Science Review* 63 (1969): 57–73. For a review of party influence in the federal courts, see Robert A. Carp and Ronald Stidham, *The Federal Courts* (Washington, DC: CQ Press, 1985), pp. 142–148.

25. See Randall D. Lloyd, "Separating Partisanship from Party in Judicial Research: Reapportionment in the U.S. District Courts," *American Political Science Review* 89 (1995): 413–420.

26. On judicial patronage, see Herbert Jacob, *Justice in America* (Boston: Little, Brown, 1965), pp. 87–89; and Martin and Susan Tolchin, *To the Victor ...: Political Patronage from Clubhouse to White House* (New York: Random House, 1971), pp. 131–186.

27. The Roosevelt letter is quoted more fully in Walter F. Murphy and C. Herman Pritchett, *Courts, Judges, and Politics* (New York: Random House, 1961), pp. 82–83.

28. Sheldon Goldman, "The Bush Imprint on the Judiciary: Carrying on a Tradition," *Judicature* 74 (1991), 294–306.

29. Sheldon Goldman, "Judicial Selection under Clinton: a midterm examination," *Judicature* 78 (1995): 276–291.

30. These data on judicial selection in the states come from the *Book of the States: 1996–1997* (Lexington, KY: Council of State Governments, 1996), pp. 133–135.

31. On the political effects of different state selection systems, see Henry R. Glick and Craig F. Emmert, "Selection Systems and Judicial Characteristics: The Recruitment of State Supreme Court Judges," *Judicature* 70 (1987), 228–235.

CHAPTER 15

1. Austin Ranney, *The Doctrine of Responsible Party Government* (Urbana: University of Illinois Press, 1962).

2. Committee on Political Parties of the American Political Science Association, *Toward a More Responsible Two-Party System* (New York: Rinehart, 1950).

3. The distinguished British observer of American politics, Lord Bryce, long ago made the same complaint about American parties. See James Bryce, *The American Commonwealth* (New York: Macmillan, 1916).

4. See Ranney, *The Doctrine of Responsible Party Government,* Chaps. 1 and 2, for an analysis of what party government presumes about democracy.

5. See the Committee on Political Parties, *Toward a More Responsible Two-Party System,* p. 15.

6. E. E. Schattschneider, *Party Government* (New York: Rinehart, 1942), p. 208.

7. This point is made in E. E. Schattschneider, *The Semi-Sovereign People* (New York: Holt, Rinehart, and Winston, 1960).

8. The literature critical of the concept of party responsibility is a large one. Pendleton Herring's *The Politics of Democracy* (New York: Rinehart, 1940) presented an early argument against the reformers. Also see Julius Turner, "Responsible Parties: A Dissent from the Floor," *American Political Science Review* 45 (1951): 143–152. An excellent evaluation of this debate is provided in APSA Committee on Political Parties member Evron Kirkpatrick's "Toward a More Responsible Two-Party System: Political Science, Policy Science, or Pseudo-Science?" *American Political Science Review* 65 (1971): 965–990. A discussion of responsible parties in the American context may be found in the various chapters of John Kenneth White and Jerome M. Mileur, eds., *Challenges to Party Government* (Carbondale and Edwardsville: Southern Illinois University Press, 1992).

9. See Leon D. Epstein, "A Comparative Study of Canadian Parties," *American Political Science Review* 58 (1964): 46–59; Leon D. Epstein, *Political Parties in Western Democracies* (New Brunswick, NJ: Transaction Books, 1980; originally published in 1967); and Austin Ranney, "Candidate Selection and Party Cohesion in Britain and the U.S.," in William J. Crotty, ed., *Approaches to the Study of Party Organization* (Boston: Allyn and Bacon, 1968), pp. 139–168.

10. Otto Kircheimer, "The Transformation of the Western European Party Systems," in Joseph LaPalombara and Myron Weiner, eds., *Political Parties and Political Development* (Princeton, NJ: Princeton University Press, 1966), pp. 184–192.

11. On the consensus among Americans on the basic principles of politics, see Louis Hartz, *The Liberal Tradition in America* (New York: Harcourt, Brace, 1955).

12. Ian Budge and Richard I. Hofferbert have demonstrated that, for the 1948–1985 period, important differences existed between the platforms of the two major American parties and the policies the parties enacted, as measured by federal expenditures when they controlled the presidency. See their "Mandates and Policy Outputs: U.S. Party Platforms and Federal Expenditures," *American Political Science Review* 84 (1990): 111–132.

13. On the importance of racial issues in the changing nature of the party coalitions among both voters and political leaders, see Edward G. Carmines and James A. Stimson, *Issue Evolution: Race and the Transformation of American Politics* (Princeton, NJ: Princeton University Press, 1989).

14. Leading examples of the view that the American public alternates between different ideological postures are Arthur M. Schlesinger, Jr., *The Cycles of American History* (Boston: Houghton Mifflin, 1986); and Samuel P. Huntington, *American Politics: The Promise of Disharmony* (Cambridge, MA: Harvard University Press, 1981.) For a more contemporary account based on systematic empirical analysis, see James A. Stimson, *Public Opinion: Moods, Cycles, and Swings* (Boulder, CO: Westview, 1991).

15. The seminal study, based on surveys conducted in 1956, 1958, and 1960, is Philip E. Converse, "The Nature of Belief Systems in Mass Publics," in David Apter, ed., *Ideology and Discontent* (New York: Free Press, 1964), pp. 206–261. For subsequent years, see Norman H. Nie, Sidney Verba, and John R. Petrocik, *The Changing American Voter* (Cambridge, MA: Harvard University Press, 1976), Chaps. 7–9; Philip E. Converse, "Public Opinion and Voting Behavior," in Fred I. Greenstein and Nelson W. Polsby, eds., *Handbook of Political Science,* Vol. 4 (Reading, MA: Addison-Wesley, 1975); and John L. Sullivan, James E. Piereson, and George E. Marcus, "Ideological Constraint in the Mass Public: A Methodological Critique and Some New Findings," *American Journal of Political Science* 23 (1978): 233–249.

16. The survey results come from CBS News's "Millennium Poll," December, 1999, available from the Interuniversity Consortium for Political and Social Research. The quotations can be found in Angus Campbell, Philip E. Converse, Warren E. Miller, and Donald E. Stokes, *The American Voter* (New York: John Wiley & Sons, 1960), 232–233. On ideological self-identification, see Pamela Conover and Stanley Feldman, "The Origins and Meaning of Liberal/Conservative Self-Identification," *American Journal of Political Science* 25 (1981): 617–645. On its relationship to positions on issues, see Lloyd A. Free and Hadley Cantril, *The Political Beliefs of Americans: A Study of Public Opinion* (New Brunswick, NJ: Rutgers University Press, 1968).

17. See Thomas Ferguson and Joel Rogers, *Right Turn: The Decline of the Democrats and the Future of American Politics* (New York: Hill and Wang, 1986), especially Chap. 1; Paul R. Abramson, John H. Aldrich, and David W. Rohde, *Change and Continuity in the 1988 Elections* (Washington, DC: CQ Press, 1989), Chap. 6; and Abramson, Aldrich, and Rohde, *Change and Continuity in the 1992 Elections* (Washington, DC: CQ Press, 1995), Chaps. 6 and 7.

18. For evidence on the ideological nature of the electorate in political systems with more responsible parties, see David Butler and Donald Stokes, *Political Change in Britain* (New York: St. Martin's, 1969), Chap. 9; and Philip E. Converse and Roy Pierce, *Political Representation in France* (Cambridge, MA: Harvard University Press, 1986), Chap. 4.

19. See Herbert McClosky, Paul J. Hoffman, and Rosemary O'Hara, "Issue Conflict and Consensus among Party Leaders and Followers," *American Political Science Review* 54 (1960): 406–427; Jeane Kirkpatrick, "Representation in the American National Conventions: The Case of 1972," *British Journal of Political Science* 5 (1975): 265–322; Robert S. Montjoy,

William R. Shaffer, and Ronald E. Weber, "Policy Preferences of Party Elites and Masses: Conflict or Consensus?" *American Politics Quarterly* 8 (1980): 319–344; John S. Jackson III, Barbara L. Brown, and David Bositis, "Herbert McClosky and Friends Revisited: 1980 Democratic and Republican Party Elites Compared to the Mass Public," *American Politics Quarterly* 10 (1982): 158–180; Warren E. Miller and M. Kent Jennings, *Parties in Transition* (New York: Russell Sage Foundation, 1986), pp. 189–219; and Denise L. Baer and David A. Bositis, *Elite Cadres and Party Coalitions* (New York: Greenwood Press, 1988), pp. 100–107. Evidence that party activists have become even more polarized ideologically is found in John M. Bruce, John A. Clark, and John H. Kessel, "Advocacy Politics in Presidential Parties," *American Political Science Review* 85 (1991): 1089–1105.

20. On the use of ambiguity as a political strategy, see Benjamin Page, *Choices and Echoes in Presidential Elections* (Chicago: University of Chicago Press, 1978).

21. The tendency for candidates seeking office in the general elections to converge on the center in a two-party system is given theoretical expression in Anthony Downs, *An Economic Theory of Democracy* (New York: Harper & Row, 1957). Rebecca B. Morton has shown that ideological candidates and parties will still diverge to some degree in spite of the pressures to converge; see her "Incomplete Information and Ideological Explanations of Platform Divergence," *American Political Science Review* 87 (1993): 382–392.

22. David Nice, "Ideological Stability and Change at the Presidential Nominating Conventions," *Journal of Politics* 42 (1980): 847–853; and Howard L. Reiter, "Party Factionalism: National Conventions in the New Era," *American Politics Quarterly* 8 (1980): 303–318.

23. For a discussion of the British responsible party model as an ideal and a reality, see Leon D. Epstein, "What Happened to the British Party Model?" *American Political Science Review* 74 (1980): 9–22.

24. This is largely the point V. O. Key makes in *The Responsible Electorate* (Cambridge, MA: Harvard University Press, 1966). Alternatively, retrospective policy-voting may be viewed from the Downsian perspective in which the past is the best rational guide to the future. See Downs, *An Economic Theory of Democracy.* For a contrast between these two types of retrospective voting and a powerful application of the Downsian approach, see Morris P. Fiorina, *Retrospective Voting in American National Elections* (New Haven, CT: Yale University Press, 1981).

25. See Paul Allen Beck, "The Electoral Cycle and Patterns of American Politics," *British Journal of Political Science* 9 (1979): 129–156; and James L. Sundquist, *Dynamics of the Party System* (Washington, DC: Brookings Institution, 1983).

26. For further development of these points, see Paul Allen Beck, "The Electoral Cycle and Patterns of American Politics"; and Jerome M. Clubb, William H. Flanagan, and Nancy H. Zingale, *Partisan Realignment* (Beverly Hills, CA: Sage, 1980), pp. 155–188.

27. On divided government in the states, see Morris Fiorina, *Divided Government* (New York: MacMillan, 1992), Chap. 3; and "Divided Government in the American States: A Byproduct of Legislative Professionalism," *American Political Science Review* 88 (1994): 304–316.

28. On the causes of divided government, see the essays by Gary C. Jacobson, John Petrocik, Martin Wattenberg, Morris Fiorina, and Charles Stewart in Gary Cox and Samuel Kernell, eds., *The Politics of Divided Government* (Boulder, CO: Westview, 1991); Gary Jacobson, *The Electoral Origins of Divided Government: Competition in U.S. House Elections, 1946–1988* (Boulder, CO: Westview, 1990); and Paul Allen Beck, Lawrence Baum, Aage Clausen, and Charles E. Smith, Jr., "Patterns and Sources of Split-Ticket Voting," *American Political Science Review* 86 (1992): 916–928.

29. James L. Sundquist, "Needed: A Political Theory for the New Era of Coalition Government in the United States," *Political Science Quarterly* 103 (1988): 613–635.

30. On the consequences of divided government, see Alberto Alesina and Howard Rosenthal, *Partisan Politics, Divided Government, and the Economy* (New York: Cambridge University Press, 1994); James E. Alt and Robert C. Lowery, "Divided Government, Fiscal Institutions, and Budget Deficits: Evidence from the States," *American Political Science Review* 88 (1994): 811–828; the essays by Samuel Kernell, Mathew McCubbins, and Gary Cox and Mathew McCubbins in Cox and Kernell, eds., *The Politics of Divided Government;* John J. Coleman, "Unified Government, Divided Government, and Party Responsiveness," *American Political Science* Review 93 (1999): 821–835; and Fiorina, *Divided Government,* Chap. 6. For a contrary view that divided government has not made much difference for federal policy-making, see David R. Mayhew, *Divided We Govern* (New Haven, CT: Yale University Press, 1991).

31. See Fiorina, *Divided Government,* Chap. 5. Also see Richard Born, "Split-Ticket Voters, Divided Government, and Fiorina's Policy-Balancing Model," *Legislative Studies Quarterly* 19 (1994): 95–115.

32. The reform-minded commitment of the 1950 APSA Committee on Political Parties lives on in state and national chapters of the Committee for Party Renewal, which has joined scholars and political leaders in the quest for more responsible parties. Also the bipartisan blue-ribbon Committee on the Constitutional System, deeply concerned about the deadlock produced by divided government, offered a number of recommendations to strengthen parties in its 1987 report. The recommendations included increased collaboration between Congress and the president through, among other things, scheduling all congressional elections in presidential election years and allowing members of Congress to serve simultaneously in the executive branch; public financing of congressional campaigns with party leaders controlling half of the funds; and a presidential nomination system in which congressional nominees had more influence over who the presidential nominee would be. For more on the Committee's report, see an article by Stuart Taylor, Jr., in the *New York Times,* January 11, 1987, p. 1.

33. See John Aldrich, *Why Parties? The Origin and Transformation of Party Politics in America* (Chicago: University of Chicago Press, 1995), Chap. 9; and Walter Dean Burnham, "Critical Realignment: Dead or Alive," in Byron E. Shafer, ed., *The End of Realignment? Interpreting American Electoral Eras* (Madison, WI: University of Wisconsin Press, 1991), pp. 101–139

CHAPTER 16

1. For a systematic discussion, see Robert Harmel and Kenneth Janda, *Parties and Their Environments: Limits to Reform* (New York: Longman, 1982).

2. Note, however, that change has occurred in American electoral districts, even beyond the decennial battles over redistricting. For example, multimember districts were once common in American state legislatures but their number has dwindled in recent years. See Richard Niemi, Simon Jackman, and Laura Winsky, "Candidates and Competitiveness in Multimember Districts," *Legislative Studies Quarterly* 16 (1991): 91–109; and Theodore J. Lowi, "Toward a More Responsible Three-Party System," *PS* 16 (1983): 699–706.

3. These figures are taken from Harold W. Stanley and Richard G. Niemi, *Vital Statistics on American Politics 1999–2000* (Washington, DC: CQ Press, 2000), Tables 3.12 (on split-ticket voting, p. 133) and 1.13 (on split-district outcomes, p. 44).

4. See Bruce E. Cain, John Ferejohn, and Morris P. Fiorina, *The Personal Vote: Constituency Service and Electoral Independence* (Cambridge, MA: Harvard University Press, 1987).

5. The extensive literature on the "decline of parties" during the 1960s and 1970s has been cited in earlier chapters. Most representative of these works are David S. Broder, *The Party's Over* (New York: Harper & Row, 1972); Nelson W. Polsby, *Consequences of Party Reform* (New York: Oxford University Press, 1983); Alan Ware, *The Breakdown of the*

Democratic Party Organization: 1940–1980 (New York: Oxford University Press, 1985); and Martin P. Wattenberg, *The Rise of Candidate-Centered Politics* (Cambridge, MA: Harvard University Press, 1991).

6. For a discussion of these characteristics of dealignment and how they might serve as necessary though not sufficient conditions for a later realignment, see Paul Allen Beck, "The Electoral Cycle and Patterns of American Politics," *British Journal of Political Science* 9 (1979): 129–156.

7. On the argument that recent signs of realignment do not meet the conditions traditionally required of a realignment, see Martin P. Wattenberg, "The Hollow Realignment: Partisan Change in a Candidate-Centered Era," *Public Opinion Quarterly* 51 (1987): 58–74; and Paul Allen Beck, "Incomplete Realignment: The Reagan Legacy for Parties and Elections," in Charles O. Jones, ed., *The Reagan Legacy* (Chatham, NJ: Chatham House, 1988), pp. 145–171. In *Critical Elections and the Mainsprings of American Politics* (New York: Norton, 1970), Chap. 5, Walter Dean Burnham contends that antiparty political reforms probably keep present or future realignments from becoming as complete as past realignments. A similar point is made in John H. Aldrich, *Why Parties: The Origin and Transformation of Party Politics in America* (Chicago: University of Chicago Press, 1995), Chap. 9.

8. For a discussion of information sources in American campaigns, see Robert Huckfeldt and Paul Allen Beck, "Contexts, Intermediaries, and Political Activity," in Lawrence C. Dodd and Calvin Jillson, eds., *The Dynamics of American Politics: Approaches and Interpretations* (Boulder, CO: Westview Press, 1994), Chap. 11.

9. For an elaboration of this view, see W. Phillips Shively, "The Development of Party Identification among Adults: Exploration of a Functional Model," *American Political Science Review* 73 (1979): 1039–1054.

10. Such skepticism about the ability of the new "service" party to restore the party organization to its earlier prominence is best expressed in John J. Coleman, "The Resurgence of Party Organization: A Dissent from the New Orthodoxy," in Daniel M. Shea and John C. Green, eds., *The State of the Parties: The Changing Role of Contemporary American Parties* (Lanham, MD: Rowman and Littlefield, 1994), Chap. 20.

11. See Cornelius P. Cotter, James L. Gibson, John F. Bibby, and Robert J. Huckshorn, *Party Organization in American Politics* (New York: Praeger, 1984); Xandra Kayden and Eddie Mahe, Jr., *The Party Goes On* (New York: Basic Books, 1985); David E. Price, *Bringing Back the Parties* (Washington, DC: CQ Press, 1984); Larry J. Sabato, *The Party's Just Begun* (Glenview, IL: Scott Foresman/Little, Brown, 1988); and Joseph A. Schlesinger, "The New American Political Party," *American Political Science Review* 79 (1985): 1152–1169.

12. Marjorie Randon Hershey, "If 'The Party's in Decline,' Then What's That Filling the News Columns?" in Nelson W. Polsby and Raymond E. Wolfinger, *On Parties* (Berkeley, CA: Institute of Governmental Studies, 1999), 257–278. Doris A. Graber discusses media treatment of politics in *Mass Media and American Politics*, 5th ed. (Washington, DC: CQ Press, 1997).

13. On the greater sophistication and politicization of Western electorates and the resulting decline of "blind" party loyalties, see Ronald Inglehart, *Culture Shift* (Princeton, NJ: Princeton University Press, 1990), especially Chaps. 10 and 11. See Kay Lawson and Peter H. Merkl, *When Parties Fail: Emerging Alternative Organizations* (Princeton, NJ: Princeton University Press, 1988), on the growing strength of competitors to the parties throughout the Western world.

14. On the centrality of the organization in these working-class parties, especially the British Labour Party, see Leon D. Epstein, *Political Parties in Western Democracies* (New York: Praeger, 1967), Chap. 11.

15. The conservative coalition became conspicuous as early as the 1930s and reached its pinnacle in the 1950s and 1960s. Formed on about a quarter of all votes in the 1970s, its appearance has declined to less than 10 percent of all votes in recent years.

16. In most other democracies the parties rather than the candidates receive the public financing for campaigns and control television time for campaign advertising as well. In American politics the only parallels are found in the few states that give public financing to the party organizations, not the candidates, and in the (now dwindling) coverage television networks give to the national party conventions.

17. See Paul S. Herrnson and John C. Green, *Multiparty Politics in America* (Lanham, MD: Rowman & Littlefield, 1997), and Steven J. Rosenstone, Roy L. Behr, and Edward H. Lazarus, *Third Parties in America*, 2nd ed. (Princeton, NJ: Princeton University Press, 1994).

18. Burnham, *Critical Elections and the Mainsprings of American Politics,* p. 133.

19. Willis D. Hawley, *Nonpartisan Elections and the Case for Party Politics* (New York: Wiley, 1973).

20. A slight SES bias of the decline in turnout in recent decades is described in Ruy A. Teixeira, *The Disappearing American Voter* (Washington, DC: Brookings Institution, 1992), Chap. 3. Broader studies of voter participation in the United States and elsewhere demonstrate the importance of the political parties for mobilizing lower-status groups into politics. See Steven J. Rosenstone and John Mark Hansen, *Mobilization, Participation, and Democracy in America* (New York: Macmillan, 1993), especially Chap. 8; and Sidney Verba, Norman H. Nie, and Jae-On Kim, *Participation and Political Equality* (Cambridge, U.K.: Cambridge University Press, 1978).

21. One alternative form of politics without parties could be a plebiscitary democracy in which a dominant national leader (today a president; a popular monarch in an earlier day) faces an up or down vote at regular intervals. Voters in these plebiscites might be especially swayed by the leader's command of television as well as how the country was faring at the time. At the other extreme large numbers of narrow interests might try for political dominance, with none of them strong enough to govern alone or pragmatic enough to join with other interests in lasting governing coalitions. Both these alternatives seem likely to do the work of parties—for example, selecting candidates for office, mobilizing voters, coordinating government, and simplifying policy alternatives—in ways that give unwarranted advantages to a few and that undermine democratic principles.

Index

Page numbers followed by *italicized* letters *f* and *t* indicate figures and tables, respectively